The Everyday Writer

6TH EDITION

The Everyday Writer

Andrea A. Lunsford

STANFORD UNIVERSITY

Coverage for multilingual writers with

Paul Kei Matsuda

ARIZONA STATE UNIVERSITY

Christine M. Tardy

UNIVERSITY OF ARIZONA

Bedford/St. Martin's

A Macmillan Education Imprint

BOSTON ◆ NEW YORK

For Bedford/St. Martin's

Vice President, Editorial, Macmillan Higher Education Humanities: Edwin Hill
Editorial Director, English and Music: Karen S. Henry
Publisher for Composition, Business and Technical Writing, Developmental Writing: Leasa Burton
Executive Editors: Carolyn Lengel and Brendan Baruth
Editorial Assistant: Dmitriy Rapoport
Senior Production Editor: Ryan Sullivan
Production Manager: Joe Ford
Marketing Manager: Emily Rowin
Copy Editor: Wendy Polhemus-Annibell
Indexer: Ellen Kuhl Repetto
Director of Rights and Permissions: Hilary Newman
Senior Art Director: Anna Palchik
Text Design: Claire Seng-Niemoeller
Illustrator: GB Tran
Cover Design: Donna Lee Dennison and William Boardman
Composition: Graphic World, Inc.
Printing and Binding: RR Donnelley and Sons

0   9   8   7   6   5
f   e   d   c   b   a

For information, write: Bedford/St. Martin's, 75 Arlington Street, Boston, MA 02116   (617-399-4000)

ISBN 978-1-4576-9847-7 (Student Edition, comb-bound. Manufactured in China.)
ISBN 978-1-319-02705-6 (Student Edition, spiral-bound. Manufactured in China.)
ISBN 978-1-319-02703-2 (Instructor's Edition. Manufactured in the U.S.)

Acknowledgments

Text acknowledgments and copyrights appear at the back of the book on page 655, which constitutes an extension of the copyright page. Art acknowledgments and copyrights appear on the same page as the art selections they cover. It is a violation of the law to reproduce these selections by any means whatsoever without the written permission of the copyright holder.

How to Use This Book

The Everyday Writer provides a writing reference you can use easily on your own—at work, in class, even on the run. Brief enough to tuck into a backpack or briefcase, this text has been designed to help you find information quickly, efficiently, and easily. I hope that this book will prove to be an everyday reference and that the following tips will lead you to any information you need.

You'll find additional resources—video prompts, tutorials, LearningCurve adaptive quizzing, model student writing with activities, and more—on LaunchPad Solo for *The Everyday Writer* at **macmillanhighered.com/everyday6e**.

Finding help in the print book

Quick Access Menu   On the inside front cover you'll find a brief overview of the book's contents, divided into twelve color-coded sections that correspond to the book's tabs. If you're looking for a particular chapter or a general topic, this is the simplest place to start.

Contents   The inside back cover has a table of contents that includes chapter titles and most major headings. It gives a closer look inside each chapter.

Tab Contents   On the back of each tabbed divider, you'll find the contents of that tab listed in depth, with page numbers.

True Tales of *The Everyday Writer*   This comic-style insert features seven real students sharing their own experiences of using the book successfully.

The Top Twenty   Chapter 1 provides guidelines for recognizing, understanding, and editing the most commonly identified issues in student writing today. This section includes brief explanations, hand-edited examples, and cross-references to other places in the book where you'll find more detail on each topic.

Documentation Tabs   Each documentation section has its own color-coded tab—gold for MLA style, blue for APA style, and white for *Chicago* style. Look for directories within each section to find models for citing sources. Easy-to-follow source maps walk you step-by-step through the processes of selecting, evaluating, using, and citing sources.

Glossaries and Index   The index lists everything covered in the book. You can look up a topic either by its formal name (*ellipses*, for example) or, if you're not sure what the formal name is, by a familiar word you use to describe it (such as *dots*). The index includes definitions of important terms, so look there first for help with writing terminology you don't understand. A glossary of usage, which helps with commonly confused words, appears in the glossary/index tab at the back of the book as well.

Directories   At the end of the book, you'll find several directories to help you locate special categories of content quickly, including a directory of storyboard art and other online activities such as quizzing, tutorials, and LearningCurve; a list of the student writing models available online; a directory of content of particular interest to multilingual writers; and directories to the "Considering Disabilities" and "Talking the Talk" boxes.

Revision Symbols   The list of symbols at the back of the book can help you learn more about marks or comments that an instructor or reviewer may make on your draft.

Page navigation help

1 **Guides at the top of every page.** Headings on left-hand pages tell you what chapter you're in, while headings on the right identify the section. Tabs identify the chapter number and section letter, and the page number appears at the outside edge of each page.

2 **"Multilingual" icons.** Help for speakers of all kinds of English, and from all educational backgrounds, is integrated throughout the book. Content that may be of particular interest to international students and other English language learners is identified with a "Multilingual" icon. **Boxed tips for multilingual writers** set off additional help. A directory to all content for multilingual writers appears at the back of the book.

3 **Hand-edited examples.** Many examples are hand-edited, allowing you to see an error or unconventional usage and its revision at a glance. Pointers and boldface type make examples easy to spot on the page.

4 **Cross-references to media content.** Cross-references at the bottom of a page point you to video prompts, quizzing, student writing models, tutorials, and more in LaunchPad Solo for *The Everyday Writer*.

5 **Boxed tips.** Many chapters include **"Quick Help"** boxes that provide an overview of important information. Look under "Quick Help" in the index to find a list. **"Talking the Talk"** boxes offer help with academic language and concepts. **"Considering Disabilities"** boxes offer tips on making your work accessible to audiences with different abilities.

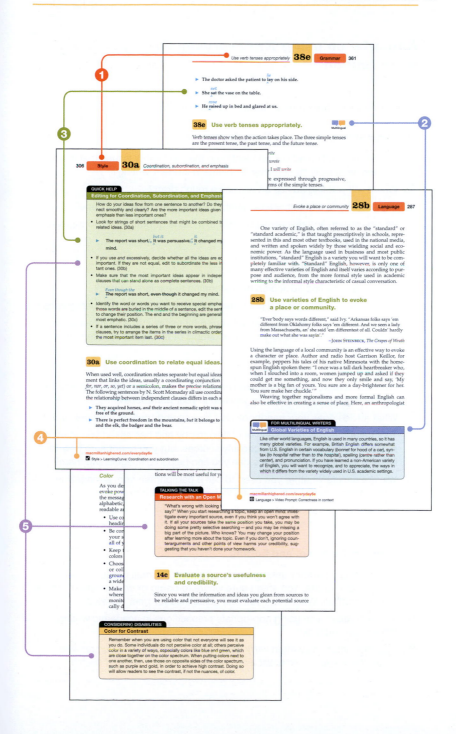

1

Use verb tenses appropriately **38e** Grammar 361

 ► The doctor asked the patient to lay on his side.

 ► She sat the vase on the table.

 ► He raised up in bed and glared at us.

38e Use verb tenses appropriately.

Verb tenses show when the action takes place. The three simple tenses
are the present tense, the past tense, and the future tense.

3

306 Style **30a** Coordination, subordination, and emphasis

QUICK HELP

Editing for Coordination, Subordination, and Emphasis

How do your ideas flow from one sentence to another? Do they connect smoothly and clearly? Are the more important ideas given
emphasis than less important ones?

• Look for strings of short sentences that might be combined to
related ideas. (30a)

 ► The report was short, but it was persuasive; it changed my
mind.

• If you use and excessively, decide whether all the ideas are e
important. If they are not equal, edit to subordinate the less in
tant ones. (30b)

• Make sure that the most important ideas appear in indepen
clauses that can stand alone as complete sentences. (30b)

 ► Even though the report was short, even though it changed my mind.

• Identify the word or words you want to receive special empha
those words are buried in the middle of a sentence, edit the sen
to change their position. The end and the beginning are genera
most emphatic. (30c)

• If a sentence includes a series of three or more words, phrase
clauses, try to arrange the items in the series in climactic orde
the most important item last. (30c)

30a Use coordination to relate equal ideas.

When used well, coordination relates separate but equal ideas
ment that links the ideas, usually a coordinating conjunction
for, nor, or, so, yet) or a semicolon, makes the precise relations
The following sentences by N. Scott Momaday all use coordin
the relationship between independent clauses differs in each s

 ► They acquired horses, and their ancient nomadic spirit was s
free of the ground.

 ► There is perfect freedom in the mountains, but it belongs to
and the elk, the badger and the bear.

4

macmillanhighered.com/everyday6e
☑ Style > LearningCurve: Coordination and subordination

Color

As you de
evoke pow
the messag
alphabetic
readable a

• Use co
headir

• Be con
your s
all of y

• Keep t
colors

• Choos
or col
groun
a wide

• Make
where
monit
cally d

tions will be most useful for y

TALKING THE TALK

Research with an Open M

"What's wrong with looking f
say?" When you start researching a topic, keep an open mind: investigate every important source, even if you think you won't agree with
it. If all your sources take the same position you take, you may be
doing some pretty selective searching — and you may be missing a
big part of the picture. Who knows? You may change your position
after learning more about the topic. Even if you don't, ignoring counterarguments and other points of view harms your credibility, suggesting that you haven't done your homework.

5

Evoke a place or community **28b** Language 287

One variety of English, often referred to as the "standard" or
"standard academic," is that taught prescriptively in schools, represented in this and most other textbooks, used in the national media,
and written and spoken widely by those wielding social and economic power. As the language used in business and most public
institutions, "standard" English is a variety you will want to be completely familiar with. "Standard" English, however, is only one of
many effective varieties of English and itself varies according to purpose and audience, from the more formal style used in academic
writing to the informal style characteristic of casual conversation.

**28b Use varieties of English to evoke
a place or community.**

"Ever'body says words different," said Ivy. "Arkansas folks says 'em
different from Oklahomy folks says 'em different. And we seen a lady
from Massachusetts, an' she said 'em differentest of all. Couldn' hardly
make out what she was sayin'."
—JOHN STEINBECK, *The Grapes of Wrath*

Using the language of a local community is an effective way to evoke
a character or place. Author and radio host Garrison Keillor, for
example, peppers his tales of his native Minnesota with the homespun English spoken there: "I once was a tall dark heartbreaker who,
when I slouched into a room, women jumped up and asked if they
could get me something, and now they only smile and say, 'My
mother is a big fan of yours. You sure are a day-brightener for her.
You sure make her chuckle.'"
Weaving together regionalisms and more formal English can
also be effective in creating a sense of place. Here, an anthropologist

FOR MULTILINGUAL WRITERS

Global Varieties of English

Like other world languages, English is used in many countries, so it has
many global varieties. For example, British English differs somewhat
from U.S. English in certain vocabulary (*bonnet* for hood of a car), syntax (*to hospital* rather than *to the hospital*), spelling (*centre* rather than
center), and pronunciation. If you have learned a non-American variety
of English, you will want to recognize, and to appreciate, the ways in
which it differs from the variety widely used in U.S. academic settings.

macmillanhighered.com/everyday6e
☐ Language > Video Prompt: Correctness in context

**14c Evaluate a source's usefulness
and credibility.**

Since you want the information and ideas you glean from sources to
be reliable and persuasive, you must evaluate each potential source

CONSIDERING DISABILITIES

Color for Contrast

Remember when you are using color that not everyone will see it as
you do. Some individuals do not perceive color at all; others perceive
color in a variety of ways, especially colors like blue and green, which
are close together on the color spectrum. When putting colors next to
one another, then, use those on opposite sides of the color spectrum,
such as purple and gold, in order to achieve high contrast. Doing so
will allow readers to see the contrast, if not the nuances, of color.

2

A tutorial on using *The Everyday Writer*, Sixth Edition

For this book to serve you well, you need to know what's inside and how to find it. This tutorial will help you familiarize yourself with *The Everyday Writer*.

Getting Started with *The Everyday Writer*

1. Where will you find advice on identifying the top twenty issues that instructors are most likely to consider problems in student writing?
2. Where will you find advice on revising a rough draft?
3. Where can you find out what a comma splice is and how to fix one?
4. Where will you find guidelines on how to include quotations in your project without plagiarizing?

Planning and Drafting

5. Where can you find advice on brainstorming to explore a topic?
6. Where can you find general guidelines for developing effective paragraphs?
7. Your instructor wants you to adapt your print essay into a multimodal presentation. Where would you find an example of this kind of presentation?

Doing Research

8. You have a topic for your research project, but your instructor asks you to narrow it down. What help can you find in your handbook?
9. What advice does your handbook give for keeping track of your research?
10. Your instructor has reviewed your bibliography and has asked you to replace some popular sources with scholarly sources, but you're not sure how to identify the differences. Where can you find help in distinguishing them?
11. You are unsure whether you need to cite a paraphrase from a magazine article. Where can you find the answer in your handbook?
12. Your instructor has asked you to use APA style. Where can you find guidelines for documenting information from an article on a website?

Reviewing, Revising, and Editing

13. Your writing instructor asks your class to work in small groups to review each others' drafts. You aren't sure where to begin or what kinds of issues to comment on. Where can you find guidelines for peer review?
14. You need advice on using appropriate prepositions in academic writing. Where can you look?
15. Your instructor has written *wrdy* next to this sentence: *The person who wrote the article is a scientist who makes the argument that it seems as*

though the scientific phenomenon of global warming is becoming a bigger issue at this point in time. Where do you look in your handbook for help responding to your instructor's comment?

16. As you edit a final draft, you stop at the following passage: *Because the actor had a reputation for delivering Oscar-worthy performances. He received the best roles.* How do you find out if this is a sentence fragment and what you should do if it is?

17. You have finished your essay and now decide to use an unusual font to make your essay more visually appealing. Is it a good idea to use this font? What information does your handbook provide?

Meeting Your Instructor's Expectations

18. Your instructor returns a draft to you and says that your paper contains mostly summary and that you need to do more critical thinking and analysis. Where can you look for information on how to read and write critically?

19. You've learned a lot by looking at the samples of good writing that your instructor has shared with the class. Where in your handbook can you find more sample student work?

20. Your professor has created a blog with a discussion forum, and you are required to comment on the week's discussion topic. You're not sure how to write online as part of a class requirement. Where can you look for help?

Writing in Any Discipline

21. You've never written a sociology project before, and you're unsure what kind of evidence to use. Where can you look for help in your handbook?

22. You're writing a report about your field research, and your instructor wants you to include a table to detail your findings. Where can you look in your handbook for help incorporating visuals?

23. You're used to writing online for social media sites, but you aren't sure what "normal" academic writing should look like. Where can you look in your handbook to help you figure out how to write for an academic audience?

Using LaunchPad Solo for *The Everyday Writer*

24. The tutor at your school's writing center suggested that you work on using active verbs in your writing. Where can you find quizzes that will help you?

25. You can't decide on a topic for your research project. Where can you find a video that might help you figure out what topic would work for you?

26. Before you write a research essay, you want to see how another student has incorporated sources. Where can you find an interactive activity that will help you analyze how a student uses evidence?

Answer key

1. "The Top Twenty" in Chapter 1. (Searching for *common errors* in the index also points students toward "The Top Twenty.")

2. Chapter 7, "Reviewing, Revising, and Editing."

3. Chapter 45, "Comma Splices and Fused Sentences." (*Comma splice* in the index also helps you find this information quickly.) Or look at "The Top Twenty" — "comma splice" is item 16.

4. Chapter 15, "Integrating Sources and Avoiding Plagiarism," gives advice on how to use quotations correctly.

5. Looking up *brainstorming* in the index leads you to section 4a. Cross-references later in the chapter direct you to videos of students talking about their writing processes, accessible by logging into LaunchPad Solo at **macmillanhighered .com/everyday6e**.

6. Looking up *paragraphs* in the index leads you to Chapter 6, on developing paragraphs. (Check the "Quick Help" box at the beginning of the chapter for a list of questions that will help you compose effective paragraphs and that will direct you to other sections in Chapter 6 where you can get more help.)

7. Looking for *presentations* in the index will lead you to Chapter 23, on presentations. LaunchPad Solo at **macmillanhighered.com/everyday6e** includes both the print essay Shuqiao Song wrote about *Fun Home* and the multimodal presentation she created from her essay.

8. Searching for *narrowing a topic* in the index will lead you to section 5a, "Narrow your topic."

9. Skim the table of contents on the "Research" tab. Chapter 14, for example, explains how to keep a working bibliography and take notes.

10. Consulting the index under either *popular sources* or *scholarly sources* leads you to section 13a, "Understand different kinds of sources," where you can find information on identifying the two types of sources.

11. For guidance on whether to cite the article, use the index to find *acknowledgment required for* under *paraphrases*, which points you to section 15f, "Know which sources to acknowledge." To be sure you've paraphrased acceptably, look under *paraphrases* in the index for *acceptable and unacceptable*. This will lead you to section 14f, which shows you how to paraphrase without inadvertently plagiarizing your source.

12. The table of contents leads you to the APA tab, which provides a full discussion of APA documentation conventions. The directory to APA style for a list of references in Chapter 63 points you to the models for documenting website sources on a references page, as well as a source map that provides a visual guide to locating the information you need.

13. Looking up *peer review* in the index will lead you to the "Quick Help" box in section 7b that provides guidelines for reviewers.

14. In Chapter 44, "Prepositions and Prepositional Phrases," a "Quick Help" box gives strategies for using prepositions idiomatically. A cross-reference in the chapter also lets you know that there is a LearningCurve activity on prepositions and prepositional phrases in LaunchPad Solo at **macmillanhighered.com/everyday6e**. To find help especially suited for multilingual writers, consult the directory of content for multilingual writers at the back of the book.

15. A list of revision symbols appears in the directory at the back of your handbook. Consulting this list tells you that *wrdy* refers to "wordy" and that wordy writing is addressed in Chapter 34, on conciseness.

16. The table of contents in the inside back cover leads you to Chapter 46, "Sentence Fragments," where you will find examples of sentence fragments and several options for revising them.

17. Looking up *fonts* or *type* in the index will take you to an entry on choosing appropriate formats in section 22c, on formatting print and digital texts. The information under "Type sizes and fonts" in this section points out that most college writing requires a standard font and that unusual fonts may be difficult to read.

18. Tab 2 (Chapters 9–11) addresses critical thinking and argument, and Chapter 9, "Critical Reading," includes sections on summarizing texts (9d) and analyzing texts (9e). These include instructions and student writing samples to help you distinguish between summarizing and analyzing.

19. Student writing is listed in small capital letters in the table of contents in the inside back cover. Searching for *student writing* in the index will also lead you to the directory of student writing in the back of your book. This lists all the samples you can find in your text, as well as those available in LaunchPad Solo at **macmillanhighered.com/everyday6e**.

20. Chapter 2, "Expectations for College Writing," has helpful advice you can use for any college writing. In particular, section 2e on using media effectively provides guidelines for writing comments and posts in online discussion lists and forums.

21. Tab 4 (Chapters 17–25) covers writing in the disciplines. Section 17e focuses on using appropriate evidence in all academic work, and Chapter 19 is dedicated to writing for the social sciences. Searching for *social sciences* in the index will also lead you to this chapter. Check the APA tab (Tab 10, Chapters 61–64) for instruction in using APA style, which includes examples of the types of evidence you might cite in a social science project.

22. Check the index for *tables* or *visuals and media* to find section 22d, on considering visuals and media. (You can learn more about conducting field research in section 13e.)

23. Browsing the table of contents in the inside back cover, you'll see that Chapter 2 covers expectations for college writing; section 2a discusses moving between social and academic writing. For more help in thinking about writing for a specific audience, check the index for *audience*.

24. Check the directory of online activities at the back of the book to find a list of topics for LearningCurve adaptive quizzes (you can also look in the Resources tab of LaunchPad Solo at **macmillanhighered.com/everyday6e**). The LearningCurve activities on "Active and passive voice" and "Verbs" can both help you practice.

25. If you navigate to LaunchPad Solo at **macmillanhighered.com/everyday6e**, clicking on the "Prewriting" and "Research" folders will lead you to a list of content that includes videos of student writers discussing relevant topics, including "Pay attention to what you're interested in" and "Researching something exciting." In the print book, topics with accompanying videos are indicated with a cross-reference at the bottom of the page.

26. Go to LaunchPad Solo at **macmillanhighered.com/everyday6e**, and look for the "Student Writing" folder. You'll find several models that ask you to consider a student research project, including an analysis activity that allows you to evaluate Benjy Mercer-Golden's use of sources in his argument paper.

Preface

Look around you, almost anywhere — on the bus, at a diner, in a park or shopping center, or just walking down the street — and you'll see people writing away on their various devices. It's not an exaggeration to say that people today are writing (and reading) *more than ever before.* The ongoing development of new communication technologies and an explosion in social media mean that writers have more ways to communicate with more people in more places than would have been imaginable even ten years ago. So today, students are no longer just consumers of information; rather, they are active producers of knowledge. More than ever before, students today are *writers* — every day, every night, all the time; writing is all around them, like the air they breathe, so much so that they don't even notice. From contributing entries to Wikipedia to blogging, texting, tweeting, and posting to YouTube, Facebook, Tumblr, and other sites, student writers are participating widely in what philosopher Kenneth Burke calls "the conversation of humankind." As access to new writing spaces grows, so too do the potential audiences: many writers, for example, are in daily contact with people around the world, and their work goes out to millions. In such a time, writers need to think more carefully than ever about how to craft effective messages and how best to represent themselves to others.

These ever-expanding opportunities for writers, as well as the challenges that inevitably come with them, have inspired this edition of *The Everyday Writer* — from the focus on thinking carefully about audience and purposes for writing and on attending to the design or "look" of writing; to an emphasis on moving smoothly between informal social-media writing and academic writing; to attention to the ways student writers can now create multimodal compositions; to a focus on writing to make something happen in the world; to an emphasis on the ways writing works across disciplines; to the questions that new genres and forms of writing raise about citing and documenting sources and about understanding and avoiding plagiarism. What remains constant is the focus on the "everydayness" of writing and on friendly, down-to-earth, practical advice for how to write well in a multitude of situations as well as across a range of genres and media.

What also remains constant is the focus on rhetorical concerns. In a time of so many challenges and possibilities, taking a rhetorical perspective is particularly important. Why? Because a rhetorical perspective rejects either/or, right/wrong, black/white approaches to writing in favor of asking what choices will be most appropriate, effective, and ethical in a given writing situation. A rhetorical perspective also means paying careful attention to the purposes you want to achieve and the audiences you want to address. Writers today need to maintain such a rhetorical perspective every single day, and *The Everyday Writer*, Sixth Edition, gives every writer the tools to make good decisions—in an accessible, usable, friendly format.

What's different about this edition?

Integrated advice on U.S. academic English Following best practices in the field of composition and rhetoric, including advice from experts Paul Kei Matsuda and Christine Tardy, who have advised me on several editions of this handbook, this edition of *The Everyday Writer* integrates the information for multilingual writers throughout the book so that it is accessible to students from all language and educational backgrounds. This change recognizes the growing numbers of multilingual students in U.S. college classes, a trend that will surely continue as the U.S. becomes a more truly multilingual country. Integrating this advice also acknowledges that international students and Generation 1.5 English speakers aren't the only students puzzled by English structures and academic genres; for many students, academic discourse itself is "another language," one they struggle to acquire and use effectively. All college writers can benefit from learning more about academic genres and formal English structures—and from understanding more about other Englishes used by their classmates, coworkers, and neighbors. And even students whose home language is English may have difficulty with idiomatic aspects of language such as prepositions. Look for the "Multilingual" icon [Multilingual] to find content of particular use to multilingual writers, or see the directory at the back of the book.

An awareness that academic writing today is multimodal For some time now, I have created the rhetorical advice in *The Everyday Writer* with the assumption that students are producing writing that goes beyond traditional word-based print essays. Research bears out the idea that multimodal assignments are becoming increasingly common in academic contexts. New coverage in this edition specifically addresses the rhetorical considerations of tasks such as planning an online text, turning a print text into a presentation, and creating multimodal compositions such as websites, wikis, blogs, and PechaKucha—while also recognizing that multimodal assignments can include nondigital content such as scrapbooks. Even more importantly, *The Everyday Writer* points out again and again—in its coverage of the writing process, of critical reading, of research, and even of sentence style and punctuation—that creating a rhetorically effective text requires students to examine their context and make good choices, and that those choices are at least as important in digital and multimodal contexts as in traditional print essays.

New research-based tips on writing moves that experts make to establish authority   Informed by the corpus linguistics research and good advice of Laura Aull, this edition of *The Everyday Writer* helps students recognize how expert writers present themselves as credible and fair. Tips based on corpus linguistics analysis identify differences in the ways student writers and experts use transitions, treat opposing points of view, restate evidence from sources, and comment on those sources. I've also included a new section, based on Laura's work with her own students, that introduces students to corpora as powerful tools that *all* writers can use to check their own usage against the moves made in academic writing.

Ideas from real students in a friendly visual guide to using *The Everyday Writer*   A comic-style insert, "True Tales of *The Everyday Writer*," tells seven real students' stories about using *The Everyday Writer* to find help in various contexts. The comic, illustrated by award-winning comics artist GB Tran (author and illustrator of the Eisner-nominated *Vietnamerica*), reports what these students told me about situations when *The Everyday Writer* had come in handy. I think students will enjoy the way words and images work together to create memorable messages about the help this handbook can provide, and I hope it will encourage students to explore the book when they need to find answers.

More multimodal and interactive elements   Content on LaunchPad Solo for *The Everyday Writer* offers resources beyond those that a print book can provide, including LearningCurve adaptive quizzing, video prompts featuring student writers, tutorials, Top Twenty editing quizzes, student work in many genres, and reflective questions.

What hasn't changed?

The world's friendliest handbook   *The Everyday Writer*'s friendly design and the plentiful illustrations by GB Tran encourage students to open and try out their handbook. The only useful tools are the tools that are *used*, so we've worked hard to make sure that information in the book is easy to find and inviting to read. (For more ideas on introducing students to their handbook, see the tutorial in the "How to Use This Book" section.)

Attention to good writing, not just to surface correctness   Effective texts in every genre and medium follow conventions that always depend on their audience, situation, and discipline. No rule can apply in every possible situation, so *The Everyday Writer* asks students to examine their rhetorical contexts and make appropriate choices.

Help for the most common writing problems   A nationwide study that I conducted with Karen Lunsford — revisiting the original 1986 research that Bob Connors and I did on student writing — shows the problems instructors are most likely to point out in first-year college writing. This book's first chapter presents a quick guide to troubleshooting the Top Twenty — with examples, explanations, and information on where to turn in the book for more detailed information.

Recognition that the literacy revolution has arrived   Students today are writing more than any generation ever has, and they are using writing not only to communicate with friends but also to reach a wider public. This "literacy revolution" has brought with it opportunities for student writers to make their voices heard by audiences never before accessible to them; to create texts that include images, sound, and video as well as words; and to present these texts across a range of genres, from brochures and posters to blogs and web-based reports. My research shows that students often make well-informed decisions in their everyday writing — so *The Everyday Writer* includes new features to help students understand the skills they already have as social writers and use those skills in their academic writing.

More student writing in more genres   Many students define good writing as active and participatory; they tell me that their most important writing aims to "make something happen in the world." Sample student writing in *The Everyday Writer* reflects the writing students are doing today, both in and out of class — from tweets and fundraising websites to reports and literary analyses.

Up-to-date advice on research and documentation   As best practices for research continue to evolve, so does *The Everyday Writer*. Integrated coverage of library and online research helps students find authoritative and credible information in any medium, along with advice on integrating sources, avoiding plagiarism, and citing sources in MLA, APA, and *Chicago* documentation styles. Visual source maps show students how to evaluate, use, and document print and online sources.

Comprehensive coverage of critical thinking, critical reading, and argument   *The Everyday Writer* provides all the information student writers need to respond effectively to their writing assignments, including practical advice on critical reading and analysis of all kinds of texts and instruction on composing arguments.

Unique coverage of language and style   Unique chapters on language help students think about language in context and about the consequences that language choices have on writers and readers. Tips throughout the book help students communicate effectively across cultures and use varieties of language both wisely and well.

A user-friendly, all-in-one glossary and index   Entries include both everyday words (such as *that* or *which*) and grammatical terms (such as *pronoun*, which appears with a definition), so students can find what they're looking for quickly and easily.

Get the most out of your course with *The Everyday Writer*

Bedford/St. Martin's offers resources and format choices that help you and your students get even more out of your book and course. To learn more about or to order any of the following products, contact your Bedford/St. Martin's sales representative, email sales support (**sales_support@bfwpub.com**), or visit the website at **macmillanhighered.com/everyday6e/catalog**.

LaunchPad Solo for The Everyday Writer: *Where students learn*

LaunchPad Solo for *The Everyday Writer* provides engaging content and new ways to get the most out of your course. Get **unique, book-specific materials** in a fully customizable course space; then assign and mix our resources with yours.

- *Multimedia selections.* LaunchPad Solo for *The Everyday Writer* offers videos of student writers talking about their own processes, with reflective prompts for low-stakes writing; student writing in many genres with activities; and tutorials on topics like citing sources and using tools to create multimodal projects.
- **Pre-built units** — including readings, videos, quizzes, discussion groups, and more — are **easy to adapt and assign** by adding your own materials and mixing them with our high-quality multimedia content and ready-made assessment options, such as **LearningCurve** adaptive quizzing.

- LaunchPad Solo also offers access to a **Gradebook** that provides a clear window on the performance of your whole class, individual students, and even individual assignments.

- A **streamlined interface** helps students focus on what's due, and social commenting tools let them **engage**, make connections, and learn from each other. Use LaunchPad Solo on its own or integrate it with your school's learning management system so that your class is always on the same page.

To get the most out of your course, order LaunchPad Solo for *The Everyday Writer* packaged with the print book. (LaunchPad Solo for *The Everyday Writer* can also be purchased on its own.) An activation code is required.

To order LaunchPad Solo for *The Everyday Writer* with the print book, use the following ISBNs:

- with *The Everyday Writer* (comb-bound): ISBN 978-1-319-06125-8

- with *The Everyday Writer* (spiral-bound): ISBN 978-1-319-06122-7

- with *The Everyday Writer with Exercises* (comb-bound): ISBN 978-1-319-06123-4

LaunchPad Solo media contents for The Everyday Writer

To see a detailed list of the media activities available with this book, go to **macmillanhighered.com/everyday6e**.

STUDENT WRITING MODELS

Annotated bibliography: Chan

Annotated scholarly article: Sanchez and Lum

APA-style research project: Bell

Argument project: Mercer-Golden

Biology literature review: Hays

Blog post: Nguyen

Chemistry lab report: Goldberg

Chicago-style research project: Rinder

Close reading of poetry: Sillay

Critical analysis: Song

Early draft: Lesk

Final draft: Lesk

Fundraising web page: Dart

MLA-style research project: Craig

Pitch package: Jane and Burke

Portfolio cover letter: Kung

Presentation: Song

Psychology literature review: Redding

Reflective annotated bibliography: Sriram

Résumés: Lange

Rhetorical analysis: Ateyea

Synthesis project: Warner

VIDEOS OF STUDENT WRITERS

Brain mapping [on clustering]: Nguyen

Correctness in context: Bridgewater, Chen, Cuervels, Murray, Quarta, Vanjani

Developing a sense of audience: Garry, Harris, Lima, Matalucci, McElligott, Murray, Sherman, Vanjani

Facing a challenging argument: Chilton

Filling in the gaps [on drafting]: Chilton

Getting ideas from social media: Chilton

If I were in the audience [on presenting]: Chilton

Improving with practice: Ly

It's hard to delete things: Song

Lessons from being a peer reviewer: Edwards, Nguyen

Lessons from informal writing: Song

Lessons from peer review: Mercer-Golden

Looking for the essential points [on genres and media]: Song

Pay attention to what you're interested in: Song

Presentation is performance: Song

Researching something exciting: Chilton

Revision happens: Cuervels, Diaz, Harris, Mackler, Murray, Ramirez

Something to learn from each other: Nguyen

This will take longer than I thought [on planning]: Mercer-Golden

When to stop researching: Song

Working with other people: Edwards, Ly

Writing for the real world: Song

Writing processes: Bridgewater, Chen, Murray, Quarta, Ramirez, Sherman, Vanjani

You just have to start: Nguyen

You want them to hear you [on slide design]: Song

LEARNINGCURVE ADAPTIVE QUIZZING

Active and passive voice

Apostrophes

Argument

Articles and nouns

Capitalization

Commas

Comma splices and fused (run-on) sentences

Coordination and subordination

Critical reading

Evaluating, integrating, and acknowledging sources (APA)

Evaluating, integrating, and acknowledging sources (MLA)

Fragments

Modifiers

Nouns and pronouns

Parallelism

Prepositions and conjunctions

Prepositions and prepositional phrases

Pronouns

Semicolons and colons

Sentence structure for multilingual writers

Shifts

Subject-verb agreement

Topics and main ideas

Topic sentences and supporting details

Verbs

Verbs, adjectives, and adverbs

Verbs for multilingual writers

Word choice

EDITING QUIZZES, VISUAL EXERCISES, AND TUTORIALS

Top Twenty contextualized editing quizzes

Storyboard visual exercises on rhetorical situations, creating a working thesis, being a peer reviewer, getting help from peer reviewers, revising and editing, critical reading, and synthesis

Tutorials on active reading, word processing, reading visuals, online research tools, citation, audio editing, photo editing, presentations, and searching for a job

Choose from alternative formats of The Everyday Writer

Bedford/St. Martin's offers a range of affordable formats, allowing students to choose the one that works best for them. For details, visit **macmillanhighered.com/everyday6e/catalog**.

- *Comb- or spiral-bound.* To order the comb-bound version of *The Everyday Writer*, use ISBN 978-1-4576-9847-7. To order the spiral-bound version of *The Everyday Writer*, use ISBN 978-1-319-02705-6.

- *Comb-bound with exercises.* To order *The Everyday Writer with Exercises*, use ISBN 978-1-319-02704-9.

- *Other popular e-book formats.* For details, visit **macmillanhighered .com/everyday6e/formats**.

Select value packages

Add value to your text by packaging one of the following resources with *The Everyday Writer*. To learn more about package options for any of the following products, contact your Bedford/St. Martin's sales representative or visit **macmillanhighered.com/everyday6e/catalog**.

Writer's Help 2.0 is a powerful online writing resource that helps students find answers, whether they are searching for writing advice on their own or as part of an assignment.

- *Smart search.* Built on research with more than 1,600 student writers, the smart search in *Writer's Help 2.0* provides reliable results even when students use novice terms, such as *flow* and *unstuck*.

- *Trusted content.* Choose *Writer's Help 2.0 for Lunsford Handbooks* and ensure that students have clear advice and examples for all of their writing questions — and a pedagogical approach that matches *The Everyday Writer*'s approach.

- *Adaptive exercises that engage students.* *Writer's Help 2.0* includes LearningCurve, game-like online quizzing that adapts to what students already know and helps them focus on what they need to learn.

Student access is packaged with *The Everyday Writer* at a significant discount. To ensure your students have easy access to online writing support, use the following ISBNs:

- with *The Everyday Writer* (comb-bound): ISBN 978-1-319-06360-3

- with *The Everyday Writer* (spiral-bound): ISBN 978-1-319-06361-0

- with *The Everyday Writer with Exercises* (comb-bound): ISBN 978-1-319-06362-7

Students who rent a book or buy a used book can purchase access to *Writer's Help 2.0* at **macmillanhighered.com/writershelp2**.

Instructors may request free access by registering as an instructor at **macmillanhighered.com/writershelp2**. For technical support, visit **macmillanhighered.com/getsupport**.

LaunchPad Solo for Readers and Writers allows students to work on whatever they need help with the most. At home or in class, students learn at their own pace, with instruction tailored to each student's unique needs.

- *Pre-built units that support a learning arc.* Each easy-to-assign unit is comprised of a pre-test check, multimedia instruction and assessment, and a post-test that assesses what students have learned about critical reading, writing process, using sources, grammar, style, mechanics, and help for multilingual writers.

- *A video introduction to many topics.* Introductions offer an overview of the unit's topic, and many include a brief, accessible video to illustrate the concepts at hand.

- *Adaptive quizzing for targeted learning.* Most units include LearningCurve, game-like adaptive quizzing that focuses on the areas in which each student needs the most help.

- *The ability to monitor student progress.* Use our gradebook to see which students are on track and which need additional help with specific topics.

LaunchPad Solo for Readers and Writers can be **packaged at a significant discount**. Visit **macmillanhighered.com/catalog/readwrite** for more information.

Get instructor resources

macmillanhighered.com/everyday6e/catalog

You have a lot to do in your course. Bedford/St. Martin's wants to make it easy for you to find the support you need—and to get it quickly.

Teaching with Lunsford Handbooks, **Second Edition (2016 Update),** is available as a PDF that can be downloaded from the Bedford/St. Martin's online catalog at the URL above. In addition to chapter overviews and teaching tips, the instructor's manual includes sample syllabi, correlations to the Council of Writing Program Administrators' Outcomes Statement, and classroom activities. If you prefer a print copy, use ISBN 978-1-319-03622-5.

Visit the catalog for this and additional instructor resources, including downloadable answer keys for *The Everyday Writer with Exercises* and for the supplemental exercise book available with *The Everyday Writer.*

Teaching Central offers the entire list of Bedford/St. Martin's print and online professional resources in one place. You'll find landmark reference works, sourcebooks on pedagogical issues, award-winning collections, and practical advice for the classroom—all free for instructors. Visit **macmillanhighered.com/teachingcentral**.

Be a part of Andrea's teaching community

- **Andrea Lunsford's "Teacher to Teacher" channel** on the award-winning *Bits* blog brings you new suggestions for the classroom and invites you to discuss ideas and events that are important to teachers of writing. When classes are in session, look for multi-modal composition ideas on Andrea's **"Multimodal Mondays"** channel. Join the *Bits* community to discuss revision, research, grammar and style, technology, peer review, and much more. Take, use, adapt, and pass the ideas around. Then come back to the site to comment or share your own suggestions. Visit **community.macmillan.com**.

- Andrea is on **Twitter**! Follow **@LunsfordHandbks** to keep up with Andrea's tweets.

- Andrea Lunsford's **author page on Facebook** also provides regular updates and links for teachers. You can find Andrea at **facebook .com/AndreaALunsford**.

Acknowledgments

As always, I am most grateful to Carolyn Lengel, my editor for this and two other handbooks as well: her patience, fortitude, and sheer hard work, her astute judgment, her wellspring of good ideas, her meticulous attention to detail, and most of all her great wit and sense of humor are gifts that just keep on giving. I am also thankful to Leah Rang for editorial assistance in the early stages of this edition and for continuing skillful management of my "Teacher to Teacher" blog on *Bits*; to Kathleen Wisneski, whose editorial help on print and digital products repeatedly saved the day; to Dmitriy Rapoport, who stepped into the editorial assistant role in the final stages of *The Everyday Writer*; to Barbara Flanagan and Adam Whitehurst for their heroic work on handbook media; to Allison Hart for managing the endlessly multiplying media production tasks; to Claire Seng-Niemoeller and Anna Palchik for their brilliant contributions to art and design; to William Boardman for another beautiful cover; to Wendy Polhemus-Annibell for her meticulous copyediting; and to Ryan Sullivan, the best project editor ever.

Many thanks, also, to the unfailingly generous and supportive members of the Bedford/St. Martin's team: Edwin Hill, Leasa Burton, Brendan Baruth, Karen Henry, Erica Appel, Jane Smith, Jimmy Fleming, Sandy Lindelof, Emily Rowin, Tracey Kuehn, Elise Kaiser, Nick Carbone, Dennis Conroy, and Joe Ford.

For this edition, I am once again tremendously grateful to GB Tran, comics artist extraordinaire, whose simple, elegant, yet "everyday" drawings add immeasurably to the visual appeal of *The Everyday Writer* and who worked with us to develop the student comic. I am also indebted to Paul Kei Matsuda and Christine Tardy for their extraordinarily helpful additions to the multilingual writer coverage of this book; to Laura Aull for her fascinating research with corpora linguistics and her useful advice on using these tools with students; to Lisa Ede for her ongoing support and advice; and to Lisa Dresdner at Norwalk Community College for her fine work on *Teaching with Lunsford Handbooks*. I have also benefited greatly from the excellent advice of some very special colleagues: Colin Gifford Brooke, Syracuse University; Patrick Clauss, Butler University; Dànielle Nicole DeVoss, Michigan State University; Barbara Fister, Gustavus Adolphus College; Beverly Moss, Ohio State University; Arnold Zwicky, Stanford University; and Marilyn Moller.

I owe special thanks to the group of student writers whose work and voices appear in and enrich this book and the digital content: Michelle Abbott, Carina Abernathy, Milena Ateyea, Martha Bell, Brett Bittiger, Alec Braun, Jamie Bridgewater, Tony Chan, Yishi Chen,

Cyana Chilton, David Craig, Matteo Cuervels, Justin Dart, Ayadhiri Diaz, Brittany Dirks, Halle Edwards, John Garry, Allyson Goldberg, Ashley Harris, Joanna Hays, Kiara James, Jackson Kim, James Kung, Megan Lange, Emily Lesk, Isaias Lima, Sarah Lum, Brandon Ly, Keith Mackler, Luisa Matalucci, Liz McElligott, Benjy Mercer-Golden, William Murray, Thanh Nguyen, Stephanie Parker, Rachel Quarta, Rachel Ramirez, Tawnya Redding, Amanda Rinder, Fernando Sanchez, David Sherman, Bonnie Sillay, Shuqiao Song, Nandita Sriram, Apeksha Vanjani, He Wanhua, and Caroline Warner.

Once again, I have been guided by a group of hardworking and meticulous reviewers, including Brenda Abbott, Bay Path University; Sherri Agee, Virginia Western Community College; Laura Aull, Wake Forest University; Dona Bailey, University of Arkansas at Little Rock; Ann Biswas, University of Dayton; Melissa Bradshaw, Loyola University Chicago; Matthew Bryan, University of Central Florida; William Carney, Cameron University; Barbara Ching, Iowa State University; Darren DeFrain, Wichita State University; Violet Dutcher, Eastern Mennonite University; Sue Fox, Central New Mexico Community College; Susan Gebhardt-Burns, Norwalk Community College; David Hammontree, Oakland University; Elizabeth Harger, Colorado Christian University; James Harger, Colorado Christian University; Melanie Jenkins, Snow College; Elizabeth Kimball, Drew University; Katherine Knutson, Gustavus Adolphus College; Kathryn Lane, Northwestern Oklahoma State University; Ben Lauren, Florida International University; Tom Lindsley, Iowa State University; Janet Little, Virginia Western Community College; Loren Marquez, Salisbury University; Dennis Negron, Southern Adventist University; Angela Petit, Idaho State University; Jonathan Purkiss, Pulaski Technical College; Lisa Ruch, Bay Path College; Kay Siebler, Missouri Western State University; James Sodon, St. Louis Community College–Florissant Valley; Andrew Stout, Pace University; Verne Underwood, Rogue Community College; Samuel Waddell, York College of Pennsylvania; and Concetta Williams, Chicago State University.

Finally, and always, I continue to learn from my students, who serve as the major inspiration for just about everything I do; from the very best sisters, nieces, and nephews anyone has ever had; and from my spectacular grand-nieces, Audrey and Lila: this book is for all of you.

Andrea A. Lunsford

Our writing center promotes learning through doing, so the explanations and examples in *The Everyday Writer* are really helpful.

The Top Twenty* is always a great starting place.

*See Ch. 1.

One student wanted to cite a presentation by a Disney executive to a campus club. The transcript and slides weren't available.

We tried Purdue OWL, but we didn't know what search terms to use. The APA handbook is incredibly hard to use—there was no way to decipher it in time.

So I opened *The Everyday Writer*, flipped to the APA tab, and skimmed through the directory.* It was specific and helpful.

The format makes everything so easy!

*See Ch. 63.

I have tutored so much with the help of this handbook that I know any issues I might encounter are covered.

I'm Fernando Sanchez.

I'm a sophomore at San José State studying graphic design.

SAN JOSÉ STATE UNIVERSITY

I'm from a small country town called Arbuckle, near Sacramento.

When I grew up, it was normal for me to see people walking lambs down the street.

It's a different world here in Silicon Valley. I'm surrounded by companies that need design, that need new ideas.

Once I had to write an essay pointing out fallacies in an advertisement. There was so much I could say.

I go beyond the question. I have TOO MANY ideas.

So I ended up on clustering in *The Everyday Writer*,* for generating ideas.

*See 4d.

It took me a while to try clustering. But when I actually tried it, I could see how useful it is.

It kept me from dragging in information that didn't belong.

I could SEE when I was getting to something that wasn't related to my topic.

The Everyday Writer saved my grade for that class.

It's a friendly book. It's like sitting down with a teacher who's actually showing you: "Try this out!"

My name is He Wanhua. This is my first semester in the US.

I'm studying mathematics at Kennesaw State University in Marietta, Georgia.

KENNESAW STATE UNIVERSITY

I like music and dance, so I am always dancing with the local students.

I dance ballet, but they dance hip-hop. They are willing to help me learn.

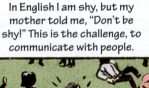

In English I am shy, but my mother told me, "Don't be shy!" This is the challenge, to communicate with people.

All Chinese students study English in primary school, but in China we don't get real practice.

Personal pronouns are different between Chinese and English. Sometimes I mix them up.

In China *she* and *her* are one word. I use LearningCurve with my handbook, and after I practice, I have improved.

Her is going
She cup of

Communicating in writing gives me time to think about my words.

When I write in English, I'm blunt in my description.

I never think about how to make my essay more vivid.

But *The Everyday Writer* explains different ways to develop writing, like definition or comparison.*

Learning these techniques improved my essay quality.

*See 6c.

My professor tells us, "Submit all your drafts in a folder."

The first draft always has many mistakes. I do a lot of revising and know I can finish better.

I'm Brett Bittiger from northeast Pennsylvania, a senior at Pace University.

I'm an English major and a business management minor—kind of a weird combination!

PACE UNIVERSITY

I'm hoping to play baseball professionally and then segueway to a career in a major league front office. My business classes require me to analyze different business situations, and I'm doing literary analysis for my English major. It's a challenge to navigate the different discourse communities.

BRETT BITTIGER 14

I also move between different spheres as a baseball player and a writing tutor.

I leave baseball practice, put on a nice shirt, and then go to the writing center.

I speak Spanish as a second language. As a tutor, I deal with a lot of multilingual students.

Many of them are grappling not only with a second language but with the expectations that accompany academic writing in the United States.

One of my early tutoring experiences was with a student who had a lot of trouble with the order of her words,* in making the transition from Spanish to English.

*See 37a.

She had a very strong voice as a writer.

I told her, "If you follow the advice in *The Everyday Writer* and get more comfortable with English word order...

...you can meet the conventions of US academic writing so you don't lose the meaning."

I think that session made a lightbulb come on for both of us.

SMACK

Writing is a way we define ourselves and make meaning out of the world.

Whether they're spoken or written, I'm a firm believer in the power of words.

My name is Jackson Kim, and I'm from Winchester, Virginia.

VIRGINIA MILITARY INSTITUTE

I really hated writing in elementary and middle school—I didn't think I was any good at it. But in high school I had a really good teacher who got me into English.

Now I'm a junior working on a degree in English at Virginia Military Institute.

I've spent a lot of time in the grammar section of *The Everyday Writer*. I needed to learn some basic grammar again when I came to college. Sentence-level issues can shape the way your argument is perceived, so I really love working with this section of the book.

I'm taking a legal writing class, and we're supposed to be really direct. The information on passive and active voice* in the book was really helpful.

*See 38g.

I have one instructor who is very strict with first drafts...

...but he allows us to keep revising until we get the grades we want. I got an essay back from him covered in comments, with a grade I was not happy with yet.

I brought it to a workshop in class. Looking through the feedback from other students was very intimidating.

I had no clue where to start. Some people liked a certain part of the essay, and other people said it was irrelevant.

The chapter "Reviewing, Revising, and Editing"* in *The Everyday Writer* helped me a ton.

I made a list of where the reviewers agreed and where they disagreed...

*See Ch. 7.

...so I was able to rank the comments in order of what I thought was most important.

It ended up being one of the essays that I'm most proud of writing.

Then I revised my essay, focusing on advancing and supporting the thesis.

I'm Kiara James.

I'm a sophomore at North Carolina Agricultural and Technical State University.

NORTH CAROLINA AGRICULTURAL & TECHNICAL STATE UNIVERSITY

Someday I want to be an inspector for the USDA, and I know I'll have to write reports about what I see and whether animals are being treated correctly.

When I got my first research assignment, I had never written a research paper before.

I didn't know what I should do and how I should set it up. So I used the research tab in *The Everyday Writer* to help me.

A lot of things were going in my mind—should I write about this subject? Should I write about that?

But then I read you should write about something you know something about, that you want to explore more fully.* That's what helped me the most.

*See 12a.

I already knew something about the topic I chose, but I also ended up learning a lot from my research.

I had never had to write in APA style, so I struggled with my resources section and citing everything correctly.

It's hard to remember what exactly you need to put in there—publisher, city, where everything goes, how it's formatted.

I referred to the handbook,* and it helped me a lot. I didn't have any points deducted for improperly citing my references!

*See Ch. 63.

I use it so much.

When I have a question, I know I can always look up the answer.

My name is Alec Braun, and I'm a sophomore at Iowa State University.

I'm studying business marketing and management.

IOWA STATE UNIVERSITY

My father runs a company that makes stock car parts and sells them across the nation.

After working with him, I thought that was something I might be interested in.

The Everyday Writer has been beneficial in making sure I'm writing effectively and getting the grades I want in my business classes.

The number one thing for me is the Top Twenty.* It's like a cheat sheet.

*See Ch. 1.

I wasn't sure where to put my commas, and that section of the book really helped me out.

It's such an easy fix if you know what you're doing, but if you don't, it's a bad error to have in your writing.

When I have questions, I go to this book, and it helps me figure out the answers.

Once I was creating a poem to put in a card for this girl, and my friends were making fun of me because my poem was so wrong.

We argued about what to capitalize and how to put the poem together. If I switched to a new line, should I capitalize the first word?

So I looked it up.*

*See 53a.

The card went over well!

Thanks, Everyday Writer!

The
Everyday
Writer

Writing Processes

There may be people who like various aspects of the writing process. For some, it may be the excitement of facing a blank page. (Hate them!) For others, it could be a sense of getting a sentence just right. (Jerks!) There may be those who like the revision process, who can go over what they've produced with a cold eye and a keen ear and feel a satisfaction in making it better. (Liars!)

— RACHEL TOOR

Writing Processes

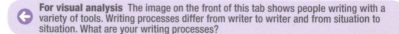

For visual analysis The image on the front of this tab shows people writing with a variety of tools. Writing processes differ from writer to writer and from situation to situation. What are your writing processes?

1 The Top Twenty: A Quick Guide to Troubleshooting Your Writing

Surface errors—grammar, punctuation, word choice, and other small-scale matters—don't always disturb readers. Whether your instructor marks an error in any particular assignment will depend on personal judgments about how serious and distracting it is and about what you should be focusing on in the draft. In addition, not all surface errors are consistently viewed as errors: some of the patterns identified in the research for this book are considered errors by some instructors but as stylistic options by others. Such differing opinions don't mean that there is no such thing as correctness in writing—only that *correctness always depends on some context,* on whether the choices a writer makes seem appropriate to readers.

Research for this book reveals a number of changes that have occurred in student writing over the past thirty years. First, writing assignments in first-year composition classes now focus less on personal narrative and much more on research essays and argument. As a result, students are now writing longer essays than they did twenty years ago and working much more often with sources, both print and digital. Thus it's no surprise that students today are struggling with the conventions for using and citing sources, a problem that did not show up in most earlier studies of student writing.

What else has changed? For starters, wrong-word errors are *by far the most common* errors among first-year student writers today. Thirty years ago, spelling errors were most common by a factor of more than three to one. The use of spell checkers has reduced the number of spelling errors in student writing—but spell checkers' suggestions may also be responsible for some (or many) of the wrong words students are using.

All writers want to be considered competent and careful. You know that your readers judge you by your control of the conventions you have agreed to use, even if the conventions change from time to time. To help you in producing writing that is conventionally correct, you should become familiar with the twenty most common error patterns among U.S. college students today, listed here in order of frequency. A brief explanation and examples of each error are provided in the following sections, and each error pattern is cross-referenced to other places in this book where you can find more detailed information and additional examples.

QUICK HELP

The Top Twenty

1. Wrong word
2. Missing comma after an introductory element
3. Incomplete or missing documentation
4. Vague pronoun reference
5. Spelling (including homonyms)
6. Mechanical error with a quotation
7. Unnecessary comma
8. Unnecessary or missing capitalization
9. Missing word
10. Faulty sentence structure
11. Missing comma with a nonrestrictive element
12. Unnecessary shift in verb tense
13. Missing comma in a compound sentence
14. Unnecessary or missing apostrophe (including *its/it's*)
15. Fused (run-on) sentence
16. Comma splice
17. Lack of pronoun-antecedent agreement
18. Poorly integrated quotation
19. Unnecessary or missing hyphen
20. Sentence fragment

---

1   Wrong word

> Religious texts, for them, take ~~prescience~~ *precedence* over other kinds of sources.

Prescience means "foresight," and *precedence* means "priority."

▶ The child suffered from a severe ~~allegory~~ *allergy* to peanuts.

Allegory is a spell checker's replacement for a misspelling of *allergy*.

▶ The panel discussed the ethical implications ~~on~~ *of* the situation.

Wrong-word errors can involve using a word with the wrong shade of meaning, using a word with a completely wrong meaning, or using a wrong preposition or another wrong word in an idiom. Selecting a word from a thesaurus without knowing its meaning, or allowing a spell checker to correct spelling automatically, can lead to wrong-word errors, so use these tools with care. If you have trouble with prepositions and idioms, memorize the standard usage. (See Chapter 29 on word choice and spelling and Chapter 44 on prepositions and idioms.)

2 Missing comma after an introductory element

▶ Determined to get the job done, we worked all weekend.

▶ Although the study was flawed, the results may still be useful.

Readers usually need a small pause—signaled by a comma—between an introductory word, phrase, or clause and the main part of the sentence. Use a comma after every introductory element. When the introductory element is very short, you don't always need a comma, but including it is never wrong. (See 47a.)

3 Incomplete or missing documentation

▶ Satrapi says, "When we're afraid, we lose all sense of analysis and reflection." *(263).*

This quotation comes from a print source, so a page number is needed.

▶ Some experts agree that James Joyce wrote two of the five best novels of all time. *("100 Best Novels").*

The source of this information should be identified (this online source has no page numbers).

Cite each source you refer to in the text, following the guidelines of the documentation style you are using. (The preceding examples follow MLA style—see Chapters 57–60; for other styles, see Chapters 61–67.) Omitting documentation can result in charges of plagiarism (see Chapter 15).

4 Vague pronoun reference

POSSIBLE REFERENCE TO MORE THAN ONE WORD

▶ Transmitting radio signals by satellite is a way of overcoming the

the airwaves
problem of scarce airwaves and limiting how ~~they~~ are used.

In the original sentence, *they* could refer to the signals or to the airwaves.

REFERENCE IMPLIED BUT NOT STATED

a policy
▶ The company prohibited smoking, ~~which~~ many employees

resented.

What does *which* refer to? The editing clarifies what employees resented.

A pronoun should refer clearly to the word or words it replaces (called the *antecedent*) elsewhere in the sentence or in a previous sentence. If more than one word could be the antecedent, or if no specific antecedent is present, edit to make the meaning clear. (See Chapter 41.)

5 Spelling (including homonyms)

Reagan
▶ Ronald ~~Regan~~ won the election in a landslide.

Everywhere
▶ ~~Every where~~ we went, we saw crowds of tourists.

The most common misspellings today are those that spell checkers cannot identify. The categories that spell checkers are most likely to miss include homonyms, compound words incorrectly spelled as separate words, and proper nouns, particularly names. After you run the spell checker, proofread carefully for errors such as these—and be sure to run the spell checker to catch other kinds of spelling mistakes. (See 29f.)

6 Mechanical error with a quotation

▶ "I grew up the victim of a disconcerting confusion$_{\wedge}$"/Rodriguez says (249).

The comma should be placed *inside* the quotation marks.

Follow conventions when using quotation marks with commas (47h), colons (52d), and other punctuation (51f). Always use quotation marks in pairs, and follow the guidelines of your documentation style for block quotations (51b). Use quotation marks for titles of short works (51c), but use italics for titles of long works (55a).

7 Unnecessary comma

BEFORE CONJUNCTIONS IN COMPOUND CONSTRUCTIONS THAT ARE NOT COMPOUND SENTENCES

▶ This conclusion applies to the United States/and to the rest of the world.

No comma is needed before *and* because it is joining two phrases that modify the same verb, *applies*.

WITH RESTRICTIVE ELEMENTS

▶ Many parents/of gifted children/do not want them to skip a grade.

No comma is needed to set off the restrictive phrase *of gifted children*, which is necessary to indicate which parents the sentence is talking about.

Do not use commas to set off restrictive elements that are necessary to the meaning of the words they modify. Do not use a comma before a coordinating conjunction (*and, but, for, nor, or, so, yet*) when the conjunction does not join parts of a compound sentence. Do not use a comma before the first or after the last item in a series, between a subject and verb, between a verb and its object or complement, or between a preposition and its object. (See 47j.)

8 Unnecessary or missing capitalization

▶ Some ~~Traditional~~ *traditional* Chinese ~~Medicines~~ *medicines* containing ~~Ephedra~~ *ephedra* remain legal.

Capitalize proper nouns and proper adjectives, the first words of sentences, and important words in titles, along with certain words indicating directions and family relationships. Do not capitalize most other words. When in doubt, check a dictionary. (See Chapter 53.)

9 Missing word

> *against*
> ▶ The site foreman discriminated ^ women and promoted men with less
>
> experience.

Proofread carefully for omitted words, including prepositions (44a), parts of two-part verbs (44b), and correlative conjunctions (36g). Be particularly careful not to omit words from quotations.

10 Faulty sentence structure

> *High*
> ▶ ~~The information which high~~ school athletes are presented with
>
> *they*
> ~~mainly includes~~ information on what credits needed to graduate, ~~and~~
>
> *colleges to try*
> ~~thinking about the college~~ which ~~athletes are trying~~ to play for,
>
> *how to*
> and apply.
> ^

A sentence that starts out with one kind of structure and then changes to another kind can confuse readers. Make sure that each sentence contains a subject and a verb (37a), that subjects and predicates make sense together (31b), and that comparisons have clear meanings (31e). When you join elements (such as subjects or verb phrases) with a coordinating conjunction, make sure that the elements have parallel structures (see Chapter 32).

11 Missing comma with a nonrestrictive element

> ▶ Marina, who was the president of the club, was first to speak.
>   ^   ^

The clause *who was the president of the club* does not affect the basic meaning of the sentence: Marina was first to speak.

A nonrestrictive element gives information not essential to the basic meaning of the sentence. Use commas to set off a nonrestrictive element (47c).

12   Unnecessary shift in verb tense

▶ Priya was watching the great blue heron. Then she ~~slips~~ *slipped* and ~~falls~~ *fell* into

the swamp.

Verbs that shift from one tense to another with no clear reason can confuse readers (33a).

13   Missing comma in a compound sentence

▶ Meredith waited for Samir**,** and her sister grew impatient.

> Without the comma, a reader may think at first that Meredith waited for both Samir and her sister.

A compound sentence consists of two or more parts that could each stand alone as a sentence. When the parts are joined by a coordinating conjunction, use a comma before the conjunction to indicate a pause between the two thoughts (47b).

14   Unnecessary or missing apostrophe (including *its/it's*)

▶ Overambitious parents can be very harmful to a ~~childs~~ *child's* well-being.

▶ The car is lying on ~~it's~~ *its* side in the ditch. ~~Its~~ *It's* a white 2004 Passat.

To make a noun possessive, add either an apostrophe and an *-s* (*Ed's book*) or an apostrophe alone (*the boys' gym*). Do not use an apostrophe in the possessive pronouns *ours*, *yours*, and *hers*. Use *its* to mean *belonging to it*; use *it's* only when you mean *it is* or *it has*. (See Chapter 50.)

15   Fused (run-on) sentence

▶ Klee's paintings seem simple**,** *but* they are very sophisticated.

▶ *Although* ~~She~~ *she* doubted the value of meditation**,** she decided to try it once.

A fused sentence (also called a *run-on*) joins clauses that could each stand alone as a sentence with no punctuation or words to link them. Fused sentences must either be divided into separate sentences or joined by adding words or punctuation. (See Chapter 45.)

16 Comma splice

for
▶ I was strongly attracted to her, she was beautiful and funny.

that
▶ We hated the meat loaf/the cafeteria served ~~it~~ every Friday.

A comma splice occurs when only a comma separates clauses that could each stand alone as a sentence. To correct a comma splice, you can insert a semicolon or period, connect the clauses with a word such as *and* or *because*, or restructure the sentence. (See Chapter 45.)

17 Lack of pronoun-antecedent agreement

All students   *uniforms.*
▶ ~~Every student~~ must provide their own ~~uniform.~~

its
▶ Each of the puppies thrived in ~~their~~ new home.

Pronouns must agree with their antecedents both in gender (male or female) and in number (singular or plural). Many indefinite pronouns, such as *everyone* and *each*, are always singular. When a singular antecedent can refer to a man or a woman, either rewrite the sentence to make the antecedent plural or to eliminate the pronoun, or use *his or her*, *he or she*, and so on. When antecedents are joined by *or* or *nor*, the pronoun should always agree with the closer antecedent. A collective noun such as *team* can be either singular or plural, depending on whether the members are seen as a group or as individuals. (See 41f.)

18 Poorly integrated quotation

showed how color affects taste:
▶ Schlosser cites a 1970s study that "Once it became apparent that the

steak was actually blue and the fries were green, some people became

ill" (565).

According to Lars Eighner,
▶ "Dumpster diving has serious drawbacks as a way of life" (~~Eighner~~

383). Finding edible food is especially tricky.

Quotations should fit smoothly into the surrounding sentence structure. They should be linked clearly to the writing around them (usually with a signal phrase) rather than dropped abruptly into the writing. (See 15b.)

> **QUICK HELP**

Taking a Writing Inventory

One way to learn from your mistakes is to take a writing inventory. It can help you think critically and analytically about how to improve your writing skills.

1. Collect two or three pieces of your writing to which either your instructor or other students have responded.

2. Read through these writings, adding your own comments about their strengths and weaknesses. How do your comments compare with those of others?

3. Group all the comments into three categories — *broad content issues* (use of evidence and sources, attention to purpose and audience, and overall impression), *organization and presentation* (overall and paragraph-level organization, sentence structure and style, and formatting), and *surface errors* (problems with wrong words, spelling, grammar, punctuation, and mechanics).

4. Make an inventory of your own strengths in each category.

5. Study your errors. Mark every instructor and peer comment that suggests or calls for an improvement, and put all these comments in a list. Consult the relevant part of this book or speak with your instructor if you don't understand a comment.

6. Make a list of the top problem areas you need to work on. How can you make improvements? Then note at least two strengths that you can build on in your writing. Reflect on your findings in a writing log that you can add to as the class proceeds.

19 Unnecessary or missing hyphen

▶ This paper looks at fictional and real‸life examples.

A compound adjective modifying a noun that follows it requires a hyphen.

▶ The buyers want to fix⁄up the house and resell it.

A two-word verb should not be hyphenated.

A compound adjective that appears before a noun needs a hyphen. However, be careful not to hyphenate two-word verbs or word groups that serve as subject complements. (See Chapter 56.)

20 Sentence fragment

NO SUBJECT

▶ Marie Antoinette spent huge sums of money on herself and her

Her extravagance
favelites. ~~And~~ helped bring on the French Revolution.

NO COMPLETE VERB

was
▶ The old aluminum boat sitting on its trailer.

BEGINNING WITH A SUBORDINATING WORD

where
▶ We returned to the drugstore/, ~~Where~~ we waited for our buddies.

A sentence fragment is part of a sentence that is written as if it were a complete sentence. Reading your draft out loud, backwards, sentence by sentence, will help you spot sentence fragments. (See Chapter 46.)

Expectations for College Writing

Your college instructors—and your future colleagues and supervisors—will expect you to demonstrate your ability to think critically, to consider ethical issues, to find as well as solve problems, to do effective research, to work productively with people of widely different backgrounds, and to present the knowledge you construct in a variety of ways and in a variety of genres and media. Your success will depend on communicating clearly and on making appropriate choices for the context.

2a Move between social and academic writing.

Social connections today involve so much writing that you probably write more out of class than in class. In fact, social writing has opened doors for writers like never before. Writing on social networking sites allows writers to get almost instant feedback, and anticipating responses from an audience often has the effect of making online writers very savvy: they know the importance of analyzing the audience and of using an appropriate style, level of formality, and tone to suit the online occasion.

As you know, writers on Twitter compose in short bursts of no more than 140 characters. By tagging content, tweeting at groups and individuals, and pointing toward links, they can start discussions, participate in ongoing conversations, and invite others to join in. Here are two representative tweets from the Twitter feed of Stephanie Parker, a college student whose interests include technology and Korean pop culture.

sparker2

Rain's over, going to Trader Joe's to buy some healthy stuff to fight this cold . . . suggestions?

Watching Queen Seon Duk/선덕여왕 on **@dramafever**, love it so far! **http://www.dramafever.com/drama/56/ #nowplaying**

In these tweets, Stephanie Parker shows a keen awareness both of the audiences she is trying to reach on Twitter and of two very common purposes for this kind of informal writing—to seek information (in the first tweet, about foods to fight off a cold) and to share information (in the second tweet, about her view of a popular Korean drama, with a link so readers can check it out for themselves).

Like Parker, many young writers today are adept at informal social writing across a range of genres and media. You may not think consciously about the audience you'll reach in a Facebook post or a tweet, or about your purpose for writing in such spaces, but you are probably more skilled than you give yourself credit for when it comes to making appropriate choices for your informal writing.

Of course, informal writing is not the only writing skill a student needs to master. You'll also need to move back and forth between informal social writing and formal academic writing, and to write across a whole range of genres and media. Look closely at your informal writing: What do you assume about your audience? What is your purpose? How do you achieve a particular tone? In short, why do you write the way you do in these situations? Analyzing the choices you make in a given writing context will help you develop the ability to make good choices in other contexts as well—an ability that will allow you to move between social and academic writing.

2b Position yourself as an academic writer.

If you're like most students, you probably have less familiarity with academic writing contexts than you do with informal contexts. You may not have written anything much longer than five pages of formal academic writing before coming to college, and you may have done only minimal research. The contexts for your college writing will require you to face new challenges and even new definitions of *writing*; you may be asked, for example, to create a persuasive website or to research, write, and deliver a multimedia presentation. If you grew up speaking and writing in other languages, the transition to producing effective college work can be especially complicated. Not only do you have to learn new information and new ways of thinking and arguing in unfamiliar rhetorical situations, but you also have to do it in a language that may not come naturally to you.

Expectations for U.S. academic writing

Instructors sometimes assume that students are already familiar with their expectations for college writing. To complicate the matter further, there is no single "correct" style of communication in any country, including the United States. Effective oral styles differ from effective written styles, and what is considered good writing in one field of study is not necessarily appropriate in another. Within a field, different rhetorical situations and genres may require different ways of writing. In business, for example, memos are usually short and simple, while a

---

TALKING THE TALK

Conventions

"Aren't conventions just rules with another name?" Not entirely. Conventions — agreed-on language practices of grammar, punctuation, and style — convey shorthand information from writer to reader. In college writing, you will generally want to follow the conventions of standard academic English unless you have a good reason to do otherwise. But unlike hard-and-fast rules, conventions are flexible; a convention appropriate for one time or situation may be inappropriate for another. You may also choose to ignore conventions at times to achieve a particular effect. (You might, for example, write a sentence fragment rather than a full sentence, such as the *Not entirely* at the beginning of this box.) As you become more experienced and confident in your writing, you will develop a sense of which conventions to apply in different writing situations.

---

market analysis report may require complex paragraphs with tables, graphs, and diagrams. Even the variety of English often referred to as "standard" covers a wide range of styles (see Chapter 28). In spite of this wide variation, several features are often associated with U.S. academic English in general:

- conventional grammar, spelling, punctuation, and mechanics
- organization that links ideas explicitly (5d)
- an easy-to-read type size and typeface, conventional margins, and double spacing
- explicitly stated claims supported by evidence (Chapter 11)
- careful documentation of all sources (Chapters 57–67)
- consistent use of an appropriate level of formality (28c and 29a)
- conventional use of idioms (Chapter 44)
- use of conventional academic formats, such as literature reviews, research essays, lab reports, and research proposals

New contexts often require the use of different sets of conventions, strategies, and resources, so ask your instructor for advice, or check with your writing center, local library, or friends for examples of the kind of text you need to create.

Authority

In the United States, most college instructors expect student writers to begin to establish their own authority—to become constructive critics who can analyze and interpret the work of others. But what does establishing authority mean in practice?

- Assume that your opinions count (as long as they are informed rather than tossed out with little thought) and that your audience expects you to present them in a well-reasoned manner.
- Show your familiarity with the ideas and works of others, both from the assigned course reading and from good points your instructor and classmates have made.

Directness and clarity

Your instructors will most often expect you to get to the point quickly and to be direct throughout an essay or other project. Research for this book confirms that readers depend on writers to organize and present their material—using sections, paragraphs, sentences, arguments, details, and source citations—in ways that aid understanding. Good academic writing prepares readers for what is coming next, provides definitions, and includes topic sentences. (See 26c for a description of the organization that instructors often prefer in student essays.) To achieve directness in your writing, try the following strategies:

- State your main point early and clearly.

- Avoid hedging your statements. Instead of writing *I think the facts reveal*, come right out and say *The facts reveal*.

- Avoid digressions. If you use an anecdote or example from personal experience, be sure it relates directly to the point you are making.

- Use appropriate evidence, such as examples and concrete details, to support each point.

- Make transitions from point to point obvious and clear. The first sentence of a new paragraph should reach back to the paragraph before and then look forward to what is to come (see Chapter 6).

- Guide readers by using effective and varied sentences that link together smoothly (see Chapter 6).

- Follow logical organizational patterns (see Chapter 6).

- Design and format the project appropriately for the audience and purpose you have in mind (see Chapter 22).

- If your project is lengthy, you may also want to use brief summary statements between sections, but avoid unnecessary repetition.

2c Read and listen actively.

Your instructors expect you to be an active reader and listener—to offer informed opinions. Stating your opinion doesn't require you to be negative or combative, just engaged with the class and the text.

Active reading and listening

The following strategies (and the detailed advice in Chapter 9) will help you read and listen actively.

- Note the name of the author and the date and place of publication, or the title and author of the presentation; these items can give you clues to the writer's purpose and intended audience.

- Understand the overall content of a text or presentation well enough to summarize it (15a).

- Formulate critical questions, and bring these questions up in class.

- Understand each sentence, and make direct connections between sentences and paragraphs. Keep track of repeated themes or images, and figure out how they contribute to the entire piece.
- Note the author's attitude toward and assumptions about the topic. Then you can speculate on how the attitude and assumptions may have affected the author's thinking.
- Note the writer's sources: what evidence does the writer rely on, and why?
- Distinguish between the author's stance and the author's reporting on the stances of others. Watch for key phrases that signal an opposing argument: *while some have argued that*, *in the past*, and so on.
- Go beyond content to notice organizational patterns, use of sources, and choice of words.
- Annotate important readings (9b and c). Make notes that record your questions, challenges, or counter-examples to the text.
- If the readings allow you to post a comment, take advantage of this opportunity to get your voice into the conversation.

Class participation

Speaking up in class is viewed as inappropriate or even rude in some cultures. In U.S. academic settings, however, doing so is expected and encouraged. Indeed, some instructors assign credit for participation in class discussions. The challenge is to contribute without losing track of the overall conversation or aims of the class and without monopolizing the discussion. These guidelines can help:

- Be prepared.
- Follow the flow of conversation. Taking notes can help you listen purposefully in a classroom.
- Make sure your comments are relevant. Ask a key question, take the conversation in a new direction, or summarize or analyze what others have said.
- Be specific in your comments: *The passage in the middle of page 42 backs up what you're saying* is more useful than *I agree*.

2d   Plan research.

Much of the work you do in college may turn an informal curiosity into various kinds of more formal research: you might start by wondering how many students on your campus are vegetarians, for example, and end up with a research project for a sociology class that then becomes part of a multimedia presentation for a campus organization. Many of your writing assignments will require extensive formal research with a wide range of sources from various media as well as information drawn from observations, interviews, or surveys.

Research can help you access important information that you didn't know, even if you know a topic very well. And no matter what you discover, college research is an important tool for establishing credibility with your audience members and thus gaining their confidence. Often, what you write will be only as good as the research on which it is based. (For more on research, see Chapters 12–16.)

2e Use digital tools effectively.

Your instructors will probably expect you to communicate both in and out of class using a variety of media. You may be asked to post to course management systems, lists, blogs, and wikis, and you may respond to the work of others on such sites. In addition, you will probably contact your instructor and classmates using email and text messages. Because electronic communication is so common, it's easy to fall into the habit of  writing very informally. If you forget to adjust style and voice for different occasions and readers, you may undermine your own intentions.

Best practices for formal messages and posts

Email was once seen as highly informal, but you will probably use it today mainly for more formal purposes, particularly to communicate for work and for school. When writing most academic and professional messages, then, or when posting to a public list that may be read by people you don't know well, follow the conventions of standard academic English (2a), and be careful not to offend or irritate your audience—remember that jokes may be read as insults and that ALL CAPS may look like shouting. Finally, proofread to make sure your message is clear and free of errors, and that it is addressed to your intended audience, before you hit SEND.

DISCUSSION LISTS AND COMMENTS

- Avoid unnecessary criticism of others' spelling or language. If a message is unclear, ask politely for a clarification. If you disagree with an assertion, offer what you believe to be the correct information, but don't insult the writer.

- If you think you've been insulted, give the writer the benefit of the doubt. Replying with patience establishes your credibility and helps you appear mature and fair.

- For email discussion lists, decide whether to reply off-list to the sender of a message or to the whole group, and be careful to use REPLY or REPLY ALL accordingly to avoid potential embarrassment.

- Keep in mind that more people than you think may be reading your messages.

EMAIL

- Use a subject line that states your purpose clearly.

- Use a formal greeting and closing (*Dear Ms. Aulie* rather than *Hi*).

- Keep messages as concise as possible.

- Conclude your message with your name and email address.

- Ask for permission before forwarding a sensitive message from someone else.

- Consider your email messages permanent and always findable, even if you delete them. Many people have been embarrassed (or worse, prosecuted) because of email trails.

- Make sure that the username on the email account you use for formal messages does not present a poor impression. If your username is *Party2Nite*, consider changing it, or use your school account for academic and professional communication.

Best practices for informal situations

Sometimes audiences expect informality. When you write in certain situations—Twitter posts, for example, and most text messages—you can play with (or ignore) the conventions you would probably follow in formal writing. Most people receiving text messages expect shorthand such as *u* for "you," but be cautious about using such shortcuts with an employer or instructor. You may want to stick to a more formal method of contact if your employer or instructor has not explicitly invited you to send text messages—or texted you first.

Even when you think the situation calls for an informal tone, be attuned to your audience's needs and your purpose for writing. And when writing for any online writing space that allows users to say almost anything about themselves or to comment freely on the postings of others, bear in mind that anonymity sometimes makes online writers feel less inhibited than they would be in a face-to-face discussion. Don't say anything you want to remain private, and even if you disagree with another writer, avoid personal attacks.

Rhetorical Situations **3**

What do a documented essay on recent global warming research, a Facebook message objecting to the latest change to the site's privacy policy, a tweet to other students in your psychology class, a comment on a blog post, a letter to the editor of your local newspaper, and a website devoted to sustainability all have in common? To communicate effectively, the writers of these texts must analyze their particular situation and then respond to it in appropriate ways.

3a Make good choices for your rhetorical situation.

If it is true that "no man [or woman!] is an island," then it is equally true that no piece of writing is an island, isolated and alone. Instead, writing is connected to a web of other writings as a writer extends, responds to, or challenges what others say. All writing exists within a rich and broad context, and all writers listen and respond to what others have said, even as they shape messages about particular topics and for particular purposes that help them connect to their audiences.

A *rhetorical situation* is the full set of circumstances surrounding any communication. When you communicate, whether you're posting on a social networking site, creating a video, or writing an essay for your psychology class, you need to consider and make careful choices about all the elements of your situation.

Elements of the rhetorical situation

The rhetorical situation is often depicted as a triangle to present the idea that three important elements are closely connected—your *text*, including your topic and the message you want to convey (3b); your role as *communicator*, including your purpose and your stance, or attitude toward the text (3c); and your *audience* (3d). If all the pieces making up the larger triangle don't work together, the communication will not be effective. But important as these elements are, they are connected to a *context* that shapes all the angles of the triangle. Considering context fully requires you to consider many other questions about the rhetorical situation, such as what kind of text you should create (3e) and what conventions you should follow to meet audience expectations for creating and delivering the text (3f).

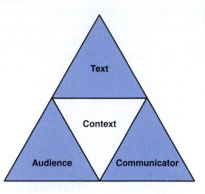

Informal and formal rhetorical situations

Most people are accustomed to writing in some rhetorical situations without analyzing them closely. When you post something on a friend's social networking page, for example, you probably spend little time pondering what your friend values or finds funny, how to phrase your words, which links or photos would best emphasize your point, or why you're taking the time to post. However, academic and other formal rhetorical situations may seem less familiar than the social writing you share with friends. Until you understand clearly what such situations demand of you, allow extra time to analyze the overall context, the topic and message, the purpose and stance, the audience, and other elements carefully.

The opportune moment (kairos)

In ancient Greece, Kairos, the god of opportunity, was depicted as running, with a prominent lock of hair on his forehead but a bald head in back. Seizing the opportune moment meant grabbing the hair as Kairos approached; once he passed, the moment was gone.

RHETORICAL SITUATIONS: Choose Your Topic

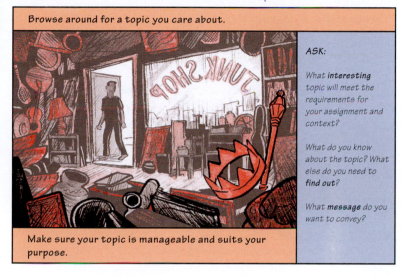

Browse around for a topic you care about.

ASK:

What **interesting** topic will meet the requirements for your assignment and context?

What do you know about the topic? What else do you need to **find out**?

What **message** do you want to convey?

Make sure your topic is manageable and suits your purpose.

Considering rhetorical situations means thinking hard about *kairos*, the appropriate time and the most opportune ways to get your point across. Take advantage of *kairos* to choose appropriate timing and current examples and evidence for your rhetorical situation.

3b Plan your text's topic and message.

An instructor or employer may tell you what topic to write about, but sometimes the choice will be yours. When the topic is left open, you may be tempted to put off getting started because you can't decide what to do. Experienced writers say that the best way to choose a topic is literally to let it choose you. Look to the topics that compel, puzzle, confuse, or pose a problem for you: these are more likely to engage your interest and hence produce your best writing.

Deciding on a broad topic is an essential step before beginning to write, but you need to go further than that to decide what you want to say about your topic and how you will shape what you want to say into a clear, powerful message.

RHETORICAL SITUATIONS: Consider Your Purpose and Stance

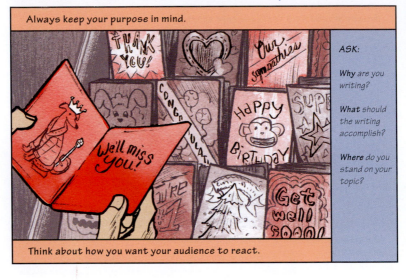

Always keep your purpose in mind.

ASK:

Why are you writing?

What should the writing accomplish?

Where do you stand on your topic?

Think about how you want your audience to react.

3c Consider your purpose and stance as a communicator.

Whether you choose to communicate for purposes of your own or have that purpose set for you by an instructor or employer, you should consider the purpose for any communication carefully. For the writing you do that is not connected to a class or work assignment, your purpose may be very clear to you: you may want to convince neighbors to support a community garden, get others in your office to help keep the kitchen clean, or tell blog readers what you like or hate about your new phone. Even so, analyzing exactly what you want to accomplish and why can make you a more effective communicator.

Purposes for academic assignments

An academic assignment may clearly explain why, for whom, and about what you are supposed to write. But sometimes college assignments seem to come out of the blue, with no specific purpose, audience, or topic. Because comprehending the assignment fully and accurately is crucial to your success in responding to it, make every effort to understand what your instructor expects. Discuss any questions you have with your instructor or your classmates.

TALKING THE TALK

Assignments

"How do instructors come up with these assignments?" Assignments, like other kinds of writing, reflect particular rhetorical contexts that vary from instructor to instructor. Assignments also change over time. The assignment for an 1892 college writing contest was to write an essay "on coal." In the twentieth century, many college writing assignments asked students to write about their own experiences; in research conducted for this textbook in the 1980s, the most common writing assignment was a personal narrative. As expectations for college students — and the needs of society — change over time, assignments also change. Competing effectively in today's workforce calls for high-level thinking, for being able to argue convincingly, and for knowing how to do the research necessary to support a claim — so it's no surprise that college writing courses today give students assignments that allow them to develop such skills. A recent study of first-year college writing in the United States found that by far the most common assignment today asks students to compose a researched argument. (See Chapters 9–11.)

- What is the primary purpose of the piece of writing — to explain? to persuade? to entertain? to achieve some other purpose?

- What purpose did the person who gave you the assignment want to achieve — to make sure you have understood something? to evaluate your thinking and writing abilities? to test your ability to think outside the box?

- What are your own purposes in this piece of writing — to respond to a question? to learn about a topic? to communicate your ideas? to express feelings? How can you achieve these goals?

- What, exactly, does the assignment ask you to do? Look for such words as *analyze*, *classify*, *compare*, *define*, *describe*, *explain*, *prove*, and *survey*. Remember that these words may differ in meaning from discipline to discipline.

Stances for academic assignments

Thinking about your own position as a communicator and your attitude toward your text — your rhetorical stance — is just as important as making sure you communicate effectively.

- Where are you coming from on this topic? What is your overall attitude toward your topic? How strong are your opinions?

- What social, political, religious, personal, or other influences account for your attitude? Will you need to explain any of these influences?

RHETORICAL SITUATIONS: Imagine Your Audience

Think about a target audience for this text.

ASK:

Who are they? How are they **like** you? How are they **different**?

How will you **reach** this audience?

What do they already know and **care** about?

Remember to focus on getting your message across.

- What is most interesting to you about the topic? Why do you care about it?
- What conclusions do you think you might reach as you complete your text?
- How will you establish your credibility? How will you show you are knowledgeable and trustworthy?
- How will you convey your stance? Should you use words alone, combine words and images, include sound, or include something else?

3d Analyze your audience.

Every communicator can benefit from thinking carefully about who the audience is, what the audience already knows or thinks, and what the audience needs and expects to find out. One of the characteristics of an effective communicator is the ability to write for a variety of audiences, using language, style, and evidence appropriate to particular readers, listeners, or viewers. Even if your text can theoretically reach people all over the world, focus your analysis on those you most want or need to reach and those who are most likely to take an interest.

Informal and formal audiences

For some informal writing, you know exactly who your audience is, and communicating appropriately may be a simple matter. It's still worth remembering that when you post in a public space, you may not be aware of how large and varied your online audience can be. Can your friend's parents, or her prospective employer, see your posts on her Facebook page? Who's reading the blogs you comment on?

Even if you write with intuitive ease in tweets and texts to friends, you may struggle when asked to write for an instructor or for a "general audience." You may wonder, for example, what a general audience might know about your topic, what they value, or what evidence they will find persuasive. When you are new to academic writing, making assumptions about such questions can be tricky. If you can identify samples of writing that appeal to a similar audience, look for clues about what that audience expects; if still in doubt, check with your instructor or drop by your campus writing center.

Appropriate language for an audience

- Is the language of your text as clear as it needs to be for your audience? If your readers can't understand what you mean, they're not likely to accept your points.

- For academic writing, should you use any vernacular or specialized varieties of English along with academic English? any occupational, professional, regional, or ethnic varieties? any words from a different language? any dialogue? (See Chapter 28.) How will these choices help you connect to your audience?

As you think about your audience, consider how you want them to respond to both the words and the images you use. And remember that sound and images can evoke very strong responses in your audience and can affect the tone of your writing (3f), so choose them with special care.

 FOR MULTILINGUAL WRITERS

Bringing In Other Languages

Even when you write in English, you may want or need to include words, phrases, or whole passages in another language. If so, consider whether your readers will understand that language and whether you need to provide a translation. See 28d for more on bringing in other languages.

CONSIDERING DISABILITIES

Your Whole Audience

Remember that considering your whole audience means thinking about members with varying abilities and special needs. Approximately one in five Americans was living with a disability in the year 2010. All writers need to think carefully about how their words reach out and connect with such very diverse audiences.

3e Think about genres and media.

You no doubt are familiar with the word *genre* in terms of movies (comedy, action) or music (hip-hop, punk). But *genre* is also used to describe forms of writing, such as research essays and lab reports. Genres and media are not the same—the genre of a research project or promotional flyer might be created using either digital or print media, for example—but the two categories are related. Over time, genres develop conventions—such as the types of content, rhetorical strategies, and kinds of language used. Most audiences begin to expect those conventional features in the genre. But genres are flexible, not cookie-cutter templates.

Features of genres

If you are not sure what kind of text you are supposed to write, ask your instructor, classmates, or a writing center tutor for clarification and examples. Look carefully at the samples to make sure you understand the conventional expectations, and ask questions like these about the genre's typical features.

- What does the genre look like? How is the text laid out? How are headings, sidebars, footnotes, and other elements incorporated into the main text? If visuals or media elements are included, how and why are they used? (See Chapter 22.)

- How long is a typical work in this genre? How long is each paragraph or section?

- What topics are usually found in this genre? What type of content is rare?

- How does the text introduce the topic? Is the main point stated explicitly or implicitly?

- How does each section contribute to the main point? How is the main point of each section supported?

TALKING THE TALK

Genre Names

"What does my instructor mean by 'essay'?" Writing assignments often mention a specific genre, such as *essay* or *report*, but genre names can be confusing. The same genre may work differently in different contexts, or people may use the same term in various ways. Depending on the field, an essay might be a personal narrative, a critical analysis, or even a journal article. Even when the name of the genre sounds familiar to you, look for specific instructions for each assignment or analyze examples provided by the instructor.

- How are the key terms defined? What background information is provided?

- Are sentences short, long, simple, complicated? Is passive voice common?

- What is the level of formality? Does the text use contractions such as *he's* and *can't* instead of *he is* and *cannot*? (50b)

- Does the text take a personal stance (*I, we*), address the audience directly (*you*), or talk about the subject without explicitly referring to the writer or the reader?

- Does the genre use technical terms (jargon)? If so, how common are they? Does the genre use slang or other common conversational expressions?

- How many sources are used in the text? How are they introduced? Are sources mentioned in the text, cited in parentheses, or both?

- What medium is typically used for this genre? Are visual images or audio commonly used? If so, for what purposes?

- Who reads this genre, and why? Does the genre usually aim to inform, to persuade, to entertain, or to serve some other purpose?

- How are the characteristics of the text similar to or different from similar genres that you have encountered elsewhere?

- How much latitude do you have in ignoring or stretching some of the boundaries of the genre?

Preparation

Plan ahead to allow the amount of time necessary for composing your text, and make sure that you understand limitations—such as time or word count—for the length of the final product. Consider the media you will need to use, and make sure you have access to any technology required—and any training necessary to use it well. If the genre will require you to contact or collaborate with other people, allow time to find and work with them effectively. Do you need to make any other preparations to create a text that fulfills the demands of the genre?

Multimodal genres for academic work

Much college writing is still done on paper in traditional genres, but this is changing. You may be asked, or may be able to choose, to create multimodal writing using audio, video, images, and words as well as written-word projects. Make sure that your choices are appropriate for your topic, purpose, audience, and genre. You may start off planning to write a traditional print-based academic essay and then discover as you proceed that a different genre or medium may offer more effective ways to communicate your point. One student, Will Rogers, who had been assigned to write an essay about something that most people took for granted, focused on a giant construction crane. When he interviewed the crane's operator, who had left his first year in college to take this job, the student decided that his project would work better—and be more powerful—as a video. That way, viewers could actually see the crane operator and hear his voice as he described the decisions he had made.

You may be asked to create a work in one genre or medium, such as a print-based research project, and translate it to another type of writing, such as a multimedia presentation, podcast, or scrapbook. Such translations may not be as straightforward as they seem. Just as filmmakers may omit content, streamline plot, and conflate characters when they create a movie version of a book, developing a solid thesis and supporting it effectively may require different strategies if you are turning a paper-based work into a video, a PowerPoint presentation, or some digital form.

3f   Consider language and style.

Although most of your college writing will be in standard academic English, you may also need to use specialized occupational or professional varieties of English—those characteristic of medicine, say, or music. You may wish to use regional, communal, or other varieties of English to connect with certain audiences or to catch the sound of someone's spoken words. You may even need to use words from a language other than English—in quoting someone, perhaps, or in using certain technical terms. Think about what languages and varieties of English will be most appropriate for reaching your audience and accomplishing your purposes (see Chapter 28).

You will also want to think carefully about style: should you be casual and breezy, somewhat informal, formal, or extremely formal? The style you choose will call for certain kinds of sentence structures, organizational patterns, and word choices. And your style will be important in creating the tone you want, one that is appropriate to your assignment, audience, topic, purpose, and genre.

Remember that visual and audio elements can influence the tone of your writing as much as the words you choose. Such elements create associations in viewers' minds: one audience may react more positively than another to an element such as a rap or heavy metal soundtrack, for example—and a presentation with a heavy metal accompaniment will make a far different impression than the same presentation with an easy-listening soundtrack. Writers can influence the way their work is perceived by carefully analyzing their audience and choosing audio and visual elements that set a mood appropriate to the point they want to make.

3g A sample rhetorical situation

Let's take an example of how one writer analyzes a rhetorical situation. Emily Lesk, a student in a first-year English course, gets an assignment that asks her to "explore the ways in which one or more media have affected an aspect of American identity." (More examples of Emily's work appear in the following chapters.) Because Emily is interested in advertising, she plans first to investigate how advertising might help shape American identity. Deciding that such a broad topic is not manageable in the time she has available, however, she shifts her focus to advertising for one company that seems particularly "American," Coca-Cola.

Since Emily's primary audience includes her instructor and her classmates, she needs to find ways to connect with them on an emotional as well as a logical level. She will do so, she decides, first by telling a story about being drawn into buying Coca-Cola products (even though she didn't really like the soft drink) because of the power of the advertising. She thinks that others in her audience may have had similar experiences. Here is a portion of her story and the visual she chose to illustrate it:

macmillanhighered.com/everyday6e

ⓓ Drafting > Video Prompt: Looking for the essential points

ⓔ Presentations > Student Writing: Presentation, Shuqiao Song

Even before setting foot in the Promised Land three years ago, I knew exactly where I could find the Coke T-shirt. The shop in the central block of Jerusalem's Ben Yehuda Street did offer other shirt designs, but the one with the bright white "Drink Coca-Cola Classic" written in Hebrew cursive across the chest was what drew in most of the dollar-carrying tourists. While waiting almost twenty minutes for my shirt (depicted in Fig. 1), I watched nearly everyone ahead of me say "the Coke shirt, *todah rabah* [thank you very much]."

Fig. 1. Hebrew Coca-Cola T-shirt. Personal photograph.

At the time, I never thought it strange that I wanted one, too. Yet, I *had* absorbed sixteen years of Coca-Cola propaganda.

Thinking about how she relates to her audience brings Emily to reflect more deeply on herself as the writer: Why has she chosen this topic? What does it say about her beliefs and values? What is her attitude toward her topic and toward her audience? What does she need to do to establish her credentials to write on this topic and to this audience?

Finally, Emily knows she will need to pay careful attention to the context in which she is writing: the assignment is due in two weeks, so she needs to work fast; the assignment calls for an essay written in academic English, though she plans to include some dialogue and a number of visuals to keep it lively; and since she knows she tends to sound like a know-it-all, she determines to work carefully on her tone and style.

4   Exploring Ideas

The point is so simple that we often forget it: we write best about topics we know well. So among the most important parts of the entire writing process are choosing a topic that will engage your interest, exploring that topic by surveying what you know about it, and determining what you need to find out. You can explore a topic in many ways; the goal is to find strategies that work well for you.

4a Try brainstorming.

Used widely in business and industry, brainstorming involves tossing out your ideas—either orally or in writing—to discover new ways to approach a topic. You can brainstorm with others or by yourself.

1. Within a time limit of five or ten minutes, list every word or phrase that comes to mind about the topic. Jot down key words and phrases, not sentences. No one has to understand the list but you. Don't worry about whether or not something will be useful—just list as much as you can in this brief span of time.
2. If little occurs to you, try coming up with thoughts about the opposite side of your topic. If you are trying, for instance, to think of reasons to raise tuition and are coming up blank, try concentrating on reasons to lower tuition. Once you start generating ideas in one direction, you'll find that you can usually move back to the other side fairly easily.
3. When the time is up, stop and read over the lists you have made. If anything else comes to mind, add it to your list. Then reread the list, looking for patterns of interesting ideas or one central idea.

4b Try freewriting or looping.

Freewriting is a method of exploring a topic by writing about it for a period of time *without stopping*.

1. Write for ten minutes or so. Think about your topic, and let your mind wander; write down whatever occurs to you. Don't worry about grammar or spelling. If you get stuck, write anything—just don't stop.
2. When the time is up, look at what you have written. You may discover some important insights and ideas.

If you like, you can continue the process by looping: find the central or most intriguing thought from your freewriting, and then

---

CONSIDERING DISABILITIES

Freespeaking

If you are better at talking out than writing out your ideas, try freespeaking, which is basically the talking version of freewriting. Speak into a tape recorder or into a computer with voice-recognition software, and keep talking about your topic for at least seven to ten minutes. Say whatever comes to your mind — don't stop talking. You can then listen to or read the results of your freespeaking and look for an idea to pursue at greater length.

---

summarize it in a single sentence. Freewrite for five more minutes on the summary sentence, and then find and summarize the central thought from the second "loop." Keep this process going until you discover a clear angle or something about the topic that you can pursue.

4c   Try drawing or creating word pictures.

If you're someone who prefers visual thinking, you might either create a drawing about the topic or use figurative language — such as similes and metaphors — to describe what the topic resembles. Working with pictures or verbal imagery can sometimes also help illuminate the topic or uncover some of your unconscious ideas or preconceptions about it.

1. If you like to draw, try sketching your topic. What images do you come up with? What details of the drawing attract you most? What would you most like to expand on? Even abstract doodling can lead you to important insights about the topic and to focus your topic productively.

2. Look for figurative language — metaphors and similes — that your topic resembles. Try jotting down three or four possibilities, beginning with "My subject is _____" or "My subject is like _____." A student working on the subject of genetically modified crops came up with this: "Genetically modified foods are like empty calories: they do more harm than good." This exercise made one thing clear to this student writer: she already had a very strong bias that she would need to watch out for while developing her topic.

FOR MULTILINGUAL WRITERS

Using Your Best Language to Explore Ideas

For generating and exploring ideas — the work of much brainstorming, freewriting, looping, and clustering — you may be most successful at coming up with good ideas quickly and spontaneously if you work in your best language. Later in the process of writing, you can choose the best of these ideas and begin working with them in English.

Play around a bit with your topic. Ask, for instance, "If my topic were a food (or a song or a movie or a video game), what would it be, and why?" Or write a Facebook status update about your topic, or send a tweet about why this topic appeals to you. Such exercises can get you out of the rut of everyday thinking and help you see your topic in a new light.

4d   Try clustering.

Clustering is a way of generating ideas using a visual scheme or chart. It is especially helpful for understanding the relationships among the parts of a broad topic and for developing subtopics. You may have a software program for clustering. If not, follow these steps:

1. Write down your topic in the middle of a blank piece of paper or screen and circle it.
2. In a ring around the topic circle, write what you see as the main parts of the topic. Circle each part, and then draw a line from it to the topic.
3. Think of more ideas, examples, facts, or other details relating to each main part. Write each of these near the appropriate part, circle each one, and draw a line from it to the part.
4. Repeat this process with each new circle until you can't think of any more details. Some trails may lead to dead ends, but you will still have many useful connections among ideas.

Here is an example of the clustering Emily Lesk did for her essay about Coca-Cola and American identity:

EMILY LESK'S CLUSTERING

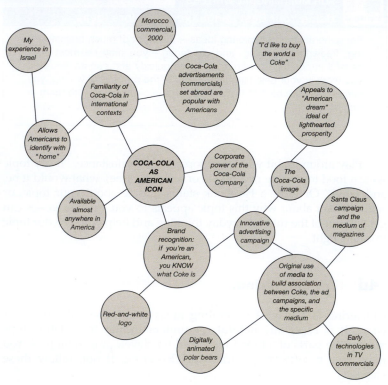

4e Look at images and videos.

Searching images or browsing videos may spark topic ideas or inspire questions that you want to explore. If you plan to create a highly visual project—a video essay or slide presentation, for instance—you will probably need to decide what you want to show your audience before you plan the words that will accompany the images.

4f Keep a reflective journal or private blog.

Writers often get their best ideas by jotting down or recording thoughts that come to them randomly. You can write in a notebook, record audio notes on a phone, store pictures and video files on a private blog—some writers even keep a marker and writing board on the shower wall so that they can write down the ideas that come to them while bathing! As you begin thinking about your assignment, taking time to record what you know about your topic and what still puzzles you may lead you to a breakthrough or help you articulate your main idea.

4g Ask questions.

Another basic strategy for exploring a topic and generating ideas is simply to ask and answer questions. Here are several widely used sets of questions to get you started, either on your own or with one or two others.

Questions to describe a topic

Originally developed by Aristotle, the following questions can help you explore a topic by carefully and systematically describing it:

- *What is it?* What are its characteristics, dimensions, features, and parts? What do your senses tell you about it?
- *What caused it?* What changes occurred to create your topic? How is it changing? How will it change?
- *What is it like or unlike?* What features differentiate your topic from others? What analogies can you make about your topic?
- *What larger system is the topic a part of?* How does your topic relate to this system?
- *What do people say about it?* What reactions does your topic arouse? What about the topic causes those reactions?

Questions to explain a topic

The well-known questions *who*, *what*, *when*, *where*, *why*, and *how*, widely used by news reporters, are especially helpful for explaining a topic.

- *Who* is doing it?
- *What* is at issue?
- *When* does it take place?
- *Where* is it taking place?
- *Why* does it occur?
- *How* is it done?

Questions to persuade

When your purpose is to persuade or convince, the following questions, developed by philosopher Stephen Toulmin, can help you think analytically about your topic (10d and 11j):

- What *claim* are you making about your topic?
- What *good reasons* support your claim?
- What valid *underlying assumptions* support the reasons for your claim?
- What *backup evidence* can you find for your claim?
- What *refutations* of your claim should you anticipate?
- In what ways should you *qualify* your claim?

4h   Browse sources.

At the library and on the Internet, browse for a topic you want to learn more about. If you have a short list of ideas, follow links from one interesting article to another to see what you can find, or do a quick check of reference works to get overviews of the topics. You can begin with a general encyclopedia or a specialized reference work that focuses on a specific area, such as music or psychology. You can also use Wikipedia as a starting point: take a look at entries that relate to your topic, especially noting the sources they list. While you should not rely on Wikipedia alone, it is a highly accessible way to begin your research.

4i   Collaborate.

As you explore your topic, remember that you can gain valuable insights from others. Many writers say that they get their best ideas in conversation with other people. If you talk with friends or roommates about your topic, at the very least you will hear yourself describe the topic and your interest in it; this practice will almost certainly sharpen your understanding of what you are doing. If those you talk to are not familiar with the topic, their questions will help you see what you need to explain. You can also use conversation with others to analyze your own assumptions. In addition, you can seek out online discussions on social media as places to share your thinking on a topic and find inspiration.

Planning and Drafting 5

Some writers just plunge right into their work and develop it as they go along. Others find that they work more effectively by making detailed blueprints before they begin drafting. Your planning and drafting may fall anywhere along this spectrum. As you plan and draft, you narrow your topic, decide on your thesis, organize materials to support that central idea, and sketch out a plan for your writing. As one student said, this is the time in the writing process "when the rubber meets the road."

5a Narrow your topic.

After exploring ideas, you may have found a topic that interests you and that you think would also be interesting to your readers. The topic, however, may be too large to be manageable. If that is the case, narrow your topic using any exploring technique that works for you (see Chapter 4).

WORKING THESIS: Plan Your Approach

Survey what you know about the topic.

ASK:

What is your **connection** to the topic?

What does your audience need to **know**?

How can you make your topic **manageable**?

Remember that there are many possible paths to approaching a topic.

▶ Drafting > Video Prompt: This will take longer than I thought

Emily Lesk planned to discuss how advertising affects American identity, but she knew that such a topic was far too broad. After thinking about products that are pitched as particularly "American" in their advertising, she posted a Facebook status update asking friends to "name products that seem super-American." She quickly got seventeen responses ranging from Hummers and Winchester rifles to "soft toilet paper," Spam, Wheaties, and apple pie. One friend identified Coca-Cola and Pepsi-Cola, two products that Emily associated with many memorable and well-documented advertising campaigns.

5b   Craft a working thesis.

Academic and professional writing in the United States often contains an explicit thesis statement. The thesis functions as a promise to readers, letting them know what the writer will discuss. Your readers may (or may not) expect you to craft the thesis as a single sentence near the beginning of the text. If you want to suggest a thesis implicitly rather than stating one explicitly, if you plan to convey your main argument somewhere other than in your introduction, or if you prefer to make your thesis longer than a single sentence, consider

WORKING THESIS: Refine Your Topic

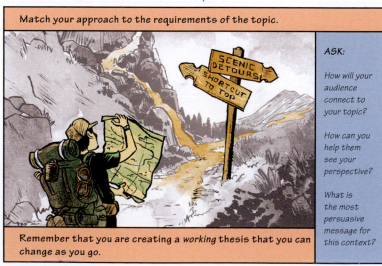

Match your approach to the requirements of the topic.

SCENIC DETOURS

SHORTCUT TO TOP

ASK:

How will your audience connect to your topic?

How can you help them see your perspective?

What is the most persuasive message for this context?

Remember that you are creating a *working* thesis that you can change as you go.

whether the rhetorical situation allows such flexibility. For an academic project, also consult with your instructor about how to meet expectations.

Whether you plan to use an implicit or explicit thesis statement in your text, you should establish a tentative working thesis early in your writing process. The word *working* is important here because your thesis may well change as you write—your final thesis may be very different from the working thesis you begin with. Even so, a working thesis focuses your thinking and research, and helps keep you on track.

A working thesis should have two parts: a topic, which indicates the subject matter the writing is about, and a comment, which makes an important point about the topic.

▶ **In the graphic novel *Fun Home*, illustrations and words combine to make meanings that are more subtle than either words alone or images alone could convey.**

A successful working thesis has three characteristics:

1. It is potentially *interesting* to the intended audience.
2. It is as *specific* as possible.
3. It limits the topic enough to make it *manageable*.

WORKING THESIS: Craft Your Message

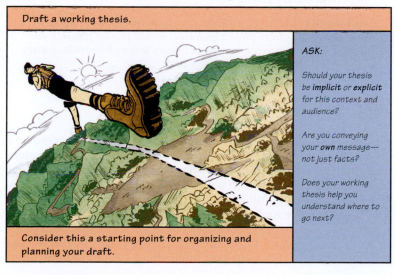

Draft a working thesis.

ASK:

Should your thesis be **implicit** or **explicit** for this context and audience?

Are you conveying your **own** message—not just facts?

Does your working thesis help you understand where to go next?

Consider this a starting point for organizing and planning your draft.

FOR MULTILINGUAL WRITERS

Stating a Thesis Explicitly

In some cultures, stating the main point explicitly may be considered rude or inelegant. In U.S. academic and business practices, however, readers often expect the writer to make key points and positions explicit. Unless your main point is highly controversial or hard for the reader to accept (such as a rejection letter), state your main point early — before presenting the supporting details.

You can evaluate a working thesis by checking it against each of these characteristics, as in the following examples:

▶ **Graphic novels combine words and images.**

> **INTERESTING?** The topic of graphic novels could be interesting, but this draft of a working thesis has no real comment attached to it—instead, it states a bare fact, and the only place to go from here is to more bare facts.

▶ **In graphic novels, words and images convey interesting meanings.**

> **SPECIFIC?** This thesis is not specific. What are "interesting meanings," exactly? How are they conveyed?

▶ **Graphic novels have evolved in recent decades to become an important literary genre.**

> **MANAGEABLE?** This thesis would not be manageable for a short-term project because it would require research on several decades of history and on hundreds of texts from all over the world.

5c Gather information.

Writing often calls for research. Your curiosity may be triggered by a found object or image that you want to learn more about. An assignment may specify that you conduct research on your topic and cite your sources. Even if you're writing about a topic on which you're an expert, you may still find that you don't know enough about some aspect of the topic to write about it effectively without doing research.

You may need to do research at various stages of the writing process—early on, to help you understand or define your topic, and later on, to find additional examples and illustrations to support your thesis. Once you have developed a working thesis, consider what additional information, opinions, visuals, and media you might need.

Basically, you can do three kinds of research to support your thesis: library research, which includes books, periodicals, and databases (and perhaps archives of other kinds of sources, such as music, films, posters, photographs, and so on); online research, which gives you access to texts, visuals, media, and people on the Internet; and field research, which includes personal observation, interviews, surveys, and other means of gathering information directly. (For more information on conducting research, see Chapter 13.)

5d Organize information.

While you're finding information on your topic, think about how you will group or organize that information to make it accessible and persuasive to readers. At the simplest level, writers most often group information in their writing projects according to four principles—space, time, logic, and association.

Spatial organization

Spatial organization of texts allows the reader to "walk through" your material, beginning at one point and moving around in an organized manner—say, from near to far, left to right, or top to bottom. It can be especially useful when you want the audience to understand the layout of a structure or the placement of elements and people in a scene: texts such as a museum visitors' audio guide, a written-word description of a historic battlefield, or a video tour of a new apartment might all call for spatial organization. Remember that maps, diagrams, and other graphics may help readers visualize your descriptions more effectively.

Chronological organization

Organization can also indicate *when* events occur, usually chronologically from first to last. Chronological organization is the basic method used in cookbooks, lab reports, instruction manuals, and many stories and narrative films. You may find it useful to organize information by describing or showing the sequence of events or the steps in a process.

Logical organization

Organizing according to logic means relating pieces of information in ways that make sense. Following is an overview of some of the most commonly used logical patterns: *illustration, definition, division and classification, comparison and contrast, cause and effect, problem and solution, analogy,* and *narration.* For examples of paragraphs organized according to these logical patterns, see 6c.

ILLUSTRATION

You will often gather examples to illustrate a point. If you write an essay discussing how one novelist influenced another, you might cite examples from the second writer's books that echo themes or characters from the first writer's works. For a pamphlet appealing for donations to the Red Cross, you might use photographs showing situations in which donations helped people in trouble, along with appropriate descriptions. For maximum effect, you may want to arrange examples in order of increasing importance unless your genre calls for an attention-grabbing initial illustration.

DEFINITION

Often a topic can be developed by definition—by saying what something is (or is not) and perhaps by identifying the characteristics that distinguish it from things that are similar or in the same general category. If you write about poverty in your community, for example, you would have to define very carefully what level of income, assets, or other measure defines a person, family, or household as "poor." In an essay about Pentecostalism, you might explain what characteristics separate Pentecostalism from related religious movements.

DIVISION AND CLASSIFICATION

Division means breaking a single topic into separate parts; classification means grouping many separate items of information about a topic according to their similarities. An essay about military recruiting policies might divide the military into different branches—army, navy, air force, and so on—and examine how each recruits volunteers. For a project on women's roles in the eighteenth century, you could organize your notes by classification: information related to women's education, occupations, legal status, and so on.

COMPARISON AND CONTRAST

Comparison focuses on the similarities between two things, whereas contrast highlights their differences, but the two are often used together.

If you were asked to analyze two case studies in an advertising text (one on Budweiser ads and the other on ads for the latest iPhone), you might well organize the response by presenting all the information on Budweiser advertising in one section and all the information on iPhone ads in another (block comparison) or by alternating between Budweiser and iPhone ads as you look at particular characteristics of each (alternating comparison).

CAUSE AND EFFECT

Cause-effect analysis may deal with causes, effects, or both. If you examine why something happens or happened, you are investigating causes. If you explain what has occurred or is likely to occur from a set of conditions, you are discussing effects. An environmental impact study of the probable consequences of building a proposed dam, for instance, would focus on effects. On the other hand, a video essay on the breakdown of authority in inner-city schools might begin with the effects of the breakdown and trace them back to their causes.

PROBLEM AND SOLUTION

Moving from a problem to a solution is a natural way to organize certain kinds of information. For example, a student studying motorcycle parking on campus decided to organize his writing in just this way: he identified a problem (the need for more parking) and then offered two possible solutions, along with visuals to help readers imagine the solutions (his outline appears on p. 47). Many assignments in engineering, business, and economics call for a similar organizational strategy.

ANALOGY

An analogy establishes connections between two things or ideas. Analogies are particularly helpful in explaining something new in terms of something very familiar. Likening the human genome to a map, for example, helps explain the complicated concept of the genome to those unfamiliar with it.

NARRATION

Narration involves telling a story of some kind. You might, for example, tell the story of how deer ravaged your mother's garden as a way of showing why you support population control measures for wildlife. Narrating calls on the writer to set the story in a context readers can understand, providing any necessary background and descriptive details as well as chronological markers and transitions (*later that day, the following morning*, and so on) to guide readers through the story.

Association

Some writers organize information through a series of associations that grow directly out of their own experiences and memories. In doing so, they may rely on a sensory memory, such as an aroma, a sound, or a scene. Thus, associational organization is common in personal narrative, where the writer follows a chain of associations to render an experience vividly for readers, as in this description:

> Flying from San Francisco to Atlanta, I looked down to see the gentle roll of the Smoky Mountains begin to appear. Almost at once, I was transported back to my granny's porch, sitting next to her drinking iced tea and eating peaches. Those fresh-picked peaches were delicious—ripened on the tree, skinned, and eaten with no regard for the sticky juice trickling everywhere. And on special occasions, we'd make ice cream, and Granny would empty a bowl brimming with chopped peaches into the creamy dish. Now—that was the life!

QUICK HELP

Organizing Visuals and Media in Academic Writing

- Use video and still images to capture your readers' attention and interest in a vivid way, to emphasize a point you make in words, to present information that is difficult to convey in words, or to communicate with audiences with different language skills.

- Consider whether you want to use images alone to convey your message, or whether words are also needed to help readers understand.

- For presentations, consider what your audience should look at as they listen to you. Make sure that the visuals enhance rather than compete with what you say. (Chapter 23)

- If you are using visuals and words together, consider both the way each image or video works on its own and the way it works in combination with the words you use.

- If you are using visuals to illustrate a written-word text, place each visual as near as possible to the words it illustrates. Introduce each visual clearly (*As the map to the right depicts . . .*). Comment on the significance or effect of the visual (*Figure 1 corroborates the firefighters' statements . . .*). Label each visual appropriately, and cite the source.

Combined organizational patterns

In much of your writing, you will want to use two or more principles of organization. You might, for example, combine several passages of narration with vivid examples to make a striking comparison, as one student did in an essay about the dramatic differences between her life in her Zuñi community and her life as a teacher in Seattle. In addition, you may want to include not only visuals but sound and other multimedia effects as well.

5e Make a plan.

At this point, you will find it helpful to write out an organizational plan, outline, or storyboard. To do so, simply begin with your thesis; review your exploratory notes, research materials, and visual or multimedia sources; and then list all the examples and other good reasons you have to support the thesis. (For more information on paragraph-level organization, see Chapter 6.)

An informal plan

One informal way to organize your ideas is to figure out what belongs in your introduction, body paragraphs, and conclusion. A student who was writing about solutions to a problem used the following plan:

WORKING THESIS

▶ **Increased motorcycle use demands the reorganization of campus parking lots.**

INTRODUCTION

give background and overview (motorcycle use up dramatically), and include photograph of overcrowded lot

state purpose — to fulfill promise of thesis by offering solutions

BODY

describe current situation (tell of my research at area parking lots)

describe problem in detail (report on statistics; cars vs. cycles), and graph my findings

present two possible solutions (enlarge lots or reallocate space)

CONCLUSION

recommend against first solution because of cost and space

recommend second solution, and summarize advantages

A formal outline

Even if you have created an informal written plan before drafting, you may wish (or be required) to prepare a more formal outline, which can help you see exactly how the parts of your writing will fit together—how your ideas relate, where you need examples, and what the overall structure of your work will be. Even if your instructor doesn't ask you to make an outline or you prefer to use some other method of sketching out your plans, you may want to come back to an outline later: doing a retrospective outline—one you do after you've already drafted your project—is a great way to see whether you have any big logical gaps or whether parts of the essay are in the wrong place.

Most formal outlines follow a conventional format of numbered and lettered headings and subheadings, using roman numerals, capital letters, arabic numerals, and lowercase letters to show the levels of importance of the various ideas and their relationships. Each new level is indented to show its subordination to the preceding level.

Thesis statement
I. First main idea
    A. First subordinate idea
        1. First supporting detail or idea
        2. Second supporting detail or idea
        3. Third supporting detail
    B. Second subordinate idea
        1. First supporting detail or idea
        2. Second supporting detail or idea
II. Second main idea
    A. (continues as above)

Note that each level contains at least two parts, so there is no A without a B, no 1 without a 2. Comparable items are placed on the same level—the level marked by capital letters, for instance, or arabic numerals. Keep in mind that headings should be stated in parallel form—either all sentences or all grammatically parallel topics.

A storyboard

The technique of storyboarding—working out a narrative or argument in visual form—can be a good way to come up with an organizational plan, especially if you are developing a video essay, website, or other media project. You can find storyboard templates online to help you get started, or you can create your own storyboard by using note cards or sticky notes. Even if you're writing a more traditional word-based college essay, however, you may find storyboarding helpful; take advantage of different colors to keep track of threads of argument, subtopics, and so on. Flexibility is a strong feature of storyboarding: you can move the cards and notes around, trying out different arrangements, until you find an organization that works well for your writing situation.

Use linear organization when you want readers to move in a particular order through your material. An online report might use the following linear organization:

LINEAR ORGANIZATION

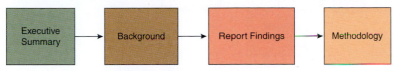

A hierarchy puts the most important material first, with subtopics branching out from the main idea. A website on dog bite prevention might be arranged like this:

HIERARCHICAL ORGANIZATION

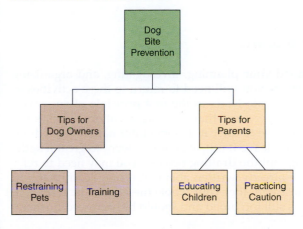

A spoke-and-hub organization allows readers to move from place to place in no particular order. Many portfolio websites are arranged this way:

SPOKE-AND-HUB ORGANIZATION

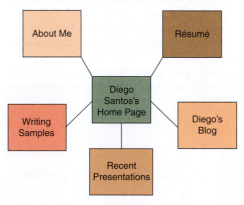

Whatever form your plan takes, you may want or need to change it along the way. Writing has a way of stimulating thought, and the process of drafting may generate new ideas. Or you may find that you need to reexamine some data or information or gather more material.

5f Create a draft.

No matter how good your planning, investigating, and organizing have been, chances are you will need to return to these activities as you draft. This fact of life leads to the first principle of successful drafting: be flexible. If you see that your organizational plan is not working, do not hesitate to alter it. If some information or medium now seems irrelevant, leave it out, even if you went to great lengths to obtain it. Throughout the drafting process, you may need to refer to points you have already written about. You may learn that you need to do more research, that your whole thesis must be reshaped, or that your topic is still too broad and should be narrowed further.

macmillanhighered.com/everyday6e

ⓔ Reviewing and Revising > Student Writing: Early draft, Emily Lesk
▣ Drafting > Tutorial: Word processing
Drafting > Video Prompt: It's hard to delete things
Drafting > Video Prompt: You just have to start

QUICK HELP

Guidelines for Drafting

- *Set up a computer folder or file for your essay.* Give the file a clear and relevant name, and save to it often. Name your files to distinguish among drafts. Since you will likely change your text over time, save a copy of each version. If you are sending a copy to classmates for review, give the file a new but related name.

- *Track changes within a document file to try out new versions.* This function is useful when you are working on a piece of writing with another writer or when you aren't sure which version of your draft you like best.

- *Have all your information close at hand and arranged according to your organizational plan.* Stopping to search for a piece of information can break your concentration or distract you.

- *Try to write in stretches of at least thirty minutes.* Writing can provide momentum, and once you get going, the task becomes easier.

- *Don't let small questions bog you down.* Just make a note of them in brackets — or in all caps — or make a tentative decision and move on.

- *Remember that first drafts aren't perfect.* Concentrate on getting all your ideas written down, and don't worry about anything else.

- *Stop writing at a place where you know exactly what will come next.* Doing so will help you start easily when you return to the draft.

Developing Paragraphs **6**

Paragraphs serve as signposts — pointers that help guide readers through a piece of writing. A look through a popular magazine will show paragraphs working this way: the first paragraph of an article almost always aims to get our attention and to persuade us to read on, and subsequent ones often indicate a new point or a shift in focus or tone.

Put most simply, a paragraph is a group of sentences or a single sentence set off as a unit. All the sentences in a paragraph usually revolve around one main idea.

QUICK HELP

Editing Paragraphs

- What is the topic sentence of each paragraph? Is it stated or implied? Is the main idea of the paragraph clear? (6a)
- Does the first sentence of each paragraph let readers know what that paragraph is about? Does the last sentence in some way conclude that paragraph's discussion? If not, does it need to?
- Within each paragraph, how does each sentence relate to the main idea? Revise or eliminate any that do not. (6a)
- How completely does each paragraph develop its main idea? What details and images are included? Are they effective? Do any paragraphs need more detail? (6b)
- What other methods of development might make the paragraph more effective? (6c)
- Is each paragraph organized in a way that is easy to follow? Are sentences within each paragraph clearly linked? Do any of the transitions try to create links between ideas that do not really exist? (6e)
- Are the paragraphs clearly linked? Do any links need to be added? Are any of the transitions from one paragraph to another artificial? (6e)
- How does the introductory paragraph catch readers' interest? How does the last paragraph draw the piece to a conclusion? (6f)

6a   Focus on a main idea.

An effective paragraph often focuses on one main idea. A good way to achieve such paragraph unity is to state the main idea clearly in one sentence and then relate all the other sentences in the paragraph to that idea. The sentence that presents the main idea is called the topic sentence.

Topic sentence

The following paragraph opens with a clear topic sentence, and the rest of the paragraph builds on the idea stated in that sentence:

> *Our friendship was the source of much happiness and many memories.* We grooved on every new recording from Jay-Z. We sweated together in the sweltering summer sun, trying to win the championship for our softball team. I recall the taste of pepperoni pizza as we discussed the highlights of our team's victory. Once we even became attracted to the same person, but luckily we were able to share his friendship.

FOR MULTILINGUAL WRITERS

Being Explicit

Native readers of English generally expect that paragraphs will have an explicitly stated main idea and that the connections between points in a paragraph will also be stated explicitly. Such step-by-step explicitness may strike you as unnecessary or ineffective, but it follows the traditional paragraph conventions of English.

A topic sentence does not always come at the beginning of a paragraph; it may come at the end. Occasionally a paragraph's main idea is so obvious that it need not be stated explicitly in a topic sentence.

Other related sentences

Whether the main idea of a paragraph is stated in a topic sentence or is implied, make sure that all other sentences in the paragraph contribute to the main idea. In the preceding example about friendship, all of the sentences clearly relate to the point that is made in the first sentence. The result is a unified paragraph.

6b   Provide details.

An effective paragraph develops its main idea by providing enough details—including visual details—to hold the reader's interest. Without such development, a paragraph may seem lifeless and abstract.

A POORLY DEVELOPED PARAGRAPH

No such thing as human nature compels people to behave, think, or react in certain ways. Rather, from our infancy to our death, we are constantly being taught, by the society that surrounds us, the customs, norms, and mores of a distinct culture. Everything in culture is learned, not genetically transmitted.

This paragraph is boring. Although its main idea is clear and its sentences hold together, it fails to gain our interest or hold our attention because it lacks any specific examples or details. Now look at the paragraph revised to include needed specifics.

THE SAME PARAGRAPH, REVISED

A child in Los Angeles decorates a Christmas tree with shiny red ornaments and sparkling tinsel. A few weeks later, a child in Beijing celebrates the Chinese New Year with feasting, firecrackers, and gift money in lucky red envelopes. It is not by instinct that one child knows how to

---

TALKING THE TALK

Paragraph Length

"How long should a paragraph be?" In college writing, paragraphs should address a specific topic or idea and develop that idea with examples and evidence. There is no set rule about how many sentences are required to make a complete paragraph. So write as many sentences as you need — and no more.

---

decorate the tree while the other knows how to celebrate the New Year. No such thing as human nature compels people to behave, think, or react in certain ways. Rather, from the time of our infancy to our death, we are constantly being taught, by the society that surrounds us, the customs, norms, and mores of one or more distinct cultures. Everything in culture is learned, not genetically transmitted.

Though both paragraphs present the same point, only the second one comes to life. It does so by bringing in specific details *from* life, including images that show readers what the paragraph describes. We want to read this paragraph because it appeals to our senses and our curiosity (why are red envelopes considered lucky?).

Details in visual texts

Details are important in both written and visual texts. If you decide to use an image because of a particular detail, make sure your readers will notice what you want them to see. Crop out any unnecessary information, and clarify what's important about the image in your text or with a caption. If you are taking a photo to illustrate a blog post on street food, for example, you will need to decide whether you should frame (or crop) the image to focus on the food or whether your discussion calls for the photo to include more of the surroundings.

6c   Use effective methods of development.

The patterns discussed in 5d for organizing essays can also help you develop paragraphs.

Narrative

A narrative paragraph uses the chronological elements of a story to develop a main idea. The following is one student's narrative paragraph that tells a personal story to support a point about the dangers of racing bicycles with flimsy alloy frames:

> People who have been exposed to the risk of dangerously designed bicycle frames have paid too high a price. I saw this danger myself in last year's Putney Race. An expensive graphite frame failed, and the rider was catapulted onto Vermont pavement at fifty miles per hour. The pack of riders behind him was so dense that other racers crashed into a tangled, sliding heap. The aftermath: four hospitalizations. I got off with some stitches, a bad road rash, and severely pulled tendons. My Italian racing bike was pretzeled, and my racing was over for that summer. Others were not so lucky. An Olympic hopeful, Brian Stone of the Northstar team, woke up in a hospital bed to find that his cycling was over—and not just for that summer. His kneecap had been surgically removed. He couldn't even walk.

Description

A descriptive paragraph uses specific details to create a clear impression. Notice how the following paragraph includes details to describe the appearance of the skyscraper and its effect on those who see it.

> The Chrysler Building, completed in 1930, still attracts the eyes of tourists and New Yorkers alike with its shiny steel exterior. The Chrysler cars of the era are incorporated into the design: the eagle-head gargoyles on the upper vertices of the building are shaped like the automobiles' hood ornaments, and winged details imitate Chrysler radiator caps. At night, an elaborate lighting scheme spotlights the sleek, powerful eagles from below—turning them into striking silhouettes—and picks out each of the upper stories' famed triangular windows, arching up into the darkness like the rays of a stylized sun.

Definition

You may often need to write an entire paragraph in order to define a word or concept, as in the following example:

> Economics is the study of how people choose among the alternatives available to them. It's the study of little choices ("Should I take the chocolate or the strawberry?") and big choices ("Should we require a reduction in energy consumption in order to protect the environment?"). It's the study of individual choices, choices by firms, and choices by governments. Life presents each of us with a wide range of alternative uses of our time and other resources; economists examine how we choose among those alternatives.
>
> – TIMOTHY TREGARTHEN, *Economics*

Example

One of the most common ways of developing a paragraph is by illustrating a point with one or more examples.

> The Indians made names for us children in their teasing way. Because our very busy mother kept my hair cut short, like my brothers', they called me Short Furred One, pointing to their hair and making the sign for short, the right hand with fingers pressed close together, held upward, back out, at the height intended. With me this was about two feet tall, the Indians laughing gently at my abashed face. I am told that I was given a pair of small moccasins that first time, to clear up my unhappiness at being picked out from the dusk behind the fire and my two unhappy shortcomings made conspicuous.
>
> – MARI SANDOZ, "The Go-Along Ones"

Division and classification

Division breaks a single item into parts. Classification groups many separate items according to their similarities. A paragraph evaluating a history course might divide the course into several segments—textbooks, lectures, assignments—and examine each one in turn. A paragraph giving an overview of many history courses might classify the courses in a number of ways—by time periods, by geographic areas, by the kinds of assignments demanded, by the number of students enrolled, or by some other principle.

DIVISION

> We all listen to music according to our separate capacities. But, for the sake of analysis, the whole listening process may become clearer if we break it up into its component parts, so to speak. In a certain sense, we all listen to music on three separate planes. For lack of a better terminology, one might name these: (1) the sensuous plane, (2) the expressive plane, (3) the sheerly musical plane. The only advantage to be gained from mechanically splitting up the listening process into these hypothetical planes is the clearer view to be had of the way in which we listen.
>
> – AARON COPLAND, *What to Listen For in Music*

CLASSIFICATION

> Two types of people are seduced by fad diets. Those who have always been overweight turn to them out of despair; they have tried everything, and yet nothing seems to work. A second group of people to succumb appear perfectly healthy but are baited by slogans such as "look good, feel good." These slogans prompt self-questioning and insecurity—do I really look good and feel good?—and as a direct result, many healthy people fall prey to fad diets. With both types of

people, however, the problems surrounding such diets are numerous and dangerous. In fact, these diets provide neither intelligent nor effective answers to weight control.

Comparison and contrast

When you compare two things, you look at their similarities; when you contrast two things, you focus on their differences. You can structure paragraphs that compare or contrast in two basic ways. One way is to present all the information about one item and then all the information about the other item, as in the following paragraph:

> You could tell the veterans from the rookies by the way they were dressed. The knowledgeable ones had their heads covered by kerchiefs, so that if they were hired, tobacco dust wouldn't get in their hair; they had on clean dresses that by now were faded and shapeless, so that if they were hired they wouldn't get tobacco dust and grime on their best clothes. Those who were trying for the first time had their hair freshly done and wore attractive dresses; they wanted to make a good impression. But the dresses couldn't be seen at the distance that many were standing from the employment office, and they were crumpled in the crush.
>
> – MARY MEBANE, "Summer Job"

Or you can switch back and forth between the two items, focusing on particular characteristics of each in turn.

> Malcolm X emphasized the use of violence in his movement and employed the biblical principle of "an eye for an eye and a tooth for a tooth." King, on the other hand, felt that blacks should use nonviolent civil disobedience and employed the theme "turning the other cheek," which Malcolm X rejected as "beggarly" and "feeble." The philosophy of Malcolm X was one of revenge, and often it broke the unity of black Americans. More radical blacks supported him, while more conservative ones supported King. King thought that blacks should transcend their humanity. In contrast, Malcolm X thought they should embrace it and reserve their love for one another, regarding whites as "devils" and the "enemy." The distance between Martin Luther King Jr.'s thinking and Malcolm X's was the distance between growing up in the seminary and growing up on the streets, between the American dream and the American reality.

Analogy

Analogies (comparisons that explain an unfamiliar thing in terms of a familiar one) can also help develop paragraphs.

> Since the advent of Hollywood editing, back in the earliest days of cinema, the goal of filmmakers has been for us to feel the movement of the camera but not to be aware of it, to look past the construction of the

media, to ignore the seams in the material. Just as an Olympic diver smiles and hides the effort as she catapults skyward and manages to pull off multiple flips while seemingly twisting in both directions, good storytelling—whether oral, in print, or visual—typically hides the construction and the hard work that go into making it. Both the medal-winning dives and the best stories are more intricate than they appear.

— STEPHEN APKON, *The Age of the Image: Redefining Literacy in a World of Screens*

Cause and effect

You can often develop paragraphs by explaining the causes of something or the effects that something brings about. The following paragraph discusses the causes that led pediatrician Phil Offit to study science and become a physician:

> To understand exactly why Offit became a scientist, you must go back more than half a century, to 1956. That was when doctors in Offit's hometown of Baltimore operated on one of his legs to correct a club foot, requiring him to spend three weeks recovering in a chronic care facility with 20 other children, all of whom had polio. Parents were allowed to visit just one hour a week, on Sundays. His father, a shirt salesman, came when he could. His mother, who was pregnant with his brother and hospitalized with appendicitis, was unable to visit at all. He was five years old. "It was a pretty lonely, isolating experience," Offit says. "But what was even worse was looking at these other children who were just horribly crippled and disfigured by polio." That memory, he says, was the first thing that drove him toward a career in pediatric infectious diseases.   — AMY WALLACE, "An Epidemic of Fear"

Process

Paragraphs that explain a process often use the principle of time or chronology to order the stages in the process.

> In July of 1877, Eadweard Muybridge photographed a horse in motion with a camera fast enough to capture clearly the split second when the horse's hooves were all off the ground—a moment never before caught on film. His next goal was to photograph a sequence of such rapid images. In June of 1878, he set up twelve cameras along a track, each connected to a tripwire. Then, as a crowd watched, a trotting horse raced down the track pulling a two-wheeled carriage. The carriage wheels tripped each camera in quick succession, snapping a dozen photographs. Muybridge developed the negatives and displayed them to an admiring public that same morning. His technical achievement helped to pave the way for the first motion pictures a decade later.

Problem and solution

Another way to develop a paragraph is to open with a topic sentence that states a problem or asks a question about a problem and then to offer a solution or answers in the sentences that follow—a technique used in this paragraph from a review of Ted Nordhaus and Michael Shellenberger's book *Break Through: From the Death of Environmentalism to the Politics of Possibility*:

> Unfortunately, at the moment growth means burning more fossil fuel. . . . How can that fact be faced? How to have growth that Americans want, but without limits that they instinctively oppose, and still reduce carbon emissions? [Nordhaus and Shellenberger's] answer is: investments in new technology. Acknowledge that America "is great at imagining, experimenting, and inventing the future," and then start spending. They cite examples ranging from the nuclear weapons program to the invention of the Internet to show what government money can do, and argue that too many clean-energy advocates focus on caps instead.
>
> – BILL McKIBBEN, "Can Anyone Stop It?"

Reiteration

Reiteration is a method of development you may recognize from political speeches or some styles of preaching. In this pattern, the writer states the main point of a paragraph and then restates it, hammering home the point and often building in intensity as well. In the following passage from Barack Obama's 2004 speech at the Democratic National Convention, Obama contrasts what he identifies as the ideas of "those who are preparing to divide us" with memorable references to common ground and unity, including repeated references to the United States as he builds to his climactic point:

> Now even as we speak, there are those who are preparing to divide us—the spin masters, the negative ad peddlers who embrace the politics of anything goes. Well, I say to them tonight, there is not a liberal America and a conservative America—there is the United States of America. There is not a black America and a white America and Latino America and an Asian America—there's the United States of America. The pundits like to slice and dice our country into Red States and Blue States: Red States for Republicans, Blue States for Democrats. But I've got news for them, too. We worship an awesome God in the Blue States, and we don't like federal agents poking around in our libraries in the Red States. We coach Little League in the Blue States and yes, we've got some gay friends in the Red States. There are patriots who opposed the war in Iraq and there are patriots who supported the war in Iraq. We are one people, all of us pledging allegiance to the stars and stripes, all of us defending the United States of America.
>
> – BARACK OBAMA

6d Consider paragraph length.

Paragraph length is determined by content and purpose. Paragraphs should develop an idea, create any desired effects (such as suspense or humor), and advance the larger piece of writing. Fulfilling these aims will sometimes require short paragraphs, sometimes long ones. For example, if you are writing a persuasive piece, you may put all your evidence into one long paragraph to create the impression of a solid, overwhelmingly convincing argument. In a story about an exciting event, on the other hand, you may use a series of short para-graphs to create suspense, to keep the reader rushing to each new paragraph to find out what happens next.

REASONS TO START A NEW PARAGRAPH

- to turn to a new idea
- to emphasize something (such as an idea or an example)
- to change speakers (in dialogue)
- to get readers to pause
- to take up a subtopic
- to start the conclusion

6e Make paragraphs flow.

A paragraph has coherence—or flows—if its details all fit together clearly in a way that readers can easily follow. When you arrange information in a particular order (as described in 5d and 6c), you help readers move from one point to another. Regardless of your organiza-tion, however, be aware of several other ways to achieve paragraph coherence.

Repetition of key words and phrases

Weaving in repeated key words and phrases—or pronouns pointing to them—not only links sentences but also alerts readers to the importance of those words or phrases in the larger piece of writing. Notice in the following example how the repetition of the italicized key words and the use of pronouns that refer to those words help hold the paragraph together:

> Over the centuries, *shopping* has changed in function as well as in style. Before the Industrial Revolution, most consumer goods were sold in open-air *markets*, *customers* who went into an actual *shop* were expected to *buy* something, and *shoppers* were always expected to *bargain* for the

best possible *price*. In the nineteenth century, however, the development of the department *store* changed the relationship between buyers and sellers. Instead of visiting several *market* stalls or small *shops*, *customers* could now *buy* a variety of merchandise under the same roof; instead of feeling expected to *buy*, they were welcome just to look; and instead of *bargaining* with several merchants, they paid a fixed *price* for each *item*. In addition, *they* could return an *item* to the *store* and exchange *it* for a different one or get their money back. All of these changes helped transform *shopping* from serious requirement to psychological recreation.

Parallelism

Parallel structures can help connect the sentences within a paragraph. As readers, we feel pulled along by the force of the parallel structures in the following example:

> William Faulkner's "Barn Burning" tells the story of a young boy trapped in a no-win situation. If he betrays his father, he loses his family. If he betrays justice, he becomes a fugitive. In trying to free himself from his trap, he does both.

Transitions

Transitions are words such as *so*, *however*, and *thus* that signal relationships between sentences and paragraphs. Transitions help guide the reader from one idea to another. To understand how important transitions are in directing readers, try reading the following paragraph, from which all transitions have been removed.

A PARAGRAPH WITH NO TRANSITIONS

> In "The Fly," Katherine Mansfield tries to show us the real personality of the boss beneath his exterior. The fly helps her to portray this real self. The boss goes through a range of emotions and feelings. He expresses these feelings to a small but determined fly, whom the reader realizes he unconsciously relates to his son. The author basically splits up the story into three parts, with the boss's emotions and actions changing quite measurably. With old Woodifield, with himself, and with the fly, we see the boss's manipulativeness. Our understanding of him as a hard and cruel man grows.

If we work at it, we can figure out the relationship of these sentences to one another, for this paragraph is essentially unified by one major idea. But the lack of transitions results in an abrupt, choppy rhythm; the paragraph lurches from one detail to the next, dragging the confused reader behind. See how much easier the passage is to read and understand with transitions added.

QUICK HELP

Making Connections with Transitions

Writers use transitions to show a variety of relationships between ideas: to show contrast (*on the other hand*); to put ideas in sequence (*first, next, finally*); to counter an idea (*however, nevertheless*); to show a causal relationship (*due to, as a result*); to compare (*in the same way, likewise, similarly*); to add an idea (*also, in addition*); or to illustrate a point (*for example*). Professor Laura Aull's research shows that expert academic writers use a wider range and variety of transitions than student writers do and that the transitions are closely tied to their purpose. Experts are most likely to use transitional markers to show contrast, sequence, addition, comparison, and illustration. Look closely at the transitional words and phrases in your writing. Is their purpose clear and appropriate? Overusing causal transitions can make your writing seem to jump to conclusions too quickly, while overusing countering transitions can make your writing seem more aggressive than you intend. Take a tip from expert writers and take particular care with transitions that show cause and effect and countering.

THE SAME PARAGRAPH WITH TRANSITIONS

In "The Fly," Katherine Mansfield tries to show us the real personality of the boss beneath his exterior. The fly in the story's title helps her to portray this real self. In the course of the story, the boss goes through a range of emotions. At the end, he finally expresses these feelings to a small but determined fly, whom the reader realizes he unconsciously relates to his son. To accomplish her goal, the author basically splits up the story into three parts, with the boss's emotions and actions changing measurably throughout. First with old Woodifield, then with himself, and last with the fly, we see the boss's manipulativeness. With each part, our understanding of him as a hard and cruel man grows.

Commonly used transitions

TO SIGNAL SEQUENCE AND TIME

after a while, afterward, again, and then, as long as, as soon as, at last, at that time, before, besides, earlier, finally, first . . . second . . . third, immediately, in the meantime, in the past, last, lately, later, meanwhile, next, now, presently, simultaneously, since, so far, soon, still, then, thereafter, until, when

TO ADD IDEAS

again, also, furthermore, in the same way, likewise, moreover, similarly, too

TO SHOW CONTRAST OR COUNTERARGUMENT

although, but, despite, even though, however, in contrast, indeed, in spite of, instead, nevertheless, nonetheless, on one hand . . . on the other hand, on the contrary, regardless, still, though, while, yet

TO SIGNAL EXAMPLES AND ILLUSTRATIONS

for example, for instance, in fact, of course, specifically, such as, the following example, to illustrate

TO SIGNAL CAUSE AND EFFECT

accordingly, as a result, because, consequently, due to, hence, so, then, therefore, thereupon, thus, to this end

TO SIGNAL PLACE

above, adjacent to, below, beyond, closer to, elsewhere, far, farther on, here, near, nearby, opposite to, there, to the left, to the right

TO SIGNAL SUMMARY, REPETITION, OR CONCLUSION

as a result, as has been noted, as I have said, as mentioned earlier, as we have seen, in any event, in conclusion, in other words, in short, on the whole, therefore, to summarize

6f Work on opening and closing paragraphs.

Opening paragraphs

Even a good piece of writing may remain unread if it has a weak opening paragraph. In addition to announcing your topic, an introductory paragraph must engage readers' interest and focus their attention on what is to follow. One common kind of opening paragraph follows a general-to-specific sequence, in which the writer opens with a general statement and then gets more and more specific, concluding with the thesis. The following paragraph illustrates such an opening:

> The human organism is adapted to function in face-to-face encounters. We know that face-to-face is the most effective way to pitch woo. And face-to-face is obviously the best way to transact an intimate relationship long term. But while we know this, there's much more to face-to-face interaction than meets the naked eye. And it is of grave importance. We risk losing a great deal in any heavy shift of social traffic onto exclusively electronic media. — MARIAM THALOS, "Why I Am Not a Friend"

In this paragraph, the opening sentence introduces a general subject, and the last sentence presents the thesis, which the rest of the essay will develop.

OTHER EFFECTIVE WAYS OF OPENING

- with a quotation: *There is a bumper sticker that reads, "Too bad ignorance isn't painful." –* NIKKI GIOVANNI, "Racism 101"

- with an anecdote: *Social networking pioneer Howard Rheingold begins his digital journalism course each year with a participatory experiment. Shut off your cell phones, he tells his students. Shut your laptop. Now, shut your eyes. –* CATHY DAVIDSON, *Now You See It*

- with a question: *Why are Americans terrified of using nuclear power as a source of energy?*

- with a strong opinion: *Men need a men's movement about as much as women need chest hair. –* JOHN RUSZKIEWICZ, *The Presence of Others*

Concluding paragraphs

A good conclusion wraps up a piece of writing in a satisfying and memorable way. A common and effective strategy for concluding is to restate the central idea (but not word for word), perhaps specifying it in several sentences, and then ending with a much more general statement.

> Lastly, and perhaps greatest of all, there was the ability, at the end, to turn quickly from war to peace once the fighting was over. Out of the way these two men [Generals Grant and Lee] behaved at Appomattox came the possibility of a peace of reconciliation. It was a possibility not wholly realized, in the years to come, but which did, in the end, help the two sections to become one nation again . . . after a war whose bitterness might have seemed to make such a reunion wholly impossible. No part of either man's life became him more than the part he played in this brief meeting in the McLean house at Appomattox. Their behavior there put all succeeding generations of Americans in their debt. Two great Americans, Grant and Lee—very different, yet under everything very much alike. Their encounter at Appomattox was one of the great moments of American history.
> – BRUCE CATTON, "Grant and Lee: A Study in Contrasts"

OTHER EFFECTIVE WAYS OF CONCLUDING

- with a quotation
- with a question
- with a vivid image
- with a call for action
- with a warning

Reviewing, Revising, and Editing

The ancient Roman poet Horace once advised aspiring writers to get distance from their work by putting it away for *nine years*. Although impractical for college writers, to say the least, Horace's advice holds a nugget of truth: putting your draft aside even for a short while will help clear your mind and give you more objectivity about your writing.

Make time to review your work (by yourself or with others) and to revise, edit, and proofread. Reviewing calls for reading your draft with a critical eye and asking others to look over your work. Revising involves reworking your draft on the basis of the review, making sure that the draft is clear, effective, complete, and well organized. Editing involves fine-tuning, attending to all the details.

7a Reread.

After giving yourself and your draft a rest, review the draft by rereading it carefully for meaning; recalling your purpose and audience; reconsidering your stance; and evaluating your organization and use of visuals.

Meaning

When you pick up the draft again, don't sweat the small stuff. Instead, concentrate on your message and on whether you have expressed it clearly. Note any places where the meaning seems unclear.

Purpose

If you responded to an assignment, make sure that you have produced what was asked for. If you set out to prove something, have you succeeded? If you intended to propose a solution to a problem, have you set forth a well-supported solution rather than just an analysis of the problem?

Audience

How appropriately do you address your audience members, given their experiences and expectations? Will you catch their interest, and will they be able to follow your discussion?

Stance

Ask yourself one central question: where are you coming from in this draft? Consider whether your stance appropriately matches the stance you started out with, or whether your stance has legitimately evolved.

Organization

One way to check the organization of your draft is to outline it. After numbering the paragraphs, read through each one, jotting down its main idea. Do the main ideas clearly relate to the thesis and to one another? Can you identify any confusing leaps from point to point? Have you left out any important points?

Genre and media

You decided to write in a particular genre, so think again about why you made that choice. Is writing in this genre the best way to achieve your purpose and reach your audience? Does the draft fulfill the requirements of the genre? Would any content in your draft be more effective presented in another medium—for example, as a print handout instead of a PowerPoint slide? Should you consider "translating" your work into another medium (see Chapters 5 and 24)? Do you need to take any additional steps to make your work as effective as it can be in this medium?

Look closely at any images, audio, and video you have chosen to use. How do they contribute to your draft? Make sure that all visuals and media files are labeled with captions and sources, and remember to refer to visuals and media and to comment on their significance to the rest of your text. Would any information in your draft work better in visual than in verbal form?

 FOR MULTILINGUAL WRITERS

Multilingual **Asking an Experienced Writer to Review Your Draft**

One good way to make sure that your writing is easy to follow is to have someone else read it. You might ask someone who is experienced in the kind of writing you are working on to read over your draft and to point out any words or patterns that are unclear or ineffective.

7b Get the most from peer review.

In addition to your own critical appraisal and that of your instructor (7c), you will probably want to get responses to your draft from friends, classmates, or colleagues. In a writing course, you may be asked to respond to the work of your peers as well as to seek responses from them.

The role of peer reviewers

One of the main goals of a peer reviewer is to help a writer see a draft differently. When you review a draft, you want to *show* the writer

---

QUICK HELP

Guidelines for Peer Response

- *Initial thoughts.* What are the main strengths and weaknesses of the draft? What might confuse readers? What is the most important thing the writer says in the draft? What will readers want to know more about?

- *Assignment.* Does the draft carry out the assignment?

- *Title and introduction.* Do the title and introduction tell what the draft is about and catch readers' interest? How else might the draft begin?

- *Thesis and purpose.* Paraphrase the thesis: *In this paper, the writer will . . .* Does the draft fulfill that promise?

- *Audience.* How does the draft interest and appeal to its audience?

- *Rhetorical stance.* Where does the writer stand? What words indicate the stance?

- *Supporting points.* List the main points, and review them one by one. How well does each point support the thesis? Do any need more explanation? Do any seem confusing or boring?

- *Visuals, media, and design.* Do visuals, if any, add to the key points? Do media files play properly and serve their intended purpose? Is the design clear and effective?

- *Organization and flow.* Is the writing easy to follow? How effective are transitions within sentences, between sentences, and between paragraphs?

- *Conclusion.* Does the draft conclude memorably? Is there another way it might end?

FOR MULTILINGUAL WRITERS
Understanding Peer Review

If you are not used to giving or receiving criticisms directly, you may be uneasy with a classmate's challenges to your work. However, constructive criticism is appropriate to peer review. Your peers will also expect you to offer your questions, suggestions, and insights.

what does and doesn't work about particular aspects of the draft. Visually marking the draft can help the writer absorb at a glance the revisions you suggest.

REVIEWING A PRINT DRAFT

When working with a hard copy of a draft, write compliments in the left margin and critiques, questions, and suggestions in the right margin. As long as you explain what your symbols mean, you can also use boxes, circles, single and double underlining, highlighting, or other visual annotations as shorthand for what you have to say about the draft.

PEER REVIEW: Work with a Writer

Give your full attention to offering as much help as you can.

ASK:

What does the writer want you to **focus** on for this stage of the draft?

Can you restate the **main points** as you see them?

What **specific** suggestions do you think will improve the draft?

Make sure that the writer can move forward when you're finished.

macmillanhighered.com/everyday6e

🄴 Reviewing and Revising > Storyboard Activity: Being a peer reviewer
🄲 Reviewing and Revising > Video Prompt: Lessons from being a peer reviewer

REVIEWING A DIGITAL DRAFT

If the draft is a digital file, the reviewer should save the document in a peer-review folder under an easy-to-recognize name. It's wise to include the writer's name, the assignment, the number of the draft, and the reviewer's initials. For example, the reviewer Ann G. Smith might name the file for the first draft of Javier Jabari's first essay *jabari.essay1.d1.ags*.

The reviewer can then use the word-processing program to add comments, questions, and suggestions to the text. Most such programs have a TRACK CHANGES tool that can show changes to the document in a different color and a COMMENT function that allows you to type a note in the margin. If your word processor doesn't have a COMMENT function, you can comment in footnotes instead.

You should also consider using highlighting in written-word texts. If you explain to the writer what the colors mean and use only a few colors, highlighting can make a powerful visual statement about what needs to be revised.

For media drafts that are difficult to annotate visually, ask the writer about preferred ways to offer suggestions. Can you include audio annotations? If not, try written notes that indicate the time stamp, so the writer will know which part of the file you are commenting on. Does the writer prefer written notes? Can you comment privately on a posted file? Should you discuss the draft in person?

BASING RESPONSES ON THE STAGE OF THE DRAFT

Different stages in the writing process call for different strategies and areas of focus on the part of the peer reviewer.

- Writers of early-stage drafts need direction and options, not editing that focuses on grammar or punctuation. Pointing out surface errors such as misspellings and missing commas will not be a good use of either your time or the writer's if the writer later decides to delete the whole sentence. Your goal as a peer reviewer of an early draft is to help the writer think of ways to expand on the ideas. Pose questions and offer examples that will help the writer think of new ways to approach the topic. Try to help the writer imagine what the final draft might be like.

- Writers of intermediate-stage drafts need to know where their claims lack sufficient evidence, what ideas confuse readers, and how their approach misses its target audience. They also need to know which parts of their drafts are clear and well written, so remember to praise as well as to criticize.

- Writers of late-stage drafts need help with first and last impressions, sentence construction, word choice, tone, and format.

Your job as a peer reviewer is to call attention to the sorts of problems writers need to solve before submitting their final work. Identify the overall strengths of the draft as well as one or two weaknesses that the writer can reasonably improve in a short amount of time.

Reviews of Emily Lesk's draft

On the following pages are the first paragraphs of Emily Lesk's draft, as reviewed by two students, Beatrice Kim and Nastassia Lopez. Beatrice and Nastassia reviewed the draft separately and combined their comments on the draft they returned to Emily. As this review shows, Nastassia and Bea agreed on some of the major problems—and good points—in Emily's draft. Their comments on the draft, however, revealed some different responses. You, too, will find that different readers do not always agree on what is effective or ineffective. In addition, you may find that you simply do not agree with their advice. In examining responses to your writing, you can often proceed efficiently by looking first for areas of agreement (*everyone was confused by this sentence—I'd better revise it*) or strong disagreement (*one person said my conclusion was "perfect," and someone else said it "didn't conclude"—better look carefully at that paragraph again*).

All-Powerful Coke

> **Comment (NL):** I'm not sure the title says enough about your argument.

I don't drink Coke. Call me picky for disliking the soda's saccharine aftertaste. Call me cheap for choosing a water fountain over a twelve-ounce aluminum can that costs a dollar from a vending machine but only pennies to produce. Even call me unpatriotic for rejecting the potable god that over the last century has come to represent all the enjoyment and ease to be found in our American way of life. But don't call me a hypocrite when I admit that I still identify with Coke and the Coca-Cola culture.

> **Comment (NL):** The first sentence is a good attention-getter.

> **Comment (BK):** The beginning seems kind of abrupt.

> **Comment (BK):** What does this mean? Will other members of your audience know?

> **Comment (NL):** The style of repeating "call me" is good, but I'm not sure the first three have much to do with the rest of the essay.

I have a favorite T-shirt that says "Drink Coca-Cola Classic" in Hebrew. It's Israel's standard tourist fare, like little nested dolls in Russia or painted horses in Scandinavia, and before setting foot in the Promised

> **Comment (NL):** Do you need these details? Will any of this be important later?

Land three years ago, I knew where I could find one.
The T-shirt shop in the central block of a Jerusalem
shopping center did offer other shirt designs ("Maccabee
Beer" was a favorite), but that Coca-Cola shirt was what
drew in most of the dollar-carrying tourists. I waited
almost twenty minutes for mine, and I watched nearly
everyone ahead of me say "the Coke shirt" (and "thanks"
in Hebrew).

> **Comment (NL):** One of what? A doll or a horse?

> **Comment (BK):** Saying it in Hebrew would be cool here.

At the time, I never asked why I wanted the shirt. I
do know, though, that the reason I wear it often, despite
a hole in the right sleeve, has to do with its power as
a conversation piece. Few people notice it without asking
something like, "Does that say Coke?" I usually smile
and nod. They mumble a compliment and we go our
separate ways. But rarely does anyone want to know what
language the world's most famous logo is written in. And
why should they? Perhaps because Coca-Cola is a cultural
icon that shapes American identity.

> **Comment (NL):** This transition works really well. I wasn't sure where this was going, but here you are starting to clue the reader in.

> **Comment (NL):** Good detail! Lots of people can relate to a "conversation piece" shirt.

> **Comment (NL):** Good question! But I don't think the next sentence really answers it.

> **Comment (BK):** Is this the thesis? It kind of comes out of nowhere.

Throughout the company's history, marketing
strategies have centered on putting Coca-Cola in scenes
of the happy, carefree American life we never stop
striving for. What 1950s teenage girl wouldn't long to
see herself in the soda shop pictured in a Coca-Cola ad
appearing in a 1958 issue of *Seventeen* magazine? A
clean-cut, handsome man flirts with a pair of smiling
girls as they laugh and drink Coca-Colas. And any girls
who couldn't put themselves in that perfect, happy
scene could at least buy a Coke for consolation. The
malt shop — complete with a soda jerk in a white jacket
and paper hat — is a theme that, even today, remains a
symbol of Americana.

> **Comment (BK):** OK, here I am beginning to understand where your argument is going.

> **Comment (NL):** Maybe this is a little too broad?

> **Comment (BK):** *Any* girls? Really?

Reviewing and Revising > Video Prompt: Something to learn from each other

PEER REVIEW: Work with Reviewers

Seek good advice about your draft.

ASK:

What issues do you want reviewers to **focus** on?

What do they think **works** and **doesn't work** in your draft?

Do you need more information to understand their suggestions?

Think about what reviewers want you to do next.

The writer's role in peer review

Remember that your reviewers should be acting as coaches, not judges, and that their job is to help you improve your essay as much as possible. Listen to and read their comments carefully. If you don't understand a particular suggestion, ask for clarification, examples, and so on. Remember, too, that reviewers are commenting on your writing, not on *you*, so be open and responsive to what they recommend. But you are the final authority on your essay; you will decide which suggestions to follow and which to disregard.

7c   Consult instructor comments.

Instructor comments on any work that you have done can help you identify mistakes, particularly ones that you make repeatedly, and can point you toward larger issues that prevent your writing from being as effective as it could be. Whether or not you will have an opportunity to revise a particular piece of writing, you should look closely at the comments from your instructor.

macmillanhighered.com/everyday6e

Reviewing and Revising > Storyboard Activity: Getting help from peer reviewers

Reviewing and Revising > Video Prompt: Lessons from peer review

In responding to student writing, however, instructors sometimes use phrases or comments that are a kind of shorthand—comments that are perfectly clear to the instructor but may be less clear to the students reading them. The instructor comments in the following chart, culled from over a thousand first-year student essays, are among those that you may find most puzzling. Alongside each comment you'll find information intended to allow you to revise as your instructor recommends. If your paper includes a puzzling comment that is not listed here, be sure to ask your instructor what the comment means and how you can fix the problem.

Instructor Comment	Actions to Take in Response
thesis not clear	Make sure that you have a main point, and state it directly. The rest of the paper will need to support the main point, too—this problem cannot be corrected by adding a sentence or two.
trying to do too much *covers too much ground*	Focus your main point more narrowly (5a) so that you can explain your topic fully in a project of the assigned length. You may need to cut back on some material and then provide evidence and details to expand what remains.
hard to follow *not logical* *incoherent* *jumps around* *parts not connected* *transition*	If overall organization is unclear, try mapping or outlining and rearranging your work. (5d) See if transitions and signals or additional explanation will solve the problem.
too general *vague*	Use concrete language and details, and make sure that you have something specific and interesting to say. (29c) If not, reconsider your topic.
underdeveloped *thin* *sparse*	Add examples and details, and be as specific as possible. (29c) You may need to do more research. (Chapters 12–14)
what about the *opposition?* *one-sided* *condescending* *overbearing*	Add information on why some people disagree with you, and represent their views fairly and completely before you refute them. Recognize that reasonable people may hold views that differ from yours. (11f)

continued

Instructor Comment	Actions to Take in Response
repetitive *you've already said this*	Revise any parts of your writing that repeat an argument, point, word, or phrase; avoid using the same evidence over and over.
awk *awkward*	Ask a peer or your instructor for suggestions about revising awkward sentences. (Chapters 30–35)
syntax *awkward syntax* *convoluted*	Read the sentence aloud to identify the problem; revise or replace the sentence. (Chapters 30–35)
unclear	Find another way to explain what you mean; add any background information or examples that your audience may need to follow your reasoning.
tone too conversational *not an academic voice* *too informal* *colloquial*	Consider your audience and genre, and revise material that may suggest that you are not serious about the topic, audience, or assignment. (Chapter 29)
pompous *stilted* *stiff*	Make sure you understand the connotations of the words that you use. Revise material that adds nothing to your meaning, no matter how impressive it sounds. (29a and b)
set up quotation *integrate quotation*	Read the sentence containing the quotation aloud; revise it if it does not make sense as a sentence. Introduce every quotation with information about the source. Explain each quotation's importance to your work. (Chapter 15)
your words? *source?* *cite*	Mark all quotations clearly. Cite paraphrases and summaries of others' ideas. Give credit for help from others, and remember that you are responsible for your own work. (Chapters 14 and 15)
doc	Check the citations to be sure that you include all of the required information, that you punctuate correctly, and that you omit information not required by the documentation style. (Chapters 57–67)

7d Revise.

Approach comments from peer reviewers or from your instructor in several stages. First, read straight through the comments. Take a few minutes to digest the feedback and get some distance from your work. Then make a revision plan—as elaborate or as simple as you want—that prioritizes the changes needed in your next draft.

If you have comments from more than one reviewer, you may want to begin by making two lists: (1) areas in which reviewers agree on needed changes, and (2) areas in which they disagree. You will then have to make choices about which advice to heed and which to ignore from both lists. Next, rank the suggestions you've chosen to address.

Focus on comments about your purpose, audience, stance, thesis, and support. Leave any changes to sentences, words, punctuation, and format for later in the process; your revision of bigger-picture issues comes first.

Prepare a file for your revised draft. Use your previous draft as a starting point, renaming it to indicate that it is a revision. (For example, Javier Jabari might rename his file *jabari essay1 d2*, using his name, assignment number, and draft number.)

REVISING AND EDITING: Read All Comments Carefully

Analyze feedback from your instructor and other readers.

Remember: how you respond to suggestions is up to you.

ASK:

What additional questions do you have about the feedback?

Which comments are most important and **useful**?

Which comments will point you toward the most improved **next** draft?

REVISING AND EDITING: Plan Your Next Draft

Make big-picture changes.

ASK:

Do you need to rethink your **purpose** or **audience**?

How could you improve your **thesis** or **organization**?

What other **support** do you need?

Keep working until you have a coherent draft.

In the new file, make the changes you identified in your revision plan. Be prepared to revise heavily, if necessary; if comments suggest that your thesis isn't working, for example, you may need to change the topic or the entire direction of your text. Heavy revision is not a sign that there's something wrong with your writing; on the contrary, major revision is a common feature of serious, goal-oriented writing.

Once you are satisfied that the revisions adequately address your major concerns, make corrections to sentences, words, and punctuation.

TALKING THE TALK

Revision

"I thought I had revised my assignment, but my instructor said I'd just corrected the typos." It's always a good idea to clarify what *revision* means with a particular instructor. Generally, though, when a writing teacher asks for a revision, minor corrections will not be enough. Plan to review your entire draft, and be prepared to make major changes if necessary. Look for sentence-level errors and typos later, during the editing stage, since these may disappear or change as you revise.

Thesis

Make sure that your thesis states the topic clearly and comments on what is particularly significant about the topic (5b). In addition, ask yourself whether the thesis is narrowed and focused enough to be thoroughly supported. If not, take time now to refine or limit your thesis further.

When you revise your thesis, remember also to revise the rest of the draft accordingly.

Support

Make sure that each paragraph relates to or supports the thesis and that each paragraph has sufficient detail to support the point it is making. Eliminate unnecessary material, and identify sections that need further details or examples.

Organization

Should any sections or paragraphs be moved to clarify your point or support your thesis more logically? Are there any paragraphs or parts of paragraphs that don't fit with the essay now or that are unnecessary? Look for confusing leaps or omissions, and identify places where transitions would make the writing easier to follow.

Title, introduction, and conclusion

Does the title give information and draw readers in? Does the introduction attract their interest and present the topic in a way that makes them want to keep reading? Does the conclusion leave readers satisfied or fired up and ready to take action? Because readers notice beginnings and endings more than other parts of a piece of writing, pay special attention to how you introduce and conclude your work.

Visuals, media, and design

As you check what you've written about your topic, you also need to take a close look at the way your text looks and works. Do your visuals, audio, and video (if any) help you make your points? How can you make this content more effective? Do you use design effectively for your genre and medium? Is your text readable and inviting?

7e Edit.

Once you have revised a draft for content and organization, look closely at your sentences and words. Turning a "blah" sentence into a memorable one—or finding exactly the right word to express a thought—can result in writing that is really worth reading. As with life, variety is the spice of sentences. You can add variety to your sentences by looking closely at their length, structure, and opening patterns.

Sentence length

Too many short sentences, especially one following another, can sound like a series of blasts on a car horn, whereas a steady stream of long sentences may tire or confuse readers. Most writers aim for some variety in the length of their sentences.

Sentence structure

Using only simple sentences can make your writing sound choppy, but overusing compound sentences can result in a singsong rhythm, and strings of long complex sentences may sound—well, overly complex. Try to vary your sentence structure!

REVISING AND EDITING: Polish Your Draft

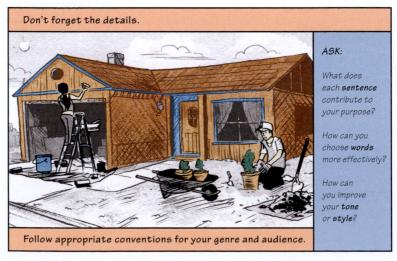

Don't forget the details.

ASK:

What does each **sentence** contribute to your purpose?

How can you choose **words** more effectively?

How can you improve your **tone** or **style**?

Follow appropriate conventions for your genre and audience.

Sentence openings

Most sentences in English follow subject-predicate order and hence open with the subject of an independent clause, as does the sentence you are now reading. But opening sentence after sentence this way results in a jerky, abrupt, or choppy rhythm. You can vary sentence openings by beginning with a dependent clause, a phrase, an adverb, a conjunctive adverb, or a coordinating conjunction (35b).

Emily Lesk's second paragraph (see pp. 70–71) tells the story of how she got her Coke T-shirt in Israel. Before she revised her draft, every sentence in this paragraph opened with the subject: *I have a favorite T-shirt, It's Israel's standard tourist fare, I waited.* . . . In her revision, Emily deleted some examples and varied her sentence openings for a dramatic and easy-to-read paragraph:

> *Even before* setting foot in Israel three years ago, I knew exactly where I could find the Coke T-shirt. The tiny shop in the central block of Jerusalem's Ben Yehuda Street did offer other designs, but the one with a bright white "Drink Coca-Cola Classic" written in Hebrew cursive across the chest was what drew in most of the dollar-carrying tourists. *While waiting* almost twenty minutes for my shirt, I watched nearly every customer ahead of me ask for "the Coke shirt, *todah rabah* [thank you very much]."

Sentences beginning with it and there

As you go over the opening sentences of your draft, look especially at those beginning with *it* or *there*. Sometimes these words can create a special emphasis, as in *It was a dark and stormy night.* But they can also appear too often. Another, more subtle problem with these openings is that they may be used to avoid taking responsibility for a statement. The following sentence can be improved by editing:

▶ ~~It is necessary to~~ raise student fees.
   ^The university must

Tone

Tone refers to the attitude that a writer's language conveys toward the topic and the audience. In examining the tone of your draft, think about the nature of the topic, your own attitude toward it, and that of your intended audience. Does your language create the tone you want to achieve (humorous, serious, impassioned, and so on), and is that tone an appropriate one, given your audience and topic?

e Reviewing and Revising > Storyboard Activity: Revising and editing

Word choice

Word choice—or diction—offers writers an opportunity to put their personal stamp on a piece of writing. Becoming aware of the kinds of words you use should help you get the most mileage out of each word. Check for connotations, or associations, of words and make sure you consider how any use of slang, jargon, or emotional language may affect your audience (see 29a and b).

Spell checkers

While these software tools won't catch every spelling error or identify all problems of style, they can be very useful. Most professional writers use their spell checkers religiously. Remember, however, that spell checkers are limited; they don't recognize most proper names, foreign words, or specialized language, and they do not recognize homonym errors (misspelling *there* as *their*, for example). (See 29f.)

Document design

Before you produce a copy for final proofreading, reconsider one last time the format and the "look" you want your text to have. This is one last opportunity to think carefully about the visual appearance of your final draft. (For more on document design, see Chapter 22. For more on the design conventions of different disciplines, see Chapters 17–23.)

QUICK HELP

Word Choice

- Are the nouns primarily abstract and general or *concrete* and *specific*? Too many abstract and general nouns can result in boring prose.

- Are there too many nouns in relation to the number of verbs? This sentence is heavy and boring: *The effect of the overuse of nouns in writing is the placement of strain on the verbs.* Instead, say this: *Overusing nouns places a strain on the verbs*.

- How many verbs are forms of *be* — *be, am, is, are, was, were, being, been*? If *be* verbs account for more than about a third of your total verbs, you are probably overusing them.

- Are verbs *active* wherever possible? Passive verbs are harder to read and remember than active ones. Although the passive voice has many uses, your writing will gain strength and energy if you use active verbs.

- Are your words *appropriate*? Check to be sure they are not too fancy — or too casual.

Proofreading the final draft

Take time for one last, careful proofreading, which means reading to correct any typographical errors or other inconsistencies in spelling and punctuation. To proofread most effectively, read through the copy aloud, making sure that you've used punctuation marks correctly and consistently, that all sentences are complete (unless you've used intentional fragments or run-ons for special effects)—and that no words are missing. Then go through the copy again, this time reading backward so that you can focus on each individual word and its spelling.

A student's revised draft

Following are the first three paragraphs from Emily Lesk's edited and proofread draft that she submitted to her instructor. Compare these paragraphs with those from her reviewed draft in 7b.

Student Writer

Emily Lesk

Emily Lesk
Professor Arraéz
Electric Rhetoric
November 15, 2013

Red, White, and Everywhere

America, I have a confession to make: I don't drink Coke. But don't call me a hypocrite just because I am still the proud owner of a bright red shirt that advertises it. Just call me an American.

Even before setting foot in Israel three years ago, I knew exactly where I could find the Coke T-shirt. The tiny shop in the central block of Jerusalem's Ben Yehuda Street did offer other designs, but the one with a bright white "Drink Coca-Cola Classic" written in Hebrew cursive across the chest was what drew in most of the dollar-carrying tourists. While waiting almost twenty minutes for my shirt (depicted in Fig. 1), I watched nearly every customer ahead of me ask for "the Coke shirt, *todah rabah* [thank you very much]."

At the time, I never thought it strange that I wanted one, too. After having absorbed sixteen years of Coca-Cola propaganda through everything from NBC's Saturday morning cartoon lineup to the concession stand at Camden Yards (the Baltimore Orioles' ballpark), I associated the shirt with singing along to the "Just for the Taste of It" jingle and with America's favorite pastime, not with a brown fizzy beverage I refused to consume. When I later realized the immensity of Coke's corporate power, I felt

Fig. 1. Hebrew Coca-Cola T-shirt. Personal photograph by author.

somewhat manipulated, but that didn't stop me from wearing the shirt. I still don it often, despite the growing hole in the right sleeve, because of its power as a conversation piece. Few Americans notice it without asking something like "Does that say Coke?" I usually smile and nod. Then they mumble a one-word compliment, and we go our separate ways. But rarely do they want to know what language the internationally recognized logo is written in. And why should they? They are interested in what they can relate to as Americans: a familiar red-and-white logo, not a foreign language. Through nearly a century of brilliant advertising strategies, the Coca-Cola Company has given Americans not only a thirst-quenching beverage but a cultural icon that we have come to claim as our own.

8 Reflecting

Research demonstrates a connection between careful reflection and learning: thinking back on what you've learned and assessing it help make that learning stick. As a result, first-year college writing courses are increasingly encouraging students to take time for such reflection. Whether or not your instructor asks you to write a formal reflection, whenever you finish a major piece of writing or a writing course, you should make time to think back over the experience and see what lessons you can learn from it.

8a   Reflect to present your work effectively.

You may find it useful (or you may be required) to reflect on the work you have done for a course as part of your preparation for submitting a portfolio of your best work.

Portfolio guidelines

In preparing a portfolio, use these tips:

- *Consider your purpose and audience.* Do you want to fulfill course requirements for an instructor, show work to a prospective employer, keep a record of what you've done for personal reasons, or something else? Answering these questions will help you decide what to include in the portfolio and whether it should be in print or electronic form.

- *Based on the portfolio's purpose, decide on the number of entries.* You may decide to include a wide range of materials—from essays, problem sets, and photos to web texts, multimedia presentations, a résumé, or anything else that is relevant—if readers can select only the pieces that interest them. For a portfolio that will be read from beginning to end, however, you should limit yourself to five to seven examples of your writing. You might include an academic essay that argues a claim, a personal essay, a brief report, writing based on research, significant correspondence, timed writing, or other work that you think shows your strengths as a writer.

- *Consider organization.* What arrangement—in chronological order, by genre, by topic—will make most sense to readers?

- *Think carefully about layout and design.* Will you include a menu, a table of contents, or appendices? How will you use color, font and type size, and other elements of design to enhance your portfolio (see Chapter 22)? Remember to label and date each piece of writing in the portfolio to help readers follow along easily. For print portfolios, number pages in consecutive order.

- *Edit and proofread* each piece in your portfolio and the reflective statement. Ask for responses from peers or an instructor.

Reflective statements

One of the most common writing assignments today is a reflective statement—often in the form of a letter, memo, or home page—that explains and analyzes a student's work in a writing course.

To create a reflective statement, think carefully about the impression it should give, and make sure your tone and style set the stage appropriately. Reflect on the strengths and weaknesses of your writing, using specific examples to provide evidence for each point you make. What are the most important things you have learned about writing—and about yourself as a writer—during the course?

If the reflective statement introduces your portfolio, follow your instructor's guidelines carefully. Unless asked to do otherwise, describe the portfolio's contents and explain why you have chosen each piece.

A STUDENT'S REFLECTIVE STATEMENT

Here is a shortened version of the cover letter that James Kung wrote to accompany his first-year writing portfolio.

Student Writer

James Kung

December 6, 2015

Dear Professor Ashdown:

"Writing is difficult and takes a long time." This simple yet powerful statement has been uttered so many times in our class that it has essentially become our motto. During this class, my persuasive writing skills have improved dramatically, thanks to many hours spent writing, revising, polishing, and thinking about my topic. The various drafts, revisions, and other materials in my portfolio show this improvement.

I entered this first-quarter Writing and Rhetoric class with both strengths and weaknesses. I have always written fairly well-organized essays. However, despite this strength, I struggled throughout the term to narrow and define the various aspects of my research-based argument.

The first aspect of my essay that I had trouble narrowing and defining was my major claim, or my thesis statement. In my "Proposal for Research-Based Argument," I proposed to argue about the case of Wen Ho Lee, the Los Alamos scientist accused of copying restricted government documents. I stated, "The Wen Ho Lee incident deals with the persecution of not only one man, but a whole ethnic group." You commented that the statement was a "sweeping claim" that would be "hard to support."

I spent weeks trying to rework that claim. Finally, as seen in my "Writer's Notebook 10/16/15," I realized that I had chosen the Lee case because of my belief that the political inactivity of Asian Americans contributed to the case against Lee. Therefore, I decided to focus on this issue in my thesis. Later I once again revised my claim, stating that the political inactivity did not cause but rather contributed to racial profiling in the Wen Ho Lee case.

I also had trouble defining my audience. I briefly alluded to the fact that my audience was a "typical American reader." However, I later decided to address my paper to an Asian American audience for two reasons. First, it would establish a greater ethos for myself as a Chinese American. Second, it would enable me to target the people the Wen Ho Lee case most directly affects: Asian Americans. As a result, in my final research-based argument, I was much more sensitive to the needs and concerns of my audience, and my audience trusted me more.

I hope to continue to improve my writing of research-based arguments.

Sincerely,

James Kung

James Kung

8b Reflect to learn.

Research shows that reflection is a key element in the move from writing for social reasons to writing for a wider public to accomplish bigger goals. When you reflect on your writing, you help ensure that what you have learned *transfers*—that is, that you will be able to use what you've learned in other disciplines and situations. Without time for reflection, you may feel that you are plunging from one assignment to the next, trying desperately to keep ahead of the syllabus, without being able to assimilate what you are learning. Try to make time to think about questions like these after every important piece of writing you do, either for school or for other purposes.

- What lessons have you learned from writing—from an individual piece of writing or an entire course?

- From what you have learned, what can you apply to the work you will do for other classes and to the writing you do for personal reasons?
- What about your writing do you feel most confident about—and why do you feel this way?
- What about your writing do you think needs additional work, and what plans do you have for improving?
- What confusions did you have while writing, and what did you do to resolve them?
- What major questions do you still have?
- How has writing helped you clarify your thinking, extend your knowledge, or deepen your understanding?
- Identify a favorite passage in your writing, and then try to articulate what you like about it. Can you apply what you learn from this analysis to other pieces of writing?
- How would you describe your development as a writer?
- What goals do you have for yourself as a writer?

A STUDENT'S REFLECTIVE BLOG POST

Student Thanh Nguyen created a political poster for a course on immigration. On his personal blog, he posted the image that he created with a few reflective notes about what he had learned. Here is the image, along with a portion of his post:

It's not too obvious what I was trying to get at in the poster, which is my own fault in the design process. I replaced the cherubs/angels from Michelangelo's *Creation of Adam* with ICE agents and politicians to comment on their anti-immigrant practices. I guess I just wanted to address

popular rhetoric dehumanizing undocumented folks in this country. They're people, too, you know? With families, lives, hopes, dreams, fears, and

Student Writing

beating hearts. Yet so many families are fractured because some children are forbidden to join their parents when deported, so many people are denied due process and proper trials because apparently you don't get them if you don't have a sheet of paper to legitimize your existence, and a lot of other messed-up stuff. As an artistic response to that, I just threw in a decapitated Statue of Liberty (lol stole/appropriated it from Cloverfield) and what I think she should say. . . .

Critical Thinking and Argument

To repeat what others have said requires
education; to challenge it requires brains.

— MARY PETTIBONE POOLE

Critical Thinking and Argument

Critical Thinking and Argument
89–144

For visual analysis The image on the front of this tab shows a person noticing a variety of transportation options. Which option would you choose in this situation, and why? Critical thinking requires you to analyze and make choices, and effective argument provides good reasons for making a particular choice.

Critical Reading **9**

I f you list all the reading you do in the course of a day, you will no doubt find that you are reading a lot—and that you are reading in many different ways for many different reasons, and using different tools and media. Reading critically means questioning, commenting, analyzing, and reflecting thoughtfully on a text—whether it's a white paper for a psychology class, a graphic novel, a Super Bowl ad, a business email, or a YouTube video. Any method you use to keep track of your questions and make yourself concentrate on a text can help you become a better critical reader.

9a Consider print and digital differences.

Onscreen reading is often social and collaborative, allowing you to connect with other readers, discuss what you've read, and thus turn reading into writing. Research suggests that onscreen readers tend to take shortcuts, scanning and skimming and jumping from link to link. Because screen reading can help you find content that relates to what you're looking for, it can be a powerful tool that you can use effectively in your college work.

But students today tell researchers that they still prefer to read print works when the reading needs to be absorbed and remembered. Psychologists find that students reading onscreen don't do nearly as much "metacognitive learning"—that is, learning that reflects on what has been learned and makes connections among the things learned—as readers of print texts do.

If you have a choice of media when you're asked to read a text, then, consider whether reading onscreen or in print will work better for your purposes. And if you must read a complex text onscreen rather than in print, be aware that you may need to try harder than usual to focus. Get in the habit of working through the steps described in this chapter—previewing (9b), annotating (9c), summarizing (9d), and analyzing (9e and f)—to ensure that you are reflecting and making appropriate connections, whether you're reading a printed page or a digital text.

9b   Preview the text.

Find out all you can about a text before beginning to look closely at it, considering its context, author, subject, genre, and design.

PREVIEWING THE CONTEXT

- Where have you encountered the work? Are you encountering the work in its original context? For example, an essay in a collection of readings may have been previously published in a magazine; a speech you watch on YouTube may have been delivered originally to a live or televised audience; a painting on a museum wall may have been created for a wealthy patron in a distant country centuries earlier.

CRITICAL READING: Preview

What do you expect to happen in this text?

Prepare to engage the text.

ASK:

What does the **title** tell you? Who **created** this work?

When, where, and how are you **encountering** the text?

How do genre, media, and design affect your expectations?

- What can you infer from the original or current context of the work about its intended audience and purpose?

LEARNING ABOUT THE AUTHOR OR CREATOR

- What information can you find about the author or creator of the text?
- What purpose, expertise, and possible agenda might you expect this person to have? Where do you think the author or creator is coming from in this text?

PREVIEWING THE SUBJECT

- What do you know about the subject of the text?
- What opinions do you have about the subject, and on what are your opinions based?
- What would you like to learn about the subject?
- What do you expect the main point to be? Why?

CONSIDERING THE TITLE, MEDIUM, GENRE, AND DESIGN

- What does the title (or caption or other heading) indicate?
- What do you know about the medium (or media) in which the work appears? Is it a text on the web, a printed advertising brochure, a speech stored in iTunes, an animated cartoon on television, or some combination of media? What role does the medium play in achieving the purpose and connecting to the audience?
- What is the genre of the text—and what can it help illuminate about the intended audience or purpose? Why might the authors or creators have chosen this genre?
- How is the text presented? What do you notice about its formatting, use of color, visuals or illustrations, overall design, general appearance, and other design features?

Student preview of an assigned text

Fernando Sanchez and Sarah Lum, students in a first-year writing class, read and analyzed an academic article, "'Mistakes Are a Fact of Life': A National Comparative Study," by Andrea A. Lunsford and Karen J. Lunsford. Some of the preview notes they made before reading the article

Student Writer

Fernando Sanchez

Student Writer

Sarah Lum

appear below. (See 9c–e for additional steps in the critical reading from these students.)

This essay was published in *College Composition and Communication* in June 2008. According to the journal's website, "*College Composition and Communication* publishes research and scholarship in rhetoric and composition studies that supports college teachers in reflecting on and improving their practices in teaching writing and that reflects the most current scholarship and theory in the field." So the original audience was probably college writing teachers.

Information on context

The essay begins with these words from essayist Nikki Giovanni: "Mistakes are a fact of life. It is the response to the error that counts." The introduction explains that the article will talk about a study of first-year college writing and compare it to "a similar study conducted over twenty years ago."

Andrea A. Lunsford was an English professor and the director of the Program in Writing and Rhetoric at Stanford University when this article appeared in 2008. She is also the author of the book we are using in our writing class. Karen J. Lunsford is an associate professor of writing at the University of California, Santa Barbara.

About the authors

According to Google Scholar, both authors have published many articles and conducted a lot of research on writing, so they have experience that relates to this article.

Information on the authors' credibility

The authors will study writing from students across the country and see whether problems are increasing or whether mistakes are just "a fact of life." I am the subject of this study without even knowing it! My high school teachers used to tell me to be careful not to include any "Internet lingo" in my writing. . . . I wonder if students really are losing the ability to write because of technology?

Subject of article

I see that the authors are replicating a study done by Andrea Lunsford and Robert Connors in 1984, and they will give a detailed comparison between the two studies. This essay may say that making mistakes in writing may not be such a bad thing.

The title includes a quotation from the epigraph that opens the essay and that sets the theme for the whole article, indicating that the authors will focus on the mistakes that others point out in this generation of student writing.

Other preview information

The genre of this essay is a scholarly article published in a journal. This journal requires MLA documentation style for endnotes and for the list of works cited. The essay also uses headings to signal changes in topics within the essay. Eight tables provide data to back up what the authors are saying.

Information about genre and design

9c Read and annotate.

As you read a text for the first time, mark it up or take notes. Consider the text's content, author, intended audience, and genre and design.

READING FOR CONTENT

- What do you find confusing or unclear about the text? Where can you look for explanations or more information? Do you need background information in order to understand fully?
- What key terms and ideas—or key patterns—do you see? What key images stick in your mind?
- What sources or other works does this text cite, refer to, or allude to?

TALKING THE TALK

Critical Thinking

"Are criticizing and thinking critically the same thing?" *Criticize* can sometimes mean "find fault with," and you certainly don't have to be relentlessly negative to think critically. Instead, critical thinking means, first and foremost, asking good questions — and not simply accepting what you see at face value. By asking not only what words and images mean, but also how meaning gets across, critical thinkers consider why a text makes a particular claim, what writers may be leaving out or ignoring, and how to tell whether evidence is accurate and believable. If you're considering questions like these, then you're thinking critically.

CRITICAL READING: Read Carefully

What do you find out by going through the text from start to finish?

ASK:

How does the text **fit** with your expectations?

What are the **major points** in the text? How are they supported?

How well do you **understand** the content?

Get everything you can from your first reading.

- How does the content fit with what you already know?
- Which points do you agree with? Which do you disagree with? Why?

READING FOR AUTHOR/CREATOR AND AUDIENCE

- Do the authors or creators present themselves as you anticipated in your preview?
- For what audience was this text created? Are you part of its intended audience?
- What underlying assumptions can you identify in the text?
- Are the medium and genre appropriate for the topic, audience, and purpose?

READING FOR DESIGN, COMPOSITION, AND STYLE

- Is the design appropriate for the subject and genre?
- Does the composition serve a purpose—for instance, does the layout help you see what is more and less important in the text?
- Do words, images, sound, and other media work together well?
- How would you describe the style of the text? What contributes to this impression—word choice? references to research or popular culture? formatting? color? something else?

Student annotation of an assigned text

Following is an excerpt from Andrea A. Lunsford and Karen J. Lunsford's essay "'Mistakes Are a Fact of Life': A National Comparative Study," with annotations made by Sarah Lum and Fernando Sanchez. To read the full article with Sarah and Fernando's annotations, go to **macmillanhighered.com/everyday6e**.

"Mistakes Are a Fact of Life": A National Comparative Study

BY ANDREA A. LUNSFORD AND KAREN J. LUNSFORD

> Mistakes are a fact of life. It is the response to the error that counts.
> —NIKKI GIOVANNI, *Black Feeling, Black Talk, Black Judgment*

Perhaps it is the seemingly endless string of what have come to be called "Bushisms" ("We shouldn't fear a world that is more interacted") and the complex response to them from both right and left. Perhaps it is the hype over Instant Messaging lingo cropping up in formal writing and the debate among teachers over how to respond (Farmer 48). Perhaps it is the long series of attempts to loosen the grip of "standard" English on the public imagination, from the 1974 special issue of *College Composition and Communication* (*Students' Right to Their Own Language*) to a 2006 special issue of *College English* devoted to *Cross-Language Relations in Composition*. Or perhaps it is the number of recent reports, many of them commissioned by the government, that have bemoaned the state of student literacy and focused attention on what they deem significant failures at the college level (see especially the recent reports from the Spellings Commission and Derek Bok's *Our Underachieving Colleges*).

> **Fernando Sanchez:** To an older audience, this is a good reference. To a much younger audience reading and researching this, "Bushisms" might not be a word in their vocabulary.

> **Sarah Lum:** Perhaps text message lingo is not the main problem of student writing; rather it is the subjects students are currently interested in. They are reading less formal texts and are more engaged in social media. In the past, I read an essay in which a student had quoted the lyrics of a rapper rather than an author.

Whatever the reasons, and they are surely complex and multilayered, forms of language use have been much in the news, with charges of what student writers can and cannot (or should and should not) do all around us. The times seemed ripe, then, for taking a close look at a national sample of student writing to see what it might tell us about the current state of affairs. With that goal in mind, we drew up plans to conduct a national study of first-year college student writing and to compare our findings to those of a similar study conducted over twenty years ago.

"The Frequency of Formal Errors," or Remembering Ma and Pa Kettle

But we are getting a bit ahead of ourselves here. For now, flash back to the mid-1980s. Some readers may remember receiving a letter from Robert Connors and Andrea Lunsford asking them to participate in a national study of student writing by submitting a set of marked student papers from a first-year composition course. That call brought in

> **FS:** This article will contain much content that older readers are already familiar with. It also includes phrases like "for now, flash back to the mid-1980s," implying the audience can easily remember those times.

well over 21,000 papers from 300 teachers around the country, and in fairly short order Andrea and Bob drew a random sample of 3,000 student papers stratified to be representative in terms of region of the country, size of institution, and type of institution. While they later analyzed patterns of teacher response to the essays as well as the particular spelling patterns that emerged (in that study, spelling was the most frequent student mistake by some 300 percent), they turned first to an analysis of which formal errors (other than spelling) were most common in this sample of student writing.

> **SL:** As frequent as misspelling is, I would expect that percentage to decrease in this age because we rely on computers to autocorrect our mistakes.

CRITICAL READING: Summarize

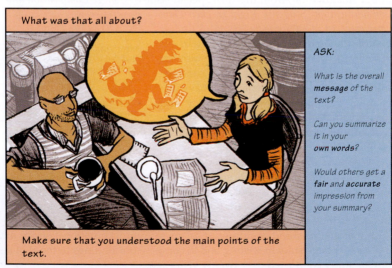

What was that all about?

ASK:

What is the overall **message** of the text?

Can you summarize it in your **own words**?

Would others get a **fair** and **accurate** impression from your summary?

Make sure that you understood the main points of the text.

☑ Critical Reading > LearningCurve: Critical reading
   Critical Reading > LearningCurve: Topics and main ideas

9d Summarize the main ideas.

When you feel that you have read and thoroughly understood the text, try to summarize the contents in your own words. A summary *briefly* captures the main ideas of a text and omits information that is less important. Try to identify the key points in the text, find the essential evidence supporting those points, and explain the contents concisely and fairly, so that a reader unfamiliar with the original can make sense of it all. Deciding what to leave out can make summarizing a tricky task—but mastering this skill can serve you well in all the reading you do in your academic, professional, and civic life. To test your understanding—and to avoid unintentional plagiarism—it's wise to put the text aside while you write your summary. (For more information on writing a summary, see 14f.)

Student summary of an assigned text

Students Fernando Sanchez and Sarah Lum, whose critical reading notes appear in this chapter, summarized the "Mistakes" article. Here is Sarah's summary:

Student Writing

In "'Mistakes Are a Fact of Life': A National Comparative Study," Andrea and Karen Lunsford investigate the claim that students today can't write as well as students in the past. To determine how writing has changed over time, they replicated the 1984 Connors and Lunsford study of errors in student writing to find similarities and differences between the formal errors made by first-year writing students in 2006. Their findings reveal that the number of mistakes made two decades ago are consistent with the number of errors made today and that actually the rate of mistakes has stayed stable for a hundred years. The authors found that slang and shorthand commonly used by young adults do not interfere with college writing. The major difference between writing then and now is that students are writing more argument essays as opposed to personal narratives and that typical papers are two-and-a-half times longer now. We can't avoid making mistakes, but we can document them and figure out means of improvement.

Annotations:

Begins by identifying authors, title, and date of article, and by stating main goal of study

Summarizes major findings

Closes with comment that captures main point of article

9e Analyze and reflect on the text.

When you feel that you understand the meaning of the text, move on to your analysis by asking additional questions about the text.

ANALYZING IDEAS AND EXAMPLES

- What are the main points in this text? Are they implied or explicitly stated?
- Which points do you agree with? Which do you disagree with? Why?
- Does anything in the text surprise you? Why, or why not?
- What kinds of examples does the text use? What other kinds of evidence does the text offer to back up the main points? Can you think of other examples or evidence that should have been included?
- Are viewpoints other than those of the author or creator included and treated fairly?
- How trustworthy are the sources the text cites or refers to?
- What assumptions does the text make? Are those assumptions valid? Why, or why not?

CRITICAL READING: Analyze

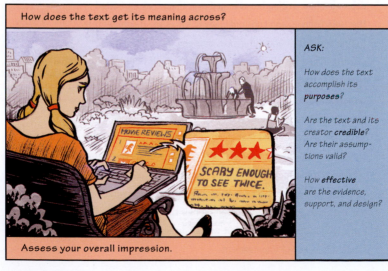

How does the text get its meaning across?

ASK:

How does the text accomplish its *purposes*?

Are the text and its creator **credible**? Are their assumptions valid?

How **effective** are the evidence, support, and design?

Assess your overall impression.

TALKING THE TALK

Visual Texts

"How can an image be a text?" In its traditional sense, a *text* involves words on paper. But now we spend at least as much time reading and analyzing images — including moving images — as we spend on printed words. So it makes sense to broaden the definition of "text" to include anything that sends a message. That's why images, ads, videos, films, and the like are often called *visual texts*.

ANALYZING FOR OVERALL IMPRESSION

- Do the authors or creators achieve their purpose? Why, or why not?
- What intrigues, puzzles, or irritates you about the text? Why?
- What else would you like to know?

Student analysis of an assigned text

After previewing, reading, annotating, and summarizing the article, students Sarah Lum and Fernando Sanchez analyzed the text. Here is Fernando's analysis:

Student Writing

Reading the first page gives the audience a good overview of what they are about to dive into. Andrea and Karen Lunsford clearly imply what side of the argument they will defend and expand on — that student errors have not increased over time. As I read, I noticed that the title quotation slowly and eloquently ties in with the argument. The authors' word choice (*positivity*, *optimism*, etc.) reminded me of this, and the phrase "mistakes are a fact of life" is also repeated several times to underline the main point.

States major finding of article

Shows how title quotation guides argument of entire essay

While a lot of people today think that students just can't write as well as we used to, this study proves the fear to be false. I am convinced by the results, which are based on careful analysis of a large number of student essays. One factor that did surprise me was an increase in student essay length. What happened between 1986 and 2006 that caused

Notes surprising aspect of essay and speculates on causes

such a huge change in length? The authors suggest that the change is related to use of technology, and this explanation makes sense to me.

Explains why he agrees with major point of essay

The authors use clear and direct examples from other studies over a century, and the tables they use really help readers understand the differences between the studies. In fact, this was a major goal: the authors want readers to see for themselves the similarities and differences in student errors that studies have shown over the past hundred years.

Notes effect of good examples and of tables representing findings

They have done a lot of research in order to find similar studies of error. In addition, one of the authors, Andrea Lunsford, was a researcher on a previous study. In my estimation, the authors achieved their purpose and have the evidence to support their conclusion. This article was well written, well explained, and well researched.

Notes how authors establish credibility

9f Think critically about visual texts.

You can use the steps given in 9b–e to read any kind of text, from a scholarly article for a research project to an Instagram image. You may be at least as accustomed to reading visual texts as you are to reading words, whether or not you take time to make a formal analysis of what you see. But pausing to look closely and reflect on how a visual text works can make you more aware of how visuals convey information.

On p. 103, a Pulitzer Prize–winning photograph (by Craig F. Walker of the *Denver Post*) appears with its caption. This image appeared as part of a series documenting the experiences of a Colorado teenager, Ian Fisher, who joined the U.S. Army to fight in Iraq. An analysis of this photograph made the following points:

The couple are in the center of the photo — and at the center of our attention. But at this moment of choosing an engagement ring, they do not look "engaged" with each other. Kayla looks excited but uncertain, as if she knows that Ian feels doubts, but she hopes he will change his mind. She is looking right at him, with her body leaning toward him but her head leaning away: she looks very

Notes what is foregrounded in image and relates it to "main point" of visual

© CRAIG F. WALKER/GETTY IMAGES

During a weekend home from his first assignment at Fort Carson, Colorado, Ian walked through a Denver-area mall with his new girlfriend, Kayla Spitzlberger, on December 15, 2007, and asked whether she wanted to go ring shopping. She was excited, but working out the financing made him nervous. They picked out the engagement ring in about five minutes, but Ian wouldn't officially propose until Christmas Day in front of her family. The couple had met in freshman math class but never really dated until now. The engagement would end before Valentine's Day.

tentative. Ian is looking away from Kayla, and the expression on his face suggests that he's already having second thoughts about the expense of the ring (we see his wallet on the counter by his elbow) and perhaps even about asking Kayla to marry him. The accompanying caption helps us interpret the image, telling us about the couple's brief history together and noting that the engagement will last less than two months after this moment. But the message comes through pretty clearly without words.

Analyzes why they "do not look 'engaged' with each other"

Shows how caption underscores image's main point

Ian and Kayla look as if they're trying on roles in this photograph. She looks ready to take the plunge, and he is resisting. These attitudes conform to stereotypical gender roles for a man and woman considering marriage (or going shopping, for that matter). The woman is expected to want the marriage and the ring; the man knows that he shouldn't show too much enthusiasm about weddings and shopping.

Analysis suggests that people in the image conform to stereotypical gender roles

It's hard for the reader to tell whether Ian and Kayla really feel that they are making good or careful choices for their situation at this moment or whether they're just doing what they think they're supposed to do under the circumstances.

The reader also can't tell how the presence of the photographer, Craig F. Walker, affected the couple's actions. The photo is part of a series of images documenting Ian Fisher's life after joining the military, so Walker had probably spent a lot of time with Ian before this photo was taken. Did Ian want to give a particular impression of himself on this day? Were he and Kayla trying on "adult" roles in this situation? Were they feeling pressure to produce a memorable moment for the camera? And what was Walker thinking when he accompanied them to the mall and took this photograph? Did he foresee the end of their engagement when he captured this revealing moment? What was his agenda?

> Notes that photographer's perspective may affect readers' understanding of image

> Raises questions for further analysis

9g   A student's critical reading of a text

Student Writer

Shuqiao Song

Following is an excerpt of a student essay written by Shuqiao Song, based on her critical reading of Alison Bechdel's graphic novel *Fun Home: A Family Tragicomic*. Shuqiao's critical reading involved looking closely at the words, at the images, and at how the words and images together create a very complex story. For Shuqiao Song's PowerPoint presentation of this essay, see 23f.

Shuqiao Song

Dr. Andrea Lunsford

English 87N

13 March 2014

Residents of a Dys*FUN*ctional *HOME*

In a 2008 online interview, comic artist Alison Bechdel remarked, "I love words, and I love pictures. But especially, I love them together — in a mystical way that I can't even explain" ("Interview"). Indeed, in her graphic novel memoir, *Fun Home: A Family Tragicomic,* text and image work together in a mystical way: text *and* image. But using both image and text results not in a simple summation but in a strange relationship — as strange as the relationship between Alison Bechdel and her father. These strange pairings have an alluring quality that makes Bechdel's *Fun Home* compelling; for her, both text and image are necessary. As Bechdel tells and shows us, alone, words can fail; alone, images deceive. Yet her life story ties both concepts inextricably to her memories and revelations such that only the interplay of text and image offers the reader the rich complexity, honesty, and possibilities in Bechdel's quest to understand and find closure for the past.

The idea that words are insufficient is not new — certainly we have all felt moments when language simply fails us and we are at a loss for words, moments like being "left . . . wordless" by "the infinite gradations of color in a fine sunset" (Bechdel, *Fun* 150). In those wordless moments, we strain to express just what we mean. Writers are especially aware of what is lost between word and meaning; Bechdel's comment on the translation of Proust's *À la Recherche du Temps Perdu* is a telling example of the troubling gap:

> After Dad died, an updated translation of Proust came out. *Remembrance of Things Past* was retitled *In Search of Lost Time*. The new title is a more literal translation

Introduces author of the work she is discussing, along with her major topic

First example in support of thesis

The Bechdels' elaborately restored house is the gilded, but tense, context of young Alison's familial relationships and a metaphor for her father's deceptions. "He used his skillful artifice not to make things, but to make things appear to be what they were not," Bechdel notes alongside an image of her father taking a photo of their family, shown in Fig. 2 (*Fun* 16). The scene represents the nature of her father's artifice; her father is *posing* a photo, an image of their family.

Fig. 2. Alison's father posing a family photo (Bechdel, *Fun* 16).

Second example in support of thesis

In that same scene, Bechdel also shows her own sleight of hand; she manipulates the scene and reverses her father's role and her own to show young Alison taking the photograph of the family and her father posing in Alison's place (Fig. 3). In the image, young Alison symbolizes Bechdel in the present—looking back through the camera lens to create a portrait of her family. But unlike her father, she isn't using false images to deceive. Bechdel overcomes the treason of images by confessing herself as an "artificer" to her audience (*Fun* 16). Bechdel doesn't villainize the illusory nature of images; she repurposes their illusory power to . . .

Fig. 3. Alison and her father trade places (Bechdel, *Fun* 17).

Song 8 | **Student Writing**

Works Cited

Bechdel, Alison. *Fun Home: A Family Tragicomic*. Boston:
    Houghton, 2006. Print.

- - -. Interview with Eva Sollberger. "Stuck in Vermont 109: Alison
    Bechdel." *YouTube*. YouTube, 13 Dec. 2008. Web. 6 Feb.
    2014.

Chabani, Karim. "Double Trajectories: Crossing Lines in *Fun Home*."
    GRAAT 1 Mar. 2007: 1-14. Print.

Chute, Hillary. "An Interview with Alison Bechdel." *MFS Modern
    Fiction Studies* 52.4 (2006): 1004-13. *Project Muse*. Web.
    30 Jan. 2014.

Gardner, Jared. "Autography's Biography, 1972-2007." *Biography*
    31.1 (Winter 2008). *Project Muse*. Web. 11 Feb. 2014.

Magritte, René. *The Treason of Images*. 1929. Los Angeles County
    Museum of Art. *lacma.org*. Web. 11 Feb. 2014.

Uses
MLA style
appropriately

Analyzing Arguments **10**

I n one important sense, all language has an argumentative edge. When you greet friends, you wish to convince them that you're glad to see them. Even apparently objective news reporting has strong argumentative overtones: when a news outlet highlights a particular story, for example, the editors are arguing that this subject is more important than others. Since argument is so pervasive, you need to be able to recognize and use it effectively—and to question your own arguments as well as those put forth by others.

QUICK HELP

Analyzing an Argument

Here are some questions that can help you judge the effectiveness of an argument:

- What conclusions about the argument can you reach by playing both the believing and the doubting game? (10a)
- What cultural contexts inform the argument, and what do they tell you about where the writer is coming from? (10b)
- What emotional, ethical, and logical appeals is the writer making in support of the argument? (10c)
- How has the writer established credibility to write about the topic? (10c)
- What is the claim (or arguable statement)? Is the claim qualified in any way? (10d)
- What reasons and assumptions support and underlie the claim? (10d)
- What additional evidence backs up the assumption and claim? How current and reliable are the sources? (10d)
- How does the writer use visuals and media to support the argument?
- What fallacies can you identify, and what effect do they have on the argument's persuasiveness? (10e)
- What is the overall impression you get from analyzing the argument? Are you convinced?

10a Think critically about argument.

Critical thinking is a crucial component of argument, for it guides you in recognizing, formulating, and examining arguments. Here are some ways to think critically about argument:

- *Check understanding.* First, make sure you understand what is being argued and why. If you need to find out more about an unfamiliar subject to grasp the argument, do the research.
- *Play the believing—and the doubting—game.* Begin by playing the *believing game:* put yourself in the position of the person creating the argument to see the topic from that person's point of view as much as possible. Once you have given the argument sympathetic attention, play the *doubting game:* look skeptically at each claim, and examine each piece of evidence to see how well (or poorly) it supports the claim. Eventually, this process of believing and doubting will become natural.

- *Ask pertinent questions.* Whether you are thinking about others' ideas or your own, you should question unstated purposes and assumptions, the writer's qualifications, the context, the goal of the argument, and the evidence presented. What objections might be made to the argument?

- *Interpret and assess information.* All information that comes to you has a perspective—a spin. Your job is to identify the perspective and assess it, examining its sources and finding out what you can about its context.

- *Assess your own arguments.* The ultimate goal of all critical thinking is to reach your own conclusions. These, too, you must question and assess.

10b Recognize cultural contexts.

To understand as fully as possible the arguments of others, pay attention to clues to cultural context and to where the writer or creator is coming from. Put yourself in the position of the person creating the argument before looking skeptically at every claim and examining the evidence. Above all, watch out for your own assumptions as you analyze what you read or see. For example, just because you assume that the use of statistics as support for your argument holds more water than, say, precedent drawn from religious belief, you can't assume that all writers agree with you. Take a writer's cultural beliefs into account before you analyze an argument. (See Chapter 26.)

10c Identify an argument's basic appeals.

Aristotle categorized argumentative appeals into three types: emotional appeals that speak to readers' hearts and values (known to the ancient Greeks as *pathos*), ethical appeals that support the writer's character (*ethos*), and logical appeals that use facts and evidence (*logos*).

Emotional appeals

Emotional appeals stir your emotions and remind you of deeply held values. When politicians argue that the country needs more tax relief, they almost always use examples of one or more families they have met, stressing the concrete ways in which a tax cut would improve the quality of their lives. Doing so creates a strong emotional appeal. Some have criticized the use of emotional appeals in argument, claiming that they are a form of manipulation intended to mislead an audience. But emotional appeals are an important part of almost every argument. Critical readers are perfectly capable of "talking back" to such appeals by analyzing them, deciding which are acceptable and which are not.

Ethical appeals

Ethical appeals support the credibility, moral character, and goodwill of the argument's creator. These appeals are especially important for critical readers to recognize and evaluate. We may respect and admire an athlete, for example, but should we invest in the mutual funds the athlete promotes? To identify ethical appeals in arguments, ask yourself these questions: How does the creator of the argument show that he or she has really done the homework on the subject and is knowledgeable and credible about it? What sort of character does he or she build, and how? More important, is that character trustworthy? What does the creator of the argument do to show that he or she has the best interests of an audience in mind? Do those best interests match your own, and, if not, how does that alter the effectiveness of the argument?

Logical appeals

Logical appeals are viewed as especially trustworthy: "The facts don't lie," some say. Of course, facts are not the only type of logical appeals, which also include firsthand evidence drawn from observations, interviews, surveys and questionnaires, experiments, and personal experience; and secondhand evidence drawn from authorities, the testimony of others, statistics, and other print and online sources. Critical readers need to examine logical appeals just as carefully as emotional and ethical ones. What is the source of the logical appeal—and is that source trustworthy? Are all terms clearly defined? Has the logical evidence presented been taken out of context, and, if so, does that change its meaning?

Appeals in a visual argument

The poster on p. 111, from TurnAround, an organization devoted to helping victims of domestic violence, is "intended to strike a chord with abusers as well as their victims." The dramatic combination of words and image builds on an analogy between a child and a target and makes strong emotional and ethical appeals.

The bull's-eye that draws your attention to the center of the poster is probably the first thing you notice about the image. Then you may observe that the "target" is, in fact, a child's body; it also has arms, legs, and a head with wide, staring eyes. The heading "A child is not a target" reinforces the bull's-eye/child connection.

This poster's stark image and headline appeal to viewers' emotions, offering the uncomfortable reminder that children are often the victims of domestic violence. The design causes viewers to see a target first and only afterward recognize that the target is actually a child—an unsettling experience. But the poster also offers ethical appeals ("TurnAround can help") to show that the organization is

Critical Reading > Tutorial: Reading visuals for audience

Critical Reading > Tutorial: Reading visuals for purpose

credible and that it supports the worthwhile goal of ending "the cycle of domestic violence" by offering counseling and other support services. Finally, it uses the logical appeal of a statistic, noting that TurnAround has served "more than 10,000 women, children and men each year" and giving specific information about where to get help.

10d   Analyze the elements of argument.

According to philosopher Stephen Toulmin's framework for analyzing arguments, most arguments contain common features: a *claim* or *claims*; *reasons* for the claim; *assumptions*, whether stated or unstated, that underlie the argument (Toulmin calls these *warrants*); *evidence* or *backing*, such as facts, authoritative opinions, examples, and statistics; and *qualifiers* that limit the claim in some way.

ELEMENTS OF A TOULMIN ARGUMENT

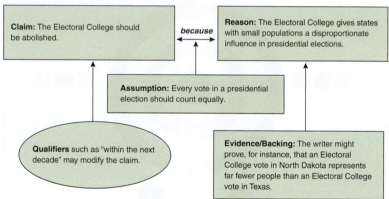

Claim: The Electoral College should be abolished.

because

Reason: The Electoral College gives states with small populations a disproportionate influence in presidential elections.

Assumption: Every vote in a presidential election should count equally.

Qualifiers such as "within the next decade" may modify the claim.

Evidence/Backing: The writer might prove, for instance, that an Electoral College vote in North Dakota represents far fewer people than an Electoral College vote in Texas.

Claims

Claims (also referred to as arguable statements) are statements that the writer wants to prove. In longer essays, you may detect a series of linked claims or even several separate claims that you need to analyze before you agree to accept them. Claims worthy of arguing are those that are debatable: to say "Ten degrees Fahrenheit is cold" is a claim, but it is probably not debatable—unless you are describing northern Alaska, where ten degrees might seem balmy. In the example shown above, the claim that the Electoral College should be abolished is certainly arguable; a Google search will turn up numerous arguments for and against this claim.

Reasons

A claim is only as good as the reasons attached to it. If a student claims that course portfolios should be graded pass or fail because so many students in the class work full-time jobs, critical readers may question whether that reason is sufficient to support the claim. In the example on the preceding page, the writer gives a reason—that states with small populations have too much influence over the Electoral College—to support the claim of abolishing the institution. As you analyze claims, test each reason by asking how directly it supports the claim, how timely it is, and what counter-reasons you could offer to question it.

Assumptions

Putting a claim and reasons together often results in what Aristotle called an *enthymeme*, an argument that rests on an assumption the writer expects the audience to hold. These assumptions (which Toulmin calls *warrants*) that connect claim and reasons are often the hardest to detect in an argument, partly because they are often unstated, sometimes masking a weak link. As a result, it's especially important to identify the assumptions in arguments you are analyzing. Once the assumption is identified, you can test it against evidence and your own experience before accepting it. If a writer argues that the Electoral College should be abolished because states with small populations have undue influence on the outcome of presidential elections, what is the assumption underlying this claim and reason? It is that *presidential elections should give each voter the same amount of influence*. As a critical reader, remember that such assumptions are deeply affected by culture and belief: ask yourself, then, what cultural differences may be at work in your response to any argument.

Evidence or backing

Evidence, which Toulmin calls *backing*, also calls for careful analysis in arguments. In an argument about abolishing the Electoral College, the writer may offer as evidence a statistical analysis of the number of voters represented by an Electoral College vote in the least populous states and in the most populous states, a historical discussion of why the Founding Fathers developed the Electoral College system, or psychological studies showing that voters in states where one political party dominates feel disengaged from presidential elections. As a critical reader, you must evaluate each piece of evidence the writer offers, asking specifically how it relates to the claim, whether it is appropriate and timely, and whether it comes from a credible source.

Qualifiers

Qualifiers offer a way of limiting or narrowing a claim so that it is as precise as possible. Words or phrases that signal a qualification include *many, sometimes, in these circumstances*, and so on. Claims having no qualifiers can sometimes lead to overgeneralizations. For example, the statement *The Electoral College should be abolished* is less precise than *The Electoral College should be abolished by 2024*. Look carefully for qualifiers in the arguments you analyze, since they will affect the strength and reach of the claim.

Elements of a visual argument

Visual arguments can also be analyzed using these Toulmin methods. Look closely at the advertisement to the right. If you decide that this advertisement is claiming that people should adopt shelter pets, you might word a reason like this: *Dogs and cats need people, not just shelter.* You might note that the campaign assumes that people make pets happier (and that all pets deserve happiness)—and that the image backs up the overall message that this inquisitive, well-cared-for dog is happier living in a home with a human than in a

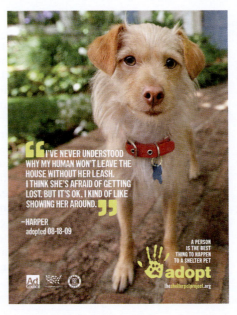

shelter. Considering unstated qualifiers (should *every* person consider adopting a shelter pet?) and thinking about potential evidence for the claim would help you complete an analysis of this visual argument.

10e   Think critically about fallacies.

Fallacies have traditionally been viewed as serious flaws that damage the effectiveness of an argument. But arguments are ordinarily fairly complex in that they always occur in some specific rhetorical situation and in some particular place and time; thus what looks like a fallacy in one situation may appear quite different in another. The best advice is to learn to identify fallacies but to be cautious in jumping to quick conclusions about them. Rather than thinking of them as errors you can use to discredit an arguer, you might think of them as barriers to common ground and understanding, since they often shut off rather than engender debate.

Verbal fallacies

AD HOMINEM

Ad hominem charges make a personal attack rather than focusing on the issue at hand.

▶ **Who cares what that fat loudmouth says about the health care system?**

GUILT BY ASSOCIATION

Guilt by association attacks someone's credibility by linking that person with a person or activity the audience considers bad, suspicious, or untrustworthy.

▶ **She does not deserve reelection; her husband had extramarital affairs.**

FALSE AUTHORITY

False authority is often used by advertisers who show famous actors or athletes testifying to the greatness of a product about which they may know very little.

▶ **He's today's greatest NASCAR driver—and he banks at National Mutual!**

BANDWAGON APPEAL

Bandwagon appeal suggests that a great movement is underway and the reader will be a fool or a traitor not to join it.

▶ **This new phone is everyone's must-have item. Where's yours?**

FLATTERY

Flattery tries to persuade readers by suggesting they are thoughtful, intelligent, or perceptive enough to agree with the writer.

▶ **You have the taste to recognize the superlative artistry of Bling diamond jewelry.**

IN-CROWD APPEAL

In-crowd appeal, a special kind of flattery, invites readers to identify with an admired and select group.

▶ **Want to know a secret that more and more of Middletown's successful young professionals are finding out about? It's Mountainbrook Manor condominiums.**

VEILED THREAT

Veiled threats try to frighten readers into agreement by hinting that they will suffer adverse consequences if they don't agree.

▶ **If Public Service Electric Company does not get an immediate 15 percent rate increase, its services to you may be seriously affected.**

FALSE ANALOGY

False analogies make comparisons between two situations that are not alike in important respects.

▶ **The volleyball team's sudden descent in the rankings resembled the sinking of the *Titanic*.**

BEGGING THE QUESTION

Begging the question is a kind of circular argument that treats a debatable statement as if it had been proved true.

▶ **Television news covered that story well; I learned all I know about it by watching TV.**

POST HOC FALLACY

The post hoc fallacy (from the Latin *post hoc, ergo propter hoc*, which means "after this, therefore caused by this") assumes that just because B happened *after* A, it must have been *caused* by A.

▶ **We should not rebuild the town docks because every time we do, a big hurricane comes along and damages them.**

NON SEQUITUR

A non sequitur (Latin for "it does not follow") attempts to tie together two or more logically unrelated ideas as if they were related.

▶ **If we can send a spaceship to Mars, then we can discover a cure for cancer.**

EITHER-OR FALLACY

The either-or fallacy insists that a complex situation can have only two possible outcomes.

▶ **If we do not build the new highway, businesses downtown will be forced to close.**

HASTY GENERALIZATION

A hasty generalization bases a conclusion on too little evidence or on bad or misunderstood evidence.

▶ **I couldn't understand the lecture today, so I'm sure this course will be impossible.**

OVERSIMPLIFICATION

Oversimplification claims an overly direct relationship between a cause and an effect.

▶ **If we prohibit the sale of alcohol, we will get rid of binge drinking.**

STRAW MAN

A straw-man argument misrepresents the opposition by pretending that opponents agree with something that few reasonable people would support.

▶ **My opponent believes that we should offer therapy to the terrorists. I disagree.**

Visual fallacies

Fallacies can also take the form of misleading images. The sheer power of images can make them especially difficult to analyze—people tend to believe what they see. Nevertheless, photographs and other visuals can be manipulated to present a false impression.

MISLEADING PHOTOGRAPHS

Faked or altered photos have existed since the invention of photography, and fakes continue to surface. On p. 118, for example, are an original photograph of an Iranian missile launch and the doctored image, showing a fourth launching missile, that Iran released to demonstrate its military might.

© AP PHOTO/SEPAHNEWS.COM

Today's technology makes such photo alterations easier than ever, if also easier to detect. But photographs need not be altered to try to fool viewers. Think of all the photos that make a politician look misleadingly bad or good. In these cases, you should closely examine the motives of those responsible for publishing the images.

MISLEADING CHARTS AND GRAPHS

Facts and statistics, too, can be presented in ways that mislead readers. For example, the following bar graph purports to deliver an argument about how differently Democrats, on the one hand, and Republicans and Independents, on the other, felt about a particular issue:

DATA PRESENTED MISLEADINGLY

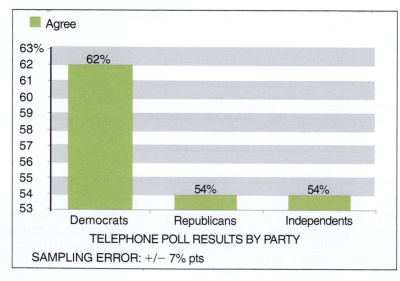

Look closely and you'll see a visual fallacy: the vertical axis starts not at zero but at 53 percent, so the visually large difference between the groups is misleading. In fact, a majority of all respondents agree about the issue, and only eight percentage points separate Democrats from Republicans and Independents (in a poll with a margin of error of +/− seven percentage points). Here's how the graph would look if the vertical axis began at zero:

DATA PRESENTED MORE ACCURATELY

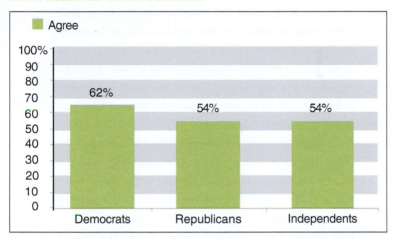

10f A student's rhetorical analysis

For a class assignment, Milena Ateyea was asked to analyze the emotional, ethical, and logical appeals in "Protecting Freedom of Expression at Harvard," an essay by Harvard president Derek Bok arguing that colleges should seek to persuade rather than to censor students who use speech or symbols that offend others.

Student Writer

Milena Ateyea

A Curse and a Blessing

In 1991, when Derek Bok's essay "Protecting Freedom of Expression at Harvard" was first published in the *Boston Globe*, I had just come to America to escape the oppressive Communist regime in Bulgaria. Perhaps my background explains why I support Bok's argument that we should not put arbitrary limits on freedom of expression. Bok wrote the essay in response to a public display of Confederate flags and a swastika at Harvard, a situation that created a heated controversy among the students. As Bok notes, universities have struggled to achieve a balance between maintaining students' right of free speech and avoiding racist attacks. When choices must be made, however, Bok argues for preserving freedom of expression.

In order to support his claim and bridge the controversy, Bok uses a variety of rhetorical strategies. The author first immerses the reader in the controversy by vividly describing the incident: two Harvard students had hung Confederate flags in public view, thereby "upsetting students who equate the Confederacy with slavery" (51). Another student, protesting the flags, decided to display an even more offensive symbol—the swastika. These actions provoked heated discussions among students. Some students believed that school officials should remove the offensive symbols, whereas others suggested that the symbols "are a form of free speech and should be protected" (51). Bok establishes common ground between the factions: he regrets the actions of the offenders but does not believe we should prohibit such actions just because we disagree with them.

The author earns the reader's respect because of his knowledge and through his logical presentation of the issue. In partial support of his position, Bok refers to U.S. Supreme Court rulings, which remind us that "the display of swastikas or Confederate flags clearly falls within the protection of the free-speech clause of the First Amendment" (52). The author also emphasizes the danger of

---

Provocative title suggests mixed response to Bok

Connects article to her own experience to build credibility (ethical appeal)

Brief overview of Bok's argument

Identifies Bok's central claim

Links Bok's claim to strategies he uses to support it

Direct quotations show appeals to emotion through vivid description

Bok establishes common ground between two positions

Emphasizes Bok's credibility (ethical appeal)

the slippery slope of censorship when he warns the reader, "If we begin to forbid flags, it is only a short step to prohibiting offensive speakers" (52). Overall, however, Bok's work lacks the kinds of evidence that statistics, interviews with students, and other representative examples of controversial conduct could provide. Thus, his essay may not be strong enough to persuade all readers to make the leap from this specific situation to his general conclusion.

Links Bok's credibility to use of logical appeals

Comments critically on kinds of evidence Bok's argument lacks

Throughout, Bok's personal feelings are implied but not stated directly. As a lawyer who was president of Harvard for twenty years, Bok knows how to present his opinions respectfully without offending the feelings of the students. However, qualifying phrases like "I suspect that" and "Under the Supreme Court's rulings, as I read them" could weaken the effectiveness of his position. Furthermore, Bok's attempt to be fair to all seems to dilute the strength of his proposed solution. He suggests that one should either ignore the insensitive deeds in the hope that students might change their behavior, or talk to the offending students to help them comprehend how their behavior is affecting other students.

Reiterates Bok's credibility

Identifies qualifying phrases that may weaken claim

Analyzes weaknesses of Bok's proposed solution

Nevertheless, although Bok's proposed solution to the controversy does not appear at first reading to be very strong, it may ultimately be effective. There is enough flexibility in his approach to withstand various tests, and Bok's solution is general enough that it can change with the times and adapt to community standards.

Raises possibility that Bok's imperfect solution may work

In writing this essay, Bok faced a challenging task: to write a short response to a specific situation that represents a very broad and controversial issue. Some people may find that freedom of expression is both a curse and a blessing because of the difficulties it creates. As one who has lived under a regime that permitted very limited, censored expression, I am all too aware that I could not have written this response in 1991 in Bulgaria. As a result, I feel, like Derek Bok, that freedom of expression is a blessing, in spite of any temporary problems associated with it.

Summarizes Bok's task

Ties conclusion back to title

Returns to own experience, which argues for accepting Bok's solution

Work Cited

Bok, Derek. "Protecting Freedom of Expression at Harvard." Rpt.
in *Current Issues and Enduring Questions*. Ed. Sylvan Barnet
and Hugo Bedau. 6th ed. Boston: Bedford, 2002. 51–52.
Boston Globe 25 May 1991. Print.

11 Constructing Arguments

Y ou respond to arguments all the time. When you see a stop sign and come to a halt, you've accepted the argument that stopping at such signs is a sensible thing to do. Unfortunately, constructing an effective argument of your own is not as easy as putting up a stop sign. Creating a thorough and convincing argument requires careful reasoning and attention to your audience and purpose.

11a Understand purposes for argument.

Although winning is an important purpose of argument, it is by no means the only purpose.

TO WIN The most traditional purpose of academic argument, arguing to win, is common in campus debating societies, in political debates, in trials, and often in business. The writer or speaker aims to present a position that will prevail over some other position.

TO CONVINCE Often, out-and-out defeat of another's position is not only unrealistic but undesirable. Instead, the goal might be to convince another person to change his or her mind. Doing so calls on a writer to provide *compelling reasons* for an audience to accept some or all of the writer's conclusions.

QUICK HELP

Reviewing Your Argument

- What is the purpose of your argument — to win? to convince others? to explore an issue? (11a)
- Is the point you want to make arguable? (11b)
- Have you formulated a strong working thesis that includes a clear claim and good reasons? (11c)
- Have you considered your audience sufficiently in shaping your appeals? (11e)
- How have you fully established your own credibility in the argument? (11f)
- How have you incorporated logical and emotional appeals into your argument? (11g and h)
- If you use sources, how effectively are they integrated into your argument? (11i)
- How is your argument organized? (11j)
- What design elements help you make your argument? (11k)

TO UNDERSTAND A writer often enters into a conversation with others to seek the best understanding of a problem, explore all approaches, and choose the best options. Argument to understand does not seek to control or conquer others or even to convince them. A writer's purpose in many situations — from trying to decide which job to pursue to exploring the best way to care for an elderly relative — will be to share information and perspectives in order to make informed political, professional, and personal choices.

TALKING THE TALK

Arguments

"Argument seems so negative — I don't want to attack anybody or contradict what someone else says." Sometimes — in law courts, for example — argument may call for attacking an opponent's credibility, and you may have used the word *argument* to describe a conversation in which the speakers said little more than "I did not!" and "You did, too!" But in college writing, argument usually means something much broader. Instead of attacking or contradicting, you will be expected to explore ideas and to work toward convincing yourself as well as others that these ideas are valuable.

11b Determine whether a statement can be argued.

At school, at home, or on the job, you will often need to convince someone or decide something. To do so, start with an arguable statement, which should meet three criteria:

1. It attempts to convince readers of something, change their minds about something, or urge them to do something—or it explores a topic in order to make a wise decision.
2. It addresses a problem for which no easily acceptable solution exists or asks a question to which no absolute answer exists.
3. It presents a position that readers might realistically have varying perspectives on.

ARGUABLE STATEMENT	Advertising in women's magazines contributes to the poor self-image that afflicts many young women.

This statement seeks to convince, addresses a problem—poor self-image among young women—that has no clear-cut solution, and takes a position many could disagree with.

UNARGUABLE STATEMENT	Women's magazines earn millions of dollars every year from advertising.

This statement does not present a position; it states a fact that can easily be verified and thus offers a poor basis for argument.

11c Make a claim and formulate a working thesis.

Once you have an arguable statement, you need to develop it into a working thesis (5b). One way to do so is to identify the elements of an argument (10d): the claim or arguable statement; one or more reasons for the claim; and assumptions—sometimes unstated—that underlie the claim and reasons.

To turn a claim into a working thesis for an argument, include at least one good reason to support the arguable statement.

REASON	Pesticides endanger the lives of farmworkers.
WORKING THESIS (CLAIM WITH REASON ATTACHED)	Because they endanger the lives of farmworkers, pesticides should be banned.

11d Examine your assumptions.

Once you have a working thesis, examine your assumptions to help test your reasoning and strengthen your argument. Begin by identifying underlying assumptions that support the working thesis.

WORKING THESIS	Because they endanger the lives of farmworkers, pesticides should be banned.
ASSUMPTION 1	Workers have a right to a safe working environment.
ASSUMPTION 2	Substances that endanger the lives of workers deserve to be banned.

Once you have a working thesis, you may want to use qualifiers to make it more precise and thus less susceptible to criticism. The preceding thesis might be qualified in this way:

▶ Because they *often* endanger the lives of farmworkers, *most* pesticides should be banned.

QUICK HELP

Showing Certainty in an Argument

How much certainty should you show when you're making an arguable claim? You may know that it's safer to say "*most* students believe" than "*all* students believe," but think carefully about when you should qualify or downplay a claim and when you can show greater confidence. Research conducted by Professor Laura Aull shows that expert academic writers in all disciplines tend to qualify their claims by using "hedges" — words such as *seems*, *might*, *may*, *generally*, *relatively*, *some*, or *likely* — and that expert writers are less likely to use intensifiers or "boosters" that show a high level of certainty — words such as *clearly*, *always*, *never*, and *must*. In contrast, student writers use many more "boosters" than "hedges." Learn from the experts: guard against overconfidence and aggressive critique of others' perspectives; overstating the truth of your claim can make you seem unfair or less credible to readers. Academic claims usually make room for alternative points of view, and they are more often qualified and cautious than absolutely certain.

11e   Shape your appeal to your audience.

Arguments and the claims they make are effective only if they appeal to the appropriate audience. For example, if you want to argue for increased lighting in parking garages on campus, you might appeal to students by citing examples drawn from their experiences of the safety problems in such dimly lit garages. If you are writing to university administrators, however, you might focus on the negative publicity associated with past attacks in campus garages and evoke the anger that such attacks cause in parents, alumni, and other influential groups.

11f   Establish credibility through ethical appeals.

To make your argument convincing, you must first gain the respect and trust of your readers, or establish credibility with them. In general, writers can establish credibility by making ethical appeals (10c) in four ways.

Knowledge

A writer can establish credibility first by establishing credentials. To decide whether you know enough to argue an issue credibly, consider the following questions:

- Can you provide information about your topic from sources other than your own knowledge?
- How reliable are your sources?
- If sources contradict one another, can you account for or resolve the contradictions?
- Would a personal experience relating to the issue help support your claim?

These questions may well show that you must do more research, check sources, resolve contradictions, refocus your working thesis, or even change your topic.

Common ground

Many arguments between people or groups are doomed to end without resolution because the two sides seem to occupy no starting

QUICK HELP

Building Ethos through Careful Restatement

Expert writers, says linguist Laura Aull, use "reformulation" or restatement to help build credibility and signal their own take on the evidence they're presenting. Phrases like *in other words*, *that is to say*, and *to be precise* show that a writer is interpreting information for the reader; *especially* or *in particular* emphasize what the writer finds particularly important; *in fact* or *indeed* or *as a matter of fact* show that a writer is contrasting an existing view. Expert writers use such phrases to restate and underscore their interpretation and introduce their own voices into their writing far more often than student writers do. Like transitions, these restatements help showcase the writer's reason for organizing the text in a particular way or emphasize the relation between ideas or parts of a text. How can you use restatement to build your ethos, or credibility? Look for — and ask peer reviewers to point out — opportunities to restate and clarify ideas.

point of agreement. The following questions can help you find common ground in presenting an argument. (See also Chapter 27.)

- What are the differing perspectives on this issue?
- What common ground can all sides agree on?
- How can you express such agreement clearly to all sides?
- How can you discover — and consider — opinions on this issue that differ from your own?
- How can you use language — occupational, regional, or ethnic varieties of English or languages other than English (28b–d) — to establish common ground with those you address?

   FOR MULTILINGUAL WRITERS

Counting Your Own Experience

You may have been told that your personal experience doesn't count in making academic arguments. If so, reconsider this advice, for showing an audience that you have relevant personal experience with a topic can carry strong persuasive appeal with many English-speaking readers.

Fairness

In arguing a position, writers must deal fairly with opposing arguments (also called counterarguments). Audiences are more inclined to listen to writers who seem to consider their opponents' views fairly than to those who ignore or distort such views. The following questions can help you discover ways of establishing yourself as open-minded and evenhanded:

- How can you show that you are taking into account all significant points of view?
- How can you demonstrate that you understand and sympathize with points of view other than your own?
- What can you do to show that you have considered evidence carefully, even when it does not support your position?

Some writers, instead of demonstrating fairness, may make unjustified attacks on an opponent's credibility. Avoid such attacks in your writing.

Visuals that make ethical appeals

In arguments and other kinds of writing, visuals can combine with text to help present a writer or an organization as trustworthy and credible. Like businesses, many institutions and individuals are using logos and other images to brand themselves as they wish the public to see them. The Sustainable Food Laboratory logo, seen here, suggests that the organization is concerned about both food production and the environment.

Visuals that make ethical appeals add to your credibility and fairness as a writer. Just as you probably consider the impression your Facebook profile photo makes on your audience, you should think about what kind of case you're making for yourself when you choose images and design elements for your argument.

11g   Use effective logical appeals.

Credibility alone cannot and should not carry the full burden of convincing readers. Indeed, many are inclined to think that the logic of the argument—the reasoning behind it—is as important as its ethos.

Examples, precedents, and narratives

Just as a picture can sometimes be worth a thousand words, so can a well-conceived example be extremely valuable in arguing a point. Examples are used most often to support generalizations or to bring abstractions to life. In making the general statement that popular media send the message that a woman must be thin to be attractive, you might include these examples:

> At the supermarket checkout, a tabloid publishes unflattering photographs of a young singer and comments on her apparent weight gain in shocked captions that ask "What happened?!?" Another praises a star for quickly shedding "ugly pounds" after the recent birth of a child. The cover of *Cosmopolitan* features a glamorously made-up and airbrushed actress in an outfit that reveals her remarkably tiny waist and flat stomach. Every woman in every advertisement in the magazine is thin—and the context makes it clear that readers are supposed to think that she is beautiful.

Precedents are examples taken from the past. If, as part of a proposal for increasing lighting in the library garage, you point out that the university has increased lighting in four other garages in the past year, you are arguing on the basis of precedent.

The following questions can help you check any use of example or precedent:

- How representative are the examples?
- Are the examples sufficient in strength or number to lead to a generalization?
- In what ways do they support your point?
- How closely does a precedent relate to the point you're trying to make? Are the situations really similar?
- How timely is the precedent? (What would have been applicable in 1920 is not necessarily applicable today.)

Because storytelling is universal, *narratives* can be very persuasive in helping readers understand and accept the logic of an argument. Narratives that use video and audio to capture the faces and voices of the people involved are often particularly compelling.

Stories drawn from your own experience can appeal particularly to readers, for they not only help make your point in true-to-life, human terms but also help readers know you better and therefore identify with you more closely.

When you include stories in an argument, ask yourself the following questions:

- Does the narrative support your thesis?

- Will the story's significance to the argument be clear to your readers?
- Is the story one of several good reasons or pieces of evidence — or does it have to carry the main burden of the argument?

In research writing, you must identify your sources for any examples, precedents, or narratives not based on your own knowledge.

Authority and testimony

Another way to support an argument logically is to cite an authority. The use of authority has figured prominently in the controversy over smoking. Since the U.S. surgeon general's 1964 announcement that smoking is hazardous to health, many Americans have quit smoking, largely persuaded by the authority of the scientists offering the evidence.

Ask the following questions to be sure you are using authorities effectively:

- Is the authority *timely*? (The argument that the United States should pursue a policy that was supported by Thomas Jefferson will probably fail since Jefferson's time was so radically different from ours.)
- Is the authority *qualified* to judge the topic at hand? (To cite a movie star in an academic essay on linguistics may not help your argument.)
- Is the authority likely to be *known and respected* by readers? (To cite an unfamiliar authority without identification will reduce the impact of the evidence.)
- Are the authority's *credentials* clearly stated and verifiable? (Especially with web-based sources, it is crucial to know whose authority guarantees the reliability of the information.)

Testimony — the evidence that an authority presents in support of a claim — is a feature of much contemporary argument. If testimony is timely, accurate, representative, and provided by a respected authority, then it, like authority itself, can add powerful support.

In research writing (see Chapters 12–16), you should cite your sources for authority and for testimony not based on your own knowledge.

Causes and effects

Showing that one event is the cause or the effect of another can help support an argument. Suppose you are trying to explain, in a petition to change your grade in a course, why you were unable to take the final examination. You would probably trace the causes of your failure to appear—your illness or the theft of your car, perhaps—so that the committee reading the petition would reconsider the effect—your not taking the examination.

Tracing causes often lays the groundwork for an argument, particularly if the effect of the causes is one we would like to change. In an environmental science class, for example, a student may argue that a national law regulating smokestack emissions from utility plants is needed because (1) acid rain on the East Coast originates from emissions at utility plants in the Midwest, (2) acid rain kills trees and other vegetation, (3) utility lobbyists have prevented Midwestern states from passing strict laws controlling emissions from such plants, and (4) if such laws are not passed, acid rain will soon destroy most eastern forests. In this case, the fourth point ties all of the previous points together to provide an overall argument from effect: if X, then Y.

Inductive and deductive reasoning

Traditionally, logical arguments are classified as using either inductive or deductive reasoning; in practice, the two almost always work together. Inductive reasoning is the process of making a generalization based on a number of specific instances. If you find you are ill on ten occasions after eating seafood, for example, you will likely draw the inductive generalization that seafood makes you ill. It may not be an absolute certainty that seafood is to blame, but the probability lies in that direction.

Deductive reasoning, on the other hand, reaches a conclusion by assuming a general principle (known as a major premise) and then applying that principle to a specific case (the minor premise). In practice, this general principle is usually derived from induction. The inductive generalization *Seafood makes me ill*, for instance, could serve as the major premise for the deductive argument *Since all seafood makes me ill, the shrimp on this buffet is certain to make me ill.*

Deductive arguments have traditionally been analyzed as syllogisms: reasoning that contains a major premise, a minor premise, and a conclusion.

MAJOR PREMISE	All people die.
MINOR PREMISE	I am a person.
CONCLUSION	I will die.

Syllogisms, however, are too rigid and absolute to serve in arguments about questions that have no absolute answers, and they often lack any appeal to an audience. Aristotle's more flexible alternative, the enthymeme, asks the audience to supply the implied major premise. Consider the following example:

> Because children who are bullied suffer psychological harm, schools should immediately discipline students who bully others.

You can analyze this enthymeme by restating it in the form of two premises and a conclusion.

MAJOR PREMISE	Schools should immediately discipline students who harm other children.
MINOR PREMISE	Being bullied causes psychological harm to children.
CONCLUSION	Schools should immediately discipline students who bully other children.

Note that the major premise is one the writer can count on an audience agreeing with or supplying: safety and common sense demand that schools should discipline children who harm other students. By implicitly asking the audience to supply this premise to the argument, the writer engages the audience's participation.

Toulmin's system (10d) looks for claims, reasons, and assumptions instead of major and minor premises.

CLAIM	Schools should immediately discipline students who bully other children.
REASON(S)	Being bullied causes psychological harm to children.
ASSUMPTION	Schools should discipline students who harm other children.

Note that in this system the assumption—which may be unstated—serves the same function as the assumed major premise in an enthymeme.

Whether it is expressed as a syllogism, an enthymeme, or a claim, a deductive conclusion is only as strong as the premise or reasons on which it is based.

Visuals that make logical appeals

Visuals that make logical appeals can be especially useful in arguments, since they present factual information that can be taken in at a glance. *Mother Jones* used this simple chart to carry a big message about income distribution in the United States. Consider how long it would take to explain all the information in this chart with words alone.

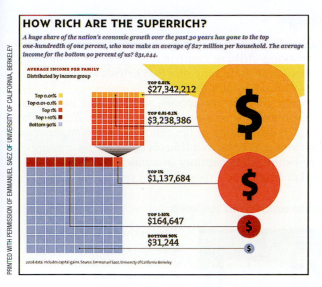

HOW RICH ARE THE SUPERRICH?

A huge share of the nation's economic growth over the past 30 years has gone to the top one-hundredth of one percent, who now make an average of $27 million per household. The average income for the bottom 90 percent of us? $31,244.

AVERAGE INCOME PER FAMILY
Distributed by income group

Top 0.01%
Top 0.01-0.1%
Top 1%
Top 1-10%
Bottom 90%

TOP 0.01%
$27,342,212

TOP 0.01-0.1%
$3,238,386

TOP 1%
$1,137,684

TOP 1-10%
$164,647

BOTTOM 90%
$31,244

2008 data. Includes capital gains. Source: Emmanuel Saez, University of California-Berkeley

11h Use appropriate emotional appeals.

Most successful arguments appeal to our hearts as well as to our minds—as is vividly demonstrated by the campaign to send aid to Nepal after a series of devastating earthquakes. Facts and figures (logical appeals) convince us that the problem is real and serious. What elicits an outpouring of support, however, is the arresting emotional power of stories and images of people affected by the disaster. But credible writers take particular care when they use emotional appeals; audiences can easily begin to feel manipulated when an argument tries too hard to appeal to their pity, anger, or fear.

Concrete descriptive details

Like photographs, vivid words can bring a moving immediacy to any argument. A student may amass facts and figures, including diagrams and maps, to illustrate the problem of wheelchair access to the library. But only when the student asks a friend who uses a wheelchair to accompany her to the library does the student writer discover the concrete details necessary to move readers. The student can then write, "Marie inched her heavy wheelchair up the steep entrance ramp, her arms straining, her face pinched with the sheer effort."

Figurative language

Figurative language, or figures of speech, can paint a detailed and vivid picture by making striking comparisons between something you are writing about and something else that helps a reader visualize, identify with, or understand it (29d).

Figures of speech include metaphors, similes, and analogies. Most simply, metaphors compare two things directly: *Richard the Lion-Hearted; old age is the evening of life.* Similes make comparisons using *like* or *as: Richard is as brave as a lion; old age is like the evening of life.* Analogies are extended metaphors or similes that compare an unfamiliar concept or process to a more familiar one.

Visuals that make emotional appeals

© RICK FRIEDMAN/CORBIS

Visuals that make emotional appeals can also add substance to your argument. To make sure that such visual appeals will enhance your argument, test them out with several potential readers to see how they interpret the appeal. Consider, for example, this photograph depicting a Boston rally of gun-rights advocates. The image includes a group of protesters, one of whom is holding a sign saying "More gun laws will not stop mad men from killing," with a large yellow Gadsden flag in the foreground. Readers who generally oppose laws regulating gun ownership in the United States may feel very differently about this image than readers who tend to support restrictions on guns in private hands.

11i   Consult sources.

In constructing an academic argument, it is often essential to use sources. The key to persuading people to accept your argument is providing good reasons; and even if your assignment doesn't specify that you must consult outside sources, they are often the most effective way of finding and establishing these reasons. Sources can help you to do the following:

- provide background information on your topic
- demonstrate your knowledge of the topic to readers

- cite authority and testimony in support of your thesis
- find opinions that differ from your own, which can help you sharpen your thinking, qualify your thesis if necessary, and demonstrate fairness to opposing arguments

For a more thorough discussion of finding, gathering, and evaluating sources, see Chapters 12–16.

11j Organize your argument.

Once you have assembled good reasons and evidence in support of an argumentative thesis, you must organize your material to present the argument convincingly. Although there is no universally favored, one-size-fits-all organizational framework, you may find it useful to try one of the following patterns.

The classical system

The system of argument often followed by ancient Greek and Roman orators is now referred to as *classical*. You can adapt the ancient format to written arguments as follows:

1. Introduction

   - Gain readers' attention and interest.
   - Establish your qualifications to write about your topic.
   - Establish common ground with readers.
   - Demonstrate fairness.
   - State or imply your thesis.

2. Background

   - Present any necessary background information, including relevant personal narrative.

3. Lines of argument

   - Present good reasons (including logical and emotional appeals) in support of your thesis.
   - Present reasons in order of importance, with the most important ones generally saved for last.
   - Demonstrate ways your argument may be in readers' best interest.

4. Alternative arguments

   - Examine alternative points of view.
   - Note advantages and disadvantages of alternative views.
   - Explain why one view is better than other(s).

5. Conclusion
   - Summarize the argument if you choose.
   - Elaborate on the implication of your thesis.
   - Make clear what you want readers to think or do.
   - Reinforce your credibility.

The Toulmin system

This simplified form of the Toulmin system (10d and 11g) can help you organize an argumentative essay:

1. Make your claim (arguable statement).
   ▶ **The federal government should ban smoking.**

2. Qualify your claim if necessary.
   ▶ **The ban would be limited to public places.**

3. Present good reasons to support your claim.
   ▶ **Smoking causes serious diseases in smokers.**
   ▶ **Nonsmokers are endangered by others' smoke.**

4. Explain the assumptions that underlie your claim and your reasons. Provide additional explanations for any controversial assumptions.

ASSUMPTION	The Constitution was established to "promote the general welfare."
ASSUMPTION	Citizens are entitled to protection from harmful actions by others.
ADDITIONAL EXPLANATION	The United States is based on a political system that is supposed to serve the basic needs of its people, including their health.

5. Provide additional evidence to support your claim (such as facts, statistics, testimony, and other logical, ethical, or emotional appeals).

STATISTICS	Cite the incidence of deaths attributed to secondhand smoke.
FACTS	Cite lawsuits won against large tobacco companies, including one that awarded billions of dollars to states in reparation for smoking-related health care costs.
FACTS	Cite bans on smoking already imposed on indoor public spaces in many cities.
AUTHORITY	Cite the surgeon general.

6. Acknowledge and respond to possible counterarguments.

COUNTER-ARGUMENT   Smokers have rights, too.

RESPONSE   The suggested ban applies only to public places; smokers are free to smoke in private.

7. Finally, state your conclusion in the strongest way possible.

Rogerian or invitational argument

The psychologist Carl Rogers argued that people should not enter into disputes until they can thoroughly and fairly understand the other person's (or persons') perspectives. From Rogers's theory, rhetoricians Richard Young, Alton Becker, and Kenneth Pike adapted a four-part structure that is now known as "Rogerian argument":

- The introduction describes the issue, problem, or conflict in enough detail to demonstrate that the writer fully grasps and respects alternative points of view.

- The writer then fairly describes the contexts in which such alternative positions might be valid.

- The writer offers his or her position on the issue and explains in what circumstances and why that position would be valid.

- Finally, the writer explains how those who hold alternative positions can benefit from adopting the writer's position.

Like Rogerian argument, invitational rhetoric has as its goal getting people to work together effectively and to identify with each other; it aims for connection and collaboration. Such arguments call for structures that are closer to good two-way conversations or freewheeling dialogues than a linear march from thesis to conclusion. If you try developing such a conversational structure, you may find that it opens up a space in your argument for new perceptions and fresh ideas.

11k   Consider design and delivery.

When someone asked the ancient orator Demosthenes to name the three most important parts of rhetoric, he said: *delivery, delivery, delivery.* In short, while what speakers said was important, the way they said it was of even greater importance. Today, we live in a time of information overload, when many powerful messages are vying for our attention. Getting and keeping an audience's attention is all about delivery. Figuring out the medium of delivery (print? digital? in-person?) and the appropriate genre is important, and so is designing the argument to appeal to your target audience.

- What medium will best get and hold your audience's attention? print? video? in-person or web presentation? social media site? Choosing just the right one is important to your success.

- What genre is most appropriate for your message? a report? a narrative? an essay? a brochure?

- What word choice, style, and tone will be most successful in delivering your message?

- Are any conventions expected in the kind of argument you are writing? Look for examples of similar arguments, or ask your instructor for information.

- What visual style will appeal to your intended readers, set a clear tone for your argument, and guide readers through your text? Spend time thinking about how the argument will look, and aim for a consistent visual design and for appealing fonts and colors.

- Are visual and media elements clearly integrated into your argument? Place images close to the text they illustrate, and label each one clearly. Make sure that audio and video files appear in appropriate places and are identified for users.

After you have a rough plan for delivering your argument, test it on friends and classmates, asking them what you need to change to make it more effective.

11l   A student's argument essay

Student Writer

Benjy Mercer-Golden

In this argument essay, Benjy Mercer-Golden argues that socially conscious businesses and traditional for-profit businesses can learn from each other in ways that benefit businesses, consumers, and the environment. His essay has been annotated to point out the various parts of his argument as well as his use of good reasons, evidence, and appeals to logic and emotion.

Benjy Mercer-Golden

28 Nov. 2012

Lessons from Tree-Huggers and Corporate Mercenaries:

A New Model of Sustainable Capitalism

Televised images of environmental degradation—seagulls with oil coating their feathers, smokestacks belching gray fumes—often seem designed to shock, but these images also represent very real issues: climate change, dwindling energy resources like coal and oil, a scarcity of clean drinking water. In response, businesspeople around the world are thinking about how they can make their companies greener or more socially beneficial to ensure a brighter future for humanity. But progress in the private sector has been slow and inconsistent. To accelerate the move to sustainability, for-profit businesses need to learn from the hybrid model of social entrepreneurship to ensure that the company is efficient and profitable while still working for social change, and more investors need to support companies with long-term, revolutionary visions for improving the world.

In fact, both for-profit corporations and "social good" businesses could take steps to reshape their strategies. First, for-profit corporations need to operate sustainably and be evaluated for their performance with long-term measurements and incentives. The conventional argument against for-profit companies deeply embedding environmental and social goals into their corporate strategies is that caring about the world does not go hand in hand with lining pockets. This morally toxic case is also problematic from a business standpoint. A 2012 study of 180 high-profile companies by Harvard Business School professors Robert G. Eccles and George Serafeim and London Business School professor Ioannis Ioannou shows that "high sustainability companies," as defined by

Provocative word choice for title

Emotional appeals through use of vivid imagery

Thesis establishing purpose

Claim related to thesis

Opposing viewpoint to establish writer's credibility

Rebuttal

　　　　　　　　　　　　　　　　　Mercer-Golden 2

environmental and social variables, "significantly outperform their counterparts over the long term, both in terms of stock market and accounting performance." The study argues that the better financial returns of these companies are especially evident in sectors where "companies' products significantly depend upon extracting large amounts of natural resources" (Eccles, Ioannou, and Serafeim).

Such empirical financial evidence to support a shift toward using energy from renewable sources to run manufacturing plants argues that executives should think more sustainably, but other underlying incentives need to evolve in order to bring about tangible change. David Blood and Al Gore of Generation Investment Management, an investment firm focused on "sustainable investing for the long term" ("About Us"), wrote a groundbreaking white paper that outlined the perverse incentives company managers face. For public companies, the default practice is to issue earnings guidances—announcements of projected future earnings—every quarter. This practice encourages executives to manage for the short term instead of adding long-term value to their company and the earth (Gore and Blood). Only the most uncompromisingly green CEOs would still advocate for stricter carbon emissions standards at the company's factories if a few mediocre quarters left investors demanding that they be fired. Gore and Blood make a powerful case against requiring companies to be subjected to this "What have you done for me lately?" philosophy, arguing that quarterly earnings guidances should be abolished in favor of companies releasing information when they consider it appropriate. And to further persuade managers to think sustainably, companies need to change the way the managers get paid. Currently, the CEO of ExxonMobil is rewarded for a highly profitable year but is not held accountable for depleting nonrenewable oil reserves. A new model

Margin notes:

Transition referring to ideas in previous paragraph

Details of claim

Logical appeals using information and evidence in white paper

Ethical appeal to companies

Partial solution proposed

should incentivize thinking for the long run. Multiyear milestones for performance evaluation, as Gore and Blood suggest, are essential to pushing executives to manage sustainably.

But it's not just for-profit companies that need to rethink strategies. Social good–oriented leaders also stand to learn from the people often vilified in environmental circles: corporate CEOs. To survive in today's economy, companies building sustainable products must operate under the same strict business standards as profit-driven companies. Two social enterprises, Nika Water and Belu, provide perfect examples. Both sell bottled water in the developed world with the mission of providing clean water to impoverished communities through their profits. Both have visionary leaders who define the lesson that all environmental and social entrepreneurs need to understand: financial pragmatism will add far more value to the world than idealistic dreams. Nika Water founder Jeff Church explained this in a speech at Stanford University:

> Social entrepreneurs look at their businesses as nine parts cause, one part business. In the beginning, it needs to be nine parts business, one part cause, because if the business doesn't stay around long enough because it can't make it, you can't do anything about the cause.

When U.K.-based Belu lost £600,000 ($940,000) in 2007, it could only give around £30,000 ($47,000) to charity. Karen Lynch took over as CEO, cutting costs, outsourcing significant parts of the company's operations, and redesigning the entire business model; the company now donates four times as much to charity (Hurley). The conventional portrayal of do-gooders is that they tend to be terrible businesspeople, an argument often grounded in reality. It is easy to criticize the Walmarts of the world for caring little about

Margin notes:

Claim extended to socially responsible businesses

Logical appeals

Additional logical appeals

Mercer-Golden 4

Return to thesis: businesses should learn from one another

sustainability or social good, but the idealists with big visions who do not follow through on their promises because their businesses cannot survive are no more praiseworthy. Walmart should learn from nonprofits and social enterprises on advancing a positive environmental and social agenda, but idealist entrepreneurs should also learn from corporations about building successful businesses.

Transition to second part of thesis signaled

The final piece of the sustainable business ecosystem is the investors who help get potentially world-changing companies off the ground. Industries that require a large amount of money to build complex products with expensive materials, such as solar power companies, rely heavily on investors—often venture capitalists based in California's Silicon Valley (Knight). The problem is that venture capitalists are not doing enough to fund truly groundbreaking companies. In an oft-cited blog post titled "Why Facebook Is Killing Silicon Valley," entrepreneur Steve Blank argues that the financial returns on social media companies have been so quick and so outsized that the companies with the *really* big ideas—like providing efficient, cheap, scalable solar power— are not being backed: "In the past, if you were a great [venture capitalist], you could make $100 million on an investment in 5–7 years. Today, social media startups can return hundreds of millions or even billions in less than 3 years." The point Blank makes is that what is earning investors lots of money right now is not what is best for the United States or the world.

Problem explained

Reasons in support of claim

Transition signaling reason for optimism

There are, however, signs of hope. PayPal founder Peter Thiel runs his venture capital firm, the Founders Fund, on the philosophy that investors should support "flying cars" instead of new social media ventures (Packer). While the next company with the mission of making photo-sharing cooler or communicating with friends easier might be both profitable and valuable, Thiel and a select few others fund technology that has the potential to solve the huge problems essential to human survival.

> Reason presented

The world's need for sustainable companies that can build products from renewable energy or make nonpolluting cars will inevitably create opportunities for smart companies to make money. In fact, significant opportunities already exist for venture capitalists willing to step away from what is easy today and shift their investment strategies toward what will help us continue to live on this planet tomorrow—even if seeing strong returns may take a few more years. Visionaries like Blank and Thiel need more allies (and dollars) in their fight to help produce more pioneering, sustainable companies. And global warming won't abate before investors wise up. It is vital that this shift happen now.

> Emotional appeal

When we think about organizations today, we think about nonprofits, which have long-term social missions, and corporations, which we judge by their immediate financial returns like quarterly earnings. That is a treacherous dichotomy. Instead, we need to see the three major players in the business ecosystem—corporations, social enterprises, and investors—moving toward a *single* model of long-term, sustainable capitalism. We need visionary companies that not only set out to solve humankind's biggest problems but also have the business intelligence to accomplish these goals, and we need investors willing to fund these companies. Gore and Blood argue that "the imperative for change has never been greater." We will see this change when the world realizes that sustainable capitalism shares the same goals as creating a sustainable environment. Let us hope that this realization comes soon.

> Logical appeal
>
> Thesis revisited
>
> Quotation, restatement of thesis, and emotional appeal close argument

Mercer-Golden 6

Works Cited

"About Us." *Generation*. Generation Investment Management LLC,
        2012. Web. 26 Nov. 2012.

Blank, Steve. "Why Facebook Is Killing Silicon Valley." *Steveblank
        .com*. N.p., 21 May 2012. Web. 23 Nov. 2012.

Church, Jeff. "The Wave of Social Entrepreneurship."
        Entrepreneurial Thought Leaders Seminar. NVIDIA Auditorium,
        Stanford U, Stanford, CA. 11 Apr. 2012. Lecture.

Eccles, Robert G., Ioannis Ioannou, and George Serafeim. "The
        Impact of a Corporate Culture of Sustainability on Corporate
        Behavior and Performance." Working Paper 12-035. Harvard
        Business School, 9 May 2012. PDF file.

Gore, Al, and David Blood. "A Manifesto for Sustainable
        Capitalism." *Generation*. Generation Investment Management,
        14 Dec. 2011. PDF file.

Hurley, James. "Belu Boss Shows Bottle for a Turnaround." *Daily
        Telegraph*. Telegraph Media Group, 28 Feb. 2012. Web. 26
        Nov. 2012.

Knight, Eric R. W. "The Economic Geography of Clean Tech
        Venture Capital." Oxford University Working Paper Series in
        Employment, Work, and Finance, 13 Apr. 2010. *Social Science
        Research Network*. Web. 23 Nov. 2012.

Packer, George. "No Death, No Taxes: The Libertarian Futurism of
        a Silicon Valley Billionaire." *New Yorker*. New Yorker, 28 Nov.
        2011. Web. 24 Nov. 2012.

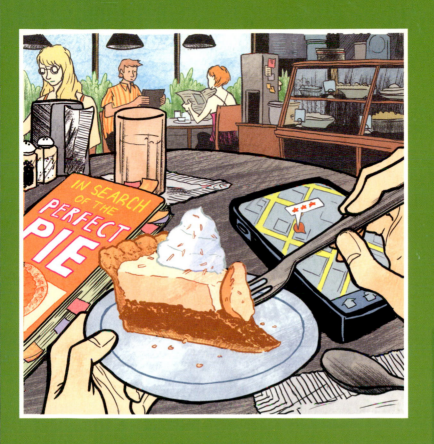

Research

Research is formalized curiosity. It is poking and prying with a purpose.

— ZORA NEALE HURSTON

Research

Research   145–198

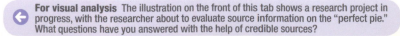

For visual analysis The illustration on the front of this tab shows a research project in progress, with the researcher about to evaluate source information on the "perfect pie." What questions have you answered with the help of credible sources?

Preparing for a Research Project

12

Your employer asks you to recommend the best software for a particular project. You want to plan a spring break trip to the beach. Your instructor assigns a research project about a jazz musician. Each of these situations calls for research, for examining various kinds of sources. Preparing to begin your research means taking a long look at what you already know, the best way to proceed, and the amount of time you have to find out what you need to know. For success in college and beyond, you need to understand how to start the process of academic research.

12a Analyze the research assignment.

In an introductory writing course, you might receive an assignment like this one:

> Choose a subject of interest to you, and use it as the basis for a research essay of approximately two thousand words that makes and substantiates a claim. You should use a minimum of five credible, authoritative sources.

Topic

If your assignment doesn't specify a topic, consider the following questions (see also 3b):

- What subjects do you already know something about? Which of them would you like to explore more fully?

- What subjects do you care about? What might you like to become an expert on?

- What subjects evoke a strong reaction from you, whether positive or negative?

Be sure to get responses about your possible topic from your instructor, classmates, and friends. Ask them whether they would be interested in reading about the topic, whether it seems manageable, and whether they know of any good sources for information on the topic.

Situation

Be sure to consider the rhetorical situation (see Chapter 3) of any research project. Here are detailed questions to think about:

AUDIENCE

- Who will be the audience for your research project (3d)?
- Who will be interested in the information you gather, and why? What will they want to know? What will they already know?
- What do you know about their backgrounds? What assumptions might they hold about the topic?
- What response do you want from them?
- What kinds of evidence will you need to convince them?
- What will your instructor expect?

PURPOSE

- If you can choose the purpose, what would you like to accomplish (3c)?
- If you have been assigned a specific research project, keep in mind the key words in that assignment. Does the assignment ask that you *describe, survey, analyze, persuade, explain, classify, compare,* or *contrast*? What do such words mean in this field?

YOUR POSITION ON THE TOPIC (STANCE)

- What is your attitude toward your topic? Are you curious about it? critical of it? Do you like it? dislike it? find it confusing?
- What influences have shaped your position (3c)?

TALKING THE TALK

Reaching an Audience

"Isn't my audience just my teacher?" To write effectively, you must think of your writing as more than just an assignment you have to complete to get a grade. Recognize that you have something to say — and that in order to get others to pay attention, you have to think about who they are and how to reach them. Of course, your instructor is part of your audience. But who else will be interested in your topic and the unique perspective you bring to it? What does that audience need from you?

SCOPE

- How long is the project supposed to be? Base your research and writing schedule on the scale of the finished project (a short versus a long paper or presentation, a brief oral report or a longer multimedia presentation, a simple versus a complex website) and the amount of time you have to complete it.

- How many and what kind(s) of sources should you use (13a)? What kind(s) of visuals — charts, maps, photographs, and so on — will you need? Will you use sound or video files? Will you do any field research — interviewing, surveying, or observing (13e)?

Here is a sample schedule for a research project:

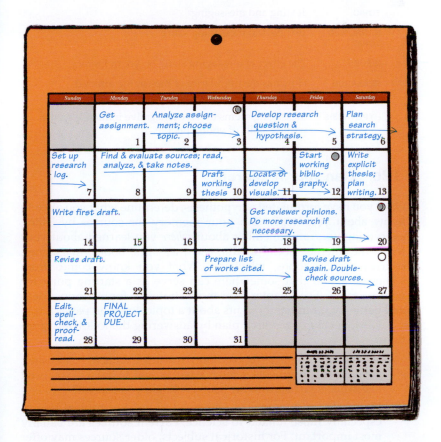

12b Formulate a research question and hypothesis.

Once you have analyzed your task, chosen your topic, and narrowed the topic to make it manageable (see 5a), formulate a research question that you can tentatively answer with a hypothesis. The hypothesis, a statement of what you anticipate your research will show, needs to be manageable, interesting, and specific (see 5b). In addition, it must be a debatable proposition that you can prove or disprove with a reasonable amount of research evidence.

David Craig, the student whose research paper appears in Chapter 60, made the following move from general topic to a narrowed topic and then to a research question and hypothesis:

TOPIC	Texting and messaging
NARROWED TOPIC	Texting and messaging slang
ISSUE	The effect of messaging slang on youth literacy
RESEARCH QUESTION	How has the popularity of messaging affected literacy among today's youth?
HYPOTHESIS	Messaging seems to have a negative influence on the writing skills of young people.

12c Plan your research.

Once you have formulated a hypothesis, determine what you already know about your topic. Tap your memory for sources by listing everything you can remember about *where* you learned about your topic: the Internet, social media, text messages, books, magazines, courses, conversations, television. What you know comes from somewhere, and that somewhere can serve as a starting point for your research. (See Chapter 4 for more strategies for exploring ideas and getting your initial thoughts about a topic down on paper.)

Next, develop a research plan by answering the following questions:

- What kinds of sources (books, journal articles, databases, websites, government documents, reference works, and so on) will you need to consult (13a)? How many sources should you consult?

- How current do your sources need to be? For topical issues, especially those related to science, current sources are usually most important. For historical subjects, older sources may offer the best information.

- How can you determine the location and availability of the kinds of sources you need?

One goal of your research plan is to build a strong working bibliography (14b). Carrying out systematic research and keeping careful notes on your sources will make developing your works-cited list or bibliography easier.

12d   Set up a research log.

Keeping a research log will make the job of writing and documenting your sources more efficient and accurate. Use your research log to jot down ideas about possible sources and to keep track of print and online materials.

- A private blog or other online site can be a good place to record your thoughts on the reading you are doing and to add links to websites, documents, and articles that you find online.

- If you are keeping a computer research log, create a new folder and label it with a name that will be easy to identify, such as *Research Log for Project on Messaging*. Within this folder, create subfolders that will help you manage your project, such as *Assignment info, Working bibliography, Image ideas, Drafts*, and so on.

- If you prefer to keep a print research log, set up a binder with dividers similar to the subfolders listed above.

Be sure to carefully distinguish the notes and comments you make from quoted passages you record (see Chapter 14).

12e   Move from hypothesis to working thesis.

As you gather information, search catalogs and databases, and read and evaluate sources, you will probably refine your research question and change your hypothesis significantly. Only after you have explored your hypothesis, tested it, and sharpened it by reading, writing, and talking with others does it become a working thesis.

David Craig, the student whose hypothesis appears in 12b, did quite a bit of research on messaging language, youth literacy, and the possible connection between the two. The more he read, the more he felt that the hypothesis suggested by his discussion with instructors—that messaging had contributed to a decline in youth literacy—did not hold

For David Craig's research essay, see Chapter 60.

up. Thus, he shifted his attention to the positive effects of messaging on communication skills and developed the following working thesis: "Although some educators criticize messaging, it may aid literacy by encouraging young people to use words and to write—even if messaging requires a different kind of writing."

In doing your own research, you may find that your interest shifts, that a whole line of inquiry is unproductive, or that your hypothesis is simply wrong. The process of research pushes you to learn more about your hypothesis and to make it more precise.

13 Doing Research

Whether you are researching Heisenberg's uncertainty principle or haircuts, you need to be familiar with the kinds of sources you are likely to use, the searches you can perform, and the types of research you will do most often: library, Internet, and field research.

13a Understand different kinds of sources.

Sources can include data from interviews and surveys, books and articles in print and online, websites, film, video, images, and more. Consider these important differences among sources.

Primary and secondary sources

Primary sources provide firsthand knowledge, and secondary sources report on or analyze the research of others. Primary sources are basic sources of raw information, including your own field research; films, works of art, or other objects you examine; literary works you read; and eyewitness accounts, photographs, news reports, and historical documents (such as letters and speeches). Secondary sources are descriptions or interpretations of primary sources, such as researchers' reports, reviews, biographies, and encyclopedia articles. Often what constitutes a primary or secondary source depends on the purpose of your research. A critic's evaluation of a film, for instance, serves as a secondary source if you are writing about the film but as a primary source if you are studying the critic's writing.

Scholarly and popular sources

While nonacademic sources like magazines can help you get started on a research project, you will usually want to depend more heavily on authorities in a field, whose work generally appears in scholarly journals in print or online. The following list will help you distinguish scholarly and popular sources:

SCHOLARLY	POPULAR

Title often contains the word *Journal*	*Journal* usually does not appear in title
Available mainly through libraries and library databases	Available outside of libraries (at newsstands or from a home Internet connection)
Few commercial advertisements	Many advertisements
Authors identified with academic credentials	Authors are usually journalists or reporters hired by the publication, not academics or experts
Summary or abstract appears on first page of article; articles are fairly long	No summary or abstract; articles are fairly short
Articles cite sources and provide bibliographies	Articles may include quotations but do not cite sources or provide bibliographies

Older and more current sources

Most projects can benefit from both older, historical sources and more current ones. Some older sources are classics, essential for understanding later scholarship. Others are simply dated. Whether a source appeared hundreds of years ago or this morning, evaluate it carefully to determine how useful it will be for you.

13b   Use the library to get started.

Many beginning researchers are tempted to assume that all the information they could possibly need is readily available on the Internet from a home connection. However, it is a good idea to begin almost any research project with the sources available in your college library.

Reference librarians

The purpose of a college reference library is to help students find information—and the staff of your library, especially reference librarians, will willingly help you figure out how to get started, what resources to choose for your project, and how to research more effectively. When in doubt, ask your librarian! You can make an appointment to talk with a librarian about your research project and get specific recommendations about databases and other helpful places to begin your research. In addition, many libraries have online tours and chat environments where students can ask questions about their research and have them answered, in real time, by a reference librarian. To get the most helpful advice, whether online or in person, pose *specific* questions—not "Where can I find information about computers?" but "Where can I find information on the history of messaging technologies?" If you are having difficulty asking precise questions, you probably need to do some background research on your topic and formulate a sharper hypothesis. A librarian may be helpful in this regard as well.

Catalogs and databases

Your library's computers hold many resources not available on the web or not accessible to students except through the library's system. One of these resources is the library's own catalog of books and other holdings, but most college libraries also subscribe to a large number of databases—digital collections of information, such as indexes to journal and magazine articles, texts of news stories and legal cases, lists of sources on particular topics, and compilations of statistics—that students can access for free. Many of these databases have been screened or compiled by editors, librarians, or other scholars. Your library may also have metasearch software that allows you to search several databases at once.

Reference works

Consulting general reference works, such as encyclopedias, biographical dictionaries, and almanacs, is another good way to get started on a research project. These works are especially helpful for getting an overview of a topic, identifying subtopics, finding more specialized sources, and identifying useful keywords for electronic searches.

TALKING THE TALK

Wikis as Sources

"Why doesn't my instructor want me to use Wikipedia as a source?" Wikis are sites that users can add to and edit as they see fit. Although many instructors now consider Wikipedia a good place to begin research on a subject you don't know much about, it's nevertheless possible for a wiki's contributors to make mistakes or even to add deliberately false information. Use wikis to get started with research, and then make sure that you double-check any information you find there.

13c Find library resources.

The library is one of a researcher's best friends, especially in an age of digital communication. Your college library houses a great number of print materials and gives you access to electronic catalogs, indexes, and databases. Check your library's website or ask a librarian for an introduction to the available resources.

Search options

The most important tools your library offers are its online databases and catalogs. Searching these tools will always be easier and more efficient if you use carefully chosen words to limit the scope of your research.

KEYWORD SEARCH

Searches using keywords make use of the computer's ability to look for any term in any field of the electronic record, including not just subject but also author, title, series, and notes. In article databases, a keyword search will look in abstracts and summaries of articles as well. Keyword searching requires you to put some thought into choosing your search terms in order to get the best results.

SUBJECT WORD SEARCH

Library holdings usually index their contents not only by author and title, but also by subject headings—standardized words and phrases used to classify the subject matter of books and articles. Most U.S. academic libraries classify their material using the *Library of Congress Subject Headings,* or LCSH. When you find a library source that seems especially relevant, you can use the subject headings for that source as search terms to browse for related titles.

ADVANCED SEARCH OPTIONS

Many library search engines offer advanced search options (sometimes on a separate page) to help you combine keywords, search for an exact phrase, or exclude items containing particular keywords. Often they can limit your search in other ways as well, such as by date or language. If you don't see a way to conduct an advanced search, note that simply entering terms in the search box may bring up advanced search options. Note, too, that search engines vary in the exact terms they use to refine searches; for instance, some use phrases such as "all these words," while others may use the word AND or something else. Most search tools offer tips on how to use the tool effectively, but these general tips can help:

- Enter at least two keywords in an "all these words" search box (or use AND) to limit your results. Entering *messaging* and *language,* for example, would bring up only results that include both terms.

- Search for an exact phrase, usually by putting the phrase in quotation marks, to limit your results. Searching for *"messaging language"* would include results containing "text messaging language" but would exclude those containing "messaging as a language."

- Enter at least two keywords in an "any of these words" search box (or use OR) to expand your results. Entering *messaging* or *language* would bring up every result that included either term.

- Enter unwanted keywords in a "none of these words" search box (or use NOT) to exclude irrelevant results. Searching for *messaging* and *language* but not *popular* would omit results focusing on popular messaging slang.

Articles

Some libraries use web-based discovery tools that allow you to search all available materials at once and that may even rank your results. If your library does not have such tools, however, you will need to use a periodical index to find articles relating to your topic. Ask a reference librarian for guidance about the most likely index for the subject of your research.

GENERAL AND SPECIALIZED INDEXES

Different indexes cover different groups of periodicals; articles written before 1990 may be indexed only in a print volume. General indexes of periodicals list articles from general-interest magazines (such as *Time*), newspapers, and perhaps some scholarly journals. General indexes are useful for finding current sources on a topic. Specialized indexes, which tend to include mainly scholarly periodicals, may focus on one discipline (as the education index ERIC does) or on a group of related disciplines (as Social Sciences Abstracts does).

FULL TEXT AND ABSTRACTS

Some periodical indexes offer the full text of articles, and some offer abstracts (short summaries) of the articles. Be sure not to confuse an abstract with a complete article. Full-text databases can be extremely convenient—you can read and print out articles directly from the computer, without the extra step of tracking down the periodical in question. However, don't limit yourself to full-text databases, which may not contain graphics and images that appeared in the print version of the periodical—and which may not include the sources that would benefit your research most. Take advantage of abstracts, which give you a very brief overview of the article's contents so you can decide whether you need to spend time finding and reading the full text.

To locate a promising article that is not available in a full-text digital version, check to see whether a print version is available in your library's periodicals room.

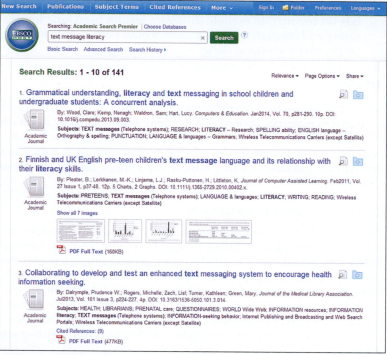

David Craig's search on the keywords text message *and* literacy *gave him the results you see here. After clicking on an entry, he was able to read an abstract. He found the full-text article in his library's journals collection.*

Books

Libraries categorize books by the *author's name*, by the *title*, and by one or more *subjects*. If you can't find a particular source under any of these headings, you can search by using a combination of subject headings and keywords. Such searches may turn up other useful titles as well.

More and more library holdings are digitized, but many books are available only in print. Catalog entries for print books list not only the author, title, subject, and publication information but also a call number that indicates how the book is classified and where it is shelved. (Many also indicate whether a book has been checked out and, if so, when it is due.)

Once you have the call number for a book, look for a library map or shelving plan to tell you where the book is housed. Take the time to browse through the books near the call number you are looking for—often you will find other books related to your topic in the immediate area.

Another strategy for finding books is to check a review index, which will help you find reviews so that you can check the relevance of a book to your project or get a thumbnail sketch of its contents before you track it down. Ask a reference librarian for guidance on review indexes.

Bibliographies

Look at any bibliographies (lists of sources) in books or articles you are using for your research; they can lead you to other valuable resources. In addition, check with a reference librarian to find out whether your library has more extensive bibliographies devoted to the area of your research.

Other library resources

In addition to books and periodicals, libraries give you access to many other useful materials that might be appropriate for your research.

- *Special collections and archives.* Your library may house archives (collections of valuable papers) and other special materials that are often available to student researchers. One student, for example, learned that her university owned a vast collection of twentieth-century posters. With help from a librarian, she was able to use some of these posters as primary sources for her research project on German culture after World War II.

- *Audio, video, multimedia, and art collections.* Many libraries have areas devoted to media and art, where they collect films, videos, paintings, and sound recordings.

- *Government documents.* Many libraries have collections of historical documents produced by local or state government offices. Check with a librarian if government publications would be useful sources for your topic. You can also look at the online version of the U.S. Government Printing Office, known as the Federal Digital System (FDsys), for electronic versions of government publications.

- *Interlibrary loans.* To borrow books, videos, or audio materials from another library, use an interlibrary loan. You can also request copies of journal articles from other libraries. Some loans—especially of books—can take time, so plan ahead.

13d   Search the Internet effectively.

The Internet is many college students' favorite way of accessing information, and it's true that much information—including authoritative sources identical to those your library provides—can be found online, sometimes for free. However, information in library databases comes from identifiable and professionally edited sources; because no one is responsible for regulating information on the web, you need to take special care to find out which information online is reliable and which is not. (See Chapter 14 for more on evaluating sources.)

Internet searches

Research using a search tool such as Google usually begins with a keyword search. Because the Internet contains vastly more material than the largest library catalog or database, Internet searching requires care in the choice of keywords. For example, if you need information on legal issues regarding the Internet and enter *Internet* and *law* as keywords in a Google search, you will get over three million hits. You may find what you need on the first page of hits, but if not, you will need to choose new keywords that lead to more specific sources.

Bookmarking tools

Today's powerful bookmarking tools can help you browse, sort, and track resources online. Social bookmarking sites allow users to tag information and share it with others. Once you register on a social bookmarking site, you can tag an online resource with any words you choose. Users' tags are visible to all other users. If you find a helpful site, you can check to see how others have tagged it and quickly browse similar tags to find related information. You can sort and group information according to your tags. Fellow users whose tags you like and trust can become part of your network so that you can follow their sites of interest.

Web browsers can also help you bookmark and return to online resources that you have found. However, unlike the bookmarking tools in a web browser, which are tied to one machine, social bookmarking tools are available from any computer with an Internet connection.

Authoritative sources online

You can find many sources online that are authoritative and reliable. For example, the Internet enables you to enter virtual libraries that allow access to some collections in libraries other than your own. Online collections housed in government sites can also be reliable and useful sources. The Library of Congress, the National Institutes of Health, and the U.S. Census Bureau, for example, have large online collections of articles. For current national news, consult online versions of reputable newspapers such as the *Washington Post* or the *Chicago Tribune*, or electronic sites for news services such as C-SPAN. To limit your searches to scholarly works, try Google Scholar.

Some scholarly journals (such as those from Berkeley Electronic Press) and general-interest magazines (including *Slate* and *Salon*) are published only on the web, and many other publications, like *Newsweek*, the *New Yorker*, and the *New Republic*, make at least some of their contents available online for free.

13e   Conduct field research appropriately.

For many research projects, particularly those in the social sciences and business, you will need to collect field data. The "field" may be many things—a classroom, a church, a laboratory, or the corner grocery store. As a field researcher, you will need to discover *where* you can find relevant information, *how* to gather it, and *who* might be your best providers of information.

Interviews

Some information is best obtained by interviewing—asking direct questions of other people. If you can talk with an expert in person, on the telephone, or online, you might get information you could not have obtained through any other kind of research.

Your first step is to find interview subjects. Has your research generated the names of people you might contact directly? Brainstorm for additional names, looking for authorities on your topic and people in your community, and then write, telephone, or email them to try to arrange an interview.

When you have identified someone to interview, prepare your questions. You will probably want to ask several kinds of questions. Questions about facts and figures (*How many employees do you have?*) elicit specific answers and don't invite expansion or opinion. You can lead the interviewee to think out loud and to give additional details by asking open-ended questions: *How do you feel now about deciding to enlist in the military after 9/11?*

Avoid questions that would encourage vague answers (*What do you think of youth today?*) or yes/no answers (*Should the laws governing corporate accounting practices be changed?*). Instead, ask questions that must be answered with supporting details (*Why should the laws governing corporate accounting practices be changed?*).

Conducting an Interview

- Determine your exact purpose, and be sure it relates to your research question and hypothesis.
- Set up the interview well in advance. Specify how long it will take, and if you wish to record the session, ask permission to do so.
- Prepare a written list of factual and open-ended questions. Brainstorming or freewriting can help you come up with questions (4a and b). Leave plenty of space for notes after each question. If the interview proceeds in a direction that seems fruitful, do not feel that you have to ask all of your prepared questions.
- Record the subject, date, time, and place of the interview.
- Even if you are taping, take notes. Ask your interviewee for permission to use video, audio, or quotations that will appear in print.
- Thank those you interview, either in person or in a letter or email.

Observations

Trained observers tell us that making a faithful record of an observation requires intense concentration and mental agility. Moreover, observation is never neutral. Just as a photographer has a particular angle on a subject, so an observer always has an angle on what he or she is looking at.

Before you conduct any observation, decide exactly what you want to find out, and anticipate what you are likely to see. Are you going to observe an action repeated by many people (such as pedestrians crossing a street), a sequence of actions (such as a medical procedure), or the interactions of a group (such as a church congregation)? Also decide exactly what you want to record and how.

Conducting an Observation

- Determine the purpose of the observation, and be sure it relates to your research question and hypothesis.
- Brainstorm about what you are looking for, but don't be rigidly bound to your expectations. (4a)
- If necessary, make appointments and gain permission to observe.
- Develop an appropriate system for recording data. Consider using a "split" notebook or screen: on one side, record your observations directly; on the other, record your thoughts and interpretations.
- Record the date, time, and place of the observation.

Surveys

To do survey research, all you need is a representative sample of people and a questionnaire that will elicit the information you need.

On any questionnaire, the questions should be clear and easy to understand and designed so that you will be able to analyze the answers easily. Questions that ask respondents to say yes or no or to rank items on a five-point scale are particularly easy to tabulate.

As you design your questionnaire, think about ways your respondents might misunderstand you or your questions. Adding a category called "other" to a list of options you are asking people about, for example, allows them to fill in information you would not otherwise get.

Because tabulating the responses takes time and because people often resent answering long questionnaires, limit the number of questions to no more than twenty. After tabulating your results, put them in an easily readable format, such as a chart or spreadsheet.

QUICK HELP

Designing a Survey Questionnaire

- Write out your purpose, and review your research question and hypothesis to determine the kinds of questions to ask.
- Figure out how to reach respondents.
- Draft questions that call for short, specific answers.
- Test the questions on several people, and revise questions that seem unfair, ambiguous, too hard to answer, or too time consuming.
- Draft a cover letter or invitation email. Be sure to state your deadline.
- If you are using a print questionnaire, leave adequate space for answers.
- Proofread the questionnaire carefully.

Data analysis and interpretation

To make sense of the information you have gathered, first try to find a focus, since you can't pay equal attention to everything. This step is especially important in analyzing results from observations or survey questionnaires.

Next, synthesize the data by looking for recurring words or ideas that fall into patterns. Establish a system for coding your information, labeling each pattern you identify—a plus sign for every positive response on a questionnaire, for example. If you ask classmates to review your notes or data, they may notice other patterns.

Finally, interpret your data by summing up the meaning of what you have found. What is the significance of your findings? Be careful not to make large generalizations.

14   Evaluating Sources and Taking Notes

The difference between a useful source and a poor one depends to a great extent on your topic, purpose, and audience. On almost any topic you can imagine (Why do mosquitoes bite? Who reads fan fiction?), you will need research—looking into sources, gathering data, and thinking critically about these sources—to answer the question. With most topics, in fact, your problem will not be so much finding sources as figuring out *which* sources to consult in the limited time you have available. Learning how to tell which sources are best for you allows you to use your time wisely, and taking effective notes allows you to put the sources to work for you.

14a   Understand the purpose of sources.

Why do writers decide to use one source rather than another? Sources serve different purposes, so part of evaluating sources involves deciding what you need the source to provide for your research projects. You may need background information or context that your audience will need to follow your writing; explanations of concepts unfamiliar to your audience; verbal and visual emphasis for your points; authority or evidence for your claims, which can help you create your own authority; other perspectives on your topic; or counter-examples or counter-evidence that you need to consider.

As you begin to work with your sources, make notes in your research log about why you plan to use a particular source. You should also begin your working bibliography.

14b   Create a working bibliography.

A working bibliography is a list of sources that you may potentially use for your project. As you find and begin to evaluate research sources—articles, books, websites, and so on—you should record source information for every source you think you might use. (Relevant information includes everything you need to find the source again and cite it correctly; the information you will need varies based on the type of source, whether you found it in a library or not, and whether you consulted it in print or online.) The emphasis here is on *working* because the list will probably include materials that end up not being useful. For this reason, you don't absolutely need to put all entries into the documentation style you will use (see Chapters 57–67). If you do follow the required documentation style, however, that part of your work will be done when you prepare the final draft.

The following chart will help you keep track of the sorts of information you should try to find:

Type of Source	Information to Collect (if applicable)
Print book	Library call number, author(s) or editor(s), title and subtitle, place of publication, publisher, year of publication, any other information (translator, edition, volume)
Part of a book	Call number, author(s) of part, title of part, author(s) or editor(s) of book, title of book, place of publication, publisher, year of publication, inclusive page numbers for part
Print periodical article	Call number of periodical, author(s) of article, title of article, name of periodical, volume number, issue number, date of issue, inclusive page numbers for article
Electronic source	Author(s), title of document, title of site, editor(s) of site, sponsor of site, publication information for print version of source, name of database or online service, date of electronic publication or last update, date you accessed the source, URL

For other kinds of sources (films, recordings, visuals), you should also list the information required by the documentation style you are using (see Chapters 57–67) and note where you found the information.

Annotated bibliography

You might wish to annotate your working bibliography to include a summary of the source's contents as well as publishing information (whether or not annotations are required) because annotating can help you understand and remember what the source says, as in the following excerpt from Tony Chan's annotated bibliography.

ANNOTATED BIBLIOGRAPHY ENTRY

Diamond, Edwin, and Stephen Bates. *The Spot: The Rise of Political Advertising on Television.* 3rd ed. Cambridge, MA: MIT Press, 1992. Diamond and Bates illustrate the impact of television on political strategy and discourse. The two argue that Lyndon Johnson's "Daisy Girl" ad succeeded by exploiting the nascent television medium, using violent images and sounds and the words "nuclear bomb" to sway the audience's emotions. Emphasizing Johnson's direct control over the production of the ad, the authors illustrate the crucial role the ad played in portraying Goldwater as a warmonger.

Customized bibliography

Some annotated bibliographies can go beyond a summary of the main points in a source to examine research methods, evaluate the credibility of the source, reflect on its usefulness for a particular project, and more. Writing professor Mark McBeth asks his students to include new vocabulary and potential quotations from the source as part of a reflective annotated bibliography assignment. Annotations that go beyond summaries can help you think critically about your sources and their place in your overall research project. What kind of annotations will be most useful for your annotated bibliography?

TALKING THE TALK

Research with an Open Mind

"What's wrong with looking for sources that back up what I want to say?" When you start researching a topic, keep an open mind: investigate every important source, even if you think you won't agree with it. If all your sources take the same position you take, you may be missing a big part of the picture. Who knows? You may change your position after learning more about the topic. Even if you don't, ignoring counterarguments and other points of view harms your credibility, suggesting that you haven't done your homework.

14c   Evaluate a source's usefulness and credibility.

Since you want the information and ideas you glean from sources to be reliable and persuasive, you must evaluate each potential source

carefully. The following guidelines can help you assess the usefulness and credibility of sources you are considering:

- *Your purpose.* What will this source add to your research project? Does it help you support a major point, demonstrate that
  you have thoroughly researched your topic, or help establish
  your own credibility through its authority?

- *Relevance.* How closely related is the source to the narrowed
  topic you are pursuing? You may need to read beyond the title
  and opening paragraph to check for relevance.

- *Level of specialization and audience.* General sources can be
  helpful as you begin your research, but you may then need the
  authority or currency of more specialized sources. On the other
  hand, extremely specialized works may be very hard to understand. Who was the source originally written for — the general
  public? experts in the field? advocates or opponents? How does
  this fit with your concept of your own audience?

- *Credentials of the publisher or sponsor.* What can you learn
  about the publisher or sponsor of the source? For example, is it a
  newspaper known for integrity, or is it a tabloid? Is it a popular
  source, or is it sponsored by a professional or governmental
  organization or academic institution? No hard-and-fast rules
  exist for deciding what kind of source to use. But knowing the
  sponsor's or publisher's credentials can help you determine if a
  source is appropriate for your project.

- *Credentials of the author.* Note names that come up from one
  source to another, since these references may indicate that the
  author is influential in the field. An author's credentials may
  also be presented in the article, book, or website, or you can
  search the Internet for information about the author. In U.S. academic writing, experts and those with significant experience in a
  field have more authority on the subject than others.

- *Date of publication.* Recent sources are often more useful than
  older ones, particularly in the sciences or other fields that change
  rapidly. However, in some fields — such as the humanities — the
  most authoritative works may be older ones. The publication
  dates of Internet sites can often be difficult to pin down. And
  even for sites that include dates of posting, remember that the
  material posted may have been composed some time earlier.

- *Accuracy of the source.* How accurate and complete is the information in the source? How thorough is the bibliography or list

macmillanhighered.com/everyday6e
Research > Student Writing: Annotated bibliography, Tony Chan
Research > Student Writing: Reflective annotated bibliography, Nandita Sriram

of works cited that accompanies the source? Can you find other sources that corroborate what your source is saying?

- *Stance of the source.* Identify the source's point of view or rhetorical stance, and scrutinize it carefully. Does the source present facts, or does it interpret or evaluate them? If it presents facts, what is included and what is omitted, and why? If it interprets or evaluates information that is not disputed, the source's stance may be obvious, but at other times, you will need to think carefully about the source's goals (14d). What does the author or sponsoring group want? to convince you of an idea? sell you something? call you to action in some way?

- *Cross-references to the source.* Is the source cited in other works? If you see your source cited by others, notice how they cite it and what they say about it to find additional clues to its credibility.

For more on evaluating web sources and periodical articles, see the Source Maps on pp. 172–75.

14d Read critically, and interpret sources.

For those sources that you want to analyze more closely, reading with a critical eye can make your research process more efficient. Use the following tips to guide your critical reading.

Your research question

As you read, keep your research question in mind, and ask yourself the following questions:

- How does this material address your research question and support your hypothesis?

- What quotations from this source might help support your thesis?

- Does the source include counterarguments to your hypothesis that you will need to answer? If so, what answers can you provide?

The author's stance and tone

Even a seemingly factual report, such as an encyclopedia article, is filled with judgments, often unstated. Read with an eye for the author's overall rhetorical stance, or perspective, as well as for facts or explicit opinions. Also pay attention to the author's tone, the way his or her attitude toward the topic and audience is conveyed. The following questions can help:

- Is the author a strong advocate or opponent of something? a skeptical critic? a specialist in the field?
- Are there any clues to why the author takes this stance?
- How does this stance affect the author's presentation and your reaction to it?
- What facts does the author include? Can you think of any important fact that is omitted?
- What is the author's tone? Is it cautious, angry, flippant, serious, impassioned? What words indicate this tone?

QUICK HELP

Guidelines for Examining Potential Sources

Looking quickly at the various parts of a source can provide useful information and help you decide whether to explore that particular source more thoroughly. You are already familiar with some of these basic elements: title and subtitle, title page and copyright page, home page, table of contents, index, footnotes, and bibliography. Be sure to check other items as well.

- *Abstracts* — concise summaries of articles and books — routinely precede journal articles and are often included in indexes and databases.
- A *preface* or *foreword* generally discusses the writer's purpose and thesis.
- *Subheadings* can alert you to how much detail is given on a topic.
- A *conclusion* or *afterword* may summarize or draw the strands of an argument together.
- For a digital source, click on some of the *links* to see if they're useful, and see if the overall *design* of the site is easy to navigate.

The author's argument and evidence

Every piece of writing takes a position. Even a scientific report implicitly "argues" that we should accept it and its data as reliable. As you read, look for the main point or the main argument the author is making. Try to identify the reasons the author gives to support his or her position. Then try to determine *why* the author takes this position.

- How persuasive is the evidence? Can you think of a way to refute it?
- Can you detect any questionable logic or fallacious thinking (10e)?

☑ Research > LearningCurve: Evaluating, integrating, acknowledging sources (APA)
  Research > LearningCurve: Evaluating, integrating, acknowledging sources (MLA)

- Does this author disagree with arguments you have read elsewhere? If so, what causes the disagreements—differences about facts or about how to interpret facts?

14e Synthesize sources.

When you read and interpret a source—for example, when you consider its purpose and relevance, its author's credentials, its accuracy, and the kind of argument it is making—you are analyzing the source. Analysis requires you to take apart something complex (such as an article in a scholarly journal) and look closely at the parts to understand the whole better. For academic writing you also need to *synthesize*—group similar pieces of information together and look for patterns—so you can put your sources (and your own knowledge and experience) together in an original argument. Synthesis is the flip side of analysis: you already understand the parts, so your job is to assemble them into a new whole.

To synthesize sources for a research project, try the following tips:

- ***Read the material carefully.*** For tips on reading with a critical eye, see Chapter 9.

SYNTHESIS: Finding Patterns

Look through your sources carefully to find what you need.

ASK:

What are the **key** ideas in each source?

What **patterns** can you identify?

How do the sources' **perspectives** relate to your own perspective?

Acknowledge that the related ideas you find may not fit smoothly together.

- *Determine the important ideas in each source.* Take notes on each source (14f). Identify and summarize the key ideas of each piece.

- *Formulate a position.* Review the key ideas of each source and figure out how they fit together. Look for patterns: discussions of causes and effects, specific parts of a larger issue, background information, and so on. Be sure to consider the complexity of the issue, and demonstrate that you have considered more than one perspective.

- *Summon evidence to support your position.* You might use paraphrases, summaries, or direct quotations from your sources as evidence (15a), or your personal experience or prior knowledge. Integrate quotations properly (see Chapter 15), and keep your ideas central to the piece of writing.

- *Deal with counterarguments.* You don't have to use every idea or every source available—some will be more useful than others. However, ignoring evidence that opposes your position makes your argument weaker. You should acknowledge the existence of valid opinions that differ from yours, and try to explain why they are incorrect or incomplete.

- *Combine your source materials effectively.* Be careful to avoid simply summarizing or listing your research. Think carefully about how the ideas in your reading support your argument. Try to weave the various sources together rather than discussing your sources one by one.

SYNTHESIS: Combining Ideas

Weave your sources into your text.

ASK:

Why are you using each source?

How do your sources **fit** with what you want to say?

How can you **arrange** your ideas and others' ideas for the best effect?

Make sure your sources support your own voice and message.

SOURCE MAP: Evaluating Web Sources

Is the sponsor credible?

1 Who is the **sponsor or publisher** of the source? See what information you can get from the URL. The domain names for government sites may end in *.gov* or *.mil* and for educational sites in *.edu*. The ending *.org* may — but does not always — indicate a nonprofit organization. If you see a tilde (~) or percent sign (%) followed by a name, or if you see a word such as *users* or *members*, the page's creator may be an individual, not an institution. In addition, check the header and footer, where the sponsor may be identified. The web page shown here comes from a site sponsored by the nonprofit Nieman Foundation for Journalism at Harvard University.

2 Look for an ***About*** page or a link to a home page for background information on the sponsor. Is a mission statement included? What are the sponsoring organization's purpose and point of view? Does the mission statement seem balanced? What is the purpose of the site (to inform, to persuade, to advocate for a cause, to advertise, or something else)? Does the information on the site come directly from the sponsor, or is the material reprinted from another source? If it is reprinted, check the original.

Is the author credible?

3 What are the **author's credentials**? Look for information accompanying the material on the page; in this case, the credit is a link to the author's Twitter profile, which also directs readers to his website. You can run a search on the author to find out more. Does the author seem qualified to write about this topic?

Is the information credible and current?

4 When was the information **posted or last updated**? Is it recent enough to be useful?

5 Does the page document sources with **footnotes or links**? If so, do the sources seem credible and current? Does the author include any additional resources for further information? Look for ways to corroborate the information the author provides.

1 Sponsor or Publisher

2 *About* Page

4 Date Posted

3 Author Information

Nieman Foundation   Fellowships   Reports   Lab   Storyboard

NiemanReports

Exploring the Rise of Live Journalism: new projects are taking narrative from the page to the stage http://t.co/vbMA6Ji2z5

Home   Articles   Watchdog   Magazine   Archives   About   Subscribe

December 11, 2014

Nieman Reports
Fall 2014

COVER STORY: THE FUTURE OF FOREIGN NEWS

Embracing Encryption in an Age of Surveillance

Surveillance technologies make it more important for journalists abroad to protect sources

M odern communications and the rise of the surveillance state make it harder than ever for journalists abroad to protect their sources. The consequences for sources can be dire, even fatal.

Journalists going abroad need to start by asking if encryption is legal where they will be. Does the government forbid certain kinds of apps? Do you need to show your ID to get a SIM card for your cell phone? "Find out the answers to these questions before you go," advises Susan E. McGregor, assistant director of Columbia's Tow Center for Digital Journalism. She adds that reporters also need to know if the telecommunications companies are state-owned. "If they are, you will need to be careful never to send specifics about people or locations via text message or e-mail especially."

Technology can also help journalists defend those who would talk to them. In countries that don't ban encryption, journalists can use encrypted e-mail tools, like Pretty Good Privacy, encrypted hard disks (FileVault2 for the Mac, PGP or

ARTICLE BY

MICHAEL FITZGERALD
@riparian

Tweet
Share
Email
Like
Comment
Print

TAGGED WITH

SOURCE MAP: Evaluating Articles

Determine the relevance of the source.

1 Look for an ==abstract==, or article summary. Is this source directly related to your research? Does it provide useful information and insights? Will your readers consider it persuasive support for your thesis?

Determine the credibility of the publication.

2 Consider the publication's ==title==. Words in the title such as *Journal*, *Review*, and *Quarterly* may indicate that the periodical is a scholarly source. Most research projects rely on authorities in a particular field, whose work usually appears in scholarly journals. For more on distinguishing between scholarly and popular sources, see 13a.

3 Try to determine the ==publisher or sponsor==. This journal is published by the University of Illinois Press. Academic presses such as this one generally review articles carefully before publishing them and bear the authority of their academic sponsors.

Determine the credibility of the author.

4 Evaluate the ==author's credentials==. In this case, they are given in a note, which indicates that the author is a college professor.

Determine the currency of the article.

5 Look at the ==publication date==, and think about whether your topic and your credibility depend on your use of very current sources.

Determine the accuracy of the article.

6 Look at the ==sources cited== by the author of the article. Here, they are documented in a reference list. Ask yourself whether the works the author has cited seem credible and current. Are any of these works cited in other articles you've considered?

In addition, consider the following questions:

- What is the article's stance or point of view? What are the author's goals? What does the author want you to know or believe?

- How does this source fit in with your other sources? Does any of the information it provides contradict or challenge other sources?

ELIZABETH TUCKER

Changing Concepts of Childhood: Children's Folklore Scholarship since the Late Nineteenth Century

1 Abstract

This essay examines children's folklore scholarship from the late nineteenth century to the present, tracing key concepts from the Gilded Age to the contemporary era. These concepts reflect significant social, cultural, political, and scientific changes. From the "savage child" to the "secret-keeping child," the "magic-making child," the "cerebral child," the "taboo-breaking child," the "monstrous child," and others, scholarly representations of young people have close connections to the eras in which they developed. Nineteenth-century children's folklore scholarship relied on evolutionism; now evolutionary biology provides a basis for children's folklore research, so we have re-entered familiar territory.

SINCE 1977, WHEN THE American Folklore Society decided to form a new section for scholars interested in young people's traditions, I have belonged to the Children's Folklore Section. It has been a joy to contribute to this dynamic organization, which has significantly influenced children's folklore scholarship and children's book authors' focus on folk tradition. This essay examines children's folklore scholarship from the late nineteenth century to the present, tracing key concepts from the Gilded Age to the contemporary era in the English language. These concepts reflect significant social, cultural, political, and scientific changes that have occurred since William Wells Newell, the first secretary of the American Folklore Society and the first editor of the *Journal of American Folklore*, published *Games and Songs of American Children* in 1883. They also reveal some very interesting commonalities. Those of us who pursue children's folklore scholarship today may consider ourselves to be light years away from nineteenth-century scholars' research but may find, when reading nineteenth-century works, that we have stayed fairly close to our scholarly "home base."

Before examining concepts of childhood that folklorists have developed, I will offer a working definition of this life stage and briefly explain the beginning of childhood [Title of Publication] summarize the Children's Folklore Section's work during the past [2] according to the *Oxford English Dictionary*, childhood consists of "the state or stage of life of a child; the time during which one is a child; the time from birth to **4** [Author's Credentials] erty" (2011). Scholars of childhood tend to draw a line between childhood and adolescence, which begins at puberty and follows pre-adolescence. The folklore

ELIZABETH TUCKER is Professor of English at Binghamton University

Journal of American Folklore 125(498):389–410

5 Publication Date

3 Publisher

6 Sources Cited

and Humanities 3:145–60.
Carpenter, Carole H. 2011. Why Children's Studies? *Centre for Research in Young People's Texts and Cultures.* crytc.uwinnipeg.ca/pdf/papers/Carole.Carpenter.pdf.
Chamberlain, Alexander Francis. 1896. *The Child and Childhood in Folk-Thought.* New York: Macmillan.
Cline, Foster W., and Jim Fay. 1990. *Parenting with Love and Logic: Teaching Children Responsibility.* Colorado Springs, CO: Pinon Press.
Conrad, JoAnn. 2002. The War on Youth: A Modern Oedipal Tragedy. *Children's Folklore Review* 24(1–2):33–42.
Crandall, Bryan Ripley. 2009. *Cow Project.* bryanripleycrandall.files.wordpress.com/2009/05/slbscow-project.pdf.
Darwin, Charles. 1859. *On the Origin of Species by Means of Natural Selection, or the Preservation of Favoured Races in the Struggle for Life* (1st edition). London: John Murray.
Dégh, Linda. 2001. *Legend and Belief.* Bloomington: Indiana University Press.
Dorson, Richard M. 1968. *The British Folklorists: A History.* Chicago: University of Chicago Press.
Douglas, Norman. [1916] 1968. *London Street Games.* Detroit: Singing Tree Press.

175

14f   Take notes and annotate sources.

Note-taking methods vary greatly from one researcher to another, so you may decide to use a computer file, a notebook, or index cards. Regardless of the method, however, you should (1) record enough information to help you recall the major points of the source; (2) put the information in the form in which you are most likely to incorporate it into your research essay, whether a summary, a paraphrase, or a quotation; and (3) note all the information you will need to cite the source accurately. The following example shows the major items a note should include:

ELEMENTS OF AN ACCURATE NOTE

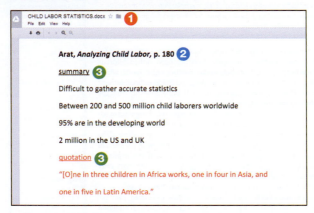

1. *Use a subject heading.* Label or title each note about your source with a brief, descriptive heading so that you can group similar subtopics together.

2. *Identify the source.* List the author's name, a shortened title of the source, and a page number, if available. Your working-bibliography entry (14b) for the source will contain the full bibliographic information, so you don't need to repeat it in each note.

3. *Indicate whether the note is a direct quotation, paraphrase, or summary.* Make sure quotations are copied accurately. Put square brackets around any change you make, and use ellipses if you omit material.

Taking complete notes will help you digest the source information as you read and incorporate the material into your text without inadvertently plagiarizing the source (see Chapter 15). Be sure to reread each note carefully, and recheck it against the source to make sure quotations, statistics, and specific facts are accurate.

Quotations

Some of the notes you take will contain quotations, which give the *exact words* of a source. Here is a note with a quotation that student Benjy Mercer-Golden used in his research paper:

QUOTATION NOTE

1. Name of document indicates subject
2. Author and short title of source (no page number for electronic source)
3. Direct quotation

QUICK HELP

Guidelines for Quoting

- Copy quotations carefully, with punctuation, capitalization, and spelling *exactly* as in the original.

- Enclose the quotation in quotation marks; don't rely on your memory to distinguish your own words from those of the source.

- Use square brackets if you introduce words of your own into a quotation or make changes in it, and use ellipses if you omit material. If you later decide to incorporate the quotation into your essay, copy it faithfully — brackets, ellipses, and all. (52b)

- Record the author's name, the shortened title, and the page number(s) on which the quotation appears. If the note refers to more than one page, use a slash (/) within the quotation to indicate where one page ends and another begins. For sources without page numbers, record the paragraph or other section number(s), if any.

- Make sure you have a corresponding working-bibliography entry with complete source information. (14b)

- Label the note with a subject heading, and identify it as a quotation.

Paraphrases

A paraphrase accurately states all the relevant information from a passage *in your own words and sentence structures*, without any additional comments or elaborations. A paraphrase is useful when the main points of a passage, their order, and at least some details are important but—unlike passages worth quoting—the exact wording is not. Unlike a summary, a paraphrase always restates *all* the main points of a passage in the same order and often in about the same number of words.

ORIGINAL

Language play, the arguments suggest, will help the development of pronunciation ability through its focus on the properties of sounds and sound contrasts, such as rhyming. Playing with word endings and decoding the syntax of riddles will help the acquisition of grammar. Readiness to play with words and names, to exchange puns and to engage in nonsense talk, promotes links with semantic development. The kinds of dialogue interaction illustrated above are likely to have consequences for the development of conversational skills. And language play, by its nature, also contributes greatly to what in recent years has been called *metalinguistic awareness*, which is turning out to be of critical importance in the development of language skills in general and of literacy skills in particular.

– DAVID CRYSTAL, *Language Play* (180)

UNACCEPTABLE PARAPHRASE: STRAYING FROM THE AUTHOR'S IDEAS

Crystal argues that playing with language—creating rhymes, figuring out how riddles work, making puns, playing with names, using invented words, and so on—helps children figure out a great deal about language, from the basics of pronunciation and grammar to how to carry on a conversation. Increasing their understanding of how language works in turn helps them become more interested in learning new languages and in pursuing education (180).

This paraphrase starts off well enough, but it moves away from paraphrasing the original to inserting the writer's ideas; Crystal says nothing about learning new languages or pursuing education.

UNACCEPTABLE PARAPHRASE: USING THE AUTHOR'S WORDS

Crystal suggests that language play, including rhyme, helps children improve pronunciation ability, that looking at word endings and decoding the syntax of riddles allows them to understand grammar, and that other kinds of dialogue interaction teach conversation. Overall, language play may be of critical importance in the development of language and literacy skills (180).

Because the highlighted phrases are either borrowed from the original without quotation marks or changed only superficially, this paraphrase plagiarizes.

UNACCEPTABLE PARAPHRASE: USING THE AUTHOR'S SENTENCE STRUCTURES

Language play, Crystal suggests, will improve pronunciation by zeroing in on sounds such as rhymes. Having fun with word endings and analyzing riddle structure will help a person acquire grammar. Being prepared to play with language, to use puns and talk nonsense, improves the ability to use semantics. These playful methods of communication are likely to influence a person's ability to talk to others. And language play inherently adds enormously to what has recently been known as *metalinguistic awareness*, a concept of great magnitude in developing speech abilities generally and literacy abilities particularly (180).

Here is a paraphrase of the same passage that expresses the author's ideas accurately and acceptably:

ACCEPTABLE PARAPHRASE: IN THE STUDENT WRITER'S OWN WORDS

Crystal argues that playing with language—creating rhymes, figuring out riddles, making puns, playing with names, using invented words, and so on—helps children figure out a great deal, from the basics of pronunciation and grammar to how to carry on a conversation. This kind of play allows children to understand the overall concept of how language works, a concept that is key to learning to use—and read— language effectively (180).

QUICK HELP

Guidelines for Paraphrasing

- Include all main points and any important details from the original source, in the same order in which the author presents them.
- State the meaning in your own words and sentence structures. If you want to include especially memorable language from the original, enclose it in quotation marks.
- Save your comments, elaborations, or reactions on another note.
- Record the author's full name, the shortened title, and the page number(s) on which the original material appears. For sources without page numbers, record the paragraph, screen, or other section number(s), if any.
- Make sure you have a corresponding working-bibliography entry with complete source information. (14b)
- Label the note with a subject heading, and identify it as a paraphrase.

Summaries

A summary is a significantly shortened version of a passage or even of a whole chapter or work that captures main ideas *in your own words*. Unlike a paraphrase, a summary uses just enough information to record the main points you wish to emphasize. To summarize a short passage, read it carefully and, without looking at the text, write a one- or two-sentence summary. Here is David Craig's note recording a summary of the Crystal passage on p. 178. Notice that it states the author's main points selectively—and without using his words.

SUMMARY NOTE

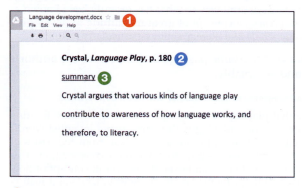

1   Subject heading
2   Author, title, page reference
3   Summary of source

For a long passage or an entire chapter, skim the headings and topic sentences, and make notes of each; then write your summary in a paragraph or two. For a whole book, you may want to refer to the preface and introduction as well as chapter titles, headings, and topic sentences—and your summary may take a page or more.

QUICK HELP

Guidelines for Summarizing

- Include just enough information to recount the main points you want to cite. A summary is usually far shorter than the original.
- Use your own words. If you include any language from the original, enclose it in quotation marks.
- Record the author, shortened title, and page number(s) on which the original material appeared. For sources without page numbers, record the paragraph, screen, or other section number(s), if any.
- Make sure you have a corresponding working-bibliography entry with complete source information. (14b)
- Label the note with a subject heading, and identify it as a summary.

FOR MULTILINGUAL WRITERS

Identifying Sources

While some language communities and cultures expect audiences to recognize the sources of important documents and texts, thereby eliminating the need to cite them directly, conventions for writing in North America call for careful attribution of any quoted, paraphrased, or summarized material. When in doubt, explicitly identify your sources.

Source annotations

Sometimes you may photocopy or print out a source you intend to use. In such cases, you can annotate the photocopies or printouts with your thoughts and questions and highlight interesting quotations and key terms.

You can copy online sources electronically, paste them into a computer file, and annotate them there. Try not to rely too heavily on copying or printing out whole pieces, however; you still need to read the material very carefully. And resist the temptation to treat copied material as notes, an action that could lead to inadvertent plagiarizing. (In a computer file, using a different color for text pasted from a source will help prevent this problem.)

Integrating Sources and Avoiding Plagiarism **15**

The process of absorbing your sources and integrating them gracefully into your own writing is one of the challenges but also the pleasures of research. When you integrate sources appropriately into your work, they don't take over your writing or drown out your voice. Instead, they work in support of your own good ideas.

Your writing is always influenced in some way by what you have read and experienced. As a writer, you need to understand current definitions of plagiarism, which have changed over time and vary from culture to culture, as well as the concept of intellectual property—works protected by copyright or by alternatives such as a Creative Commons license—so you can give credit where credit is due. An age of instant copying and linking may someday lead to revised understandings about who can "own" a text. But in college today, you should cite your sources carefully and systematically to avoid plagiarism, the use of someone else's words and ideas as if they were your own.

15a Decide whether to quote, paraphrase, or summarize.

You tentatively decided to quote, paraphrase, or summarize material when you took notes on your sources (14f). As you choose some of these sources for your research project and decide how to use them, however, you may reevaluate those decisions. The following guidelines can help you decide whether to quote, paraphrase, or summarize.

QUOTE

- wording that is so memorable or powerful, or expresses a point so perfectly, that you cannot change it without weakening its meaning
- authors' opinions you wish to emphasize
- authors' words that make clear you are considering varying perspectives
- respected authorities whose opinions support your ideas
- authors whose opinions challenge or vary greatly from those of others in the field

PARAPHRASE

- passages you do not wish to quote but that use details important to your point

SUMMARIZE

- long passages in which the main point is important to your point but the details are not

15b Integrate quotations, paraphrases, and summaries effectively.

Following are some general guidelines for integrating source materials into your writing.

macmillanhighered.com/everyday6e

☑ Research > LearningCurve: Evaluating, integrating, acknowledging sources (APA)
   Research > LearningCurve: Evaluating, integrating, acknowledging sources (MLA)

Quotations

Quotations from respected authorities can help establish your credibility and show that you are considering various perspectives. However, because your essay is primarily your own work, limit your use of quotations.

BRIEF QUOTATIONS

Short quotations should run in with your text, enclosed by quotation marks (51a).

> In Miss Eckhart, Welty recognizes a character who shares with her "the love of her art and the love of giving it, the desire to give it until there is no more left" (10).

LONG QUOTATIONS

If you are following the style of the Modern Language Association (MLA), set off a prose quotation longer than four lines. If you are following the style of the American Psychological Association (APA), set off a quotation of more than forty words or more than one paragraph. If you are following *Chicago* style, set off a quotation of more than one hundred words or more than one paragraph. Begin such a quotation on a new line. For MLA style, indent every line one inch; for APA style, five to seven spaces; for *Chicago* style, indent the text or use a smaller font (check your instructor's preference). Quotation marks are unnecessary. Introduce longer quotations with a signal phrase or a sentence followed by a colon.

The following long quotation follows MLA style:

A good seating arrangement can prevent problems; however, *withitness*, as defined by Woolfolk, works even better:

> Withitness is the ability to communicate to students that you are aware of what is happening in the classroom, that you "don't miss anything." With-it teachers seem to have "eyes in the back of their heads." They avoid becoming too absorbed with a few students, since this allows the rest of the class to wander. (359)

This technique works, however, only if students actually believe that their teacher will know everything that goes on.

INTEGRATING QUOTATIONS SMOOTHLY INTO YOUR TEXT

Carefully integrate quotations into your text so that they will flow smoothly and clearly into the surrounding sentences. Use a signal phrase or verb, such as those identified in the following examples and listed below.

> As writer Eudora Welty notes, "learning stamps you with its moments. Childhood's learning," she continues, "is made up of moments. It isn't steady. It's a pulse" (9).

> In her essay, Haraway strongly opposes those who condemn technology outright, arguing that we must not indulge in a "demonology of technology" (181).

Notice that the examples alert readers to the quotations by using signal phrases that include the author's name. When you cite a quotation in this way, you need put only the page number in parentheses.

SIGNAL VERBS

acknowledges	concludes	emphasizes	replies
advises	concurs	expresses	reports
agrees	confirms	interprets	responds
allows	criticizes	lists	reveals
answers	declares	objects	says
asserts	describes	observes	states
believes	disagrees	offers	suggests
charges	discusses	opposes	thinks
claims	disputes	remarks	writes

QUICK HELP

Commenting On or Evaluating Your Source Material

Your choice of signal verbs often reveals your attitude toward or relationship to your sources. Signal verbs like *proves*, *demonstrates*, *shows*, or *establishes* suggest that you take a positive view of the information in the source, while signal verbs like *fails*, *lacks*, *refuses*, *overlooks*, or *ignores* suggest that you take a critical view. In between are more neutral verbs (*argues*, *indicates*, *suggests*, *states*, *notes*) indicating an objective relationship to the source material. Professor Laura Aull's research shows that advanced academic writers favor neutral signal verbs, which build the writer's ethos as fair and evenhanded. She also finds that these expert writers rarely use verbs associated with opinions or feelings (*feels*, *believes*, *thinks*), while student writers use them a great deal. You can learn from the experts to look very closely at the verbs you choose when you are reporting what your sources say.

BRACKETS AND ELLIPSES

In direct quotations, enclose in brackets any words you change or add, and indicate any deletions with ellipsis points (52f).

> "There is something wrong in the [Three Mile Island] area," one farmer told the Nuclear Regulatory Commission soon after the plant accident ("Legacy" 33).

> Economist John Kenneth Galbraith has pointed out that "large corporations cannot afford to compete with one another. . . . In a truly competitive market someone loses" (qtd. in Key 17).

Paraphrases and summaries

Introduce paraphrases and summaries clearly, usually with a signal phrase that includes the author of the source, as the highlighted words preceding the summary in this example indicate.

> Professor of linguistics Deborah Tannen says that she offers her book *That's Not What I Meant!* to "women and men everywhere who are trying their best to talk to each other" (19). Tannen goes on to illustrate how communication between women and men breaks down and then to suggest that a full awareness of "genderlects" can improve relationships (297).

15c Integrate visuals and media effectively.

Choose visuals and media wisely, whether you use video, audio, photographs, illustrations, charts and graphs, or other kinds of images. Integrate all visuals and media smoothly into your text.

- *Does each visual or media file make a strong contribution to the written message?* Tangential or purely decorative visuals and media may weaken the power of your writing.

- *Is each visual or media file appropriate and fair to your subject?* An obviously biased perspective may seem unfair or manipulative to your audience.

- *Is each visual or media file appropriate for and fair to your audience?* Visuals and media should appeal to various members of your likely audience.

Whenever you post documents containing visuals or media to the web, make sure you check for copyright information. While it is considered "fair use" to use such materials in an essay or other project for a college class, once that project is published on the web, you might infringe on copyright protections if you do not ask the copyright holder for permission to use the visual or media file. U.S. copyright law considers the reproduction of works for purposes of teaching and scholarship to be "fair use" not bound by copyright, but the law is open to multiple interpretations. If you have questions about whether your work might infringe on copyright, ask your instructor for help.

Like quotations, paraphrases, and summaries, visuals and media need to be introduced and commented on in some way.

- Refer to the visual, audio, or video in the text (*As Fig. 3 demonstrates . . .*) and position it as close as possible after the first reference.

- Explain or comment on the relevance of the visual or media file. This can be done after the insertion point.

- Check the documentation system you are using to make sure you label visuals and media appropriately; MLA, for instance, asks that you number and title tables and figures (*Table 1: Average Amount of Rainfall by Region*).

- If you are posting your document or essay on a website, make sure you have permission to use any visuals or media files that are covered by copyright.

For more on using visuals, see 22d.

15d Check for excessive use of source material.

Your text needs to synthesize your research in support of your own argument; it should not be a patchwork of quotations, paraphrases, and summaries from other people. You need a rhetorical stance that represents you as the author. If you cite too many sources, your own voice will disappear, a problem the following passage demonstrates:

> The United States is one of the countries with the most rapid population growth. In fact, rapid population increase has been a "prominent feature of American life since the founding of the republic" (Day 31). In the past, the cause of the high rate of population growth was the combination of large-scale immigration and a high birth rate. As Day notes, "Two facts stand out in the demographic history of the United States: first, the single position as a receiver of immigrants; second, our high rate of growth from natural increase" (31).
>
> Nevertheless, American population density is not as high as in most European countries. Day points out that the Netherlands, with a density of 906 persons per square mile, is more crowded than even the most densely populated American states (33).

TALKING THE TALK
Saying Something New

"What can I say about my topic that experts haven't already said?" All writers — no matter how experienced — face this problem. As you read more about your topic, you will soon see areas of disagreement among experts, who may not be as expert as they first appear. Notice what your sources say and, especially, what they don't say. Consider how your own interests and experiences give you a unique perspective on the topic. Slowly but surely you will identify a claim that you can make about the topic, one related to what others say but taking a new angle or adding something different to the discussion.

15e Understand why acknowledging sources matters.

Acknowledging sources says to your reader that you have done your homework, that you have gained expertise on your topic, and that you are credible. Acknowledging your sources can also demonstrate fairness — that you have considered several points of view. In addition, recognizing your sources can help provide background for your research by placing it in the context of other thinking. Most of all, you should acknowledge sources to help your readers follow your thoughts, understand how your ideas relate to the thoughts of others, and know where to go to find more information on your topic.

15f Know which sources to acknowledge.

As you carry out research, it is important to understand the distinction between materials that require acknowledgment (in in-text citations, footnotes, or endnotes; and in the works-cited list or bibliography) and those that do not.

Materials that do not require acknowledgment

- *Common knowledge.* If most readers already know a fact, you probably do not need to cite a source for it. You do not need to credit a source for the statement that Barack Obama was reelected president in 2012, for example.

- *Facts available in a wide variety of sources.* If a number of encyclopedias, almanacs, or textbooks include a certain piece of information, you usually need not cite a specific source for it.

- *Your own findings from field research.* If you conduct observations or surveys, simply announce your findings as your own. Acknowledge people you interview as individuals rather than as part of a survey.

Materials that require acknowledgment

Some of the information you use may need to be credited to a source.

- *Quotations, paraphrases, and summaries.* Whenever you use another person's words, ideas, or opinions, credit the source. Even though the wording of a paraphrase or summary is your own, you should still acknowledge the source.

- *Facts not widely known or claims that are arguable.* If your readers would be unlikely to know a fact, or if an author presents as fact a claim that may or may not be true, cite the source. If you are not sure whether a fact will be familiar to your readers or whether a statement is arguable, cite the source.

- *Visuals from any source.* Credit all visual and statistical material not derived from your own field research, even if you yourself create a graph or table from the data provided in a source.

- *Help provided by others.* If an instructor gave you a good idea or if friends responded to your draft or helped you conduct surveys, give credit.

15g Recognize patchwriting.

Integrating sources into your writing can be a significant challenge. In fact, as a beginning researcher, you might do what Professor Rebecca Howard calls "patchwriting"; that is, rather than integrate sources smoothly and accurately, you patch together words, phrases, and even structures from sources into your own writing, sometimes without citation. The author of this book remembers doing such "patchwriting" for a middle-school report on her hero, Dr. Albert Schweitzer. Luckily, she had a teacher who sat patiently with her, showing her how to paraphrase, summarize, and quote from sources correctly and effectively. So it takes time and effort—as well as good instruction—to learn to integrate sources appropriately rather than patchwriting, which is sometimes considered plagiarism even if you didn't mean to plagiarize.

15h Adapt structures and phrases from a genre without plagiarizing.

If you are not accustomed to writing in a particular academic genre, you may find it useful to borrow and adapt transitional devices and pieces of sentence structure from other people's writing in the genre you are working in. Be careful to borrow only structures that are generic and not ideas or sentences that come from a particular, identifiable writer. You should not copy any whole sentences or sentence structures verbatim, or your borrowing may seem like plagiarism.

ORIGINAL ABSTRACT FROM A SOCIAL SCIENCE PAPER

Using the interpersonal communications research of J. K. Brilhart and G. J. Galanes, and W. Wilmot and J. Hocker, along with T. Hartman's personality assessment, I observed and analyzed the leadership roles and group dynamics of my project collaborators in a communications course. Based on results of the Hartman personality assessment, I predicted that a single leader would emerge. However, complementary individual strengths and gender differences encouraged a distributed leadership style, in which the group experienced little confrontation and conflict. Conflict, because it was handled positively, was crucial to the group's progress.

EFFECTIVE BORROWING OF STRUCTURES FROM A GENRE

Drawing on the research of Deborah Tannen on men's and women's conversational styles, I analyzed the conversational styles of six first-year students at DePaul University. Based on Tannen's research, I expected that the three men I observed would use features typical of male conversational style and the three women would use features typical of female conversational style. In general, these predictions were accurate; however, some exceptions were also apparent.

The example above illustrates effective borrowing. The student writer borrows phrases (such as "drawing on" and "based on") that are commonly used in academic writing in the social sciences to perform particular functions. Notice how the student also modifies these phrases to suit her needs.

---

macmillanhighered.com/everyday6e

☑ Research > LearningCurve: Evaluating, integrating, acknowledging sources (APA)
  Research > LearningCurve: Evaluating, integrating, acknowledging sources (MLA)

15i Uphold your academic integrity, and avoid plagiarism.

One of the cornerstones of intellectual work is academic integrity. This principle accounts for our being able to trust those sources we use and to demonstrate that our own work is equally trustworthy. While there are many ways to damage academic integrity, two that are especially important are inaccurate or incomplete acknowledgment of sources in citations—sometimes called unintentional plagiarism—and plagiarism that is deliberately intended to pass off one writer's work as another's.

Whether it is intentional or not, plagiarism can result in serious consequences. At some colleges, students who plagiarize fail the course automatically; at others, they are expelled. Instructors who plagiarize, even inadvertently, have had their degrees revoked and their books withdrawn from publication. And outside academic life, eminent political, business, and scientific leaders have been stripped of candidacies, positions, and awards because of plagiarism.

Inaccurate or incomplete citation of sources

If your paraphrase is too close to the wording or sentence structure of a source (even if you identify the source), if you do not identify the source of a quotation (even if you include the quotation marks), or if you fail to indicate clearly the source of an idea that you obviously did not come up with on your own, you may be accused of plagiarism even if your intent was not to plagiarize. Inaccurate or incomplete acknowledgment of sources often results either from carelessness or from not learning how to borrow material properly in the first place

---

 FOR MULTILINGUAL WRITERS

Plagiarism as a Cultural Concept

Many cultures do not recognize Western notions of plagiarism, which rest on a belief that language and ideas can be owned by writers. Indeed, in many countries other than the United States, and even within some communities in the United States, using the words and ideas of others without attribution is considered a sign of deep respect as well as an indication of knowledge. In academic writing in the United States, however, you should credit all materials except those that are common knowledge, that are available in a wide variety of sources, or that are your own creations (photographs, drawings, and so on) or your own findings from field research.

> **QUICK HELP**
>
> **Avoiding Plagiarism**
>
> - Maintain an accurate and thorough working bibliography. (14b)
> - Establish a consistent note-taking system, listing sources and page numbers and clearly identifying all quotations, paraphrases, summaries, statistics, and visuals. (14f)
> - Identify all quotations with quotation marks — both in your notes and in your essay. Be sure your summaries and paraphrases use your own words and sentence structures. (15b)
> - Give a citation or note for each quotation, paraphrase, summary, arguable assertion or opinion, statistic, and visual that is from a source. Prepare an accurate and complete list of sources cited according to the required documentation style. (See Chapters 57–67.)
> - Plan ahead on writing assignments so that you can avoid the temptation to take shortcuts.

(15g and h). Still, because the costs of even unintentional plagiarism can be severe, it's important to understand how it can happen and how you can guard against it.

As a writer of academic integrity, you will want to take responsibility for your research and for acknowledging all sources accurately. One easy way to keep track is to keep photocopies, printouts, or unaltered digital copies as you do your research; then you can identify needed quotations by highlighting them on each source.

Deliberate plagiarism

Deliberate plagiarism—handing in an essay written by a friend or purchased (or simply downloaded) from an essay-writing company; cutting and pasting passages directly from source materials without marking them with quotation marks and acknowledging your sources; failing to credit the source of an idea or concept in your text—is what most people think of when they hear the word *plagiarism*. This form of plagiarism is particularly troubling because it represents dishonesty and deception: those who intentionally plagiarize present the hard thinking and hard work of someone else as their own, and they claim knowledge they really don't have, thus deceiving their readers.

Deliberate plagiarism is also fairly simple to spot: your instructor will be well acquainted with your writing and likely to notice any sudden shifts in the style or quality of your work. In addition, by typing a few words from an essay into a search engine, your instructor can identify "matches" very easily.

16   Writing a Research Project

Everyday decisions often call for research and writing. In trying to choose between colleges in different towns, for example, one student made a long list of questions to answer: Which location had the lower cost of living? Which school offered more financial aid? Which program would be more likely to help graduates find a job? After conducting careful research, he was able to write a letter of acceptance to one place and a letter of regret to the other. In much the same way, when you are working on an academic project, there comes a time to draw the strands of your research together and articulate your conclusions in writing.

16a   Refine your writing plans.

You should by now have notes containing facts, opinions, paraphrases, summaries, quotations, and other material; you probably have some images or media to include as well. You may also have ideas about how to synthesize these many pieces of information. And you should have some sense of whether your hypothesis has sufficient support. Now is the time to reconsider your purpose, audience, stance, and working thesis.

- What is your central purpose? What other purposes, if any, do you have?
- What is your stance toward your topic? Are you an advocate, a critic, a reporter, an observer?
- What audience(s) are you addressing?
- How much background information or context does your audience need?
- What supporting information will your readers find convincing?
- Should your tone be that of a colleague, an expert, a friend?
- How can you establish common ground with your readers and show them that you have considered points of view other than your own? (See 11f and Chapter 27.)
- What is your working thesis trying to establish? Will your audience accept it?

Explicit thesis

Writing out an explicit thesis statement allows you to articulate your major points and to see how well they carry out your purpose and appeal to your audience. Before you begin a full draft, then, try to develop your working thesis into an explicit statement, which you may or may not decide to include, in your final draft.

David Craig developed the following explicit thesis statement:

> Instant messaging seems to be a positive force in the development of youth literacy because it promotes regular contact with words, the use of a written medium for communication, and the development of an alternative form of literacy.

For David Craig's research essay, see Chapter 60.

Questions to test your thesis

Although writing out an explicit thesis will often confirm your research, you may find that your hypothesis is invalid, inadequately supported, or insufficiently focused. In such cases, you need to rethink your original research question and perhaps do further research. To test your thesis, consider the following questions:

- How can you state your thesis more precisely or more clearly (5b)? Should the wording be more specific?
- In what ways will your thesis interest your audience? What can you do to increase that interest?
- Will your thesis be manageable, given your limits of time and knowledge? If not, what can you do to make the thesis more manageable?
- What evidence from your research supports each aspect of your thesis? What additional evidence do you need?

 FOR MULTILINGUAL WRITERS
Multilingual **Asking Experienced Writers to Review a Thesis**

You might find it helpful to ask one or two classmates who have more experience with the particular type of academic writing to look at your explicit thesis. Ask if the thesis is as direct and clear as it can be, and revise accordingly.

Design considerations

As you move toward producing a draft, take some time to think about how you want your research essay or project to look. What font size will you use? Should you use color? Do you plan to insert text boxes, visuals, or media files? Will you need headings and sub-headings? (See Chapter 22.)

16b Organize and draft.

Experienced writers differ considerably in the ways they go about organizing ideas and information, and you will want to experiment until you find a method that works well for you. (For more on orga-nizational strategies, see 5d.)

Subject organization

You may find it useful to have physical notes to arrange—note cards or sticky notes, for example, or printouts of your slides or of notes you have been keeping online that you mark in some way to make the subject categories easy to identify. You can group the pieces around subject headings and reorder the parts until they seem to make sense.

Grouping your notes will help you see how well you can sup-port your thesis and help you see if you have missed any essential points. Do you need to omit any ideas or sources? Do you need to find additional evidence for a main or supporting point? Once you have gathered everything together and organized your materials, you can see how the many small pieces of your research fit together. Make sure that your evidence supports your explicit thesis; if not, you may need to revise it or do additional research—or both.

Once you have established initial groups, skim through the notes and look for ways to organize your draft. Figure out what background your audience needs, what points you need to make first, how much detail and support to offer for each point, and so on.

Outlines

You can use outlines in various ways and at various stages. Some writers group their notes, write a draft, and then outline the draft to study its tentative structure. Others develop an informal working outline from their notes and revise it as they go along. Still other writers prefer to plot out their organization early on in a formal out-line. (For more on outlines, see 5e.)

Drafting

For most college research projects, drafting should begin *at least* two weeks before the instructor's deadline in case you need to gather more information or do more drafting. Set a deadline for having a complete draft, and structure your work with that date in mind. Gather your notes, outline, and sources, and read through them, getting involved in your topic. Most writers find that some sustained work (two or three hours at a time) pays off at this point. Begin drafting a section that you feel confident about. For example, if you are not sure how you want to introduce the draft but do know how you want to approach a particular point, begin with that, and return to the introduction later. The most important thing is to get started.

WORKING TITLE AND INTRODUCTION

The title and introduction play special roles, for they set the stage for what is to come. Ideally, the title announces the subject of the research essay or project in an intriguing or memorable way. The introduction should draw readers in and provide any background they will need to understand your discussion. Here are some tips for drafting an introduction to a research essay:

- It is often effective to *open with a question*, especially your research question. Next, you might explain what you will do to answer the question. Then *end with your explicit thesis statement* — in essence, the answer.

- Help readers by *forecasting your main points*.

- *Establish your own credibility* by revealing how you have become knowledgeable about the topic.

- A quotation can be a good attention-getter, but you may not want to open with a quotation if doing so will give that source too much emphasis.

CONCLUSION

A good conclusion to a research project helps readers know what they have learned. Its job is not to persuade (the body of the essay or project should already have done that) but to contribute to the overall effectiveness of your argument. Here are some strategies that may help:

- Refer to your thesis, and then expand to a more general conclusion that reminds readers of the significance of your discussion.

- If you have covered several main points, you may want to remind readers of them. Be careful, however, to provide more than a mere summary.
- Try to end with something that will have an impact—a provocative quotation or question, a vivid image, a call for action, or a warning. But guard against sounding preachy.

16c Incorporate source materials.

When you reach the point of drafting your research project, a new task awaits: weaving your source materials into your writing. The challenge is to use your sources yet remain the author—to quote, paraphrase, and summarize other voices while remaining the major voice in your work. (See Chapter 15 for tips on integrating sources.)

16d Review and get responses to your draft.

Once you've completed your draft, reread it slowly. As you do so, answer the following questions, and use them as a starting point for revision:

- What do you now see as your essay's *purpose*? How does this compare with your original purpose? Does the draft do what your assignment requires?
- What *audience* does your essay address?
- What is your *stance* toward the topic?
- What is your *thesis*? Is it clearly stated?
- What *evidence* supports your thesis? Is the evidence sufficient?

Next, ask friends, classmates, and, if possible, your instructor to read and respond to your draft. Asking specific questions of your readers will result in the most helpful advice. (See Chapter 7.)

16e Revise and edit your draft.

When you have considered your reviewers' responses and your own analysis, you can turn to revising and editing. See the box on p. 197 and sections 7d and e for more information.

QUICK HELP

Guidelines for Revising a Research Project

- *Take responses into account.* Look at specific problems that reviewers think you need to solve or strengths you might capitalize on. For example, if they showed great interest in one point but no interest in another, consider expanding the first and deleting the second.

- *Reconsider your original purpose, audience, and stance.* Have you achieved your purpose? If not, consider how you can. How well have you appealed to your readers? Make sure you satisfy any special concerns of your reviewers. If your rhetorical stance toward your topic has changed, does your draft need to change, too?

- *Assess your research.* Think about whether you have investigated the topic thoroughly and consulted materials with more than one point of view. Have you left out any important sources? Are the sources you use reliable and appropriate for your topic? Have you synthesized your research findings and drawn warranted conclusions?

- *Assess your use of visuals and media.* Make sure that each one supports your argument, is clearly labeled, and is cited appropriately.

- *Gather additional material.* If you need to strengthen any points, first check your notes to see whether you already have the necessary information. In some instances, you may need to do more research.

- *Decide what changes you need to make.* List everything you must do to perfect your draft. With your deadline in mind, plan your revision.

- *Rewrite your draft.* Many writers prefer to revise first on paper rather than on a computer. However you revise, be sure to save copies of each draft. Begin with the major changes, such as adding content or reorganizing. Then turn to sentence-level problems and word choice. Can you sharpen the work's dominant impression?

- *Reevaluate the title, introduction, and conclusion.* Is your title specific and engaging? Does the introduction capture readers' attention and indicate what the work discusses? Does your conclusion help readers see the significance of your argument?

- *Check your documentation.* Make sure you've included a citation in your text for every quotation, paraphrase, summary, visual, and media file you incorporated, following your documentation style consistently.

- *Edit your draft.* Check grammar, usage, spelling, punctuation, and mechanics. Consider the advice of computer spell checkers (29f) and grammar checkers carefully before accepting it.

16f Prepare a list of sources.

Once you have your final draft and source materials in place, you are ready to prepare a list of sources. Create an entry for each source used in your essay. Then double-check your essay against your list of sources cited; be sure that you have listed every source mentioned in the in-text citations or notes and that you have not listed any sources not cited in your essay. (For guidelines on documentation styles, see Chapters 57–67.)

16g Prepare and proofread your final copy.

To make sure that the final version of your essay puts your best foot forward, proofread it carefully. Work with a hard copy, since reading onscreen often leads to inaccuracies and missed typos. Proofread once for typographical and grammatical errors and once again to make sure you haven't introduced new errors. If you are keeping an editing checklist, look for the types of editing problems you have had in the past.

Academic, Professional, and Public Writing

Don't underestimate your readers'
intelligence, but don't overestimate their
knowledge of a particular field.

— JULIE ANN MILLER

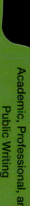

Academic, Professional, and Public Writing

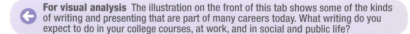

For visual analysis The illustration on the front of this tab shows some of the kinds of writing and presenting that are part of many careers today. What writing do you expect to do in your college courses, at work, and in social and public life?

17 Academic Work in Any Discipline

A recent survey confirmed that good writing plays an important role in almost every profession. One MBA wrote, "Those who advance quickly in my company are those who write and speak well—it's as simple as that." But while writing is always a valuable skill, writing well means different things in different disciplines. As you prepare written assignments for various courses, then, you will need to become familiar with the expectations, vocabularies, styles, methods of proof, and conventional formats used in each field.

17a Read and write for every discipline.

Writing is central to learning regardless of the discipline. So whether you are explaining the results of a telephone survey you conducted for a psychology class, preparing a lab report for chemistry, conducting a case study for anthropology, or working on a proposal for material sciences and engineering, writing helps you get the job done.

One good way to learn to write well in a discipline is to read the texts others write. So read a lot, and pay attention to the texts you are reading. To get started, choose an article in an important journal in the field you plan to major in and then answer the following questions:

- How does a journal article in this discipline begin?
- How is the article organized? Does it have specific sections with subheads?
- What sources are cited, and how are they used—as backup support, as counter-examples, or as an argument to refute?
- How does the article conclude?
- What audience does the text seem to address? Is it a narrow technical or disciplinary audience, or is it aimed at a broader reading public? Is it addressed to readers of a specific journal? Is it published in print or online?

Finally, make sure you know whether the articles you are reading are from juried or nonjuried journals. Juried journals use panels of expert readers to analyze proposed articles, so articles in juried journals have been recommended for publication by experts in the field. Nonjuried journals can also offer valuable information, but they may bear the stamp of the editor's biases more strongly than a juried journal. To find out whether a journal is juried or nonjuried, check the submissions guidelines for information about whether submitted articles are sent to reviewers before publication.

For additional guidelines on reading critically, see Chapter 9. For guidelines on using online databases (called "corpora") to explore conventions of writing in various academic disciplines, see 29e.

17b Consider expectations for academic assignments.

When you receive an assignment, your first job is to be sure you understand what that assignment is asking you to do. Some assignments

---

QUICK HELP

Analyzing an Assignment

- *What is the purpose of the assignment?* Are you expected to join a discussion, demonstrate your mastery of the topic in writing, or something else?

- *Who is the audience?* The instructor will be one audience, but are there others? If so, who are they?

- *What does the assignment ask of you?* Look for key terms such as *summarize, explain, evaluate, interpret, illustrate,* and *define.*

- *Do you need clarification of any terms?* If so, ask your instructor.

- *What do you need to know or find out to complete the assignment?* You may need to do background reading, develop a procedure for analyzing or categorizing information, or carry out some other kind of preparation.

- *What does the instructor expect in a written response?* How will you use sources? What kinds of sources should you use? How should you organize and develop the assignment? What is the expected format and length?

- *Can you locate a model of an effective response to a similar assignment?*

- *What do other students think the assignment requires?* Talking over an assignment with classmates is one good way to test your understanding.

may be as vague as "Write a five-page essay on one aspect of the Civil War." Others may be fairly specific: "Collect, summarize, and interpret data drawn from a sample of letters to the editor published in two newspapers, one in a small rural community and one in an urban community, over a period of three months." Whatever the assignment, use the questions on p. 203 (and the information in Chapter 3) to analyze it.

17c Learn specialized vocabularies.

Entering into an academic discipline or a profession is like going to a party where you don't know anyone. At first you feel like an outsider, and you may not understand much of what you hear or see. Before you enter the conversation, you have to listen and observe carefully. Eventually, however, you will be able to join in—and if you stay long enough, participating in the conversation becomes easy and natural.

To learn the routines, practices, and ways of knowing in a new field, you must also make an effort to enter into the conversation. A good way to get started is to study the vocabulary of the field you are most interested in.

Highlight the key terms in your reading or notes to learn how much specialized or technical vocabulary you will be expected to know. If you find only a small amount of specialized vocabulary, try to master the new terms quickly by reading your textbook carefully, looking up key words or phrases, and asking questions. If you find a great deal of specialized vocabulary, however, you may want to familiarize yourself with it methodically. Any of the following procedures may help:

- Keep a log of unfamiliar words used in context. Check definitions in your textbook's glossary or index, or consult a specialized dictionary.

- See if your textbook has a glossary of terms or sets off definitions. Study pertinent sections to master the terms.

- Work with key concepts. Even if they are not yet entirely clear to you, using them will help you understand them. For example, in a statistics class, try to work out (in words) how to do an analysis of *covariance*, step by step, even if you are not sure of the precise definition of the term. Or try to plot the narrative progression in a story even if you are still not entirely sure of the definition of *narrative progression*.

- Take special note of the ways technical language or disciplinary vocabulary is used in online information related to a particular field.

17d Study disciplinary style.

Another important way to learn about a discipline is to identify its stylistic features. Study pieces of writing in the field with the following in mind:

- *Overall tone.* How would you describe it? (See 3f.)
- *Title.* Are titles generally descriptive ("Findings from a Double-Blind Study of the Effect of Antioxidants"), persuasive ("Antioxidants Proven Effective"), or something else? How does the title shape your expectations?
- *Stance.* To what extent do writers in the field strive for distance and objectivity? What strategies help them to achieve this stance? (See 3c.)
- *Sentence length.* Are sentences long and complex? Simple and direct?
- *Voice.* Are verbs generally active or passive? Why? (See 38g.)
- *Person.* Do writers use the first-person *I* or third-person terms such as *the investigator*? Some of both? What is the effect of this choice?
- *Visuals.* Do writers typically use elements such as graphs, tables, maps, or photographs? How are visuals integrated into the text? What role, if any, do headings and other formatting elements play in the writing? (See Chapter 22.)
- *Documentation style.* Do writers use MLA, APA, or *Chicago* style? (See Chapters 57–67.)

TALKING THE TALK

The First Person

"Is it true that I should never use *I* in college writing?" In much writing in college, using the first-person *I* is perfectly acceptable to most instructors. As always, think about the context — if your own experience is relevant to the topic, you are better off saying *I* than trying too hard not to. But don't overdo it, especially if the writing isn't just autobiographical. And check with your instructor if you aren't sure: in certain academic disciplines, using *I* may be seen as inappropriate. (See 29e for other ways to research the use of *I* in your discipline.)

Of course, writings within a single discipline may have different purposes and different styles. A chemist may write a grant proposal, a lab notebook, a literature review, a research report, and a lab report, each with a different purpose and style.

17e Use evidence effectively.

As you grow familiar with an area of study, you will develop a sense of what it takes to prove a point in that field. You can speed up this process, however, by investigating and questioning. The following questions will help you think about the use of evidence in materials you read:

- How do writers in the field use precedent and authority? What or who counts as an authority in this field? How are the credentials of an authority established? (See 11f.)
- What kinds of quantitative data (countable or measurable items) are used, and for what purposes? How are the data gathered and presented?
- How are qualitative data (systematically observed items) used?
- How are statistics used and presented? Are tables, charts, graphs, or other visuals important, and why?
- How is logical reasoning used? How are definition, cause and effect, analogy, and example used?
- How does the field use primary materials—the firsthand sources of information—and secondary sources that are reported by others? (See 13a.) How is each type of source presented?
- What kinds of textual evidence are cited?
- How are quotations and other references to sources used and integrated into the text? (See Chapter 15.)

17f Use conventional patterns and formats.

To produce effective writing in a discipline, you need to know the field's generally accepted formats for organizing and presenting evidence. A typical laboratory report, for instance, follows a fairly standard organizational framework and usually has a certain look (see 20c for an example). A case study in sociology or education or anthropology likewise follows a typical organizational plan.

Ask your instructor to recommend some excellent examples of the kind of writing you will do in the course. Then analyze these examples in terms of format and organization. You might also look at major scholarly journals in the field to see what types of formats seem most common and how each is organized. Consider the following questions about organization and format:

- What types of articles, reports, or documents are common in this field? What is the purpose of each?

- What can a reader expect to find in each type of writing? What does each type assume about its readers?

- Do articles or other documents typically begin with an abstract? If so, does the abstract describe the parts of the article to come, or does it provide substantive information such as findings or conclusions?

- How is each type of text organized? What are its main parts? How are they labeled?

- How does a particular type of essay, report, or document show the connections among ideas? What assumptions does it take for granted? What points does it emphasize?

Remember that there is a close connection between the writing patterns and formats a particular area of study uses and the work that scholars in that field undertake.

17g Pay attention to ethical issues.

Writers in all disciplines face ethical questions. Those who plan and carry out research on living people, for example, must be careful to avoid harming their subjects. Researchers in all fields must be scrupulous in presenting data to make sure that others can replicate research and test claims. In whatever discipline or field you are working, you should take into consideration your own interests, those of your collaborators, and those of your employers — but you must also responsibly safeguard the interests of the general public.

Fortunately, a growing number of disciplines have adopted guidelines for ethics. The American Psychological Association has been a pioneer in this area, and many other professional organizations and companies have their own codes or standards of ethics. These guidelines can help you make decisions about day-to-day writing. Even so, you will no doubt encounter situations where the right or ethical decision is murky at best. In such situations, consult your own conscience first and then talk your choices over with colleagues you respect before coming to a decision on how to proceed.

17h   Collaborate effectively.

In contemporary academic and business environments, working with others is not just a highly valued skill—it is a necessity. Such collaboration happens when peers work together on a shared document, when classmates divide research and writing duties to create a multimedia presentation, when reviewers share advice on a draft, or when colleagues in an office offer their views on appropriate revisions for a companywide document.

Because people all over the world now have the ability to research, study, write, and work together, you must be able to communicate effectively within and across cultures. Conventions for academic writing (or for forms of digital communication) can vary from culture to culture, from discipline to discipline, and from one form of English to another. What is considered polite in one culture may seem rude in another, so those who communicate globally must take care to avoid giving offense—or taking it where none was intended. (For more information on writing across cultures, see Chapter 26.)

TALKING THE TALK

Collaborating or Cheating?

"When is asking others for help and opinions acceptable, and when is it cheating?" In academic work, the difference between collaborating and cheating depends almost entirely on context. There will be times — during exams, for example — when instructors will expect you to work alone. At other times, working with others — for a team project, perhaps, or peer review — may be required, and getting others' opinions on your writing is always a good habit. You draw the line, however, at having another person do your work for you. Submitting material under your name that you did not write is unacceptable in college writing. But collaboration is a key fact of life in today's digital world, so it's important to think carefully about how to collaborate effectively — and ethically.

Planning goes a long way toward making any group collaboration work well. Although you will probably do much of your group work online, keep in mind that face-to-face meetings can accomplish some things that virtual meetings cannot. Here are some strategies for group projects:

- Establish a regular meeting time and space (whether in person or online), and exchange contact information.
- Establish ground rules. Be sure that everyone has a responsibility to participate and to meet deadlines.
- Establish clear duties for each participant.
- With final deadlines in mind, create an overall agenda to organize the project. At each group meeting, take turns writing up notes on what was discussed and review them at the end of the meeting.
- Use group meetings to work together on difficult problems. If an assignment is complex, have each member explain one section to the others. Check with your instructor if part of the task is unclear or if members don't agree on what is required.
- Express opinions politely and respectfully. If disagreements arise, try paraphrasing to see if everyone is hearing the same thing.
- Remember that the goal is not for everyone just to get along; constructive conflict is desirable. Get a spirited debate going, and discuss all available options.
- If your project requires a group-written document, assign one member to get the writing project started. Set deadlines for each part of the project. Come to an agreement about how you will edit and change each other's contributions to avoid offending any member of the group.
- Assess the group's effectiveness periodically. Should you make changes as you go forward? What has been accomplished? What has the group done best? What has it done less successfully? What has each member contributed? What have you learned about how to work more effectively with others on future projects?

Writing for the Humanities   **18**

In humanities disciplines, the interpretation and creation of texts are central. The nature of texts can vary widely, from poems and plays to novels, articles, philosophical treatises, films, advertisements, paintings, and so on. But whether the text being studied is ancient or modern, literary or historical, verbal or visual, textual analysis plays a critical role in the reading and writing that people in the humanities undertake.

18a Read texts in the humanities.

To read critically in the humanities, you will need to pose questions and construct hypotheses as you read. You may ask, for instance, why a writer might make some points or develop some examples but omit others. Rather than finding meaning only in the surface information that texts or artifacts convey, you should use your own questions and hypotheses to create fuller meanings—to construct the significance of what you read.

QUICK HELP

Guidelines for Reading Texts in the Humanities

- **Be clear about the purpose of the text.** The two most common purposes for works in the humanities are to provide information and to argue for a particular interpretation. Pay attention to whether the text presents opinions or facts, to what is included and omitted, and to how facts are presented to the audience. (14c)

- **Get an overall impression.** What does the work make you think about — and why? What is most remarkable or memorable? What confuses you?

- **Annotate the text.** Be prepared to "talk back," ask questions, note emerging patterns or themes, and point out anything out of place or ineffective. (Chapter 9)

- **Look at the context.** Consider the time and place represented in the work as well as when and where the writer lived. You may also consider social, political, or personal forces that may have affected the writer.

- **Think about the audience.** Who are the readers or viewers the writer seems to address? Do they include you?

- **Pay attention to genre.** What category does the work fall into (graphic novel, diary, political cartoon, sermon, argumentative essay, Hollywood western)? What is noteworthy about the form? How does it conform to, stretch, or even subvert your expectations about the genre? (3e)

- **Pay attention to visual elements and design.** How does the text look? What visual elements does it include? What contribution do these make to the overall effect or argument?

- **Note the point of view.** Whose point of view is represented? How does it affect your response?

- **Notice the major themes.** Are specific claims being advanced? How are these claims supported?

- **Understand how primary and secondary sources differ.** Primary sources provide firsthand knowledge, while secondary sources report on or analyze the research of others. (13a)

To successfully engage texts, you must recognize that you are not a neutral observer, not an empty cup into which the meaning of a work is poured. If such were the case, writing would have exactly the same meanings for all of us, and reading would be a fairly boring affair. If you have ever gone to see a movie with a friend and each come away with a completely different understanding or response, you already have ample evidence that a text never has just one meaning.

Nevertheless, you may in the past have been willing to accept the first meaning to occur to you—to take a text at face value. Most humanities courses, however, will expect you to exercise your interpretive powers. The guidelines on p. 210 can help you build your strengths as a close reader of humanities texts.

18b Write texts in the humanities.

As a writer in the humanities, you will use the findings from close examination of a text or artifact to develop an argument or to construct an analysis.

Assignments

Common assignments that make use of the skills of close reading, analysis, and argument include summaries, response pieces, position papers, critical analyses of primary and secondary sources, and research-based projects. In philosophy, for example, you might need to summarize an argument, critique a text's logic and effectiveness, or discuss a moral issue from a particular philosophical perspective. A literature assignment may ask you to look very closely at a particular text ("Examine the role of chocolate in Toni Morrison's *Tar Baby*") or to go well beyond a primary text ("Discuss the impact of agribusiness on modernist novels"). Other disciplines may ask you to write articles, primary source analyses, or research papers.

For texts in literature, modern languages, and philosophy, writers often use the documentation style of the Modern Language Association; see Chapter 57 for advice on using MLA style. For projects in history and other areas of the humanities, writers often use the documentation style of the University of Chicago Press; see Chapter 65 for advice on using *Chicago* style.

Critical stance

To analyze a text, you need to develop a critical stance—the approach you will take to the work—that can help you develop a thesis or major claim (see 5b and 11c). To evaluate the text and present a critical response to it, you should look closely at the text itself, including its style; at the context in which it was produced; and at the audience the text aims to reach, which may or may not include yourself.

To look closely at the text itself, consider its genre, form, point of view, and themes, and look at the stylistic features, such as word choice, use of imagery, visuals, and design. Then consider context: ask why the text was created, note its original and current contexts, and think about how attitudes and ideas of its era may have influenced it. Consider who the intended audience might be, and think about how people outside this intended group might respond to the text. Finally, think about your personal response to the text as well. (See also Chapters 9 and 10.)

Carrying out these steps should provide you with plenty of material to work with as you begin to shape a critical thesis and write your analysis. You can begin by grounding your analysis in one or more important questions you have about the work.

Literary analysis

When you analyze or interpret a literary work, think of your thesis as answering a question about some aspect of the work. The guiding question you bring to the literary work will help you decide on a critical stance toward the work. For example, a student who is writing about Shakespeare's *Macbeth* might find her curiosity piqued by the many comic moments that appear in this tragedy. She might turn the question of why Shakespeare uses so much comedy in *Macbeth* into the following thesis statement, which proposes an answer: "The many unexpected comic moments in *Macbeth* emphasize how disordered the world becomes for murderers like Macbeth and his wife."

18c A student's close reading of poetry

Student Writer

Bonnie Sillay

Following is an excerpt from student Bonnie Sillay's close reading of two poems by E. E. Cummings. This essay follows MLA style (see Chapters 57–60). Bonnie is creating her own interpretation, so the only works she cites are the poems she analyzes.

1/2"

1"

Bonnie Sillay

Instructor Angela Mitchell

English 1102

December 4, 2011

"Life's Not a Paragraph"

Throughout his poetry, E. E. Cummings leads readers deep into a thicket of scrambled words, missing punctuation, and unconventional structure. Within Cummings's poetic bramble, ambiguity leads the reader through what seems at first a confusing and winding maze. However, this confusion actually transforms into a path that leads the reader to the center of the thicket where Cummings's message lies: readers should not allow their experience to be limited by reason and rationality. In order to communicate his belief that emotional experience should triumph over reason, Cummings employs odd juxtapositions, outlandish metaphors, and inversions of traditional grammatical structures that reveal the illogic of reason. Indeed, by breaking down such formal boundaries, Cummings's poems "since feeling is first" and "as freedom is a breakfastfood" suggest that emotion, which provides the compositional fabric for our experience of life, should never be defined or controlled.

In "since feeling is first," Cummings urges his reader to reject attempts to control emotion, using English grammar as one example of the restrictive conventions present in society. Stating that "since feeling is first / who pays any attention / to the syntax of things" (lines 1-3), Cummings suggests that emotion should not be forced to fit into some preconceived framework or mold. He carries this message throughout the poem by juxtaposing images of the abstract and the concrete—images of emotion and of English grammar. Cummings's word choice enhances his intentionally strange juxtapositions, with the poet using grammatical terms that suggest regulation or confinement. For example, in the line "And

Name, instructor, course number, date on left margin

Title centered

Present tense used to discuss poetry

Foreshadows discussion of work to come

Introductory paragraph ends with thesis statement

Quotation cited parenthetically

Double spacing throughout

Annotations indicate effective choices or MLA-style formatting.

Paper header includes last name and page number

death i think is no parenthesis" (16), Cummings uses the idea that parentheses confine the words they surround in order to warn the reader not to let death confine life or emotions.

Transition sentence connects the previous paragraph to this one

The structure of the poem also rejects traditional conventions. Instead of the final stanzas making the main point, Cummings opens his poem with his primary message, that "feeling is first" (1). Again, Cummings shows that emotion rejects order and structure. How can emotion be bottled in sentences and interrupted by commas, colons, and spaces? To Cummings, emotion is a never-ending run-on sentence that should not be diagramed or dissected.

Writer uses a metaphor that captures the spirit of Cummings's point

In the third stanza of "since feeling is first," Cummings states his point outright, noting "my blood approves, / and kisses are a better fate / than wisdom" (7-9). Here, Cummings argues for reveling in the feeling during a fleeting moment such as a kiss. He continues, "the

Quotation integrated into writer's sentence

best gesture of my brain is less than / your eyelids' flutter" (11-12). Cummings wants the reader to focus on a pure emotive response (the flutter of an eyelash)—on the emotional, not the logical—on the meanings of words instead of punctuation and grammar.

Cummings's use of words such as *kisses* and *blood* (8, 7) adds to the focus on the emotional. The ideas behind these words are difficult to confine or restrict to a single definition: kisses mean different things to different people, blood flows through the body freely and continually. The words are not expansive or free enough to encompass all that they suggest. Cummings ultimately paints language as more restrictive than the flowing, powerful force of emotion.

Paragraph reiterates Cummings's claim and sums up his argument

The poet's use of two grammatical terms in the last lines, "for life's not a paragraph / And death i think is no parenthesis," warns against attempts to format lives and feelings into conventional and rule-bound segments (15-16). Attempts to control, rather than feel, are rejected throughout "since feeling is first." Emotion should be limitless, free from any restrictions or rules.

Sillay 3

While "since feeling is first" argues that emotions should not be controlled, ordered, or analyzed, "as freedom is a breakfastfood" suggests the difficulty of defining emotion. In this poem, Cummings uses deliberately far-fetched metaphors such as "freedom is a breakfastfood" and "time is a tree" (1, 26). These metaphors seem arbitrary: Cummings is not attempting to make profound statements on time or freedom. Instead, he suggests that freedom and time are subjective, and attempts at narrow definition are ridiculous. Inversions of nature, such as "robins never welcome spring" and "water most encourage flame" (16, 7), underscore emotion's ability to defy reason. These inversions suggest the arbitrariness of what "since feeling is first" calls "the syntax of things" (3).

> Clear and explicit transition from discussion of first poem

Although most of "as freedom is a breakfastfood" defies logic, Cummings shifts the tone at the end to deliver one last metaphor: "but love is the sky" (27). The word *but* separates this definition from the rest of the poem and subtly implies that, unlike the metaphors that have come before it, "love is the sky" is an accurate comparison. In order to reach this final conclusion, however, Cummings has taken his readers on a long and often ambiguous journey.

Nevertheless, the confusion has been deliberate. Cummings wants his readers to follow him through the winding path through the thicket because he believes the path of the straight and narrow limits the possibilities of experience. Through the unconventionality of his poetic structures, Cummings urges his readers to question order and tradition. He wants his readers to realize that reason and rationality are always secondary to emotion and that emotional experience is a free-flowing force that should not be constrained. Cummings's poetry suggests that in order to get at the true essence of something, one must look past the commonsensical definition and not be limited by "the syntax of things."

> Writer returns to the image of the thicket from the introduction to create a closing that resonates with the opening

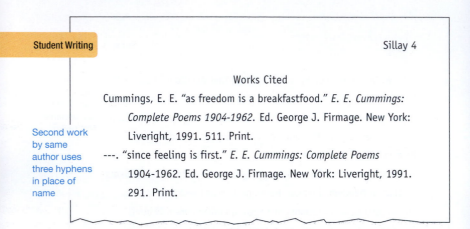

Student Writing

Sillay 4

Works Cited

Cummings, E. E. "as freedom is a breakfastfood." *E. E. Cummings: Complete Poems 1904-1962.* Ed. George J. Firmage. New York: Liveright, 1991. 511. Print.

---. "since feeling is first." *E. E. Cummings: Complete Poems 1904-1962.* Ed. George J. Firmage. New York: Liveright, 1991. 291. Print.

Second work by same author uses three hyphens in place of name

19 Writing for the Social Sciences

The social sciences share with the humanities an interest in what it means to be human. But the social sciences also share with the sciences the goal of engaging in a systematic, observable study of human behavior. When you write in the social sciences, you will attempt to identify, understand, and explain patterns of human behavior.

19a Read texts in the social sciences.

When you read in the social sciences, you ask questions, analyze, and interpret as you read, whether you are reading an academic paper that sets forth a theoretical premise or overall theory and defends it, a case study that describes a particular case and draws out inferences and implications from it, or a research report that presents the results of an investigation into an important question in the field. Most of what you read in the social sciences will attempt to prove a point, and you will need to evaluate how well that particular point is supported.

The social sciences, like other disciplines, often use specialized vocabulary as shorthand for complex ideas that otherwise would take paragraphs to explain.

Qualitative and quantitative studies

Different texts in the social and natural sciences may call for different methods and strategies. Texts that report the results of *quantitative* studies collect data represented with numerical measurements that are drawn from surveys, polls, experiments, and tests. For example, a study of voting patterns in southern states might rely on quantitative data such as statistics. Texts that report the results of *qualitative* studies rely on non-numerical methods such as interviews and observations to reveal social patterns. A study of the way children in one kindergarten class develop rules of play, for instance, would draw on qualitative data—observations of social interaction, interviews with students and teachers, and so on. Of course, some work in the social and behavioral sciences combines quantitative and qualitative data and methods: an educational report might begin with statistical data related to a problem and then move to a qualitative case study to exemplify what the statistics reveal.

In the social sciences, both quantitative and qualitative researchers must determine what they are examining and measuring in order to get answers to research questions. A researcher who studies childhood aggression, for example, must first define and measure *aggression*. If the research is qualitative, a researcher may describe types of behavior that indicate aggression and then discuss observations of children and interviews with teachers and peers about those behaviors. A quantitative researcher, on the other hand, might design an experiment that notes how often children hit a punching bag or that asks children to rate their peers' aggression on a scale of one to ten.

It's important to recognize that both quantitative and qualitative studies have points of view, and that researchers' opinions influence everything from the hypothesis and the design of the research study to the interpretation of findings. Readers must consider whether the researchers' views are sensible and solidly supported by evidence, and they must pay close attention to the kind of data the writer is using and what those data can—and cannot—prove. For example, if researchers of childhood aggression define *aggression* in a way that readers find unpersuasive, or if they observe behaviors that readers consider playful rather than aggressive, then the readers will likely not accept their interpretation of the findings.

Conventional formats

Make use of conventional disciplinary formats to help guide your reading in the social sciences. Many such texts conform to the format and documentation style of the American Psychological Association (APA). In addition, articles often include standard features—an abstract that gives an overview of the findings, followed by the introduction, review of literature, methods, results, discussion, and references. Readers who become familiar with such a format can easily find the information they need. (For more on APA style, see Chapters 61–64.)

19b   Write texts in the social sciences.

Perhaps because the social sciences share concerns with both the humanities and the sciences, the forms of writing within the social sciences are particularly varied, including summaries, abstracts, literature reviews, reaction pieces, position papers, radio scripts, briefing notes, book reviews, briefs, research papers, quantitative research reports, case studies, ethnographic analyses, and meta-analyses. You may find such an array of writing assignments overwhelming, but in fact these assignments can be organized under five main categories:

- Writing that encourages student learning, such as reaction pieces and position papers

- Writing that demonstrates student learning, such as summaries, abstracts, and research papers

- Writing that reflects common on-the-job communication tasks for members of a discipline, such as radio scripts, briefing notes, and informational reports

- Writing that requires students to analyze and evaluate the writings of others, such as literature reviews, book reviews, and briefs

- Writing that asks students to replicate the work of others or to engage in original research, such as quantitative research reports, case studies, and ethnographic analyses

Many forms of writing in the social sciences call either explicitly or implicitly for argument (see Chapter 10). If you write an essay that reports on the results of a survey you developed about attitudes among students on your campus toward physician-assisted suicide, you will make an explicit argument about the significance of your data. But even with other forms of writing, such as summaries and book reports, you will implicitly argue that your description and analysis provide a clear, thorough overview of the text(s) you have read.

Style in the social sciences

Writing in the social sciences need not be dry and filled with jargon. While you need to understand the conventions, concepts, and habits of mind typical of a discipline, you can still write clear prose that engages readers.

When discussing research sources in a paper conforming to APA style, use the past tense or the present perfect tense (38e) for the verbs: *Raditch showed* or *Raditch has shown*. Make sure that any writing you do is as clear and grammatically correct as possible so that readers see you as capable and credible.

Literature reviews

Students of the social sciences carry out literature reviews to find out the most current thinking about a topic, to learn what research has already been carried out on that topic, to evaluate the work that has been done, and to set any research they will do in context. The following guidelines are designed to help you explore and question sources, looking for flaws or gaps. Such a critical review could then lead to a discussion of how your own research will avoid such flaws and advance knowledge.

- What is your topic or dependent variable (item or characteristic studied)?
- What is already known about this topic? What characteristics does the topic or dependent variable have? How have other researchers measured the item or characteristic being studied? What other factors are involved, and how are they related to each other and to your topic or variable? What theories are used to explain the way things are now?
- How has research been done so far? Who or what has been studied? How have measurements been taken?
- Has there been change over time? What has caused any changes?
- What problems do you find in the new research? What questions have not been answered? Have researchers drawn unwarranted conclusions?
- What gaps will your research fill? How is it new? What problems do you want to correct?

19c An excerpt from a student's psychology literature review

Following is an excerpt from a psychology literature review by Tawnya Redding that adheres to the conventions for social science writing in this genre and follows the guidelines of APA style (see Chapters 61–64) to document sources.

Student Writer

Tawnya Redding

Running head: MOOD MUSIC   1

Running head
(fifty characters
or fewer)
appears flush
left on first line
of title page

Page number
appears flush
right on first
line of every
page

Title, name,
and affiliation
centered and
double-spaced

Mood Music: Music Preference and the Risk for Depression

and Suicide in Adolescents

Tawnya Redding

Psychology 480

Professor Ede

February 23, 2009

Annotations indicate effective choices or APA-style formatting.

MOOD MUSIC   2 **Student Writing**

Abstract

There has long been concern for the effects that certain genres of music (such as heavy metal and country) have on youth. While a correlational link between these genres and increased risk for depression and suicide in adolescents has been established, researchers have been unable to pinpoint what is responsible for this link, and a causal relationship has not been determined. This paper will begin by discussing correlational literature concerning music preference and increased risk for depression and suicide, as well as the possible reasons for this link. Finally, studies concerning the effects of music on mood will be discussed. This examination of the literature on music and increased risk for depression and suicide points out the limitations of previous research and suggests the need for new research establishing a causal relationship for this link as well as research into the specific factors that may contribute to an increased risk for depression and suicide in adolescents.

Heading centered

No indentation

Use of passive voice appropriate for social sciences

Clear, straightforward description of literature under review

Text is double-spaced

Conclusions indicated

Full title
centered

Mood Music: Music Preference and the Risk for Depression
and Suicide in Adolescents

Paragraphs
indented

Music is a significant part of American culture. Since the
explosion of rock and roll in the 1950s, there has been a concern
for the effects that music may have on listeners, and especially

Background
information
about review
supplied

on young people. The genres most likely to come under suspicion
in recent decades have included heavy metal, country, and blues.
These genres have been suspected of having adverse effects on the
mood and behavior of young listeners. But can music really alter
the disposition and create self-destructive behaviors in listeners?

Questions
focus reader's
attention

And if so, which genres and aspects of those genres are responsible?
The following review of the literature will establish the correlation
between potentially problematic genres of music such as heavy metal
and country and depression and suicide risk. First, correlational
studies concerning music preference and suicide risk will be
discussed, followed by a discussion of the literature concerning the
possible reasons for this link. Finally, studies concerning the effects
of music on mood will be discussed. Despite the link between genres
such as heavy metal and country and suicide risk, previous research
has been unable to establish the causal nature of this link.

Boldface
headings
help organize
review

**The Correlation Between Music and Depression
and Suicide Risk**

Studies over the past two decades have set out to answer
this question by examining the correlation between youth music
preference and risk for depression and suicide. A large portion of
these studies have focused on heavy metal and country music as the
main genre culprits associated with youth suicidality and depression

Parenthetical
references
follow APA
style

(Lacourse, Claes, & Villeneuve, 2001; Scheel & Westefeld, 1999;
Stack & Gundlach, 1992). Stack and Gundlach (1992) examined the
radio airtime devoted to country music in 49 metropolitan areas and
found that the higher the percentages of country music airtime . . .

MOOD MUSIC   9

References

Baker, F., & Bor, W. (2008). Can music preference indicate mental health status in young people? *Australasian Psychiatry, 16*(4), 284–288. Retrieved from http://www3.interscience.wiley.com /journal/118565538/home

George, D., Stickle, K., Rachid, F., & Wopnford, A. (2007). The association between types of music enjoyed and cognitive, behavioral, and personality factors of those who listen. *Psychomusicology, 19*(2), 32–56.

Lacourse, E., Claes, M., & Villeneuve, M. (2001). Heavy metal music and adolescent suicidal risk. *Journal of Youth and Adolescence, 30*(3), 321–332.

Lai, Y. (1999). Effects of music listening on depressed women in Taiwan. *Issues in Mental Health Nursing, 20,* 229–246. doi: 10.1080/016128499248637

Martin, G., Clark, M., & Pearce, C. (1993). Adolescent suicide: Music preference as an indicator of vulnerability. *Journal of the American Academy of Child and Adolescent Psychiatry, 32,* 530–535.

Scheel, K., & Westefeld, J. (1999). Heavy metal music and adolescent suicidality: An empirical investigation. *Adolescence, 34*(134). 253–273.

Siedliecki, S., & Good, M. (2006). Effect of music on power, pain, depression and disability. *Journal of Advanced Nursing, 54*(5), 553–562. doi: 10.1111/j.1365-2648.2006.03860.x

Smith, J. L., & Noon, J. (1998). Objective measurement of mood change induced by contemporary music. *Journal of Psychiatric & Mental Health Nursing, 5,* 403–408.

Stack, S. (2000). Blues fans and suicide acceptability. *Death Studies, 24,* 223–231.

Stack, S., & Gundlach, J. (1992). The effect of country music on suicide. *Social Forces, 71*(1), 211–218. Retrieved from http:// socialforces.unc.edu/

References begin on new page

Journal article from a database, no DOI

Print journal article

Journal article from a database with DOI

20   Writing for the Natural and Applied Sciences

Natural sciences such as biology, chemistry, and physics study the natural world and its phenomena; applied sciences such as nano-technology and the various fields of engineering apply knowledge from the natural sciences to practical problems. Whether you are working in the lab or the field, writing will play a key role in your courses in the natural and applied sciences.

20a   Read texts in the natural and applied sciences.

Scientists and engineers work with evidence that can be observed, ver-ified, and controlled. Though they cannot avoid interpretation, they still strive for objectivity by using the scientific method—observing or studying phenomena, formulating a hypothesis about the phenom-ena, and testing that hypothesis through controlled experiments and observations. Scientists and engineers aim to generate precise, replica-ble data; they develop experiments to account for extraneous factors. In this careful, precise way, scientists and engineers identify, test, and write persuasively about theoretical and real-world problems.

Argument in the sciences

As you read in the sciences, try to become familiar with disciplinary terms, concepts, and formats as soon as possible, and practice reading—and listening—for detail. If you are reading a first-year biology textbook, you can draw upon general critical-reading strate-gies. In addition, charts, graphs, illustrations, models, and other visuals often play an important role in scientific writing, so your ability to read and comprehend these visual displays of knowledge is particularly important.

When you read a science or engineering textbook, you can assume that the information presented there is authoritative and as objective as possible. When you read specialized materials, however, recognize that although scholarly reports undergo significant peer review, they nevertheless represent arguments (see Chapter 10). The connection between facts and claims in the sciences, as in all subject areas, is created by the author rather than simply revealed by the data. So read both facts and claims with a questioning eye: Did the scientist choose the best method to test the hypothesis? Are there other reasonable interpretations of the experiment's results? Do other studies contradict the conclusions of this experiment? When you read specialized texts in the sciences with questions like these in mind, you are reading—and thinking—like a scientist. (For additional information on assessing a source's credibility, see 14c.)

Conventional formats

As you advance in your course work, you will need to develop reading strategies for increasingly specialized texts. Many scientific texts include standard features—an abstract that gives an overview of the findings, followed by an introduction and literature review, a materials and methods section, the results of the research, discussion, and references. (This format is often called "IMRAD," for "Introduction, Methods, Results, and Discussion.")

You might expect to read a journal article for a science or engineering course from start to finish, giving equal weight to each section. However, an experienced reader in sciences and engineering might skim an abstract to see if an article warrants further reading. If it does—and this judgment is based on the reader's own research interest—he or she might then read the introduction to understand the rationale for the experiment and then skip to the results. A reader with a specific interest in the methods will read that section with particular care.

20b Write texts in the natural and applied sciences.

In the sciences and engineering, you must be able to respond to a diverse range of writing and speaking tasks. Often, you must maintain lab or engineering notebooks that include careful records of experiments. You will also write memos, papers, project proposals and reports, literature reviews, and progress reports; in addition, you may develop print and web-based presentations for both technical and lay audiences (see Chapter 23). Particularly common writing assignments in the sciences are the literature review, research proposal, and research report.

Assignments

Writing a literature review enables you to keep up with and evaluate developments in your field. Literature reviews are an essential first step in any research effort, for they enable you to discover what research has already been completed and how you might build on earlier efforts. Successful literature reviews demonstrate your ability to identify relevant research on a topic and to summarize and in some instances evaluate that research.

Most scientists spend a great deal of time writing research or grant proposals aimed at securing funds to support their research. As an undergraduate, you may have an opportunity to make similar proposals to an office of undergraduate research or to a science-based firm that supports student research, for instance. Funding agencies often have guidelines for preparing a proposal. Proposals for research funding generally include the following sections: title page, introduction, purpose(s) and significance of the study, methods, timeline, budget, and references. You may also need to submit an abstract.

Research reports, another common writing form in the sciences, may include both literature reviews and discussions of primary research, most often experiments. Like journal articles, research reports generally follow this form: title, author(s), abstract, introduction, literature review, materials and methods, results, discussion, and references. Academic journals in many fields now expect work that they publish to follow this format, known by the shorthand "IMRAD" (for "Introduction, Methods, Results, and Discussion"). The focus of many IMRAD-format articles is on the introduction (which situates the research in the context of other work in the field) and on the discussion of the results. Many instructors will ask you to write lab reports (20c), which are briefer versions of research reports and may not include a literature review.

Today, most scientific writing is collaborative. As you move from introductory to advanced courses and then to the workplace, you will increasingly find yourself working as part of a team or group. Indeed, in such areas as engineering, collaborative projects are the norm.

Style in the sciences

In general, use the present tense for most writing you do in the natural and applied sciences. Use the past tense, however, when you are describing research already carried out (by you or others) or published in the past.

As a writer in the sciences, you will need to produce complex figures, tables, images, and models and use software designed to analyze data or run computer simulations. In addition, you must present data carefully. If you create a graph, you should provide headings for columns, label axes with numbers or units, and identify data points. Caption figures and tables with a number and descriptive title. And avoid orphan data—data that you present in a figure or table but don't comment on in your text.

Finally, make sure that any writing you do is as clear, concise, and grammatically correct as possible to ensure that readers see you as capable and credible.

20c An excerpt from a student's chemistry lab report

Following is an excerpt from a lab report on a chemistry experiment by student Allyson Goldberg.

Student Writer

Allyson Goldberg

Student Writing

Introduction

Introduction explains purpose of lab and gives overview of results

The purpose of this investigation was to experimentally determine the value of the universal gas constant, R. To accomplish this goal, a measured sample of magnesium (Mg) was allowed to react with an excess of hydrochloric acid (HCl) at room temperature and pressure so that the precise amount and volume of the product hydrogen gas (H_2) could be determined and the value of R could be calculated using the ideal gas equation, $PV = nRT$.

Materials & Methods

Materials and methods section explains lab setup and procedure

Two samples of room temperature water, one about 250mL and the other about 400mL, were measured into a smaller and larger beaker respectively. 15.0mL of HCl was then transferred into a side arm flask that was connected to the top of a buret (clamped to a ringstand) through a 5/16" diameter flexible tube.

Passive voice throughout is typical of writing in the natural sciences

(This "gas buret" was connected to an adjacent "open buret," clamped to the other side of the ringstand, and left open to the atmosphere of the laboratory at its wide end, by a 1/4" diameter flexible tube. These two burets were adjusted on the ringstand so that they were vertically parallel and close together.) The HCl sample was transferred to the flask such that none came in contact with the inner surface of the neck of the flask. The flask was then allowed to rest, in an almost horizontal position, in the smaller beaker.

The open buret was adjusted on the ringstand such that its 20mL mark was horizontally aligned with the 35mL mark on the gas buret. Room temperature water was added to the open buret until the water level of the gas buret was at about 34.00mL.

A piece of magnesium ribbon was obtained, weighed on an analytical balance, and placed in the neck of the horizontal side arm flask. Next, a screw cap was used to cap the flask and form an airtight seal. This setup was then allowed to sit for 5 minutes in order to reach thermal equilibrium.

After 5 minutes, the open buret was adjusted so that the menisci on both burets were level with each other; the side arm flask was then tilted vertically to let the magnesium ribbon react with the HCl. After the brisk reaction, the flask was placed into the larger beaker and allowed to sit for another 5 minutes.

Next, the flask was placed back into the smaller beaker, and the open buret was adjusted on the ringstand such that its meniscus was level with that of the gas buret. After the system sat for an additional 30 minutes, the open buret was again adjusted so that the menisci on both burets were level.

This procedure was then repeated two more times, with the exception that HCl was not again added to the side arm flask, as it was already present in enough excess for all reactions from the first trial.

Results and Calculations

Trial #	Lab Temp. (°C)	Lab Pressure (mbar)	Mass of Mg Ribbon Used (g)	Initial Buret Reading (mL)	Final Buret Reading (mL)
1	24.4	1013	0.0147	32.66	19.60
2	24.3	1013	0.0155	33.59	N/A*
3	25.0	1013	0.0153	34.35	19.80

*See note in Discussion section.

Results and calculations show measurements and calculations of final value of R

21   Writing for Business

In today's business world, the global economy is now a common-place concept, and both corporate giants and home-office eBay oper-ations conduct business worldwide. Yet in the midst of these changes, one constant remains: written communication is still essential in iden-tifying and solving the complex problems of today's companies.

21a   Read texts for business.

In business today, you and your colleagues may have almost unlim-ited access to information and to people whose expertise can be of use to your projects. Somehow, you will need to negotiate and evalu-ate a huge stream of information.

General strategies for effective reading (Chapter 9) can help. One such strategy—keeping a clear purpose in mind when you read—is particularly important for work-related reading. Are you reading to solve a problem? to gather and synthesize information? to make a rec-ommendation? Knowing why you are reading will increase your pro-ductivity. Time constraints and deadlines will also affect your decisions about what and how to read; the ability to identify important informa-tion quickly is a skill you should cultivate as a business reader.

21b   Write texts for business.

Writing assignments in business classes generally serve two related functions. While their immediate goal is to help you master the the-ory and practice of business, these assignments also prepare you for the kinds of writing that you will one day face in the world of work. For this reason, students in *every* discipline need to know how to write effective business documents such as memos, emails, letters, résumés, and reports.

Much writing in business today is collaborative. You may find that your coworkers expect you to ask for or offer comments on drafts of important documents that will present your team's work to others in the company or to the public. For more on collaboration, see 17h.

Business writing tends to use conventional formats and to follow the conventions of standard written English. When you write to employers or prospective employers, stick to more formal communication unless you have a very good reason to do otherwise.

Remember that much or all of the writing you do at work is essentially public and that employers have easy access to email written by employees. (For more about email, see 2e.) As always, it's best to use discretion and caution in all on-the-job communication.

Business memo and business email

Memos are a common form of print or digital correspondence sent within and between organizations. Memos and business email messages both tend to be brief and direct, often dealing with only one subject.

As with any writing, consider the audience for your memo carefully. Make sure to include everyone who might need the information, but be cautious about sharing it too widely, especially when the information in your document may be sensitive.

Follow these guidelines for writing effective memos and business email:

- Clearly identify the subject.

- Begin with the most important information: depending on the memo's purpose, you may have to provide background information, define the task or problem, or clarify the goal.

- Use your opening paragraph to focus on how the information you convey affects your readers.

- Focus each of your subsequent paragraphs on one idea pertaining to the subject.

- Relate your information concisely and present it from the readers' perspective.

- Emphasize exactly what you want readers to do and when.

- Keep business email as brief and concise as possible. Use attachments for detailed supporting information.

- Adjust your style and tone to fit your audience.

- Attempt to build goodwill in your conclusion.

Student Writer

Michelle Abbott

Student Writer

Carina Abernathy

Following is a memo, written by students Michelle Abbott and Carina Abernathy, that presents an analysis and recommendation to help an employer make a decision.

MEMO

TO:	ROSA DONAHUE, SALES MANAGER
FROM:	MICHELLE ABBOTT & CARINA ABERNATHY
SUBJECT:	TAYLOR NURSERY BID

Opening provides background

As you know, Taylor Nursery has requested bids on a 25,000-pound order of private-label fertilizer. Taylor Nursery is one of the largest distributors of our Fertikil product.

Most important information put in bold

The total cost for manufacturing 25,000 pounds of the private-label brand for Taylor Nursery is $44,075. This cost includes direct material, direct labor, and variable manufacturing overhead. Although our current equipment and facilities provide adequate capacity for processing this special order, the job will require overtime labor, which has been factored into our costs.

Options presented

The minimum price that Jenco could bid for this product without losing money is $44,075 (our cost). Applying our standard markup of 40% results in a price of $61,705. You could reasonably establish a price anywhere within that range.

Final recommendation

Taylor Nursery has requested bids from several competitors. One rival, Eclipse Fertilizers, is submitting a bid of $60,000 on this order. Therefore, our recommendation is to slightly underbid Eclipse with a price of $58,000, representing a markup of approximately 32%.

Closing builds goodwill by offering further help

Please let us know if we can be of further assistance in your decision on the bid.

Cover letter or letter of inquiry

When you send a business or professional letter, you are writing either as an individual or as a representative of an organization. In either case, and regardless of your purpose, a business letter should follow certain conventions.

A cover letter often accompanies a résumé. The purpose of a cover letter is to demonstrate how the experiences and skills you outline in your résumé have prepared you for a particular job. (A letter of inquiry does similar work, but the writer typically asks more generally about openings or job leads.) Remember to focus, then, on how you can benefit the company, not how the company can help you. A well-written letter can help you stand out from a pile of applications and inquiries, even if you are new to the field and don't yet have impressive qualifications, so craft your words carefully.

If you are posting a cover letter to accompany an online application, you will probably provide your contact information elsewhere, and you may not know the address (or name or title) of the person who will ultimately read the letter. The basic contents, however, will be the same whether you print and mail a letter or post it online.

Follow these guidelines for effective business correspondence:

- Use a conventional format unless you have a specific reason to do otherwise.
- Whenever possible, write to a specific person (*Dear Mr. Robinson* or *Dear Ms. Otuteye*) rather than to a general *Dear Sir or Madam*.
- Open cordially and be polite—even if you have a complaint.
- Clearly state your reason for writing. Include whatever details will help your reader see your point and respond.
- If appropriate, make clear what you hope your reader will do.
- Express appreciation for your reader's attention.
- Make it easy for your reader to respond by including your contact information. If you are mailing a print letter and expect a reply, include a self-addressed, stamped envelope.

Résumé

While a cover letter usually emphasizes specific parts of the résumé, telling how your background is suited to a particular job, a résumé summarizes your experience and qualifications and provides support for your letter. An effective résumé is brief, usually one or two pages.

Research shows that employers generally spend less than a minute reading a résumé. Remember that they are interested not in what they can do for you but what you can do for them. They expect a résumé to be formatted neatly, and your aim is to use clear headings and adequate spacing that will make it easy to read.

A well-written résumé with a standard format and typefaces is still, in many cases, the best way to distinguish yourself, but in certain contexts, a more creative résumé that includes media links, images, and other nontraditional content may help you succeed. As with any writing situation, consider your context and purpose.

Your résumé may be arranged chronologically (from most to least recent) or functionally (based on skill or expertise). Include the following information:

- *Name, address, phone number, email address.* You may also want to include links to a career profile page or personal website, and, if the content is professionally appropriate, to social media content such as a Twitter feed.

- *Educational background.* Include degrees, diplomas, majors, and special programs or courses that pertain to your field of interest.

- *Work experience.* Identify each job — whether a paying job, an internship, or military experience — with dates and names of organizations. Describe your duties by carefully selecting strong action verbs.

- *Skills, personal interests, activities, awards, and honors.*

- *References.* Most writers simply say that references are available on request.

Some applicants also include images in their résumés. Make choices that seem appropriate for your specific situation.

Increasingly, job seekers are uploading résumés to a company website when applying for a position. In such cases, take special care to make sure that you have caught any errors or typos before submitting the form.

Student Writer

Megan N. Lange

The following pages show student Megan N. Lange's résumé in two formats, one in traditional print style and the other in a creative format optimized for digital presentation. Like many recent college graduates, she is considering possible career paths, and having two very different résumés prepared allows her to present herself appropriately to either traditional or more creative potential employers.

TRADITIONAL RÉSUMÉ

Megan N. Lange Name in bold-
1234 Kingston Pike • Knoxville, TN 37919   face and larger
Phone: 865.643.xxxx • Email: mlange1@utk.edu   type size

Education Educational
background
Exp. May 2014 **The University of Tennessee**, Knoxville. B.A. in Technical Writing
and Business Editing, Classical Studies

May 2009 **Lenoir City High School**

Work Experience

• **The Yankee Candle Company** – Store 433 August 2010 – present Relevant work
Sales Associate: assists guests in-store, answers phones, experience
restocks floor, operates cash register

• **Holston Conference of the United Methodist Church** June 2011 – August 2011
Youth and Young Adult Intern: worked in-office with team,
out-of-office with local youth workers, planned and facilitated
youth retreats and events

• **Megan Lange Photography** January 2011 – present
Head Photographer: senior portraiture, weddings, maternity

Relevant Courses

• **Technical Writing 360** Fall 2011 Courses
Focused on proper formatting of different professional relevant to
documents, teamwork, creative thinking position being

• **Technical Writing 460** Spring 2012 sought
Proofreading and formatting of professional documents,
email etiquette, international communication

Affiliations/Memberships

• **Society for Technical Communication**, East Tennessee Chapter Spring 2012 Affiliations and
experience not
Other Experience listed above

• **Great Smoky Mountain Chrysalis Board** August 2010 – present

• **University of Tennessee Singers** August 2009 – May 2011

• **Cedar Springs Presbyterian Church Choir** August 2011 – present

*References available upon request.

*Megan Lange uses this résumé to apply for most jobs. The clean, inviting,
businesslike look presents the content in expected ways — her name and
contact information, educational background, work experience, courses she
has taken in the field she hopes to enter, and other information that may help
prospective employers know more about the kind of person she is.*

CREATIVE RÉSUMÉ

Megan Lange uses this résumé to apply for positions for which her creativity would be an asset. The design is still easy to read, but reveals more of her personality. Icons under "Social Media" are live links to her feeds on various sites.

Making Design Decisions **22**

In the ancient Greek world, a speaker's delivery (known as *actio*) was an art every educated person needed to master: how a speaker delivered a speech—tone, pace, volume, use of gestures, and so on—had a great impact on the message and how it would be received. Writers now have many tools that writers and speakers in the ancient world did not have to help them get and hold an audience's attention, from font options to color and video. All these tools help bring the dimension of *visual rhetoric* to today's writing.

22a Choose a type of text.

A text can be anything that you might "read"—not just words but also images, data, audio, video, or combinations of media. A print book, for example, may include words alone or words and visuals. Texts that go online can grow much richer with the ability to include animations, video, audio, links, and interactive features. As a result, college writers today have choices that were almost unimaginable until quite recently.

Rhetorical contexts

Ultimately, the organization and look of any text you design should depend on what you are trying to achieve. You should make decisions about layout, formatting, color, fonts (for written words), non-alphabetic elements such as images or video, and other aspects of design based on rhetorical needs—your audience, purpose, topic, stance, genre conventions, and so on—and on practical constraints, such as the time and tools available.

Design choices for different genres

While you still will probably be assigned to compose traditional texts such as academic essays, you may also be asked to create course-work in other genres. Research conducted for this textbook found that today's students are encountering assignments that range from newsletters and poster presentations to PechaKuchas and video essays—and that multimodal assignments are increasingly characteristic of first-year writing courses. Whatever genre you choose for your assignment, familiarize yourself with conventions of design for that genre, and think carefully about the most appropriate and compelling design choices for your particular context.

Print or digital delivery

One of your first design decisions will be choosing between print delivery and digital delivery (or deciding to create both print and digital versions). In general, print documents are easily portable, easy to read without technical assistance, and relatively fast to produce. In addition, the tools for producing print texts are highly developed and stable. Digital texts, on the other hand, can include sound, animation, and video; updates are easy to make; distribution is fast and efficient; and feedback can be swift. Design decisions may have similar goals, such as clarity and readability, no matter what medium you are working in, but the specific choices you make to achieve those goals may differ in print and digital texts.

22b   Plan a visual structure.

Today, all writers need to think carefully about the look of any text they create and plan a visual structure for it. The design decisions you make will help guide readers by making the texts easier on the eyes and easier to understand.

Design principles

Designer Robin Williams, in her *Non-Designer's Design Book*, points out four simple principles for designing effective texts—contrast, alignment, repetition, and proximity. These principles are illustrated here with the familiar Wikipedia page design.

CONTRAST

Contrast attracts your eye to elements on a page and guides you around it, helping you follow an argument or find information. You may achieve contrast through the use of color, icons, boldface or large type size, headings, and so on. Begin with a focus point—the dominant point, image, or words where you want your reader's eye to go first—and structure the flow of your visual information from this point.

ALIGNMENT

Alignment refers to the way visuals and text on a page are lined up, both horizontally and vertically. The overall guideline is not to mix alignments arbitrarily. That is, if you begin with a left alignment, stick with it for the major parts of your page. The result will be a cleaner and more organized look. For example, the title, text, and subheadings of a Wikipedia article align with the left margin, and images align with the right margin.

Chances are that most readers will look first at either the heading or the images on this Wikipedia page. The site uses large black type against a white background for the title of each page at the upper left. On this page, color images of molecular models also draw the eye.

REPETITION

Readers are guided by the repetition of key words and elements. Use a consistent design throughout your document for such elements as color, typeface, and images. Every Wikipedia page uses the same fonts and the same layout, so readers know what to expect.

PROXIMITY

Parts of a text that are closely related should appear together (proximate to one another). Your goal is to position related points, text, and visuals near one another and to use clear headings to identify these clusters, as the Wikipedia page does.

CONSISTENT OVERALL IMPRESSION

Aim for a visual structure and design that create the appropriate overall impression or mood for your text. For example, with an academic essay, whether print or digital, you will probably make conservative choices that strike a serious scholarly note. In a newsletter for a campus group, you might choose attention-getting images. In a website designed to introduce yourself to future employers, you might favor a mix of material drawn from your current résumé, including writing, embedded video or links to digital content that relates to your skills and career goals, and at least one image of yourself—all in a carefully organized and easy-to-comprehend structure.

Templates

If designing your writing yourself seems intimidating, consider using a template. Templates are basic models that show you how to lay out a particular type of text. You may have used templates in a word-processing program to create a document such as a memo or report, in PowerPoint to create slides, or in a blog-publishing service to design your content. Templates are readily available for many genres of texts in both print and digital media. Before you create a text in a genre that is new to you, it's a good idea to look for available design templates. You can use them to familiarize yourself with conventional elements and layouts for the genre, even if you decide not to follow the template's settings for color, fonts, and other details of formatting.

22c   Format print and digital texts appropriately.

With so many options available, you should always spend some time thinking about appropriate formatting for elements of your text. Although the following guidelines often apply, remember that print documents, web pages, slide shows, videos, and so on all have their own formatting conventions.

FOR MULTILINGUAL WRITERS

Reading Patterns

In documents written in English and other Western languages, information tends to flow from left to right and top to bottom — since that is the way English texts are written and read. In some languages, which may be written from right to left or vertically, documents may be arranged from top right to bottom left. Understanding the reading patterns of the language you are working in will help you design your documents most effectively.

White space (negative space)

The parts of a page or screen left intentionally blank are called *white space* or *negative space*. Too little white space makes a page look crowded, while too much can make it seem empty. Think about the amount of white space at the page level (top and side margins), paragraph level (the space between paragraphs), and sentence level (the space between sentences). Within the page, you can also use white space around particular content, such as an image, an embedded video, or a list, to make it stand out.

Color

As you design your documents, keep in mind that some colors can evoke powerful responses, so take care that the colors you use match the message you are sending. Color can enliven texts that are mainly alphabetic, but using color poorly can also make a text seem less readable and inviting.

- Use color to draw attention to elements you want to emphasize: headings, text boxes, or graphs, for example.

- Be consistent in your use of color; use the same color for all of your subheads, for example, or the same background color for all of your PowerPoint slides.

- Keep the color palette fairly small for most projects; too many colors can create a jumbled or confused look.

- Choose color combinations that are easy to read. Ask a few peers or colleagues whether your text is legible against the background before presenting, submitting, or posting your work for a wider audience.

- Make sure all color visuals and text are legible in the format where they will be read. Colors can be sharper on a computer monitor than in a print document, and slides may look dramatically different when you project them.

CONSIDERING DISABILITIES

Color for Contrast

Remember when you are using color that not everyone will see it as you do. Some individuals do not perceive color at all; others perceive color in a variety of ways, especially colors like blue and green, which are close together on the color spectrum. When putting colors next to one another, then, use those on opposite sides of the color spectrum, such as purple and gold, in order to achieve high contrast. Doing so will allow readers to see the contrast, if not the nuances, of color.

Type sizes and fonts

For words in the body of a traditional report, essay, or web posting, an 11- or 12-point type size is conventional. (A 12-point type size is larger than an 11-point type size of the same font, but type size in different fonts can vary considerably, so aim for a size that seems neither unreadably small nor surprisingly large.)

Choose a readable font, either a serif font (used in this sentence) or a sans serif font (used in headings on this page). Although unusual fonts might seem attractive at first glance, readers may find such styles distracting and hard to read over long stretches of material. Remember that fonts help you create the tone of a document, so consider your audience and purpose when selecting type.

Different fonts convey different feelings.
Different fonts convey different feelings.
DIFFERENT FONTS CONVEY DIFFERENT FEELINGS.
Different fonts convey different feelings.

Most important, be consistent in the size and style of typeface you use, especially for the main part of your text. Unless you are striving for some special effect, shifting sizes and fonts within a document can give an appearance of disorderliness. But purposeful use of special fonts can signal imagination, humor, and even spontaneity.

Margin and line spacing

For traditional print projects, you will probably use a single column of text with standard one-inch margins for your writing, but many other kinds of projects call for text columns of variable widths or for multiple columns. Both very short and very long text lines can be difficult to read. Online readers generally prefer short, manageable chunks of text rather than long paragraphs; consider breaking up a long online piece with headings or visuals.

Computers allow you to decide whether or not you want left and right margins justified, or squared off—as they are on typical book pages (including this one). Readers will often expect you to justify the left margin, except in posters and other texts where you are trying to achieve a distinctive visual effect. However, most readers—and many instructors—prefer the right margin to be "ragged," or unjustified, as it is in the Wikipedia entry on p. 239.

For college writing assignments that are submitted in print, you will usually use double-spaced type with the first line of each paragraph indented one-half inch. Letters, memorandums, and online texts are usually single-spaced and may use spaces between paragraphs instead of paragraph indentation. Check the conventions of the genre, or ask about your instructor's preference.

Headings

For brief essays and reports, you may need no headings at all. For longer texts, however, headings call attention to the organization and thus help readers understand. Headings can help break long web texts into the short, manageable chunks that online readers expect. Some kinds of reports require conventional headings (such as *Abstract* and *Summary*), which writers must provide.

You can distinguish headings by type size and font as well as by color, as this book does—for example, by using capital letters, boldface type, italics, and so on. Position each level of heading consistently throughout the text. And remember that headings need to appear above the text they introduce; be careful, for example, not to put a heading at the bottom of a printed page.

For formal academic work, look for the most succinct and informative way to word headings. In general, state a topic in a single word, usually a noun (*Toxicity*); in a phrase, usually a noun phrase (*Levels of Toxicity*) or a gerund phrase (*Measuring Toxicity*); in a question that will be answered in the text (*How Can Toxicity Be Measured?*); or in an imperative that tells readers what steps to take (*Measure the Toxicity*). Informal texts might use more playful headings. For both informal and formal texts, use the same structure consistently for all headings of the same level.

22d Consider visuals and media.

Choose visuals and other media that will help make a point more vividly and succinctly than written words alone. In some cases, visuals and media may even be your primary text.

- Choose visual and media elements that will make your text more effective for your audience. If they don't help you accomplish your purpose, look for better options.

- Consider design principles for placement of visual and media files within a text, and aim to make your media files accessible to as many readers as possible. (22b)

- Tell the audience explicitly what a visual demonstrates, especially if it presents complex information. Do not assume readers will "read" the visual the way you do; your commentary on it is important.

- Follow established conventions for documenting visual and media sources (Chapters 57–67). Ask permission for use if someone else controls the rights.

- Get responses to your visuals and media in an early draft. If readers can't follow them or are distracted by them, revise accordingly.

- If you alter or edit visuals, audio, or video to include them in your writing, be sure to do so ethically.

Visual and media selection

Consider carefully what you want visuals, audio, or video to do for your writing. What will your audience want or need you to show? Try to choose visuals and media that will enhance your credibility, allow you to make your point more emphatically, and clarify your overall text. (See the following examples for advice on which visuals work best for particular situations.)

Use *pie charts* to compare parts to the whole.

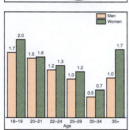

Use *bar graphs* and *line graphs* to compare one element with another, to compare elements over time, or to show correlations and frequency.

Use *tables* to draw attention to detailed numerical information.

Table 10: Commuter Rail Schedule: Reading/Haverhill Line, Boston 2004			
	Train 223	Train 227	Train 231
North Station	3:00 pm	4:36 pm	5:15 pm
Reading	3:38 pm	4:54 pm	5:42 pm
Haverhill	4:04 pm	5:31 pm	6:21 pm

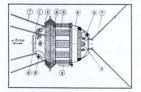

Use *diagrams* to illustrate textual information or to point out details of objects or places described.

(BOTTOM) © SOVFOTO/GETTY IMAGES

Use *maps* to show geographical locations and to emphasize spatial relationships.

Use *cartoons* to illustrate a point dramatically or comically.

Use *photographs* or *illustrations* to show particular people, places, objects, and situations described in the text or to help readers find or understand types of content.

(BOTTOM) REPRODUCED WITH PERMISSION OF MIKE ENRIGHT

Effective media content can come from many sources—your own drawings or photographs, charts or graphs you create, or recordings you make, as well as materials created by others. If you are using media from another source, be sure to give appropriate credit and to get permission before making it available to the public as part of your work.

Placement

Make sure to position visuals and media clips alongside or after the text that refers to them. In formal texts, number figures and tables separately and give them informative titles. Some documentation styles ask that you include source information in a caption.

CONSIDERING DISABILITIES

Making Media Texts Accessible

As you create media texts, take steps to make sure that all your readers can access your content — for example, by providing alternative text for all visuals so that they will make sense when read by a screen reader, and by providing captions for sound files and transcripts of longer audio content. For details on designing accessible texts, visit the Americans with Disabilities Act site at www.ada.gov.

Ethical use of visuals and media

Technical tools available to writers and designers today make it relatively easy to manipulate and edit visuals, audio, and video. As you would with any source material, carefully assess any visuals you find for effectiveness, appropriateness, and validity, and identify the source for any media files you use that you have not created yourself.

- Check the context in which the visual, video, or audio appears. Is it part of an official government, school, or library site or otherwise from a credible source (14c)?

- If the visual is a photograph, is the information about the photo believable?

- If the visual is a chart, graph, or diagram, are the numbers and labels explained? Are the sources of the data given? Will the visual representation help readers make sense of the information, or could it mislead them?

- Can you find contact information for the creator or rightsholder?

At times, you may make certain changes to visuals that you use, such as cropping an image to show the most important detail, digitally brightening a dark image, or using a short clip from a longer audio or video file. You can make digital changes as long as you do so ethically, telling your audience what you have done and making no attempt to mislead readers.

23 Creating Presentations

When the Gallup Poll reports on what U.S. citizens say they fear most, the findings are often the same: public speaking is apparently even scarier than an attack from outer space. Nevertheless, many writing courses may require you not only to compose written texts but also to give presentations in front of an audience, and it's safe to say that most jobs require you to present information orally in front of audiences of all kinds. People who are successful presenters point to four elements crucial to their effectiveness: a thorough knowledge of the subject at hand, careful attention to the interactive nature of speaking and thus to the needs of the audience, careful integration of verbal and visual information, and practice, practice, and more practice.

23a Consider assignment, purpose, and audience for presentations.

You'll be wise to begin preparing for a class presentation as soon as you get the assignment. Think about how much time you have to prepare; how long the presentation is to be; whether you will use written-out text or note cards or some other kind of cue; what kind of posters, handouts, slides, or other materials you may need; and what equipment you will need. If you are making a group presentation, you will need time to divide duties and practice. Make sure that you understand the criteria for evaluation—how will the presentation be graded or assessed?

QUICK HELP

Guidelines for Presentations

- How can your presentation accomplish the specifications of the assignment? (23a)
- How will your presentation achieve your purpose? How will it appeal to your audience's experiences and interests? (3c and d)
- What do you know about your audience, and how will you get the audience's attention? What background information do you need to provide? (23b)
- What organizational structure informs your presentation? (23b)
- Check for signposts that can guide listeners. Are there explicit transitions? Do you repeat key words or ideas? (23b)
- Have you used mostly straightforward sentences? Consider revising any long or complicated sentences to make your presentation easier to follow. Substitute concrete words for abstract ones as often as you can. (23b)
- How should you mark your script or notes for pauses and emphasis? Have you marked material that you can omit if you find yourself short of time? (23b)
- What should your audience see and hear during your presentation? How will your slides and media contribute to your presentation? (23c)
- Have you followed principles of good design for your visuals? (22b)
- Have you practiced your presentation so that you will appear confident and knowledgeable? (23d)
- Have you prepared a list of sources to accompany your presentation?

---

macmillanhighered.com/everyday6e
▶ Presentations > Tutorial: Presentations
Presentations > Video Prompt: If I were in the audience

Consider the purpose of your presentation (3c). Are you to lead a discussion? teach a lesson? give a report? engage a group in an activity? Also consider the audience (3d). If your instructor is a member of the audience, what will he or she expect you to do — and do well? What do audience members know about your topic? What opinions do they already hold about it? What do they need to know to follow your presentation and perhaps accept your point of view? If your presentation will be posted online, how much can you know about the audience? In a webinar format, you may have a list of all participants; but in other settings you may not be able to know who your words will reach. In these cases, you may want to shape or limit the audience who will have access to your presentation. Finally, consider your own stance toward your topic and audience. Are you an expert? novice? well-informed observer? peer?

Shuqiao Song got a two-part assignment for her writing class on graphic narratives: she had to write a researched argument, and then she had to turn that information into a script for a twelve-minute oral presentation with slides. After some brainstorming and talking with her instructor, Shuqiao chose her favorite graphic memoir, Alison Bechdel's *Fun Home*, as her topic.

As she thought about her assignment and topic, Shuqiao realized that she had more than one purpose. Certainly she wanted to do well on the assignment and receive a good grade. But she also wanted to convince her classmates that Bechdel's book was a complex and important one and that its power lay in the relationship between words and images. She also had to admit to at least one additional purpose: it would be great to turn in a truly *impressive* performance.

23b Write to be heard and remembered.

Getting and keeping the attention of listeners may require you to use different strategies than the ones you generally employ when writing for a reading audience. To be *remembered* rather than simply heard, consider these features of memorable presentations.

Stories

There's nothing like a good story to get and hold audience attention. In fact, presentation expert Nancy Duarte found that stories were at the heart of hundreds of great speeches she analyzed. Many speakers prefer to use personal stories that are witty and memorable. Andrew Linderman, a storytelling coach, says that the best ones are "honest and personal . . . without emoting too much or going off the rails." But a good presentation story may also be about someone else. Shuqiao Song used several stories from the book *Fun Home* to help make her argument.

Introduction and conclusion

Remember that listeners, like readers, tend to remember beginnings and endings most readily, so work extra hard to make these elements memorable. Consider, for example, using a startling statement, opinion, or question; a dramatic anecdote; a powerful quotation; or a vivid image. Shifting language, especially into a variety of language that your audience will identify with, is another effective way to catch their attention (see Chapter 28). Whenever you can link your subject to the experiences and interests of your audience, do so.

Shuqiao Song began her presentation this way:

> Welcome, everyone. I'm Shuqiao Song and I'm here today to talk about residents of a dys*FUN*ctional *HOME*.
>
> We meet these residents in a graphic memoir called *Fun Home*.

Student Writing

(Here, Shuqiao showed a three-second video clip of author Alison Bechdel saying, "I love words, and I love pictures. But especially, I love them together—in a mystical way that I can't even explain.")

> That was Alison Bechdel, author of *Fun Home*. In that clip, she conveniently introduces the topics of my presentation today: Words. Pictures. And the mystical way they work together.

Note that this presentation opened with a play on words ("dys-*FUN*ctional *HOME*"), to which Shuqiao returned later on, and with a short, vivid video clip that perfectly summed up the main topic of the presentation. Also note the use of short sentences and fragments, special effects that act like drumbeats to get and hold the attention of the audience.

Signpost language

Organize your presentation clearly and carefully, and give an overview of your main points toward the beginning of your presentation.

Accessible Presentations

Remember that some members of your audience may not be able to see your presentation or may have trouble hearing it, so do all you can to make your presentation accessible.

- Be sure to face any audience members who rely on lip-reading to understand your words. For a large audience, request an ASL (American Sign Language) interpreter.

- Do not rely on color or graphics alone to get across information — some audience members may be unable to pick up these visual cues.

- For presentations you publish on the web, provide brief textual descriptions of your visuals.

- If you use video, provide labels for captions to explain any sounds that won't be audible to some audience members, and embed spoken captions to explain images to those who cannot see them. Be sure that the equipment you'll be using is caption capable.

- Remember that students have very different learning styles and abilities. You may want to provide a written overview of your presentation or put the text of your presentation on slides or transparencies for those who learn better by reading *and* listening.

(You may wish to recall these points again toward the end of the talk.) Throughout your presentation, pause between major points, and use signpost language as you move from one topic to the next. Such signposts act as explicit transitions in your talk and should be clear and concrete: *The second crisis point in the breakup of the Soviet Union occurred hard on the heels of the first* instead of *The breakup of the Soviet Union came to another crisis point. . . .* In addition to such explicit transitions (6e) as *next*, *on the contrary*, and *finally*, you can offer signposts by repeating key words and ideas as well as by sticking to concrete topic sentences to introduce each new idea.

At the end of Shuqiao's introduction, she set forth the structure of her presentation in a very clear, straightforward, and simple way to help her audience follow what came next:

Student Writing

So, to outline the rest of my presentation: first, I'll show how *text* is insufficient — but also why it is necessary to Bechdel's story. Second, I'll show how *images* can't be trusted, but again, why they are still necessary for Bechdel's purposes. Third and finally, I'll show how the interplay of text and image in *Fun Home* creates a more complex and comprehensive understanding of the story.

Simple syntax and memorable language

Avoid long, complicated sentences, and use straightforward sentence structure (subject-verb-object) as much as possible. Listeners prefer action verbs and concrete nouns to abstractions. You may need to deal with abstract ideas, but try to provide concrete examples for them (29c). Memorable presentations often call on the power of figures of speech and other devices of language, such as careful repetition, parallelism, and climactic order.

Shuqiao Song's presentation script included the following example:

> Now, to argue my second point, I'll begin with an
> image. This is a René Magritte painting. The text means,
> *"This is not a pipe."* Is this some surrealist Jedi mind trick? Not really. Now
> listen to the title of the painting to grasp Magritte's point. The painting is
> called *The Treason of Images*. Here Magritte is showing us that "this is not a
> pipe" because it is an *image* of a pipe.

Student Writing

Shuqiao's short sentences, vivid word choice ("surrealist Jedi mind trick"), and straightforward subject-verb-object syntax all help to make the passage easy on listeners.

In a presentation on Fun Home, *Shuqiao Song uses a Magritte painting as evidence to show that "images can't be trusted."*

Script

Even though you will probably rely on some written material, you will need to adapt it for speech. Depending on the assignment, the audience, and your personal preferences, you may even speak from a full script. If so, double- or triple-space it, and use fairly large print so that it will be easy to refer to. Try to end each page with the end of a sentence so that you won't have to pause while you turn a page. In addition, you may decide to mark spots where you want to pause and to highlight words you want to emphasize.

A PARAGRAPH FROM SHUQIAO SONG'S PRINT ESSAY

Student Writing

Finally, we can see how image and text function together. On the one hand, image and text support each other in that each highlights the subtleties of the other; but on the other hand, the more interesting interaction comes when there is some degree of distance between what is written and what is depicted. In *Fun Home*, there is no one-to-one closure that mentally connects text and image. Rather, Bechdel pushes the boundaries of mental closure between image and text. If the words and pictures match exactly, making the same point, the story would read like a children's book, and that would be too simple for what Bechdel is trying to accomplish. However, text and image can't be so mismatched that meaning completely eludes the readers. Bechdel crafts her story deliberately, leaving just enough mental space for the reader to solve the rest of the puzzle and resolve the cognitive dissonance. The reader's mental closure, which brings coherence to the text and images and draws together loose ends, allows for a more complex and sophisticated understanding of the story.

SHUQIAO SONG'S PARAGRAPH REVISED FOR ORAL PRESENTATION

Finally, image and text can work together. They support each other: each highlights the subtleties of the other. But they are even more interesting when there's a gap — some distance between the story the words tell and the story the pictures tell. In *Fun Home*, text and image are never perfectly correlated. After all, if the words and pictures matched up exactly, the story would read like a kids' book. That would be way too simple for Bechdel's purposes. But we wouldn't want a complete disconnect between words and images either, since we wouldn't be able to make sense of them.

Still, Bechdel certainly pushes the boundaries that would allow us to bring closure between image and text. So what's the take-home point here?

> That in Bechdel's *Fun Home*, image and text are not just supporting actors
> of each other. Instead, each offers a *version* of the story. It's for us — the
> readers. We take these paired versions and weave them into a really rich
> understanding of the story.

Note that the revised paragraph presents the same information, but this time it is written to be heard. The revision uses helpful signpost language, some repetition, simple syntax, and informal varieties of English to help listeners follow along and remain interested.

Notes

If you decide to speak from notes rather than from a full script, here are some tips for doing so effectively:

- In general, use one note card for each point in your presentation, beginning with the introduction and then ending with the conclusion.
- Number the cards so that you can quickly find the next part of your presentation if your cards are out of order.
- On each card, include the major point you want to make in large bold text. Include subpoints in a bulleted list below the main point, again printed large enough for you to see easily. You can use full sentences or phrases, as long as you include enough information to remind you of what you have planned to say.
- Include signpost language on each note so that you will be sure to use it to guide your listeners.
- Practice your presentation using the notes at least twice.
- Time your presentation very carefully so that you will be sure not to go overtime. If you think you may run out of time, use color or brackets to mark material in your notes that you can skip. If your presentation is too long, move past the marked material so that you can end with your planned conclusion.

23c Create slides or other visuals.

Visuals are often an integral part of a presentation, carrying a lot of the message the speaker wants to convey. So think of your visuals not as add-ons but as a major means of getting your points across. Many speakers use slides created in presentation software to help keep themselves on track and to guide the audience. In addition, posters, flip charts, chalkboards, or interactive whiteboards can also help you make strong visual statements.

Guidelines for Slide Presentations

- Audiences can't read and listen to you at the same time, so make the slides support what you are saying as clearly and visually as possible. Just one or two words — or a visual without words — may back up what you are saying more effectively than a list of bullet points.

- Avoid reading from your slides. Your audience can read faster than you can talk, and you are guaranteed to bore your listeners with this technique.

- Use your media wisely, and respect your audience's time. If you feel that you need to include more than three or four bullet points (or more than fifty words of text) on a slide, you may be trying to convey information in a slide show that would make more sense in a report. Rethink your presentation so that what you say and what you show work together to win over your audience.

- Use text on your slides to guide your audience — not as a teleprompter. Be familiar enough with your material so that you don't have to rely on your slides to know what comes next.

- Make sure any text you show is big enough to read, and create a clear contrast between text or illustration and background. In general, light backgrounds work better in a darkened room, and dark backgrounds in a lighted one.

- Be careful not to depend too heavily on slide templates. The choices of color, font, and layout offered by such templates may not always match your goals or fit with your topic.

- Choose visuals that will reproduce sharply, and make sure they are large enough to be clearly visible.

- Make sure that sound or video clips are audible and that they relate directly to your topic. If you want to use sound as background, make sure it does not distract from what you are trying to say.

- Although there are no firm rules about how many slides you should use or how long each slide should be made visible, plan length and timing with your audience's needs and your purpose in mind.

- Most important, make sure your slides engage and help your listeners rather than distract them from your message.

Presentation software such as PowerPoint or Prezi allows you to prepare slides you want to display and even to enhance the images with sound. PowerPoint presentations move in a linear fashion from beginning to end, while Prezi software allows presenters to move in more circular paths (and to show the circling in the slides). To choose software for a presentation, consider what the software allows you to do and how much time you will need to learn to use it effectively. Before you begin designing your presentation, make sure that the equipment you need will be available, and keep simple design principles in mind (22b).

For her presentation, "Residents of a DysFUNctional *HOME*: Text and Image," Shuqiao Song developed a series of very simple slides aimed at underscoring her points and keeping her audience focused on them. She began by introducing the work, showing the book cover on an otherwise black slide. Throughout the presentation, she used very simple visuals—a word or two, or a large image from the book she was discussing—to keep her audience focused on what she was saying.

23d Practice the presentation.

In oral presentations, as with many other things in life, practice makes perfect. Prepare a draft of your presentation and slides or other media far enough in advance to allow for workshopping the slides with friends or classmates—just as you would workshop an essay—and for several run-throughs. If possible, make a video of yourself, and then examine the video in detail. You can also practice in front of a mirror or in front of friends. Do whatever works for you—just as long as you practice!

If you are using slides or other visuals to accompany your presentation (and most students do so), make sure your use of the visuals is smooth and on track with your script. Some student speakers like to embed all visuals or slides into their scripts so that they can coordinate easily, using a clicker to advance the slides. Others prefer to use the slides to guide them through the presentation, though to do so they must know their material so well that they don't leave awkward gaps as they move from slide to slide.

Make sure you can be heard clearly. If you are soft-spoken, concentrate on projecting your voice. If your voice tends to rise when you are in the spotlight, practice lowering your pitch. If you speak rapidly, practice slowing down and enunciating words clearly. Remember that tone of voice affects listeners, so aim for a tone that conveys interest in and commitment to your topic and listeners. If you practice with friends or classmates, ask them how well they can hear you and what advice they have for making your voice clearer and easier to listen to.

Once you are comfortable giving the presentation, make sure you will stay within the allotted time. One good rule of thumb is to allow roughly two and a half minutes per double-spaced 8½" x 11" page of text or script. The only way to be sure about your time, however, is to time yourself as you practice. Knowing that your presentation is neither too short nor too long will help you relax and gain self-confidence; and when the members of your audience sense your self-confidence, they will become increasingly receptive to your message.

23e   Deliver the presentation.

Experienced speakers always expect to feel at least some anxiety before delivering a presentation—and they develop strategies for dealing with it. Remember that a little nervousness can act to your advantage: adrenaline, after all, can help you perform well.

Having confidence in your own knowledge will go a long way toward making you a confident presenter. In addition to doing your homework, however, you may be able to use the following strategies to good advantage:

- Consider how you will dress and how you will move around. In each case, your choices should be appropriate for the situation. Most experienced speakers like to dress simply and comfortably for easy movement. But dressing up a little signals your pride in your appearance and your respect for your audience.

- Go over the scene of your presentation in your mind, and think it through completely, in order to feel more comfortable during it. In addition, check out the presentation room and double-check to make sure you have all the equipment you might need.

- If you are using handouts, decide when to distribute them. Unless they include material you want your audience to use while you speak, distribute them after the presentation.

- Get some rest before the presentation, and avoid too much caffeine.

- Try to relax while you wait to begin. You might want to do some deep-breathing exercises.

Stand or sit up straight for your presentation. Move around the room if you are comfortable doing so. If you are more comfortable in one spot, then keep both feet flat on the floor. If you are behind a lectern, rest your hands lightly on it. Many speakers find that this stance keeps them from fidgeting.

Pause before you begin your presentation, and concentrate on your opening lines. During your presentation, interact with your audience as much as possible. You can do so by facing the audience at all times and making eye contact as often as possible. You may want to choose two or three people to look at and "talk to," particularly if you are addressing a large group. In any case, make sure you are looking at your audience during the entire presentation, not at your laptop or at the screen behind you. Allow time for the audience to ask questions. Try to keep your answers short so that others may participate in the conversation. When you conclude, remember to thank your audience.

23f A student's presentation

To see Shuqiao Song's presentation, "Residents of a DysFUNctional *HOME*: Text and Image," go to the integrated media page at **macmillanhighered.com/everyday6e**.

23g Consider other kinds of presentations.

You may want or need to think about other kinds of presentations for school or work, including poster presentations, online presentations, or PechaKuchas.

Poster presentations

Many college courses and conferences now call on students to make poster presentations. During the class or conference session, the presenter will use a poster board as background while talking through the presentation and answering questions. Remember the following tips if you are preparing a poster presentation:

- Create a board that can be read from at least three feet away.
- Include a clear title (at least two inches high) at the top of the board.
- Include your name and other appropriate information: course title and number, name of instructor, conference title or session, and so on.
- Use a series of bullets or boxes to identify your major points and to lead the audience through the presentation.
- Include an arresting image or an important table or figure if it illustrates your points in a clear and memorable way.

© Presentations > Video Prompt: Presentation is performance
e Presentations > Student Writing: Presentation, Shuqiao Song

- Consider using a provocative question toward the bottom of the poster to focus attention and anticipate your conclusion.

- Remember that simple, uncluttered posters are usually easier to follow and therefore more effective than overly complex ones.

- Practice the oral part of the presentation until you are comfortable referring to the poster while keeping your full attention on the audience.

Online presentations

A webcast is essentially a presentation that is broadcast on the Internet, using streaming media to distribute the presentation to viewers, who might be anywhere in the world.

As you learn to adapt to online presentation environments, remember these commonsense guidelines:

- Practice is very important, since you need to make sure that you can immediately access everything you need online—a set of slides, for example, or a document or video clip, as well as any names, dates, or sources that you might be called on to provide during the presentation.

- Because you cannot make eye contact with audience members, you should remember to look into the camera, if you are using one. If you are using a stationary webcam, practice staying still enough to remain in the frame without looking stiff.

- Even though your audience may not be visible to you, assume that if you are on camera, the audience can see you quite well; if you slouch, they'll notice. Also assume that your microphone is always live—don't say anything that you don't want your audience to hear.

PechaKucha presentations

PechaKucha—from Japanese: ペチャクチャ, for "chit chat"—is a special form of presentation with a set structure: twenty slides, each of which advances automatically after twenty seconds, for a total time of 6:40. Astrid Klein and Mark Dytham, architects in Tokyo, invented PechaKucha in 2003 because they felt that "architects talk too much" about their own work; they wanted to design a way to keep the presentations succinct and crisp. From this professional presentation format grew "PechaKucha nights" where people can share their work in a relaxed and supportive, if sometimes also competitive, atmosphere. Some college instructors are now inviting students to try their hands at constructing a PechaKucha as a way of presenting ideas to classmates. If you have an opportunity to create a PechaKucha, here are a few tips:

- Choose your topic carefully. The best PechaKuchas feature an element of surprise; many use humor to great effect. Think of a topic you can tell a story or weave a narrative about, one that will allow you to be creative.

- Choose images that will help tell your story. These images should be simple to grasp and easy to see. Many PechaKucha experts use just one image per slide, and few use more than two on any slide.

- Use PowerPoint, Prezi, or other presentation software to develop slides of your images, and set the slides to auto-advance after twenty seconds.

- Create a script to accompany each slide, making sure that the script lasts precisely twenty seconds and includes a segue to the next slide.

- Practice, practice, practice—then practice some more!

Communicating in Other Media   **24**

Writing instructors across the country are assigning not just PowerPoint and Prezi presentations but annotated playlists, blogs, comics, product pitches, live tweets, video essays, wikis, and more. Student writers seem to like and appreciate such multimodal assignments, saying that they provide room for creative control and for self-expression. As communicating with media becomes more common and even more necessary in your life, it's important to think carefully about your goals and your audiences—as well as about how to accomplish and reach them most effectively, no matter what kind of project you are creating.

24a   Consider your rhetorical context.

As with any college assignment, you will want to make sure you consider time and technical constraints. Many online projects take much more time than a traditional writing assignment: one student, for example, told us that she spent ninety hours creating a three-minute animated video. So you need to plan carefully to make sure you have both the access to any tools you will need and the time to carry out the project (and to learn about the tools, if necessary).

As with any writing project, you will want to think about rhetorical concerns, such as your purpose for creating the text, the needs of your audience, and the main point or message you want to get across.

- Why are you creating this text, document, or project? How do you want viewers to use it? Considering purpose will help you determine what features you want to highlight.

- What potential audience(s) can you identify? Thinking about the audience for your project will help you make strong rhetorical choices about tone, word choice, graphic style and design, level of detail, and many other factors. If your intended audience is limited to people you know (such as a wiki for members of your class), you may be able to make some assumptions about their background, knowledge, and likely responses. If you are covering a particular topic, you may have ideas about the type of audience you think you'll attract. Plan your project to appeal to readers you expect — but remember that an online text may reach other, unanticipated audiences.

- What is the subject or topic of your project? The topic will certainly affect the content and design of the project. If you want to focus on the latest Hong Kong film releases, for example, you might create a blog that always places your most recent posts at the top; if you want to explore the works of 1940s detective writers, you might produce a website with pages devoted to particular writers or themes. If you prefer to show information on your topic, you might consider creating an infographic or a video essay that you can post to an existing site.

- How do you relate to your subject matter? Your rhetorical stance determines how your audience will see you. Will you present yourself as an expert, a fan, a novice seeking input from others? What information will make you seem credible and persuasive to your audience(s)?

24b Consider types of multimodal texts.

Among the common types of multimodal assignments in college writing courses are websites and web pages, blogs, microblogs, wikis, audio and video projects, and nondigital multimodal projects like comics and posters.

Websites and web pages

A website can consist of multiple individual web pages. The hypertext that makes up a website allows the writer to organize elements

CONSIDERING DISABILITIES

Accessible Web Texts

Much on the web remains hard to access and read for persons with disabilities. The website for the Americans with Disabilities Act provides guidelines on designing accessible sites, which include offering textual descriptions of any visuals and captions for any sound files. For details, visit www.ada.gov.

as a cluster of associations. Each page may cover a single topic within a larger pool of content; a menu on the page typically lets readers find related information on the site. A website is relatively easy to change in order to accommodate new information.

Keep your purpose in mind as you create, embed, or link to content for your site, and workshop your layout and navigation plan with friends or classmates. Is the layout clear and easy to navigate? Do users find what they are looking for, or are you missing content that readers need? If your instructor does not require you to follow a particular plan for a website or web page, consider following a template design, or use a site or page that you admire as a model for your own work.

Blogs

Some blogs resemble journals or diaries. Other blogs may report on a particular topic. Some bloggers write short posts or comment on links to other sites; others write essay-length analyses of issues that interest them. There are as many varieties of blogs as there are reasons for writing them. Therefore, you won't find any hard-and-fast rules about how informal your tone should be when you write (or comment on) a blog post. Many bloggers adopt a conversational tone, but blogs aimed at a general audience tend to follow the conventions of edited English unless the writer wants to achieve a special effect.

Readers expect blog content to be refreshed frequently, so blog posts are often time-stamped, and the newest content appears first. Blogs also usually invite readers to comment publicly on each post. If you are creating a blog, consider whether you want to be able to moderate comments before they appear.

- Consider how you want to represent yourself to readers. Will they expect humor, careful reasoning, personal anecdotes, expertise? What level of formality will produce the results you want from your audience?

- To comment on a blog, follow the same conventions you would for a discussion-list posting. Become familiar with the conversation before you add a comment of your own, and in general, avoid commenting on entries that are several days old.

Microblogs

Social media sites that encourage you to write very short updates, such as Twitter and Tumblr, have some additional conventions.

- In microblog posts, brevity is more important than conventionally correct grammar and spelling. As always, however, remember your audience. Posts on such sites *do* follow conventions, even though they don't always resemble those for academic writing. So learn the current standards of the community you are trying to reach—especially the conventions for sharing other users' posts.

- Use punctuation appropriately to organize posts and help others find information they want. For instance, to communicate with a particular group, you can add the symbol # (hashtag) and an identifying label to your tweets to make it easier for group members to find your posts; your Hindi study group might use a tag such as *#hin101*.

Wikis

Wikis, such as Wikipedia, are collaborative online texts that empower all users of the site to contribute content, although this content may be moderated before being posted. Wikis create communities where all content is peer reviewed and evaluated by other members; they draw on the collective knowledge of many contributors.

Wiki organization is largely left up to contributors, so you can decide when to link to existing content, create new pages, and so on. If the wiki you are working on allows you to annotate your work, you may want to explain your reasons for changing or correcting content others have posted. Many wikis allow users to add citations and create bibliographies; if you add content, you will help others by including links or identifying sources for your information.

Audio and video projects

Today's technology makes it easy for users to record, edit, and upload audio and video files to the web. Audio and video content can vary as widely as the content found in written-word media. Writers who create podcasts (which can be downloaded for playback) and streaming media (which can be played without downloading) may produce episodic content united by a common host or theme.

Creating audio and video may be a somewhat greater technical challenge than adding words and images to a blog post or website, but your school may have media experts who can help, or you may be able to turn to friends or classmates for technical advice—so don't assume that video or audio projects are necessarily too difficult. If you have the opportunity to create audio or video essays in response to an assignment, consider the following as you make choices about your project:

- Audio and video files can stand alone as online texts on sites like YouTube, but they can also be embedded on a web page or blog or included in a presentation to add dimension to still images and written words. If only part of your text needs audio or video, consider embedding a short clip instead of making the entire project a media file.

- Do you need to record your own audio or video? If so, make a plan for getting the content you need, which might include creating a script or interview questions, finding locations, and so on. Will you appear in the project? Will others also need to participate?

- Will you need sound or images from other sources? If so, where can you acquire what you need? If you use the work of others in a project that will be posted for the public, you may need to seek permission from the rightsholders. However, critiquing or analyzing someone else's work in your own project is often considered a "fair use" that does not require permission. You may also want to look for images and sounds distributed under a Creative Commons license, which allows others to use them freely.

Nondigital multimodal projects

If the idea of having to use technology to create a writing project seems intimidating, remember that you can make a multimodal or multimedia project without digital tools. To be "multimodal" or "multimedia," a project simply needs to go beyond words—but you can use pens and scissors and any other resources at hand to add images, shapes, and other features to your texts.

Comics, scrapbooks, posters, and collages are just a few of the multimodal genres that you can create with or without digital help.

Public, Professional, Digital Writing > Tutorial: Photo editing with GIMP

Public, Professional, Digital Writing > Tutorial: Audio editing with Audacity

Projects like these may incorporate words, or they may let images do most or all of the communicating. However, your instructor will still expect you to consider the rhetorical features of your projects and to convey your purpose and stance effectively to your audience, no matter what genres you choose or what tools you use.

24c Plan features of texts.

Use organization, interactivity, and links to make your web text work as effectively as possible.

Organization

Whether you are creating a layout for a web page or storyboarding a video essay, you should develop a clear structure for your text. Some types of online texts are organized in standard ways—most blogs and social media sites, for example, put the newest posts at the top. Others allow you to make choices about how to arrange materials. Choose a structure that makes sense for your purpose, audience, topic, and rhetorical stance. Arrange your text to allow readers to find what they are looking for as quickly and intuitively as possible. (For more on organizing and planning your text, see Chapter 5.)

Interaction

The possibility of interaction with readers is one of the great opportunities of online writing, but you can consider different levels of interactivity. While wikis are full-scale collaborative efforts and frequently allow contribution from users, you might also include something as simple as a thumbs-up/thumbs-down or LIKE button to allow users to register their reaction to a text. Online texts can incorporate polls, comments, and links for contacting writers.

Links

Academic and formal writing follows guidelines that tell readers the sources of other people's ideas and research through notes and bibliographic references (see Chapters 57–67). Some less formal online writing includes links to external sites. You can also link to content that helps prove a point, such as complex explanations, supporting statistics, bibliographies, referenced websites, or additional readings. Links also help readers navigate from one part of a text to another.

Each link should have a clear rhetorical purpose and be in an appropriate location. If you put a link in the middle of a paragraph, be aware that readers may go to the linked content before finishing what's before them—and if that link takes them to an external site, they may never come back! If it's important for users to read the whole paragraph, you may want to move the link to the end of it.

Writing to Make Something Happen in the World **25**

College students participating in a research study were asked, "What is good writing?" The researchers expected fairly straightforward answers like "writing that gets its message across," but the students kept coming back to one central idea: good writing "makes something happen in the world." They felt particular pride in the writing they did for family, friends, and community groups—and for many extracurricular activities that were meaningful to them. They produced newsletters for community action groups, nature guides for local parks, and websites for local emergency services. Furthermore, once these students graduated from college, they continued to create—and to value—these kinds of public writing. The writing that matters most to many students and citizens, then, is writing that has an effect in the world: writing that gets up off the page or screen, puts on its working boots, and marches out to get something done!

25a Decide what should happen.

During your college years or soon after, you are highly likely to create not just writing that you turn in for a grade, but writing that you do because you want to make a difference. You may already have found reasons for communicating with a public audience—perhaps you have invited others to an event, advertised your expertise, reported on a project you were involved in, or advocated for a cause. Often the purpose for doing this kind of writing may seem obvious to you—you have a clear idea of *what* the writing needs to accomplish. Now take the time to consider *how* to get the results that you want. Get feedback from friends and others who may be affected by your plan.

QUICK HELP

Characteristics of Writing That Makes Something Happen

- Public writing has a very clear *purpose* (to promote a local cause or event; to inform or explain an issue or problem; to persuade others to act; sometimes even to entertain). (25a)
- It is intended for a specific *audience* and addresses those people directly. (25b)
- It uses the *genre* most suited to its purpose and audience — a poster to alert people to an upcoming fund drive, a newsletter to inform members of a group, a brochure to describe the activities of a group, a letter to the editor to argue for an issue, a video to promote an upcoming musical performance — and it appears in a *medium* (print, online, or both) where the intended audience will see it. (25b)
- It generally uses straightforward, everyday *language*.
- It generally uses *design* to get and hold the audience's attention.

25b Connect with your audience.

When you have clarified the actions you want your readers to take in response to your writing, think about the people you most want to reach—audiences today can be as close as your immediate neighbors or as dispersed as global netizens. Who will be interested in the topic you are writing about? For example, if you are trying to encourage your elementary school to plant a garden, you might try to interest parents, teachers, and PTA members; if you are planning a voter registration drive, you might start with eighteen-year-olds.

Once you have a target audience in mind, think carefully about where and how you are likely to find them, how you can get their attention, and what you can say to achieve your purpose.

Appeals to an audience

What do you know about your audience's interests? Why should they appreciate what you want to communicate? If you want to convince your neighbors to contribute their time, effort, and resources to build a local playground, then you may have a head start: knowing the neighbors and their children, and understanding local concerns about safety, can help you think of effective appeals to get their attention and convince them to join in this project. If you want to create a flash mob to publicize ineffective security at chemical plants near your city, on the other hand, you will need to reach as many people as possible, most of whom you will not know. Finding ways to reach appropriate audiences and convince them to join your project will probably require you to do some research.

Genre and media

Even if you know the members of your audience, you still need to think about the genre and media that will be most likely to reach them. To get neighbors involved in a playground project, you might decide that a colorful print flyer delivered door to door and posted at neighborhood gathering places would work best, or you may put together a neighborhood Facebook page or email list in order to share information digitally. To gather a flash mob, an easily for-warded message—text, tweet, or email—will probably work best.

Appropriate language

For all public writing, think carefully about the audience you want to reach—as well as *unintended* audiences your message might reach. Doing so can help you craft writing that will be persuasive without being offensive.

Timing

Making sure your text will appear in a timely manner is crucial to the success of your project. If you want people to plan to attend an event, present your text to them at least two weeks ahead of time. If you are issuing a blog or newsletter, make sure that you create con-tent frequently enough to keep people interested (but not so often that readers can't or won't bother to keep up). If you are reporting information based on something that has already happened, make it available as soon as possible so that your audience won't consider your report "old news."

25c   Sample writing to make something happen in the world

On the following pages are some examples of the forms that public writing can take.

FUNDRAISING WEB PAGE

This fundraising web page, created by student Justin Dart, has a very clear purpose: to crowd-source the funding to help Jey, a young street vendor in Accra, Ghana, get a college education. Justin, who was studying marketing at the University of Colorado, aimed this fundraising campaign, "Teach a Man: Wisdom," at friends and acquaintances and urged them to share it on social media outlets. Using the Indiegogo template, Justin posted a video spelling out the background and purpose of the Indiegogo fundraiser; a short written description of the project, broken into easily digestible chunks with boldface headings; and a list of perks for donors at various levels. Other tabs offered updates that Justin posted over the course of the fundraising project, comments from donors, photos, and more. Justin and his team ended up raising enough to pay for Jey's university tuition for his college career, housing, and incidentals.

WEB COMIC

Student Zack Karas worked with a team of classmates on an assignment to do field research in a public space. His group chose a local coffee shop, and after conducting observations of the environment and the interactions among people there, they presented a critical analysis of the coffee-drinking scene to the rest of the class.

Zack then used his team's coffee shop experience as the basis for a comic, which he posted on a blog created to host his artwork. The final panels include a twist: Zack's comic avatar fails to recognize that he, like many of the customers, is also a "post-ironic hipster . . . with facial hair, a hoodie, and an iPhone." Turning the report into a comic allowed Zack to reach an audience beyond his classmates—readers who share his interest in humor, online comics, and the critique of the coffee-culture demographic.

PITCH PACKAGE

AMERICA LOVES MUSICALS!!!

With hit shows like *Glee* and *Smash,* musicals are becoming a bigger phenomenon and more popular than ever. Now more gritty and raw, musicals are used to explore many different elements of life. *Strange Fruit* is no exception. Using the most popular musical art form today, hip-hop, *Strange Fruit* bravely goes into uncharted territory through innovative means. *Strange Fruit* is a film that digs up the deep roots of our American past, discovering how slavery affects interracial relationships today. It's a powerful and poignant film, full of music, drama, humor, and passion. It's aimed to be a musical sensation.

SAMPLE BOX OFFICE GROSS COMPARISONS

MOVIE	COST	GROSS
The Help	25 million	169 million
Dreamgirls	70 million	100 million
The Color Purple	15 million	98 million
Chicago	45 million	306 million
Back to the Future	19 million	350 million
Precious	10 million	47 million

Deborah Jane and Jamie Burke collaborated to create this pitch package, to encourage backers to invest in a film based on Deborah's play *Strange Fruit: The Hip-Hopera.* The pitch package includes a synopsis, individual character breakdowns, character relationship dynamics, brief biographies of the production team, and the financial analysis seen here. Deborah and Jamie created the pitch package digitally for easy distribution.

NEWSLETTER

Asana Americana

Videos are up!
Joelle on About.com

I spent Memorial Day sequestered in Go Yoga shooting instructional videos for About.com. It was a hot day and my first time on film. (Second time was also this summer in a poet-bike messenger murder mystery set in NY--I play the role of a "senior editor." More about this next month!)

Some of the videos are now live. Take a look. Here's bow pose.

Thank you, Ann Pizer, former student, and current yoga adviser and blogger at About.com, for inviting me to do these videos. Read her blog post about the videos here.

After Labor Day
Back to Normal Teaching Schedule

I was fortunate to go on several retreats this summer. Thanks for your patience as I subbed out my classes. I'm now back to my normal schedule.

Curious about where I went?
I was at the Himalayan Institute, learning the magic of Tantra (it's not what you think!)--studies I'll continue over the next year. I was also in upstate New York at an inspired gathering of women called the Goddess Retreat, run by Kula teacher Alison Sinatra. Super heart-filled--and fun! And finally I attended Omega's Being Yoga conference in Rhinebeck, NY, to interview young PhD and yoga dynamo, Kelly McGonigal, who's developing compassion-based protocols sanctioned by the Dalai Lama.

My Recent Articles & Blog Posts

RECENT ARTICLES & BLOG POSTS:

YogaCityNYC
Interview with my teacher Gary Kraftsow Last Labor Day and again this summer, I interviewed Gary about his life as a student, teacher, and trainer of thousands. He was destined to become a great teacher--the stars foretold it--and has pioneered the field of yoga therapy in the US.

Anatomy Studies for Yoga Teachers: Jason R. Brown took the hard road to learn anatomy, but his new program (ASYT) makes the way much easier for the rest of us.

JOELLE'S YOGA
teaching & writing
NEWSLETTER

TEACHING SCHEDULE
Sunday, 10am open
Monday, 8:15pm basics

at Go Yoga
N6th at Berry, Williamsburg

Privates available by appointment or for trade

yoganation gmail com

INFO
If you have any questions, comments, or suggestions don't hesitate to get in touch.

Namaste!

photos of me by
timknoxphotography.com

As with the writers of the web page, flyer, and pitch package, yoga teacher Joelle Hann has a clear purpose in mind for her newsletter: to provide information to her audience—students and others interested in her yoga classes and developments in the yoga community. Emailing the newsletter to her subscribers allows her to reach an interested audience quickly and to provide links to more of the content she's discussing. This format also means she can include photos, illustrations, and color to enhance her document's design impact.

Language

Many people think of language as a set
of rules; break them, and you're wrong.
But that's not how language works.

— ROBERT LANE GREENE

Language

For visual analysis The illustration on the front of this tab shows Scrabble players trying to make the best possible use of their letters. Effective communicators choose carefully from the language tools they have available and position their ideas to make an impact. What language moves will work best for your context?

Writing to the World 26

People today often communicate instantaneously across vast distances and cultures. Businesspeople complete multinational transactions with a single click, students in Ohio take online classes at MIT or chat with hundreds of Facebook friends, and tweets from Tehran find readers in Atlanta. When the whole world can be your potential audience, it's time to step back and think about how to communicate successfully with a diverse group—how to become a world writer.

26a Think about what seems "normal."

Your judgment on what's "normal" may be based on assumptions you are not even aware of. But remember: behavior that is considered out of place in one context may appear perfectly normal in another. What's considered "normal" in a text message would be anything but in a request for an internship with a law firm. If you want to communicate with people across cultures, try to learn something about the norms in those cultures and be aware of the norms that guide your own behavior.

Like most people, you may tend to see your own way as the "normal" way to do things. How do your own values and assumptions guide your thinking and behavior? Keep in mind that if your ways seem inherently right, then—even without thinking about it—you may assume that other ways are somehow less than right.

- Know that most ways of communicating are influenced by cultural contexts and differ widely from one culture to the next.

Communicating across Cultures

- Recognize what you consider "normal." Examine your own customary behaviors and assumptions, and think about how they may affect what you think and say (and write). (26a)
- Listen closely to someone from another culture, and ask for clarification if necessary. Carefully define your terms. (26b)
- Think about your audience's expectations. How much authority should you have? What kind of evidence will count most with your audience? (26c)
- Organize your writing with your audience's expectations in mind. If in doubt, use formal style. (26c)

- Pay close attention to the ways that people from cultures other than your own communicate, and be flexible.
- Pay attention to and respect the differences among individual people within a given culture. Don't assume that all members of a community behave in the same way or value the same things.
- Remember that your audience may be made up of people from many backgrounds who have very different concepts about what is appropriate or "normal." So don't assume unanimity!

26b   Clarify meaning.

When an instructor called for "originality" in his students' essays, what did he mean? A Filipina student thought *originality* meant

going to an original source and explaining it; a student from Massachusetts thought *originality* meant coming up with an idea entirely on her own. The professor, however, expected students to read multiple sources and develop a critical point of their own about those sources. In subsequent classes, this professor defined *originality* as he was using it in his classes, and he gave examples of student work he judged original.

This brief example points to the challenges all writers face in trying to communicate across space, across languages, across cultures. While there are no foolproof rules, here are some tips for communicating with people from cultures other than your own:

- Listen carefully. Don't hesitate to ask people to explain or even repeat a point if you're not absolutely sure you understand.

- Take care to be explicit about the meanings of the words you use.

- Invite response — ask whether you're making yourself clear. This kind of back-and-forth is particularly easy (and necessary) in email.

- Remember that sometimes a picture is worth a thousand words. A visual may help make your meaning absolutely clear.

26c Meet audience expectations.

When you do your best to meet an audience's expectations about how a text should work, your writing is more likely to have the desired effect. In practice, figuring out what audiences want, need, or expect can be difficult — especially when you are writing in public spaces online and your audiences can be composed of anyone, anywhere. If you do know something about your readers' expectations, use what you know to present your work effectively. If you know little about your potential audiences, however, carefully examine your assumptions about your readers.

Expectations about your authority as a writer

In the United States, students are often asked to establish authority in their writing — by drawing on certain kinds of personal experience, by reporting on research they or others have conducted, or by taking a position for which they can offer strong evidence and support. But this expectation about writerly authority is by no means universal. Indeed, some cultures view student writers as novices whose job is to reflect what they learn from their teachers. One Japanese student, for example, said he was taught that it's rude to challenge a teacher: "Are you ever so smart that you should challenge the wisdom of the ages?"

As this student's comment reveals, a writer's tone also depends on his or her relationship with listeners and readers. As a world writer, you need to remember that those you're addressing may hold a wide range of attitudes about authority.

- What is your relationship to those you are addressing?
- What knowledge are you expected to have? Is it appropriate for or expected of you to demonstrate that knowledge — and, if so, how?

- What is your goal—to answer a question? to make a point? to agree? something else?
- What tone is appropriate? If in doubt, show respect: politeness is rarely if ever inappropriate.
- What level of control do you have over your writing? In a report, you may have the final say. But if you are writing on a wiki, where you share control with others, sensitivity to communal standards is key.

Expectations about persuasive evidence

How do you decide what evidence will best support your ideas? The answer depends, in large part, on the audience you want to persuade. American academics generally give great weight to factual evidence.

Differing concepts of what counts as evidence can lead to arguments that go nowhere. Consider, for example, how rare it is for a believer in creationism to be persuaded by what the theory of evolution presents as evidence—or for a supporter of evolutionary theory to be convinced by what creationists present as evidence. Think carefully about how you use evidence in writing, and pay attention to what counts as evidence to members of other groups you are trying to persuade.

- Should you rely on facts? concrete examples? firsthand experience? religious or philosophical texts? other sources?
- Should you include the testimony of experts? Which experts are valued most, and why?
- Should you use analogies as support? How much will they count?
- When does evidence from unedited websites such as blogs offer credible support, and when should you question or reject it?

Once you determine what counts as evidence in your own thinking and writing, think about where you learned to use and value this kind of evidence. You can ask these same questions about the use of evidence by members of other cultures.

Expectations about organization

As you make choices about how to organize your writing, remember that the patterns you find pleasing are likely to be ones that are deeply embedded in your own culture. For example, the organizational pattern favored by U.S. engineers, highly explicit and leaving little or nothing unsaid or unexplained, is probably familiar to many U.S. students: introduction and thesis, necessary background, overview of the parts to follow, systematic presentation of evidence, consideration of other viewpoints, and conclusion. If a piece of writing follows this pattern, American academic readers ordinarily find it well organized and coherent.

In the United States, many audiences (especially those in the academic and business worlds) expect a writer to get to the point as directly as possible and to take on the major responsibility of articulating that point efficiently and unambiguously. But not all audiences have such expectations. For instance, a Chinese student with an excellent command of English heard from her U.S. teachers that her writing was "vague," with too much "beating around the bush." As it turned out, her teachers in China had prized this kind of indirectness, expecting audiences to read between the lines.

When writing for audiences who may not share your expectations, then, think about how you can organize material to get your message across effectively. There are no hard-and-fast rules to help you organize your writing for effectiveness across cultures, but here are a few options to consider:

- Determine when to state your thesis—at the beginning? at the end? somewhere else? not at all?
- Consider whether digressions are a good idea, a requirement, or best avoided with your intended audience.
- Remember that electronic communication may call for certain ways of organizing. In messages or postings, you need to place the most important information first and be as succinct as possible. Or you may need to follow a template, as in submitting a résumé online or creating a blog.

Expectations about style

As with beauty, good style is most definitely in the eye of the beholder—and thus is always affected by language, culture, and rhetorical tradition. In fact, what constitutes effective style varies broadly across cultures and depends on the rhetorical situation—purpose, audience, and so on (see Chapter 3). Even so, there is one important style question to consider when writing across cultures: what level of formality is most appropriate? In most writing to a general audience in the United States, a fairly informal style is often acceptable, even appreciated. Many cultures, however, tend to value a more formal approach. When in doubt, it may be wise to err on the side of formality in writing to people from other cultures, especially to elders or to those in authority.

- Be careful to use proper titles:

  Dr. Atul Gawande　　　Professor Jaime Mejía

- Avoid slang and informal structures such as fragments.

- Do not use first names of people you do not know in correspondence (even in text messages) unless invited to do so. Note, however, that an invitation to use a first name could come indirectly; if someone signs a message to you with his or her first name, you are implicitly invited to use the first name as a term of address. (See 2e for more on electronic communication.)

- For business correspondence, use complete sentences and words; avoid contractions. Open with the salutation "Dear Mr. / Ms." or the person's title, if you know it. Write dates with the day before the month, and spell out the name of the month: *7 June 2015*.

Beyond formality, other stylistic preferences vary widely, and context matters. Long, complex sentences and ornate language may be exactly what some audiences are looking for. On Twitter, on the other hand, writers have to limit their message to 140 characters — so using abbreviated words, symbols, and fragments is expected, even desirable.

World writers, then, should take very little about language for granted. To be an effective world writer, aim to recognize and respect stylistic differences as you move from community to community and to meet expectations whenever you can.

27 Language That Builds Common Ground

The golden rule of language use might be "Speak to others the way you want them to speak to you." The words we select have power: they can praise, delight, inspire — and also hurt, offend, or even destroy. Words that offend prevent others from identifying with you and thus damage your credibility. Few absolute guidelines exist for using words that respect differences and build common ground. Two rules, however, can help: consider carefully the sensitivities and preferences of others, and watch for words that betray your assumptions, even when you have not directly stated them.

QUICK HELP

Using Language That Builds Common Ground

- Check for stereotypes and other assumptions that might come between you and your readers. Look, for instance, for language implying approval or disapproval and for the ways you use *we*, *you*, and *they*. (27a)

- Avoid potentially sexist language. (27b)

- Make sure your references to race, religion, sexual orientation, and so on are relevant or necessary to your discussion. If they are not, leave them out. (27c and d)

- Check that the terms you use to refer to groups are accurate and acceptable. (27c and d)

27a Examine assumptions and avoid stereotypes.

Unstated assumptions that enter into thinking and writing can destroy common ground by ignoring important differences between others and ourselves. For example, a student in a religion seminar who uses *we* to refer to Christians and *they* to refer to members of other religions had better be sure that everyone in the class identifies as Christian, or some may feel left out of the discussion.

At the same time, don't overgeneralize about or stereotype a group of people. Because stereotypes are often based on half-truths, misunderstandings, and hand-me-down prejudices, they can lead to intolerance, bias, and bigotry.

Sometimes stereotypes and assumptions lead writers to call special attention to a group affiliation when it is not relevant to the point, as in *a woman plumber* or *a white basketball player*. Even positive stereotypes—for example, *Jewish doctors are the best*—or neutral ones—*all college students like pizza*—can hurt, for they inevitably ignore the uniqueness of an individual. Careful writers make sure that their language doesn't stereotype any group or individual.

27b Examine assumptions about gender.

Powerful gender-related words can subtly affect our thinking and our behavior. For instance, at one time many young women were discouraged from pursuing careers in medicine or engineering at least partially because speakers commonly referred to hypothetical doctors or engineers as *he* (and then labeled a woman who worked as a doctor *a woman doctor*, as if to say, "She's an exception; doctors are normally men"). Similarly, a label like *male nurse* may offend by reflecting stereotyped assumptions about proper roles for men. Equally problematic is the traditional use of *man* and *mankind* to refer to people of both sexes and the use of *he* and *him* to refer generally to any human being. Because such usage ignores half of the people on earth, it hardly helps a writer build common ground.

Sexist language, those words and phrases that stereotype or ignore members of either sex or that unnecessarily call attention to gender, can usually be revised fairly easily. There are several alternatives to using masculine pronouns to refer to persons whose gender is unknown to the writer. One option is to recast the sentence using plural forms.

▶ A ~~lawyer~~ *Lawyers* must pass the bar exam before ~~he~~ *they* can begin to practice.

Another option is to substitute pairs of pronouns such as *he or she, him or her*, and so on.

▶ A lawyer must pass the bar exam before he *or she* can begin to practice.

Yet another way to revise the sentence is to eliminate the pronouns.

▶ A lawyer must pass the bar exam before ~~he can begin~~ *beginning* to practice.

Try to eliminate words that make assumptions about gender from your writing.

INSTEAD OF	TRY USING
anchorman, anchorwoman	anchor
businessman	businessperson, business executive
chairman, chairwoman	chair, chairperson
congressman	member of Congress, representative
fireman	firefighter
mailman	mail carrier
male nurse	nurse
man, mankind	humans, human beings, humanity, the human race, humankind
manpower	workers, personnel
mothering	parenting
policeman, policewoman	police officer
salesman	salesperson, sales associate
woman engineer	engineer

27c   Examine assumptions about race and ethnicity.

Generalizations about racial and ethnic groups can result in especially harmful stereotyping. To build common ground, then, avoid language that ignores differences not only among individual members of a race or ethnic group but also among subgroups. Writers must be aware, for instance, of the diverse places from which Americans of Spanish-speaking ancestry have come.

When writing about an ethnic or racial group, how can you refer to that group in terms that its members actually desire? Doing so is sometimes not an easy task, for terms can change often and vary widely.

The word *colored*, for example, was once widely used in the United States to refer to Americans of African ancestry. By the 1950s, the preferred term had become *Negro*. This changed in the 1960s, however, as *black* came to be preferred by most, though certainly not all, members of that community. Since the late 1980s, both *black*—sometimes capitalized (*Black*)—and *African American* have been widely used.

The word *Oriental*, once used to refer to people of East Asian descent, is now often considered offensive. At the University of California at Berkeley, the Oriental Languages Department is now known as the East Asian Languages Department. One advocate of the change explained that *Oriental* is appropriate for objects—like rugs—but not for people.

Once widely preferred, the term *Native American* is being challenged by those who argue that the most appropriate way to refer to indigenous peoples is by the specific name of the tribe or pueblo, such as *Chippewa* or *Diné*. Many indigenous peoples once referred to as *Eskimos* now prefer *Inuit* or a specific term such as *Tlingit*. It has also become fairly common for tribal groups to refer to themselves as *Indians* or *Indian tribes*.

Among Americans of Spanish-speaking descent, the preferred terms of reference are many: *Chicano/Chicana*, *Hispanic*, *Latin American*, *Latino/Latina*, *Mexican American*, *Dominican*, and *Puerto Rican*, to name but a few.

Clearly, then, ethnic terminology changes often enough to challenge the most careful writers—including writers who belong to the groups they are writing about. Consider your words carefully, seek information about ways members of groups refer to themselves (or ask about preferences), but don't expect one person to speak for all members of a group or expect unanimity on such terms. Finally, check any term you are unsure of in a current dictionary. *Random House Webster's College Dictionary* includes particularly helpful usage notes about racial and ethnic designations.

27d   Consider other kinds of difference.

Age

Mention age if it is relevant, but be aware that age-related terms (*matronly*, *well-preserved*, and so on) can carry derogatory connotations. Describing Mr. Fry as *elderly but still active* may sound polite to you, but chances are Mr. Fry would prefer being called *an active seventy-eight-year-old*—or just *a seventy-eight-year-old*, which eliminates the unstated assumption of surprise that he is active at his age.

Class

Take special care to examine your words for assumptions about class. As a writer, you should not assume that all your readers share your background or values—that your classmates all own cars, for instance. And avoid using any words—*redneck*, *blueblood*, and the like—that might alienate members of an audience.

Geographical area

You should not assume that geography determines personality or lifestyle. New Englanders are not all thrifty and tight-lipped; people in "red states" may hold liberal views; midwesterners are not always polite. Be careful not to make simplistic assumptions.

Check also that you use geographical terms accurately.

AMERICA, AMERICAN Although many people use these words to refer to the United States alone, such usage will not necessarily be acceptable to people from Canada, Mexico, and Central or South America.

BRITISH, ENGLISH Use *British* to refer to the island of Great Britain, which includes England, Scotland, and Wales, or to the United Kingdom of Great Britain and Northern Ireland. In general, do not use *English* for these broader senses.

CONSIDERING DISABILITIES
Knowing Your Readers

Nearly 10 percent of first-year college students — about 155,000 — identify themselves as having one or more disabilities. That's no small number. Effective writers consider their own and their readers' disabilities so that they can find ways to build common ground.

ARAB This term refers only to people of Arabic-speaking descent. Note that Iran is not an Arab nation; its people speak Farsi, not Arabic. Note also that *Arab* is not synonymous with *Muslim* or *Moslem* (a believer in Islam). Most (but not all) Arabs are Muslim, but many Muslims (those in Pakistan, for example) are not Arab.

Physical ability or health

When writing about a person with a serious illness or physical disability, ask yourself whether mentioning the disability is relevant to your discussion and whether the words you use carry negative connotations. You might choose, for example, to say someone *uses* a wheelchair rather than to say he or she is *confined to* one. Similarly, you might note a subtle but meaningful difference in calling someone a *person with AIDS* rather than an *AIDS victim*. Mentioning the person first and the disability second, such as referring to a *child with diabetes* rather than a *diabetic child* or a *diabetic*, is always a good idea.

Religion

Assumptions about religious groups are very often inaccurate and unfair. For example, Roman Catholics hold a wide spectrum of views on abortion, Muslim women do not all wear veils, and many Baptists are not fundamentalists. In fact, many people do not believe in or practice a religion at all, so be careful of such assumptions. As in other cases, do not use religious labels without considering their relevance to your point.

Sexual orientation

If you wish to build common ground, do not assume that readers all share one sexual orientation—that everyone is attracted to the opposite sex, for example. As with any label, reference to sexual orientation should be governed by context. Someone writing about Senator Tammy Baldwin's or Federal Reserve Chair Janet Yellen's economic views would probably have no reason to refer to either person's sexual orientation. On the other hand, someone writing about diversity in U.S. government might find it important to note that, in 2012, Baldwin became the first openly gay person elected to the Senate.

28   Language Variety

When Pulitzer Prize–winning author Junot Díaz spoke to a group of college students in California in 2008, he used colloquial English and Spanish, plus a few four-letter words—and the students loved every minute of it. When he was interviewed a month later on National Public Radio, however, Díaz addressed his nationwide audience in more formal English. As a college student, you will need to think carefully about how to make appropriate choices. Since academic English is still expected for most of your classes, you will want to use it effectively. But you may also choose to use another language or variety of English or to mix varieties of English for rhetorical purpose or special effect. Strong writers recognize these differences and learn to use all their languages and language varieties in the most appropriate and powerful ways.

28a   Use "standard" varieties of English appropriately.

How do writers decide when to use another language or switch from one variety of English to another? Even writers who are perfectly fluent in several languages must think for a moment before switching linguistic gears. The key to shifting among varieties of English and among languages is appropriateness: you need to consider when such shifts will help your audience appreciate your message and when shifts may be a mistake. Used appropriately and wisely, *any* variety of English can serve a good purpose.

QUICK HELP

Language Variety

You can use different varieties of language to good effect for the following purposes:

- to repeat someone's exact words
- to evoke a person, place, or activity
- to establish your credibility and build common ground
- to make a strong point
- to connect with an audience

One variety of English, often referred to as the "standard" or "standard academic," is that taught prescriptively in schools, represented in this and most other textbooks, used in the national media, and written and spoken widely by those wielding social and economic power. As the language used in business and most public institutions, "standard" English is a variety you will want to be completely familiar with. "Standard" English, however, is only one of many effective varieties of English and itself varies according to purpose and audience, from the more formal style used in academic writing to the informal style characteristic of casual conversation.

28b Use varieties of English to evoke a place or community.

"Ever'body says words different," said Ivy. "Arkansas folks says 'em different from Oklahomy folks says 'em different. And we seen a lady from Massachusetts, an' she said 'em differentest of all. Couldn' hardly make out what she was sayin'."

—JOHN STEINBECK, *The Grapes of Wrath*

Using the language of a local community is an effective way to evoke a character or place. Author and radio host Garrison Keillor, for example, peppers his tales of his native Minnesota with the homespun English spoken there: "I once was a tall dark heartbreaker who, when I slouched into a room, women jumped up and asked if they could get me something, and now they only smile and say, 'My mother is a big fan of yours. You sure are a day-brightener for her. You sure make her chuckle.'"

Weaving together regionalisms and more formal English can also be effective in creating a sense of place. Here, an anthropologist

FOR MULTILINGUAL WRITERS

Global Varieties of English

Like other world languages, English is used in many countries, so it has many global varieties. For example, British English differs somewhat from U.S. English in certain vocabulary (*bonnet* for hood of a car), syntax (*to hospital* rather than *to the hospital*), spelling (*centre* rather than *center*), and pronunciation. If you have learned a non-American variety of English, you will want to recognize, and to appreciate, the ways in which it differs from the variety widely used in U.S. academic settings.

writing about one Carolina community takes care to let the residents speak their minds—and in their own words:

> For Roadville, schooling is something most folks have not gotten enough of, but everybody believes will do something toward helping an individual "get on." In the words of one oldtime resident, "Folks that ain't got no schooling don't get to be nobody nowadays."
>
> —SHIRLEY BRICE HEATH, *Ways with Words*

28c Build credibility within a community with language variety.

Whether you are American Indian or trace your ancestry to Europe, Asia, Latin America, Africa, or elsewhere, your heritage lives on in the diversity of the English language.

See how one Hawaiian writer uses a local variety of English to paint a picture of young teens hearing a "chicken skin" story from their grandmother.

> "—So, rather dan being rid of da shark, da people were stuck with many little ones, for dere mistake."
>
> Then Grandma Wong wen' pause, for dramatic effect, I guess, and she wen' add, "Dis is one of dose times. . . . Da time of da sharks."
>
> Those words ended another of Grandma's chicken skin stories. The stories she told us had been passed on to her by her grandmother, who had heard them from her grandmother. Always skipping a generation.
>
> —RODNEY MORALES, "When the Shark Bites"

Notice how the narrator of the story uses varieties of English—presenting information necessary to the story line mostly in "standard" English and using a local, ethnic variety to represent spoken language. One important reason for the shift is to demonstrate that the writer is a member of the community whose language he is representing and thus to build credibility with others in the community.

Take care, however, in using the language of communities other than your own. When used inappropriately, such language can have an opposite effect, perhaps destroying credibility and alienating your audience.

28d Bring in other languages appropriately.

You might use a language other than English for the same reasons you might use different varieties of English: to represent the actual words of a speaker, to make a point, to connect with your audience, or to get their attention. See how Gerald Haslam uses Spanish to capture his great-grandmother's words and to make a point about his relationship to her.

> "*Expectoran su sangre!*" exclaimed Great-grandma when I showed her the small horned toad I had removed from my breast pocket. I turned toward my mother, who translated: "They spit blood."
>
> "*De los ojos,*" Grandma added. "From their eyes," mother explained, herself uncomfortable in the presence of the small beast.
>
> I grinned, "Awwwwwww."
>
> But my Great-grandmother did not smile. "*Son muy tóxicos,*" she nodded with finality. Mother moved back an involuntary step, her hands suddenly busy at her breast. "Put that thing down," she ordered.
>
> "His name's John," I said.
>
> – GERALD HASLAM, *California Childhood*

Word Choice and Spelling **29**

Deciding which word is the right word can be a challenge. It's not unusual to find many words that have similar but subtly different meanings, and each makes a different impression on your

---

QUICK HELP

Editing for Appropriate Language and Spelling

- Check to see that your language reflects the appropriate level of formality for your audience, purpose, and topic. (29a)
- Unless you are writing for a specialized audience that will understand jargon, either define technical terms or replace them with words that are easy to understand. (29a)
- Revise pompous language, inappropriate euphemisms, and double-speak. (29a)
- Consider the connotations of words carefully. If you say someone is *pushy*, be sure you mean to be critical; otherwise, use a word like *assertive*. (29b)
- Use both general and specific words. If you are writing about the general category *beds*, for example, do you give enough concrete detail (*an antique four-poster bed*)? (29c)
- Look for clichés, and replace them with fresher language. (29d)
- Use spell checkers with care. (29f)

audience. For instance, the "pasta with marinara sauce" presented in a restaurant may look and taste much like the "macaroni and gravy" served at an Italian family dinner, but the choice of one label rather than the other tells us not only about the food but also about the people serving it and the people they expect to serve it to.

Ensuring that you choose the correct spelling for the word you want to use is also important. Spell checkers can help you avoid some errors, but they can also make other mistakes more likely, including word choice errors, so use them with care (see 29f).

29a Choose appropriate words for the context.

Choose a level of formality that matches your audience, purpose, and topic. In an email or letter to a friend or close associate, informal language is often appropriate. For most academic and professional writing, however, more formal language is appropriate because you are addressing people you do not know well. Compare the following responses to a request for information about a job candidate:

EMAIL TO SOMEONE YOU KNOW WELL

Maisha is great—hire her if you can!

LETTER OF RECOMMENDATION TO SOMEONE YOU DO NOT KNOW

I am pleased to recommend Maisha Fisher. She will bring good ideas and extraordinary energy to your organization.

Slang and colloquial language

Slang, or extremely informal language, is often confined to a relatively small group of people and usually becomes obsolete rather

---

TALKING THE TALK

Texting Abbreviations

"Can I use text-message slang when I contact my teacher?" In a chat or text message, abbreviations such as *u* for *you* may be conventional, but using such shortcuts when communicating with an instructor can be a mistake. At least some of your instructors are likely to view them as disrespectful, unprofessional, or simply sloppy writing. Unless you are working to create a special effect for a special purpose and audience, keep to the conventions of standard English for college writing—and for contacting your instructor.

quickly, though some slang gains wide use (*selfie, duh*). Colloquial language, such as *in a bind* or *snooze*, is less informal, more widely used, and longer lasting than most slang.

Writers who use slang and colloquial language run the risk of not being understood or of not being taken seriously. If you are writing for a general audience about gun-control legislation, for example, and you use the term *gat* to refer to a weapon, some readers may not know what you mean, and others may be irritated by what they see as a frivolous reference to a deadly serious subject.

Jargon

Jargon is the special vocabulary of a trade or profession, enabling members to speak and write concisely to one another. Reserve jargon for an audience that will understand your terms. The example that follows, from a blog about fonts and typefaces, uses jargon appropriately for an interested and knowledgeable audience.

The Modern typeface classification is usually associated with Didones and display faces that often have too much contrast for text use. The Ingeborg family was designed with the intent of producing a Modern face that was readable at any size. Its roots might well be historic, but its approach is very contemporary. The three text weights (Regular, Bold, and Heavy) are functional and discreet while the Display weights (Fat and Block) catch the reader's

eye with a dynamic form and a whole lot of ink on the paper. The family includes a boatload of extras like unicase alternates, swash caps, and a lined fill. —FONTSHOP.COM BLOG

Depending on the needs of the audience, jargon can be irritating and incomprehensible—or extremely helpful. Terms that begin as jargon for specialists (such as *asynchronous* or *vertical integration*) can quickly become part of the mainstream if they provide a useful shorthand for an otherwise lengthy explanation. Before you use technical jargon, remember your readers: if they will not understand the terms, or if you don't know them well enough to judge, then say what you need to say in everyday language.

Pompous language, euphemisms, and doublespeak

Stuffy or pompous language is unnecessarily formal for the purpose, audience, or topic. It often gives writing an insincere or unintentionally humorous tone, making a writer's ideas seem insignificant or even unbelievable.

POMPOUS

Pursuant to the August 9 memorandum regarding petroleum pricing, it is incumbent upon us to endeavor to make maximal utilization of alternate methods of communication in lieu of personal visitation.

REVISED

As noted in the August 9 memo, gas costs are still high, so please use email, texting, and phone calls rather than personal visits whenever possible.

As these examples illustrate, some writers use words in an attempt to sound expert, and these puffed-up words can easily backfire.

INSTEAD OF	TRY USING	INSTEAD OF	TRY USING
ascertain	find out	optimal	best
commence	begin	parameters	boundaries
finalize	finish, complete	peruse	look at
impact (as verb)	affect	ramp up	increase
methodology	method	utilize	use

Euphemisms are words and phrases that make unpleasant ideas seem less harsh. *Your position is being eliminated* seeks to soften the blow of being fired or laid off. Other euphemisms include *pass on* or *pass away* for *die* and *plus-sized* for *fat*. Although euphemisms can sometimes appeal to an audience by showing that you are considerate of people's feelings, they can also sound insincere or evasive.

FOR MULTILINGUAL WRITERS

Multilingual **Avoiding Fancy Language**

In writing standard academic English, which is fairly formal, students are often tempted to use many "big words" instead of simple language. Although learning impressive words can be a good way to expand your vocabulary, it is usually best to avoid flowery or fancy language in college writing. Academic writing at U.S. universities tends to value clear, concise prose.

Doublespeak is language used to hide or distort the truth. During massive layoffs and cutbacks in the business world, companies speak of firings as *employee repositioning* or *proactive downsizing*, and of unpaid time off as a *furlough*. The public — and particularly those who lose their jobs — recognize these terms for what they are.

29b Consider denotations and connotations.

Thinking of a stone tossed into a pool and ripples spreading out from it can help you understand the distinction between *denotation*, the dictionary meaning of a word (the stone), and *connotation*, the associations that accompany the word (the ripples). The words *enthusiasm*, *passion*, and *obsession*, for instance, all carry roughly the same denotation. But the connotations are quite different: an *enthusiasm* is a pleasurable and absorbing interest; a *passion* has a strong emotional component and may affect someone positively or negatively; an *obsession* is an unhealthy attachment that excludes other interests.

Note the differences in connotation among the following three statements:

▶ **Students Against Racism (SAR) erected a temporary barrier on the campus oval. They say it symbolizes "the many barriers to those discriminated against by university policies."**

▶ **Left-wing agitators threw up an eyesore on the oval to stampede the university into giving in to their demands.**

▶ **Supporters of human rights for all students challenged the university's investment in racism by erecting a protest barrier on campus.**

The first statement is the most neutral, merely stating facts; the second, using words with negative connotations (*agitators, eyesore, stampede*), is strongly critical; the third, using a phrase with positive connotations (*supporters of human rights*) and presenting assertions as facts (*the university's investment in racism*), gives a favorable slant to the story.

29c Use general and specific language effectively.

Effective writers balance general words, which name or describe groups or classes, with specific words, which identify individual and particular things. Some general words are abstract; they refer to things we cannot perceive through our five senses. Specific words are often concrete; they name things we can see, hear, touch, taste, or smell. We can seldom draw a clear-cut line between general or abstract words on the one hand and specific or concrete words on the other. Instead, most words fall somewhere in between.

GENERAL	LESS GENERAL	SPECIFIC	MORE SPECIFIC
book	dictionary	abridged dictionary	*The American Heritage College Dictionary*

ABSTRACT	LESS ABSTRACT	CONCRETE	MORE CONCRETE
culture	visual art	painting	van Gogh's *Starry Night*

Strong writing usually provides readers with both an overall picture and specific examples or concrete details to fill in that picture. In the following passage, the author might have simply made a general statement—*their breakfast was always liberal and good*—or simply given the details of the breakfast. Instead, he employs both general and specific language.

> There would be a brisk fire crackling in the hearth, the old smoke-gold of morning and the smell of fog, the crisp cheerful voices of the people and their ruddy competent morning look, and the cheerful smells of breakfast, which was always liberal and good, the best meal that they had: kidneys and ham and eggs and sausages and toast and marmalade and tea.   – THOMAS WOLFE, *Of Time and the River*

29d   Use figurative language effectively.

Figurative language, or figures of speech, paint pictures in readers' minds, allowing them to "see" a point readily and clearly. Far from being merely decorative, such language is often crucial to readers' understanding.

Similes, metaphors, and analogies

Similes use *like*, *as*, *as if*, or *as though* to make explicit the similarity between two seemingly different things.

▶ You can tell the graphic-novels section in a bookstore from afar, by the young bodies sprawled around it like casualties of a localized disaster.   – PETER SCHJELDAHL

▶ The comb felt as if it was raking my skin off.
    – MALCOLM X, "My First Conk"

Metaphors are implicit comparisons, omitting the *like, as, as if*, or *as though* of similes.

▶ **The Internet is the new town square.** – JEB HENSARLING

Mixed metaphors make comparisons that are inconsistent.

▶ **The lectures were like brilliant comets streaking through the night**
 dazzling   *flashes*
sky, ~~showering~~ listeners with ~~a torrential rain~~ of insights.

The images of streaking light and heavy precipitation are inconsistent; in the revised sentence, all of the images relate to light.

Analogies compare similar features of two dissimilar things; they explain something unfamiliar by relating it to something familiar.

▶ **One way to establish that peace-preserving threat of mutual assured destruction is to commit yourself beforehand, which helps explain why so many retailers promise to match any competitor's advertised price. Consumers view these guarantees as conducive to lower prices. But in fact offering a price-matching guarantee should make it less likely that competitors will slash prices, since they know that any cuts they make will immediately be matched. It's the retail version of the doomsday machine.** – JAMES SUROWIECKI

▶ **One Hundred and Twenty-fifth Street was to Harlem what the Mississippi was to the South, a long traveling river always going somewhere, carrying something.**
 – MAYA ANGELOU, *The Heart of a Woman*

 FOR MULTILINGUAL WRITERS

Learning Idioms

Why do you wear a diamond *on* your finger but *in* your ear? See 44a for more on using prepositions idiomatically.

Clichés

A cliché is a frequently used expression such as *busy as a bee*. By definition, we use clichés all the time, especially in speech, and many serve usefully as shorthand for familiar ideas or as a way of connecting to an audience. But if you use too many clichés in your writing, readers may conclude that what you are saying is not very new or interesting—or true. To check for clichés, use this rule of thumb: if you can predict exactly what the next word in a phrase will be, the phrase stands a good chance of being a cliché.

Multilingual

29e   Check usage with search engines and online databases.

Search engines and online databases of writing (known as *corpora*) can provide a useful way of checking sentence structure and word usage.

Search engines

A search engine such as Google can be a simple way to check usage of a single word or phrase. For example, if you are not sure whether you should use an infinitive form (*to* + verb) or a gerund (*-ing*) for the verb *confirm* after the main verb *expect* (37d), you can search for both *"expected confirming"* and *"expected to confirm"* in quotation marks to see which search term yields more results. A Google search for *"expected confirming"* yields many entries with a comma between the two words, indicating that one phrase ends with *expected* and another begins with *confirming*.

On the other hand, a search for *"expected to confirm"* yields many more hits than a search for *"expected confirming."* These results indicate that *expected to confirm* is the more commonly used expression. Be sure to click through a few pages of the search engine's results to make sure that most results come from ordinary sentences rather than from headlines or phrases that may be constructed differently from standard English.

Online databases (corpora)

You can also do your own analysis of academic writing using online databases such as the Corpus of Contemporary American English (COCA), which you can find in a quick online search. COCA is a free database containing more than 450 million words written between 1990 and 2012 in fiction, academic journals, magazines, newspapers, TV, and radio. The academic writing section contains articles and essays from one hundred peer-reviewed sources balanced across a range of disciplines, which allows you to make comparisons.

Suppose you want to know the answer to a question like this: *How do different writers and speakers use the first-person pronoun* I *in academic writing?* If you type *I* into the search box on the main page of COCA and select "chart" to get the results, you see a bar graph that identifies at a glance which kinds of writing use *I* the most. A search performed in 2015 identified 4.8 million uses of *I* and revealed that spoken language (from recorded sources such as radio) and fiction used *I* by far the most often—1.7 and 1.6 million times each—while academic writing used *I* least often, just 214,000 times.

COCA allows you to break down the academic writing category further to see which disciplines use *I* most. The same 2015 search found that writers in humanities disciplines use *I* more often than writers in other disciplines, while writers in the sciences, technology, and history use *I* least often. You can even look at examples of the way your search term (in this case, *I*) is used and look for patterns. Professor Laura Aull's research using COCA has found that advanced academic writers often use first-person pronouns to indicate what and how they will argue—for instance, in phrases such as *I will show* or *I argue that*. By contrast, first-year student writers and speakers most often use *I* to narrate personal experiences—for example, in phrases such as *I will never forget*.

You can also use the COCA academic section to answer questions about the use of articles (*a, an, the*), to learn how academic experts introduce sources, or to decide on preferred usage in academic writing. If you did a COCA search comparing *in regards to* with *in regard to*, you would find that COCA academic writers used *in regard to* much more often, so you would have evidence to help you make an effective choice for your own writing.

29f Make spell checkers work for you.

Research conducted for this textbook shows that spelling errors have changed dramatically in the past twenty-five years—and the reason is spell checkers. Although these programs have weeded out many once-common misspellings, they are not foolproof. Spell checkers still allow typical kinds of errors that you should look out for.

Common errors with spell checkers

- **Homonyms.** Spell checkers cannot distinguish between words such as *affect* and *effect* that sound alike but are spelled differently.

- **Proper nouns.** A spell checker cannot tell you when you have misspelled a proper name. Proofread names with special care.

- **Compound words written as two words.** Spell checkers will not see a problem if *nowhere* is incorrectly written as *no where*. When in doubt, check a dictionary.

- **Typos.** The spell checker will not flag *heat* even if you meant to type *heart*.

Spell checker use

To make spell checkers work best for you, you need to learn to adapt them to your own needs.

- Always proofread your text carefully, even after you have used the spell checker. The more important the message or document, the more careful you should be about ensuring its accuracy and clarity.

- Use a dictionary to look up any word the spell checker highlights that you are not sure of.

- If your spell checker's dictionary allows you to add new words, enter proper names, non-English words, or specialized language you use regularly and have trouble spelling. Be careful to enter the correct spelling!

- If you know that you habitually mix up certain homonyms, such as *there* and *their*, check for these words after running your spell checker.

- Remember that spell checkers are not sensitive to capitalization. If you write "the united states," the spell checker won't question it.

- Do *not* automatically accept the spell checker's suggestions: you may end up with a word you don't really want.

TALKING THE TALK

Spell Checkers and Wrong-Word Errors

"Can I trust spell checkers to correct a word I've spelled wrong?" In a word, no. The spell checker may suggest bizarre substitutes for many proper names and specialized terms (even when you spell them correctly) and for certain typographical errors, thus introducing wrong words into your paper if you accept its suggestions automatically. For example, a student who had typed *fantic* instead of *frantic* found that the spell checker's first choice was to substitute *fanatic* — a replacement that made no sense. Wrong-word errors are the most common surface error in college writing today (see Chapter 1), and spell checkers are partly to blame. So be careful not to take a spell checker's recommendation without paying careful attention to the replacement word.

FOR MULTILINGUAL WRITERS
Recognizing American Spellings

Different varieties of English often use different spelling conventions. If you have learned British or Indian English, for example, you will want to be aware of some of the more common spelling differences in American English. For example, words ending in *-yse* or *-ise* in British/Indian English (*analyse, criticise*) usually end in *-yze* or *-ize* in American English (*analyze, criticize*); words ending in *-our* in British/Indian English (*labour, colour*) usually end in *-or* in American English (*labor, color*); and words ending in *-re* in British/Indian English (*theatre, centre*) usually end in *-er* in American English (*theater, center*).

Homonyms

A relatively small number of homonyms—just eight groups—cause writers the most frequent trouble.

accept (to take or receive)
except (to leave out)

affect (an emotion; to have an influence

effect (a result; to cause to happen)

its (possessive of *it*)
it's (contraction of *it is* or *it has*)

their (possessive of *they*)
there (in that place)
they're (contraction of *they are*)

to (in the direction of)
too (in addition; excessive)
two (number between *one* and *three*)

weather (climatic conditions)
whether (if)

who's (contraction of *who is* or *who has*)
whose (possessive of *who*)

your (possessive of *you*)
you're (contraction of *you are*)

If you tend to confuse particular homonyms, try creating a special memory device to help you remember the differences. For example, "*We* all complain about the *weather*" will remind you that *weather* (the climate) starts with *we*.

In addition, pay close attention to homonyms that may be spelled as one word or two, depending on the meaning.

▶ Of course, they did not wear *everyday* clothes *every day.*

▶ Before the six lawyers were *all ready* to negotiate, it was *already* May.

▶ The director *may be* on time. But *maybe* she'll be late.

For additional advice on commonly confused words, see the glossary of usage at the end of this book.

29g   Master spelling rules.

General spelling rules can help writers enormously, but many rules have exceptions. When in doubt, consult a dictionary.

i *before* e *except after* c

Here is a slightly expanded version of the "*i* before *e*" rule:

I BEFORE *E*	ach*ie*ve, br*ie*f, f*ie*ld, fr*ie*nd
EXCEPT AFTER *C*	c*ei*ling, rec*ei*pt, perc*ei*ve
OR WHEN PRONOUNCED *AY*	*ei*ghth, n*ei*ghbor, r*ei*gn, w*ei*gh
OR IN WEIRD EXCEPTIONS	*ei*ther, for*ei*gn, h*ei*ght, l*ei*sure, n*ei*ther, s*ei*ze

Word endings (suffixes)

FINAL SILENT *E*

Drop the final silent *e* when you add an ending that starts with a vowel.

imagine + -able = imaginable   exercise + -ing = exercising

Generally, keep the final *e* if the ending starts with a consonant. Common exceptions include *argument*, *judgment*, *noticeable*, and *truly*.

force + -ful = forceful   state + -ly = stately

FINAL *Y*

When adding an ending to a word that ends in a consonant plus *y*, change the *y* to an *i* in most cases.

try, tried   busy, busily

Keep the *y* if it is part of a proper name or if the ending begins with *i*.

Kennedy, Kennedyesque   dry, drying

FINAL CONSONANTS

When adding an ending beginning with a vowel to a word that ends with a vowel and a consonant, double the final consonant if the original word is one syllable or if the accent is on the same syllable in both the original and the new word.

   stop, stopped   begin, beginner   refer, referral

Otherwise, do not double the final consonant.

   bait, baiting   start, started   refer, reference

Plurals

ADDING -S OR -ES

For most nouns, add -s. For words ending in *s*, *ch*, *sh*, *x*, or *z*, add -es instead.

   pencil, pencils   church, churches   bus, buses

In general, add -s to nouns ending in *o* if the *o* is preceded by a vowel. Add -es if the *o* is preceded by a consonant.

   rodeo, rodeos   patio, patios   potato, potatoes   hero, heroes

For some nouns ending in *f* or *fe*, change *f* to *v*, and add -s or -es.

   calf, calves   life, lives   hoof, hooves

For compound nouns written as separate or hyphenated words, make the most important part plural, whether or not it is the last part of the compound.

   lieutenant governors   brothers-in-law

For plurals of numbers and words used as terms, see 50c.

CONSIDERING DISABILITIES

Spelling

Spelling is especially difficult for people who have trouble processing letters and sounds in sequence. Technology can help: "talking pens" can scan words and read them aloud, and voice-recognition programs can transcribe dictated text.

Style

Look: wear your black some days, and
wear your purple others. There is no
other rule besides pulling it off.

— ZADIE SMITH

Style

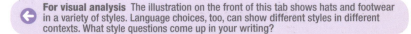

For visual analysis The illustration on the front of this tab shows hats and footwear in a variety of styles. Language choices, too, can show different styles in different contexts. What style questions come up in your writing?

Coordination, Subordination, and Emphasis   **30**

Coordination and subordination are ways of joining ideas in sentences that show relationships between ideas and emphasize more important ideas. In speech, people tend to use *and* and *so* as all-purpose connectors.

> I've requested that information for you, and I will get back in touch shortly to let you know what's going on.

If you said this sentence aloud, you could provide clues about which parts of the sentence were most important by stressing certain words and phrases and by using facial expressions and gestures to provide hints about your meaning. But if you wrote the sentence rather than saying it, your reader might not be certain what you wanted to emphasize.

By choosing subordination, you convey that one part of the sentence or the other is more important. The emphasis here is on the promise to get back in touch, not on the request that has already happened:

> Having requested that information for you, I will get back in touch shortly to let you know what's going on.

You can also use other coordinating conjunctions to clarify the relationships between equally important ideas. Notice the different impression you would give by using *but* instead of *and*:

> I've requested that information for you, but I will get back in touch shortly to let you know what's going on.

All these sentences are grammatically correct, but all of them mean slightly different things. Choosing appropriate coordination and subordination allows your meaning to come through clearly.

QUICK HELP

Editing for Coordination, Subordination, and Emphasis

How do your ideas flow from one sentence to another? Do they connect smoothly and clearly? Are the more important ideas given more emphasis than less important ones?

- Look for strings of short sentences that might be combined to join related ideas. (30a)

  ▶ The report was short/, ~~It~~ was persuasive/; ~~It~~ changed my mind.

  (with edits: "The report was short, but it was persuasive; it changed my mind.")

- If you use *and* excessively, decide whether all the ideas are equally important. If they are not equal, edit to subordinate the less important ones. (30b)

- Make sure that the most important ideas appear in independent clauses that can stand alone as complete sentences. (30b)

  ▶ *Even though the* ~~The~~ report was short, ~~even though~~ it changed my mind.

- Identify the word or words you want to receive special emphasis. If those words are buried in the middle of a sentence, edit the sentence to change their position. The end and the beginning are generally the most emphatic. (30c)

- If a sentence includes a series of three or more words, phrases, or clauses, try to arrange the items in the series in climactic order, with the most important item last. (30c)

30a Use coordination to relate equal ideas.

When used well, coordination relates separate but equal ideas. The element that links the ideas, usually a coordinating conjunction (*and, but, for, nor, or, so, yet*) or a semicolon, makes the precise relationship clear. The following sentences by N. Scott Momaday all use coordination, but the relationship between independent clauses differs in each sentence:

- ▶ They acquired horses, *and* their ancient nomadic spirit was suddenly free of the ground.

- ▶ There is perfect freedom in the mountains, *but* it belongs to the eagle and the elk, the badger and the bear.

▶ No longer were they slaves to the simple necessity of survival; they were a lordly and dangerous society of fighters and thieves, hunters and priests of the sun.

–N. Scott Momaday, *The Way to Rainy Mountain*

Momaday uses coordination in these sentences carefully in order to achieve very specific effects. In the first sentence, for example, the use of *and* gives a sense of adding on: "They acquired horses" *and*, of equal importance, "their ancient nomadic spirit was suddenly free." Momaday might have made other, equally correct choices, but they would have resulted in slightly different sentences. Compare these altered versions with Momaday's sentences. How do the changes affect your understanding?

▶ They acquired horses, *so* their ancient nomadic spirit was suddenly free of the ground.

▶ There is perfect freedom in the mountains; it belongs to the eagle and the elk, the badger and the bear.

In your own writing, think about exactly what information you want to convey with coordination. You, too, may have several correct options—so make the choice that works best for your situation and audience.

Coordination can help make explicit the relationship between two ideas.

▶ Generations have now grown up with *The Simpsons*/**;** Bart, Lisa, and
      Maggie never get older, but today's college students may have been
      watching the show since before they could talk.

Connecting these two sentences with a semicolon strengthens the connection between two closely related ideas.

When you connect ideas within a sentence, make sure the relationship between the ideas is clear.

                                                              but
▶ Surfing the Internet is a common way to spend leisure time, ~~and~~ it

   should not replace human contact.

What does a common form of leisure have to do with replacing human contact? Changing *and* to *but* better relates the two ideas.

30b   Use subordination to distinguish main ideas.

Subordination allows you to distinguish major points from minor points or to bring in supporting details. If, for instance, you put your main idea in an independent clause—words that could stand alone as a sentence (37e)—you might then put any less significant ideas in dependent clauses, phrases, or even single words. The following sentence italicizes the subordinated point:

▶ **Mrs. Viola Cullinan was a plump woman** *who lived in a three-bedroom house somewhere behind the post office.*
> – MAYA ANGELOU, "My Name Is Margaret"

The dependent clause adds important information about Mrs. Cullinan, but it is subordinate to the independent clause.

Choices about subordination

Notice that the choice of what to subordinate rests with the writer and depends on the intended meaning. Angelou might have given the same basic information differently.

▶ **Mrs. Viola Cullinan,** *a plump woman,* **lived in a three-bedroom house somewhere behind the post office.**

Subordinating the information about Mrs. Cullinan's size to that about her house would suggest a slightly different meaning, of course. When you write, think carefully about what you want to emphasize and subordinate information accordingly.

Subordination also establishes logical relationships among ideas. These relationships are often specified by relative pronouns—such as *which, who,* and *that*—and by subordinating conjunctions.

COMMON SUBORDINATING CONJUNCTIONS

after	if	though
although	in order that	unless
as	once	until
as if	since	when
because	so that	where
before	than	while
even though		

The following sentence italicizes the subordinate clause and underlines the subordinating word:

▶ She usually rested her smile until late afternoon <u>when</u> *her women friends dropped in and Miss Glory, the cook, served them cold drinks on the closed-in porch.*

— MAYA ANGELOU, "My Name Is Margaret"

Using too many coordinate structures can be monotonous and can make it hard for readers to recognize the most important ideas. Subordinating lesser ideas can help highlight the main ideas.

▶ Many people check email in the evening, and so they turn on the
computer. ~~They~~ *Though they* may intend to respond only to urgent messages, a
friend sends a link to a blog post, ~~and~~ *which* they decide to read ~~it~~ for just a
short while~~.~~/. ~~and~~ *Eventually,* they get engrossed in Facebook, and they end up

spending the whole evening in front of the screen.

▶ *Although our* ~~Our~~ new boss can be difficult, ~~although~~ she has revived and maybe

even saved the division.

The editing puts the more important information—that she has saved part of the company—in an independent clause and subordinates the rest.

Excessive subordination

When too many subordinate clauses are strung together, readers may have trouble keeping track of the main idea.

TOO MUCH SUBORDINATION

▶ Philip II sent the Spanish Armada to conquer England, which was ruled by Elizabeth, who had executed Mary because she was plotting to overthrow Elizabeth, who was a Protestant, whereas Mary and Philip were Roman Catholics.

REVISED

▶ Philip II sent the Spanish Armada to conquer England, which was ruled by Elizabeth, a Protestant. She had executed Mary, a Roman Catholic like Philip, because Mary was plotting to overthrow her.

Putting the facts about Elizabeth executing Mary into an independent clause makes key information easier to recognize.

30c   ## Use closing and opening positions for emphasis.

When you read a sentence, the part you are most likely to remember is the ending. This part of the sentence should move the writing forward by providing new information, as it does in the following example:

▶ Employers today expect college graduates to have *excellent writing skills*.

A less emphatic but still important position in a sentence is the opening, which often connects the new sentence with what has come before.

▶ Today's employers want a college-educated workforce that can communicate well. *Excellent writing skills* are high on the list of qualifications.

If you place relatively unimportant information in the memorable closing position of a sentence, you may undercut what you want to emphasize or give more emphasis to the closing words than you intend.

Last month, she   *$500,000.*
▶ She gave $500,000 to the school capital campaign last month.
  ^   ^

Moving *$500,000* to the end of the sentence emphasizes the amount.

When you arrange ideas in order of increasing importance, power, or drama, your writing builds to a climax. By saving its most dramatic item for last, the following sentence makes its point forcefully and memorably:

▶ After they've finished with the pantry, the medicine cabinet, and the attic, [neat people] will throw out the red geranium (too many leaves), sell the dog (too many fleas), and send the children off to boarding school (too many scuffmarks on the hardwood floors).
                    – SUSANNE BRITT, "Neat People vs. Sloppy People"

TALKING ABOUT STYLE

Anticlimax and Humor

Sometimes it's fun to turn the principle of climactic order upside down, opening with grand or exaggerated language only to end anti-climactically, with everyday words.

He is a writer for the ages — the ages of four to eight.
                                              – DOROTHY PARKER

Parker builds up expectations at the beginning of the sentence — only to undercut them unexpectedly by shifting the meaning of *ages*. Having led readers to expect something dramatic, she makes us laugh, or at least smile, with words that are decidedly undramatic.

Consistency and Completeness 31

In conversation, you will hear inconsistent and incomplete structures all the time. For instance, during an interview with journalist Bill Moyers, Jon Stewart discussed the supposed objectivity of news reporting.

> But news has never been objective. It's always . . . what does every newscast start with? "Our top stories tonight." That's a list. That's a subjective . . . some editor made a decision: "Here's our top stories. Number one: There's a fire in the Bronx."

Because Stewart is talking casually, some of his sentences begin one way but then move in another direction. The mixed structures pose no problem for the viewer—they sound like conversations we hear every day—but sentences such as these can be confusing in writing.

31a Revise faulty sentence structure.

One inconsistency that poses problems for writers and readers alike is a mixed structure, which results from beginning a sentence with one grammatical pattern and then switching to another one.

MIXED   The fact that I get up at 5:00 AM, a wake-up time that explains why I'm always tired in the evening.

The sentence starts out with a subject (*The fact*) followed by a dependent clause (*that I get up at 5:00 AM*). The sentence needs a predicate to complete the independent clause, but instead it moves to another phrase followed by a dependent clause (*a wake-up time that explains why I'm always tired in the evening*), and what results is a fragment.

REVISED   *The fact* that I get up at 5:00 AM *explains* why I'm always tired in the evening.

Deleting *a wake-up time that* changes the rest of the sentence into a predicate.

REVISED   *I get up* at 5:00 AM, a wake-up time that explains why I'm always tired in the evening.

Deleting *The fact that* turns the beginning of the sentence into an independent clause.

(For information about subjects and predicates, see 37b and c; for information about independent and dependent clauses, see 37e.)

31b Match up subjects and predicates.

Another kind of mixed structure, called faulty predication, occurs when a subject and predicate do not fit together grammatically or simply do not make sense together. Many cases of faulty predication result from using forms of *be* when another verb would be stronger.

▶ A characteristic that I admire is ~~a person who is generous.~~ *generosity.*

A person is not a characteristic.

▶ The rules of the corporation ~~expect~~ *require* employees to be on time.

Rules cannot expect anything.

Constructions using *is when, is where,* and *the reason . . . is because* are used frequently in informal contexts, but they may be inappropriate in academic writing because they describe a noun using an adverb clause (37e).

▶ A stereotype is ~~when someone characterizes~~ *an unfair characterization of* a group. ~~unfairly.~~

▶ A confluence is ~~where~~ *a place* two rivers join to form one.

▶ ~~The reason~~ I like to play soccer ~~is~~ because it provides aerobic exercise.

31c Use elliptical structures carefully.

Sometimes writers omit a word in a compound structure. This type of structure, known as an elliptical structure, is appropriate when the word omitted later in the compound is exactly the same as the word earlier in the compound.

> ▶ **That bell belonged to the figure of Miss Duling as though it grew directly out of her right arm, as wings grew out of an angel or a tail [grew] out of the devil.** – EUDORA WELTY, *One Writer's Beginnings*

If the omitted word does not match a word in the other part of the compound, readers might be confused, so the omission is inappropriate in formal writing.

> ▶ **His skills are weak, and his performance** *is* **only average.**

The verb *is* does not match the verb in the other part of the compound (*are*), so the writer needs to include it.

31d Check for missing words.

The best way to catch inadvertent omissions is to proofread carefully.

> ▶ **The new website makes it easier to look** *at* **and choose from the**
>
> **company's inventory.**

QUICK HELP

Editing for Consistency and Completeness

- If you find an especially confusing sentence, check to see whether it has a subject and a predicate. If not, revise as necessary. (31a) If you find both a subject and a predicate, and you are still confused, see whether the subject and verb make sense together. (31b)
- Revise any *is when*, *is where*, and *reason . . . is because* constructions. (31b)

  > ▶ **Spamming is** ~~where companies send~~ *the practice of sending* **electronic junk mail.**

- Check all comparisons for completeness. (31e)

  > ▶ **We like Lisa better than** *we like* **Margaret.**

31e   ## Make comparisons complete, consistent, and clear.

When you compare two or more things, the comparison must be complete, logically consistent, and clear.

▶ I was embarrassed because my parents were so different. *from my friends' parents.*

Different from what? Adding *from my friends' parents* tells readers what the comparison is being made with.

UNCLEAR   Aneil always felt more affection for his brother than his sister.

CLEAR   Aneil always felt more affection for his brother than his sister did.

CLEAR   Aneil always felt more affection for his brother than he did for his sister.

32   Parallelism

Parallel grammatical structures show up in many familiar phrases: *sink or swim, rise and shine, shape up or ship out*. If you look and listen for these structures, you will see parallelism in everyday use. Bumper stickers often use parallel grammatical structures to make their messages memorable (*Minds are like parachutes; both work best when open*), but the pleasing effects of parallel structures can benefit any kind of writing.

32a   ## Make items in a series parallel.

Parallelism makes a series both graceful and easy to follow.

▶ In the eighteenth century, armed forces could fight *in open fields* and *on the high seas*. Today, they can clash *on the ground anywhere, on the sea, under the sea,* and *in the air*.
     – DONALD SNOW AND EUGENE BROWN, *The Contours of Power*

> **QUICK HELP**
>
> ## Editing for Parallelism
>
> - Look for any series of three or more items, and make all of the items parallel in structure. (32a)
> - Be sure items in lists and in related headings are parallel. (32a)
> - Check for places where two ideas are paired in the same sentence. Often these ideas will appear on either side of *and*, *but*, *or*, *nor*, *for*, *so*, or *yet*, or after each part of *both . . . and*, *either . . . or*, *neither . . . nor*, *not only . . . but also*, *whether . . . or*, or *just as . . . so*. Edit to make the two ideas parallel in structure. (32b)
> - Check any parallel structures to make sure that you have included all necessary words — prepositions, the *to* of the infinitive, and so on. (32c)

The parallel phrases, as well as the parallel structure of the sentences themselves, highlight the contrast between warfare in the eighteenth century and warfare today.

In the following sentences, note how the revisions make all items in the series parallel:

► The quarter horse skipped, pranced, and ~~was sashaying.~~ *sashayed.*

► The children ran down the hill, skipped over the lawn, and *jumped* into the swimming pool.

► The duties of the job include babysitting, housecleaning, and ~~preparation of~~ *preparing* meals.

Items in a list, in a formal outline, and in headings in a writing project should be parallel.

► Kitchen rules: (1) Coffee to be made only by library staff. (2) Coffee service to be closed at 4:00 PM. (3) Doughnuts to be kept in cabinet. (4) ~~No faculty members should handle coffee materials.~~ *Coffee materials not to be handled by faculty.*

32b Make paired ideas parallel.

Parallel structures can help you pair two ideas effectively. The more nearly parallel the two structures are, the stronger the connection between the ideas will be.

▶ *History became* popular, and *historians became* alarmed.
– WILL DURANT

▶ *I type* in one place, but *I write* all over the house.
– TONI MORRISON

▶ Writers are often more interesting on the page than they are in ~~person.~~ *the flesh.*

In these examples, the parallel structures help readers see an important contrast between two ideas or acts.

Coordinating conjunctions

When you link ideas with a coordinating conjunction—*and, but, or, nor, for, so,* or *yet*—try to make the ideas parallel in structure.

▶ Consult a friend in your class or *who is* good at math.

▶ The wise politician promises the possible and ~~should accept~~ *accepts* the inevitable.

In both sentences, the editing links the two ideas by making them parallel.

Correlative conjunctions

Use the same structure after both parts of a correlative conjunction: *either . . . or, both . . . and, neither . . . nor, not . . . but, not only . . . but also, just as . . . so,* and *whether . . . or.*

▶ I wanted not only to go away to school but also to *live in* New England.

Balancing *to go* with *to live* links the two ideas and makes the sentence easier to read.

32c Include all necessary words.

In addition to making parallel elements grammatically similar, be sure to include any words—prepositions, articles, verb forms, and so on—that are necessary for clarity, grammar, or idiom.

▶ We'll move to a town in the Southwest or *in* Mexico.

To a town in Mexico or to Mexico in general? The editing makes the meaning clear.

Shifts 33

A shift in writing is an abrupt change that results in inconsistency. Sometimes a writer or speaker will shift deliberately, as linguist Geneva Smitherman does in this passage from *Word from the Mother*: "There are days when I optimistically predict that Hip Hop will survive—and thrive. . . . In the larger realm of Hip Hop culture, there is cause for optimism as we witness Hip Hop younguns tryna git they political activist game togetha."

Smitherman's shift from formal academic language to vernacular speech calls out for and holds our attention. Although writers make shifts for good rhetorical reasons, unintentional shifts in verb tenses, pronouns, and tone can be confusing to readers.

33a Revise unnecessary shifts in verb tense.

If the verbs in a passage refer to actions occurring at different times, they may require different tenses. Be careful, however, not to change tenses for no reason.

▶ A few countries produce almost all of the world's illegal drugs, but addiction *affects* ~~affected~~ many countries.

33b Revise unnecessary shifts in mood.

Be careful not to shift from one mood to another without good reason. The mood of a verb can be indicative (he *closes* the door), imperative (*close* the door), or subjunctive (if the door *were closed*) (38h).

▶ Keep your eye on the ball, and ~~you should~~ bend your knees.

33c Revise unnecessary shifts in voice.

Do not shift without reason between the active voice (she *sold* it) and the passive voice (it *was sold*). Sometimes a shift in voice is justified, but often it only confuses readers (38g).

▶ Two youths approached me/ and ~~I was~~ asked ^me^ for my wallet.

> The original sentence shifts from the active (*youths approached*) to the passive (*I was asked*), so it is unclear who asked for the wallet. Making both verbs active clears up the confusion.

33d Revise unnecessary shifts in person and number.

Unnecessary shifts in point of view among first person (*I, we*), second person (*you*), and third person (*he, she, it, they*), or between singular and plural subjects, can be very confusing to readers.

▶ ^You^ ~~Someone~~ can do well on this job if you budget your time.

> Is the writer making a general statement or giving advice? Eliminating the shift eliminates this confusion.

33e Revise shifts between direct and indirect discourse.

Multilingual

When you quote someone's exact words, you are using direct discourse: *She said, "I'm an editor."* When you report what someone says without repeating the exact words, you are using indirect discourse: *She says she is an editor.* Shifting between direct and indirect discourse in the same sentence can cause problems, especially with questions.

> QUICK HELP
>
> ## Confusing Shifts
>
> - Make sure you have a reason for shifting from one verb tense to another. (33a)
> - Revise any shifts in mood — perhaps from an indicative statement to an imperative — that are not necessary. (33b)
> - Check for shifts from active (*She asks questions*) to passive voice (*Questions are asked*). Are they intentional? (33c)
> - Make sure you have good reasons for any shifts in person or number — from *we* to *you*, for example. (33d)
> - Check your writing for consistency in tone and word choice. (33f)

         he

▶ Viet asked what ~~could he~~ do to help~~?~~.

The editing eliminates an awkward shift by reporting Viet's question indirectly. It could also be edited to quote Viet directly: *Viet asked, "What can I do to help?"*

33f Revise shifts in tone and word choice.

Tone, a writer's attitude toward a topic or audience, is related to word choice and to overall formality or informality. Watch out for tone or diction shifts that can confuse readers and leave them wondering what your real attitude is (3f).

INCONSISTENT TONE

The question of child care forces a society to make profound decisions about its economic values. Can most families with young children actually live adequately on only one salary? If some conservatives had their way, June Cleaver would still be stuck in the kitchen baking cookies for Wally and the Beaver and waiting for Ward to bring home the bacon, except that, with only one income, the Cleavers would be lucky to afford hot dogs.

In this version, the first two sentences set a serious, formal tone by discussing child care in fairly general, abstract terms. But in the third sentence, the writer shifts suddenly to sarcasm, to references to television characters of an earlier era, and to informal language like *stuck* and *bring home the bacon*. Readers cannot tell whether the writer is presenting a serious analysis or preparing for a humorous satire. The revision makes the tone consistently formal.

REVISED

The question of child care forces a society to make profound decisions about its economic values. Can most families with young children actually live adequately on only one salary? Some conservatives believe that women with young children should not work outside the home, but many mothers are forced to do so for financial reasons.

34   Conciseness

If you have a Twitter account, you know a lot about being concise—that is, about getting messages across without wasting words (Twitter limits writers to 140 characters). Recently, *New York Times* editor Bill Keller decided to start a discussion by tweeting, "Twitter makes you stupid. Discuss." That little comment drew a large number of responses, including one from his wife that read, "I don't know if Twitter makes you stupid, but it's making you late for dinner. Come home."

No matter how you feel about the effects of Twitter on the brain (or stomach!), you can make any writing more effective by using clear structures and choosing words that convey exactly what you mean to say.

34a   Eliminate unnecessary words.

Sometimes writers say that something is large *in size* or red *in color* or that two ingredients should be combined *together*. The italicized words are unnecessarily repetitive; delete such redundant words.

► ~~Compulsory attendance~~ at assemblies is required.
Attendance

► Many different forms of hazing occur, such as physical ~~abuse~~ and mental abuse.

Meaningless modifiers

Many modifiers are so overused that they have little meaning.

MEANINGLESS MODIFIERS

absolutely, awfully, definitely, fine, great, interesting, quite, really, very

---

> **QUICK HELP**
>
> ### Editing for Conciseness
>
> - Look for redundant words. If you are unsure about a certain word, read the sentence without it; if meaning is not affected, leave the word out. (34a)
> - Take out empty words — words like *aspect* or *factor*, *definitely* or *very*. (34a)
> - Replace wordy phrases with a single word. Instead of *because of the fact that*, try *because*. (34a)
> - Reconsider any sentences that begin with *it is* or *there is/are*. Unless they create special emphasis, try recasting the sentences without these words. (34b)

Wordy phrases

Wordy phrases can be reduced to a word or two with no loss in meaning.

WORDY	CONCISE
at all times	always
at that point in time	then
at the present time	now/today
due to the fact that	because
for the purpose of	for
in order to	to
in spite of the fact that	although
in the event that	if

34b   Simplify sentence structure.

Using simple grammatical structures can strengthen your sentences considerably.

▶ Hurricane Katrina, ~~which was certainly~~ one of the most powerful

storms ever to hit the Gulf Coast, caused damage*widespread*. ~~to a very wide area.~~

Deleting unnecessary words and replacing five words with one tightens the sentence and makes it easier to read.

> When ~~she was~~ questioned about her previous job, she seemed
>
> *and*
> nervous./~~She also~~ tried to change the subject.
>   ^

Combining two sentences produces one concise sentence.

There is, there are, *and* it is

Sometimes expletive constructions—*there is, there are,* and *it is*—can introduce a topic effectively; often, however, your writing will be better without them.

> *Many*
> ~~There are many~~ people ~~who~~ fear success because they believe they do
>   ^
> not deserve it.

> *Presidential*   *need*
> ~~It is necessary for presidential~~ candidates to perform well on television.
>   ^   ^

Active voice

Some writing situations call for the passive voice (38g), but it is always wordier than the active—and often makes for dull or even difficult reading.

> *Gower*
> ~~In Gower's research, it was~~ found that pythons often dwell in
>   ^
> trees.

Wordy noun forms

Forming nouns from verbs, a process sometimes called *nominalization*, can help make prose more concise—for example, using *abolition* instead of *the process of abolishing*—but it can also make a sentence wordy and hard to read.

> *assessing*
> The firm is now ~~engaged in an assessment of~~ its procedures for
>   ^
> *developing*
> ~~the development of~~ new products.
> ^

The original sentence sounds pretentious, and the noun phrases cloud the message. In contrast, the edited version is clear and forceful.

Sentence Variety   **35**

Row upon row of trees identical in size and shape may appeal to our sense of orderliness, but in spite of that appeal, the rows soon become boring. Constant uniformity in anything, in fact, soon gets tiresome. Variety is important in sentence structures because too much uniformity results in dull, listless prose. This chapter examines ways to revise sentences by creating variety in length and in openings.

35a Vary sentence length.

Is there a "just right" length for a particular sentence or idea? The answer depends partly on your purpose, intended audience, and topic. But note that after one or more long sentences with complex ideas or images, the punch of a short sentence can be refreshing.

▶ **To become a doctor, you spend so much time in the tunnels of preparation—head down, trying not to screw up, just going from one day to the next—that it is a shock to find yourself at the other end, with someone offering you a job.** *But the day comes.*

— ATUL GAWANDE, *Better*

QUICK HELP

Editing for Sentence Variety

- Count the number of words in each of your sentences. If the difference between the longest and shortest sentences is small — say, five words or fewer — try revising your sentences to create greater variety. (35a)

- If many sentences have fewer than ten words, consider whether any of them require additional detail or should be combined with other sentences.

- How do your sentences open? If all or most of them open with a subject, try recasting some sentences to begin with a transition, a phrase, or a dependent clause. (35b)

35b   Vary sentence openings.

If sentence after sentence begins with a subject, a passage may become monotonous or hard to read.

▶ The way football and basketball are played is as interesting as the
players. ~~Football~~ *Because football* is a game of precision~~.~~*/,* ~~Each~~ *each* play is diagrammed to
accomplish a certain goal. Basketball *, however,* is a game of endurance.
~~A~~ *In fact, a* basketball game looks like a track meet; the team that drops of
exhaustion first, loses. Basketball players are often compared to
artists~~.~~*/,* ~~The players'~~ *their* graceful moves and slam dunks are their
masterpieces.

The editing adds variety by using a subordinating word (*Because*) and a prepositional phrase (*In fact*) and by linking sentences. Varying sentence openings prevents the passage from seeming to jerk or lurch along.

You can add variety to your sentence openings by using transitions, various kinds of phrases, and dependent clauses.

TRANSITIONAL EXPRESSIONS

▶ *In contrast,* our approach will save time and money.

▶ *Nevertheless,* the show must go on.

▶ *However,* the report is accurate.

▶ *Additionally,* my client insists on immunity from prosecution.

PHRASES

▶ *Before dawn,* tired commuters drink their first cups of coffee.

▶ *Frustrated by the delays,* the drivers started honking their horns.

▶ *To qualify for flight training,* one must be in excellent physical condition.

▶ *Our hopes for victory dashed,* we started home.

DEPENDENT CLAUSES

▶ *What they want* is a place to call home.

▶ *Because the hills were dry,* the fire spread rapidly.

▶ *When the police appeared wearing riot gear,* the protesters stopped chanting, stared for a moment, and then scattered.

▶ *Although you may not consider a cell phone a necessity,* a homeless veteran will not be able to find a job without one.

TALKING ABOUT STYLE

Technical Writing

For some types of writing, varying sentence structure and length is not always appropriate. Many technical writers, particularly those who write manuals that will be translated into other languages, must follow stringent rules for sentence structure and length. One computer company, for example, requires writers to adhere to a strict subject-verb-object order and limit all of their sentences to no more than fifteen words. Learn the style conventions of your field as fully as possible, and then bring them to bear on your own sentence revisions.

Sentence Grammar

Most of us don't know a gerund from a gerbil and don't care, but we'd like to speak and write as though we did.

— PATRICIA T. O'CONNER

Sentence Grammar

For visual analysis The illustration on the front of this tab shows ingredients being combined into a salad—one of many possible metaphors for the way elements of language combine to form grammatical sentences. How well does this metaphor fit with your understanding of the conventions of grammar?

Parts of Speech 36

Grammatical correctness alone is not enough to ensure that a sentence is effective and artful — or that it serves an appropriate purpose in your writing. Understanding grammatical structures can, however, help you produce sentences that are appropriate and effective as well as grammatically correct. The English language includes eight different categories of words called the *parts of speech* — verbs, nouns, pronouns, adjectives, adverbs, prepositions, conjunctions, and interjections. Many English words can function as more than one part of speech. When you *book an airplane flight*, the word *book* is a verb; when you *take a good book to the beach*, it is a noun; and when you have *book knowledge*, it is an adjective.

36a Verbs

Verbs move the meaning of sentences along by showing action (*glance, speculate*), occurrence (*become, happen*), or being (*be, seem*). Verbs change form to show *time, person, number, voice,* and *mood* (Chapter 38).

TIME	we *work*, we *worked*
PERSON	I *work*, she *works*
NUMBER	one person *works*, two people *work*
VOICE	she *asks*, she *is asked*
MOOD	we *see*, if I *were to see*

Helping verbs (also called *auxiliary verbs*) combine with main verbs to create verb phrases. Auxiliaries include the forms of *be, do,* and *have*, which are also used as main verbs, and *can, could, may, might, must, shall, should, will,* and *would* (38b).

▶ I *could have danced* all night.

▶ She *would prefer* to learn Italian rather than Spanish.

▶ When *do* you *need* the spreadsheet?

36b Nouns

Nouns name persons (*aviator, child*), places (*lake, library*), things (*truck, suitcase*), or concepts (*happiness, balance*). Proper nouns, which are capitalized, name specific persons, places, things, or concepts: *Bill, Iowa, Supreme Court, Buddhism.* Collective nouns (40d) name groups: *flock, jury.*

Most nouns change from singular (one) to plural (more than one) when you add *-s* or *-es*: *horse, horses; kiss, kisses.* Some nouns, however, have irregular plural forms: *woman, women; mouse, mice; deer, deer.* Noncount nouns (39a) cannot be made plural because they name things that cannot easily be counted: *dust, peace, prosperity.*

The possessive form of a noun shows ownership. Possessive forms add an apostrophe plus *-s* to most singular nouns or just an apostrophe to most plural nouns: *the horse's owner, the boys' department.*

Nouns are often preceded by the article (or determiner) *a, an,* or *the*: *a rocket, an astronaut, the launch* (39b).

> **FOR MULTILINGUAL WRITERS**
> **Count and Noncount Nouns**
>
> Do people conduct *research* or *researches*? See 39a for a discussion of count and noncount nouns.

36c Pronouns

Pronouns often take the place of nouns or other words functioning as nouns so that you do not have to repeat words that have already been mentioned. A word or word group that a pronoun replaces or refers to is called the antecedent of the pronoun (41f).

ANTECEDENT   PRONOUN
▶ Caitlin refused the invitation even though *she* wanted to go.

Pronouns fall into several categories.

PERSONAL PRONOUNS

Personal pronouns refer to specific persons or things. Each can take several forms (*I, me, my, mine*) depending on its function in the sentence (41a).

▶ **When Keisha saw the dogs again, *she* called *them*, and *they* ran to *her*.**

POSSESSIVE PRONOUNS

Possessive pronouns (*my, mine, your, yours, her, hers, his, its, our, ours, their, theirs*) are personal pronouns that indicate ownership (41a and 50a).

▶ *My* **roommate lost *her* keys.**

REFLEXIVE PRONOUNS

Reflexive pronouns refer to the subject of the sentence or clause in which they appear. They end in *-self* or *-selves*: *myself, yourself, himself, herself, itself, oneself, ourselves, yourselves, themselves.*

▶ **The seals sunned *themselves* on the warm rocks.**

INTENSIVE PRONOUNS

Intensive pronouns have the same form as reflexive pronouns. They emphasize a noun or another pronoun.

▶ **He decided to paint the apartment *himself*.**

INDEFINITE PRONOUNS

Indefinite pronouns do not refer to specific nouns, although they may refer to identifiable persons or things. The following is a partial list:

all, another, anybody, both, each, either, everything, few, many, most, neither, none, no one, nothing, one, some, something

▶ *Everybody* **screamed, and *someone* fainted, when the lights went out.**

DEMONSTRATIVE PRONOUNS

Demonstrative pronouns (*this, that, these, those*) identify or point to specific nouns.

▶ *These* **are Peter's books.**

INTERROGATIVE PRONOUNS

Interrogative pronouns (*who, which, what*) are used to ask questions.

▶ *Who* **can help set up the chairs for the meeting?**

RELATIVE PRONOUNS

Relative pronouns (*who, which, that, what, whoever, whichever, what-ever*) introduce dependent clauses and relate the dependent clause to the rest of the sentence (37e). The interrogative pronoun *who* and the relative pronouns *who* and *whoever* have different forms depending on how they are used in a sentence (41b).

▶ **Maya,** *who* **hires interns, is the manager** *whom* **you should contact.**

RECIPROCAL PRONOUNS

Reciprocal pronouns (*each other, one another*) refer to individual parts of a plural antecedent.

▶ **The business failed because the partners distrusted** *each other.*

36d Adjectives

Adjectives modify (limit the meaning of) nouns and pronouns, usually by describing, identifying, or quantifying those words (see Chapter 42). Adjectives that identify or quantify are sometimes called *determiners* (39b).

▶ **The** *red* **Corvette ran off the road.** [describes]
▶ *That* **Corvette needs to be repaired.** [identifies]
▶ **We saw** *several other* **Corvettes race by.** [quantifies]

In addition to their basic forms, most descriptive adjectives have other forms that allow you to make comparisons: *small, smaller, small-est; foolish, more foolish, most foolish, less foolish, least foolish.*

▶ **This year's attendance was** *smaller* **than last year's.**

Adjectives usually precede the words they modify, though they may follow linking verbs: *The car was defective.* Many pronouns (36c) can function as identifying adjectives when they are followed by a noun.

▶ *That* **is a dangerous intersection.** [pronoun]
▶ *That* **intersection is dangerous.** [identifying adjective]

Other kinds of adjectives that identify or quantify are the articles *a, an,* and *the* (39b) and numbers (*three, sixty-fifth, five hundred*).

Proper adjectives, which are capitalized (53b), are formed from or relate to proper nouns (*Egyptian, Emersonian*).

36e Adverbs

Adverbs modify verbs, adjectives, other adverbs, or entire clauses (see Chapter 42). Many adverbs end in -*ly*, though some do not (*always, never, very, well*), and some words that end in -*ly* are not adverbs but adjectives (*friendly, lovely*). One of the most common adverbs is *not*.

▶ Business writers *frequently* communicate with strangers. [modifies the verb *communicate*]

▶ How can they attract customers in an *increasingly* difficult economy? [modifies the adjective *difficult*]

▶ They must work *especially* hard to avoid offending readers. [modifies the adverb *hard*]

▶ *Obviously,* they need to weigh their words with care. [modifies the independent clause that makes up the rest of the sentence]

Adverbs often answer the questions *when? where? why? how? to what extent?*

Many adverbs, like many adjectives, take different forms when making comparisons: *forcefully, more forcefully, most forcefully, less forcefully, least forcefully.*

Conjunctive adverbs modify an entire clause, and they express the connection in meaning between that clause and the preceding clause (or sentence). Common conjunctive adverbs include *however, furthermore, therefore,* and *likewise.* (See 36g.)

36f Prepositions

Prepositions express relationships—in space, time, or other senses—between nouns or pronouns and other words in a sentence.

▶ We did not want to leave *during* the game.

▶ The contestants waited nervously *for* the announcement.

A prepositional phrase (see Chapter 44) begins with a preposition and ends with the noun or pronoun it connects to the rest of the sentence.

▶ Drive *across* the bridge and go *down* the avenue *past* three stoplights.

SOME COMMON PREPOSITIONS

about	at	down	near	since
above	before	during	of	through
across	behind	except	off	toward
after	below	for	on	under
against	beneath	from	onto	until
along	beside	in	out	up
among	between	inside	over	upon
around	beyond	into	past	with
as	by	like	regarding	without

SOME COMPOUND PREPOSITIONS

according to	except for	instead of
as well as	in addition to	next to
because of	in front of	out of
by way of	in place of	with regard to
due to	in spite of	

Research for this book shows that many writers—including native speakers of English—have trouble choosing appropriate prepositions. If you are not sure which preposition to use, consult your dictionary, or use search engines or online databases to choose one (see 29e).

36g Conjunctions

Conjunctions connect words or groups of words to each other and tell something about the relationship between these words.

Coordinating conjunctions

Coordinating conjunctions (30a) join equivalent structures, such as two or more nouns, pronouns, verbs, adjectives, adverbs, prepositions, conjunctions, phrases, or clauses.

▶ A strong *but* warm breeze blew across the desert.

▶ Please print *or* type the information on the application form.

▶ Taiwo worked two shifts today, *so* she is tired tonight.

COORDINATING CONJUNCTIONS

and	but	for	nor	or	so	yet

Correlative conjunctions

Correlative conjunctions join equal elements, and they come in pairs.

▶ *Both* **Bechtel** *and* **Kaiser submitted bids on the project.**

▶ **Maisha** *not only* **sent a card** *but also* **visited me in the hospital.**

CORRELATIVE CONJUNCTIONS

both . . . and	just as . . . so	not only . . . but also
either . . . or	neither . . . nor	whether . . . or

Subordinating conjunctions

Subordinating conjunctions (30b) introduce adverb clauses and signal the relationship between the adverb clause and another clause, usually an independent clause. For instance, in the following sentence, the subordinating conjunction *while* signals a time relationship, letting us know that the two events in the sentence happened simultaneously:

▶ **Sweat ran down my face** *while* **I frantically searched for my child.**

SOME COMMON SUBORDINATING CONJUNCTIONS

after	if	unless
although	in order that	until
as	once	when
as if	since	where
because	so that	whether
before	than	while
even though	that	who
how	though	why

Conjunctive adverbs

Conjunctive adverbs connect independent clauses and often act as transitional expressions (47e) that show how the second clause relates to the first clause. As their name suggests, conjunctive adverbs can act as both adverbs and conjunctions because they modify the second clause in addition to connecting it to the preceding clause.

▶ **The cider tasted bitter;** *however,* **each of us drank a tall glass of it.**

▶ **The cider tasted bitter; each of us,** *however,* **drank a tall glass of it.**

SOME CONJUNCTIVE ADVERBS

also	however	moreover	similarly
anyway	incidentally	namely	still
besides	indeed	nevertheless	then
certainly	instead	next	therefore
finally	likewise	now	thus
furthermore	meanwhile	otherwise	undoubtedly

36h Interjections

Interjections express surprise or emotion: *oh, ouch, hey*. Interjections often stand alone. Even when they are included in a sentence, they do not relate grammatically to the rest of the sentence.

▶ *Hey*, **no one suggested that we would find an easy solution to this problem.**

37   Parts of Sentences

The grammar of your first language comes to you almost automatically. Listen in on a conversation between two four-year-olds:

AUDREY: My new bike that Aunt A got me has a red basket and a loud horn, and I love it.

LILA: Can I ride it?

AUDREY: Yes, as soon as I take a turn.

This simple conversation features sophisticated grammar—the subordination of one clause to another, a compound object, and a number of adjectives—used effortlessly. If you are like many English speakers, you may never really have reflected on the details of how the language works. Paying close attention to how you put sentences together can help you understand the choices available to you whenever you write.

37a The basic grammar of sentences

A sentence is a grammatically complete group of words that expresses a thought. Words in a sentence can be identified by parts of speech (see Chapter 36), but you should also understand how words and phrases function in sentences.

Subjects and predicates

To be grammatically complete, a sentence must contain both a subject, which identifies what the sentence is about, and a predicate, which says or asks something about the subject or tells the subject to do something.

SUBJECT	PREDICATE
I	have a dream.
The rain in Spain	stays mainly in the plain.
Her skill as an archer	makes her a formidable opponent.

TALKING THE TALK

Understanding Grammatical Terms

"I never learned any grammar." You may lack *conscious* knowledge of grammar and grammatical terms (and if so, you are not alone — American students today rarely study English grammar). But you probably understand the ideas that grammatical terms such as *auxiliary verb* and *direct object* represent, even if the terms themselves are unfamiliar. Brushing up on the terms commonly used to talk about grammar will make it easier for you and your instructor — as well as other readers and reviewers — to share a common language when you discuss the best ways to get your ideas across clearly and with few distractions.

Some sentences contain only a one-word predicate with an implied subject; for example, *Stop!* is a complete sentence, with the unspoken subject *you*. Most sentences, however, contain some words that expand upon the basic subject and predicate.

The central elements of subjects and predicates are nouns (36b) and verbs (36a).

SUBJECT ┐ ┌── PREDICATE ──┐
　　　　NOUN   VERB
▶ A solitary **figure** **waited** on the platform.

┌── SUBJECT ──┐ ┌── PREDICATE ──┐
　NOUN　　　　　　VERB
▶ Her **skill** as an archer **makes** her a formidable opponent.

Conventional English word order

Multilingual

In general, subjects, verbs, and objects must all be placed in specific positions within a sentence.

SUBJECT VERB OBJECT   ADVERB
▶ Mario left Venice reluctantly.

The only word in this sentence that you can move is the adverb *reluctantly* (*Mario reluctantly left Venice* or *Reluctantly, Mario left Venice*). The three key elements of subject, verb, and object rarely move out of their normal order.

QUICK HELP

Basic Sentence Patterns

1. Subject / verb
   ┌─ S ─┐┌ V ┐
   ▶ **Babies drool.**

2. Subject / verb / subject complement
   ┌─ S ─┐┌ V ┐┌ SC ┐
   ▶ **Babies smell sweet.**

3. Subject / verb / direct object
   ┌─ S ─┐┌ V ┐┌ DO ┐
   ▶ **Babies drink milk.**

4. Subject / verb / indirect object / direct object
   ┌─ S ─┐┌ V ┐┌── IO ──┐┌─ DO ─┐
   ▶ **Babies give grandparents pleasure.**

5. Subject / verb / direct object / object complement
   ┌─ S ─┐┌ V ┐┌ DO ┐┌ OC ┐
   ▶ **Babies keep parents awake.**

Sentence patterns

Knowing a word's part of speech (see Chapter 36) helps you understand how to use it, but you also have to look at the part it plays in a particular sentence. In the following sentences, the noun *description* plays different roles:

> SUBJECT
> ▶ This *description* conveys the ecology of the Everglades.

> DIRECT OBJECT
> ▶ I read a *description* of the ecology of the Everglades.

In the first sentence, *description* serves as the subject of the verb *conveys*, while in the second it serves as the direct object of the verb *read*.

37b Subjects

The subject of a sentence identifies what the sentence is about. The simple subject consists of one or more nouns (36b) or pronouns (36c); the complete subject consists of the simple subject with all its modifiers.

> ▶ **Baseball** is a summer game.

> ┌────── COMPLETE SUBJECT ──────┐
> ▶ Sailing over the fence, the **ball** crashed through Mr. Wilson's window.

> ┌────── COMPLETE SUBJECT ──────┐
> ▶ **Those** who sit in the bleachers have the most fun.

A compound subject contains two or more simple subjects joined with a coordinating conjunction (*and, but, or*) or a correlative conjunction (*both…and, either…or, neither…nor, not only…but also*). (See 36g.)

> ▶ **Baseball** *and* **softball** developed from cricket.
> ▶ Both **baseball** *and* **softball** developed from cricket.

Subject positions

The subject usually comes before the predicate (37a), but sometimes writers reverse this order to achieve a particular effect.

> ▶ Up to the plate stepped *Casey*.

In questions, the subject appears between the helping verb and the main verb.

▶ **Can** *statistics* **lie?**

▶ **How did the** *manager* **turn these players into a winning team?**

In sentences beginning with *there* or *here* followed by a form of the verb *be*, the subject always follows the verb. *There* and *here* are never the subject.

▶ **There was no** *joy* **in Mudville.**

Explicit subjects

Multilingual

While many languages can omit a sentence subject, English very rarely allows this. You might write *Responsible for analyzing data* on a résumé, but in most varieties of spoken and written English, you must state the subject explicitly. In fact, with only a few exceptions, all clauses in English must have an explicit subject.

it
▶ **They took the Acela Express to Boston because was fast.**

English even requires a kind of "dummy" subject to fill the subject position in certain kinds of sentences.

▶ *It* **is raining.**

▶ *There* **is a strong wind.**

Imperative sentences (37f), which express requests or commands, are an exception to the rule of explicit subjects; the subject *you* is usually implied rather than stated.

▶ *(You)* **Keep your eye on the ball.**

37c   Predicates

In addition to a subject, every sentence has a predicate, which asserts or asks something about the subject or tells the subject to do something. The key word of most predicates is a verb. The simple predicate of a sentence consists of the main verb and any auxiliaries; the complete predicate includes the simple predicate and any modifiers of the verb and any objects or complements (37a) and their modifiers.

┌────── COMPLETE PREDICATE ──────┐
▶ **Both of us are planning to major in history.**

A compound predicate contains two or more verbs that have the same subject, usually joined by a coordinating or a correlative conjunction (36g).

▶ Omar shut the book, put it back on the shelf, *and* sighed.

On the basis of how they function in predicates, verbs can be divided into three categories: linking, transitive, and intransitive.

Linking verbs

A linking verb connects a subject with a subject complement (SC), a word or word group that identifies or describes the subject.

      S   V   ┌──── SC ────┐
▶ Christine *is* an excellent teacher.

     S V SC
▶ She *is* patient.

A subject complement can be either a noun or pronoun (*teacher*) or an adjective (*patient*).

The forms of *be*, when used as main verbs, are common linking verbs. Other verbs, such as *appear, become, feel, grow, look, make, seem, smell,* and *sound,* can also function as linking verbs, depending on the sense of the sentence.

┌──── S ────┐ V   SC
▶ The neighborhood *looked* prosperous.

Transitive verbs

Multilingual

A transitive verb expresses action that is directed toward a noun or pronoun called the *direct object* (DO).

    S   V ┌──── DO ────┐
▶ He *peeled* all the rutabagas.

Here, the subject and verb do not express a complete thought. The direct object completes the thought by saying *what* he peeled.

A direct object may be followed by an object complement (OC), a word or word group that describes or identifies the direct object. Object complements may be adjectives, as in the first example below, or nouns, as in the second example.

 S V ┌──────── DO ────────┐┌──── OC ────┐
▶ I *find* cell-phone conversations in restaurants very annoying.

   S   V   DO ┌──── OC ────┐
▶ Alana *considers* Keyshawn her best friend.

Some transitive verbs may also be followed by an indirect object (IO), which is the recipient of the direct object. The indirect object tells to whom or what, or for whom or what, the verb does its action.

> ┌─────── S ───────┐ V IO ┌─────── DO ───────┐
> ▶ **The sound of the traffic** *gave* **me a splitting headache.**

Transitive verbs typically require you to state the object explicitly. For example, you can't just say *Give!* even if it is clear that you mean *Give me the phone.*

Intransitive verbs

Multilingual

An intransitive verb does not have a direct object.

> ┌── S ──┐   V
> ▶ **The Red Sox** *persevered.*

> ┌── S ──┐   V
> ▶ **Their fans** *watched* **anxiously.**

The verb *persevered* has no object (it makes no sense to ask, *persevered what?*), and the verb *watched* is directed toward an object that is implied but not expressed.

Some verbs that express action can be only transitive or only intransitive, but most can be used either way, with or without a direct object.

> ┌── S ──┐ V   ┌─ DO ─┐
> ▶ **The butler** *opened* **the door.** [transitive]

> ┌── S ──┐   V
> ▶ **The door** *opened* **silently.** [intransitive]

37d Phrases

A phrase is a group of words that lacks a subject or a predicate or both.

Noun phrases

Made up of a noun and all its modifiers, a noun phrase can function in a sentence as a subject, object, or complement.

> ┌──────── SUBJECT ────────┐
> ▶ *Delicious, gooey peanut butter* **is surprisingly healthful.**

> ┌──────────── OBJECT ────────────┐
> ▶ **I craved** *a green salad with plenty of fresh vegetables.*

> ┌ COMPLEMENT ┐
> ▶ **Soup is** *a popular lunch.*

Verb phrases

A main verb and its auxiliary verbs make up a verb phrase, which can function in a sentence only as a verb.

▶ Frank *can swim* for a long time.

▶ His headaches *might have been caused* by tension.

Prepositional phrases

A prepositional phrase begins with a preposition and includes a noun or pronoun (the object of the preposition) and any modifiers of the object. Prepositional phrases usually function as adjectives or adverbs.

              ADJECTIVE
▶ Our house *in Maine* was a cabin.

          ADVERB
▶ *From Cadillac Mountain*, you can see the northern lights.

Verbal phrases

Verbals look like verbs, but they function as nouns, adjectives, or adverbs. There are three kinds of verbals: participles, gerunds, and infinitives.

PARTICIPLES AND PARTICIPIAL PHRASES

The present participle is the *-ing* form of a verb (*spinning*). The past participle of most verbs ends in *-ed* (*accepted*), but some verbs have an irregular past participle (*worn*, *frozen*). Participles function as adjectives (42a).

▶ A kiss awakened the *dreaming* princess.

▶ The cryptographers deciphered the *hidden* meaning in the

message.

Participial phrases, which also act as adjectives, consist of a present or past participle and any modifiers, objects, or complements.

▶ *Irritated by the delay*, Luisa complained.

▶ A dog *howling at the moon* kept me awake.

GERUNDS AND GERUND PHRASES

The gerund has the same *-ing* form as the present participle but functions as a noun.

> SUBJECT
> ▶ *Writing* takes practice.

> DIRECT OBJECT
> ▶ The organization promotes *recycling.*

Gerund phrases, which function as nouns, consist of a gerund and any modifiers, objects, or complements.

> ┌──────── SUBJECT ────────┐
> ▶ *Opening their eyes to the problem* was not easy.

> ┌──────── DIRECT OBJECT ────────┐
> ▶ They suddenly heard *a loud wailing from the sandbox.*

INFINITIVES AND INFINITIVE PHRASES

The infinitive is the *to* form of a verb (*to dream*, *to be*). An infinitive can function as a noun, an adjective, or an adverb.

> ┌ NOUN ┐
> ▶ She wanted *to write.*

> ADJECTIVE
> ▶ They had no more time *to waste.*

> ADVERB
> ▶ The corporation was ready *to expand.*

Infinitive phrases consist of an infinitive and any modifiers, objects, or complements. Like infinitives, they function as nouns, adjectives, or adverbs.

> ┌──────── NOUN ────────┐
> ▶ My goal is *to be a biology teacher.*

> ┌──────── ADJECTIVE ────────┐
> ▶ A party *to end the semester* would be a good idea.

> ┌──────── ADVERB ────────┐
> ▶ *To perfect a draft,* always proofread carefully.

INFINITIVE-GERUND CONFUSION

Multilingual

In general, infinitives tend to indicate intentions, desires, or expectations, and gerunds tend to indicate facts. Knowing whether to use an infinitive or a gerund in a sentence can be a challenge for many students.

INFINITIVES TO STATE INTENTIONS

▶ Kumar *expected to get* a good job after graduation.
▶ Last year, Fatima *decided to change* her major.
▶ The strikers have *refused to go* back to work.

Verbs such as *expect*, *decide*, and *refuse*, which indicate intentions, must always be followed by an infinitive.

GERUNDS TO STATE FACTS

▶ Jerzy *enjoys going* to the theater.
▶ We *resumed working* after our coffee break.
▶ Kim *appreciated getting* a card from Sean.

Verbs like *enjoy*, *resume*, and *appreciate*, which indicate that something has actually happened, can be followed only by gerunds, not by infinitives.

OTHER RULES AND GUIDELINES

A few verbs can be followed by either an infinitive or a gerund. With some, such as *begin* and *continue*, the choice doesn't affect the meaning. With others, however, the difference is important.

▶ Carlos was working as a medical technician, but he *stopped to study* English.

The infinitive shows that Carlos quit because he intended to study English.

▶ When Carlos left the United States, he *stopped studying* English.

The gerund indicates that Carlos gave up his English studies when he left.

You can use only a gerund—never an infinitive—right after a preposition.

▶ This fruit is safe for ~~to eat.~~ *eating.*

▶ This fruit is safe ~~for~~ to eat.

▶ This fruit is safe for *us* to eat.

Consult a learner's dictionary for more information on whether to follow a verb with an infinitive or a gerund.

Absolute phrases

An absolute phrase usually includes a noun or pronoun and a participle. It modifies an entire sentence rather than a particular word and is usually set off from the rest of the sentence with commas (47c).

▶ I stood on the deck, *the wind whipping my hair.*

▶ *My fears laid to rest,* I set off on my first solo flight.

Appositive phrases

An appositive phrase is a noun phrase that renames the noun or pronoun that immediately precedes it (47c).

▶ The report, *a hefty three-volume work,* included more than ninety recommendations.

▶ We had a single desire, *to change the administration's policies.*

37e Clauses

A clause is a group of words containing a subject and a predicate. There are two kinds of clauses: independent and dependent. Independent clauses (also known as main clauses) can stand alone as complete sentences.

▶ The window is open.

Pairs of independent clauses may be joined with a comma and a coordinating conjunction (*and, but, for, nor, or, so, yet*).

▶ The window is open, so the room feels cool.

Like independent clauses, dependent clauses (also referred to as subordinate clauses) contain a subject and a predicate. They cannot stand alone as complete sentences, however, for they begin with a subordinating word—a subordinating conjunction (36g) or a relative pronoun (36c)—that connects them to an independent clause.

▶ Because the window is open, the room feels cool.

The subordinating conjunction *because* transforms the independent clause *the window is open* into a dependent clause. In doing so, it indicates a causal relationship between the two clauses.

Dependent clauses function as nouns, adjectives, or adverbs.

Noun clauses

Multilingual

Noun clauses are always contained within another clause. They usually begin with a relative pronoun (*that, which, what, who, whom, whose, whatever, whoever, whomever, whichever*) or with *when, where, whether, why,* or *how.*

▶ ⎡——— SUBJECT ———⎤
What the archeologists found was startling.

▶ ⎡——— DIRECT OBJECT ———⎤
She explained *that the research was necessary.*

▶ ⎡——— SUBJECT COMPLEMENT ———⎤
The mystery was *why the ancient city had been abandoned.*

▶ ⎡——— OBJECT OF PREPOSITION ———⎤
They were looking for *whatever information was available.*

Like a noun, a noun clause is an integral part of the sentence; for example, in the second sentence the independent clause is not just *She explained* but *She explained that the research was necessary.* This complex sentence is built out of two sentences; one of them (*The research was necessary*) is embedded in the other (*She explained [something]*). The relative pronoun *that* introduces the noun clause that is the object of *explained.*

A *that* clause can serve as the subject of a sentence, but the effect is very formal.

▶ ⎡——— SUBJECT ———⎤
That the city had been abandoned was surprising.

In less formal contexts, and in spoken English, a long noun clause is usually moved to the end of the sentence and replaced with the "dummy subject" *it.*

▶ *It* was surprising *that the city had been abandoned.*

Adjective clauses

Multilingual

Adjective clauses modify nouns and pronouns in another clause. Usually, they immediately follow the words they modify.

▶ The surgery, *which took three hours,* was a complete success.

▶ It was performed by the surgeon *who had developed the procedure.*

▶ The hospital was the one *where I was born.*

Sometimes the relative pronoun introducing an adjective clause may be omitted, as in the following examples:

▶ **That is one book** [*that*] *I intend to read.*

▶ **The company** [*that*] *the family had invested in* **grew rapidly.**

To see how the adjective clause fits into this sentence, rewrite it as two sentences: *The company grew rapidly. The family had invested in it.* To make *The family had invested in it* a relative clause, change it to a relative pronoun and move it to the beginning of the clause: *The family had invested in it* becomes *that the family had invested in.* Then position the new clause after the word it describes (in this case, *company*): *The company that the family had invested in grew rapidly.*

In very formal writing, when the pronoun you are changing is the object of a preposition, select *which* (or *whom* for people) and move the whole prepositional phrase to the beginning of the clause: *The company in which the family had invested grew rapidly.* In many American English contexts, however, such constructions may sound too formal, so consider your audience carefully.

Adverb clauses

Adverb clauses modify verbs, adjectives, or other adverbs. They begin with a subordinating conjunction (36g). Like adverbs, they usually tell when, where, why, how, or to what extent.

▶ **We hiked** *where few other hikers went.*

▶ **My backpack felt heavier** *than it ever had.*

▶ **Climbers ascend Mount Everest** *because it is there.*

37f Types of sentences

Like words, sentences can be categorized both grammatically and functionally.

Grammatical sentence structure

Grammatically, sentences may be simple, compound, complex, or compound-complex.

SIMPLE SENTENCES

A simple sentence consists of one <mark>independent clause</mark> and no dependent clause. The subject or the verb, or both, may be compound.

┌──────────── INDEPENDENT CLAUSE ────────────┐
▶ **The trailer is surrounded by a wooden deck.**

┌──────────────── INDEPENDENT CLAUSE ────────────────┐
▶ **Pompeii and Herculaneum disappeared under tons of lava and ash.**

COMPOUND SENTENCES

A compound sentence consists of two or more <mark>independent clauses</mark> and no dependent clause. The clauses may be joined by a comma and a coordinating conjunction (36g) or by a semicolon.

┌──────── INDEPENDENT CLAUSE ────────┐ ┌ INDEPENDENT CLAUSE ┐
▶ **Occasionally a car goes up the dirt trail, and dust flies everywhere.**

┌────── INDEPENDENT CLAUSE ──────┐ ┌──────── INDEPENDENT CLAUSE ────────┐
▶ **Alberto is obsessed with soccer; he eats, breathes, and lives the game.**

COMPLEX SENTENCES

A complex sentence consists of one <mark>independent clause</mark> and at least one <mark>dependent clause</mark>.

┌ INDEPENDENT CLAUSE ┐┌──── DEPENDENT CLAUSE ────┐
▶ **Many people believe that anyone can earn a living.**

┌──── DEPENDENT CLAUSE ────┐ ┌──── INDEPENDENT CLAUSE ────┐
▶ **As I awaited my interview, I sat with another candidate**

┌── DEPENDENT CLAUSE ──┐
who smiled nervously.

COMPOUND-COMPLEX SENTENCES

A compound-complex sentence consists of two or more independent clauses and at least one dependent clause.

INDEPENDENT CLAUSE ┌── DEPENDENT CLAUSE ──┐ INDEPENDENT CLAUSE
▶ **I complimented Luis when he finished the job, and he seemed pleased.**

┌──── INDEPENDENT CLAUSE ────┐ ┌──── INDEPENDENT CLAUSE ────┐
▶ **The actors performed well, but the audience hated the play,**

┌──────── DEPENDENT CLAUSE ────────┐
which was confusing and far too long.

Sentence function

In terms of function, sentences can be declarative (making a statement), interrogative (asking a question), imperative (giving a command), or exclamatory (expressing strong feeling).

DECLARATIVE	He sings with the Grace Church Boys' Choir.
INTERROGATIVE	How long has he sung with them?
IMPERATIVE	Comb his hair before the performance starts.
EXCLAMATORY	What voices those boys have!

38 Verbs and Verb Phrases

R estaurant menus often spotlight verbs in action. One famous place in Boston, for instance, offers to bake, broil, pan-fry, deep-fry, poach, sauté, fricassée, blacken, or scallop any of the fish entrées on its menu. To someone ordering—or cooking—at this restaurant, the important distinctions lie entirely in the verbs.

When used skillfully, verbs can be the heartbeat of prose, moving it along, enlivening it, carrying its action. (See Chapter 40 for advice on subject-verb agreement.)

38a Understand the five forms of verbs.

Except for *be*, all English verbs have five forms.

BASE FORM	PAST TENSE	PAST PARTICIPLE	PRESENT PARTICIPLE	-S FORM
talk	talked	talked	talking	talks
adore	adored	adored	adoring	adores

BASE FORM	We often *go* to Legal Sea Foods.
PAST TENSE	Grandpa always *ordered* bluefish.
PAST PARTICIPLE	Grandma *has tried* the oyster stew.
PRESENT PARTICIPLE	Juanita *is getting* the shrimp platter.
-S FORM	The chowder *needs* salt and pepper.

> **QUICK HELP**
>
> ## Editing the Verbs in Your Own Writing
>
> - Check verb endings that cause you trouble. (38a and c)
> - Double-check forms of *lie* and *lay*, *sit* and *set*, *rise* and *raise*. See that the words you use are appropriate for your meaning. (38d)
> - If you are writing about a literary work, remember to refer to the action in the work in the present tense. (38e)
> - If you have problems with verb tenses, use the guidelines in 38e to check your verbs.
> - Check all uses of the passive voice for appropriateness. (38g)
> - Check all verbs used to introduce quotations, paraphrases, and summaries. (15b) If you rely on *say*, *write*, and other very general verbs, try substituting more vivid, specific verbs (*claim*, *insist*, and *wonder*, for instance).

-s *and* -es *endings*

Except with *be* and *have*, the *-s* form consists of the base form plus *-s* or *-es*. In standard English, this form indicates action in the present for third-person singular subjects. All singular nouns; the personal pronouns *he*, *she*, and *it*; and many other pronouns (such as *this*, *anyone*, *everything*, and *someone*) are third-person singular.

	SINGULAR	PLURAL
FIRST PERSON	I wish	we wish
SECOND PERSON	you wish	you wish
THIRD PERSON	he/she/it *wishes*	they wish
	Joe *wishes*	children wish
	someone *wishes*	many wish

Forms of be

Be has three forms in the present tense and two in the past tense.

BASE FORM	be
PAST PARTICIPLE	been
PRESENT PARTICIPLE	being
PRESENT TENSE	I *am*, he/she/it *is*, we/you/they *are*
PAST TENSE	I/he/she/it *was*, we/you/they *were*

TALKING ABOUT STYLE

Everyday Use of *Be*

Spoken varieties of English may follow rules for the use of *be* that differ from the rules of most academic English. For instance, you may have heard speakers say "She ain't here now" (instead of *She isn't here now*) or "He be at work every Saturday" (instead of *He is at work every Saturday*). You may sometimes want to quote dialogue featuring such spoken usages when you write or to use what linguists refer to as "habitual *be*" in writing to particular audiences. In most academic and professional writing, however, you will want to follow the conventions of academic English. (For help on using varieties of English appropriately, see Chapter 28.)

38b Form verb phrases appropriately.

English sentences must have at least one verb or verb phrase that is not simply an infinitive (*to write*), a gerund (*writing*), or a participle (*written*) without any helping verbs. Use helping (also called *auxiliary*) verbs with a main verb—a base form, present participle, or past participle—to create verb phrases.

The most common auxiliaries are forms of *be*, *have*, and *do*. *Have* is used to form perfect tenses that indicate completed action (38e); *be* is used with progressive forms that show continuing action (38e) and to form the passive voice (38g).

▶ **The engineers** *have considered* **possible problems.** [completed action]

▶ **The college** *is building* **a new dormitory.** [continuing action]

▶ **The activists** *were warned* **to stay away.** [passive voice]

As an auxiliary, *do* is used to show emphasis, to form questions, and to make negative statements.

▶ **I** *do respect* **my opponent's viewpoint.** [emphasis]

▶ *Do* **you** *know* **the answer?** [question]

▶ **He** *does* **not** *like* **wearing a tie.** [negative statement]

Helping (auxiliary) verb order

Multilingual

Verb phrases can be built up out of a main verb and one or more auxiliaries.

▶ **Immigration figures** *have been rising* **every year.**

Verb phrases have strict rules of order. The only permissible change to word order is to form a question, moving the first auxiliary to the beginning of the sentence: *Have immigration figures been rising every year?*

When two or more auxiliaries appear in a verb phrase, they must follow a particular order based on the type of auxiliary:

1. A modal (*can, could, may, might, must, shall, should, will, would,* or *ought to*)
2. A form of *have* used to indicate a perfect tense (38e)
3. A form of *be* used to indicate a progressive tense (38e)
4. A form of *be* used to indicate the passive voice, followed by a past participle (38g)

Very few sentences include all four kinds of auxiliaries.

	Modal	Perfect *Have*	Progressive *Be*	Passive *Be*	Main Verb	
Sonia	—	has	—	been	invited	to visit Prague.
Her arrange-ments	will	—	—	be	made	by the relatives.
The invitation	must	have	—	been	sent	in the spring.
She	—	has	been	—	studying	Czech.
She	may	—	be	—	feeling	nervous.
She	might	have	been	—	expecting	to travel elsewhere.
The trip	will	have	been	being	planned	for months by the time she leaves.

Modals

Multilingual

The modal auxiliaries—*can, could, may, might, shall, should, will, would, must,* and *ought to*—indicate future action, possibility, necessity, or obligation.

▶ They *will explain* the procedure. [future action]
▶ You *can see* three states from the top of the mountain. [possibility]

▶ Students *must manage* their time wisely. [necessity]
▶ They *should examine* the results of the study. [obligation]

No verb phrase can include more than one modal.

▶ She will ~~can~~ speak Czech much better soon.
 be able to

USING MODALS FOR REQUESTS OR INSTRUCTIONS

Modals are often used in requests and instructions. If you use a modal such as *could* or *would*, you are politely acknowledging that the person you are talking to may be unable or unwilling to do what you ask.

▶ *Could* you bring me a pillow?

Modals appearing in instructions usually indicate whether an action is suggested or required:

1. You *can* / You *may* post your work online. [Posting online is allowed.]
2. You *should* submit your report electronically. [Posting online is recommended or required.]
3. You *must* / You *will* submit your report electronically. [Posting online is required.]

USING MODALS TO SHOW DOUBT OR CERTAINTY

Modals can also indicate how confident the writer is about his or her claims. Using *may* or *might* results in a tentative suggestion, while *will* indicates complete confidence:

▶ The study *might help explain* the findings of previous research.
▶ The study *will help explain* the findings of previous research.

Phrases with modals

Multilingual

Use the base form of a verb after a modal.

▶ Alice *can read* Latin.
▶ Sanjay *should have studied* for the test.

In many other languages, modals such as *can* and *must* are followed by an infinitive (*to* + base form). In English, only the base form follows a modal.

▶ Alice can ~~to~~ read Latin.

Notice that a modal auxiliary never changes form to agree with the subject.

For the most part, modals refer to present or future time. When you want to use a modal to refer to the past, you follow the modal with a perfect form of the main verb (see 38e).

▶ If you have a fever, you *should see* a doctor.

▶ If you had a fever, you *should have seen* a doctor.

The modal *must* is a special case. The past tense of *must* is *had to* or *needed to.*

▶ You *must renew* your visa by the end of this week.

▶ You *had to renew* / You *needed to renew* your visa by last Friday.

Note, too, the different meanings of the negative forms *must not* and *don't have to.*

▶ You *must not go* to the party. [You are forbidden to go.]

▶ You *don't have to go* to the party. [You are not required to go, but you may.]

38c   Use appropriate forms of irregular verbs.

A verb is regular when its past tense and past participle are formed by adding *-ed* or *-d* to the base form.

BASE FORM	PAST TENSE	PAST PARTICIPLE
love	loved	loved
honor	honored	honored
obey	obeyed	obeyed

A verb is irregular when it does not follow the *-ed* or *-d* pattern. If you are not sure whether a verb form is regular or irregular, or what the correct form is, consult the following list or a dictionary. Dictionaries list any irregular forms under the entry for the base form.

Some common irregular verbs

BASE FORM	PAST TENSE	PAST PARTICIPLE
arise	arose	arisen
be	was/were	been
beat	beat	beaten
become	became	become
begin	began	begun

BASE FORM	PAST TENSE	PAST PARTICIPLE
bite	bit	bitten, bit
blow	blew	blown
break	broke	broken
bring	brought	brought
broadcast	broadcast	broadcast
build	built	built
burn	burned, burnt	burned, burnt
burst	burst	burst
buy	bought	bought
catch	caught	caught
choose	chose	chosen
come	came	come
cost	cost	cost
dig	dug	dug
dive	dived, dove	dived
do	did	done
draw	drew	drawn
dream	dreamed, dreamt	dreamed, dreamt
drink	drank	drunk
drive	drove	driven
eat	ate	eaten
fall	fell	fallen
feel	felt	felt
fight	fought	fought
find	found	found
fly	flew	flown
forget	forgot	forgotten, forgot
freeze	froze	frozen
get	got	gotten, got
give	gave	given
go	went	gone
grow	grew	grown
hang (suspend)[1]	hung	hung
have	had	had

---

[1]*Hang* meaning "execute by hanging" is regular: *hang, hanged, hanged.*

BASE FORM	PAST TENSE	PAST PARTICIPLE
hear	heard	heard
hide	hid	hidden
hit	hit	hit
keep	kept	kept
know	knew	known
lay	laid	laid
lead	led	led
leave	left	left
lend	lent	lent
let	let	let
lie (recline)²	lay	lain
lose	lost	lost
make	made	made
mean	meant	meant
meet	met	met
prove	proved	proved, proven
put	put	put
read	read	read
ride	rode	ridden
ring	rang	rung
rise	rose	risen
run	ran	run
say	said	said
see	saw	scen
send	sent	sent
set	set	set
shake	shook	shaken
shoot	shot	shot
show	showed	showed, shown
shrink	shrank	shrunk
sing	sang	sung
sink	sank	sunk
sit	sat	sat
sleep	slept	slept

²*Lie* meaning "tell a falsehood" is regular: *lie, lied, lied.*

BASE FORM	PAST TENSE	PAST PARTICIPLE
speak	spoke	spoken
spend	spent	spent
spring	sprang, sprung	sprung
stand	stood	stood
steal	stole	stolen
strike	struck	struck, stricken
swim	swam	swum
swing	swung	swung
take	took	taken
tear	tore	torn
throw	threw	thrown
wake	woke, waked	waked, woken
wear	wore	worn
write	wrote	written

38d Choose between *lie* and *lay*, *sit* and *set*, *rise* and *raise*.

These pairs of verbs cause confusion because both verbs in each pair have similar-sounding forms and related meanings. In each pair, one of the verbs is transitive, meaning that it is followed by a direct object (*I laid the cloth on the table*). The other is intransitive, meaning that it does not have an object (*He lay on the floor when his back ached*). The best way to avoid confusing these verbs is to memorize their forms and meanings.

BASE FORM	PAST TENSE	PAST PARTICIPLE	PRESENT PARTICIPLE	-S FORM
lie (recline)	lay	lain	lying	lies
lay (put)	laid	laid	laying	lays
sit (be seated)	sat	sat	sitting	sits
set (put)	set	set	setting	sets
rise (get up)	rose	risen	rising	rises
raise (lift)	raised	raised	raising	raises

macmillanhighered.com/everyday6e
☑ Grammar > LearningCurve: Verbs
Grammar > LearningCurve: Verbs for multilingual writers

▶ The doctor asked the patient to ~~lay~~ *lie* on his side.

▶ She ~~sat~~ *set* the vase on the table.

▶ He ~~raised~~ *rose* up in bed and glared at us.

38e Use verb tenses appropriately.

Multilingual

Verb tenses show when the action takes place. The three simple tenses are the present tense, the past tense, and the future tense.

PRESENT TENSE	I *ask*, I *write*
PAST TENSE	I *asked*, I *wrote*
FUTURE TENSE	I *will ask*, I *will write*

More complex aspects of time are expressed through progressive, perfect, and perfect progressive forms of the simple tenses.

PRESENT PROGRESSIVE	she *is asking*, she *is writing*
PAST PROGRESSIVE	she *was asking*, she *was writing*
FUTURE PROGRESSIVE	she *will be asking*, she *will be writing*
PRESENT PERFECT	she *has asked*, she *has written*
PAST PERFECT	she *had asked*, she *had written*
FUTURE PERFECT	she *will have asked*, she *will have written*
PRESENT PERFECT PROGRESSIVE	she *has been asking*, she *has been writing*
PAST PERFECT PROGRESSIVE	she *had been asking*, she *had been writing*
FUTURE PERFECT PROGRESSIVE	she *will have been asking*, she *will have been writing*

The simple tenses locate an action only within the three basic time frames of present, past, and future. Progressive forms express continuing actions; perfect forms express actions completed before another action or time in the present, past, or future; perfect progressive forms express actions that continue up to some point in the present, past, or future.

Present tense

SIMPLE PRESENT

Use the simple present to indicate actions occurring now and those occurring habitually.

▶ I *eat* breakfast every day at 8:00 AM.

▶ Love *conquers* all.

Use the simple present when writing about action in literary works.

          realizes   *is*

▶ Ishmael slowly ~~realized~~ all that ~~was~~ at stake in the search for the

white whale.

General truths or scientific facts should be in the simple present, even when the predicate of the sentence is in the past tense.

                                 makes

▶ Pasteur demonstrated that his boiling process ~~made~~ milk safe.

When you are quoting, summarizing, or paraphrasing a work, in general use the present tense.

           writes

▶ Keith Walters ~~wrote~~ that the "reputed consequences and promised

blessings of literacy are legion."

But in an essay using APA (American Psychological Association) style, report your experiments or another researcher's work in the past tense (*wrote*, *noted*) or the present perfect (*has reported*). (See Chapter 61.)

           noted

▶ Comer (1995) ~~notes~~ that protesters who deprive themselves of food

are seen as "caring, sacrificing, even heroic" (p. 5).

PRESENT PROGRESSIVE

Use the present progressive form when an action is in progress now. The present progressive uses a present form of *be* (*am*, *is*, *are*) and the *-ing* form of the main verb.

▶ He *is directing* a new film.

In contrast, use the simple present tense for actions that frequently occur in the present, but that are not necessarily happening now.

SIMPLE PRESENT   PRESENT PROGRESSIVE
▶ **My sister *drives* a bus. She *is taking* a vacation now.**

With an appropriate expression of time, you can use the present progressive to indicate a scheduled event in the future.

▶ **We *are having* friends over for dinner tomorrow night.**

Some verbs are rarely used in progressive forms in formal writing. These verbs are said to express unchanging conditions or mental states: *believe, belong, hate, know, like, love, need, own, resemble, understand*. However, in spoken and informal written English, progressive forms like *I'm loving this* and *You're not understanding me correctly* are becoming increasingly common.

PRESENT PERFECT

The present perfect tense indicates actions begun in the past and either completed at some unspecified time in the past or continuing into the present. To form the present perfect, use a present form of *have* (*has*, *have*) and a perfect participle such as *talked*.

▶ **Uncontrolled logging *has destroyed* many tropical forests.**

PRESENT PERFECT PROGRESSIVE

Use the present perfect progressive form to indicate continuous actions begun in the past and continuing into the present. To form the present perfect progressive, use the present perfect form of *be* (*have been*, *has been*) and the *-ing* form of the main verb.

▶ **Since September, he *has been writing* a novel in his spare time.**

Past tense

In the past tense, you can use simple past, past progressive, past perfect, and past perfect progressive forms.

SIMPLE PAST

Use the simple past to indicate actions or conditions that occurred at a specific time and do not extend into the present.

▶ **Germany *invaded* Poland on September 1, 1939.**

PAST PROGRESSIVE

Use the past progressive when an action was in progress in the past. It is used relatively infrequently in English, and it focuses on duration or calls attention to a past action that went on at the same time as something else. The present progressive uses a past form of *be* (*was*, *were*) and the *-ing* form of the main verb.

▶ Lenin *was living* in exile in Zurich when the tsar was overthrown.

PAST PERFECT

Use the past perfect to indicate actions or conditions completed by a specific time in the past or before some other past action occurred. To form the past perfect, use *had* and a perfect participle such as *talked*.

▶ By the fourth century, Christianity *had become* the state religion.

PAST PERFECT PROGRESSIVE

Use the past perfect progressive form to indicate a continuing action or condition in the past that had already been happening when some other past action happened. (You will probably need the simple past tense for the other past action.) To form the past perfect progressive, use the past perfect form of *be* (*had been*) and the *-ing* form of the main verb.

▶ Carter *had been planning* a naval career until his father died.

Future tense

The future tense includes simple, progressive, perfect, and perfect progressive forms.

SIMPLE FUTURE

Use the simple future (*will* plus the base form of the verb) to indicate actions or conditions that have not yet begun.

▶ The exhibition *will come* to Washington in September.

FUTURE PROGRESSIVE

Use the future progressive to indicate continuing actions or conditions in the future. The future progressive uses the future form of *be* (*will be*) and the *-ing* form of the main verb.

▶ The loans *will be coming* due over the next two years.

FUTURE PERFECT

Use the future perfect to indicate actions or conditions that will be completed by or before some specified time in the future. To form the future perfect, use *will have* and a perfect participle such as *talked*.

▶ **By next summer, she** *will have published* **the results of the research study.**

FUTURE PERFECT PROGRESSIVE

Use the future perfect progressive to indicate continuing actions or conditions that will be completed by some specified time in the future. To form the future perfect progressive, use the future perfect form of *be* (*will have been*) and the *-ing* form of the main verb.

▶ **As of May 1, I** *will have been living* **in Tucson for five years.**

QUICK HELP

Editing Verb Tenses

If you have trouble with verb tense in standard English, make a point of checking for these common trouble spots as you proofread.

- Problems with verb form: writing *seen* for *saw*, for example, which confuses the past-participle and past-tense forms. (38c)
- Problems with tense: using the simple past (*Uncle Charlie arrived*) when meaning requires the present perfect (*Uncle Charlie has arrived*). (38e)
- Think carefully before using a regional or ethnic variety of English in situations calling for standard academic English. (See Chapter 28.)

38f Sequence verb tenses effectively.

Careful and accurate use of tenses is important for clear writing. Even the simplest narrative describes actions that take place at different times; when you use the appropriate tense for each action, readers can follow such time changes easily.

▶ **By the time he** *lent* **her the money, she** *had declared* **bankruptcy.**

Use an infinitive (*to* plus a base form: *to go*) to indicate actions occurring at the same time as or later than the action of the predicate verb.

▶ **Each couple** *hopes to win* **the dance contest.**

The hoping is in the present; the winning is in the future.

Use a present participle (base form plus *-ing*) to indicate actions occurring at the same time as that of the predicate verb.

> ▶ *Seeking to relieve unemployment,* **Roosevelt established several public works programs.**

A past participle or a present-perfect participle (*having* plus a past participle) indicates actions occurring before that of the predicate verb.

> *Flown*
> ▶ ~~Flying~~ **to the front, the troops joined their hard-pressed comrades.**
> ⌃

The past participle *flown* shows that the flying occurred before the joining.

> *Having crushed*
> ▶ ~~Crushing~~ **all opposition at home, he launched a war of conquest.**
> ⌃

He launched the war after he crushed the opposition.

One common error is to use *would* in both clauses of a sentence with an *if* clause. Use *would* only in one clause.

> *had*
> ▶ **If I ~~would have~~ played harder, I would have won.**
> ⌃

38g Use active and passive voice effectively.

Voice tells whether the subject is acting (*he questions us*) or being acted upon (*he is questioned*). When the subject is acting, the verb is in the active voice; when the subject is being acted upon, the verb is in the passive voice.

ACTIVE VOICE The storm *uprooted* huge pine trees.

PASSIVE VOICE Huge pine trees *were uprooted* by the storm.

The passive voice uses the appropriate form of the auxiliary verb *be* followed by the past participle of the main verb: *he is being questioned, he was questioned, he will be questioned, he has been questioned.*

Most contemporary writers use the active voice as much as possible because it livens up their prose. Passive-voice verbs often make a passage hard to understand and remember. In addition, writers sometimes use the passive voice to avoid taking responsibility for what they have written. A government official who admits that "mistakes were made" skirts the question: who made them?

To shift a sentence from the passive to the active voice, make the performer of the action the subject of the sentence, and make the recipient of the action an object.

▶ ~~The~~ prizewinning photograph. ~~was taken by my sister.~~
    My sister took the

The passive voice can work to good advantage in some situations. Journalists often use the passive voice when the performer of an action is unknown or less important than the recipient.

▶ **Colonel Muammar el-Qaddafi** *was killed* **during an uprising.**

Much technical and scientific writing uses the passive voice to highlight what is being studied.

▶ **The volunteers' food intake** *was* **closely** *monitored.*

38h   Understand mood and conditional sentences.

The mood of a verb indicates the attitude of the writer. The indicative mood states facts and opinions or asks questions. The imperative mood gives commands and instructions. The subjunctive mood (used mainly in clauses beginning with *that* or *if*) expresses wishes or conditions that are contrary to fact.

INDICATIVE	I *did* the right thing.
IMPERATIVE	*Do* the right thing.
SUBJUNCTIVE	If I *had done* the right thing, I would not be in trouble now.

Subjunctives

The present subjunctive uses the base form, no matter what the subject of the verb is.

▶ **It is important that children** *be* **psychologically ready for a new sibling.**

The past subjunctive is the same as the simple past except for the verb *be*, which uses *were* for all subjects.

▶ **He spent money as if he** *had* **infinite credit.**
▶ **If the store** *were* **better located, it would attract more customers.**

Subjunctive mood

Because the subjunctive can create a rather formal tone, many people today tend to substitute the indicative mood in informal conversation.

▶ **If I *was* a better swimmer, I would try out for the team.** [informal]

For academic and professional writing, use the subjunctive in the following contexts:

CLAUSES EXPRESSING A WISH

▶ **He wished that his mother *were* still living nearby.**

AS IF AND *AS THOUGH* CLAUSES

▶ **He started down the trail as if he *were* walking on ice.**

THAT CLAUSES EXPRESSING A REQUEST OR DEMAND

▶ **The job requires that the employee *be* in good physical condition.**

IF CLAUSES EXPRESSING A CONDITION THAT DOES NOT EXIST

▶ **If the sale of tobacco *were* banned, tobacco companies would suffer a great loss.**

One common error is to use *would* in both clauses. Use the subjunctive in the *if* clause and *would* in the main clause.

▶ **If I ~~would have~~ played harder, I would have won.**
   had

Conditional sentences

Multilingual

Sentences that use an *if* clause don't always require subjunctive forms. Each of the following conditional sentences makes different assumptions about whether or not the *if* clause is true.

▶ **If you *practice* writing frequently, you *know* what your chief problems are.**

This sentence assumes that what is stated in the *if* clause is probably true. Any tense that is appropriate may be used in both the *if* clause and the main clause.

▶ **If you *practice* writing for the rest of this term, you *will understand* the process better.**

This sentence makes a prediction. The main clause uses the future tense (*will understand*) or a modal that can indicate future time (*may understand*). The *if* clause uses the present tense.

▶ **If you *practiced* writing every single day, it *would* eventually *seem* much easier to you.**

This sentence indicates doubt. In the *if* clause, the verb is past subjunctive, even though it refers to future time. The main clause contains *would* + the base form of the main verb.

▶ **If you *practiced* writing on Mars, you *would find* no one to read your work.**

This sentence imagines an impossible situation. The past subjunctive is used in the *if* clause, although past time is not being referred to, and *would* + the base form is used in the main clause.

▶ **If you *had practiced* writing in ancient Egypt, you *would have used* hieroglyphics.**

This sentence shifts the impossibility to the past; obviously, you aren't going to find yourself in ancient Egypt. But a past impossibility demands a form that is "more past": the past perfect in the *if* clause and *would* + the perfect form of the verb in the main clause.

Nouns and Noun Phrases **39**

Although all languages have nouns, English nouns differ from those in some other languages in various ways, such as their division into count and noncount nouns and the use of plural forms, articles, and other modifiers.

39a Use count and noncount nouns appropriately.

Multilingual

Nouns in English can be either count nouns or noncount nouns. Count nouns refer to distinct individuals or things that can be directly counted: *a doctor, an egg, a child; doctors, eggs, children*. Noncount nouns refer to masses, collections, or ideas without distinct parts: *milk, rice, courage*. You cannot count noncount nouns except with a preceding phrase: *a glass of milk, three grains of rice, a little courage*.

Count nouns usually have singular and plural forms: *tree, trees.* Noncount nouns usually have only a singular form: *grass.*

COUNT	NONCOUNT
people (plural of person)	humanity
tables, chairs, beds	furniture
letters	mail
pebbles	gravel
suggestions	advice

Some nouns can be either count or noncount, depending on their meaning.

COUNT   Before video games, children played with *marbles.*

NONCOUNT   The palace floor was made of *marble.*

When you learn a new noun in English, you need to determine whether it is count, noncount, or both. Many dictionaries provide this information.

39b Use determiners appropriately.

Multilingual

Determiners are words that identify or quantify a noun, such as <u>*this*</u> *study,* <u>*all*</u> *people,* <u>*his*</u> *suggestions.*

COMMON DETERMINERS
- the articles *a, an, the*
- *this, these, that, those*
- *my, our, your, his, her, its, their*
- possessive nouns and noun phrases (<u>*Sheila's*</u> *paper,* <u>*my friend's*</u> *book*)
- *whose, which, what*
- *all, both, each, every, some, any, either, no, neither, many, much, (a) few, (a) little, several, enough*
- the numerals *one, two,* etc.

These determiners . . .	. . . can precede these noun types	Examples
a, an, each, every	singular count nouns	*a* book *an* American *each* word *every* Buddhist
this, that	singular count nouns noncount nouns	*this* book *that* milk
(*a*) *little, much*	noncount nouns	*a little* milk *much* affection
some, any, enough	noncount nouns plural count nouns	*some* milk *any* fruit *enough* trouble *some* books *any* questions *enough* problems
the	singular count nouns plural count nouns noncount nouns	*the* doctor *the* doctors *the* information
these, those, (*a*) *few, many, both, several*	plural count nouns	*these* books *those* plans *a few* ideas *many* students *both* hands *several* trees

Determiners with singular count nouns

Every singular count noun must be preceded by a determiner. Place any adjectives between the determiner and the noun.

▶ *my*
   sister
   ^

▶ *the*
   growing population
   ^

▶ *that*
   old neighborhood
   ^

Determiners with plural or noncount nouns

Noncount and plural nouns sometimes have determiners and sometimes do not. For example, *This research is important* and *Research is important* are both acceptable but have different meanings.

39c   Use articles conventionally.

Multilingual

Articles (*a, an,* and *the*) are a type of determiner. In English, choosing which article to use—or whether to use an article at all—can be challenging. Although there are exceptions, the following general guidelines can help.

The articles a or an

Use the indefinite articles *a* and *an* with singular count nouns. Use *a* before a consonant sound (*a car*) and *an* before a vowel sound (*an uncle*). Consider sound rather than spelling: *a house, an hour.*

A or *an* tells readers they do not have enough information to identify specifically what the noun refers to. Compare these sentences:

▶ I need *a* new coat for the winter.

▶ I saw *a* coat that I liked at Dayton's, but it wasn't heavy enough.

The coat in the first sentence is hypothetical. Since it is indefinite to the writer and the reader, it is used with *a*, not *the*. The second sentence refers to an actual coat, but since the writer cannot expect the reader to know which one, it is used with *a* rather than *the*.

If you want to speak of an indefinite quantity rather than just one indefinite thing, use *some* or *any* with a noncount noun or a plural count noun. Use *any* in negative sentences and questions.

▶ This stew needs *some* more salt.

▶ I saw *some* plates that I liked at Gump's.

▶ This stew doesn't need *any* more salt.

▶ Do you have *any* sandwiches left?

The article the

Use the definite article *the* with both count and noncount nouns whose identity is known or is about to be made known to readers. The necessary information for identification can come from the noun phrase itself, from elsewhere in the text, from context, from general knowledge, or from a superlative.

> *the*
> ▶ Let's meet at ⌃fountain in front of Dwinelle Hall.

The phrase *in front of Dwinelle Hall* identifies the specific fountain.

> ▶ Last Saturday, a fire that started in a restaurant spread to a nearby
> *The store*
> clothing store. ~~Store~~ was saved, although it suffered water damage.
> ⌃

The word *store* is preceded by *the*, which directs our attention to the information in the previous sentence, where the store is first identified.

> *the*
> ▶ She asked him to shut ⌃door when he left her office.

The context shows that she is referring to her office door.

> *The pope*
> ▶ ~~Pope~~ is expected to visit Africa in October.
> ⌃

There is only one living pope.

> *the*
> ▶ Bill is now ⌃best singer in the choir.

The superlative *best* identifies the noun *singer*.

No article (the zero article)

Noncount and plural count nouns can be used without an article or any other determiner when making generalizations:

> ▶ In this world nothing is certain but death and taxes.
> – BENJAMIN FRANKLIN

Franklin refers not to a particular death or specific taxes but to death and taxes in general, so no article is used with *death* or with *taxes*.

English differs from many other languages that use the definite article to make generalizations. In English, a sentence like *The ants live in colonies* can refer only to particular, identifiable ants, not to ants in general.

It is sometimes possible to make general statements with *the* or *a/an* and singular count nouns.

> ▶ *First-year college students* are confronted with many new experiences.

> ▶ *A first-year student* is confronted with many new experiences.

> ▶ *The first-year student* is confronted with many new experiences.

These sentences all make the same general statement, but the emphasis of each sentence is different. The first sentence refers to first-year college students as a group, the second focuses on a hypothetical student taken at random, and the third sentence, which is characteristic of formal written style, projects the image of a typical student as representative of the whole class.

40 Subject-Verb Agreement

I n everyday terms, the word *agreement* refers to an accord of some sort: friends agree to go to a movie; the United States and Russia negotiate an agreement about reducing nuclear arms. In most sentences, making subjects and verbs agree is fairly simple; only a few subject-verb constructions cause confusion.

40a Understand subject-verb agreement.

In academic varieties of English, verbs must agree with their subjects in number (singular or plural) and in person (first, second, or third).

To make a verb in the present tense agree with a third-person singular subject, add *-s* or *-es* to the base form.

▶ A vegetarian diet lowers the risk of heart disease.

To make a verb in the present tense agree with any other subject, use the base form of the verb.

▶ I *miss* my family.
▶ They *live* in another state.

The verbs *have* and *be* do not follow the *-s* or *-es* pattern with third-person singular subjects. *Have* changes to *has; be* has irregular forms in both the present and past tenses and in the first person as well as the third person. (See Chapter 38.)

▶ War *is* hell.
▶ The soldier *was* brave beyond the call of duty.

In some varieties of proper African American or regional English, third-person singular verb forms do not end with *-s* or *-es: She go to*

Editing for Subject-Verb Agreement

- Identify the subject that goes with each verb. Cover up any words between the subject and the verb to identify agreement problems more easily. (40b)
- Check compound subjects. Those joined by *and* usually take a plural verb form. With those subjects joined by *or* or *nor*, however, the verb agrees with the part of the subject closest to the verb. (40c)
- Check collective-noun subjects. These nouns take a singular verb form when they refer to a group as a single unit but a plural form when they refer to the multiple members of a group. (40d)
- Check indefinite-pronoun subjects. Most take a singular verb form. *Both*, *few*, *many*, *others*, and *several* take a plural form; and *all*, *any*, *enough*, *more*, *most*, *none*, and *some* can be either singular or plural, depending on the noun they refer to. (40e)

work every day. In most academic writing, however, your audience will expect third-person singular verb forms to end in *-s* or *-es* (38a).

40b Make separated subjects and verbs agree.

Make sure the verb agrees with the subject and not with another noun that falls in between.

▶ A **vase** of flowers **makes** a room attractive.

▶ Many **books** on the best-seller list ~~has~~ *have* little literary value.

The simple subject is *books*, not *list*.

Be careful when you use phrases beginning with *as well as, along with, in addition to, together with,* or similar prepositions. They do not make a singular subject plural.

▶ A passenger, as well as the driver, ~~were~~ *was* injured in the accident.

Though this sentence has a grammatically singular subject, it suggests the idea of a plural subject. The sentence makes better sense with a compound subject: *The driver and a passenger were injured in the accident.*

40c Make verbs agree with compound subjects.

Two or more subjects joined by *and* generally require a plural verb form.

▶ Tony and his friend commute from Louisville.

▶ A backpack, a canteen, and a rifle ~~was~~ *were* issued to each recruit.

When subjects joined by *and* are considered a single unit or refer to the same person or thing, they take a singular verb form.

▶ George W. Bush's older brother and political ally was the governor of Florida.

▶ Drinking and driving ~~remain~~ *remains* a major cause of highway fatalities.

> In this sentence, *drinking and driving* is considered a single activity, and a singular verb is used.

If the word *each* or *every* precedes subjects joined by *and*, the verb form is singular.

▶ Each boy and girl chooses one gift to take home.

With subjects joined by *or* or *nor*, the verb agrees with the part closest to the verb.

▶ Neither my roommate nor my neighbors *like* my loud music.

▶ Either the witnesses or the defendant ~~are~~ *is* lying.

If you find this sentence awkward, put the plural noun closest to the verb: *Either the defendant or the witnesses are lying.*

40d Make verbs agree with collective nouns.

Collective nouns—such as *family, team, audience, group, jury, crowd, band, class,* and *committee*—refer to a group. Collective nouns can take either singular or plural verb forms, depending on whether they refer to the group as a single unit or to the multiple members of the group. The meaning of a sentence as a whole is your guide to whether a collective noun refers to a unit or to the multiple parts of a unit.

▶ **After deliberating, the jury *reports* its verdict.**

The jury acts as a single unit.

▶ **The jury still *disagree* on a number of counts.**

The members of the jury act as multiple individuals.

scatter
▶ **The duck family s̶c̶a̶t̶t̶e̶r̶s̶ when the cat approaches.**

Family here refers to the many ducks; they cannot scatter as one.

Treat fractions that refer to singular nouns as singular and those that refer to plural nouns as plural.

SINGULAR   Two-thirds of the park *has* burned.

PLURAL   Two-thirds of the students *were* commuters.

Even though *eyeglasses, scissors, pants,* and other such words refer to single items, they take plural verbs because they are made up of pairs.

▶ **Where *are* my reading glasses?**

Treat phrases starting with *the number of* as singular and with *a number of* as plural.

SINGULAR   The number of applicants for the internship *was* amazing.

PLURAL   A number of applicants *were* put on the waiting list.

40e   Make verbs agree with indefinite pronouns.

Indefinite pronouns do not refer to specific persons or things. Most take singular verb forms.

SOME COMMON INDEFINITE PRONOUNS

another	each	much	one
any	either	neither	other
anybody	everybody	nobody	somebody
anyone	everyone	no one	someone
anything	everything	nothing	something

▶ Of the two jobs, neither *holds* much appeal.

         depicts
▶ Each of the plays ~~depict~~ a hero undone by a tragic flaw.

Both, *few*, *many*, *others*, and *several* are plural.

▶ Though many *apply*, few *are* chosen.

All, *any*, *enough*, *more*, *most*, *none*, and *some* can be singular or plural, depending on the noun they refer to.

▶ All of the cake *was* eaten.

▶ All of the candidates *promise* to improve the schools.

40f   Make verbs agree with *who, which,* and *that.*

When the relative pronouns *who*, *which*, and *that* are used as a subject, the verb agrees with the antecedent of the pronoun.

▶ Fear is an ingredient that *goes* into creating stereotypes.

▶ Guilt and fear are ingredients that *go* into creating stereotypes.

Problems often occur with the words *one of the*. In general, *one of the* takes a plural verb, while *only one of the* takes a singular verb.

                       work
▶ Carla is one of the employees who always ~~works~~ overtime.

    Some employees always work overtime. Carla is among them. Thus *who* refers to *employees*, and the verb is plural.

                              works
▶ Ming is the only one of the employees who always ~~work~~ overtime.

    Only one employee always works overtime, and that employee is Ming. Thus *one*, and not *employees*, is the antecedent of *who*, and the verb form is singular.

40g   Make linking verbs agree with subjects.

A linking verb should agree with its subject, which usually precedes the verb, not with the subject complement, which follows it (37a).

▶ Three key treaties ~~is~~ *are* the topic of my talk.

The subject is *treaties*, not *topic*.

▶ Nero Wolfe's passion ~~were~~ *was* orchids.

The subject is *passion*, not *orchids*.

40h   Make verbs agree with subjects ending in -s.

Some words that end in *-s* appear plural but are singular and thus take singular verb forms.

▶ Measles still ~~strike~~ *strikes* many Americans.

Some nouns of this kind (such as *statistics* and *politics*) may be either singular or plural, depending on context.

SINGULAR   Statistics *is* a course I really dread.

PLURAL   The statistics in that study *are* highly questionable.

40i   Make verbs agree with subjects that follow.

In English, verbs usually follow subjects. When this order is reversed, make the verb agree with the subject, not with a noun that happens to precede it.

▶ Beside the barn ~~stands~~ *stand* silos filled with grain.

The subject is *silos*; it is plural, so the verb must be *stand*.

In sentences beginning with *there is, there are, there was,* or *there were,* the word *there* serves only as a placeholder; the subject follows the verb.

▶ There **are** five basic **positions** in classical ballet.

The subject, *positions,* is plural, so the verb must also be plural.

40j **Make verbs agree with titles and words used as words.**

▶ *One Writer's Beginnings* ~~describe~~ _{describes} Eudora Welty's childhood.

▶ *Steroids* _{is} ~~are~~ a little word that packs a big punch in the world of sports.

41 Pronouns

As words that stand in for nouns, pronouns carry a lot of weight in everyday language. These directions show one of the reasons why it's important to use pronouns clearly:

> When you see a dirt road turning left off Winston Lane, follow it for two more miles.

The listener may not know whether *it* means the dirt road or Winston Lane. Pronouns can improve understanding, but only when they're used carefully and accurately.

41a **Consider a pronoun's role in the sentence.**

Most speakers of English know intuitively when to use *I, me,* and *my.* Our choices reflect differences in case, the form a pronoun takes to indicate how it acts in a sentence. Pronouns acting as subjects are in the subjective case (*I*); those acting as objects are in the objective case (*me*); those acting as possessives are in the possessive case (*my*).

SUBJECTIVE PRONOUNS	OBJECTIVE PRONOUNS	POSSESSIVE PRONOUNS
I	me	my/mine
we	us	our/ours
you	you	your/yours
he/she/it	him/her/it	his/her/hers/its
they	them	their/theirs
who/whoever	whom/whomever	whose

QUICK HELP

Editing Pronouns

- Are all pronouns after forms of the verb *be* in the subjective case? *It's me* is common in spoken English, but in formal writing use *It is I.* (41a)

- To check for use of *who* and *whom* (and *whoever* and *whomever*), try substituting *he* or *him*. If *he* is correct, use *who* (or *whoever*); if *him*, use *whom* or *whomever*. (41b)

- In compound structures, make sure any pronouns are in the same case they would be in if used alone (*She and Jake were living in Spain*). (41c)

- When a pronoun follows *than* or *as*, complete the sentence mentally. If the pronoun is the subject of an unstated verb, it should be subjective (*I like her better than he [likes her]*). If it is the object of an unstated verb, make it objective (*I like her better than [I like] him*). (41d)

- If you have used *he*, *his*, or *him* to refer to *everyone* or another singular indefinite pronoun that includes both males and females, revise the sentence. (41f)

- For each pronoun, identify the specific word that it refers to in the sentence (its antecedent). If you cannot find one specific word, supply one. If the pronoun refers to more than one word, revise the sentence. (41g)

- Check each use of *it*, *this*, *that*, and *which* to be sure the pronoun refers to a specific word. (41g)

- Be sure that any use of *you* refers to your specific reader or readers. (41g)

Subjective case

A pronoun should be in the subjective case (*I, we, you, he/she/it, they, who, whoever*) when it is a subject, a subject complement, or an appositive renaming a subject or subject complement.

SUBJECT

She was passionate about recycling.

SUBJECT COMPLEMENT

The main supporter of the recycling program was *she*.

APPOSITIVE RENAMING A SUBJECT OR SUBJECT COMPLEMENT

Three colleagues—Peter, John, and *she*—worked on the program.

Americans routinely use the objective case for subject complements, especially in conversation: *Who's there? It's me.* If the subjective case for a subject complement sounds stilted or awkward (*It's I*), try rewriting the sentence using the pronoun as the subject (*I'm here*).

▶ *She was the* ~~was she.~~
The first person to see Kishore after the awards. ~~was she.~~

Objective case

Use the objective case (*me, us, you, him/her/it, them*) when a pronoun functions as a direct or indirect object, an object of a preposition, an appositive renaming an object, or a subject of an infinitive.

DIRECT OBJECT

The boss surprised *her* with a big raise.

INDIRECT OBJECT

The owner gave *him* a reward.

OBJECT OF A PREPOSITION

Several friends went with *me*.

APPOSITIVE RENAMING AN OBJECT

The students elected two representatives, Joan and *me*.

SUBJECT OF AN INFINITIVE

The students convinced *him* to vote for the school bond.

Possessive case

Use the possessive case when a pronoun shows possession or ownership. The adjective forms of possessive pronouns (*my, our, your, his/her/its, their, whose*) are used before nouns or gerunds, and noun forms (*mine, ours, yours, his/hers/its, theirs, whose*) take the place of a possessive noun. Possessive pronouns do not include apostrophes (50a).

BEFORE A NOUN

The sound of *her* voice came right through the walls.

IN PLACE OF A POSSESSIVE NOUN

The responsibility is *hers*.

Pronouns before a gerund should be in the possessive case.

▶ I remember ~~him~~ *his* singing.

His modifies the gerund *singing*.

41b   Use *who, whoever, whom,* and *whomever* appropriately.

A common problem with pronoun case is deciding whether to use *who* or *whom*. Even when traditional grammar requires *whom*, many Americans use *who* instead, especially in informal writing and speech. Nevertheless, you should understand the difference between *who* and *whom* so that you can make informed choices in situations such as formal college writing. The most common confusion with *who* and *whom* occurs when they begin a question and when they introduce a dependent clause.

TALKING THE TALK

Correctness or Stuffiness?

"I think *Everyone has their opinion* sounds better than *Everyone has his or her opinion.* And nobody says *whom.* Why should I write that way?" Over time, the conventions governing certain usages — such as *who* versus *whom*, or *their* versus *his or her* when it refers to an indefinite pronoun like *everyone* — have become much more relaxed. To many Americans, *Whom did you talk to?* and *No one finished his or her test* — both of which are technically "correct" — sound unpleasantly fussy. However, other people object to less formal constructions such as *Who did you talk to?* and *No one finished their test*. Unfortunately, you can't please everyone. Use whatever you are most comfortable with in speaking, but be more careful in formal writing. If you don't know whether your audience will prefer more or less formality, try recasting your sentence.

Questions

You can determine whether to use *who* or *whom* at the beginning of a question by answering the question using a personal pronoun. If the answer is *he*, *she*, or *they*, use *who*; if it is *him*, *her*, or *them*, use *whom*.

> *Whom*
> ▶ ~~Who~~ did you visit?

> I visited *them*. *Them* is objective; thus *whom* is correct.

> *Who*
> ▶ ~~Whom~~ do you think wrote the story?

> I think *she* wrote the story. *She* is subjective; thus *who* is correct.

Dependent clauses

The case of a pronoun in a dependent clause is determined by its purpose in the clause, no matter how that clause functions in the sentence. If the pronoun acts as a subject or subject complement in the clause, use *who* or *whoever*. If the pronoun acts as an object in the clause, use *whom* or *whomever*.

> *whoever*
> ▶ The center is open to ~~whomever~~ wants to use it.

> *Whoever* is the subject of the clause *whoever wants to use it*. (The clause is the object of the preposition *to*, but the clause's function in the sentence does not affect the case of the pronoun.)

> *whom*
> ▶ The new president was not ~~who~~ she had expected.

> Here, *whom* is the object of the verb *had expected* in the clause *whom she had expected*.

If you are not sure which case to use, try separating the dependent clause from the rest of the sentence. Rewrite the clause as a new sentence, and substitute a personal pronoun for *who(ever)* or *whom(ever)*. If the pronoun is in the subjective case, use *who* or *whoever*; if it is in the objective case, use *whom* or *whomever*.

> ▶ The minister glared at (*whoever/whomever*) made any noise.

> Isolate the clause *whoever/whomever made any noise*. Substituting a personal pronoun gives you *they made any noise*. *They* is in the subjective case; therefore, *The minister grimaced at <u>whoever</u> made any noise.*

▶ The minister glared at whoever ~~she thought~~ made any noise.

Ignore such expressions as *he thinks* and *she says* when you isolate the clause.

41c Consider case in compound structures.

When a pronoun is part of a compound subject, complement, object, or appositive, put it in the same case you would use if the pronoun were alone.

▶ When ~~him~~ *he* and Zelda were first married, they lived in New York.

▶ The boss invited ~~she~~ *her* and her family to dinner.

▶ This morning saw yet another conflict between my sister and ~~I.~~ *me.*

▶ Both panelists—Javonne and ~~me~~ *I*—were stumped.

To decide whether to use the subjective or objective case in a compound structure, mentally delete the rest of the compound and try the pronoun alone.

▶ Come to the park with Anh and ~~I.~~ *me.*

Mentally deleting *Anh and* results in *Come to the park with I*. Rewrite as *Come to the park with Anh and me.*

41d Consider case in elliptical constructions.

In elliptical constructions, some words are understood but left out. When an elliptical construction ends in a pronoun, put the pronoun in the case it would be in if the construction were complete.

▶ His sister has always been more athletic than *he* [is].

In some elliptical constructions, the case of the pronoun depends on the meaning intended.

▶ Willie likes Lily more than *she* [likes Lily].

She is the subject of the omitted verb *likes.*

▶ **Willie likes Lily more than [he likes]** *her*.

Her is the object of the omitted verb *likes*.

41e   Use *we* and *us* appropriately before a noun.

If you are unsure about whether to use *we* or *us* before a noun, recast the sentence without the noun. Use whichever pronoun would be correct if the noun were omitted.

▶ *We*
Us fans never give up hope.

Without *fans*, *we* would be the subject.

▶ The Rangers depend on *us* we fans.

Without *fans*, *us* would be the object of a preposition.

41f   Make pronouns agree with antecedents.

The antecedent of a pronoun is the word the pronoun refers to. The antecedent usually appears before the pronoun—earlier in the sentence or in the prior sentence. Pronouns and antecedents are said to agree when they match up in person, number, and gender.

SINGULAR   The choirmaster raised *his* baton.

PLURAL   The boys picked up *their* music.

Compound antecedents

Compound antecedents joined by *and* require plural pronouns.

▶ *My parents and I tried to resolve* our *disagreement.*

When *each* or *every* precedes a compound antecedent, however, it takes a singular pronoun.

▶ *Every plant and animal has* its *own ecological niche.*

With a compound antecedent joined by *or* or *nor*, the pronoun agrees with the nearer or nearest antecedent. If the parts of the antecedent are of different genders, however, this kind of sentence can be awkward or ambiguous and may need to be revised.

AWKWARD	Neither Annie nor Barry got *his* work done.
REVISED	Annie didn't get *her* work done, and neither did Barry.

When a compound antecedent contains both singular and plural parts, the sentence may sound awkward unless the plural part comes last.

▶ Neither the newspaper nor the radio stations would reveal *their* sources.

Collective-noun antecedents

A collective noun that refers to a single unit (*herd*, *team*, *audience*) requires a singular pronoun.

▶ The audience fixed *its* attention on center stage.

When such an antecedent refers to the multiple parts of a unit, however, it requires a plural pronoun.

▶ The director chose this cast because *they* had experience in the roles.

Indefinite-pronoun antecedents

Indefinite pronouns are those that do not refer to specific persons or things. Most indefinite pronouns are always singular; a few are always plural. Some can be singular or plural depending on the context.

▶ *One* of the ballerinas lost *her* balance.

▶ *Many* in the audience jumped to *their* feet.

SINGULAR	Some of the furniture was showing *its* age.
PLURAL	Some of the farmers abandoned *their* land.

Sexist pronouns

Indefinite pronouns often serve as antecedents that may be either male or female. Writers used to use a masculine pronoun, known as the generic *he*, to refer to such indefinite pronouns. However, such wording ignores or even excludes females.

> **QUICK HELP**

> ### Editing Out Generic *He*, *His*, *Him*

> *Everyone should know* his *legal rights.*
>
> Here are three ways to express the same idea without *his*:

> 1. Revise to make the antecedent a plural noun.
>   *All citizens should know* their *legal rights.*
> 2. Revise the sentence altogether.
>   *Everyone should have some knowledge of basic legal rights.*
> 3. Use both masculine and feminine pronouns.
>   *Everyone should know* his *or* her *legal rights.*

> This third option, using both masculine and feminine pronouns, can be awkward, especially when repeated several times in a passage.

> A fourth option replaces *his* with the plural *their*. Although this gender-neutral solution is increasingly common, some audiences will consider it unacceptably informal.

When the antecedent is *anybody*, *each*, *everybody*, or *everyone*, some people avoid the generic *he* by using a plural pronoun.

▶ **Everyone should know *their* legal rights.**

You will hear such sentences in conversation and see them in writing. However, if you are writing for situations in which formal choices are expected, be aware that many people believe that it's a mistake to use the plural *their* with singular antecedents such as *anybody*, *each*, and *everyone*.

41g Make pronouns refer to clear antecedents.

The antecedent of a pronoun is the word the pronoun substitutes for. If a pronoun is too far from its antecedent, readers will have trouble making the connection between the two.

Ambiguous antecedents

Readers have trouble when a pronoun can refer to more than one antecedent.

▶ **The car went over the bridge just before ~~it~~ *the bridge* fell into the water.**

What fell into the water—the car or the bridge? The revision makes the meaning clear.

▶ Kerry told Ellen, ~~she~~ should be ready soon."
  "I

Reporting Kerry's words directly, in quotation marks, eliminates the ambiguity.

Vague use of it, this, that, *and* which

The words *it*, *this*, *that*, and *which* often function as a shortcut for referring to something mentioned earlier. But such shortcuts can cause confusion for readers. Like other pronouns, each must refer to a specific antecedent.

▶ When the senators realized the bill would be defeated, they tried to
  postpone the vote but failed. ~~It~~ was a fiasco.
  The entire effort

▶ Nancy just found out that she won the lottery, ~~which~~ explains her
  and that news

  sudden resignation from her job.

Indefinite use of *you, it, and* they

In conversation, we frequently use *you, it,* and *they* in an indefinite sense in such expressions as *you never know; in the paper, it said;* and *they say.* In academic and professional writing, however, use *you* only to mean "you, the reader," and *they* or *it* only to refer to a clear antecedent.

▶ Commercials try to make ~~you~~ buy without thinking.
  people

▶ ~~On the~~ Weather Channel/~~it~~ reported that an earthquake devastated
  The

  parts of Pakistan.

▶ ~~In France, they~~ allow dogs. ~~in many restaurants.~~
  Many restaurants in France

Possessive antecedents

A possessive may *suggest* a noun antecedent but does not serve as a clear antecedent.

▶ In ~~Alexa's~~ formal complaint, ~~she~~ showed why the test question was
  her   *Alexa*

  wrong.

42 Adjectives and Adverbs

As words that describe other words, adjectives and adverbs can add liveliness and color to writing, helping writers show rather than just tell. In addition, adjectives and adverbs often provide indispensable meanings to the words they modify. In basketball, for example, there is an important difference between a *flagrant* foul and a *technical* foul, or an *angry* coach and an *abusively angry* coach. In each instance, the modifiers are crucial to accurate communication.

42a Understand adjectives and adverbs.

Adjectives modify nouns and pronouns, answering the question *which? how many?* or *what kind?* Adverbs modify verbs, adjectives, other adverbs, or entire clauses; they answer the question *how? when? where?* or *to what extent?* Many adverbs are formed by adding *-ly* to adjectives (*slight, slightly*), but many are not (*outdoors, very*). And some words that end in *-ly* are adjectives (*lovely, homely*). To tell adjectives and adverbs apart, identify the word's function in the sentence.

QUICK HELP

Editing Adjectives and Adverbs

- Scrutinize each adjective and adverb. Consider synonyms for each one to see whether you have chosen the best word possible.
- See if a more specific noun would eliminate the need for an adjective (*mansion* rather than *enormous house*, for instance); do the same with verbs and adverbs.
- Consider adding an adjective or adverb that might make your writing more vivid or specific.
- Make sure all adjectives modify nouns or pronouns and all adverbs modify verbs, adjectives, or other adverbs. Check especially for proper use of *good* and *well*, *bad* and *badly*, *real* and *really*. (42c)
- Make sure all comparisons are complete. (42d)
- If English is not your first language, check that adjectives are in the right order. (42g)
- Avoid using too many adverbs and adjectives in your writing. (42h)

42b Use adjectives after linking verbs.

When adjectives come after linking verbs, they usually describe the subject: *I am patient*. Note that in specific sentences, some verbs may or may not act as linking verbs—*look, appear, sound, feel, smell, taste, grow,* and *prove,* for instance. When a word following one of these verbs modifies the subject, use an adjective; when the word modifies the verb, use an adverb.

ADJECTIVE **Fluffy** looked **angry.**

ADVERB **Fluffy** looked **angrily** at the poodle.

Linking verbs suggest a state of being, not an action. In the preceding examples, *looked angry* suggests the state of being angry; *looked angrily* suggests an angry action.

42c Use adverbs to modify verbs, adjectives, and adverbs.

In everyday conversation, you will often hear (and perhaps use) adjectives in place of adverbs. When you write in formal academic English, however, use adverbs to modify verbs, adjectives, and other adverbs.

▶ You can feel the song's meter if you listen ~~careful.~~ *carefully.*

▶ The audience was ~~real~~ *really* disappointed by the show.

Good *and* well, bad *and* badly

The modifiers *good, well, bad,* and *badly* cause problems for many writers because the distinctions between *good* and *well* and between *bad* and *badly* are often not observed in conversation. *Good* and *bad* are always adjectives, and both can be used after a linking verb. In formal writing, do not use them to modify a verb, an adjective, or an adverb; use *well* or *badly* instead.

▶ The weather looks *good* today.

▶ He plays the trumpet ~~good~~ *well* and the trombone ~~bad.~~ *badly.*

Badly is an adverb and can modify a verb, an adjective, or another adverb. Do not use it after a linking verb in formal writing; use *bad* instead.

>   bad
> ▶ I feel ~~badly~~ for the Cubs' fans.
>   ^

Problems also arise because *well* can function as either an adjective or an adverb. As an adjective, *well* means "in good health"; as an adverb, it means "in a good manner" or "thoroughly."

     ADJECTIVE   After a week of rest, Julio felt *well* again.

     ADVERB   She plays *well* enough to make the team.

Regional modifiers (right *smart*, wicked *fun*)

Most regions have certain characteristic adjectives and adverbs. Some of the most colorful are intensifiers, adverbs meaning *very* or *absolutely*. In parts of the South, for example, and particularly in Appalachia, you are likely to hear the following: *He paid a right smart price for that car* or *She was plumb tuckered out*. In New England, you might hear *That party was wicked fun*. In each of these cases, the adverb (*right*, *plumb*, *wicked*) acts to intensify the meaning of the adjective (*smart*, *tuckered out*, *fun*).

     As with all language, use regional adjectives and adverbs when they are appropriate (28c). In writing about a family member in Minnesota, for example, you might well quote her, bringing midwestern expressions into your writing. For most academic writing, however, you should use academic English.

 FOR MULTILINGUAL WRITERS

Adjectives with Plural Nouns

In Spanish, Russian, and many other languages, adjectives agree in number with the nouns that they modify. In English, however, adjectives do not change their number this way: *her kittens are cute* (not *cutes*).

42d Choose appropriate comparative and superlative forms.

Most adjectives and adverbs have three forms: positive, comparative, and superlative.

POSITIVE	COMPARATIVE	SUPERLATIVE
large	larger	largest
early	earlier	earliest
careful	more careful	most careful
delicious	more delicious	most delicious
happily	more happily	most happily

▶ Canada is *larger* than the United States.

▶ My son needs to be *more careful* with his money.

▶ This is the *most delicious* coffee we have tried.

▶ They are the *most happily* married couple I know.

The comparative and superlative of most short (one-syllable and some two-syllable) adjectives are formed by adding *-er* and *-est*. With some two-syllable adjectives, longer adjectives, and most adverbs, use *more* and *most*: *scientific, more scientific, most scientific; elegantly, more elegantly, most elegantly*. If you are not sure whether a word has *-er* and *-est* forms, consult the dictionary entry for the simple form.

Irregular forms

A number of adjectives and adverbs have irregular comparative and superlative forms.

POSITIVE	COMPARATIVE	SUPERLATIVE
good	better	best
well	better	best
bad	worse	worst
badly	worse	worst
little (quantity)	less	least
many, some, much	more	most

Comparatives or superlatives

In academic writing, use the comparative to compare two things; use the superlative to compare three or more.

▶ Rome is a much *older* city than New York.

▶ Damascus is one of the ~~older~~ cities in the world.
  oldest

▶ Which of the two candidates is the ~~strongest~~ for the job?
  stronger

Double comparatives and superlatives

Double comparatives and superlatives, used in some informal contexts, use both *more* or *most* and the *-er* or *-est* ending. Occasionally they can act to build a special emphasis, as in the title of Spike Lee's movie *Mo' Better Blues*. In college writing, however, double comparatives and superlatives may count against you. Make sure not to use *more* or *most* before adjectives or adverbs ending in *-er* or *-est* in formal situations.

▶ Paris is the ~~most~~ loveliest city in the world.

Incomplete comparisons

Even if you think your audience will understand an implied comparison, you will be safer if you make sure that comparisons in formal writing are complete and clear (31e).

▶ The patients taking the drug appeared healthier.
  than those receiving a placebo.

Absolute concepts

Some readers consider modifiers such as *perfect* and *unique* to be absolute concepts; according to this view, a construction such as *more unique* is illogical because a thing is either unique or it isn't, so modified forms of the concept don't make sense. However, many seemingly absolute words have multiple meanings, all of which are widely accepted as correct. For example, *unique* may mean *one of a kind* or *unequaled*, but it can also simply mean *distinctive* or *unusual*.

If you think your readers will object to a construction such as *more perfect* (which appears in the U.S. Constitution) or *somewhat unique*, then avoid such uses.

Multiple negatives

Multiple negatives such as *I can't hardly see you* have a long history in English (and in other languages) and can be found in the works of Chaucer and Shakespeare. In the eighteenth century, however, in an effort to make English more logical, double negatives came to be labeled as incorrect. In college writing, you may well have reason to quote passages that include them (whether from Shakespeare, Toni Morrison, or your grandmother), but it is safer to avoid other uses of double negatives in academic writing.

42e Consider nouns as modifiers.

Sometimes a noun can function as an adjective by modifying another noun, as in *chicken soup* or *money supply*. If noun modifiers pile up, however, they can make your writing harder to understand.

> AWKWARD   The cold war–era Rosenberg espionage trial and
>   execution continues to arouse controversy.
>
> REVISED   The Rosenbergs' trial and execution for espionage
>   during the cold war continues to arouse controversy.

42f Understand adjectives ending in *-ed* and *-ing*.

Multilingual

Many verbs refer to feelings—for example, *bore, confuse, excite, frighten, interest*. The present participles of such verbs, which end in *-ing*, and the past participles, which end in *-ed*, can be used as adjectives (36d).
    Use the *-ed* (past participle) form to describe a person having the feeling.

▶ The *frightened* boy started to cry.

Use the *-ing* (present participle) form to describe the thing or person causing the feeling.

▶ The *frightening* movie gave him nightmares.

Be careful not to confuse the two types of adjectives.

▶ I am ~~interesting~~ *interested* in African literature.

▶ African literature seems ~~interested.~~ *interesting.*

42g Put adjectives in order.

Multilingual

Modifiers are words that give more information about a noun; that is, they *modify* the meaning of the noun in some way. Some modifiers precede the noun, and others follow it, as indicated in the chart below.

If there are two or more adjectives, their order is variable, but English has strong preferences, described below.

- Subjective adjectives (those that show the writer's opinion) go before objective adjectives (those that merely describe): *these old-fashioned kitchen tiles.*
- Adjectives of size generally come early: *these large old-fashioned kitchen tiles.*
- Adjectives of color generally come late: *these beautiful blue kitchen tiles.*
- Adjectives derived from proper nouns or from nouns that refer to materials generally come after color terms and right before noun modifiers: *these beautiful blue Portuguese ceramic kitchen tiles.*
- All other objective adjectives go in the middle, separated by commas (see 47d): *these decorative, heat-resistant, old-fashioned blue Portuguese ceramic kitchen tiles.*

Very long noun phrases are usually out of place in most kinds of writing. Academic and professional types of writing tend to avoid long strings of adjectives.

Modifier Type	Arrangement	Examples
determiners	at the beginning of the noun phrase	*these* old-fashioned tiles
all or *both*	before any other determiners	*all* these tiles
numbers	after any other determiners	these *six* tiles
noun modifiers	directly before the noun	these *kitchen* tiles
adjectives	between determiners and noun modifiers	these *old-fashioned* kitchen tiles
phrases or clauses	after the noun	the tiles *on the wall* the tiles *that we bought*

42h Avoid overuse of adverbs and adjectives.

In formal academic writing, expert writers tend to use adverbs and adjectives sparingly. So take a tip from the experts: using fewer modifiers can ensure that each adjective or adverb has a greater impact on your writing.

Adverbs

In his memoir *On Writing*, novelist Stephen King says, "I believe the road to hell is paved in adverbs, and I will shout it from the rooftops." Note that he doesn't say he will shout it *loudly*, since readers already know that shouting is loud. Many adverbs are simply redundant:

▶ Tourists meandered ~~aimlessly~~ in the garden.

> The verb *meandered* means "wandered aimlessly," so *aimlessly* is unnecessary.

In academic writing, avoid redundant adverbs, and omit adverbs that are so overused that they have little meaning anymore, such as *definitely*, *absolutely*, and *extremely*.

Adjectives

Adjectives can also lead to redundancy. Ask yourself whether you need to say "the *large* mountain" or whether your readers will know that a mountain is large. When you overuse adjectives, you can simply bog down readers.

▶ The author responded to the ~~wonderful cheery~~ smiles lighting up all of the ~~happy, delighted~~ faces in the ~~listening~~ audience.

Adjectives and adverbs in informal writing

As always, consider the context when deciding whether you are overusing adjectives and adverbs. Repetition that would be inappropriate in formal contexts can add effective emphasis in informal writing, as in the hashtag *#sosososcared* or a status update saying "I'm massively, insanely psyched for the show tonight."

43   Modifier Placement

Consider the following notice in a guidebook:

> Visit the old Dutch cemetery where early settlers are buried from noon to five daily.

Does the old cemetery really bury early settlers for five hours every day? Repositioning the modifier *from noon to five daily* eliminates the confusion and makes it clear when the cemetery is open: *From noon to five daily, visit the old Dutch cemetery where early settlers are buried.* To be effective, modifiers should refer clearly to the words they modify and be placed close to those words.

43a   Revise misplaced modifiers.

Modifiers can cause confusion or ambiguity if they are not close enough to the words they modify or if they seem to modify more than one word in the sentence.

QUICK HELP

Editing for Misplaced or Dangling Modifiers

1. Identify all the modifiers in each sentence, and draw an arrow from each modifier to the word it modifies.

2. If a modifier is far from the word it modifies, try to move the two closer together. (43a)

3. Does any modifier seem to refer to a word other than the one it is intended to modify? If so, move the modifier so that it refers clearly to only the intended word. (43a and b)

4. If you cannot find the word to which a modifier refers, revise the sentence: supply such a word, or revise the modifier itself so that it clearly refers to a word already in the sentence. (43c)

▶ She teaches a seminar this term ~~on voodoo~~ at Skyline College.
                   on voodoo

The voodoo was not at the college; the seminar is.

▶ ~~Billowing from every window, he~~ saw clouds of smoke.
                 He   *billowing from every window.*

People cannot billow from windows.

▶ *After he lost the 1962 gubernatorial race,* Nixon told reporters that he planned to get out of politics. ~~after he lost the 1962 gubernatorial race.~~

The unedited sentence implies that Nixon planned to lose the race.

Limiting modifiers

Be especially careful with the placement of limiting modifiers such as *almost*, *even*, *just*, *merely*, and *only*. In general, these modifiers should be placed right before or after the words they modify. Putting them in other positions may produce not just ambiguity but a completely different meaning.

> **AMBIGUOUS** The court *only* hears civil cases on Tuesdays.
>
> **CLEAR** The court hears *only* civil cases on Tuesdays.
>
> **CLEAR** The court hears civil cases on Tuesdays *only*.

In the first sentence, placing *only* before *hears* makes the meaning ambiguous. Does the writer mean that civil cases are the only cases heard on Tuesdays or that those are the only days when civil cases are heard?

▶ The city ~~almost~~ spent $20 million on the new stadium.
          almost

The original sentence suggests the money was almost spent; moving *almost* makes clear that the amount spent was almost $20 million.

Squinting modifiers

If a modifier can refer to either the word before it or the word after it, it is a squinting modifier. Put the modifier where it clearly relates to only a single word.

> **SQUINTING** Students who practice writing *often* will benefit.
>
> **REVISED** Students who *often* practice writing will benefit.
>
> **REVISED** Students who practice writing will *often* benefit.

43b Revise disruptive modifiers.

Disruptive modifiers interrupt the connections between parts of a grammatical structure or a sentence, making it hard for readers to follow the progress of the thought.

▶ *If they are cooked too long, vegetables will*
~~Vegetables will, if they are cooked too long,~~ lose most of their
^

nutritional value.

A modifier placed between the *to* and verb of an infinitive (*to boldly go*) is known as a split infinitive. Once considered a serious writing error, split infinitives are no longer taboo. Few readers will object to a split infinitive in a clear and understandable sentence.

▶ Students need to *really* know the material to pass the exam.

Sometimes, however, split infinitives can be distracting to readers—especially when more than one word comes between the parts of the infinitive. In such cases, move the modifier before or after the infinitive, or reword the sentence, to remove the distracting interruption.

▶ *surrender*
Hitler expected the British to fairly quickly. ~~surrender.~~
^   ^

43c Revise dangling modifiers.

Dangling modifiers modify nothing in particular in the rest of a sentence. They often *seem* to modify something that is implied but not actually present in the sentence. Dangling modifiers frequently appear at the beginnings or ends of sentences.

DANGLING	Driving nonstop, Salishan Lodge is located two hours from Portland.
REVISED	Driving nonstop from Portland, you can reach Salishan Lodge in two hours.

To revise a dangling modifier, often you need to add a subject that the modifier clearly refers to. In some cases, however, you have to revise the modifier itself, turning it into a phrase or a clause.

▶ *our family gave away*
Reluctantly, the hound ~~was given away~~ to a neighbor.
^

In the original sentence, was the dog reluctant, or was someone else who is not mentioned reluctant?

> *When he was*
> ~~As~~ a young boy, his grandmother told stories of her years as a country
>
> schoolteacher.

His grandmother was never a young boy.

> *My*
> ~~Thumbing through the magazine, my~~ eyes automatically noticed the
> *as I was thumbing through the magazine.*
> perfume ads./

Eyes cannot thumb through a magazine.

Prepositions and Prepositional Phrases

44

Words such as *to, from, over,* and *under* show the relations between other words; these words are prepositions, and they are one of the more challenging elements of English writing. You will need to decide which preposition to use for your intended meaning and understand how to use verbs that include prepositions, such as *take off, pick up,* and *put up with.*

44a Use prepositions idiomatically.

Multilingual

Even if you know where to use a preposition, it can be difficult to determine which preposition to use. Each of the most common prepositions has a wide range of applications, and this range never coincides exactly from one language to another. See, for example, how *in* and *on* are used in English.

> The peaches are *in* the refrigerator.
> The peaches are *on* the table.
> Is that a diamond ring *on* your finger?

The Spanish translations of these sentences all use the same preposition (*en*), a fact that might lead you astray in English.

> *on*
> Is that a ruby ring ~~in~~ your finger?

QUICK HELP

Using Prepositions Idiomatically

1. Keep in mind typical examples of each preposition.

IN   The peaches are *in* the refrigerator.

There are still some pickles *in* the jar.

The book you are looking for is *in* the bookcase.

Here the object of the preposition *in* is a container that encloses something.

ON   The peaches are *on* the table.

There are still some pickles *on* the plate.

The book you are looking for is *on* the top shelf.

Here the object of the preposition *on* is a horizontal surface with which something is in direct contact.

2. Learn other examples that show some similarities and some differences in meaning.

IN   You shouldn't drive *in* a snowstorm.

Here there is no container, but like a container, the falling snow surrounds the driver. The preposition *in* is used for other weather-related expressions as well: *in a tornado, in the sun, in the rain*.

ON   Is that a diamond ring *on* your finger?

The preposition *on* is used to describe things we wear: *the hat on his head*, *the shoes on her feet, the tattoo on his back*.

3. Use your imagination to create mental images that can help you remember figurative uses of prepositions.

IN   Michael is *in* love.

The preposition *in* is often used to describe a state of being: *in love*, *in pain*, *in a panic*. As a way to remember this, you might imagine the person immersed *in* this state of being.

4. Try to learn prepositions not in isolation but as part of a system. For example, in identifying the location of a place or an event, you can use the three prepositions *at, in,* and *on*.

At specifies the exact point in space or time.

AT   There will be a meeting tomorrow *at* 9:30 AM *at* 160 Main Street.

Expanses of space or time within which a place is located or an event takes place might be seen as containers and so require *in*.

IN   I arrived *in* the United States *in* January.

On must be used in two cases: with the names of streets (but not the exact address) and with days of the week or month.

ON   The airline's office is *on* Fifth Avenue.

I'll be moving to my new apartment *on* September 30.

There is no easy solution to the challenge of using English prepositions idiomatically. Digital tools, such as search engines and online
databases of English usage (29e), can help you see how other writers
have expressed a particular idiom. You can also try the strategies in
the box on p. 402.

44b Use two-word verbs idiomatically.

Multilingual

Some words that look like prepositions do not always function as prepositions. Consider the following two sentences:

▶ The balloon rose *off* the ground.

▶ The plane took *off* without difficulty.

In the first sentence, *off* is a preposition that introduces the prepositional phrase *off the ground*. In the second, *off* does not function as a
preposition. Instead, it combines with *took* to form a two-word verb
with its own meaning. Such a verb is called a phrasal verb, and the
word *off*, when used this way, is called an adverbial particle. Many
prepositions can function as particles to form phrasal verbs.

Phrasal verbs

The verb + particle combination that makes up a phrasal verb is a
single entity that often cannot be torn apart.

▶ The plane took *off* without difficulty. ~~off~~.

However, when a phrasal verb takes a direct object (37a), the particle
may sometimes be separated from the verb by the object.

▶ I *picked up my baggage* at the terminal.

▶ I *picked my baggage up* at the terminal.

If a personal pronoun (such as *it, her,* or *him*) is used as the direct
object, that pronoun must separate the verb from its particle.

▶ I *picked it up* at the terminal.

Prepositional verbs

Some idiomatic two-word verbs are not phrasal verbs.

▶ We *ran into* our neighbor on the train.

Here, *into* is a preposition, and *our neighbor* is its object. You can't separate the verb from the preposition (*We ran our neighbor into on the train* does not make sense in English). Verbs like *run into* are called prepositional verbs.

Notice that *run into our neighbor* is different from a normal verb and prepositional phrase, such as *run into a room*. The combination *run + into* has a special meaning, "meet by chance," that you could not guess from the meanings of *run* and *into*.

English has many idiomatic prepositional verbs. Here is a small sample.

PREPOSITIONAL VERB	MEANING
take after	resemble (usually a parent or older relative)
get over	recover from
count on	trust

Other prepositional verbs have predictable meanings but require you to use a particular preposition that you should learn along with the verb: *depend on, look at, listen to, approve of*.

Finally, look out for phrasal-prepositional verbs such as the following, which include a verb, a particle, and a preposition in a set order.

PHRASAL-PREPOSITIONAL VERB	MEANING
put up with	tolerate
look forward to	anticipate with pleasure
get away with	avoid punishment for

45 Comma Splices and Fused Sentences

Writers sometimes use comma splices for special effects. In advertising and other slogans, comma splices can provide a catchy rhythm.

Dogs have owners, cats have staff.   – BUMPER STICKER

45a Identify comma splices and fused sentences.

A comma splice results from placing only a comma between two independent clauses, as in this tweet:

▶ One thing is certain, girls everywhere need education.

A related construction is a fused, or run-on, sentence, which results from joining two independent clauses with no punctuation or connecting word between them. As a fused sentence, the tweet above would read *One thing is certain girls everywhere need education.*

Using comma splices is increasingly common in writing that aims for a casual, informal feel, but comma splices and fused sentences in academic writing are likely to draw an instructor's criticism. If you use comma splices and fused sentences in formal writing, be sure your audience can tell that you are doing so for a special effect.

45b Separate the clauses into two sentences.

The simplest way to revise comma splices or fused sentences is to separate them into two sentences.

COMMA SPLICE

My mother spends long hours every spring tilling the soil and moving manure/. *This* ~~this~~ part of gardening is nauseating.

FUSED SENTENCE

My mother spends long hours every spring tilling the soil and moving manure. *This* ~~this~~ part of gardening is nauseating.

If the two clauses are very short, making them two sentences may sound abrupt and terse, so some other method of revision is probably preferable.

QUICK HELP

Editing for Comma Splices and Fused Sentences

If you find no punctuation between two of your independent clauses —
groups of words that can stand alone as sentences — you have identified a fused sentence. If you find two such clauses joined only by a
comma, you have identified a comma splice. Revise comma splices
and fused sentences with one of these methods.

1. Separate the clauses into two sentences. (45b)

   ▶   Education is an elusive idea,. *It* it means different things to
   different people.

2. Link the clauses with a comma and a coordinating conjunction (*and,*
   but, or, nor, for, so, or *yet*). (45c)

   ▶   Education is an elusive idea, *for* it means different things to
   different people.

3. Link the clauses with a semicolon. (45d)

   ▶   Education is an elusive idea,; it means different things to
   different people.

   If the clauses are linked with only a comma and a conjunctive adverb —
   a word like *however, then, therefore* — add a semicolon.

   ▶   Education is an elusive idea,; *indeed,* it means different things to
   different people.

4. Recast the two clauses as one independent clause. (45e)

   ▶   *An elusive idea, education*
   ~~Education is an elusive idea, it~~ means different things to
   different people.

5. Recast one independent clause as a dependent clause. (45f)

   ▶   Education is an elusive idea, *because* it means different things to
   different people.

6. In informal writing, link the clauses with a dash. (45g)

   ▶   Education is an elusive idea,—it means different things to
   different people.

45c Link the clauses with a comma and a coordinating conjunction.

If the two clauses are closely related and equally important, join them with a comma and a coordinating conjunction (*and, but, or, nor, for, so,* or *yet*). (See 30a.)

COMMA SPLICE
I got up feeling bad, *and* I feel even worse now.

FUSED SENTENCE
I should pay my tuition, *but* I need a new car.

45d Link the clauses with a semicolon.

If the ideas in the two clauses are closely related and you want to give them equal emphasis, link them with a semicolon.

COMMA SPLICE
This photograph is not at all realistic; it even uses dreamlike images to convey its message.

FUSED SENTENCE
The practice of journalism is changing dramatically; advances in technology have sped up news cycles.

Be careful when you link clauses with a conjunctive adverb or a transitional phrase. You must precede such words and phrases with a semicolon (see Chapter 48), with a period, or with a comma combined with a coordinating conjunction (30a).

COMMA SPLICE
Many developing countries have very high birthrates; therefore, most of their citizens are young.

FUSED SENTENCE
Many developing countries have very high birthrates. Therefore, most of their citizens are young.

FUSED SENTENCE
Many developing countries have very high birthrates, *and* therefore, most of their citizens are young.

SOME CONJUNCTIVE ADVERBS AND TRANSITIONAL PHRASES

also	in contrast	next
anyway	indeed	now
besides	in fact	otherwise
certainly	instead	similarly
finally	likewise	still
furthermore	meanwhile	then
however	moreover	therefore
in addition	namely	thus
incidentally	nevertheless	undoubtedly

FOR MULTILINGUAL WRITERS

Judging Sentence Length

In U.S. academic contexts, readers sometimes find a series of short sentences "choppy" and undesirable. If you want to connect two independent clauses into one sentence, be sure to join them using one of the methods discussed in this chapter so that you avoid creating a comma splice or fused sentence. Another useful tip for writing in American English is to avoid writing several very long sentences in a row. If you find this pattern in your writing, try breaking it up by including a shorter sentence occasionally.

TALKING ABOUT STYLE

Comma Splices in Context

Spliced and fused sentences appear frequently in literary and journalistic writing, where they can create momentum with a breathless rush of details:

> Bald eagles are common, ospreys abound, we have herons and mergansers and kingfishers, we have logging with Percherons and Belgians, we have park land and nature trails, we have enough oddballs, weirdos, and loons to satisfy anybody.
>
> – Anne Cameron

Context is critical. Depending on audience, purpose, and situation, structures commonly considered errors can actually be appropriate and effective.

45e Rewrite the clauses as one independent clause.

Sometimes you can reduce two spliced or fused independent clauses to a single independent clause.

COMMA SPLICE *Most* ~~A large part~~ of my mail is advertisements/*and* ~~most of the rest is bills.~~

45f Rewrite one independent clause as a dependent clause.

When one independent clause is more important than the other, try converting the less important one to a dependent clause (30b).

COMMA SPLICE The arts and crafts movement, *which reacted against mass production,* called for handmade objects/. ~~it reacted against mass production.~~

In the revision, the writer chooses to emphasize the first clause, the one describing what the movement advocated, and to make the second clause, the one describing what it reacted against, into a dependent clause.

FUSED SENTENCE *Although* Zora Neale Hurston is regarded as one of America's major novelists, she died in obscurity.

In the revision, the writer chooses to emphasize the second clause and to make the first one into a dependent clause by adding the subordinating conjunction *although.*

45g Link the two clauses with a dash.

In informal writing, you can use a dash to join the two clauses, especially when the second clause elaborates on the first clause.

COMMA SPLICE Exercise trends come and go/—this year yoga is hot.

46 Sentence Fragments

S entence fragments are often used to make writing sound conversational, as in this Facebook status update:

> Realizing that there are no edible bagels in this part of Oregon. Sigh.

Fragments—groups of words that are punctuated as sentences but are not sentences—are often seen in intentionally informal writing and in public writing, such as advertising, that aims to attract attention or give a phrase special emphasis. But you should think carefully before using fragments in academic or professional writing, where some readers might regard them as errors.

46a Identify sentence fragments.

A group of words must meet three criteria to form a complete sentence. If it does not meet all three, it is a fragment. Revise a fragment by combining it with a nearby sentence or by rewriting it as a complete sentence.

1. A sentence must have a subject (37b).
2. A sentence must have a verb, not just a verbal. A verbal cannot function as a sentence's verb without an auxiliary verb (37d).

   VERB   The terrier is *barking.*

   VERBAL   The terrier *barking.*

3. Unless it is a question, a sentence must have at least one clause that does not begin with a subordinating word (36g). Following are some common subordinating words:

although	if	when
as	since	where
because	that	whether
before	though	which
how	unless	who

46b Revise phrase fragments.

Phrases are groups of words that lack a subject, a verb, or both (37d). When verbal phrases, prepositional phrases, noun phrases, and appositive phrases are punctuated like sentences, they become fragments. To revise these fragments, attach them to an independent clause, or make them a separate sentence.

▶ NBC is broadcasting the debates. *with* ~~With~~ discussions afterward.

> *With discussions afterward* is a prepositional phrase, not a sentence. The editing combines the phrase with an independent clause.

▶ The town's growth is controlled by zoning laws. *a* ~~A~~ strict set of regulations for builders and corporations.

> *A strict set of regulations for builders and corporations* is an appositive phrase renaming the noun *zoning laws*. The editing attaches the fragment to the sentence containing that noun.

▶ Kamika stayed out of school for three months after Linda was born. *She did so to* ~~To~~ recuperate and to take care of the baby.

> *To recuperate and to take care of the baby* includes verbals, not verbs. The revision—adding a subject (*she*) and a verb (*did*)—turns the fragment into a separate sentence.

Fragments beginning with transitions

If you introduce an example or explanation with one of the following transitions, be certain you write a sentence, not a fragment.

also	for example	like
as a result	for instance	such as
besides	instead	that is

▶ Joan Didion has written on many subjects. *such* ~~Such~~ as the Hoover Dam and migraine headaches.

> The second word group is a phrase, not a sentence. The editing combines it with an independent clause.

46c   Revise compound-predicate fragments.

A compound predicate consists of two or more verbs, along with their modifiers and objects, that have the same subject. Fragments occur when one part of a compound predicate lacks a subject but is punctuated as a separate sentence. These fragments usually begin with *and*, *but*, or *or*. You can revise them by attaching them to the independent clause that contains the rest of the predicate.

▶ They sold their house. ~~And~~ *and* moved into an apartment.

46d   Revise dependent-clause fragments.

Dependent clauses contain both a subject and a verb, but they cannot stand alone as sentences; they depend on an independent clause to complete their meaning. Dependent clauses usually begin with words such as *after*, *because*, *before*, *if*, *since*, *though*, *unless*, *until*, *when*, *where*, *while*, *who*, *which*, and *that*. You can usually combine dependent-clause fragments with a nearby independent clause.

▶ When I decided to work part-time, I gave up a lot of my earning potential.

If you cannot smoothly attach a clause to a nearby independent clause, try deleting the opening subordinating word and turning the dependent clause into a sentence.

▶ The majority of injuries in automobile accidents occur in two ways. ~~When an~~ *An* occupant either is hurt by something inside the car or is thrown from the car.

Punctuation and Mechanics

The function of most punctuation . . . is to add precision and complexity to meaning. It increases the information potential of strings of words.

— LOUIS MENAND

Punctuation and Mechanics

For visual analysis The illustration on the front of this tab shows tools in use. Writers use punctuation and mechanical devices such as capital letters to connect and separate information. How can you use these tools effectively?

47 Commas

Commas often play a crucial role in meaning. See how important the comma is in the following directions for making hot cereal:

> Add Cream of Wheat slowly, stirring constantly.

That sentence tells the cook to *add the cereal slowly*. If the comma came before the word *slowly*, however, the cook might add all of the cereal at once and *stir slowly*. Using commas correctly can help you communicate more effectively.

47a Use commas to set off introductory words, phrases, and clauses.

▶ However, health care costs keep rising.

▶ In the end, only you can decide.

▶ Wearing new running shoes, Logan prepared for the race.

▶ To win the contest, Connor needed skill and luck.

▶ Pencil poised in anticipation, Audrey waited for the drawing contest to begin.

▶ While her friends watched, Lila practiced her gymnastics routine.

QUICK HELP

Editing for Commas

Research for this book shows that five of the twenty most common errors in college writing involve commas. Check your writing for the following errors:

1. Check every sentence that doesn't begin with the subject to see whether it opens with an introductory element (a word, phrase, or clause that describes the subject or tells when, where, how, or why the main action of the sentence occurs). In these cases, use a comma to separate the introductory material from the main part of the sentence. (47a)

2. Look at every sentence that contains one of the conjunctions *and*, *but*, *or*, *nor*, *for*, *so*, or *yet*. If the groups of words both before and after the conjunction function as complete sentences, you have a compound sentence. Make sure to use a comma before the conjunction. (47b)

3. Look at each adjective clause beginning with *which*, *who*, *whom*, *whose*, *when*, or *where*, and at each phrase and appositive. (37e) Is the element essential to the meaning of the sentence? If the sentence would be unclear without it, do not set off the element with commas. (47c)

4. Make sure that adjective clauses beginning with *that* are not set off with commas. Do not use commas between subjects and verbs, verbs and objects or complements, or prepositions and objects; to separate parts of compound constructions other than compound sentences; to set off restrictive clauses; or before the first or after the last item in a series. (47c and d)

5. Do not use a comma alone to separate sentences; this would create a comma splice (see Chapter 45).

▶ **If candidates expect to be taken seriously‚ they should suggest solutions for the problems of ordinary Americans.**

Some writers omit the comma if the introductory element is short and does not seem to require a pause after it.

▶ *At the racetrack* **Henry lost his entire paycheck.**

However, you will seldom be wrong if you use a comma after an introductory element.

47b Use commas with conjunctions that join clauses in compound sentences.

A comma usually precedes a coordinating conjunction (*and, but, or, nor, for, so,* or *yet*) that joins two independent clauses in a compound sentence (37e).

▶ The title sounds impressive, but *administrative clerk* is just another word for *photocopier.*

▶ The show started at last, and the crowd grew quiet.

With very short clauses, you can sometimes omit the comma.

▶ She saw her chance and she took it.

Always use the comma if there is any chance the sentence will be misread without it.

▶ I opened the junk drawer, and the cabinet door jammed.

Use a semicolon rather than a comma when the clauses are long and complex or contain their own commas.

▶ When these early migrations took place, the ice was still confined to the lands in the far north; but eight hundred thousand years ago, when man was already established in the temperate latitudes, the ice moved southward until it covered large parts of Europe and Asia.
— ROBERT JASTROW, *Until the Sun Dies*

47c Use commas to set off nonrestrictive elements.

Nonrestrictive elements are word groups that do not limit, or restrict, the meaning of the noun or pronoun they modify. Setting nonrestrictive elements off with commas shows your readers that the information is not essential to the meaning of the sentence. Restrictive elements, on the other hand, *are* essential to meaning and should *not* be set off with commas. The same sentence may mean different things with and without the commas:

▶ The bus drivers rejecting the management offer remained on strike.
▶ The bus drivers, rejecting the management offer, remained on strike.

The first sentence says that only *some* bus drivers, the ones rejecting the offer, remained on strike. The second says that *all* the drivers did.

Since the decision to include or omit commas affects how readers interpret your sentence, you should think especially carefully about what you mean and use commas (or omit them) accordingly.

> **RESTRICTIVE**   Drivers *who have been convicted of drunken driving* should lose their licenses.

In the preceding sentence, the clause *who have been convicted of drunken driving* is essential because it explains that only drivers who have been convicted of drunken driving should lose their licenses. Therefore, it is *not* set off with commas.

> **NONRESTRICTIVE**   The two drivers involved in the accident, *who have been convicted of drunken driving,* should lose their licenses.

In the second sentence, however, the clause *who have been convicted of drunken driving* is not essential to the meaning because it merely provides more information about what it modifies, *The two drivers involved in the accident.* Therefore, the clause is set off with commas.

To decide whether an element is restrictive or nonrestrictive, read the sentence without the element, and see if the deletion changes the meaning of the rest of the sentence.

- If the deletion does change the meaning, the element is probably restrictive, and you should not set it off with commas.
- If it does not change the meaning, the element is probably nonrestrictive and requires commas.

Adjective and adverb clauses

An adjective clause that begins with *that* is always restrictive; do not set it off with commas. An adjective clause beginning with *which* may be either restrictive or nonrestrictive; however, some writers prefer to use *which* only for nonrestrictive clauses, which they set off with commas.

RESTRICTIVE CLAUSES

▶ **The claim *that men like seriously to battle one another to some sort of finish* is a myth.**
> – John McMurtry, "Kill 'Em! Crush 'Em! Eat 'Em Raw!"

The *that* clause is necessary to the meaning because it explains which claim is a myth; therefore, the clause is not set off with commas.

▶ **The man/who rescued Jana's puppy/won her eternal gratitude.**

The *who* clause is necessary to the meaning because only the man who rescued the puppy won the gratitude; therefore, the clause takes no commas.

NONRESTRICTIVE CLAUSES

▶ **I borrowed books from the rental library of Shakespeare and Company,** *which was the library and bookstore of Sylvia Beach at 12 rue de l'Odeon.*   – ERNEST HEMINGWAY, *A Moveable Feast*

The clause describing Shakespeare and Company is not necessary to the meaning of the sentence and therefore is set off with a comma.

In general, set off an adverb clause that follows a main clause only if it begins with *although, even though, while,* or another subordinating conjunction expressing contrast.

▶ **He uses semicolons frequently, while she prefers periods and short sentences.**

The clause *while she prefers periods and short sentences* expresses contrast; therefore, it is set off with a comma.

Do *not* set off any other adverb clause that follows a main clause.

▶ **Remember to check your calculations/before you submit the form.**

Phrases

Participial phrases may be restrictive or nonrestrictive. Prepositional phrases are usually restrictive, but sometimes they are not essential to the meaning of a sentence and are set off with commas (37d).

NONRESTRICTIVE PHRASES

▶ **Frédéric Chopin, in poor health, still composed prolifically.**

The phrase *in poor health* does not limit the meaning of *Frédéric Chopin* and so is set off with commas.

Appositives

An appositive renames a nearby noun (37d). When an appositive is not essential to identify what it renames, it is set off with commas.

NONRESTRICTIVE APPOSITIVES

▶ Jon Stewart, an actor and comic, became a respected political commentator.

Jon Stewart's name identifies him; the appositive *an actor and comic* provides extra information.

RESTRICTIVE APPOSITIVES

▶ Mozart's opera/*The Marriage of Figaro*/was considered revolutionary.

The appositive is restrictive because Mozart wrote more than one opera.

47d Use commas with items in a series.

▶ He has plundered our seas, ravaged our coasts, burnt our towns, and destroyed the lives of our people.   – Declaration of Independence

You may see a series with no comma after the next-to-last item, particularly in newspaper writing. Occasionally, however, omitting the comma can cause confusion.

▶ All the cafeteria's vegetables—broccoli, green beans, peas, and carrots—were cooked to a gray mush.

Without the comma after *peas,* you wouldn't know if there were three choices (the third being a *mixture* of peas and carrots) or four.

When the items in a series contain commas of their own or other punctuation, separate them with semicolons rather than commas (48b).

Coordinate adjectives, those that relate equally to the noun they modify, should be separated by commas.

▶ The long, twisting, muddy road led to a shack in the woods.

In a sentence like *The cracked bathroom mirror reflected his face,* however, *cracked* and *bathroom* are not coordinate because *bathroom mirror* is the equivalent of a single word, which is modified by *cracked.* Hence, they are *not* separated by commas.

You can usually determine whether adjectives are coordinate by inserting *and* between them. If the sentence makes sense with the *and,* the adjectives are coordinate and should be separated by commas.

▶ **They are sincere *and* talented *and* inquisitive researchers.**

The sentence makes sense with the *and*s, so the adjectives should be separated by commas: *They are sincere, talented, inquisitive researchers.*

▶ **Byron carried an elegant *and* pocket watch.**

The sentence does not make sense with *and,* so the adjectives *elegant* and *pocket* should not be separated by commas: *Byron carried an elegant pocket watch.*

47e Use commas to set off parenthetical and transitional expressions.

Parenthetical expressions add comments or information. Because they often interrupt the flow of a sentence or digress, they are usually set off with commas.

▶ **Some studies have shown that chocolate, of all things, helps to prevent tooth decay.**

▶ **Roald Dahl's stories, it turns out, were often inspired by his own childhood.**

Transitional expressions, conjunctive adverbs (words such as *however* and *furthermore*), and other words and phrases used to connect parts of sentences are usually set off with commas (6e).

▶ **Ozone is a by-product of dry cleaning, for example.**

▶ **Ceiling fans are, moreover, less expensive than air conditioners.**

47f Use commas to set off contrasting elements, interjections, direct address, and tag questions.

CONTRASTING ELEMENTS

▶ **On official business it was she, *not my father*, one would usually hear on the phone or in stores.**
> — Richard Rodriguez, "Aria: A Memoir of a Bilingual Childhood"

INTERJECTIONS

▶ ***My God***, **who wouldn't want a wife?**
> — Judy Brady, "I Want a Wife"

▶ Remember, *sir*, that you are under oath.

▶ The governor did not veto the unemployment bill, *did she*?

47g Use commas with dates, addresses, titles, and numbers.

Dates

Use a comma between the day of the week and the month, between the day of the month and the year, and between the year and the rest of the sentence, if any.

▶ The attacks on the morning of Tuesday, September 11, 2001, took the United States by surprise.

Do not use commas with dates in inverted order or with dates consisting of only the month and the year.

▶ She dated the letter *26 August 2015*.
▶ Thousands of Germans swarmed over the wall in *November 1989*.

Addresses and place-names

Use a comma after each part of an address or place-name, including the state if there is no ZIP code. Do not precede a ZIP code with a comma.

▶ Forward my mail to the Department of English, The Ohio State University, Columbus, Ohio 43210.

▶ Portland, Oregon, is much larger than Portland, Maine.

Titles

Use commas to set off a title such as *MD* or *PhD* from the name preceding it and from the rest of the sentence. The titles *Jr.* and *Sr.,* however, often appear without commas.

▶ Oliver Sacks, MD, has written about the way the mind works.

▶ Martin Luther King Jr. was one of the twentieth century's greatest orators.

Numbers

In numerals of five digits or more, use a comma between each group of three, starting from the right.

▶ The city's population rose to *158,000* in the 2000 census.

The comma is optional within numerals of four digits but never occurs in four-digit dates, street addresses, or page numbers.

▶ The college had an enrollment of *1,789* [or *1789*] in the fall of 2008.

▶ My grandparents live at *2428* Loring Place.

▶ Turn to page *1566*.

47h Use commas to set off most quotations.

Commas set off a quotation from words used to introduce or identify the source of the quotation. A comma following a quotation goes inside the closing quotation mark. (See 52d for advice about using colons instead of commas to introduce quotations.)

▶ A German proverb warns, "Go to law for a sheep, and lose your cow."

▶ "All I know about grammar, " said Joan Didion, "is its infinite power."

Do not use a comma after a question mark or exclamation point.

▶ "What's a thousand dollars?/" asks Groucho Marx in Cocoanuts. "Mere chicken feed. A poultry matter."

▶ "Out, damned spot!/" cries Lady Macbeth.

Do not use a comma when you introduce a quotation with *that*.

▶ The writer of Ecclesiastes concludes that/"all is vanity."

Do not use a comma before an indirect quotation—one that does not use the speaker's exact words.

▶ Patrick Henry declared/that he wanted either liberty or death.

47i Use commas to prevent confusion.

Sometimes commas are necessary to make sentences easier to read or understand.

▶ The members of the dance troupe strutted in, in matching costumes.

▶ Before, I had planned to major in biology.

47j Eliminate unnecessary commas.

Excessive use of commas can spoil an otherwise fine sentence.

Around restrictive elements

Do not use commas to set off restrictive elements—elements that limit, or define, the meaning of the words they modify or refer to (47c).

▶ I don't let my children watch films/that are violent.

▶ A law/reforming campaign financing/was passed in 2002.

▶ My only defense/against my allergies/is to stay indoors.

▶ The actor/Chiwetel Ejiofor/might win this award.

Between subjects and verbs, verbs and objects or complements, and prepositions and objects

Do not use a comma between a subject and its verb, a verb and its object or complement, or a preposition and its object. This rule holds true even if the subject, object, or complement is a long phrase or clause.

▶ Watching movies late at night/is a way for me to relax.

▶ Parents must decide/how much television their children may watch.

▶ The winner of/the community-service award stepped forward.

In compound constructions

In compound constructions (other than compound sentences—see 47b), do not use a comma before or after a coordinating conjunction that joins the two parts.

▶ Improved health care/and more free trade were two of the administration's goals.

The *and* here joins parts of a compound subject, which should not be separated by a comma.

▶ **Donald Trump was born rich,/ and used his money to make more money.**

The *and* here joins parts of a compound predicate, which should not be separated by a comma.

Before the first or after the last item in a series

▶ **The auction included,/ furniture, paintings, and china.**

▶ **The swimmer took slow, elegant, powerful,/ strokes.**

48 Semicolons

The following public-service announcement, posted in New York City subway cars, reminded commuters what to do with a used newspaper at the end of the ride:

Please put it in a trash can; that's good news for everyone.

The semicolon in the subway announcement separates two clauses that could have been written as separate sentences. Semicolons, which create a pause stronger than that of a comma but not as strong as the full pause of a period, show close connections between related ideas.

48a Use semicolons to link independent clauses.

Though a comma and a coordinating conjunction often join independent clauses, semicolons provide writers with subtler ways of signaling closely related clauses. The clause following a semicolon often restates an idea expressed in the first clause; it sometimes expands on or presents a contrast to the first.

▶ **Immigration acts were passed; newcomers had to prove, besides moral correctness and financial solvency, their ability to read.**
— MARY GORDON, "More Than Just a Shrine"

Gordon uses a semicolon to join the two clauses, giving the sentence an abrupt rhythm that suits the topic: laws that imposed strict requirements.

A semicolon should link independent clauses joined by conjunctive adverbs such as *therefore, however,* and *indeed* or transitional expressions such as *in fact, in addition,* and *for example* (36g).

▶ **The circus comes as close to being the world in microcosm as anything I know; in a way, it puts all the rest of show business in the shade.**
— E. B. WHITE, "The Ring of Time"

If two independent clauses joined by a coordinating conjunction contain commas, you may use a semicolon instead of a comma before the conjunction to make the sentence easier to read.

▶ **Every year, whether the Republican or the Democratic party is in office, more and more power drains away from the individual to feed vast reservoirs in far-off places; and we have less and less say about the shape of events which shape our future.**
— WILLIAM F. BUCKLEY JR., "Why Don't We Complain?"

48b Use semicolons to separate items in a series containing other punctuation.

Ordinarily, commas separate items in a series (47d). But when the items themselves contain commas or other marks of punctuation, using semicolons to separate the items will make the sentence clearer and easier to read.

▶ **Anthropology encompasses archeology, the study of ancient civilizations through artifacts; linguistics, the study of the structure and development of language; and cultural anthropology, the study of language, customs, and behavior.**

QUICK HELP

Editing for Semicolons

- If you use semicolons, be sure they appear only between independent clauses — groups of words that can stand alone as sentences (48a) — or between items in a series. (48b)
- If you find few or no semicolons in your writing, ask yourself whether you should add some. Would any closely related ideas in two sentences be better expressed in one sentence with a semicolon? (48a)

48c Revise misused semicolons.

A comma, not a semicolon, should separate an independent clause from a dependent clause or phrase.

▶ The police found fingerprints; which they used to identify the thief.

▶ The new system would encourage students to register for courses online; thus streamlining registration.

A colon, not a semicolon, should introduce a series or list.

▶ The reunion tour includes the following bands; Urban Waste, Murphy's Law, Rapid Deployment, and Ism.

49 End Punctuation

Periods, question marks, and exclamation points often appear in advertising to create special effects or draw readers along from line to line.

You have a choice to make.
Where can you turn for advice?
Ask our experts today!

QUICK HELP

Editing for End Punctuation

- If all or almost all of your sentences end with periods, see if some of them might be phrased more effectively as questions or exclamations. (49a–c)
- Check to be sure you use question marks appropriately. (49b)
- If you use exclamation points, consider whether each is justified. Does the sentence call for extra emphasis? If in doubt, use a period instead. (49c)

End punctuation tells us how to read each sentence—as a matter-of-fact statement, a query, or an emphatic request. Making appropriate choices with end punctuation allows readers to understand exactly what you mean.

49a Use periods appropriately.

Use a period to close sentences that make statements or give mild commands.

▶ **All books are either dreams or swords.** – AMY LOWELL

▶ **Don't use a fancy word if a simpler word will do.**
– GEORGE ORWELL, "Politics and the English Language"

A period also closes indirect questions, which report rather than ask questions.

▶ **I asked how old the child was.**

▶ **We all wonder who will win the election.**

Until recently, periods have been used with most abbreviations in American English (see Chapter 54). However, more and more abbreviations are appearing without periods.

Mr.	MD	BC *or* B.C.
Ms.	PhD	BCE *or* B.C.E.
Mrs.	MBA	AD *or* A.D.
Jr.	RN	AM *or* a.m.
Dr.	Sen.	PM *or* p.m.

Some abbreviations rarely if ever appear with periods. These include the postal abbreviations of state names, such as *FL* and *TN* (though the traditional abbreviations, such as *Fla.* and *Tenn.*, do call for periods), and most groups of initials (*GE, CIA, AIDS, UNICEF*). If you are not sure whether a particular abbreviation should include periods, check a dictionary, or follow the style guidelines (such as those of the Modern Language Association) you are using in a research paper.

49b Use question marks appropriately.

Use a question mark to close sentences that ask direct questions.

▶ **Have you finished the essay, or do you need more time?**

Question marks do not close *indirect* questions, which report rather than ask questions.

▶ She asked whether I opposed his nomination?**.**

Do not use a comma or a period immediately after a question mark that ends a direct quotation (51f).

▶ "Am I my brother's keeper?**/**" Cain asked.

▶ Cain asked, "Am I my brother's keeper?"**/**

Questions in a series may have question marks even when they are not separate sentences.

▶ I often confront a difficult choice: should I go to practice? finish my homework? spend time with my friends?

A question mark in parentheses can be used to indicate that a writer is unsure of a date, a figure, or a word.

▶ Quintilian died in 96 CE (?).

49c   Use exclamation points appropriately.

Use an exclamation point to show surprise or strong emotion.

▶ In those few moments of geologic time will be the story of all that has happened since we became a nation. And what a story it will be!
— JAMES RETTIE, "But a Watch in the Night"

Today, we live in a world of many exclamations. But use exclamation points sparingly in academic work because they can distract your readers or suggest that you are exaggerating. In general, try to create emphasis through diction and sentence structure rather than with exclamation points.

▶ This university is so large, so varied, that attempting to tell someone everything about it would take three years**!.**

Do not use a comma or a period after an exclamation point that ends a direct quotation.

▶ On my last visit, I looked out the sliding glass doors and ran breathlessly to Connor in the kitchen: "There's a *huge* black pig in the backyard!"**/**   — ELLEN ASHDOWN, "Living by the Dead"

49d **Consider end punctuation in informal writing.**

In informal writing, especially texts and tweets with character limits, writers today are increasingly likely to omit end punctuation entirely. In informal writing that does use end punctuation, research shows that ellipses (. . .), or "dots," are on the rise; they can signal a trailing off of a thought or leave open the possibility of further communication. Exclamation marks can convey an excited or a chatty tone, so they are used more frequently in social media and other informal writing situations than in academic writing. And some writers have argued that ending informal writing with a period rather than no punctuation at all can suggest that the writer is irritated. The meaning of end punctuation is changing in informal contexts, so pay attention to how others communicate, and use what you learn in your own social writing.

Apostrophes **50**

The little apostrophe can make a big difference in meaning. The following sign at a neighborhood swimming pool, for instance, says something different from what the writer probably intended:

> Please deposit your garbage (and your guests) in the trash receptacles before leaving the pool area.

The sign indicates that guests should be put in the trash. Adding a single apostrophe would offer a more neighborly statement: *Please deposit your garbage (and your guests') in the trash receptacles before leaving the pool area* asks that the guests' garbage, not the guests themselves, be thrown away.

50a **Use apostrophes appropriately to show possession.**

The possessive case denotes ownership or possession of one thing by another.

> **QUICK HELP**
>
> **Editing for Apostrophes**
>
> - Check each noun that ends in *-s* and shows possession. Is the apostrophe in the right place, either before or after the *-s*? (50a)
> - Check the possessive form of each indefinite pronoun, such as *someone's*. Be sure the apostrophe comes before the *-s*. (50a)
> - Check each personal pronoun that ends with *-s* (*yours, his, hers, its, ours, theirs*) to make sure it does not include an apostrophe. (50a)
> - Does each *it's* mean *it is* or *it has*? If not, remove the apostrophe. (50b)
> - Make sure other contractions use apostrophes correctly. (50b)

Singular nouns and indefinite pronouns

Add an apostrophe and *-s* to form the possessive of most singular nouns, including those that end in *-s,* and of indefinite pronouns (36c). Do not use apostrophes with the possessive forms of personal pronouns: *yours, his, hers, its, ours, theirs.*

▶ The *bus's* fumes overpowered her.

▶ *Star Wars* made George *Lucas's* fortune.

▶ *Anyone's* guess is as good as mine.

Plural nouns

To form the possessive case of plural nouns not ending in *-s,* add an apostrophe and *-s.*

▶ The *men's* department sells business attire.

For plural nouns ending in *-s,* add only the apostrophe.

▶ The three *clowns'* costumes were bright green and orange.

Compound nouns

For compound nouns, make the last word in the group possessive.

▶ The *secretary of state's* speech was televised.

▶ My *in-laws'* disapproval dampened our enthusiasm for the new house.

Two or more nouns

To signal individual possession by two or more owners, make each noun possessive.

▶ **Great differences exist between** *Jerry Bruckheimer's* **and** *Ridley Scott's* **films.**

Bruckheimer and Scott have produced different films.

To signal joint possession, make only the last noun possessive.

▶ *Wallace and Gromit's* **creator is Nick Park.**

Wallace and Gromit have the same creator.

50b Use apostrophes in contractions.

Contractions are two-word combinations formed by leaving out certain letters, which are indicated by an apostrophe.

it is, it has/it's	I would, I had/I'd	will not/won't
was not/wasn't	he would, he had/he'd	let us/let's
I am/I'm	would not/wouldn't	cannot/can't
he is, he has/he's	do not/don't	who is, who
you will/you'll	does not/doesn't	has/who's

Contractions are common in conversation and informal writing. Academic and professional work, however, often calls for greater formality.

Use of it's and its

Its is the possessive form of *it*. *It's* is a contraction for *it is* or *it has*.

▶ **This disease is unusual;** *its* **symptoms vary from person to person.**

▶ *It's* **a difficult disease to diagnose.**

50c Avoid apostrophes in most plural forms.

Many style guides now advise against using apostrophes for any plurals.

▶ **The gymnasts need marks of** *8s* **and** *9s* **to qualify for the finals.**

Others use an apostrophe and *-s* to form the plural of numbers, letters, and words referred to as terms.

▶ **The five** *Shakespeare's* **in the essay were spelled five different ways.**

Check your instructor's preference.

51 Quotation Marks

As a way of bringing other people's words into your own, quotations can be a powerful writing tool.

Mrs. Macken encourages parents to get books for their children, to read to them when they are "li'l," and when they start school to make certain they attend regularly. She holds herself up as an example of "a millhand's daughter who wanted to be a schoolteacher and did it through sheer hard work."
– SHIRLEY BRICE HEATH, *Ways with Words*

The writer lets her subject speak for herself—and lets readers hear Mrs. Macken's voice.

51a Use quotation marks to identify direct quotations.

▶ The president asked Congress to "try common sense."
▶ She smiled and said, "Son, this is one incident that I will never forget."

Use quotation marks to enclose the words of each speaker within running dialogue. Mark each shift between speakers with a new paragraph.

> "I want no proof of their affection," said Elinor; "but of their engagement I do."
> "I am perfectly satisfied of both."
> "Yet not a syllable has been said to you on the subject, by either of them." – JANE AUSTEN, *Sense and Sensibility*

Use single quotation marks for a quotation within a quotation. Open and close the quoted passage with double quotation marks, and change any quotation marks that appear *within* the quotation to single quotation marks.

▶ Baldwin says, "The title 'The Uses of the Blues' does not refer to music; I don't know anything about music."

> **QUICK HELP**

Editing for Quotation Marks

- Use quotation marks around direct quotations and titles of short works. (51a and c)
- Do not use quotation marks around set-off quotations of more than four lines of prose or more than three lines of poetry, or around titles of long works. Consult a style guide, such as that of the Modern Language Association (MLA), for guidelines. (51b and c)
- Use quotation marks to signal irony and invented words, but do so sparingly. (51e)
- Check other punctuation used with closing quotation marks. (51f)

  Periods and commas should be *inside* the quotation marks.

  Colons, semicolons, and footnote numbers should be *outside*.

  Question marks, exclamation points, and dashes should be *inside* if they are part of the quoted material, *outside* if they are not.
- Never use quotation marks around indirect quotations. (51g)
- Do not use quotation marks just to add emphasis to words. (51g)

51b Punctuate block quotations and poetry appropriately.

If the prose passage you wish to quote is more than four typed lines, set the quotation off by starting it on a new line and indenting it one inch from the left margin. This format, known as block quotation, does not require quotation marks.

> In "Suspended," Joy Harjo tells of her first awareness of jazz as a child:
>
>> My rite of passage into the world of humanity occurred then, via jazz. The music made a startling bridge between the familiar and strange lands, an appropriate vehicle, for . . . we were there when jazz was born. I recognized it, that humid afternoon in my formative years, as a way to speak beyond the confines of ordinary language. I still hear it. (84)

This block quotation, including the ellipsis dots and the page number in parentheses at the end, follows the style of the Modern Language Association (MLA). The American Psychological Association (APA) has different guidelines for setting off block quotations. (See Chapters 57 and 61.)

When quoting poetry, if the quotation is brief (fewer than four lines), include it within your text. Separate the lines of the poem with slashes, each preceded and followed by a space, in order to tell the reader where one line of the poem ends and the next begins.

> In one of his best-known poems, Robert Frost remarks, "Two roads diverged in a yellow wood, and I — / I took the one less traveled by / And that has made all the difference" (lines 18–20).

To quote more than three lines of poetry, indent the block one inch from the left margin. Do not use quotation marks. Take care to follow the spacing, capitalization, punctuation, and other features of the original poem.

> The duke in Robert Browning's poem "My Last Duchess" is clearly a jealous, vain person, whose arrogance is illustrated through this statement:
>
> > She thanked men — good! but thanked
> > Somehow — I know not how — as if she ranked
> > My gift of a nine-hundred-years-old name
> > With anybody's gift. (lines 31–34)

51c Use quotation marks for titles of short works.

Quotation marks are used to enclose the titles of short poems, short stories, articles, essays, songs, sections of books, and episodes of television and radio programs.

▶ **"Dover Beach" moves from calmness to sadness.** [poem]

▶ **Alice Walker's "Everyday Use" is about more than just quilts.** [short story]

▶ **The *Atlantic* published an article entitled "Illiberal Education."** [article]

▶ **In "Photography," Susan Sontag considers the role of photography in our society.** [essay]

▶ **The *Nature* episode "Echo of the Elephants" portrays ivory hunters unfavorably.** [television series episode]

Use italics rather than quotation marks for the titles of television series, magazines, movies, and other long works (see 55a).

51d Use quotation marks appropriately for definitions.

▶ In social science, the term *sample size* means "the number of individuals being studied in a research project."
– KATHLEEN STASSEN BERGER AND ROSS A. THOMPSON, *The Developing Person through Childhood and Adolescence*

Use italics for words used as a term, like *sample size* above (see 55b).

51e Use quotation marks to identify irony and invented terms.

To show readers that you are using a word or phrase ironically or that you made it up, enclose it in quotation marks.

▶ The "banquet" consisted of dried-out chicken and canned vegetables.

The quotation marks suggest that the meal was anything but a banquet.

▶ Your whole first paragraph or first page may have to be guillotined in any case after your piece is finished: it is a kind of "forebirth."
– JACQUES BARZUN, "A Writer's Discipline"

The writer made up the term *forebirth*.

51f Follow conventions for other punctuation with quotation marks.

Periods and commas go *inside* closing quotation marks.

▶ "Don't compromise yourself," said Janis Joplin. "You are all you've got."

When you follow MLA style for documenting a short quotation, place the period *after* the parentheses with source information (see Chapter 58).

▶ In places, de Beauvoir "sees Marxists as believing in subjectivity" (Whitmarsh 63).

For more information on using a comma with a quotation, see 47h.

Colons, semicolons, and footnote numbers go *outside* closing quotation marks.

▶ **I felt one emotion after finishing "Eveline": sorrow.**

▶ **Everything is dark, and "a visionary light settles in her eyes"; this vision, this light, is her salvation.**

▶ **Tragedy is defined by Aristotle as "an imitation of an action that is serious and of a certain magnitude."[1]**

Question marks, exclamation points, and dashes go *inside* if they are part of the quoted material, *outside* if they are not.

PART OF THE QUOTATION

▶ **The cashier asked, "Would you like to super-size that?"**

▶ **"Jump!" one of the firefighters shouted.**

NOT PART OF THE QUOTATION

▶ **What is the theme of "The Birth-Mark"?**

▶ **"Break a leg" — that phrase is supposed to bring good luck.**

51g   Revise misused quotation marks.

Do not use quotation marks for indirect quotations — those that do not use someone's exact words.

▶ **Our mother told us that ⸝she was sure she would never forget the incident.⸜**

Do not use quotation marks just to add emphasis to particular words or phrases.

▶ **Michael said that his views might not be ⸝politically correct⸜ but that he wasn't going to change them for anything.**

▶ **Much time was spent speculating about their ⸝relationship.⸜**

Do not use quotation marks around slang or colloquial language; they create the impression that you are apologizing for using those words. If you have a good reason to use slang or a colloquial term, use it without quotation marks.

▶ **After our twenty-mile hike, we were ready to ⸝turn in.⸜**

FOR MULTILINGUAL WRITERS

Quoting in American English

Remember that the way you mark quotations in American English (" ") may not be the same as in other languages. In French, for example, quotations are marked with *guillemets* or angle quotes (« »), while in German, quotations take split-level marks („ "). Writers of British English use single quotation marks first and, when necessary, double quotation marks for quotations within quotations. If you are writing for an American audience, be careful to follow the U.S. conventions governing quotation marks.

Other Punctuation Marks 52

Parentheses, brackets, dashes, colons, slashes, and ellipses are everywhere. Every URL includes colons and slashes, and dashes and ellipses are increasingly common in writing that expresses conversational informality.

You can also use these punctuation marks for more formal purposes: to signal relationships among parts of sentences, to create particular rhythms, and to help readers follow your thoughts.

52a Use parentheses appropriately.

Use parentheses to enclose material that is of minor or secondary importance in a sentence—material that supplements, clarifies, comments on, or illustrates what precedes or follows it.

▶ Inventors and men of genius have almost always been regarded as fools at the beginning (and very often at the end) of their careers.
　　　　　　　　　　　　　　　　　　　　– FYODOR DOSTOYEVSKY

▶ During my research, I found problems with the flat-rate income tax (a single-rate tax with no deductions).

Textual citations

▶ Freud and his followers have had a most significant impact on the ways abnormal functioning is understood and treated (Joseph, 1991).
　　　　　　　　　　　　　　– RONALD J. COMER, *Abnormal Psychology*

▶ Zamora notes that Kahlo referred to her first self-portrait, given to a close friend, as "your Botticelli" (110).

The first in-text citation shows the style of the American Psychological Association (APA); the second, the style of the Modern Language Association (MLA).

Numbers or letters in a list

▶ Five distinct styles can be distinguished: (1) Old New England, (2) Deep South, (3) Middle American, (4) Wild West, and (5) Far West or Californian.   – ALISON LURIE, *The Language of Clothes*

Other punctuation marks with parentheses

A period may be placed either inside or outside a closing parenthesis, depending on whether the parenthetical text is part of a larger sentence. A comma, if needed, is always placed *outside* a closing parenthesis (and never before an opening one).

▶ Gene Tunney's single defeat in an eleven-year career was to a flamboyant and dangerous fighter named Harry Greb ("The Human Windmill"), who seems to have been, judging from boxing literature, the dirtiest fighter in history.   – JOYCE CAROL OATES, "On Boxing"

Parentheses, commas, and dashes

In general, use commas when the material to be set off is least interruptive (47c, e, and f), parentheses when it is more interruptive, and dashes when it is the most interruptive (52c).

52b   Use brackets appropriately.

Use brackets to enclose parenthetical elements in material that is itself within parentheses and to enclose explanatory words or comments that you are inserting into a quotation.

Material within parentheses

▶ Eventually the investigation had to examine the major agencies (including the previously sacrosanct National Security Agency [NSA]) that were conducting covert operations.

Material within quotations

▶ Massing notes that "on average, it [Fox News] attracts more than eight million people daily—more than double the number who watch CNN."

The bracketed words *Fox News* clarify what *it* refers to in the original quotation.

In the quotation in the following sentence, the artist Gauguin's name is misspelled. The bracketed word *sic,* which means "so," tells readers that the person being quoted—not the writer who has picked up the quotation—made the mistake.

▶ **One admirer wrote, "She was the most striking woman I'd ever seen—a sort of wonderful combination of Mia Farrow and one of Gaugin's [*sic*] Polynesian nymphs."**

52c Use dashes appropriately.

Dashes give more emphasis than parentheses to the material they enclose. Many word-processing programs automatically convert two typed hyphens into a solid dash.

▶ **The pleasures of reading itself—who doesn't remember?—were like those of Christmas cake, a sweet devouring.**
> – EUDORA WELTY, "A Sweet Devouring"

Explanatory material

▶ **Indeed, several of modern India's greatest scholars—such as the Mughal historian Muzaffar Alam of the University of Chicago—are madrasa graduates.** – WILLIAM DALRYMPLE

Material at the end of a sentence

▶ **In the twentieth century it has become almost impossible to moralize about epidemics—except those which are transmitted sexually.**
> – SUSAN SONTAG, *AIDS and Its Metaphors*

A sudden change in tone

▶ **New York is a catastrophe—but a magnificent catastrophe.**
> – LE CORBUSIER

Summary or explanation

▶ **In walking, the average adult person employs a motor mechanism that weighs about eighty pounds—sixty pounds of muscle and twenty pounds of bone.** – EDWIN WAY TEALE

Hesitation in speech

▶ As the officer approached his car, the driver stammered, "What—what have I done?"

52d Use colons appropriately.

Use a colon to introduce explanations or examples and to separate some elements from one another.

Explanation, example, or appositive

▶ The men may also wear the getup known as Sun Belt Cool: a pale beige suit, open-collared shirt (often in a darker shade than the suit), cream-colored loafers and aviator sunglasses.

– ALISON LURIE, *The Language of Clothes*

Series, list, or quotation

▶ At the baby's one-month birthday party, Ah Po gave him the Four Valuable Things: ink, inkslab, paper, and brush.

– MAXINE HONG KINGSTON, *China Men*

▶ The teachers wondered: "Do boys and girls really learn differently?"

The preceding example could have taken a comma instead of a colon (see 47h). Use a colon rather than a comma to introduce a quotation when the lead-in is a complete sentence on its own.

▶ The State of the Union address contained one surprising statement: "America is addicted to oil."

Colons with other elements

SALUTATIONS IN FORMAL LETTERS
▶ Dear Dr. Chapman:

HOURS, MINUTES, AND SECONDS
▶ 4:59 PM
▶ 2:15:06

RATIOS
▶ a ratio of 5:1

BIBLICAL CHAPTERS AND VERSES
▶ I Corinthians 3:3–5

TITLES AND SUBTITLES
▶ *The Joy of Insight:*
Passions of a Physicist

CITIES AND PUBLISHERS IN BIBLIOGRAPHIC ENTRIES
▶ Boston: Bedford, 2015

Unnecessary colons

Do not put a colon between a verb and its object or complement—unless the object is a quotation.

▶ Some natural fibers are: cotton, wool, silk, and linen.

Do not put a colon between a preposition and its object or after such expressions as *such as, especially,* and *including.*

▶ In poetry, additional power may come from devices such as: simile,
metaphor, and alliteration.

52e Use slashes appropriately.

Use a slash to separate alternatives.

▶ Then there was Daryl, the cabdriver/bartender.
                                    – JOHN L'HEUREUX, *The Handmaid of Desire*

Use slashes to mark line divisions between two or three lines of poetry quoted within running text. When using a slash to separate lines of poetry, precede and follow it with a space (51b).

▶ In Sonnet 29, the persona states, "For thy sweet love rememb'red
such wealth brings / That then I scorn to change my state with kings."

Slashes also separate parts of fractions and Internet addresses.

52f Use ellipses appropriately.

Ellipses, or ellipsis points, are three equally spaced dots. Ellipses usually indicate that something has been omitted from a quoted passage, but they can also signal a pause or hesitation in speech in the same way that a dash can.

Omissions

Just as you should carefully use quotation marks around any material that you quote directly from a source, so you should carefully use ellipses to indicate that you have left out part of a quotation that otherwise appears to be a complete sentence.

The ellipses in the following example indicate two omissions—one in the middle of the sentence and one at the end. When you omit the last part of a quoted sentence, add a period after the ellipses, for a total of four dots. Be sure a complete sentence comes before and after the four points. If you are adding your own ellipses to a quotation that already has other ellipses, enclose yours in brackets.

ORIGINAL TEXT

▶ **The quasi-official division of the population into three economic classes called high-, middle-, and low-income groups rather misses the point, because as a class indicator the amount of money is not as important as the source.**   – PAUL FUSSELL, "Notes on Class"

WITH ELLIPSES

▶ **As Paul Fussell argues, "The quasi-official division of the population into three economic classes . . . rather misses the point. . . ."**

If your shortened quotation ends with a source (such as a page number, a name, or a title), follow these steps:

1. Use three ellipsis points but no period after the quotation.
2. Add the closing quotation mark, closed up to the third ellipsis point.
3. Add the source documentation in parentheses.
4. Use a period to indicate the end of the sentence.

▶ **Packer argues, "The Administration is right to reconsider its strategy . . ." (34).**

Hesitation

▶ **Then the voice, husky and familiar, came to wash over us—"The winnah, and still heavyweight champeen of the world . . . Joe Louis."**
   – MAYA ANGELOU, *I Know Why the Caged Bird Sings*

53 Capital Letters

Capital letters are a key signal in everyday life. Look around any store to see their importance: you can shop for Levi's or *any* blue jeans, for Coca-Cola or *any* cola, for Kleenex or *any* tissue. As these examples show, one of the most common reasons for capitalizing a word is to indicate that it is part of a name or title—of a brand, person, article, or something else.

QUICK HELP

Editing for Capitalization

- Capitalize the first word of each sentence. If you quote a poem, follow its original capitalization. (53a)
- Check to make sure you have appropriately capitalized proper nouns and proper adjectives. (53b)
- Review where you have used titles of people or of works to be sure you have capitalized them correctly. (53b and c)
- Double-check the capitalization of geographical directions (*north* or *North*?), family relationships (*dad* or *Dad*?), and seasons of the year (*winter*, not *Winter*). (53d)

53a Capitalize the first word of a sentence or line of poetry.

Capitalize the first word of a sentence. If you are quoting a full sentence, capitalize the first word of the quotation.

▶ **Kennedy said, "Let us never negotiate out of fear."**

Capitalization of a sentence following a colon is optional.

▶ **Gould cites the work of Darwin: The [*or* the] theory of natural selection incorporates the principle of evolutionary ties among all animals.**

Capitalize a sentence within parentheses unless the parenthetical sentence is inserted into another sentence.

▶ **Gould cites the work of Darwin. (Other researchers cite more recent evolutionary theorists.)**

▶ **Gould cites the work of Darwin (see page 150).**

When citing poetry, follow the capitalization of the original poem. Though most poets capitalize the first word of each line in a poem, some poets do not.

▶ **Morning sun heats up the young beech tree**
leaves and almost lights them into fireflies

— JUNE JORDAN, "Aftermath"

53b Capitalize proper nouns and proper adjectives.

Capitalize proper nouns (those naming specific persons, places, and things) and most proper adjectives (those formed from proper nouns). All other nouns are common nouns and are not capitalized unless they begin a sentence or are used as part of a proper noun: *a street* or *the street where you live,* but *Elm Street.* The following list shows proper nouns and adjectives on the left and related common nouns and adjectives on the right.

PEOPLE

Ang Lee	the film's director
Nixonian	political

NATIONS, NATIONALITIES, ETHNIC GROUPS, AND LANGUAGES

Brazil, Brazilian	their native country, his citizenship
Italian American	an ethnic group

PLACES

Pacific Ocean	an ocean
Hawaiian Islands	tropical islands

STRUCTURES AND MONUMENTS

the Lincoln Memorial	a monument
the Eiffel Tower	a landmark

SHIPS, TRAINS, AIRCRAFT, AND SPACECRAFT

the *Queen Mary*	a cruise ship
the *City of New Orleans*	the 6:00 train

ORGANIZATIONS, BUSINESSES, AND GOVERNMENT INSTITUTIONS

United Auto Workers	a trade union
Library of Congress	certain federal agencies

ACADEMIC INSTITUTIONS AND COURSES

University of Maryland	a state university
Political Science 102	my political science course

HISTORICAL EVENTS AND ERAS

the Easter Uprising	a rebellion
the Renaissance	the fifteenth century

RELIGIONS AND RELIGIOUS TERMS

God	a deity
the Qur'an	a holy book
Catholicism, Catholic	a religion, their religious affiliation

TRADE NAMES

Nike	running shoes
Cheerios	cereal

Product names

Some contemporary companies use capitals called *InterCaps* in the middle of their own or their product's names. Follow the style you see in company advertising or on the product itself—*eBay, FedEx, iTunes*.

Titles of individuals

Capitalize titles used before a proper name. When used alone or following a proper name, most titles are not capitalized. One common exception is the word *president,* which many writers capitalize whenever it refers to the president of the United States.

Chief Justice Roberts	John Roberts, the chief justice
Professor Lisa Ede	my English professor
Dr. Edward A. Davies	Edward A. Davies, our doctor

 FOR MULTILINGUAL WRITERS
Learning English Capitalization

Capitalization systems vary considerably among languages, and some languages (Arabic, Chinese, Hindi, and Hebrew, for example) do not use capital letters at all. English may be the only language to capitalize the first-person singular pronoun (*I*), but Dutch and German capitalize some forms of the second-person pronoun (*you*). German capitalizes all nouns; English used to capitalize more nouns than it does now (see, for instance, the Declaration of Independence).

53c   Capitalize titles of works.

Capitalize most words in titles of books, articles, stories, speeches, essays, plays, poems, documents, films, paintings, and musical compositions. Do not capitalize an article (*a, an, the*), a preposition, a conjunction, or the *to* in an infinitive unless it is the first or last word in a title or subtitle.

Walt Whitman: A Life	Declaration of Independence
"As Time Goes By"	*Charlie and the Chocolate Factory*
"Shooting an Elephant"	*Rebel without a Cause*

53d   Revise unnecessary capitalization.

Do not capitalize a compass direction unless the word designates a specific geographic region.

▶ Voters in the **South** and much of the **West** tend to favor socially conservative candidates.

▶ John Muir headed ~~West,~~ *west,* motivated by the need to explore.

Do not capitalize a word indicating a family relationship unless the word is used as part of the name or as a substitute for the name.

▶ I could always tell when **Mother** was annoyed with **Aunt Rose.**

▶ When she was a child, my ~~Mother~~ *mother* shared a room with my ~~Aunt.~~ *aunt.*

Do not capitalize seasons of the year and parts of the academic or financial year.

spring	fall semester
winter	winter term
autumn	third-quarter earnings

Capitalizing entire words and phrases in online writing gives them emphasis. On social media, writers may capitalize a few words or phrases for comic effect (*"I am shocked, SHOCKED to hear you say that!"*). But note that using all capital letters makes writing in digital environments feel like shouting. In email and professional writing, use italics, boldface, or underlining for emphasis.

Abbreviations and Numbers **54**

Any time you look up an address, you see an abundance of abbreviations and numbers, as in the following movie theater listing from a Google map of Berkeley, California:

Oaks Theater   1875 Solano Av   Brk

Abbreviations and numbers allow writers to present detailed information in a small amount of space.

54a Abbreviate some titles before and all titles after proper names.

Ms. Susanna Moller   Henry Louis Gates Jr.

Mr. Aaron Oforlea   Karen Lancry, MD

Dr. Cheryl Gold   Samuel Cohen, PhD

Other titles—including religious, academic, and government titles—should be spelled out in academic writing. In other writing, they can be abbreviated before a full name but should be written out when used with only a last name.

Rev. Fleming Rutledge   Reverend Rutledge

Prof. Vershawn Young   Professor Young

Gen. Colin Powell   General Powell

QUICK HELP

Editing Abbreviations and Numbers

- Use abbreviations and numbers according to the conventions of a specific field (see p. 452): for example, *57%* might be acceptable in a math paper, but *57 percent* may be more appropriate in a sociology essay. (54f)

- If you use an abbreviation readers might not understand, spell out the term the first time you use it, and give the abbreviation in parentheses. (54c)

Do not use both a title and an academic degree with a person's name. Use one or the other. Instead of *Dr. Beverly Moss, PhD,* write *Dr. Beverly Moss* or *Beverly Moss, PhD.* (Note that academic degrees such as *RN* and *PhD* often appear without periods; see 49a.)

54b Abbreviate years and hours appropriately.

You can use the following abbreviations with numerals. Notice that AD precedes the numeral; all other abbreviations follow the numeral. Today, BCE and CE are generally preferred over BC and AD, and periods in all four of these abbreviations are optional.

399 BCE ("before the common era") *or* 399 BC ("before Christ")

49 CE ("common era") *or* AD 49 (*anno Domini,* Latin for "year of our Lord")

11:15 AM (*or* a.m.)

9:00 PM (*or* p.m.)

For these abbreviations, you may use full-size capital letters or small caps, a typographical option in word-processing programs.

54c Abbreviate some business, government, and science terms.

As long as you can be sure your readers will understand them, use common abbreviations such as *PBS, NASA, DNA,* and *CIA.* If an abbreviation may be unfamiliar, however, spell out the full term the first time you use it, and give the abbreviation in parentheses. After that, you can use the abbreviation by itself.

▶ The Comprehensive Test Ban (CTB) Treaty was first proposed in the 1950s. For those nations signing it, the CTB would bring to a halt all nuclear weapons testing.

54d Use abbreviations in official company names.

Use such abbreviations as *Co., Inc., Corp.,* and *&* if they are part of a company's official name. Do not, however, use these abbreviations in most other contexts.

▶ Sears, Roebuck & Co. was the only large ~~corp.~~ in town.
corporation

▶ Paola has a part-time job at the Warner ~~Brothers~~ store in the mall.
Bros.

54e Use Latin abbreviations appropriately.

In general, avoid these Latin abbreviations except when citing sources:

cf.	compare (*confer*)
e.g.	for example (*exempli gratia*)
et al.	and others (*et alia*)
etc.	and so forth (*et cetera*)
i.e.	that is (*id est*)
N.B.	note well (*nota bene*)
P.S.	postscript (*postscriptum*)

▶ Many firms have policies to help working parents—~~e.g.,~~ flexible
for example,

hours, parental leave, and day care.

▶ Before the conference began, Haivan unpacked the name tags,

programs, pens, ~~etc.~~
and so forth.

54f Use symbols and unit abbreviations appropriately.

Symbols such as %, +, $, and = are acceptable in charts and graphs. Dollar signs are acceptable with figures: *$11* (but not with words: *eleven dollars*). Units of measurement can be abbreviated in charts and graphs (*4 in.*) but not in the body of a paper (*four inches*).

54g Use other abbreviations according to convention.

Some abbreviations required in notes and in source citations are not appropriate in the body of a paper.

TALKING ABOUT STYLE

Abbreviations and Numbers in Different Fields

Use of abbreviations and numbers varies in different fields. See a typical example from a biochemistry textbook:

> The energy of a green photon . . . is 57 kilocalories per mole (kcal/mol). An alternative unit of energy is the joule (J), which is equal to 0.239 calorie; 1 kcal/mol is equal to 4.184 kJ/mol.
>
> – LUBERT STRYER, *Biochemistry*

These two sentences demonstrate how useful figures and abbreviations can be; reading the same sentences would be very difficult if the numbers and units of measurement were all written out.

Become familiar with the conventions governing abbreviations and numbers in your field. The following reference books provide guidelines:

MLA Handbook for Writers of Research Papers for literature and the humanities

Publication Manual of the American Psychological Association for the social sciences

Scientific Style and Format: The CSE Manual for Authors, Editors, and Publishers for the natural sciences

The Chicago Manual of Style for the humanities

AIP Style Manual for physics and the applied sciences

CHAPTER AND PAGES	chapter, page, pages (*not* ch., p., pp.)
MONTHS	January, February (*not* Jan., Feb.)
STATES AND NATIONS	California, Mexico (*not* Calif., Mex.)
	Two exceptions are Washington, D.C., and U.S.

54h Spell out numbers expressed in one or two words.

If you can write out a number in one or two words, do so. Use figures for longer numbers.

thirty-eight

▶ Her screams were heard by ~~38~~ *thirty-eight* people, none of whom called the police.

▶ A baseball is held together by ~~two hundred sixteen~~ *216* red stitches.

If one of several numbers *of the same kind* in the same sentence requires a figure, you should use figures for all the numbers in that sentence.

> *$100*
> ▶ An audio system can range in cost from ~~one hundred dollars~~ to $2,599.
> ^

54i Spell out numbers that begin sentences.

When a sentence begins with a number, either spell out the number or rewrite the sentence.

> *One hundred nineteen*
> ▶ ~~119~~ years of CIA labor cost taxpayers sixteen million dollars.
> ^

Most readers find it easier to read figures than three-word numbers; thus the best solution may be to rewrite this sentence: *Taxpayers spent sixteen million dollars for 119 years of CIA labor.*

54j Use figures according to convention.

ADDRESSES	23 Main Street; 175 Fifth Avenue
DATES	September 17, 1951; 6 June 1983; 4 BCE; the 1860s
DECIMALS AND FRACTIONS	65.34; 8½
PERCENTAGES	77 percent (*or* 77%)
EXACT AMOUNTS OF MONEY	$7,348; $1.46 trillion; $2.50; thirty-five (*or* 35) cents
SCORES AND STATISTICS	an 8–3 Red Sox victory; a verbal score of 600; an average age of 22; a mean of 53
TIME OF DAY	6:00 AM (*or* a.m.)

FOR MULTILINGUAL WRITERS

Using the Term *Hundred*

The term *hundred* is used idiomatically in English. When it is linked with numbers like two, eight, and so on, the word *hundred* remains singular: *Eight hundred years have passed and still old animosities run deep.* Add the plural *-s* to *hundred* only when no number precedes the term: *Hundreds of priceless books were lost in the fire.*

55   Italics

The slanted type known as *italics* is more than just a pretty typeface. Indeed, italics give words special meaning or emphasis. In the sentence "Many people read *People* on the subway every day," the italics (and the capital letter) tell readers that *People* is a publication.

QUICK HELP

Editing for Italics

- Check that all titles of long works are italicized. (55a)
- If you use any words, letters, or numbers as terms, make sure they are in italics. (55b)
- Italicize any non-English words or phrases that are not in an English dictionary. (55c)

55a   Italicize titles of long works.

In general, use italics for titles of long works; use quotation marks for shorter works (51c).

BOOKS	*Fun Home: A Family Tragicomic*
CHOREOGRAPHIC WORKS	Agnes de Mille's *Rodeo*
FILMS AND VIDEOS	*Selma*
LONG MUSICAL WORKS	*Brandenburg Concertos*
LONG POEMS	*Bhagavad Gita*
MAGAZINES AND JOURNALS	*Ebony,* the *New England Journal of Medicine*
NEWSPAPERS	the *Cleveland Plain Dealer*
PAINTINGS AND SCULPTURE	Georgia O'Keeffe's *Black Iris*
PAMPHLETS	Thomas Paine's *Common Sense*
PLAYS	*The Book of Mormon*
RADIO SERIES	*All Things Considered*

| RECORDINGS | *Nevermind* |
| TELEVISION SERIES | *House of Cards* |

55b Italicize words, letters, and numbers used as terms.

▶ On the back of his jersey was the famous *24*.

▶ One characteristic of some New York speech is the absence of postvocalic *r*—for example, pronouncing the word *four* as "fouh."

55c Italicize non-English words and phrases.

Italicize words from other languages unless they have become part of English—like the French "bourgeois" or the Italian "pasta," for example. If a word is in an English dictionary, it does not need italics.

▶ At last one of the phantom sleighs gliding along the street would come to a stop, and with gawky haste Mr. Burness in his fox-furred *shapka* would make for our door. — VLADIMIR NABOKOV, *Speak, Memory*

Hyphens 56

Hyphens are undoubtedly confusing to many people—hyphen problems are now one of the twenty most common surface errors in student writing. The confusion is understandable. Over time, the conventions for hyphen use in a given word can change (*tomorrow* was once spelled *to-morrow*). New words, even compounds such as *firewall*, generally don't use hyphens, but controversy continues to rage  over whether to hyphenate *email* (or is it *e-mail*?). And some words are hyphenated when they serve one kind of purpose in a sentence and not when they serve another.

> **QUICK HELP**
>
> **Editing for Hyphens**
>
> - Double-check compound words to be sure they are properly closed up, separated, or hyphenated. If in doubt, consult a dictionary. (56a)
> - Check all terms that have prefixes or suffixes to see whether you need hyphens. (56b)
> - Do not hyphenate two-word verbs or word groups that serve as subject complements. (56c)

56a Use hyphens with compound words.

Some compounds are one word (*rowboat, pickup*), some are separate words (*hard drive*), and some require hyphens (*sister-in-law*). You should consult a dictionary to be sure. However, the following conventions can help you decide when to use hyphens with compound words.

Compound adjectives

Hyphenate most compound adjectives that precede a noun but not those that follow a noun.

| a *well-liked* boss | My boss is *well liked.* |
| a *six-foot* plank | The plank is *six feet long.* |

In general, the reason for hyphenating compound adjectives is to facilitate reading.

▶ Designers often use potted plants as living-room dividers.

Without the hyphen, *living* may seem to modify *room dividers.*

Never hyphenate an -*ly* adverb and an adjective.

▶ They used a widely-distributed mailing list.

Fractions and compound numbers

Use a hyphen to write out fractions and to spell out compound numbers from twenty-one to ninety-nine.

| one-seventh | thirty-seven |
| two and seven-sixteenths | three hundred fifty-four thousand |

56b Use hyphens with prefixes and suffixes.

Most words containing prefixes or suffixes are written without hyphens: *antiwar, gorillalike.* Here are some exceptions:

BEFORE CAPITALIZED BASE WORDS	un-American, non-Catholic
WITH FIGURES	pre-1960, post-1945
WITH CERTAIN PREFIXES AND SUFFIXES	all-state, ex-partner, self-possessed, quasi-legislative, mayor-elect, fifty-odd
WITH COMPOUND BASE WORDS	pre-high school, post-cold war
FOR CLARITY OR EASE OF READING	re-cover, anti-inflation, troll-like

Re-cover means "cover again"; the hyphen distinguishes it from the word *recover,* meaning "get well." In *anti-inflation* and *troll-like,* the hyphens separate confusing clusters of vowels and consonants.

56c Avoid unnecessary hyphens.

Unnecessary hyphens are at least as common a problem as omitted ones. Do not hyphenate the parts of a two-word verb such as *depend on, turn off,* or *tune out* (44b).

▶ Every player must pick‑up a medical form before football tryouts.

The words *pick up* act as a verb and should not be hyphenated.

However, be careful to check that two words do indeed function as a verb in the sentence (36a); if they function as an adjective, a hyphen may be needed.

▶ Let's sign up for the early class.

The verb *sign up* should not have a hyphen.

▶ Where is the sign-up sheet?

The compound adjective *sign-up,* which modifies the noun *sheet,* needs a hyphen.

Do not hyphenate a subject complement—a word group that follows a linking verb (such as a form of *be* or *seem*) and describes the subject (37b).

▶ Audrey is almost eleven‑years‑old.

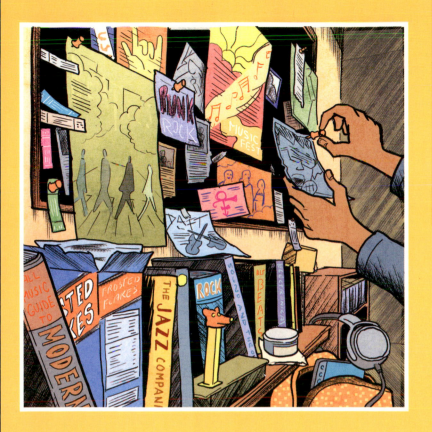

MLA Documentation

Careful citation shows your reader that
you've done your homework. . . . It amounts to
laying your intellectual cards on the table.

— JACK LYNCH

MLA Documentation

For visual analysis The illustration on the front of this tab suggests just a few possibilities for sources—from reference works to live performances—that you might cite in MLA style. Which sources will you include?

The Basics of MLA Style 57

Different rhetorical situations call for different approaches to citing sources—that is, for different ways of answering the question "Says who?" If you're reading a popular magazine, you probably won't expect the writer to provide careful source citations or a list of references at the end of an article. If you're posting material on a blog, you might follow conventions for citation by simply linking to the material you're talking about. But in other situations, including most academic writing, you will be expected to follow a more rigorous system for citing the information you use. Many courses in English ask writers to follow MLA style, the system developed by the Modern Language Association. For further reference, consult Chapters 58–60 or the *MLA Handbook for Writers of Research Papers,* Seventh Edition (2009).

57a Think about what readers need from you.

Why does academic work call for very careful citation practices when writing for the general public may not? The answer to that question is pretty easy: readers of your academic work (your instructor, other students, perhaps even researchers and professionals in your field) expect to get certain information from source citations:

- Source citations demonstrate that while you may not yet be a recognized expert on the topic, you've nevertheless done your homework, and you are a part of the conversation surrounding it. You include sources that you find credible and that provide evidence and good reasons to back up your claims, as well as sources that you need to respond to or refute (see 14a). Careful citation shows your readers what you know, where you stand, and what you think is important.

- Source citations show that you understand the need to give credit when you make use of someone else's intellectual property. Especially in academic writing, when it's better to be safe than sorry, include a citation for any source you think you might need to cite. (See Chapter 15 for details.)

- Source citations give explicit directions to guide readers who want to look for themselves at the works you're using.

The guidelines for MLA style (or APA or *Chicago*—if you are asked to use these systems, see Chapters 61–67) help you with this last purpose, giving you instructions on exactly what information to include in your citation and how to format that information.

57b   Identify the type of source you are using.

Before you can decide how to cite your source following MLA guidelines, you need to determine what kind of source you're using. This task can be surprisingly difficult. Citing a print book may seem relatively easy (though dizzying complications can arise—such as if the book has an editor or a translator, multiple editions, or chapters written by different people, to name a few possibilities). But citing digital sources may be especially mystifying. How, for instance, can you tell a website from a database you access online? What if your digital source reuses material from another source? Who publishes a digital text? Taking a step-by-step approach can help you solve such puzzles.

Print and digital sources

If your source has printed pages—a book or a newspaper, for instance—and you read the print version, you should look at the Directory to MLA Style on pp. 476–77 for information on citing a print source. If the print source is a regularly issued journal, magazine, or newspaper (look for a date or seasonal information such as "Spring" on the cover or first page), consider it a periodical rather than a book.

Be careful, however. If you access the digital version of an article, or if you read a book on an e-reader device such as a Kindle, then you should cite your source not as a print text but as a digital one. A digital version of a source may include updates or corrections that the print version lacks, so MLA guidelines require you to indicate your mode of access and to cite print and digital sources differently. If you can't find a model exactly like the source you've selected, see the box on p. 475.

Magazine and journal sources

MLA style treats magazines and journals slightly differently. To determine whether a print source is a magazine (a popular source) or a journal (a scholarly source), see 13a.

Web and database sources

Many students wonder how to distinguish between a web source and a source from a database. Both, after all, can be reached from a computer (if you have home access to your school library's online resources, you may be able to reach databases from any wired location). But guidelines for citing articles from the two types of sources are different, and so are considerations for using each type of writing.

DATABASE SOURCES

You need a subscription to look through most databases, so individual researchers almost always gain access to articles in databases through the computer system of a school or community library that pays to subscribe. The easiest way to tell whether a source comes from a database, then, is that its information is *not* available for free to anyone with an Internet connection. Many databases are digital collections of articles that originally appeared in print periodicals. The articles generally have the same written-word content as they did in print form, without changes or updates (some databases omit illustrations that appear in the print versions of articles, but others upload articles as PDFs that show not just words and illustrations but also the original print layout and page numbering). Print periodicals have editors, and some journals are peer-reviewed by experts in a field, ensuring that an authority vouches for the accuracy of the information. Finding information in an article from a database does *not* guarantee its credibility, but such information often has more authority behind it than much of what you find for free on the web.

David Craig, whose research writing appears in Chapter 60, found the source shown on p. 464 in Academic Search Premier, a database he accessed through a library website. From this page he was able to click through to the full text of the article. He printed this computer screen in case he needed to cite the article; the image includes all the information (other than his date of access) that he would need to create a complete MLA citation for an article from a database. Including the original print publication information for the article and the name of the database allows any reader who can access the database to locate the same article.

A SOURCE FROM A DATABASE

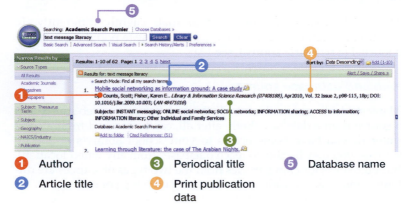

1 Author   **3** Periodical title   **5** Database name

2 Article title   **4** Print publication data

WEB SOURCES

Almost anyone can create a page on the web, and information posted there often has not been verified by anyone. Therefore, MLA guidelines ask you to identify the publisher or sponsor for any work from a website that you cite in your writing. Information about sponsors and publishers often appears at the bottom of a page, on a home page, or in a separate "About" section on a reputable website (see pp. 172–75 in Chapter 14 for details on evaluating web sources).

If the site doesn't identify a sponsor or publisher, you may still use it, but you should do more digging to find out about the site's creator, and you would be wise to verify information on such a site before including it in your own text. David Craig looked at a website called "Text Message 101" while doing his preliminary research; although no author was identified, the information seemed useful. But when he noticed that the site's sponsor was a cell phone provider using the site to sell phone plans, he decided against using the source in his writing project.

Web sources for content beyond the written word

Many sources used in academic writing consist mainly of written words, presented either in print or in digital form. But you may also want to include sources in which images and other media are at least as important as written words. Figuring out which model to follow for media sources that appear online can pose additional questions.

While researching her PowerPoint presentation on Alison Bechdel's graphic memoir *Fun Home* (see Chapter 23), Shuqiao Song came across a brief video interview with Bechdel on YouTube that she wanted to play for her audience. However, the YouTube post noted that the interview had originally appeared on a video log called *Stuck in Vermont* and that this interview grew out of, and included passages from, a print interview from a small local print publication. (This kind of complicated backstory is by no means unusual for online media.) Shuqiao had to decide whether the video clip was most like a video, an interview, a work from a website, or something else entirely. After consulting with her instructor, she decided to give the full citation for the source as a work from a website (see the source map on pp. 496–97), since a YouTube citation seemed likely to make the source most accessible to those who saw her presentation. (For advice on making such decisions when no exact model is available, see the box on p. 475.)

57c Plan and connect your citations.

MLA citations appear in two connected parts — the brief in-text citation, usually in parentheses in the body of your written text, and the full citation in the list of works cited, to which the in-text citation directs your readers. The most straightforward in-text citations include the author's name and the page number, but many variations on this basic format are discussed in Chapter 58.

In the text of his research essay (see Chapter 60), David Craig paraphrases material from the print book *Language Play* by linguist David Crystal. As shown here, he cites the book page on which the original information appears in a parenthetical reference that points readers to the entry for "Crystal, David" in his list of works cited. He also cites statistics from a report with four named authors that he found on a website sponsored by the nonprofit Pew Internet & American Life Project. The report, like many online texts, does not include page numbers. These examples show just two of the many ways to cite sources using in-text citations and a list of works cited. You'll need to make case-by-case decisions based on the types of sources you include.

for good reason. According to David Crystal, an internationally
recognized scholar of linguistics at the University of Wales, as
young children develop and learn how words string together to
express ideas, they go through many phases of language play.
The singsong rhymes and nonsensical chants of preschoolers are
vital to learning language, and a healthy appetite for wordplay
leads to a better command of language later in life (182).

Craig 10

*Ten-Year Trend in SAT Scores
Math Is Yielding Results:
Reading and Writing Are Causes for Concern*. New York: College
Board, 2002. Print.

College Board. "2011 SAT Trends." *Collegeboard.org*. College Board,
14 Sept. 2011. Web. 6 Dec. 2014.

Crystal, David. *Language Play*. Chicago: U of Chicago P, 1998. Print.

The Discouraging Word. "Re: Messaging and Literacy." Message to
the author. 13 Nov. 2014. E-mail.

Ferguson, Niall. "Texting Makes U Stupid." *Newsweek* 158.12
(2011): 11. *Academic Search Premier*. Web. 7 Dec. 2014.

Leibowitz, Wendy R. "Technology Transforms Writing and the
Teaching of Writing." *Chronicle of Higher Education* 26 Nov.
1999: A67-A68. Print.

Lenhart, Amanda. *Teens, Smartphones, & Texting*. Pew Research
Center, 19 Mar. 2012. PDF file.

Lenhart, Amanda, Sousan Arafeh, Aaron Smith, and Alexandra
Macgill. *Writing, Technology & Teens*. Pew Research Center, 24
Apr. 2008. Web. 6 Dec. 2014.

is rising among the young. According to the Pew Internet &
American Life Project, 85 percent of those aged twelve to
seventeen at least occasionally write text messages, instant
messages, or comments on social networking sites (Lenhart,
Arafeh, Smith, and Macgill). In 2001, the most conservative

s. *Teenage Life Online: The Rise of
...tion and the Internet's Impact on
...tionships*. Pew Research Center, 21
...14.

...y to Prove Text-Messaging Skills
Can Score SAT Points. *Christian Science Monitor* 11 Mar. 2005.
Web. 10 Dec. 2014.

57d   Include notes as needed.

MLA citation style asks you to include explanatory notes for information or comments that don't readily fit into your text but are needed
for clarification or further explanation. In addition, MLA permits bibliographic notes for offering information about or evaluation of a
source, or to list multiple sources that relate to a single point. Use
superscript numbers in the text to refer readers to the notes, which
may appear as endnotes (under the heading *Notes* on a separate page
immediately before the list of works cited) or as footnotes at the bottom of each page where a superscript number appears.

EXAMPLE OF SUPERSCRIPT NUMBER IN TEXT

Although such communication relies on the written word, many messagers disregard standard writing conventions. For example, here is a snippet from an IM conversation between two teenage girls:[1]

EXAMPLE OF EXPLANATORY NOTE

1. This transcript of an IM conversation was collected on 20 Nov. 2014. The teenagers' names are concealed to protect privacy.

57e Format MLA manuscripts appropriately.

The MLA recommends the following format for the manuscript of a research-based print project. If you are creating a nonprint project or have formatting questions, it's always a good idea to check with your instructor before preparing your final draft.

For detailed guidelines on formatting a list of works cited, see Chapter 59. For a sample student essay in MLA style, see Chapter 60.

- *First page and title page.* The MLA does not require a title page. Type each of the following items on a separate line on the first page, beginning one inch from the top and flush with the left margin: your name, the instructor's name, the course name and number, and the date. Double-space between each item; then double-space again and center the title. Double-space between the title and the beginning of the text.

- *Margins and spacing.* Leave one-inch margins at the top and bottom and on both sides of each page. Double-space the entire text, including set-off quotations, notes, and the list of works cited. Indent the first line of a paragraph one-half inch.

- *Page numbers.* Include your last name and the page number on each page, one-half inch below the top and flush with the right margin.

- *Long quotations.* Set off a long quotation (one with more than four typed lines) in block format by starting it on a new line and indenting each line one inch from the left margin. Do not enclose the passage in quotation marks (15b).

- *Headings.* MLA style allows, but does not require, headings. Many students and instructors find them helpful.

- *Visuals.* Place tables, photographs, drawings, charts, graphs, and other figures as near as possible to the relevant text. (See 15c for guidelines on incorporating visuals into your text.) Tables should have a label and number (*Table 1*) and a clear caption.

The label and caption should be aligned on the left, on separate lines. Give the source information below the table. All other visuals should be labeled *Figure* (abbreviated *Fig.*), numbered, and captioned. The label and caption should appear on the same line, followed by the source information. Remember to refer to each visual in your text, indicating how it contributes to the point you are making.

58   MLA Style for In-Text Citations

I n MLA style, a citation in the text of an essay is required for every quotation, paraphrase, summary, or other material requiring documentation (see 15f). In-text citations document material from other sources with both signal phrases and parenthetical references. Parenthetical references should include the information your readers need to locate the full reference in the list of works cited at the end of the text (Chapter 59). An in-text citation in MLA style aims to give the reader two kinds of information: (1) it indicates *which source* on the works-cited page the writer is referring to, and (2) it explains *where in the source* the material quoted, paraphrased, or summarized can be found, if the source has page numbers or other numbered sections.

The basic MLA in-text citation includes the author's last name either in a signal phrase introducing the source material (15b) or in parentheses at the end of the sentence. For sources with stable page numbers, it also includes the page number in parentheses at the end of the sentence.

SAMPLE CITATION USING A SIGNAL PHRASE

In his discussion of Monty Python routines, Crystal notes that the group relished "breaking the normal rules" of language (107).

SAMPLE PARENTHETICAL CITATION

A noted linguist explains that Monty Python humor often relied on "bizarre linguistic interactions" (Crystal 108).

(For digital sources without print page numbers, see model 3.)

In-text citations

1. Author named in a signal phrase, *469*
2. Author named in a parenthetical reference, *469*
3. Digital or nonprint source, *470*
4. Two or three authors, *470*
5. Four or more authors, *470*
6. Organization as author, *471*
7. Unknown author, *471*
8. Author of two or more works cited in the same project, *471*
9. Two or more authors with the same last name, *471*
10. Indirect source (author quoting someone else), *471*
11. Multivolume work, *472*
12. Work in an anthology or collection, *472*
13. Government source, *472*
14. Entire work, *472*
15. Two or more sources in one citation, *472*
16. Personal communication or social media source, *473*
17. Literary work, *473*
18. Sacred text, *473*
19. Encyclopedia or dictionary entry, *474*
20. Visual, *474*

Note in the following examples where punctuation is placed in relation to the parentheses.

1. AUTHOR NAMED IN A SIGNAL PHRASE

The MLA recommends using the author's name in a signal phrase to introduce the material and citing the page number(s), if any, in parentheses.

> Lee claims that his comic-book creation, Thor, was actually "the first regularly published superhero to speak in a consistently archaic manner" (199).

2. AUTHOR NAMED IN A PARENTHETICAL REFERENCE

When you do not mention the author in a signal phrase, include the author's last name before the page number(s), if any, in parentheses. Do not use punctuation between the author's name and the page number(s).

> The word *Bollywood* is sometimes considered an insult because it implies that Indian movies are merely "a derivative of the American film industry" (Chopra 9).

469

3. DIGITAL OR NONPRINT SOURCE

Give enough information in a signal phrase or in parentheses for readers to locate the source in your list of works cited. Many works found online or in electronic databases lack stable page numbers; you can omit the page number in such cases. However, if you are citing a work with stable pagination, such as an article in PDF format, include the page number in parentheses.

DIGITAL SOURCE WITHOUT STABLE PAGE NUMBERS

As a *Slate* analysis has noted, "Prominent sports psychologists get praised for their successes and don't get grief for their failures" (Engber).

DIGITAL SOURCE WITH STABLE PAGE NUMBERS

According to Whitmarsh, the British military had experimented with using balloons for observation as far back as 1879 (328).

If the source includes numbered sections, paragraphs, or screens, include the abbreviation (*sec.*), paragraph (*par.*), or screen (*scr.*) and the number in parentheses.

Sherman notes that the "immediate, interactive, and on-the-spot" nature of Internet information can make nondigital media seem outdated (sec. 32).

4. TWO OR THREE AUTHORS

Use all the authors' last names in a signal phrase or in parentheses.

Gortner, Hebrun, and Nicolson maintain that "opinion leaders" influence other people in an organization because they are respected, not because they hold high positions (175).

5. FOUR OR MORE AUTHORS

To give credit to all authors, name all the authors in a signal phrase or in parentheses. Alternatively, use the first author's name and *et al.* ("and others").

Similarly, as Belenky, Clinchy, Tarule, and Goldberger assert, examining the lives of women expands our understanding of human development (7).

Similarly, as Belenky et al. assert, examining the lives of women expands our understanding of human development (7).

6. ORGANIZATION AS AUTHOR

Give the group's full name or a shortened form of it in a signal phrase or in parentheses.

> Any study of social welfare involves a close analysis of "the impacts, the benefits, and the costs" of its policies (Social Research Corporation iii).

7. UNKNOWN AUTHOR

Use the full title, if it is brief, in your text—or a shortened version of the title in parentheses.

> One analysis defines *hype* as "an artificially engendered atmosphere of hysteria" (*Today's Marketplace* 51).

8. AUTHOR OF TWO OR MORE WORKS CITED IN THE SAME PROJECT

If your list of works cited has more than one work by the same author, include a shortened version of the title of the work that you are citing in a signal phrase or in parentheses to prevent reader confusion.

> Gardner shows readers their own silliness in his description of a "pointless, ridiculous monster, crouched in the shadows, stinking of dead men, murdered children, and martyred cows" (*Grendel* 2).

9. TWO OR MORE AUTHORS WITH THE SAME LAST NAME

Include the author's first *and* last names in a signal phrase or first initial and last name in a parenthetical reference.

> Children will learn to write if they are allowed to choose their own subjects, James Britton asserts, citing the Schools Council study of the 1960s (37-42).

10. INDIRECT SOURCE (AUTHOR QUOTING SOMEONE ELSE)

Use the abbreviation *qtd. in* to indicate that you are quoting from someone else's report of a source.

> As Arthur Miller says, "When somebody is destroyed everybody finally contributes to it, but in Willy's case, the end product would be virtually the same" (qtd. in Martin and Meyer 375).

11. MULTIVOLUME WORK

In a parenthetical reference, note the volume number first and then the page number(s), with a colon and one space between them.

> Modernist writers prized experimentation and gradually even sought to blur the line between poetry and prose, according to Forster (3: 150).

If you name only one volume of the work in your list of works cited, include only the page number in the parentheses.

12. WORK IN AN ANTHOLOGY OR COLLECTION

For an essay, short story, or other piece of prose reprinted in an anthology, use the name of the author of the work, not the editor of the anthology, but use the page number(s) from the anthology.

> Narratives of captivity play a major role in early writing by women in the United States, as demonstrated by Silko (219).

13. GOVERNMENT SOURCE

Because entries for sources authored by government agencies will appear on your list of works cited under the name of the country (see Chapter 59, item 79), your in-text citation for such a source should include the name of the country as well as the name of the agency responsible for the source.

> To reduce the agricultural runoff into the Chesapeake Bay, the United States Environmental Protection Agency has argued that "[h]igh nutrient loading crops, such as corn and soybean, should be replaced with alternatives in environmentally sensitive areas" (26).

14. ENTIRE WORK

Include the reference in the text, without any page numbers.

> In *Into the Wild,* Krakauer both criticizes and admires the solitary impulses of its young hero, which end up killing him.

15. TWO OR MORE SOURCES IN ONE CITATION

Separate the information with semicolons.

> Economists recommend that *employment* be redefined to include unpaid domestic labor (Clark 148; Nevins 39).

16. PERSONAL COMMUNICATION OR SOCIAL MEDIA SOURCE

Provide information that will allow readers to locate the source in your list of works cited, such as a name (if you know it) or username.

> George Hahn posted a self-portrait with a Citibike on Instagram with the caption, "Citibike is fabulous. Don't let anyone tell you differently."

17. LITERARY WORK

Because literary works are often available in many different editions, cite the page number(s) from the edition you used followed by a semicolon; then give other identifying information that will lead readers to the passage in any edition. Indicate the act and/or scene in a play (*37; sc. 1*). For a novel, indicate the part or chapter (*175; ch. 4*).

> In utter despair, Dostoyevsky's character Mitya wonders aloud about the "terrible tragedies realism inflicts on people" (376; bk. 8, ch. 2).

For a poem, cite the part (if there is one) and line(s), separated by a period.

> Whitman speculates, "All goes onward and outward, nothing collapses, / And to die is different from what anyone supposed, and luckier" (6.129-30).

If you are citing only line numbers, use the word *line(s)* in the first reference (*lines 21–22*) and the line numbers alone in subsequent references.

> The duke criticizes his late wife for having a "heart . . . too soon made glad" (line 22).

For a verse play, give only the act, scene, and line numbers, separated by periods.

> The witches greet Banquo as "Lesser than Macbeth, and greater" (1.3.65).

18. SACRED TEXT

To cite a sacred text such as the Qur'an or the Bible, give the title of the edition you used, then the book, chapter, and verse (or their equivalent), separated by a period. In your text, spell out the names of books. In parenthetical references, use abbreviations for books with names of five or more letters (*Gen.* for *Genesis*).

> He ignored the admonition "Pride goes before destruction, and a haughty spirit before a fall" (*New Oxford Annotated Bible,* Prov. 16.18).

19. ENCYCLOPEDIA OR DICTIONARY ENTRY

An entry for a reference work that does not list an author's name—for example, an encyclopedia or dictionary—will appear on the works-cited list under the entry's title. Enclose the title in quotation marks and place it in parentheses. Omit the page number if the reference work arranges entries alphabetically.

> The term *prion* was coined by Stanley B. Prusiner from the words
>
> *proteinaceous* and *infectious* and a suffix meaning *particle* ("Prion").

20. VISUAL

When you include an image in your text, number it and include a parenthetical reference that precedes the image in your text (*see Fig. 2*). Number figures (photos, drawings, cartoons, maps, graphs, and charts) and tables separately. Each visual should include a caption with the figure or table number and information about the source (see the box on p. 506).

> This trend is illustrated in a chart distributed by the College Board as part of
>
> its 2011 analysis of aggregate SAT data (see Fig. 1).

Soon after the preceding sentence, readers find the following figure and caption (see Chapter 60):

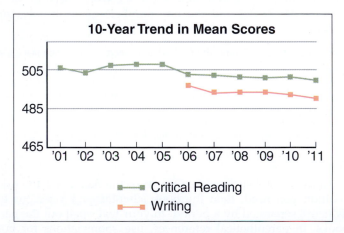

Fig. 1. Ten-year trend in mean SAT reading and writing scores (2001-2011). Data source: College Board, "2011 SAT Trends."

An image that you create might appear with a caption like this:

Fig. 4. Young woman reading a magazine. Personal photograph by author.

MLA Style for a List of Works Cited   **59**

A list of works cited is an alphabetical list of the sources you have referred to in your essay. (If your instructor asks you to list everything you have read as background, call the list *Works Consulted*.) Begin the works-cited list on a separate page or slide after the text of your project and any notes, under the centered heading *Works Cited* (not italicized or in quotation marks).

- Do not indent the first line of each entry, but indent subsequent lines for the entry one-half inch. (This makes the author names easy to scan.) Double-space the entire list.

- List sources alphabetically by authors' last names or by title for works without authors. For titles beginning with the article *A, An,* or *The,* don't count the article when alphabetizing.

QUICK HELP

Citing Sources That Don't Match Any Model Exactly

What should you do if your source doesn't match the model exactly? Suppose, for instance, that your source is a translated essay that appears in the fifth edition of an anthology.

- Identify a basic model to follow. If you decide that your source looks most like an essay in an anthology, you would start with a citation that looks like model 10.

- Look for models that show the additional elements in your source. For this example, you would need to add elements of model 13 (for the translation) and model 19 (for an edition other than the first).

- Add new elements from other models to your basic model in the order indicated.

- If you aren't sure how to arrange the pieces to create a combination model, ask your instructor.

  To cite a source for which you cannot find a model, collect as much information as you can find — about the creator, title, sponsor, date of posting or latest update, your access date, and the site's location — with the goal of helping your readers find the source for themselves, if possible. Then look at the models in this section to see which one most closely matches the type of source you are using. If possible, seek your instructor's advice to find the best model.

- List the author's last name first, followed by a comma and the first name. If a source has more than one author, subsequent authors' names appear first name first (see model 2).
- Italicize titles of books and long works. Put titles of articles and other short works in quotation marks.
- Give a medium, such as *Print* or *Web*, for each entry.

Works-cited entries, continued

Guidelines for author listings

The list of works cited is arranged alphabetically. The in-text citations in your writing point readers toward particular sources on the list (see Chapter 58).

NAME CITED IN SIGNAL PHRASE IN TEXT

Crystal explains . . .

NAME IN PARENTHETICAL CITATION IN TEXT

. . . (Crystal 107).

BEGINNING OF ENTRY IN LIST OF WORKS CITED

Crystal, David.

Models 1–6 explain how to arrange author names. The information that follows the name depends on the type of work you are citing—a print book (models 7–28); a print periodical (models 29–36); a written text from a digital source, such as an article from a website or database (models 37–54); sources from art, film, comics, or other media, including live performances (models 55–77); or academic, government, and legal sources (models 78–85). Consult the model that most closely resembles the source you are using.

1. ONE AUTHOR

Put the last name first, followed by a comma, the first name (and initial, if any), and a period.

Crystal, David.

2. MULTIPLE AUTHORS

List the first author's last name first (see model 1). Then, give the names of any other authors with the first name first. Separate authors' names with commas, and include the word *and* before the last person's name.

Martineau, Jane, Desmond Shawe-Taylor, and Jonathan Bate.

For four or more authors, either list all the names or list the first author followed by a comma and *et al.* ("and others").

Lupton, Ellen, Jennifer Tobias, Alicia Imperiale, Grace Jeffers, and Randi

Mates.

Lupton, Ellen, et al.

3. ORGANIZATION OR GROUP AUTHOR

Give the name of the group, government agency, corporation, or other organization listed as the author.

Getty Trust.

United States. Government Accountability Office.

4. UNKNOWN AUTHOR

When the author is not identified, begin the entry with the title, and alphabetize by the first important word. Italicize titles of books and long works, but put titles of articles and other short works in quotation marks.

"California Sues EPA over Emissions."

New Concise World Atlas.

5. AUTHOR USING A PSEUDONYM (PEN NAME) OR SCREEN NAME

Give the author's name as it appears in the source, followed by the real name in brackets. If you don't know the author's real name, use only the pseudonym or screen name.

Grammar Girl [Mignon Fogarty].

JennOfArk.

6. TWO OR MORE WORKS BY THE SAME AUTHOR

Arrange the entries alphabetically by title. Include the author's name in the first entry, but in subsequent entries, use three hyphens followed by a period. (For the basic format for citing a book, see model 7. For the basic format for citing an article from an online newspaper, see model 40.)

Chopra, Anupama. "Bollywood Princess, Hollywood Hopeful." *New York Times.*
New York Times, 10 Feb. 2008. Web. 13 Feb. 2008.

---. *King of Bollywood: Shah Rukh Khan and the Seductive World of Indian*
Cinema. New York: Warner, 2007. Print.

Note: Use three hyphens only when the work is by *exactly* the same author(s) as the previous entry.

Print books

7. BASIC FORMAT FOR A BOOK

Begin with the author name(s). (See models 1–6.) Then include the title and subtitle, the city of publication and the publisher, the publication year, and the medium (*Print*). The source map on pp. 482–83 shows where to find this information in a typical book.

Crystal, David. *Language Play.* Chicago: U of Chicago P, 1998. Print.

Note: Place a period and a space after the name, title, and date. Place a colon after the city and a comma after the publisher, and shorten the publisher's name—omit *Co.* or *Inc.*, and abbreviate *University Press* to *UP*.

8. AUTHOR AND EDITOR BOTH NAMED

Bangs, Lester. *Psychotic Reactions and Carburetor Dung.* Ed. Greil Marcus. New York: Knopf, 1988. Print.

To cite the editor's contribution instead, begin the entry with the editor's name.

Marcus, Greil, ed. *Psychotic Reactions and Carburetor Dung.* By Lester Bangs. New York: Knopf, 1988. Print.

9. EDITOR, NO AUTHOR NAMED

Wall, Cheryl A., ed. *Changing Our Own Words: Essays on Criticism, Theory, and Writing by Black Women.* New Brunswick: Rutgers UP, 1989. Print.

10. ANTHOLOGY

Cite an entire anthology the same way you would cite a book with an editor and no named author (see model 9).

Walker, Dale L., ed. *Westward: A Fictional History of the American West.* New York: Forge, 2003. Print.

11. WORK IN AN ANTHOLOGY OR CHAPTER IN A BOOK WITH AN EDITOR

List the author(s) of the selection; the selection title, in quotation marks; the title of the book, italicized; the abbreviation *Ed.* and the name(s) of the editor(s); publication information; the selection's page numbers; and the medium (*Print*).

Komunyakaa, Yusef. "Facing It." *The Seagull Reader.* Ed. Joseph Kelly. New York: Norton, 2000. 126-27. Print.

Note: Use the following format to provide original publication information for a reprinted selection:

Byatt, A. S. "The Thing in the Forest." *New Yorker* 3 June 2002: 80-89. Rpt. in *The O. Henry Prize Stories 2003*. Ed. Laura Furman. New York: Anchor, 2003. 3-22. Print.

---

12. TWO OR MORE ITEMS FROM THE SAME ANTHOLOGY

List the anthology as one entry (see model 10). Also list each of the selections separately with a cross-reference to the anthology.

Estleman, Loren D. "Big Tim Magoon and the Wild West." Walker 391-404.

Salzer, Susan K. "Miss Libbie Tells All." Walker 199-212.

13. TRANSLATION

Bolaño, Roberto. *2666*. Trans. Natasha Wimmer. New York: Farrar, 2008. Print.

14. BOOK WITH BOTH TRANSLATOR AND EDITOR

List the editor's and translator's names after the title, in the order they appear on the title page.

Kant, Immanuel. *"Toward Perpetual Peace" and Other Writings on Politics, Peace, and History*. Ed. Pauline Kleingeld. Trans. David L. Colclasure. New Haven: Yale UP, 2006. Print.

15. TRANSLATION OF A SECTION OF A BOOK

If different translators have worked on various parts of the book, identify the translator of the part you are citing.

García Lorca, Federico. *"The Little Mad Boy."* Trans. W. S. Merwin. *The Selected Poems of Federico García Lorca*. Ed. Francisco García Lorca and Donald M. Allen. London: Penguin, 1969. Print.

16. TRANSLATION OF A BOOK BY AN UNKNOWN AUTHOR

Place the title first unless you wish to emphasize the translator's work.

Grettir's Saga. Trans. Denton Fox and Hermann Palsson. Toronto: U of Toronto P, 1974. Print.

17. BOOK IN A LANGUAGE OTHER THAN ENGLISH

Include a translation of the title in brackets, if necessary.

Benedetti, Mario. *La borra del café* [*The Coffee Grind*]. Buenos Aires: Sudamericana, 2000. Print.

Take information from the book's title page and copyright page (on the reverse side of the title page), not from the book's cover or a library catalog.

1 **Author.** List the last name first. End with a period. For variations, see models 2–6.

2 **Title.** Italicize the title and any subtitle; capitalize all major words. End with a period.

3 **City of publication and publisher.** If more than one city is given, use the first one listed. For foreign cities, add an abbreviation of the country or province (*Cork, Ire.*). Follow it with a colon and a shortened version of the publisher's name (*Oxford UP* for *Oxford University Press*). Follow it with a comma.

4 **Year of publication.** If more than one copyright date is given, use the most recent one. End with a period.

5 **Medium of publication.** End with the medium (*Print*) followed by a period.

A citation for the book on p. 483 would look like this:

Patel, Raj. *The Value of Nothing: How to Reshape Market Society and Redefine Democracy.* New York: Picador, 2009. Print.

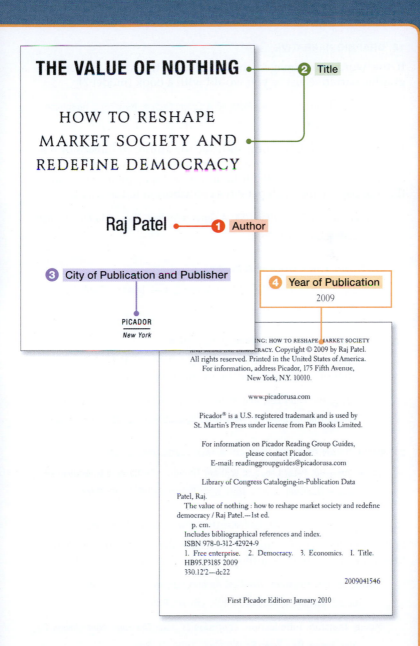

THE VALUE OF NOTHING — ❷ Title

HOW TO RESHAPE MARKET SOCIETY AND REDEFINE DEMOCRACY

Raj Patel — ❶ Author

❸ City of Publication and Publisher

PICADOR
New York

❹ Year of Publication
2009

...NG: HOW TO RESHAPE MARKET SOCIETY AND REDEFINE DEMOCRACY. Copyright © 2009 by Raj Patel. All rights reserved. Printed in the United States of America. For information, address Picador, 175 Fifth Avenue, New York, N.Y. 10010.

www.picadorusa.com

Picador® is a U.S. registered trademark and is used by St. Martin's Press under license from Pan Books Limited.

For information on Picador Reading Group Guides, please contact Picador.
E-mail: readinggroupguides@picadorusa.com

Library of Congress Cataloging-in-Publication Data

Patel, Raj.
The value of nothing : how to reshape market society and redefine democracy / Raj Patel.—1st ed.
p. cm.
Includes bibliographical references and index.
ISBN 978-0-312-42924-9
1. Free enterprise. 2. Democracy. 3. Economics. I. Title.
HB95.P3185 2009
330.12'2—dc22

2009041546

First Picador Edition: January 2010

18. GRAPHIC NARRATIVE

If the words and images are created by the same person, cite a graphic narrative just as you would with a book (model 7).

> Bechdel, Alison. *Are You My Mother? A Comic Drama.* New York: Houghton, 2012. Print.

If the work is a collaboration, indicate the author or illustrator who is most important to your research before the title of the work. List other contributors after the title, in the order of their appearance on the title page. Label each person's contribution to the work.

> Stavans, Ilan, writer. *Latino USA: A Cartoon History.* Illus. Lalo Arcaraz. New York: Basic, 2000. Print.

19. EDITION OTHER THAN THE FIRST

> Walker, John A. *Art in the Age of Mass Media.* 3rd ed. London: Pluto, 2001. Print.

20. ONE VOLUME OF A MULTIVOLUME WORK

Give the number of the volume cited after the title. Including the total number of volumes after the publication date is optional.

> Ch'oe, Yong-Ho, Peter Lee, and William Theodore De Barry, eds. *Sources of Korean Tradition.* Vol. 2. New York: Columbia UP, 2000. Print. 2 vols.

21. MORE THAN ONE VOLUME OF A MULTIVOLUME WORK

> Ch'oe, Yong-Ho, Peter Lee, and William Theodore De Barry, eds. *Sources of Korean Tradition.* 2 vols. New York: Columbia UP, 2000. Print.

22. PREFACE, FOREWORD, INTRODUCTION, OR AFTERWORD

Following the writer's name, describe the contribution. After the title, indicate the book's author (with *By*) or editor (with *Ed.*).

> Atwan, Robert. Foreword. *The Best American Essays 2002.* Ed. Stephen Jay Gould. Boston: Houghton, 2002. viii-xii. Print.

> Moore, Thurston. Introduction. *Confusion Is Next: The Sonic Youth Story.* By Alec Foege. New York: St. Martin's, 1994. xi. Print.

23. ENTRY IN A REFERENCE BOOK

For a well-known encyclopedia, note the edition (if identified) and year of publication. If the entries are alphabetized, omit publication information and page number.

Kettering, Alison McNeil. "Art Nouveau." *World Book Encyclopedia*. 2002 ed. Print.

24. BOOK THAT IS PART OF A SERIES

After the medium (*Print*), cite the series name (and number, if any) from the title page.

Nichanian, Marc, and Vartan Matiossian, eds. *Yeghishe Charents: Poet of the Revolution*. Costa Mesa: Mazda, 2003. Print. Armenian Studies Ser. 5.

25. REPUBLICATION (MODERN EDITION OF AN OLDER BOOK)

Indicate the original publication date after the title.

Austen, Jane. *Sense and Sensibility*. 1813. New York: Dover, 1996. Print.

26. PUBLISHER'S IMPRINT

If the title page gives a publisher's imprint, hyphenate the imprint and the publisher's name.

Hornby, Nick. *About a Boy*. New York: Riverhead-Penguin Putnam, 1998. Print.

27. BOOK WITH A TITLE WITHIN THE TITLE

Do not italicize a book title within a title. For an article title within a title, italicize as usual and place the article title in quotation marks.

Mullaney, Julie. *Arundhati Roy's The God of Small Things: A Reader's Guide*. New York: Continuum, 2002. Print.

Rhynes, Martha. *"I, Too, Sing America": The Story of Langston Hughes*. Greensboro: Morgan, 2002. Print.

28. SACRED TEXT

To cite any individual published editions of sacred books, begin the entry with the title.

Qur'an: The Final Testament (Authorized English Version) with Arabic Text. Trans. Rashad Khalifa. Fremont: Universal Unity, 2000. Print.

Formatting Print Periodical Entries

- Place the *title of the article* from a periodical (journal, magazine, or newspaper) in quotation marks. Put the period inside the closing quotation mark.
- Give the *title of the periodical* as it appears on the magazine's or journal's cover or the newspaper's front page; omit any initial *A*, *An*, or *The*. Italicize the title.
- For *journals*, include the volume number, a period, the issue number (if given), and the year in parentheses.
- For *magazines and newspapers*, give the date in this order: day (if given), month, year. Abbreviate months except for May, June, and July.
- List inclusive *page numbers* if the article appears on consecutive pages. If it skips pages, give only the first page number and a plus sign (*34 +*).
- End with the *medium* (*Print*).

Articles and short works in print periodicals

Begin with the author name(s). (See models 1–6.) Then include the article title, the title of the periodical, the date or volume information, the page numbers, and the medium (*Print*). The source map on pp. 488–89 shows where to find all of this information in a sample periodical.

29. ARTICLE IN A PRINT JOURNAL

Follow the journal title with the volume number, a period, the issue number (if given), and the year (in parentheses).

> Gigante, Denise. "The Monster in the Rainbow: Keats and the Science of Life." *PMLA* 117.3 (2002): 433-48. Print.

30. ARTICLE IN A PRINT MAGAZINE

Provide the date from the magazine cover, and do not include volume or issue numbers.

> Sanneh, Kelefa. "Skin in the Game." *New Yorker* 24 Mar. 2014: 48-55. Print.

> Taubin, Amy. "All Talk?" *Film Comment* Nov.-Dec. 2007: 45-47. Print.

31. ARTICLE IN A PRINT NEWSPAPER

Include the edition (if listed) and the section number or letter (if listed).

> Fackler, Martin. "Japan's Foreign Minister Says Apologies to Wartime Victims
>
> Will Be Upheld." *New York Times* 9 Apr. 2014, late ed.: A6. Print.

Note: For locally published newspapers, add the city in brackets after the name if it is not part of the name: *Globe and Mail [Toronto].*

32. EDITORIAL IN A PRINT PERIODICAL

Include the writer's name, if given, and the title, if any, followed by the label *Editorial.*

> "California Dreaming." Editorial. *Nation* 25 Feb. 2008: 4. Print.

33. LETTER TO THE EDITOR OF A PRINT PERIODICAL

Include the writer's name, if given, and the title, if any, followed by the label *Letter.* Provide relevant information for the type of source (journal, magazine, newspaper).

> MacEwan, Valerie. Letter. *Believer* Jan. 2014: 4. Print.

34. REVIEW IN A PRINT PERIODICAL

Include the writer's name and the title of the review, if given, then *Rev. of* and the title of the work under review.

> Nussbaum, Emily. "Change Agents." Rev. of *Silicon Valley*, by Mike Judge. *New*
>
> *Yorker* 31 Mar. 2014: 68. Print.

> Schwarz, Benjamin. Rev. of *The Second World War: A Short History*, by
>
> R. A. C. Parker. *Atlantic Monthly* May 2002: 110-11. Print.

35. INTERVIEW IN A PRINT PERIODICAL

List the person interviewed and either the title of the interview (if any) or the label *Interview*, along with the interviewer's name, if relevant.

> Blume, Judy. Interview by Lena Dunham. *Believer* Jan. 2014: 39+. Print.

36. UNSIGNED ARTICLE IN A PRINT PERIODICAL

> "Performance of the Week." *Time* 6 Oct. 2003: 18. Print.

MLA SOURCE MAP: Articles in Print Periodicals

1 **Author.** List the last name first. End with a period. For variations, see models 2–6.

2 **Article title.** Put the title and any subtitle in quotation marks; capitalize all major words. Place a period inside the closing quotation mark.

3 **Periodical title.** Italicize the title; capitalize all major words. Omit any initial *A*, *An*, or *The*.

4 **Volume and issue / Date of publication.** For journals, give the volume number and issue number (if any), separated by a period; then list the year in parentheses and follow it with a colon.

For magazines, list the day (if given), month, and year.

5 **Page numbers.** List inclusive page numbers. If the article skips pages, put the first page number and a plus sign. End with a period.

6 **Medium.** Give the medium (*Print*). End with a period.

A citation for the article on p. 489 would look like this:

Quart, Alissa. "Lost Media, Found Media: Snapshots from the Future of Writing." *Columbia Journalism Review* May/June 2008: 30-34. Print.

3 Periodical Title

COLUMBIA
JOURNALISM REVIEW
May / June 2008 · cjr.org

4 Date of Publication
May/June 2008

The Future of
Writing

Nonfiction's
ALISSA QUART

Kindle isn't
EZRA KLEIN

UNDER TH
A reporter r
that got him
CAMERON MC

LOVE THY
The religion
TIM TOWNSE

$4.95

2 Article Title

Lost Media, Found Media

Snapshots from the future of writing

BY ALISSA QUART

1 Author
ALISSA QUART

If there were an ashram for people who worship contemplative long-form journalism, it would be the Nieman Conference on Narrative Journalism. This March, at the Sheraton Boston Hotel, hundreds of journalists, authors, students, and aspirants came for the weekend event. Seated on metal chairs in large conference rooms, we learned about muscular storytelling (the Q-shaped narrative structure—who knew?). We sipped cups of coffee and ate bagels and heard about reporting history through letters and public documents and how to evoke empathy for our subjects, particularly our most marginal ones. As we listened to reporters discussing great feats—exposing Walter Reed's fetid living quarters for wounded soldiers, for instance—we also renewed our pride in our profession. In short, the conference exemplified the best of the older media models, the ones that have so recently fallen into economic turmoil.

Yet even at the weekend's strongest lectures on interview techniques or the long-form profile, we couldn't ignore the digital elephant in the room. We all knew as writers that the kinds of pieces we were discussing require months of work to be both deep and refined, and that we were all hard-pressed for the time and the money to do that. It was always hard for nonfiction writers, but something seems to have changed. For those of us who believed in the value of the journalism and literary nonfiction of the past, we had become like the people at the ashram after the guru has died.

Right now, journalism is more or less divided into two camps, which I will call Lost Media and Found Media. I went to the Nieman conference partially because I wanted to see how the forces creating this new division are affecting and afflicting the Lost Media world that I love best, not on the institutional level, but for reporters and writers themselves. This world includes people who write for all the newspapers and magazines that are currently struggling with layoffs, speedups, hiring freezes, buyouts, the death or shrinkage of film- and book-review sections, limits on expensive investigative work, the erasure of foreign bureaus, and the general narrowing of institutional ambition. It includes freelance writers competing with hordes of ever-younger competitors willing to write and publish online for free, the fade-out of established journalistic career paths, and, perhaps most crucially, a muddled sense of the meritorious, as blogs level and scramble the value and status of print publications, and of professional writers. The glamour and influence once associated with a magazine elite seem to have faded, becoming a sort of pastiche of winsome articles about yearning and boxers and dinners at Elaine's.

Found Media-ites, meanwhile, are the bloggers, the contributors to Huffington Post-type sites that aggregate blogs, as well as other work that somebody else paid for, and the new non-profits and pay-per-article schemes that aim to save journalism from 20 percent profit-margin demands. Although these elements are often disparate, together they compose the new media landscape. In economic terms, I mean all the outlets for nonfiction writing that seem to be thriving in the new era or striving to fill niches that Lost Media is giving up in a new order. Stylistically, Found Media tends to feel spontaneous, almost accidental. It's a domain dominated by the young, where writers get points not for following traditions or burnishing them but for amateur and hybrid vigor, for creating their own venues and their own genres. It is about public expression and community—not quite John Dewey's Great Community, which the critic Eric Alterman alluded to in a recent *New Yorker* article on newspapers, but rather a fractured form of Dewey's ideal: call it Great Communities.

To be a Found Media journalist or pundit, one need not be elite, expert, or trained; one must simply produce punchy intellectual property that is in conversation with groups of

30 MAY/JUNE 2008

Illustration by Tomer Hanuka

5 Page Numbers
30–34

Citing Digital Sources

When citing sources accessed online or from a digital database, include as many of the following elements as you can find:

1. **Author.** Give the author's name, if available.
2. **Title.** Put titles of articles or short works in quotation marks. Italicize book titles.

FOR WORKS FROM DATABASES:

3. **Title of periodical,** italicized.
4. **Publication information.** After the volume/issue/year or date, include page numbers (or *n. pag.* if no page numbers are listed).
5. **Name of database,** italicized, if you used a subscription service such as Academic Search Premier.

FOR WORKS FROM THE WEB:

3. **Title of the site,** italicized.
4. **Name of the site's publisher or sponsor.** This information usually appears at the bottom of the page.
5. **Date of online publication or most recent update.** This information often appears at the bottom of the page. If no date is given, use *n.d.*

6. **Medium of publication.** Use *Web* for works from both databases and the web.
7. **Date of access.** Give the most recent date you accessed the source.

If you think your readers will have difficulty finding the source without a URL, put it after the period following the date of access, inside angle brackets, with a period after the closing bracket.

Digital written-word sources

Digital sources such as websites differ from print sources in the ease with which they can be changed, updated, or eliminated. In addition, the various digital media do not organize their works the same way. The most commonly cited digital sources are documents from websites and databases. For help determining which is which, see Chapter 57.

37. WORK FROM AN ONLINE DATABASE

The basic format for citing a work from a database appears in the source map on pp. 492–93.

For a periodical article that is available in print but that you access in an online database through a library subscription service such as Academic Search Premier, begin with the author's name (if given); the title of the work, in quotation marks; the title of the periodical, italicized; and the volume/issue and date of the print version of the work (see models 29–36). Include the page numbers from the print version; if no page numbers are available, use *n. pag.* Then give the name of the online database, italicized; the medium (*Web*); and your most recent date of access.

> Collins, Ross F. "Cattle Barons and Ink Slingers: How Cow Country Journalists Created a Great American Myth." *American Journalism* 24.3 (2007): 7-29. *Communication and Mass Media Complete.* Web. 7 Feb. 2013.

38. ARTICLE FROM A JOURNAL ON THE WEB

Begin an entry for an online journal article as you would one for a print journal article (see model 29). If an article does not have page numbers, use *n. pag.* End with the medium consulted (*Web*) and the date of access.

> Gallagher, Brian. "Greta Garbo Is Sad: Some Historical Reflections on the Paradoxes of Stardom in the American Film Industry, 1910-1960." *Images: A Journal of Film and Popular Culture* 3 (1997): n. pag. Web. 7 Aug. 2013.

39. ARTICLE FROM A MAGAZINE ON THE WEB

List the author, article title, and name of the magazine. Then identify the sponsor of the website and the date of publication, the medium (*Web*), and your date of access.

> Sullivan, Barbara Apple. "Big Data: Where Does Intuition Fit In?" *Below the Fold.* Sullivan, Apr. 2014. Web. 11 Apr. 2014.

40. ARTICLE FROM A NEWSPAPER ON THE WEB

After the name of the newspaper, give the publisher, publication date, medium (*Web*), and access date.

> Shyong, Frank. "Sriracha Showdown Intensifies as Irwindale Declares Public Nuisance." *Los Angeles Times.* Los Angeles Times, 10 Apr. 2014. Web. 16 May 2014.

Library subscriptions—such as EBSCOhost and Academic Search Premier—provide access to huge databases of articles.

1 **Author.** List the last name first. End with a period. For variations, see models 2–6.

2 **Article title.** Enclose the title and any subtitle in quotation marks.

3 **Periodical title.** Italicize it. Exclude any initial *A*, *An*, or *The*.

4 **Volume and issue / Date of publication.** List the volume and issue number, if any. Then, add the date of publication, including the day (if given), month, and year, in that order. Last, add a colon.

5 **Page numbers.** Give the inclusive page numbers. If an article has no page numbers, write *n. pag*.

6 **Database name.** Italicize the name of the database.

7 **Medium.** For an online database, use *Web*.

8 **Date of access.** Give the day, month, and year, then a period.

A citation for the article on p. 493 would look like this:

Arnett, Robert P. "*Casino Royale* and Franchise Remix: James Bond as Superhero." *Film Criticism* 33.3 (2009): 1-16. *Academic Search Premier.* Web. 16 May 2014.

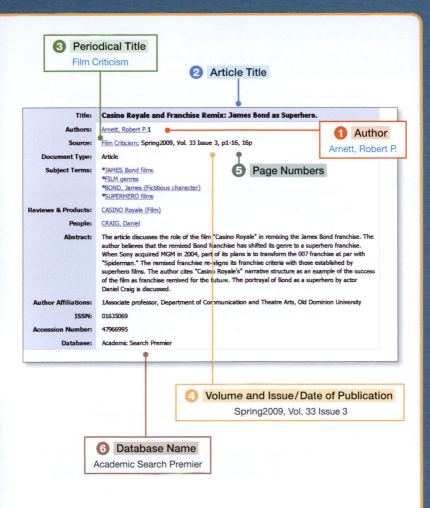

3 Periodical Title
Film Criticism

2 Article Title

Title:	Casino Royale and Franchise Remix: James Bond as Superhero.
Authors:	Arnett, Robert P.1
Source:	Film Criticism; Spring2009, Vol. 33 Issue 3, p1-16, 16p
Document Type:	Article
Subject Terms:	*JAMES Bond films *FILM genres *BOND, James (Fictitious character) *SUPERHERO films
Reviews & Products:	CASINO Royale (Film)
People:	CRAIG, Daniel
Abstract:	The article discusses the role of the film "Casino Royale" in remixing the James Bond franchise. The author believes that the remixed Bond franchise has shifted its genre to a superhero franchise. When Sony acquired MGM in 2004, part of its plans is to transform the 007 franchise at par with "Spiderman." The remixed franchise re-aligns its franchise criteria with those established by superhero films. The author cites "Casino Royale's" narrative structure as an example of the success of the film as franchise remixed for the future. The portrayal of Bond as a superhero by actor Daniel Craig is discussed.
Author Affiliations:	1Associate professor, Department of Communication and Theatre Arts, Old Dominion University
ISSN:	01635069
Accession Number:	47966995
Database:	Academic Search Premier

1 Author
Arnett, Robert P.

5 Page Numbers

4 Volume and Issue/Date of Publication
Spring2009, Vol. 33 Issue 3

6 Database Name
Academic Search Premier

41. DIGITAL BOOK (ONLINE OR E-READER)

Provide information as for a print book (see models 7–28); then give the digital publication information, the medium, and the date of access.

> Euripides. *The Trojan Women*. Trans. Gilbert Murray. New York: Oxford UP,
>
>   1915. *Internet Sacred Text Archive*. Web. 12 Oct. 2014.

If you read the book on an e-reader such as a Kindle or Nook, the medium should specify the type of reader file you used. No access date is required.

> Schaap, Rosie. *Drinking with Men: A Memoir*. New York: Riverhead-Penguin,
>
>   2013. Kindle file.

42. PART OF A DIGITAL BOOK

Cite as you would a part of a print book (see models 11 and 22). Give the print (if any) and digital publication information, the medium (*Web*), and the date of access.

> Riis, Jacob. "The Genesis of the Gang." *The Battle with the Slum*. New York:
>
>   Macmillan, 1902. N. pag. *Bartleby.com: Great Books Online*. Web.
>
>   31 Mar. 2014.

43. ONLINE POEM

Include the poet's name, the title of the poem, and the print publication information (if any). End with the electronic publication information, the medium (*Web*), and the date of access.

> Geisel, Theodor. "Too Many Daves." *The Sneetches and Other Stories*. New York:
>
>   Random House, 1961. N. pag. *Poetry Foundation*. Web. 2 Feb. 2014.

44. ONLINE EDITORIAL OR LETTER TO THE EDITOR

Include the author's name (if given) and the title (if any). Then give the label *Editorial* or *Letter*. Follow the appropriate model for the type of source you are using. (Check the directory on pp. 476–77.)

> "Shorter Drug Sentences." Editorial. *New York Times*. New York Times, 10 Apr.
>
>   2014. Web. 5 May 2014.

> Starr, Evva. "Local Reporting Thrives in High Schools." Letter. *Washington
>
>   Post*. Washington Post, 4 Apr. 2014. Web. 16 Apr. 2014.

45. ONLINE REVIEW

Cite an online review as you would a print review (see model 34), and include information about the work under review. End with the name of the website, the sponsor, the date of publication, the medium, and the date of access.

> O'Hehir, Andrew. "Aronofsky's Deranged Biblical Action Flick." Rev. of *Noah*,
>
> dir. Darren Aronofsky. *Salon*. Salon Media Group, 27 May 2014. Web.
>
> 24 Apr. 2014.

46. SHORT WORK FROM A WEBSITE

For basic information for citing a work on a website that is not part of a regularly published journal, magazine, or newspaper, see the source map on pp. 496–97. Include all of the following elements that are available: the author; the title of the document, in quotation marks; the name of the website, italicized; the name of the publisher or sponsor (if none is available, use *N.p.*); the date of publication (if not available, use *n.d.*); the medium consulted (*Web*); and the date of access.

> Bali, Karan. "Kishore Kumar." *Upperstall.com*. Upperstall, n.d. Web. 7 May 2014.

> "Our Mission." *Trees for Life International*. Trees for Life International, 2011.
>
> Web. 31 May 2014.

47. ENTIRE WEBSITE

Follow the guidelines for a specific work from the web, beginning with the name of the author or editor (if any), followed by the title of the website, italicized; the name of the sponsor or publisher (if none, use *N.p.*); the date of publication or last update; the medium of publication (*Web*); and the date of access.

> Glazier, Loss Pequeño, dir. *Electronic Poetry Center*. SUNY Buffalo, 2014. Web.
>
> 26 Sept. 2014.

> *Weather.com*. Weather Channel Interactive, 2014. Web. 13 Mar. 2014.

For a personal website, include the name of the person who created the site; the title, in quotation marks if it is part of a larger work or italicized if it is not, or (if there is no title) a description such as *Home page*, not italicized; the name of the larger site, if different from the personal site's title; the publisher or sponsor of the site (if none, use

MLA SOURCE MAP: Works from Websites

You may need to browse other parts of a site to find some of the following elements, and some sites may omit elements. Uncover as much information as you can.

1 **Author.** List the last name first. End with a period. If no author is given, begin with the title. For variations, see models 2–6.

2 **Title of work.** Enclose the title and any subtitle of the work in quotation marks.

3 **Title of website.** Give the title of the entire website, italicized.

4 **Publisher or sponsor.** Look for the sponsor's name at the bottom of the home page. If no information is available, write *N.p.* Follow it with a comma.

5 **Date of publication or latest update.** Give the most recent date, followed by a period. If no date is available, use *n.d.*

6 **Medium.** Use *Web* and follow it with a period.

7 **Date of access.** Give the date you accessed the work. End with a period.

A citation for the work on p. 497 would look like this:

Tønnesson, Øyvind. "Mahatma Gandhi, the Missing Laureate." *Nobelprize.org.* Nobel Media AB, 2015. Web. 4 May 2015.

① **Author**
Øyvind
Tønnesson

③ **Title of Website**

② **Title of Work**

⑤ **Date of Publication**
2015

④ **Publisher or Sponsor**
Nobel Media AB

N.p.); the date of the last update (if there is no date, use *n.d.*); the medium of publication (*Web*); and the date of access.

> Enright, Mike. Home page. *Menright.com*. N.p., n.d. Web. 17 May 2014.

48. ENTRY IN AN ONLINE REFERENCE WORK OR WIKI

Begin with the title unless the author is named. (A wiki, which is collectively edited, will not include an author.) Treat an online reference entry as you would a short work from a website (see model 46). Include the title of the entry; the name of the work, italicized; the sponsor or publisher (use *N.p.* if none is named); the date of the latest update; the medium (*Web*); and the date of access. Before using a wiki as a source, check with your instructor.

> "Gunpowder Plot." *Wikipedia*. Wikimedia Foundation, 28 Mar. 2014. Web. 10 Apr. 2014.

49. ACADEMIC COURSE OR DEPARTMENT WEBSITE

For a course site, include the name of the instructor, the title of the course in quotation marks, the title of the site in italics, the department (if relevant) and institution sponsoring the site, the date (or *n.d.* if none is given), the medium consulted (*Web*), and the access information.

> Creekmur, Corey K., and Philip Lutgendorf. "Topics in Asian Cinema: Popular Hindi Cinema." *University of Iowa*. Depts. of English, Cinema, and Comparative Literature, U of Iowa, 2007. Web. 13 Mar. 2014.

For a department website, give the department name, the description *Dept. home page*, the institution (in italics), the site sponsor, the date (or *n.d.*), the medium (*Web*), and the access information.

> English Dept. home page. *Amherst College*. Amherst Coll., n.d. Web. 5 Apr. 2014.

50. BLOG

For an entire blog, give the author's name, if any; the title of the blog, italicized; the sponsor or publisher of the blog (if there is none, use *N.p.*); the date of the most recent update; the medium (*Web*); and the date of access.

> Levy, Carla Miriam. *Filmi Geek*. N.p., 2 Apr. 2014. Web. 14 Apr. 2014.

> *Little Green Footballs*. Little Green Footballs, 14 Apr. 2014. Web. 14 Apr. 2014.

Note: To cite a blogger who writes under a pseudonym, begin with the pseudonym and then put the writer's real name (if you know it) in square brackets. (See model 5, p. 479.)

> Atrios [Duncan Black]. *Eschaton*. N.p., 27 Apr. 2014. Web.
>
> 27 Apr. 2014.

51. POST OR COMMENT ON A BLOG OR DISCUSSION GROUP

Give the author's name; the title of the post, in quotation marks (if there is no title, use the description *Online posting*, not italicized); the title of the site, italicized; the sponsor (if there is none, use *N.p.*); the date of the most recent update; the medium (*Web*); and the date of access.

> Edroso, Roy. "Friends in High Places." *Alicublog*. N.p., 16 Apr. 2014. Web.
>
> 18 Apr. 2014.

For a comment on an online post, give the writer's name or screen name (see model 5); the title of the comment or a label such as *Online comment*, not italicized; the title of the article commented on, in quotation marks; and the label *by* and the article author's name. End with the citation information for the type of article.

> JennOfArk. Online comment. "Friends in High Places," by Roy Edroso.
>
> *Alicublog*. N.p., 16 Apr. 2014. Web. 18 Apr. 2014.

52. TWEET

Include the writer's real name, if known, with the user name (if different) in parentheses. If you don't know the real name, give just the user name. Include the entire tweet, in quotation marks. End with the date and time of the message and the medium *Tweet*.

> Patterson, Amy (amycep). "So many cool student projects at the @
>
> BedfordPub Celebration of Multimodal Composition! #4c14 pic.twitter.
>
> com/pZpxYgmpbj." 21 Mar. 2014, 4:46 p.m. Tweet.

53. POSTING ON A SOCIAL NETWORKING SITE

To cite a posting on Facebook, Instagram, or another social networking site, include the writer's name; up to 140 characters of the posting, in quotation marks (or a description such as *Photograph*, not italicized and not in quotation marks, if no text appears); the date of the post; and the medium of delivery (such as *Facebook post*). (The MLA does not provide guidelines for citing postings or messages on such sites; this model is based on the MLA's guidelines for citing a tweet.)

> Cannon, Kevin. "Portrait of Norris Hall in #Savannah, GA — home (for a few more months, anyway) of #SCAD's sequential art department." Mar. 2014. Instagram post.

54. EMAIL OR MESSAGE ON A SOCIAL NETWORKING SITE

Include the writer's name; the subject line, in quotation marks, if one is provided; *Message to* (not italicized or in quotation marks) followed by the recipient's name; the date of the message; and the medium of delivery (such as *E-mail* or *Facebook message*—note that MLA style hyphenates *e-mail*).

> Carbone, Nick. "Screen vs. Print Reading." Message to the author. 17 Apr. 2013. E-mail.

> Natiello, Michael. Message to the author. 31 Mar. 2014. Facebook message.

Visual, audio, multimedia, and live sources

55. FILM (THEATRICAL, DVD, OR OTHER FORMAT)

If you cite a particular person's work, start with that name. If not, start with the title of the film; then name the director, distributor, and year of release. Other contributors, such as writers or performers, may follow the director. If you cite a DVD or Blu-ray disc instead of a theatrical release, include the original film release date and the label *DVD* or *BD*. Treat a film that you viewed streaming online as a theatrical release.

> *Spirited Away*. Dir. Hayao Miyazaki. 2001. Walt Disney Video, 2003. DVD.

> *Twelve Years a Slave*. Dir. Steve McQueen. Perf. Chiwetel Ejiofor. Fox Searchlight, 2013. Film.

56. ONLINE VIDEO CLIP

Cite an online video as you would a short work from a website (see model 46).

> Weber, Jan. "As We Sow, Part 1: Where Are the Farmers?" *YouTube*. YouTube, 15 Mar. 2008. Web. 27 Sept. 2014.

57. TELEVISION BROADCAST

Begin with the title of the program, italicized (for an entire series), or the title of the episode, in quotation marks. Then list important contributors (narrator, writer, director, actors); the network; the local station and city, if the show appeared on a local channel; the broadcast date(s); and the medium. To cite a particular person's work, begin with that name. When citing an entire series, give inclusive dates.

> *Breaking Bad.* Creator Vince Gilligan. Perf. Bryan Cranston, Aaron Paul, Anna Gunn. AMC, 2008-2013. Television.

> "Time Zones." *Mad Men.* Writ. Matthew Weiner. Dir. Scott Hornbacher. AMC, 13 Apr. 2014. Television.

58. TELEVISION ON THE WEB

For a show accessed on a network website, begin as for a television broadcast (model 57). After the network, include the date of posting, the website title, the medium (*Web*), and the access date.

> "Time Zones." *Mad Men.* Writ. Matthew Weiner. Dir. Scott Hornbacher. AMC, 13 Apr. 2014. *AMCTV.com.* Web. 15 Apr. 2014.

59. RADIO BROADCAST

If you are citing a particular episode or segment, begin with the title, in quotation marks. Then give the program title in italics. List important contributors (narrator, writer, director, actors); the network; the local station and city, if the show appeared locally; the broadcast date(s); and the medium (*Radio*). To cite a particular person's work, begin with that name.

> "Tarred and Feathered." *This American Life.* Narr. Ira Glass. WNYC, New York, 11 Apr. 2013. Radio.

60. RADIO ON THE WEB

For a show or segment accessed on the web, begin as for a radio broadcast (model 59). After the network, include the date of posting, the website title, the medium (*Web*), and the access date. (For downloaded versions, see model 73.)

> "Obama's Failures Have Made Millennials Give Up Hope." *The Rush Limbaugh Show.* Narr. Rush Limbaugh. Premiere Radio Networks, 14 Apr. 2014. *RushLimbaugh.com.* Web. 15 Apr. 2014.

61. TELEVISION OR RADIO INTERVIEW

List the person interviewed and then the title, if any. If the interview has no title, use the label *Interview* and name the interviewer, if relevant. Then identify the source. End with information about the program, the date(s) the interview took place, and the medium.

> Russell, David O. Interview by Terry Gross. *Fresh Air.* WNYC, New York, 20 Feb.
>
>   2014. Radio.

Note: If you found an archived version of a television or radio interview online, provide the site's sponsor (if known), the date of the interview, the name of the website, the medium (*Web*), and the access date. For a podcast interview, see model 72.

> Revkin, Andrew. Interview by Terry Gross. *Fresh Air.* NPR, 14 June 2006. *NPR*
>
>   *.org.* Web. 12 Jan. 2014.

62. ONLINE INTERVIEW

Start with the name of the person interviewed. Give the title or the label *Interview* and the interviewer (if named), then the title of the site, the sponsor or publisher (or *N.p.* if none is identified), the date of publication, the medium (*Web*), and the access date.

> Ladd, Andrew. "What Ends: An Interview with Andrew Ladd." *Looks & Books.*
>
>   N.p., 25 Feb. 2014. Web. 10 Apr. 2014.

63. PERSONAL INTERVIEW

List the person interviewed; the label *Telephone interview*, *Personal interview*, or *E-mail interview*; and the date the interview took place.

> Freedman, Sasha. Personal interview. 10 Nov. 2014.

64. SOUND RECORDING

List the name of the person or group you wish to emphasize (such as the composer, conductor, or band); the title of the recording or composition; the artist, if appropriate; the manufacturer; the year of issue; and the medium (such as *CD*, *MP3 file*, or *LP*). If you are citing a particular song or selection, include its title, in quotation marks, before the title of the recording.

> Bach, Johann Sebastian. *Bach: Violin Concertos.* Perf. Itzhak Perlman and
>
>   Pinchas Zukerman. English Chamber Orch. EMI, 2002. CD.
>
> Sonic Youth. "Incinerate." *Rather Ripped.* Geffen, 2006. MP3 file.

Note: If you are citing instrumental music that is identified only by form, number, and key, do not underline, italicize, or enclose it in quotation marks.

> Grieg, Edvard. Concerto in A minor, op. 16. Cond. Eugene Ormandy.
> Philadelphia Orch. RCA, 1989. LP.

65. MUSICAL COMPOSITION

When you are not citing a specific published version, first give the composer's name, followed by the title.

> Mozart, Wolfgang Amadeus. *Don Giovanni*, K527.

> Mozart, Wolfgang Amadeus. Symphony no. 41 in C major, K551.

66. PUBLISHED SCORE

Cite a published score as you would a book. If you include the date the composition was written, do so immediately after the title.

> Schoenberg, Arnold. *Chamber Symphony No. 1 for 15 Solo Instruments, Op. 9.*
> 1906. New York: Dover, 2002. Print.

67. VIDEO GAME

Start with the developer or author (if any). After the title, give the version (*Vers.*), if given, then the distributor, the date of publication, and the medium.

> Harmonix. *Rock Band Blitz.* MTV Games, 2012. Xbox 360.

Note: If you play the game on the web, give the name of the site, the medium *Web*, and the date after the game publication information.

68. COMPUTER SOFTWARE OR APP

Cite as a video game (see model 67), giving the available information about the version, distributor, date, and platform.

> *Angry Birds.* Vers. 4.1.0. Rovio, 2014. Android 4.0.4.

69. LECTURE OR SPEECH (LIVE)

List the speaker; the title (if any), in quotation marks; the sponsoring institution or group; the place; and the date. If the speech is untitled, use a label such as *Lecture.*

> Eugenides, Jeffrey. Portland Arts and Lectures. Arlene Schnitzer Concert Hall,
> Portland, OR. 30 Sept. 2003. Lecture.

70. LECTURE OR SPEECH ON THE WEB

Cite as you would a short work from a website (model 46).

> Burden, Amanda. "How Public Spaces Make Cities Work." *TED.com*. TED
>
> Conferences, Mar. 2014. Web. 15 Apr. 2014.

71. LIVE PERFORMANCE

List the title, the appropriate names (such as the writer or performer), the place, and the date. To cite a particular person's work, begin the entry with that name.

> The Sea Ranch Songs. By Aleksandra Vrebalov. Perf. The Kronos Quartet.
>
> White Barn, The Sea Ranch, CA. 23 May 2015. Performance.

72. PODCAST (STREAMING)

Cite a podcast that you view or listen to online as you would a short work from a website (model 46). For a downloaded podcast, see model 73.

> Fogarty, Mignon. "Begs the Question: Update." *QuickandDirtyTips.com*.
>
> Macmillan, 6 Mar. 2014. Web. 27 June 2014.

73. DOWNLOADED DIGITAL FILE

A citation for a file that you can download — one that exists independently, not only on a website — begins with citation information required for the type of source (a photograph or sound recording, for example). For the medium, indicate the type of file (*MP3 file*, *JPEG file*).

> *Officers' Winter Quarters, Army of Potomac, Brandy Station*. Mar. 1864. Prints
>
> and Photographs Div., Lib. of Cong. TIFF file.

> "Return to the Giant Pool of Money." *This American Life*. Narr. Ira Glass. NPR,
>
> 25 Sept. 2009. MP3 file.

74. WORK OF ART OR PHOTOGRAPH

List the artist's or photographer's name; the work's title, italicized; the date of composition (if unknown, use *n.d.*); and the medium of composition (*Oil on canvas*, *Bronze*). Then cite the name of the museum or other location and the city. To cite a reproduction in a book, add the publication information (see the second model below). To cite artwork found online, omit the medium of composition, and after the location, add the title of the database or website, italicized; the medium consulted (*Web*); and the date of access.

Bronzino, Agnolo. *Lodovico Capponi*. 1550-55. Oil on poplar panel. Frick Collection, New York.

General William Palmer in Old Age. 1810. National Army Museum, London. *White Mughals: Love and Betrayal in Eighteenth-Century India*. By William Dalrymple. New York: Penguin, 2002. 270. Print.

Theotolopoulos, Domenikos. *Christ Driving the Money Changers from the Temple*. c. 1570. Minneapolis Inst. of Arts. *artsmia.org*. Web. 6 Oct. 2014.

75. MAP OR CHART

Cite a map or chart as you would a book or a short work within a longer work, and include the word *Map* or *Chart* after the title. Then, add the medium of publication. For an online source, end with the date of access.

"Australia." Map. *Perry-Castañeda Library Map Collection*. U of Texas, 1999. Web. 4 Nov. 2014.

California. Map. Chicago: Rand, 2002. Print.

76. CARTOON OR COMIC STRIP

List the artist's name; the title (if any) of the cartoon or comic strip, in quotation marks; the label *Cartoon* or *Comic strip*; and the usual publication information for a print periodical (see models 29–36) or a short work from a website (model 46).

Flake, Emily. Cartoon. *New Yorker* 13 Apr. 2015: 66. Print.

Munroe, Randall. "Heartbleed Explanation." Comic strip. *xkcd.com*. N.p., n.d. Web. 15 Apr. 2014.

77. ADVERTISEMENT

Include the label *Advertisement* after the name of the item or organization being advertised.

Ameritrade. Advertisement. *Wired* Jan. 2014: 47. Print.

Lufthansa. Advertisement. *New York Times*. New York Times, 16 Apr. 2014. Web. 16 Apr. 2014.

QUICK HELP

Citing Visuals That Appear in Your Text

If you choose to include images in your text, you need to cite and caption them correctly (see p. 474).

- For a work that you have created, the works-cited entry should begin with a descriptive phrase from the image's caption ("L.A. Bus Stop"), a label ("Photograph by author"), and the date.

- For a visual reproduced from another source, you can include the complete citation information in the caption, or you can indicate the source to allow readers to find it on the list of works cited. If you give the complete citation in the caption and do not cite the visual elsewhere in your text, you can omit the visual from your works-cited page.

Other sources (including digital versions)

If an online version is not shown in this section, use the appropriate model for the source and then end with the medium and date of access.

78. REPORT OR PAMPHLET

Follow the guidelines for a print book (models 7–28) or a digital book (model 41).

> Allen, Katherine, and Lee Rainie. *Parents Online*. Washington: Pew Internet and Amer. Life Project, 2002. Print.

> Environmental Working Group. *Dead in the Water*. Washington: Environmental Working Group, 2006. Web. 24 Apr. 2014.

79. GOVERNMENT PUBLICATION

Begin with the author, if identified. Otherwise, start with the name of the government, followed by the agency. For congressional documents, cite the number, session, and house of Congress (*S* for Senate, *H* for House of Representatives); the type (*Report, Resolution, Document*) in abbreviated form; and the number. End with the publication information. The print publisher is often the Government Printing Office (GPO). For online versions, follow the models for a short work from a website (model 46), an entire website (model 47), or a downloadable file (model 73).

> Gregg, Judd. *Report to Accompany the Genetic Information Act of 2003*. US 108th Cong., 1st sess. S. Rept. 108-22. Washington: GPO, 2003. Print.

Kinsella, Kevin, and Victoria Velkoff. *An Aging World: 2001*. US Bureau of the Census. Washington: GPO, 2001. Print.

United States. Dept. of Health and Human Services. *Keep the Beat Recipes: Deliciously Healthy Dinners*. National Institutes of Health, Oct. 2009. PDF file.

80. PUBLISHED PROCEEDINGS OF A CONFERENCE

Cite the proceedings as you would a book.

Cleary, John, and Gary Gurtler, eds. *Proceedings of the Boston Area Colloquium in Ancient Philosophy 2002*. Boston: Brill Academic, 2003. Print.

81. DISSERTATION

Enclose the title in quotation marks. Add the label *Diss.*, the school, and the year the work was accepted.

Thompson, Brian. "I'm Better Than You and I Can Prove It: Games, Expertise, and the Culture of Competition." Diss. Stanford U, 2015. Print.

Note: Cite a published dissertation as a book, adding the identification *Diss.* and the university after the title.

82. DISSERTATION ABSTRACT

Cite the abstract as you would an unpublished dissertation (see model 81). For the abstract of a dissertation that uses *Dissertation Abstracts International* (*DAI*), include the *DAI* volume, year, and page number.

Huang-Tiller, Gillian C. "The Power of the Meta-Genre: Cultural, Sexual, and Racial Politics of the American Modernist Sonnet." Diss. U of Notre Dame, 2000. *DAI* 61 (2000): 1401. Print.

83. UNPUBLISHED LETTER

Cite a published letter as a work in an anthology (see model 11). If the letter is unpublished, follow this form:

Anzaldúa, Gloria. Letter to the author. 10 Sept. 2002. MS.

84. MANUSCRIPT OR OTHER UNPUBLISHED WORK

List the author's name; the title (if any) or a description of the material; the form of the material (such as *MS* for manuscript or *TS* for typescript) and any identifying numbers; and the name and location of the library or research institution housing the material, if applicable.

> Woolf, Virginia. "The Searchlight." N.d. TS. Ser. III, Box 4, Item 184. Papers
> of Virginia Woolf, 1902-1956. Smith Coll., Northampton.

85. LEGAL SOURCE

To cite a court case, give the names of the first plaintiff and defendant, the case number, the name of the court, and the date of the decision. To cite an act, give the name of the act followed by its Public Law (*Pub. L.*) number, the date the act was enacted, and its Statutes at Large (*Stat.*) cataloging number.

> Eldred v. Ashcroft. No. 01-618. Supreme Ct. of the US. 15 Jan. 2003. Print.

> Museum and Library Services Act of 2003. Pub. L. 108-81. 25 Sept. 2003.
> Stat. 117.991. Print.

Note: You do not need an entry in the list of works cited when you cite articles of the U.S. Constitution and laws in the U.S. Code.

60   A Student Research Essay, MLA Style

Student Writer

David Craig

David Craig's research project appears on the following pages. In preparing this essay, he followed the MLA guidelines described in this chapter. His complete project appears with an activity at **macmillanhighered.com/everyday6e**.

David Craig

Professor Turkman

English 219

18 December 2014

Messaging: The Language of Youth Literacy

The English language is under attack. At least, that is what many people seem to believe. From concerned parents to local librarians, everyone seems to have a negative comment on the state of youth literacy today. They fear that the current generation of grade school students will graduate with an extremely low level of literacy, and they point out that although language education hasn't changed, kids are having more trouble reading and writing than in the past. When asked about the cause of this situation, many adults pin the blame on technologies such as texting and instant messaging, arguing that electronic shortcuts create and compound undesirable reading and writing habits and discourage students from learning conventionally correct ways to use language. But although the arguments against messaging are passionate, evidence suggests that they may not hold up.

The disagreements about messaging shortcuts are profound, even among academics. John Briggs, an English professor at the University of California, Riverside, says, "Americans have always been informal, but now the informality of precollege culture is so ubiquitous that many students have no practice in using language in any formal setting at all" (qtd. in McCarroll). Such objections are not new; Sven Birkerts of Mount Holyoke College argued in 1999 that "[students] read more casually. They strip-mine what they read" online and consequently produce "quickly generated, casual prose" (qtd. in Leibowitz A67). However, academics are also among the defenders of texting and instant messaging (IM), with

Name, instructor, course, and date aligned at left

Title centered

Opens with attention-getting statement

Background on the problem of youth literacy

Explicit thesis statement concludes introductory paragraph

Indirect quotation uses "qtd. in" and name of web source on list of works cited

---

Marginal annotations indicate effective choices or MLA-style formatting.

Craig 2

Writer's last
name and
page number
at upper right
corner of every
page

some suggesting that messaging may be a beneficial force in the development of youth literacy because it promotes regular contact with words and the use of a written medium for communication.

Definition and
example of
messaging

Texting and instant messaging allow two individuals who are separated by any distance to engage in real-time, written communication. Although such communication relies on the written word, many messagers disregard standard writing conventions. For example, here is a snippet from an IM conversation between two teenage girls:[1]

> Teen One: sorry im talkinto like 10 ppl at a time
>
> Teen Two: u izzyful person
>
> Teen Two: kwel
>
> Teen One: hey i g2g

As this brief conversation shows, participants must use words to communicate via texting and messaging, but their words do not have to be in standard English.

Writer consid-
ers argument
that youth
literacy is in
decline

The issue of youth literacy does demand attention because standardized test scores for language assessments, such as the verbal and writing sections of the College Board's SAT, have declined in recent years. This trend is illustrated in a chart distributed by the College Board as part of its 2011 analysis of aggregate SAT data (see Fig. 1).

Figure
explained in
text and cited
in parenthetical
reference

Discussion of
Figure 1

The trend lines illustrate a significant pattern that may lead to the conclusion that youth literacy is on the decline. These lines display the ten-year paths (from 2001 to 2011) of reading and writing scores, respectively. Within this period, the average verbal score dropped a few points—and appears to be headed toward a further decline in the future.

Explanatory
note adds
information not
found on list of
works cited

1. This transcript of an IM conversation was collected on 20 Nov. 2014. The teenagers' names are concealed to protect privacy.

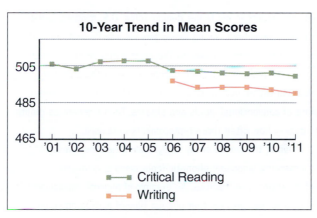

Fig. 1. Ten-year trend in mean SAT reading and writing scores (2001-2011). Data source: College Board, "2011 SAT Trends."

Based on the preceding statistics, parents and educators appear to be right about the decline in youth literacy. And this trend coincides with another phenomenon: digital communication is rising among the young. According to the Pew Internet & American Life Project, 85 percent of those aged twelve to seventeen at least occasionally write text messages, instant messages, or comments on social networking sites (Lenhart, Arafeh, Smith, and Macgill). In 2001, the most conservative estimate based on Pew numbers showed that American youths spent, at a minimum, nearly three million hours per day on instant messaging services (Lenhart and Lewis 20). These numbers are now exploding thanks to texting, which was "the dominant daily mode of communication" for teens in 2012 (Lenhart), and messaging on popular social networking sites such as Facebook and Tumblr.

In the interest of establishing the existence of a messaging language, I analyzed 11,341 lines of text from IM conversations

Figure labeled, titled, and credited to source; inserted at appropriate point in text

Writer accepts part of critics' argument; transition to next point

For a web source with no page numbers, only author names appear in parentheses

Writer's field research described

Craig 4

between youths in my target demographic: U.S. residents aged
twelve to seventeen. Young messagers voluntarily sent me chat
logs, but they were unaware of the exact nature of my research.
Once all of the logs had been gathered, I went through them,
recording the number of times messaging language was used in
place of conventional words and phrases. Then I generated graphs
to display how often these replacements were used.

During the course of my study, I identified four types
of messaging language: phonetic replacements, acronyms,
abbreviations, and inanities. An example of phonetic replacement is
using *ur* for *you are*. Another popular type of messaging language
is the acronym; for a majority of the people in my study, the most
common acronym was *lol*, a construction that means *laughing*
out loud. Abbreviations are also common in messaging, but I
discovered that typical IM abbreviations, such as *etc.*, are not
new to the English language. Finally, I found a class of words that
I call "inanities." These words include completely new words or
expressions, combinations of several slang categories, or simply
nonsensical variations of other words. My favorite from this category
is *lolz*, an inanity that translates directly to *lol* yet includes a
terminating *z* for no obvious reason.

In the chat transcripts that I analyzed, the best display of
typical messaging lingo came from the conversations between two
thirteen-year-old Texan girls, who are avid IM users. Figure 2 is a
graph showing how often they used certain phonetic replacements
and abbreviations. On the *y*-axis, frequency of replacement is
plotted, a calculation that compares the number of times a word
or phrase is used in messaging language with the total number of
times that it is communicated in any form. On the *x*-axis, specific
messaging words and phrases are listed.

Findings of
field research
presented

Figure
introduced and
explained

My research shows that the Texan girls use the first ten phonetic replacements or abbreviations at least 50 percent of the time in their normal messaging writing. For example, every time one of them writes *see*, there is a parallel time when *c* is used in its place. In light of this finding, it appears that the popular messaging culture contains at least some elements of its own language. It also seems that much of this language is new: no formal dictionary yet identifies the most common messaging words and phrases. Only in the heyday of the telegraph or on the rolls of a stenographer would you find a similar situation, but these "languages" were never a popular medium of youth communication. Texting and instant messaging, however, are very popular among young people and continue to generate attention and debate in academic circles.

Discussion of findings presented in Figure 2

My research shows that messaging is certainly widespread, and it does seem to have its own particular vocabulary, yet these two factors alone do not mean it has a damaging influence on youth literacy. As noted earlier, however, some people claim that

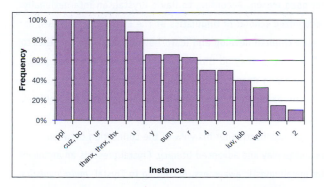

Fig. 2. Usage of phonetic replacements and abbreviations in messaging.

Figure labeled and titled

Writer returns to opposition argument

the new technology is a threat to the English language. In an article provocatively titled "Texting Makes U Stupid," historian Niall Ferguson argues, "The good news is that today's teenagers are avid readers and prolific writers. The bad news is that what they are reading and writing are text messages." He goes on to accuse texting of causing the United States to "[fall] behind more literate societies."

For author of web source named in signal phrase, no parenthetical citation needed

Transition to support of thesis and refutation of critics

The critics of messaging are numerous. But if we look to the field of linguistics, a central concept — metalinguistics — challenges these criticisms and leads to a more reasonable conclusion — that messaging has no negative impact on a student's development of or proficiency with traditional literacy.

Scholars of metalinguistics offer support for the claim that messaging is not damaging to those who use it. As noted earlier, one of the most prominent components of messaging language is phonetic replacement, in which a word such as *everyone* becomes *every1*. This type of wordplay has a special importance in the development of an advanced literacy, and for good reason. According to David Crystal, an internationally recognized scholar of linguistics at the University of Wales, as young children develop and learn how words string together to express ideas, they go through many phases of language play. The singsong rhymes and nonsensical chants of preschoolers are vital to learning language, and a healthy appetite for wordplay leads to a better command of language later in life (182).

Linguistic authority cited in support of thesis

Author of print source named in signal phrase, so parenthetical citation includes only page number

As justification for his view of the connection between language play and advanced literacy, Crystal presents an argument for metalinguistic awareness. According to Crystal, *metalinguistics* refers to the ability to "step back" and use words to analyze how language works:

> If we are good at stepping back, at thinking in a more
> abstract way about what we hear and what we say, then
> we are more likely to be good at acquiring those skills
> which depend on just such a stepping back in order
> to be successful — and this means, chiefly, reading
> and writing. . . . [T]he greater our ability to play with
> language, . . . the more advanced will be our command
> of language as a whole. (Crystal 181)

If we accept the findings of linguists such as Crystal that
metalinguistic awareness leads to increased literacy, then it seems
reasonable to argue that the phonetic language of messaging can
also lead to increased metalinguistic awareness and, therefore,
increases in overall literacy. As messagers develop proficiency
with a variety of phonetic replacements and other types of texting
and messaging words, they should increase their subconscious
knowledge of metalinguistics.

Metalinguistics also involves our ability to write in a variety
of distinct styles and tones. Yet in the debate over messaging and
literacy, many critics assume that either messaging or academic
literacy will eventually win out in a person and that the two
modes cannot exist side by side. This assumption is, however,
false. Human beings ordinarily develop a large range of language
abilities, from the formal to the relaxed and from the mainstream
to the subcultural. Mark Twain, for example, had an understanding
of local speech that he employed when writing dialogue for
Huckleberry Finn. Yet few people would argue that Twain's
knowledge of this form of English had a negative impact on his
ability to write in standard English.

However, just as Mark Twain used dialects carefully in
dialogue, writers must pay careful attention to the kind of language

Block format
for a quotation
of more than
four lines

Ellipses and
brackets
indicate
omissions and
changes in
quotation

Writer links
Crystal's views
to thesis

Another refuta-
tion of critics'
assumptions

Example from
well-known
work of
literature used
as support

they use in any setting. The owner of the language website *The Discouraging Word*, who is an anonymous English literature graduate student at the University of Chicago, backs up this idea in an e-mail to me:

Email correspondence cited in support of claim

> What is necessary, we feel, is that students learn how to shift between different styles of writing—that, in other words, the abbreviations and shortcuts of messaging should be used online . . . but that they should not be used in an essay submitted to a teacher. . . . Messaging might even be considered . . . a different way of reading and writing, one that requires specific and unique skills shared by certain communities.

The analytical ability that is necessary for writers to choose an appropriate tone and style in their writing is, of course, metalinguistic in nature because it involves the comparison of two or more language systems. Thus, youths who grasp multiple languages will have a greater natural understanding of metalinguistics. More specifically, young people who possess both messaging and traditional skills stand to be better off than their peers who have been trained only in traditional or conventional systems. Far from being hurt by their online pastime, instant messagers can be aided in standard writing by their experience with messaging language.

Writer synthesizes evidence for claim

Transition to final point

Alternative explanation for decline in literacy

The fact remains, however, that youth literacy seems to be declining. What, if not messaging, is the main cause of this phenomenon? According to the College Board, which collects data on several questions from its test takers, course work in English composition and grammar classes has decreased by 14 percent between 1992 and 2002 (Carnahan and Coletti 11). The possibility of messaging causing a decline in literacy seems inadequate when statistics on English education for US youths provide other evidence of the possible causes. Simply put, schools in the United States are not teaching English as much as they used to. Rather than blaming texting and messaging language alone for the decline in literacy and test scores, we must also look toward our schools' lack of focus on the teaching of standard English skills.

My findings indicate that the use of messaging poses virtually no threat to the development or maintenance of formal language skills among American youths aged twelve to seventeen. Diverse language skills tend to increase a person's metalinguistic awareness and, thereby, his or her ability to use language effectively to achieve a desired purpose in a particular situation. The current decline in youth literacy is not due to the rise of texting and messaging. Rather, fewer young students seem to be receiving an adequate education in the use of conventional English. Unfortunately, it may always be fashionable to blame new tools for old problems, but in the case of messaging, that blame is not warranted. Although messaging may expose literacy problems, it does not create them.

Transition to conclusion

Concluding paragraph sums up argument and reiterates thesis

Craig 10

Works Cited

Heading centered

Carnahan, Kristin, and Chiara Coletti. *Ten-Year Trend in SAT Scores*

Report

Indicates Increased Emphasis on Math Is Yielding Results:
Reading and Writing Are Causes for Concern. New York: College
Board, 2002. Print.

Graph source

College Board. "2011 SAT Trends." *Collegeboard.org*. College Board,
14 Sept. 2011. Web. 6 Dec. 2014.

Print book

Crystal, David. *Language Play*. Chicago: U of Chicago P, 1998. Print.

Email

The Discouraging Word. "Re: Messaging and Literacy." Message to
the author. 13 Nov. 2014. E-mail.

Article from database

Ferguson, Niall. "Texting Makes U Stupid." *Newsweek* 158.12
(2011): 11. *Academic Search Premier*. Web. 7 Dec. 2014.

Print newspaper article

Leibowitz, Wendy R. "Technology Transforms Writing and the
Teaching of Writing." *Chronicle of Higher Education* 26 Nov.
1999: A67-A68. Print.

Downloaded file

Lenhart, Amanda. *Teens, Smartphones, & Texting*. Pew Research
Center, 19 Mar. 2012. PDF file.

Online report

Lenhart, Amanda, Sousan Arafeh, Aaron Smith, and Alexandra
Macgill. *Writing, Technology & Teens*. Pew Research Center, 24
Apr. 2008. Web. 6 Dec. 2014.

Lenhart, Amanda, and Oliver Lewis. *Teenage Life Online: The Rise of*
the Instant-Message Generation and the Internet's Impact on
Friendships and Family Relationships. Pew Research Center, 21
June 2001. Web. 6 Dec. 2014.

Subsequent lines of each entry indented

Online newspaper article

McCarroll, Christina. "Teens Ready to Prove Text-Messaging Skills
Can Score SAT Points." *Christian Science Monitor* 11 Mar. 2005.
Web. 10 Dec. 2014.

APA
Documentation

Documentation styles in different disciplines vary according to what information is valued most highly. Thus in the social sciences, where timeliness of publication is crucial, the date of publication comes up front, right after the author's name.

— ANDREA A. LUNSFORD

APA Documentation

For visual analysis The illustration on the front of this tab suggests the kinds of disciplines in which you might use APA style and some of the kinds of research you might do. What sources will you need to cite?

The Basics of APA Style **61**

C hapters 61–64 discuss the basic formats prescribed by the American Psychological Association (APA), guidelines that are widely used in the social sciences. For further reference, consult the *Publication Manual of the American Psychological Association*, Sixth Edition (2010).

61a Think about what readers need from you.

Why does academic work call for very careful citation practices when writing for the general public may not? The answer to that question is pretty easy: readers of your academic work (your instructor, other students, perhaps even researchers and professionals in your field) expect to get certain information from source citations:

- Source citations demonstrate that while you may not yet be a recognized expert on the topic, you've nevertheless done your homework, and you are a part of the conversation surrounding it. You include sources that you find credible and that provide evidence and good reasons to back up your claims, as well as sources that you need to respond to or refute (see 14a). Careful citation shows your readers what you know, where you stand, and what you think is important.

- Source citations show that you understand the need to give credit when you make use of someone else's intellectual property. Especially in academic writing, when it's better to be safe than sorry, include a citation for any source you think you might need to cite. (See Chapter 15 for details.)

- Source citations give explicit directions to guide readers who want to look for themselves at the works you're using.

The guidelines for APA style help you with this last purpose, giving you instructions on exactly what information to include in your citation and how to format that information.

61b   Identify the type of source you are using.

Before you can decide how to cite your source following APA guidelines, you need to determine what kind of source you're using. This task can be surprisingly difficult. Citing a print book may seem relatively easy (though dizzying complications can arise—such as if the book has an editor or a translator, multiple editions, or chapters written by different people, to name a few possibilities). But citing digital sources may be especially mystifying. How, for instance, can you tell a website from a database you access online? What if your digital source reuses material from another source? Who publishes a digital text? Taking a step-by-step approach can help you solve such puzzles.

Print and digital sources

If your source has printed pages—a book or a newspaper, for instance—and you read the print version, you should look at the Directory to APA Style on pp. 532–33 for information on citing a print source. If the print source is a regularly issued journal, magazine, or newspaper (look for a date or seasonal information such as "Spring" on the cover or first page), consider it a periodical rather than a book.

If you access the digital version of a magazine or newspaper article, or if you read a book on an e-reader device such as a Kindle, then you should cite your source not as a print text but as a digital one. A digital version of a source may include updates or corrections that the print version lacks, so APA guidelines require you to indicate your mode of access and to cite print and digital sources differently.

Magazine and journal sources

APA style treats magazines and journals slightly differently. To determine whether a print source is a magazine (a popular source) or a journal (a scholarly source), see 13a.

Web and database sources

You need a subscription to look through most databases, so individual researchers almost always gain access to articles in databases through the computer system of a school or community library that pays to subscribe. The easiest way to tell whether a source comes from a database, then, is that its information is *not* generally available for free to anyone with an Internet connection. Many databases are digital collections of articles that originally appeared in edited print periodicals, ensuring that an authority has vouched for the accuracy of the information. Such sources often have more credibility than much of what is available for free on the web.

61c Plan and connect your citations.

APA citations appear in two connected parts of your text—a brief in-text citation in the body of your written text and a full citation in the list of references, to which the in-text citation directs readers. The most straightforward in-text citations include the author's name, the publication year, and the page number, but many variations on this basic format are discussed in Chapter 62.

In the text of her research essay (see 19c), Tawnya Redding includes a paraphrase of material from an online journal that she accessed through the publisher's website. She cites the authors' names and the year of publication in a parenthetical reference, pointing readers to the entry for "Baker, F., & Bor, W. (2008)" in her references list, shown below.

MOOD MUSIC   9

References

Baker, F., & Bor, W. (2008). Can music preference indicate mental
health status in young people? *Australasian Psychiatry, 16*(4),
284–288. Retrieved from http://www3.interscience.wiley.com/
journal/118565538/home

types of music can alter the mood of at-risk youth in a negative
way. This view of the correlation between music and suicide risk
is supported by a meta-analysis done by Baker and Bor (2008), in
which the authors assert that most studies reject the notion that
music is a causal factor and suggest that music preference is more

sociation
and
19(2),

tal music

and adolescent suicidal risk. *Journal of Youth and Adolescence,*
30(3), 321–332.

Lai, Y. (1999). Effects of music listening on depressed women in

61d Include notes as needed.

APA style allows you to use content notes, either at the bottom of the page or on a separate page at the end of the text, to expand or supplement your text. Indicate such notes in the text by superscript numerals (^{1}). Double-space all entries. Indent the first line of each note five spaces, but begin subsequent lines at the left margin.

SUPERSCRIPT NUMBER IN TEXT

The age of the children involved in the study was an important factor in the selection of items for the questionnaire.[1]

FOOTNOTE

[1] Marjorie Youngston Forman and William Cole of the Child Study Team provided great assistance in identifying appropriate items for the questionnaire.

61e Format APA manuscripts appropriately.

The following formatting guidelines are adapted from the APA recommendations for preparing manuscripts for publication in journals. However, check with your instructor before preparing the final draft of a print text.

- *Title page.* If your instructor wants you to include a running head, place it flush left on the first line. Write the words *Running head*, a colon, and a short version of the title (fifty characters or fewer, including spaces) using all capital letters. On the same line, flush with the right margin, type the number *1*.

  Center the title and include your name and school affiliation. An author's note at the bottom of the page can give the course name and contact information, if desired.

- *Margins and spacing.* Leave margins of one inch at the top and bottom and on both sides of the page. Do not justify the right margin. Double-space the entire text, including any headings, set-off quotations (15b), content notes, and the list of references. Indent one-half inch for the first line of a paragraph and all lines of a quotation over forty words long.

- *Short title and page numbers.* Place the short title in the upper left corner of each page. Place the page number in the upper right corner of each page, in the same position as on the title page.

- **Long quotations.** To set off a long quotation (more than forty words), indent it one-half inch from the left margin. Do not use quotation marks. Place the page reference in parentheses one space after the final punctuation.

- **Abstract.** If your instructor asks for an abstract, the abstract should go immediately after the title page, with the word *Abstract* centered an inch from the top of the page. Double-space the text. In most cases, a one-paragraph abstract of 150–250 words will be sufficient to introduce readers to your topic and provide a brief summary of your major thesis and supporting points.

- **Headings.** Headings are used within the text of many APA-style projects. In a text with only one or two levels of headings, use boldface type; center the main headings, and position the subheadings flush with the left margin. Capitalize all major words; however, do not capitalize articles, short prepositions, and coordinating conjunctions unless they are the first word or follow a colon.

- **Visuals.** Tables should be labeled *Table*, numbered, and captioned. All other visuals (such as charts, graphs, photographs, and drawings) should be labeled *Figure*, numbered, and captioned with a description and the source information. Remember to refer to each visual in your text, stating how it contributes to the point(s) you are making. Tables and figures should generally appear near the relevant text; check with your instructor or see 13e for guidelines on the placement of visuals.

APA Style for In-Text Citations 62

An in-text citation in APA style always indicates which source on the references page the writer is referring to, and it explains in what year the material was published; for quoted material, the in-text citation also indicates where in the source the quotation can be found.

Note that APA style generally calls for using the past tense or present perfect tense for signal verbs: *Baker (2003) showed* or *Baker (2003) has shown.* Use the present tense only to discuss results (*the experiment demonstrates*) or widely accepted information (*researchers agree*).

1. BASIC FORMAT FOR A QUOTATION

Generally, use the author's name in a signal phrase to introduce the cited material, and then place the date, in parentheses, immediately following the author's name. If the source includes page numbers, the page number, preceded by *p.*, should appear in parentheses following the quotation.

> Gitlin (2001) pointed out that "political critics, convinced that the media are rigged against them, are often blind to other substantial reasons why their causes are unpersuasive" (p. 141).

If the author is not named in a signal phrase, place the author's name, the year, and the page number in parentheses after the quotation: (Gitlin, 2001, p. 141). For a long, set-off quotation (more than forty words), place the page reference in parentheses one space after the final word in the quotation.

For quotations from works without page numbers, you may use paragraph numbers, if the source includes them, preceded by the abbreviation *para.*

> Driver (2007) has noticed "an increasing focus on the role of land" in policy debates over the past decade (para. 1).

2. BASIC FORMAT FOR A PARAPHRASE OR SUMMARY

Include the author's last name and the year as in model 1, but omit the page or paragraph number unless the reader will need it to find the material in a long work.

> Gitlin (2001) has argued that critics sometimes overestimate the influence of the media on modern life.

3. TWO AUTHORS

Use both names in all citations. Use *and* in a signal phrase, but use an ampersand (&) in parentheses.

> Babcock and Laschever (2003) have suggested that many women do not negotiate their salaries and pay raises as vigorously as their male counterparts do.

> A recent study has suggested that many women do not negotiate their salaries and pay raises as vigorously as their male counterparts do (Babcock & Laschever, 2003).

4. THREE TO FIVE AUTHORS

List all the authors' names for the first reference.

> Safer, Voccola, Hurd, and Goodwin (2003) reached somewhat different conclusions by designing a study that was less dependent on subjective judgment than were previous studies.

In subsequent references, use just the first author's name followed by *et al.*

> Based on the results, Safer et al. (2003) determined that the apes took significant steps toward self-expression.

5. SIX OR MORE AUTHORS

Use only the first author's name and *et al.* in every citation.

> As Soleim et al. (2002) demonstrated, advertising holds the potential for manipulating "free-willed" consumers.

6. CORPORATE OR GROUP AUTHOR

If the name of the organization or corporation is long, spell it out the first time you use it, followed by an abbreviation in brackets. In later references, use the abbreviation only.

FIRST CITATION   (Centers for Disease Control and Prevention [CDC], 2006)

LATER CITATIONS   (CDC, 2006)

7. UNKNOWN AUTHOR

Use the title or its first few words in a signal phrase or in parentheses. A book's title is italicized, as in the following example; an article's title is placed in quotation marks.

The employment profiles for this time period substantiated this trend (*Federal Employment,* 2001).

8. TWO OR MORE AUTHORS WITH THE SAME LAST NAME

Include the authors' initials in each citation.

S. Bartolomeo (2000) conducted the groundbreaking study on teenage childbearing.

9. TWO OR MORE WORKS BY AN AUTHOR IN A SINGLE YEAR

Assign lowercase letters (*a*, *b*, and so on) alphabetically by title, and include the letters after the year.

Gordon (2004b) examined this trend in more detail.

10. TWO OR MORE SOURCES IN ONE PARENTHETICAL REFERENCE

List any sources by different authors in alphabetical order by the authors' last names, separated by semicolons: (Cardone, 1998; Lai, 2002). List works by the same author in chronological order, separated by commas: (Lai, 2000, 2002).

11. SOURCE REPORTED IN ANOTHER SOURCE

Use the phrase *as cited in* to indicate that you are reporting information from a secondary source. Name the original source in a signal phrase, but list the secondary source in your list of references.

Amartya Sen developed the influential concept that land reform was necessary for "promoting opportunity" among the poor (as cited in Driver, 2007, para. 2).

12. PERSONAL COMMUNICATION

Cite personal letters, email messages, electronic postings, telephone conversations, or interviews as shown. Do not include personal communications in the reference list.

> R. Tobin (personal communication, November 4, 2014) supported his claims about music therapy with new evidence.

13. DIGITAL SOURCE

Cite a web or electronic document (including social media) as you would a print source, using the author's name and date.

> Link and Phelan (2005) argued for broader interventions in public health that would be accessible to anyone, regardless of individual wealth.

The APA recommends the following for electronic sources without names, dates, or page numbers:

AUTHOR UNKNOWN

Use a shortened form of the title in a signal phrase or in parentheses (see model 7). If an organization is the author, see model 6.

DATE UNKNOWN

Use the abbreviation *n.d.* (for "no date") in place of the year: (*Hopkins, n.d.*).

NO PAGE NUMBERS

Many works found online or in electronic databases lack stable page numbers. (Use the page numbers for an electronic work in a format, such as PDF, that has stable pagination.) If paragraph numbers are included in such a source, use the abbreviation *para.*: (*Giambetti, 2014, para. 7*). If no paragraph numbers are included but the source includes headings, give the heading and identify the paragraph in the section:

> Jacobs and Johnson (2007) have argued that "the South African media is still highly concentrated and not very diverse in terms of race and class" (South African Media after Apartheid, para. 3).

14. ENTIRE WEBSITE

If you are citing an entire website, not simply a page or document from a site, list the URL in parentheses in the text of your writing project. Do not include it in the list of references.

15. TABLE OR FIGURE REPRODUCED IN THE TEXT

Number figures (illustrations, graphs, charts, and photographs) and tables separately.

For a table, place the label (*Table 1*) and an informative heading (*Hartman's Key Personality Traits*) above the table; below, provide information about its source.

Table 1
Hartman's Key Personality Traits

Trait category	Color			
	Red	Blue	White	Yellow
Motive	Power	Intimacy	Peace	Fun
Strengths	Loyal to tasks	Loyal to people	Tolerant	Positive
Limitations	Arrogant	Self-righteous	Timid	Uncommitted

Note: Adapted from *The Hartman Personality Profile*, by N. Hayden. Retrieved February 24, 2013, from http://students.cs.byu.edu/~nhayden/Code/index.php

For a figure, place the label (*Figure 3*) and a caption indicating the source below the image. If you do not cite the source of the table or figure elsewhere in your text, you do not need to include the source in your list of references.

63 APA Style for a List of References

A list of references is an alphabetical list of the sources you have referred to in your essay. (If your instructor asks you to list everything you have read, not just the sources you cite, call the list *Bibliography*.) Begin the references list on a separate page or slide after the text of your project and any notes, under the centered heading *References* (not italicized or in quotation marks).

- Do not indent the first line of each entry, but indent subsequent lines for the entry one-half inch. (This makes the author names easy to scan.) Double-space the entire list.

- List sources alphabetically by authors' last names or by the title for any works without an author. For titles beginning with the article *A, An,* or *The,* don't count the article when alphabetizing the entries.

- List the author's last name first, followed by a comma and initials. For more than one author, use an ampersand (&) before the name of the last author, and separate the names with commas.

- Italicize titles of books and long works. Do not italicize titles of articles and other short works, and do not enclose them in quotation marks.

- For titles of books and articles, capitalize only the first word of the title and subtitle and any proper nouns or proper adjectives. For titles of periodicals, capitalize all major words.

QUICK HELP

Citing Sources That Don't Match Any Model Exactly

What should you do if your source doesn't match the model exactly? Suppose, for instance, that your source is a translation of a republished book with an editor.

- Identify a basic model to follow. If you decide that your source looks most like a republished book, start with a citation that looks like model 18.

- Look for models that show the additional elements in your source. For this example, you would need to add elements of model 13 (for the translation) and model 8 (for the editor).

- Add new elements from other models to your basic model in the order indicated.

- If you aren't sure how to arrange the pieces to create a combination model, ask your instructor.

 To cite a source for which you cannot find a model, collect as much information as you can find about the creator, title, sponsor, date, and so on, with the goal of helping your readers find the source for themselves. Then look at the models in this section to see which one most closely matches the type of source you are using. If possible, seek your instructor's advice to find the best model.

References

References, continued

Visual, audio, multimedia, and live sources

48. Film (theatrical, DVD, or other format), *551*
49. Video or audio on the web, *551*
50. Transcript of video or audio file, *551*
51. Television episode broadcast, *551*
52. Television series, *552*
53. Television episode on the web, *552*
54. Podcast (downloaded file), *552*
55. Sound recording, *552*
56. Video game, *552*
57. Computer software or app, *552*
58. Lecture or speech (live), *553*
59. Lecture or speech viewed on the web, *553*
60. Data set or graphic representation of data, *553*
61. Presentation slides, *553*
62. Work of art or photograph, *553*
63. Map, *553*
64. Advertisement, *553*

Academic sources (including online versions)

65. Published proceedings of a conference, *554*
66. Paper presented at a meeting or symposium, unpublished, *554*
67. Poster session, *554*
68. Dissertation, *554*

Personal communications and social media

69. Tweet, *554*
70. Posting on a public social networking site, *555*
71. Email, private message, or post on a social networking site, *555*

Guidelines for author listings

The list of references is arranged alphabetically. The in-text citations in your writing point readers toward particular sources in the list (see Chapter 62).

NAME CITED IN SIGNAL PHRASE IN TEXT

Driver (2007) has noted . . .

NAME IN PARENTHETICAL CITATION IN TEXT

. . . (Driver, 2007).

BEGINNING OF ENTRY IN LIST OF REFERENCES

Driver, T. (2007).

Models 1–9 explain how to arrange author and editor names. The information that follows the name of the author depends on the type of work you are citing—a print book (models 10–22), a print periodical (models 23–29), a digital written-word source (models 30–47), a media or live source (models 48–64), an academic source (models 65–68), or a personal communication (models 69–71).

1. ONE AUTHOR

Give the last name, a comma, the initial(s), and the date in parentheses.

Zimbardo, P. G. (2007). *The Lucifer effect: Understanding how good people turn evil.* New York, NY: Random House.

2. MULTIPLE AUTHORS

List up to seven authors, last name first, with commas separating authors' names and an ampersand (&) before the last author's name.

Miller, S. J., O'Hea, E. L., Lerner, J. B., Moon, S., & Foran-Tuller, K. A. (2011).

For a work with more than seven authors, list the first six, then an ellipsis (. . .), and then the final author's name.

Lahmann, C., Henrich, G., Henningsen, P., Baessler, A., Fischer, M., Loew, T., . . . Pieh, C. (2011).

3. ORGANIZATION OR GROUP AUTHOR

Resources for Rehabilitation. (2003).

4. UNKNOWN AUTHOR

Begin with the work's title. Italicize book titles, but do not italicize article titles or enclose them in quotation marks. Capitalize only the first word of the title and subtitle (if any) and proper nouns or proper adjectives.

Safe youth, safe schools. (2009).

5. AUTHOR USING A PSEUDONYM (PEN NAME) OR SCREEN NAME

Give the author's real name, if known, and give the pen or screen name in brackets. If the real name is unknown, use only the screen name.

Psych Babbler. (2013, August 4). Blogging under a pseudonym [Web log post]. Retrieved from http://www.overacuppacoffee.com/blogging -under-a-pseudonym/

6. TWO OR MORE WORKS BY THE SAME AUTHOR

List works by the same author in chronological order. Repeat the author's name in each entry.

Goodall, J. (1999).

Goodall, J. (2002).

7. TWO OR MORE WORKS BY THE SAME AUTHOR IN THE SAME YEAR

If the works appeared in the same year, list them alphabetically by title, and assign lowercase letters (*a, b,* etc.) after the dates.

> Shermer, M. (2002a). On estimating the lifetime of civilizations. *Scientific American, 287*(2), 33.

> Shermer, M. (2002b). Readers who question evolution. *Scientific American, 287*(1), 37.

8. EDITOR

If the source has an editor but no author, alphabetize the entry under the editor's last name.

> Mishra, P. (Ed.). (2005). *India in mind.* New York, NY: Random House-Vintage.

9. AUTHOR AND EDITOR

To cite a work with both an author and an editor, place the editor's name, with a comma and the abbreviation *Ed.*, in parentheses after the title.

> Austin, J. (1995). *The province of jurisprudence determined.* (W. E. Rumble, Ed.). Cambridge, England: Cambridge University Press.

Print books

10. BASIC FORMAT FOR A BOOK

Begin with the author name(s). (See models 1–9.) Then include the publication year, title and subtitle, city of publication, country or state abbreviation, and publisher. The source map on pp. 536–37 shows where to find this information in a typical book.

> Levick, S. E. (2003). *Clone being: Exploring the psychological and social dimensions.* Lanham, MD: Rowman & Littlefield.

11. ENTIRE ANTHOLOGY OR COLLECTION

Begin with the editor's name, and use the label *Ed.* or *Eds.*

> Rudd, E., & Descartes, L. (Eds.). (2008). *The changing landscape of work and family in the American middle class: Reports from the field.* Lanham, MD: Lexington.

APA SOURCE MAP: Books

Take information from the book's title page and copyright page (on the reverse side of the title page), not from the book's cover or a library catalog.

1 **Author.** List all authors' last names first, and use only initials for first and middle names. For more about citing authors, see models 1–9.

2 **Publication year.** Enclose the year of publication in parentheses.

3 **Title.** Italicize the title and any subtitle. Capitalize only the first word of the title and subtitle and any proper nouns or proper adjectives.

4 **City and state of publication, and publisher.** List the city of publication and the country or state abbreviation, a colon, and the publisher's name, dropping any *Inc.*, *Co.*, or *Publishers*.

A citation for the book on p. 537 would look like this:

Tsutsui, W. (2004). *Godzilla on my mind: Fifty years of the king of monsters.* New York, NY: Palgrave Macmillan.

2 Publication Year

2004

GODZILLA ON MY MIND
Copyright © William Tsutsui, 2004.

First published 2004 by
PALGRAVE MACMILLAN™
175 Fifth Avenue, New York, N.Y. 10010 and
Houndmills, Basingstoke, Hampshire, England RG21 6XS
Companies and representatives throughout the world.

4 City and State of Publication

New York, N.Y.

PALGRAVE MACMILLAN is the global academic imprint of
the Palgrave Macmillan division of St. Martin's Press, LLC and of
Palgrave Macmillan Ltd. Macmillan® is a registered trademark in
the United States, United Kingdom and other countries. Palgrave
is a registered trademark in the European Union and other
countries.

ISBN 1-4039-6474-2

Library of Congress Cataloging-in-Publication Data
Tsutsui, William
Godzilla on my mind : fifty years of the king of monsters / William
Tsutsui.
    p. cm.
  Includes bibliographical references and index.
  ISBN 1-4039-6474-2
  1. Godzilla films—History and criticism. I. Title.

PN1995.9.G63T78 2004
791.43'651—dc22

A catalogue reco
Library.

Design by Letra

10 9 8 7 6

Printed in the U

3 Title

GODZILLA®
ON MY MIND

*

3 Subtitle

*Fifty Years of the
King of Monsters*

WILLIAM TSUTSUI **1** Author

palgrave
macmillan

4 Publisher

12. WORK IN AN ANTHOLOGY OR COLLECTION

Give the name of the work's author first. List editors after the work's title, and include page numbers after the collection's title.

Pash, D. M. (2008). Gay family values: Gay co-father families in straight communities. In E. Rudd & L. Descartes (Eds.), *The changing landscape of work and family in the American middle class: Reports from the field* (pp. 159–187). Lanham, MD: Lexington.

13. TRANSLATOR

After the title, give the translator's name and the abbreviation *Trans.* in parentheses.

Al-Farabi, A. N. (1998). *On the perfect state* (R. Walzer, Trans.). Chicago, IL: Kazi.

14. BOOK IN A LANGUAGE OTHER THAN ENGLISH

Include the English translation (in brackets) after the title.

Andre, C. (2004). *Psychologie de la peur* [The psychology of fear]. Paris, France: Odile Jacob.

15. EDITION OTHER THAN THE FIRST

Moore, G. S. (2002). *Living with the earth: Concepts in environmental health science* (2nd ed.). New York, NY: Lewis.

16. ONE VOLUME OF A MULTIVOLUME WORK

List the volume in parentheses after the title.

Barnes, J. (Ed.). (1995). *Complete works of Aristotle* (Vol. 2). Princeton, NJ: Princeton University Press.

17. MORE THAN ONE VOLUME OF A MULTIVOLUME WORK

List the complete span of volumes in parentheses after the title.

Barnes, J. (Ed.). (1995). *Complete works of Aristotle* (Vols. 1–2). Princeton, NJ: Princeton University Press.

18. REPUBLISHED BOOK (MORE RECENT VERSION OF AN OLDER BOOK)

Piaget, J. (1952). *The language and thought of the child*. London, England: Routledge & Kegan Paul. (Original work published 1932)

19. INTRODUCTION, PREFACE, FOREWORD, OR AFTERWORD

Klosterman, C. (2007). Introduction. In P. Shirley, *Can I keep my jersey?: 11 teams, 5 countries, and 4 years in my life as a basketball vagabond* (pp. v–vii). New York, NY: Villard-Random House.

20. GOVERNMENT PUBLICATION

Office of the Federal Register. (2003). *The United States government manual 2003/2004*. Washington, DC: U.S. Government Printing Office.

21. BOOK WITH A TITLE WITHIN THE TITLE

Do not italicize or enclose in quotation marks a title within a book title.

Klarman, M. J. (2007). Brown v. Board of Education *and the civil rights movement*. New York, NY: Oxford University Press.

22. ARTICLE IN A REFERENCE BOOK

Dean, C. (1994). Jaws and teeth. In *The Cambridge encyclopedia of human evolution* (pp. 56–59). Cambridge, England: Cambridge University Press.

If no author is listed, begin with the title.

Articles and short works in print periodicals

Begin with the author name(s). (See models 1–9.) Then include the publication date (year only for journals, and year, month, and day for all other periodicals); the article title; the periodical title; the volume number and issue number, if any; and the page numbers. The source map on pp. 540–41 shows where to find this information in a sample periodical.

23. ARTICLE IN A PRINT JOURNAL

Include the issue number (in parentheses and not italicized) after the volume number (italicized).

Hall, R. E. (2000). Marriage as vehicle of racism among women of color. *Psychology: A Journal of Human Behavior, 37*(2), 29–40.

24. ARTICLE IN A PRINT MAGAZINE

Include the month (as well as the day, if given).

Solomon, A. (2014, March 17). The reckoning. *The New Yorker, 90*(4), 36–45.

APA SOURCE MAP: Articles from Print Periodicals

1 **Author.** List all authors' last names first, and use only initials for first and middle names. For more about citing authors, see models 1–9.

2 **Publication date.** Enclose the date in parentheses. For journals, use only the year. For magazines and newspapers, use the year, a comma, the month (spelled out), and the day, if given.

3 **Article title.** Do not italicize or enclose article titles in quotation marks. Capitalize only the first word of the article title and subtitle and any proper nouns or proper adjectives.

4 **Periodical title.** Italicize the periodical title (and subtitle, if any), and capitalize all major words. Follow the periodical title with a comma.

5 **Volume and issue numbers.** Give the volume number (italicized) and, without a space in between, the issue number (if given) in parentheses. Follow with a comma.

6 **Page numbers.** Give the inclusive page numbers of the article. For newspapers only, include the abbreviation *p.* ("page") or *pp.* ("pages") before the page numbers. End the citation with a period.

A citation for the periodical article on p. 541 would look like this:

Etzioni, A. (2006). Leaving race behind: Our growing Hispanic population creates a golden opportunity. *The American Scholar, 75*(2), 20–30.

The AMERICAN
SCHOLAR

4 Periodical Title

Spring 2006 | Vol. 75, No. 2 — **5** Volume and Issue Numbers

2 Publication Date

ROBERT WILSON
Editor

JEAN STIPICEVIC
Managing Editor

SANDRA COSTICH

The AMERICAN
SCHOLAR

3 Article Title

Leaving Race Behind

Our growing Hispanic population creates a golden opportunity

AN
EDW
PHY

AMITAI ETZIONI **1** Author

JOSEPH

Some years ago the United States government asked me what my race was. I was reluctant to respond because my 50 years of practicing sociology—and some powerful personal experiences—have underscored for me what we all know to one degree or another, that racial divisions bedevil America, just as they do many other societies across the world. Not wanting to encourage these divisions, I refused to check off one of the specific racial options on the U.S. Census form and instead marked a box labeled "Other." I later found out that the federal government did not accept such an attempt to de-emphasize race, by me or by some 6.75 million other Americans who tried it. Instead the government assigned me to a racial category, one it chose for me. Learning this made me conjure up what I admit is a far-fetched association. I was in this place once before. When I was a Jewish child in Nazi Germany in the early 1930s, many Jews who saw themselves as good Germans wanted to "pass" as Aryans. But the Nazi regime would have none of it. Never mind, they told these Jews, *we determine* who is Jewish and who is not. A similar practice prevailed in the Old South, where if you had one drop of African blood you were a Negro, disregarding all other facts and considerations, including how you saw yourself.

You might suppose that in the years since my little Census-form protest

---

~ Amitai Etzioni is University Professor at George Washington University and the author of *The Monochrome Society*.

25. ARTICLE IN A PRINT NEWSPAPER

Use *p.* or *pp.* with the page numbers.

> Fackler, M. (2014, April 9). Japan's foreign minister says apologies to wartime victims will be upheld. *The New York Times,* p. A6.

26. EDITORIAL OR UNSIGNED ARTICLE IN A PRINT PUBLICATION

Add an identifying label such as *[Editorial]*.

> The tyranny of the glass boxes [Editorial]. (2014, April 22). *The New York Times,* p. A24.

27. LETTER TO THE EDITOR IN A PRINT PUBLICATION

Add an identifying label.

> MacEwan, V. (2014, January). [Letter to the editor]. *The Believer, 12*(1), 4.

28. REVIEW IN A PRINT PUBLICATION

Include the author and title of the review, if given. In brackets, give the type of work, the title, and the author (for a book) or year (for a motion picture).

> Lane, A. (2014, March 17). Double trouble [Review of the motion picture *Enemy*, 2014]. *The New Yorker, 90*(4), 78–79.

29. INTERVIEW IN A PRINT PUBLICATION

> Blume, J. (2014, January). Judy Blume in conversation with Lena Dunham [Interview by Dunham]. *The Believer, 12*(1), 39–48.

Digital written-word sources

Updated guidelines for citing digital resources are maintained at the APA's website (www.apa.org).

30. WORK FROM AN ONLINE DATABASE

Provide the author, date, title, and publication information as you would for a print document. Include both the volume and issue numbers for all journal articles. If the article has a digital object identifier (DOI), include it. If there is no DOI, write *Retrieved from* and the URL of the journal's home page (not the URL of the database). The source map on pp. 544–45 shows where to find this information for a typical article from a database.

> Hazleden, R. (2003, December). Love yourself: The relationship of the self with itself in popular self-help texts. *Journal of Sociology, 39*(4), 413–428. Retrieved from http://jos.sagepub.com

> Morley, N. J., Ball, L. J., & Ormerod, T. C. (2006). How the detection of insurance fraud succeeds and fails. *Psychology, Crime, & Law, 12*(2), 163–180. doi:10.1080/10683160512331316325

31. ARTICLE FROM A JOURNAL ON THE WEB

Give information as for an article in a print journal (see model 23). If the article has a DOI (digital object identifier), include it. If there is no DOI, include the URL for the journal's home page or for the article, if it is difficult to find from the home page.

> Cleary, J. M., & Crafti, N. (2007). Basic need satisfaction, emotional eating, and dietary restraint as risk factors for recurrent overeating in a community sample. *E-Journal of Applied Psychology, 2*(3), 27–39. Retrieved from http://ojs.lib.swin.edu.au/index.php/ejap/article/view/90/116

QUICK HELP

Citing Digital Sources

When citing sources accessed online or from an electronic database, include as many of the following elements as you can find:

- **Author.** Give the author's name, if available.

- **Publication date.** Include the date of electronic publication or of the latest update, if available. When no publication date is available, use *n.d.* ("no date").

- **Title.** If the source is not from a larger work, italicize the title.

- **Print publication information.** For articles from online journals, magazines, or reference databases, give the publication title and other publishing information as you would for a print periodical (see models 23–29).

- **Retrieval information.** For a work from a database, do the following: if the article has a DOI (digital object identifier), include that number after the publication information; do not include the name of the database. If there is no DOI, write *Retrieved from* followed by the URL for the journal's home page (not the database URL). For a work found on a website, write *Retrieved from* and include the URL. If the work seems likely to be updated, include the retrieval date. If the URL is longer than one line, break it only before a punctuation mark; do not break *http://*.

APA SOURCE MAP: Articles from Databases

1 **Author.** Include the author's name as you would for a print source. List all authors' last names first, and use initials for first and middle names. For more about citing authors, see models 1–9.

2 **Publication date.** Enclose the date in parentheses. For journals, use only the year. For magazines and newspapers, use the year, a comma, the month, and the day, if given.

3 **Article title.** Capitalize only the first word of the article title and the subtitle and any proper nouns or proper adjectives.

4 **Periodical title.** Italicize the periodical title.

5 **Volume and issue numbers.** For journals and magazines, give the volume number (italicized) and the issue number (in parentheses).

6 **Page numbers.** For journals only, give inclusive page numbers.

7 **Retrieval information.** If the article has a DOI (digital object identifier), include that number after the publication information; do not include the name of the database. If there is no DOI, write *Retrieved from* followed by the URL of the journal's home page (not the database URL).

A citation for the article on p. 545 would look like this:

Knobloch-Westerwick, S., & Crane, J. (2012). A losing battle: Effects of prolonged exposure to thin-ideal images on dieting and body satisfaction. *Communication Research, 39*(1), 79–102. doi:10.1177/0093650211400596

3 Article Title

4 Periodical Title

6 Page Numbers

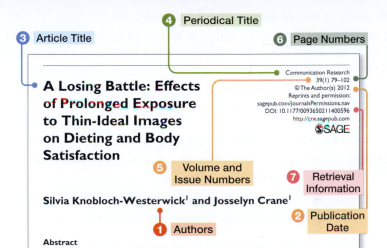

Communication Research
39(1) 79–102
© The Author(s) 2012
Reprints and permission:
sagepub.com/journalsPermissions.nav
DOI: 10.1177/0093650211400596
http://crx.sagepub.com
$SAGE

A Losing Battle: Effects of Prolonged Exposure to Thin-Ideal Images on Dieting and Body Satisfaction

5 Volume and Issue Numbers

7 Retrieval Information

Silvia Knobloch-Westerwick[1] and Josselyn Crane[1]

1 Authors

2 Publication Date

Abstract

The present study examined prolonged exposure effects of thin-ideal media messages. College-aged females participated in seven online sessions over 10 days including a baseline measures session, five daily measures, and a posttest. Two experimental groups viewed magazine pages with thin-ideal imagery. One of those groups was induced to engage in social comparisons with the thin-ideal models. The control group viewed messages with body-neutral images of women. Prolonged exposure to thin-ideal messages led to greater body satisfaction. This finding was attributed to the fact that the experimental groups reported more dieting behaviors. A mediation analysis showed that the impact of thin-ideal message exposure on body satisfaction was mediated by dieting.

Keywords

body dissatisfaction, body image, dieting, prolonged exposure, social comparison

Idealized body images in the media have been linked to unrealistic body shape aspirations and body dissatisfaction (see meta-analysis by Grabe, Ward, & Hyde, 2008), which, in turn, have been linked to numerous pathological problems, including depression, obesity, dieting, and eating disorders (e.g., Johnson & Wardle, 2005; Neumark-Sztainer, Paxton, Hannan, Haines, & Story, 2006; Ricciardelli & McCabe, 2001). However, another meta-analysis by Holmstrom (2004) found that the longer the media exposure, the *better* the individuals felt about their body. This inconsistency indicates that the factors and processes at work have not yet been fully understood and captured by the research at hand and deserve further investigation. Social comparison theory is the theoretical framework that has guided much

[1]The Ohio State University

Corresponding Author:
Silvia Knobloch-Westerwick, The Ohio State University, 154 N Oval Mall, Columbus, OH 43210
Email: knobloch-westerwick.1@osu.edu

32. ARTICLE FROM A MAGAZINE ON THE WEB

Give information as for an article from a print magazine (see model 24). If the article has a DOI (digital object identifier), include it. If there is no DOI, include the URL for the magazine's home page.

Galchen, R. (2015, April 13). Weather underground. *The New Yorker, (91)*8, 34–40. Retrieved from http://www.newyorker.com/

33. ARTICLE FROM A NEWSPAPER ON THE WEB

Include information as for a print newspaper article (see model 25). Add the URL of the searchable website.

Barringer, F. (2008, February 7). In many communities, it's not easy going green. *The New York Times.* Retrieved from http://www.nytimes.com/

34. ABSTRACT FOR A JOURNAL ARTICLE ONLINE

Include a label.

Gudjonsson, G. H., & Young, S. (2010). Does confabulation in memory predict suggestibility beyond IQ and memory? [Abstract]. *Personality & Individual Differences, 49*(1), 65–67. doi:10.1016/j.paid.2010.03.014

35. COMMENT ON AN ONLINE ARTICLE

Give the writer's real name (if known) or screen name. If both are given, follow the real name with the screen name in brackets. Use *Re:* before the title of the article, and add the label *Comment* in brackets.

The Lone Ranger. (2014, April 22). Re: The American middle class is no longer the world's richest [Comment]. *The New York Times.* Retrieved from http://www.nytimes.com/

36. DIGITAL BOOK (ONLINE OR E-READER)

For a book you read online, give the URL for the home page of the site after the book title.

Stossel, S. (2013). *My age of anxiety: Fear, hope, dread, and the search for peace of mind.* Retrieved from http://books.google.com/

If you downloaded the book to an e-reader such as a Kindle or Nook, give the version after the title. Include the DOI, if given, or the URL of the home page for the site from which you downloaded the file.

Schaap, R. (2013). *Drinking with men: A memoir* [Nook version]. Retrieved from http://www.barnesandnoble.com/

37. ONLINE EDITORIAL OR LETTER TO THE EDITOR

Include the author's name (if given) and the title (if any). For an editorial, give the label *[Editorial]*. For a letter, give the label *[Letter to the editor]*.

> Shorter drug sentences [Editorial]. (2014, April 10). *The New York Times.*
> Retrieved from http://www.nytimes.com/

> Starr, E. (2014, April 4). Local reporting thrives in high schools [Letter
> to the editor]. *The Washington Post.* Retrieved from http://www
> .washingtonpost.com/

38. ONLINE REVIEW

Cite an online review as you would a print review (see model 28), and end with a retrieval statement.

> Miller, L. (2014, April 20). How the American office worker wound up in a box
> [Review of the book *Cubed,* by N. Saval]. *Salon.* Retrieved from http://
> www.salon.com/

39. INTERVIEW PUBLISHED ONLINE

> Ladd, A. (2014, February 25). What ends: An interview with Andrew Ladd
> [Interview by J. Gallagher]. Retrieved from http://www.looksandbooks
> .com/

40. ENTRY IN AN ONLINE REFERENCE WORK OR WIKI

Begin with the title unless the author is named. (A wiki, which is collectively edited, will not include an author.)

> Gunpowder plot. (2014). In *Wikipedia.* Retrieved April 10, 2014, from http://
> www.wikipedia.org/

41. REPORT OR DOCUMENT FROM A WEB SITE

List all of the following that are available: the author's name; the publication date (or *n.d.* if no date is given); the title of the document, italicized; and the URL. If the publisher is identified and is not the same as the author, list the publisher in the retrieval statement. The source map on pp. 548–49 shows where to find this information for a report from a website.

> Institute of Medicine of the National Academies. (2011, August 25). *Adverse
> effects of vaccines: Evidence and causality.* Retrieved from http://www.iom
> .edu/Reports/2011/Adverse-Effects-of-Vaccines-Evidence-and-Causality.aspx

APA SOURCE MAP: Reports and Long Works from Websites

1 **Author.** If one is given, include the author's name (see models 1–9). List last names first, and use only initials for first names. The site's sponsor may be the author. If no author is identified, begin the citation with the title of the document.

2 **Publication date.** Enclose the date of publication or latest update in parentheses. Use *n.d.* ("no date") when no publication date is available.

3 **Title of work.** Italicize the title. Capitalize only the first word of the title and subtitle and any proper nouns or proper adjectives.

4 **Retrieval information.** Write *Retrieved from* and include the URL. For a report from an organization's website, identify the organization in the retrieval statement. If the work seems likely to be updated, include the retrieval date. If you need to break a long URL in the retrieval statement, do so before a punctuation mark.

A citation for the web document on p. 549 would look like this:

Parker, K., & Wang, W. (2013, March 14). *Modern parenthood: Roles of moms and dads converge as they balance work and family.* Retrieved from the Pew Research Center website: http://www.pewsocialtrends .org/2013/03/14/modern-parenthood-roles-of-moms-and-dads -converge-as-they-balance-work-and-family/

② Publication Date

March 14, 2013

④ Retrieval Information

④ Retrieval Information

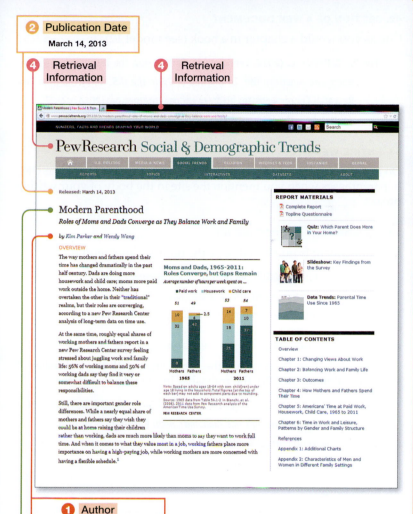

Released: March 14, 2013

Modern Parenthood

Roles of Moms and Dads Converge as They Balance Work and Family

by *Kim Parker* and *Wendy Wang*

OVERVIEW

The way mothers and fathers spend their time has changed dramatically in the past half century. Dads are doing more housework and child care; moms more paid work outside the home. Neither has overtaken the other in their "traditional" realms, but their roles are converging, according to a new Pew Research Center analysis of long-term data on time use.

At the same time, roughly equal shares of working mothers and fathers report in a new Pew Research Center survey feeling stressed about juggling work and family life: 56% of working moms and 50% of working dads say they find it very or somewhat difficult to balance these responsibilities.

Still, there are important gender role differences. While a nearly equal share of mothers and fathers say they wish they could be at home raising their children rather than working, dads are much more likely than moms to say they want to work full time. And when it comes to what they value most in a job, working fathers place more importance on having a high-paying job, while working mothers are more concerned with having a flexible schedule.[1]

Moms and Dads, 1965-2011: Roles Converge, but Gaps Remain

Average number of hours per week spent on ...

■ Paid work ■ Housework ■ Child care

REPORT MATERIALS

Complete Report
Topline Questionnaire

Quiz: Which Parent Does More in Your Home?

Slideshow: Key Findings from the Survey

Data Trends: Parental Time Use Since 1965

TABLE OF CONTENTS

① Author

Kim Parker and *Wendy Wang*

③ Title of Work

42. SECTION OF A WEB DOCUMENT

Cite as you would a chapter in a book (see model 12).

> Fox, S., & Rainie, L. (2014, February 27). Part 1: How the Internet has woven itself into American life. In *The web at 25 in the U.S.* Retrieved from Pew Research Center website: http://www.pewinternet.org/2014/02/27 /part-1-how-the-internet-has-woven-itself-into-american-life/

43. ENTIRE WEBSITE

Do not cite an entire website in your list of references. Give the URL in parentheses when you mention the site in the body of your writing project.

44. GOVERNMENT SOURCE ONLINE

If the document is numbered, give the number in parentheses.

> U.S. Census Bureau. (2013, September). *Income, poverty, and health insurance coverage in the United States: 2012* (Report No. P60-245). Retrieved from http://www.census.gov/prod/2013pubs/p60-245.pdf

45. ONLINE REPORT FROM A PRIVATE ORGANIZATION

If the publisher and author are the same, start with the publisher. If they are different, identify the publisher in the retrieval statement.

> Southern Poverty Law Center. (2013, February). *Easy money, impossible debt: How predatory lending traps Alabama's poor.* Retrieved from http:// www.splcenter.org/sites/default/files/downloads/publication/Payday _Lending_Report_web.pdf

46. BLOG POST

Give the author's real name (if known) or screen name; the date of the post (or *n.d.* if no date is given); the title, followed by the label *Blog post* in brackets; and the URL.

> Black, D. (2014, April 22). Wealthy white people from good backgrounds are never involved in crime [Blog post]. Retrieved from http://www .eschatonblog.com/2014/04/wealthy-white-people-from-good.html

47. BLOG COMMENT

Follow model 46 for a blog post, but put *Re:* before the title of the article commented on, and use the label *Blog comment* in brackets.

JennOfArk. (2014, April 16). Re: Friends in high places [Blog comment]. Retrieved from http://alicublog.blogspot.com/2014/04/friends-in-high -places.html

Visual, audio, multimedia, and live sources

48. FILM (THEATRICAL, DVD, OR OTHER FORMAT)

Begin with the director, the producer, and other relevant contributors.

Bigelow, K. (Director, Producer), Boal, M. (Producer), & Ellison, M. (Producer). (2012). *Zero dark thirty* [Motion picture]. United States: Annapurna.

If you watched the film in another medium, such as on a DVD or Blu-ray disc, indicate the medium in brackets. If the DVD or Blu-ray and the film were not released in the same year, put *Original release* and the year in parentheses at the end of the entry.

Hitchcock, A. (Director, Producer). (2010). *Psycho* [Blu-ray disc]. United States: Universal. (Original release 1960.)

49. VIDEO OR AUDIO ON THE WEB

Use the label *Audio file* or *Video file* in brackets after the title. If the video or audio is a segment or episode of a show rather than a stand-alone file, identify the show, as in the first model below.

Buckner, T. (2013, May 7). *Last laugh* [Audio file]. In *The moth.* Retrieved from http://www.themoth.org/

Klusman, P. (2008, February 13). *An engineer's guide to cats* [Video file]. Retrieved from http://www.youtube.com/watch?v5=mHXBL6bzAR4

50. TRANSCRIPT OF VIDEO OR AUDIO FILE

Glass, I. (2014, March 28). *Bad baby* [Transcript of audio file no. 521]. In *This American life.* Retrieved from http://www.thisamericanlife.org

51. TELEVISION EPISODE BROADCAST

Weiner, M. (Writer), & Hornbacher, S. (Director). (2014, April 13). Time zones [Television series episode]. In M. Weiner (Executive producer), *Mad men.* New York, NY: AMC.

52. TELEVISION SERIES

Gilligan, V. (Executive producer). (2008–2013). *Breaking bad* [Television series]. New York, NY: AMC.

53. TELEVISION EPISODE ON THE WEB

Weiner, M. (Writer), & Hornbacher, S. (Director). (2014, April 13). Time zones [Television series episode]. In M. Weiner (Executive producer), *Mad men*. Retrieved from http://www.amctv.com/

54. PODCAST (DOWNLOADED FILE)

For an episode of a podcast series, follow model 53. For a standalone podcast, follow model 41 for a document from the web. Include an identifying label in brackets.

Britt, M. A. (Writer & Producer). (2013, December 13). Ep. 211: Is a little deception okay? Paid crowds and native advertising [Audio podcast]. In M. A. Britt (Producer), *The psych files*. Retrieved from http://www .thepsychfiles.com/

Spack, N. (2014, April 16). *How I help transgender teens become who they want to be* [Video podcast]. Retrieved from http://www.ted.com/

55. SOUND RECORDING

The Avalanches. (2001). Frontier psychiatrist. On *Since I left you* [CD]. Los Angeles, CA: Elektra/Asylum Records.

56. VIDEO GAME

Begin with the game's creator, if possible. Follow with the label *[Video game]*. If you accessed the game on the web, give the URL; if you played on a game console, identify the type.

Harmonix. (2012). *Rock band blitz* [Video game]. New York, NY: MTV Games. Xbox 360.

King. (2014). *Candy crush saga* [Video game]. Retrieved from http://www .candycrushsaga.com/

57. COMPUTER SOFTWARE OR APP

If an individual can be identified as the developer, use that person's name. Otherwise, start with the name of the product and give the version. Use the label *Computer software* or *Mobile application software* in brackets.

> MediaWiki (Version 1.22.0) [Mobile application software]. Retrieved from
> http://www.microsoft.com/web/gallery

58. LECTURE OR SPEECH (LIVE)

> Khan, S. (2014, April 16). *Education reimagined.* Address at the Stanford
> University Ventures Program, Stanford University, Stanford, CA.

59. LECTURE OR SPEECH VIEWED ON THE WEB

Cite as you would a work from a website (model 41).

> Burden, A. (2014, March). *How public spaces make cities work* [Video file].
> Retrieved from http://www.ted.com/

60. DATA SET OR GRAPHIC REPRESENTATION OF DATA

If the graphic appears as part of a larger document, do not italicize the title. Give information about the type of source in brackets.

> U.S. Census Bureau. (2012, December 20). *State-to-state migration for states
> of 8 million or more* [Graph]. Retrieved from http://www.census.gov
> /dataviz/visualizations/028/

61. PRESENTATION SLIDES

> Mader, S. L. (2007, March 27). *The Zen aesthetic* [Presentation slides].
> Retrieved from http://www.slideshare.net/slmader/the-zen-aesthetic

62. WORK OF ART OR PHOTOGRAPH

> Bronzino, A. (1550–1555). *Lodovico Capponi* [Painting]. Frick Collection, New
> York, NY.

> Theotolopoulos, D. (ca. 1570). *Christ driving the money changers from the
> temple* [Painting]. Retrieved from http://www.artsmia.org/

63. MAP

> Australia [Map]. (1999). Retrieved from the University of Texas at Austin
> Perry-Castañeda Library Map Collection website: http://www.lib.utexas
> .edu/maps/australia/australia_pol99.jpg

64. ADVERTISEMENT

> Ameritrade [Advertisement]. (2014, January). *Wired, 22*(1), 47.

Academic sources (including online versions)

65. PUBLISHED PROCEEDINGS OF A CONFERENCE

Robertson, S. P., Vatrapu, R. K., & Medina, R. (2009). YouTube and Facebook: Online video "friends" social networking. In *Conference proceedings: YouTube and the 2008 election cycle* (pp. 159–176). Amherst, MA: University of Massachusetts. Retrieved from http://scholarworks.umass .edu/jitpc2009

66. PAPER PRESENTED AT A MEETING OR SYMPOSIUM, UNPUBLISHED

Cite the month of the meeting if it is available.

Banks, A. (2015, March). *"Ain't no walls behind the sky, baby": Funk, flight, and freedom.* Paper presented at the Conference on College Composition and Communication, Tampa, FL.

67. POSTER SESSION

Barnes Young, L. L. (2003, August). *Cognition, aging, and dementia.* Poster session presented at the 2003 Division 40 APA Convention, Toronto, Ontario, Canada.

68. DISSERTATION

If you retrieved the dissertation from a database, give the database name and the accession number, if one is assigned.

Lengel, L. L. (1968). *The righteous cause: Some religious aspects of Kansas populism.* Retrieved from ProQuest Digital Dissertations. (AAT 6900033)

If you retrieve a dissertation from a website, give the type of dissertation and the institution after the title, and provide a retrieval statement. If you retrieve the dissertation from an institution's own site, omit the institution after the title.

Meeks, M. G. (2006). *Between abolition and reform: First-year writing programs, e-literacies, and institutional change* (Doctoral dissertation). Retrieved from http://dc.lib.unc.edu/etd/

Personal communications and social media

69. TWEET

Include the writer's real name, if known, with the user name (if different) in brackets. If you don't know the real name, give just the user name. Include the entire tweet as the title, followed by the label *Tweet* in brackets.

> Waldman, K. [xwaldie]. (2014, April 24). The psychology of unfriending
>   someone on Facebook: slate.com/blogs/future_t . . . [Tweet]. Retrieved
>   from https://twitter.com/xwaldie/status/459336732232912896

70. POSTING ON A PUBLIC SOCIAL NETWORKING SITE

When citing a posting on a public Facebook page or another social networking site that is visible to anyone, include the writer's name as it appears in the post. Give a few words from the post, and add an identifying label. Include the date you retrieved the post and the URL for the public page. Do not include a page on the list of references if your readers will not be able to access the source; instead, cite it as a personal communication in the text (see model 12 on p. 529).

> American Psychological Association. (2014, April 24). Why do many people do
>   their best thinking while walking? [Facebook post]. Retrieved April 24,
>   2014, from https://www.facebook.com/AmericanPsychologicalAssociation

71. EMAIL, PRIVATE MESSAGE, OR POST ON A SOCIAL NETWORKING SITE

Email messages, letters, and any personal messages or privacy-protected postings on Facebook and other social media sites are not included in the list of references because the APA stresses that all sources in your list of references should be retrievable by your readers. (See model 12 on p. 529 for information on citing personal communication in your text.)

A Student Research Essay, APA Style **64**

On the following pages is a paper by Martha Bell that conforms to the APA guidelines described in this chapter. Her project also appears with an activity at **macmillanhighered.com/everyday6e**.

Student Writer

Martha Bell

Running head: POST-LYME MYSTERY   1

Running head
(fifty characters
or fewer)
appears flush
left on first line
of title page

Page number
appears flush
right on first
line of every
page

Title, name,
and affiliation
centered and
double-spaced

The Mystery of Post-Lyme Disease Syndrome

Martha Bell

Eastern Mennonite University

Author's note
lists specific
information
about course
(and can
include contact
information)

Author Note: This paper was prepared for College Writing 130C,
taught by Professor Eads.

Annotations indicate effective choices or APA-style formatting.

POST-LYME MYSTERY   2

Abstract

Lyme disease, prevalent in parts of the United States, is a preventable illness spread by tick bites. Lyme disease is considered treatable with a course of antibiotics in the early stages of infection. In some cases, however, symptoms of Lyme disease persist in individuals who have completed antibiotic treatment. The causes of post-Lyme disease syndrome, sometimes called "chronic Lyme disease," are unknown, and treatment of those suffering post-Lyme disease syndrome is controversial, with some physicians arguing for long-term antibiotic treatment and others convinced that such treatments are harmful to patients. There is a need for more research with a focus on developing the technology to perform replicable studies and eventually an effective treatment algorithm for post-Lyme disease syndrome.

Running head appears in all capital letters flush left on each page

Heading centered

No indentation for abstract

Double-spaced text throughout

Full title centered

The Mystery of Post-Lyme Disease Syndrome

The Centers for Disease Control and Prevention (CDC)

Paragraphs indented

estimates a total of 300,000 cases of Lyme disease annually. Many medical professionals believe Lyme disease can be cured in a matter of weeks with a simple antibiotic treatment. In some cases,

Background information supplied

however, patients develop post-Lyme disease syndrome, sometimes called "chronic Lyme disease," exhibiting persistent symptoms of Lyme after initial treatment is completed. The scientific community, divided over the causes of post-Lyme disease syndrome, cannot agree on the best treatment for the syndrome. Although Lyme disease is preventable, people are still vulnerable to infection; consequently, there is a need for more research and collaboration with a focus on developing the technology to perform replicable studies, which may subsequently lead to an effective treatment algorithm for post-Lyme disease syndrome.

Boldface headings help organize review

Prevention

Ixodes ticks, also known as blacklegged and deer ticks, are infected with the bacterium *Borrelia burgdorferi*, responsible for Lyme disease (Hawker et al., 2012). Since being bitten by an

Reference to work with six or more authors uses *et al.*

infected tick is the only known way of contracting Lyme disease, evading Ixodes ticks is an effective measure. According to M'ikanatha, Lynfield, Van Beneden, and de Valk (2013), "Lyme disease is acquired peridomestically and the risk is highest in residential settings abutting areas with forests, meadows, and high prevalence of deer" (p. 168). While adult ticks are more active in the cooler months, developing Ixodes ticks, called nymphs, feed the most during the spring and summer months (Centers for

First reference to organization gives abbreviation for later references

Disease Control and Prevention [CDC], 2011b). Therefore, avoiding areas such as meadows and grasslands in the spring and summer seasons aids in preventing Lyme disease.

POST-LYME MYSTERY

4

Using permethrin repellent on clothes and 20 to 30 percent
DEET insect repellent on the skin also keeps ticks away (U.S.
Department of Health and Human Services [HHS], 2012). Other
measures include wearing light-colored clothing to make ticks
more visible, wearing long sleeves and long pants, tucking shirts
into pants and pants into socks, and taping closed open areas
of clothing when spending time outdoors in areas where ticks
are prevalent (Hawker et al., 2012; HHS, 2012). Additionally,
individuals should keep yards and houses clean to avert mammals,
such as deer and rodents, that carry Ixodes ticks, and should check
pets for ticks (HHS, 2012).

More than
one reference
included in
citation

Though all of these measures greatly reduce the chance
of receiving a tick bite, they are not foolproof. The bacterium
B. burgdorferi takes approximately 36 to 48 hours to become
infectious after the tick has bitten an individual (Hawker et al.,
2012). A bull's-eye rash called erythema migrans is the only unique
symptom of Lyme disease (HHS, 2012). It appears 3 to 32 days
after infection (Hawker et al., 2012). According to one study,
only 70 to 80 percent of Lyme disease victims develop erythema
migrans; therefore, other symptoms must be assessed (Steere &
Sikand, 2003). Other characteristics of Lyme disease include fevers,
headaches, stiff neck, swollen lymph nodes, body aches, fatigue,
facial palsy, polyarthritis, aseptic meningitis, peripheral root
lesions, radiculopathy, and myocarditis (CDC, 2011a; Hawker et al.,
2012; HHS, 2012).

On average, it takes a few weeks for infected individuals
to produce antibodies against *B. burgdorferi* (HHS, 2012).
Consequently, most cases of Lyme disease have better outcomes
and recovery rates when antibiotics are administered quickly
(Steere & Sikand, 2003). Administered in the beginning stages of

Lyme disease, antibiotics help speed recovery and prevent more serious symptoms, such as heart and nervous system problems, from developing (HHS, 2012).

Erythema migrans is not always present, and other symptoms of Lyme disease are similar to other illnesses. Therefore, Lyme disease may be misdiagnosed and untreated. Raphael B. Stricker (2007), a doctor at the University of California at San Francisco, explained that "in the absence of typical features of Lyme disease, patients may go on to develop a syndrome with multiple nonspecific symptoms that affect various organ systems, including the joints, muscles, nerves, brain, and heart" (p. 149). Conversely, even when patients receive proper antibiotic treatment for two to four weeks they can continue to experience symptoms.

Parenthetical citation for quotation from print source includes page number

Post-Lyme Disease Syndrome

The majority of Lyme disease patients are cured after multiple weeks of antibiotics; however, 10 to 15 percent of patients acquire relapsing nonspecific symptoms such as fatigue, arthritis, and short-term memory problems that can persist for months or even years (Brody, 2013). When there is no other possible origin of the nonspecific symptoms, and the individual has had proper treatment for Lyme disease, the patient is classified as having post-Lyme disease syndrome (Lantos, 2011). Adriana Marques (2008) of the Laboratory of Clinical Infectious Diseases explains, "The appearance of post-Lyme disease symptoms seems to correlate with disseminated diseases, a greater severity of illness at presentation, and delayed antibiotic therapy; but not with the duration of the initial antibiotic therapy." The medical community is unsure of how to treat the nonspecific symptoms or what causes them (Lantos, 2011).

Possible Sources of Post-Lyme Disease Syndrome

Scientists are unable to identify the exact source of post-Lyme disease syndrome for several reasons. Identifying patients is difficult because of the general nature of the symptoms. Several surveys demonstrate that a relatively high percentage of the overall population reports nonspecific symptoms, such as fatigue, chronic pain, or cognitive dysfunction after a tick bite (Lantos, 2011). In addition, researchers struggle to find participants for their studies (Marques, 2008). Study participants must have previous documentation of contracting Lyme disease, which significantly diminishes the testing population (Lantos, 2011).

Scientists and physicians suspect the source of post-Lyme disease syndrome to be multifactorial (Marques, 2008). Plausible causes of reoccurring nonspecific symptoms include persistent infection of *B. burgdorferi*, other tick-borne infections, a natural healing process after infection, post-infective fatigue syndrome, autoimmune mechanisms, and intercurrent conditions (Marques, 2008). Nevertheless, only a few ideas have been thoroughly explored thus far by the scientific community. The majority of scientists believe remaining damage to tissue and the immune system from the infection causes post-Lyme disease syndrome; however, some believe persistent infection of the bacteria is the source (CDC, 2014).

Despite complications, a majority of the medical community considers persistent symptoms to be a result of residual damage to the tissues and the immune system that occurred during the infection. These "auto-immune" reactions, which the body uses against foreign elements, occur in infections similar to Lyme disease such as Campylobacter, Chlamydia, and Strep throat (CDC, 2014). Patients report their nonspecific symptoms improving over time after the typical antibiotic treatment (Marques, 2008). Physicians who followed their patients with post-Lyme disease syndrome for extended times also see nonspecific symptoms resolve without further antibiotic treatment (Marques, 2008). Consequently, post-Lyme disease syndrome may be a natural evolution of the body healing after an intense infection.

A smaller portion of the medical community considers persistent infection of the microorganism *B. burgdorferi* as the cause of post-Lyme disease syndrome. Recently published studies performed on animals show signs of ongoing infection of the bacterium. One scientific study infected mice with *B. burgdorferi* and gave them intense treatment of antibiotics that should have wiped out the bacterium (Bockenstedt, Gonzalez, Haberman, & Belperron, 2012). Bockenstedt et al. (2012) observed the mice over a period of time and found "that infectious spirochetes are rapidly eliminated after institution of antibiotics, but inflammatory *B. burgdorferi* antigens persist adjacent to cartilage and in the enthuses" (p. 2652). This is one of the first studies to show continuous effects of the harmful microorganism in post-Lyme disease syndrome. Another recent scientific study was conducted on nonhuman primates, rhesus macaques. Once again the scientists infected the animals with *B. burgdorferi* and then four to six months later administered an antibiotic treatment to half of the monkeys (Embers et al., 2012). Their results also confirmed that *B. burgdorferi* could withstand antibiotic treatment in rhesus macaques and proceed to cause post-Lyme disease syndrome (Embers et al., 2012). Nonetheless, these results showing perpetual infection as the cause of post-Lyme disease syndrome have yet to be replicated in humans.

In contrast, many studies over the years contradict the theory of ongoing infection, though these studies have not been confirmed true in humans. Lantos (2011), an MD Medical Instructor in the Department of Medicine at Duke University School of Medicine, clarifies that "[n]o adequately controlled, hypothesis-driven study using a repeatable method has demonstrated that viable *B. burgdorferi* is found in patients with persistent post-Lyme symptoms any more frequently than in those with favorable outcomes" (p. 790). Most scientific studies trying to prove persistent infection of *B. burgdorferi* have not been replicated because their procedures and techniques are at fault (Marques, 2008). The problem derives from the technology that detects the microorganism (Lantos, 2011). PCR and *B. burgdorferi* culture are commonly used to find evidence of the bacteria in the body; however, both have "low sensitivity in most body fluids from patients with Lyme disease" (Marques, 2008). Even though other methods, such as finding antibodies in immune complexes, changes in C6 antibody levels, and PCR in urine samples, have been tried, none prove helpful (Marques, 2008). Therefore, the persistent infection of *B. burgdorferi* has not yet successfully been proven as the cause of post-Lyme disease syndrome.

Post-Lyme Disease Syndrome Treatment

Since the cause of post-Lyme disease syndrome is controversial, treatment for the infection varies from patient to patient and physician to physician. Treatment is still in the experimental stages, meaning no set treatment algorithm currently exists. Numerous patients rely on long-term antibiotic medication, despite the overwhelming defying scientific evidence against this treatment (CDC, 2014). The research studies that focus on prolonged antibiotic treatment observe no dramatic difference in benefits or recoveries of those who had the treatment and those who did not (Marques, 2008). On the contrary, many long-term antibiotic research studies found that post-Lyme disease syndrome patients develop harmful side effects (Lantos, 2011). These adverse health effects include "catheter-associated venous thromboembolism, catheter-associated septicemia, allergic reactions and ceftriaxone-induced gallbladder toxicity" (Lantos, 2011, p. 792). Therefore, most of the scientific community considers long-term antibiotic treatment for chronic Lyme disease a harmful, risky, and unbeneficial plan.

Most of the scientific community advises against the use of long-term antibiotics because of potential adverse effects. Nevertheless, a small minority of physicians have observed improvements with long-term antibiotics. Because numerous studies show a lack of benefit to long-term antibiotics, these hopeful patients may be experiencing a placebo effect, which occurs when patients improve because they believe they are receiving an effective treatment (Marques, 2008).

Solving the Mystery

Individuals can take various simple preventive measures to avoid contracting Lyme disease. If the infection is contracted, those who seek prompt treatment increase the chance of full recovery and decrease the chance of developing post-Lyme disease syndrome. However, these steps do not guarantee complete avoidance of post-Lyme disease syndrome. Finding the source of post-Lyme disease syndrome will lead to a specific treatment plan that effectively heals patients. Many scientists deem the source of post-Lyme disease syndrome to be a natural autoimmune reaction; conversely, a few other scientists consider persistent infection as the cause. Both theories, however, need better technology to prove their accuracy. Since scientists disagree about the source of post-Lyme disease syndrome, a variety of experimental treatments have arisen. Replicable studies are needed so that an effective treatment for post-Lyme disease syndrome can be found.

Conclusion indicates need for further research

References

Bockenstedt, L., Gonzalez, D., Haberman, A., & Belperron, A. (2012). Spirochete antigens persist near cartilage after murine Lyme borreliosis therapy. *The Journal of Clinical Investigation, 122*(7), 2652–2660. doi:10.1172/JCI58813

Brody, J. (2013, July 8). When Lyme disease lasts and lasts. *The New York Times*. Retrieved from http://nytimes.com/

Centers for Disease Control and Prevention. (2011a, April 12). *Signs and symptoms*. Retrieved from http://www.cdc.gov/lyme/

Centers for Disease Control and Prevention. (2011b, April 12). *Transmission*. Retrieved from http://www.cdc.gov/lyme/

Centers for Disease Control and Prevention. (2014, February 24). *Post-treatment Lyme disease syndrome*. Retrieved from http://www.cdc.gov/lyme/

Embers, M. E., Barthold, S. W., Borda, J. T., Bowers, L., Doyle, L., Hodzic, E., . . . & Philipp, M. T. (2012). Persistence of *Borrelia burgdorferi* in rhesus macaques following antibiotic treatment of disseminated infection. *PLoS ONE, 7*(1). doi:10.1371/journal.pone.0029914

Hawker, J., Begg, N., Blair, L., Reintjes, R., Weinberg, J., & Ekdahl, K. (2012). *Communicable disease control and health protection handbook* (3rd ed.). Retrieved from http://reader.eblib.com.hartzler.emu.edu

Lantos, P. (2011). Chronic Lyme disease: The controversies and the science. *Expert Review of Anti-Infective Therapy, 9*(7), 787–797. doi:10.1586/eri.11.63

Marques, A. (2008). Chronic Lyme disease: An appraisal. *Infectious Disease Clinics of North America, 22*(2), 341–360. doi:10.1016/j.idc.2007.12.011

References begin on a new page

Article from an online newspaper

Two works by the same author in the same year

Work with more than seven authors

Journal article with DOI

Electronic
book

M'ikanatha, N. M., Lynfield, R., Van Beneden, C. A., & de Valk, H.
        (2013). *Infectious disease surveillance* (2nd ed.). Retrieved from
        http://reader.eblib.com.hartzler.emu.edu

Steere, A., & Sikand, V. (2003). The presenting manifestations
        of Lyme disease and the outcomes of treatment. *The
        New England Journal of Medicine, 348*(24), 2472–2474.
        doi:10.1056/NEJM200306123482423

Stricker, R. (2007). Counterpoint: Long-term antibiotic therapy
        improves persistent symptoms associated with Lyme
        disease. *Clinical Infectious Diseases, 45*(2), 147–157.
        doi:10.1086/518853

U.S. Department of Health and Human Services, National Institutes
        of Health, National Institute of Allergy and Infectious
        Diseases. (2012, October 9). *A history of Lyme disease,
        symptoms, diagnosis, treatment, and prevention.* Retrieved
        from http://www.niaid.nih.gov/topics/lymedisease
        /understanding/pages/intro.aspx

Chicago
Documentation

Chicago style is based on the *Chicago Manual of Style*, first published in 1906 but regularly updated to keep up with changes in publishing practices and technologies. It has long been used extensively not only in the humanities but across disciplines, and it is a trusted resource used by many popular, academic, and scholarly publishers—including the publisher of this book.

— ANDREA A. LUNSFORD

Chicago Documentation

For visual analysis The illustration on the front of this tab, which depicts the 120-year-old bronze lions flanking the Art Institute of Chicago, suggests the history of *Chicago* style and its usefulness in researched writing in many disciplines.

The Basics of *Chicago* Style **65**

The style guide of the University of Chicago Press has long been used in history as well as in other areas of the arts and humanities. The Sixteenth Edition of *The Chicago Manual of Style* (2010) provides a complete guide to *Chicago* style, including two systems for citing sources. This chapter presents the notes and bibliography system. For easy reference, examples of notes and bibliographic entries are shown together in Chapter 66.

65a Consider what readers need from you.

Why does academic work call for very careful citation practices when writing for the general public may not? The answer is that readers of academic work expect to get certain information from source citations:

- Source citations demonstrate that you've done your homework on your topic or issue and that you are a part of the conversation surrounding it.

- Source citations show that you understand the need to give credit where credit is due when you make use of someone else's intellectual property. (See Chapter 15 for more details.)

- Source citations give explicit directions to guide readers who want to look for themselves at the works you're using.

Guidelines from *The Chicago Manual of Style* will tell you exactly what information you need to include in your citation and how you should format that information.

Print and digital sources

You will need to be careful to tell your readers whether you read a print version or a digital version of a source that consists mainly of written words. Digital magazine and newspaper articles may include updates or corrections that the print version lacks; digital books may not number pages or screens the same way the print book does. If you can't find a model exactly like the source you've selected, see the box on p. 575.

Magazine and journal sources

Chicago style treats magazines and journals slightly differently. To determine whether a print source is a magazine (a popular source) or a journal (a scholarly source), see 13a.

Web and database sources

You need a subscription to look through most databases, so individual researchers almost always gain access to articles in databases through the computer system of a school or public library that pays to subscribe. The easiest way to tell whether a source comes from a database, then, is that its information is *not* generally available free to anyone with an Internet connection. Many databases are digital collections of articles that originally appeared in edited print periodicals, ensuring that an authority has vouched for the accuracy of the information. Such sources may have more credibility than free material available on the web.

65b   Connect parts of citations.

Citations in *Chicago* style will appear in three places in your text—a note number in the text marks the material from the source, a footnote or an endnote includes information to identify the source (or information about supplemental material), and the bibliography provides the full citation. In her research essay (see Chapter 67), Amanda Rinder uses a footnote to link a source in her text to a numbered note and then to a bibliography entry, as shown in the figure on p. 571.

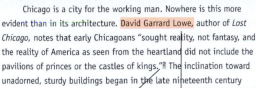

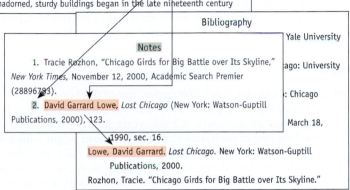

65c Format *Chicago* manuscripts appropriately.

- *Title page.* About halfway down the title page, center the full title of your project and your name. Unless otherwise instructed, at the bottom of the page also list the course name, the instructor's name, and the date submitted. Do not type a number on this page. Check to see if your instructor has a preference on whether to count the title page as part of the text (if so, the first text page will be page 2) or as part of the frontmatter (if so, the first text page will be page 1).

- *Margins and spacing.* Leave one-inch margins on all sides. Double-space the entire text, including block quotations. Single-space notes and bibliographic entries, but double-space between entries.

- *Page numbers.* Number all pages (except the title page) in the upper right-hand corner. Also use a short title or your name before page numbers.

- *Long quotations.* For a long quotation, indent one-half inch (or five spaces) from the left margin and do not use quotation marks. *Chicago* defines a long quotation as one hundred words or eight lines, though you may set off shorter quotes for emphasis.

- **Headings.** *Chicago* style allows, but does not require, headings.
- **Visuals.** Visuals (photographs, drawings, charts, graphs, and tables) should be placed as near as possible to the relevant text. (See 15c for guidelines on incorporating visuals into your text.) Tables should be labeled *Table,* numbered, and captioned. All other visuals should be labeled *Figure* (abbreviated *Fig.*), numbered, and captioned. Remember to refer to each visual in your text, pointing out how it contributes to the point(s) you are making.

Notes

Notes can be footnotes (each one appearing at the bottom of the page on which its citation appears) or endnotes (in a list on a separate page at the end of the text). (Check your instructor's preference.) Indent the first line of each note one-half inch and begin with a number, a period, and one space before the first word. All remaining lines of the entry are flush with the left margin. Single-space footnotes and endnotes, with a double space between entries, unless your instructor asks you to double-space the entire project.

Use superscript numbers ([1]) to mark citations in the text. Place the superscript number for each note just after the relevant quotation, sentence, clause, or phrase. Type the number after any punctuation mark except the dash, and do not leave a space before the superscript. Number the citations sequentially throughout the text. When you use signal phrases to introduce source material, note that *Chicago* style requires you to use the present tense (*citing Bebout's studies, Meier points out . . .*).

IN THE TEXT

Sweig argues that Castro and Che Guevara were not the only key players in the Cuban Revolution of the late 1950s.[19]

IN THE FIRST NOTE REFERRING TO THE SOURCE

　　19. Julia Sweig, *Inside the Cuban Revolution* (Cambridge, MA: Harvard University Press, 2002), 9.

After giving complete information the first time you cite a work, shorten additional references to that work: list only the author's last name, a comma, a short version of the title, a comma, and the page number. If you refer to the same source cited in the previous note, you can use the Latin abbreviation *Ibid.* ("in the same place") instead of the name and title.

IN FIRST AND SUBSEQUENT NOTES

19. Julia Sweig, *Inside the Cuban Revolution* (Cambridge, MA: Harvard University Press, 2002), 9.

20. Ibid., 13.

21. Ferguson, "Comfort of Being Sad," 63.

22. Sweig, *Cuban Revolution*, 21.

Bibliography

Begin the list of sources on a separate page after the main text and any endnotes. Continue numbering pages consecutively. Center the title *Bibliography* (without underlining, italics, or quotation marks) one inch below the top of the page. Begin each entry at the left margin. Indent the second and subsequent lines of each entry one-half inch, or five spaces.

List sources alphabetically by authors' last names or by the first major word in the title if the author is unknown. Italicize titles of books and periodicals, and enclose titles of short works in quotation marks. See p. 595 for an example of a *Chicago*-style bibliography.

In the bibliographic entry, include the same information as in the first note for that source, but omit the page reference. Give the *first* author's last name first, followed by a comma and the first name; separate the main elements of the entry with periods rather than commas; and do not enclose the publication information for books in parentheses.

IN THE BIBLIOGRAPHY

Sweig, Julia. *Inside the Cuban Revolution*. Cambridge, MA: Harvard University Press, 2002.

Chicago Style for Notes and Bibliographic Entries **66**

The following examples demonstrate how to format both notes and bibliographic entries according to *Chicago* style. The note, which is numbered, appears first; the bibliographic entry, which is not numbered, appears below the note.

Notes and bibliographic entries

Print and digital books

For the basic format for citing a print book, see the source map on pp. 576–77. The note for a book typically includes five elements: author's name, title and subtitle, city of publication and publisher, year, and page number(s) or electronic locator information for the information in the note. The bibliographic entry usually includes all these elements but the page number (and does include a URL or other locator if the book is digitally published), but it is styled differently: commas separate major elements of a note, but a bibliographic entry uses periods.

QUICK HELP

Citing Sources That Don't Match Any Model Exactly

What should you do if your source doesn't match the model exactly? Suppose, for instance, that your source is a translation of a republished book with an editor.

- Identify a basic model to follow. If you decide that your source looks most like a republished book, start with a citation that looks like model 12.

- Look for models that show the additional elements in your source. For this example, you would need to add elements of model 11 (for the translation) and either model 7 or model 8 (for the editor).

- Add new elements from other models to your basic model in the order indicated.

- If you aren't sure how to arrange the pieces to create a combination model, ask your instructor.

To cite a source for which you cannot find a model, collect as much information as you can find about the creator, title, sponsor, date, and so on, with the goal of helping your readers find the source for themselves. Then look at the models in this section to see which one most closely matches the type of source you are using. If possible, seek your instructor's advice to find the best model.

1. ONE AUTHOR

1. Nell Irvin Painter, *The History of White People* (New York: W. W. Norton, 2010), 119.

Painter, Nell Irvin. *The History of White People.* New York: W. W. Norton, 2010.

2. MULTIPLE AUTHORS

2. Margaret Macmillan and Richard Holbrooke, *Paris 1919: Six Months That Changed the World* (New York: Random House, 2003), 384.

Macmillan, Margaret, and Richard Holbrooke. *Paris 1919: Six Months That Changed the World.* New York: Random House, 2003.

With more than three authors, you may give the first-listed author followed by *et al.* in the note. In the bibliography, list all the authors' names.

2. Stephen J. Blank et al., *Conflict, Culture, and History: Regional Dimensions* (Miami: University Press of the Pacific, 2002), 276.

Blank, Stephen J., Lawrence E. Grinter, Karl P. Magyar, Lewis B. Ware, and Bynum E. Weathers. *Conflict, Culture, and History: Regional Dimensions.* Miami: University Press of the Pacific, 2002.

CHICAGO SOURCE MAP: Books

Take information from the book's title page and copyright page (on the reverse side of the title page), not from the book's cover or a library catalog. Look carefully at the differences in punctuation between the note and the bibliographic entry.

1 **Author.** In a note, list the author(s) first name first. In a bibliographic entry, list the first author last name first. List other authors first name first.

2 **Title.** Italicize the title and subtitle, and capitalize all major words.

3 **City of publication and publisher.** List the city (and country or state abbreviation for an unfamiliar city) followed by a colon. In a note only, city, publisher, and year appear in parentheses. Drop *Inc.*, *Co.*, *Publishing*, or *Publishers*. Follow with a comma.

4 **Publication year.** In a bibliographic entry, end with a period.

5 **Page number.** In a note only, end with the page number and a period.

Citations for the book on p. 577 would look like this:

ENDNOTE

1. Alex von Tunzelmann, *Red Heat: Conspiracy, Murder, and the Cold War in the Caribbean* (New York: Picador, 2011), 178.

BIBLIOGRAPHIC ENTRY

von Tunzelmann, Alex. *Red Heat: Conspiracy, Murder, and the Cold War in the Caribbean.* New York: Picador, 2011.

Publication Year

2011

RED HEAT

 Title

CONSPIRACY, MURDER, AND THE COLD WAR IN THE CARIBBEAN

ALEX VON TUNZELMANN

 Author

PICADOR

HENRY HOLT AND COMPANY
NEW YORK

 Publisher and City of Publication

577

3. ORGANIZATION AS AUTHOR

3. World Intellectual Property Organization, *Intellectual Property Profile of the Least Developed Countries* (Geneva: World Intellectual Property Organization, 2002), 43.

World Intellectual Property Organization. *Intellectual Property Profile of the Least Developed Countries.* Geneva: World Intellectual Property Organization, 2002.

4. UNKNOWN AUTHOR

4. *Broad Stripes and Bright Stars* (Kansas City, MO: Andrews McMeel, 2002), 10.

Broad Stripes and Bright Stars. Kansas City, MO: Andrews McMeel, 2002.

5. ONLINE BOOK

5. Dorothy Richardson, *Long Day: The Story of a New York Working Girl, as Told by Herself* (1906; UMDL Texts, 2010), 159, http://quod.lib.umich.edu /cgi/t/text/text-idx?c=moa;idno=AFS7156.0001.001.

Richardson, Dorothy. *Long Day: The Story of a New York Working Girl, as Told by Herself.* 1906. UMDL Texts, 2010. http://quod.lib.umich.edu/cgi/t/text /text-idx?c=moa;idno=AFS7156.0001.001.

6. ELECTRONIC BOOK (E-BOOK)

6. Manal M. Omar, *Barefoot in Baghdad* (Naperville, IL: Sourcebooks, 2010), Kindle edition, ch. 4.

Omar, Manal M. *Barefoot in Baghdad.* Naperville, IL: Sourcebooks, 2010. Kindle edition.

7. EDITED BOOK WITH NO AUTHOR

7. James H. Fetzer, ed., *The Great Zapruder Film Hoax: Deceit and Deception in the Death of JFK* (Chicago: Open Court, 2003), 56.

Fetzer, James H., ed. *The Great Zapruder Film Hoax: Deceit and Deception in the Death of JFK.* Chicago: Open Court, 2003.

8. EDITED BOOK WITH AUTHOR

8. Leopold von Ranke, *The Theory and Practice of History,* ed. Georg G. Iggers (New York: Routledge, 2010), 135.

von Ranke, Leopold. *The Theory and Practice of History.* Edited by Georg G. Iggers. New York: Routledge, 2010.

9. SELECTION IN AN ANTHOLOGY OR CHAPTER IN A BOOK WITH AN EDITOR

9. Denise Little, "Born in Blood," in *Alternate Gettysburgs,* ed. Brian Thomsen and Martin H. Greenberg (New York: Berkley Publishing Group, 2002), 245.

Give the inclusive page numbers of the selection or chapter in the bibliographic entry.

Little, Denise. "Born in Blood." In *Alternate Gettysburgs,* edited by Brian Thomsen and Martin H. Greenberg, 242–55. New York: Berkley Publishing Group, 2002.

10. INTRODUCTION, PREFACE, FOREWORD, OR AFTERWORD

10. Robert B. Reich, introduction to *Making Work Pay: America after Welfare,* ed. Robert Kuttner (New York: New Press, 2002), xvi.

Reich, Robert B. Introduction to *Making Work Pay: America after Welfare,* edited by Robert Kuttner, vii–xvii. New York: New Press, 2002.

11. TRANSLATION

11. Suetonius, *The Twelve Caesars,* trans. Robert Graves (London: Penguin Classics, 1989), 202.

Suetonius. *The Twelve Caesars.* Translated by Robert Graves. London: Penguin Classics, 1989.

12. EDITION OTHER THAN THE FIRST

12. Dee Brown, *Bury My Heart at Wounded Knee: An Indian History of the American West,* 4th ed. (New York: Owl Books, 2007), 12.

Brown, Dee. *Bury My Heart at Wounded Knee: An Indian History of the American West,* 4th ed. New York: Owl Books, 2007.

13. MULTIVOLUME WORK

13. John Watson, *Annals of Philadelphia and Pennsylvania in the Olden Time,* vol. 2 (Washington, DC: Ross & Perry, 2003), 514.

Watson, John. *Annals of Philadelphia and Pennsylvania in the Olden Time.* Vol. 2. Washington, DC: Ross & Perry, 2003.

14. REFERENCE WORK

In a note, use *s.v.,* the abbreviation for the Latin *sub verbo* ("under the word"), to help your reader find the entry. Do not list reference works such as encyclopedias or dictionaries in your bibliography.

14. *Encyclopaedia Britannica,* s.v. "carpetbagger."

15. WORK WITH A TITLE WITHIN THE TITLE

Use quotation marks around any title within a book title.

15. John A. Alford, *A Companion to "Piers Plowman"* (Berkeley: University of California Press, 1988), 195.

Alford, John A. *A Companion to "Piers Plowman."* Berkeley: University of California Press, 1988.

16. SACRED TEXT

Do not include sacred texts in the bibliography.

> 16. Luke 18:24–25 (New International Version)

> 16. Qur'an 7:40–41

17. SOURCE QUOTED IN ANOTHER SOURCE

Identify both the original and the secondary source.

> 17. Frank D. Millet, "The Filipino Leaders," *Harper's Weekly*, March 11, 1899, quoted in Richard Slotkin, *Gunfighter Nation: The Myth of the Frontier in Twentieth-Century America* (New York: HarperCollins, 1992), 110.

> Millet, Frank D. "The Filipino Leaders." *Harper's Weekly*, March 11, 1899. Quoted in Richard Slotkin, *Gunfighter Nation: The Myth of the Frontier in Twentieth-Century America* (New York: HarperCollins, 1992), 110.

Print and digital periodicals

The note for an article in a periodical typically includes the author's name, the article title, and the periodical title. The format for other information, including the volume and issue numbers (if any) and the date of publication, as well as the page number(s) to which the note refers, varies according to the type of periodical and whether you consulted it in print, on the web, or in a database. In a bibliographic entry for a journal or magazine article from a database or a print periodical, also give the inclusive page numbers.

18. ARTICLE IN A PRINT JOURNAL

> 18. Karin Lützen, "The Female World: Viewed from Denmark," *Journal of Women's History* 12, no. 3 (2000): 36.

> Lützen, Karin. "The Female World: Viewed from Denmark." *Journal of Women's History* 12, no. 3 (2000): 34–38.

19. ARTICLE IN AN ONLINE JOURNAL

Give the DOI if there is one. If not, include the article URL. If page numbers are provided, include them as well.

> 19. Jeffrey J. Schott, "America, Europe, and the New Trade Order," *Business and Politics* 11, no. 3 (2009), doi:10.2202/1469-3569 .1263.

> Schott, Jeffrey J. "America, Europe, and the New Trade Order." *Business and Politics* 11, no. 3 (2009). doi:10.2202/1469-3569.1263.

20. JOURNAL ARTICLE FROM A DATABASE

For basic information on citing a periodical article from a database in *Chicago* style, see the source map on pp. 582–83.

> 20. W. Trent Foley and Nicholas J. Higham, "Bede on the Britons," *Early Medieval Europe* 17, no. 2 (2009): 157, doi:10.1111/j.1468 -0254.2009.00258.x.

Foley, W. Trent, and Nicholas J. Higham. "Bede on the Britons." *Early Medieval Europe* 17, no. 2 (2009): 154–85. doi:10.1111/j.1468 -0254.2009.00258.x.

21. ARTICLE IN A PRINT MAGAZINE

> 21. Terry McDermott, "The Mastermind: Khalid Sheikh Mohammed and the Making of 9/11," *New Yorker,* September 13, 2010, 42.

McDermott, Terry. "The Mastermind: Khalid Sheikh Mohammed and the Making of 9/11." *New Yorker,* September 13, 2010, 38–51.

22. ARTICLE IN AN ONLINE MAGAZINE

> 22. Tracy Clark-Flory, "Educating Women Saves Kids' Lives," *Salon,* September 17, 2010, http://www.salon.com/life/broadsheet/2010/09/17 /education_women/index.html.

Clark-Flory, Tracy. "Educating Women Saves Kids' Lives." *Salon,* September 17, 2010. http://www.salon.com/life/broadsheet/2010/09/17/education _women/index.html.

23. MAGAZINE ARTICLE FROM A DATABASE

> 23. Sami Yousafzai and Ron Moreau, "Twisting Arms in Afghanistan," *Newsweek,* November 9, 2009, 8, Academic Search Premier (44962900).

Yousafzai, Sami, and Ron Moreau. "Twisting Arms in Afghanistan." *Newsweek,* November 9, 2009. 8. Academic Search Premier (44962900).

24. ARTICLE IN A NEWSPAPER

Do not include page numbers for a newspaper article, but you may include the section, if any.

> 24. Katherine Q. Seelye, "A Heinous Crime, Secret Histories, and a Sinn Fein Leader's Arrest," *New York Times,* May 2, 2014, sec. A.

Seelye, Katherine Q. "A Heinous Crime, Secret Histories, and a Sinn Fein Leader's Arrest." *New York Times,* May 2, 2014, sec. A.

If you provide complete documentation of a newspaper article in a note, you may not need to include it in the bibliography. Check your instructor's preference.

1 **Author.** In a note, list the author(s) first name first. In a bibliographic entry, list the first author last name first, comma, first name; list other authors first name first.

2 **Article title.** Enclose the title and subtitle (if any) in quotation marks, and capitalize major words. In the notes section, put a comma before and after the title. In the bibliography, put a period before and after.

3 **Periodical title.** Italicize the title and subtitle, and capitalize all major words. For a magazine or newspaper, follow with a comma.

4 **Volume and issue numbers (for journals) and date.** For journals, follow the title with the volume number, a comma, the abbreviation _no.,_ and the issue number; enclose the publication year in parentheses and follow with a comma (in a note) or with a period (in a bibliography), or with a colon when page numbers follow. For other periodicals, give the month and year or month, day, and year, not in parentheses, followed by a comma.

5 **Page numbers.** In a note, give the page where the information is found. In a bibliographic entry, give the page range.

6 **Retrieval information.** Provide the article's DOI, if one is given; the name of the database and an accession number; or a "stable or persistent" URL for the article in the database. Because you provide stable retrieval information, you do not need to identify the electronic format of the work (that is, PDF, as in the example shown here). End with a period.

Citations for the journal article on p. 583 would look like this:

ENDNOTE

1. Elizabeth Tucker, "Changing Concepts of Childhood: Children's Folklore Scholarship since the Late Nineteenth Century," _Journal of American Folklore_ 125, no. 498 (2012): 399, http://www.jstor.org/stable/10.5406/jamerfolk .125.498.0389.

BIBLIOGRAPHIC ENTRY

Tucker, Elizabeth. "Changing Concepts of Childhood: Children's Folklore Scholarship since the Late Nineteenth Century." _Journal of American Folklore_ 125, no. 498 (2012): 389–410. http://www.jstor.org/stable /10.5406/jamerfolk.125.498.0389.

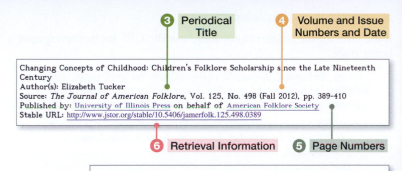

Changing Concepts of Childhood: Children's Folklore Scholarship since the Late Nineteenth Century
Author(s): Elizabeth Tucker
Source: *The Journal of American Folklore*, Vol. 125, No. 498 (Fall 2012), pp. 389-410
Published by: University of Illinois Press on behalf of American Folklore Society
Stable URL: http://www.jstor.org/stable/10.5406/jamerfolk.125.498.0389

③ Periodical Title

④ Volume and Issue Numbers and Date

⑥ Retrieval Information

⑤ Page Numbers

ELIZABETH TUCKER

② Article Title and Subtitle

① Author

Changing Concepts of Childhood: Children's Folklore Scholarship since the Late Nineteenth Century

This essay examines children's folklore scholarship from the late nineteenth century to the present, tracing key concepts from the Gilded Age to the contemporary era. These concepts reflect significant social, cultural, political, and scientific changes. From the "savage child" to the "secret-keeping child," the "magic-making child," the "cerebral child," the "taboo-breaking child," the "monstrous child," and others, scholarly representations of young people have close connections to the eras in which they developed. Nineteenth-century children's folklore scholarship relied on evolutionism; now evolutionary biology provides a basis for children's folklore research, so we have re-entered familiar territory.

SINCE 1977, WHEN THE American Folklore Society decided to form a new section for scholars interested in young people's traditions, I have belonged to the Children's Folklore Section. It has been a joy to contribute to this dynamic organization, which has significantly influenced children's folklore scholarship and children's book authors' focus on folk tradition. This essay examines children's folklore scholarship from the late nineteenth century to the present, tracing key concepts from the Gilded Age to the contemporary era in the English language. These concepts reflect significant social, cultural, political, and scientific changes that have occurred since William Wells Newell, the first secretary of the American Folklore Society and the first editor of the *Journal of American Folklore*, published *Games and Songs of American Children* in 1883. They also reveal some very interesting commonalities. Those of us who pursue children's folklore scholarship today may consider ourselves to be light years away from nineteenth-century scholars' research but may find, when reading nineteenth-century works, that we have stayed fairly close to our scholarly "home base."

Before examining concepts of childhood that folklorists have developed, I will offer a working definition of this life stage and briefly explain the beginning of childhood studies. I will also summarize the Children's Folklore Section's work during the past thirty-four years. According to the *Oxford English Dictionary*, childhood consists of "the state or stage of life of a child; the time during which one is a child; the time from birth to puberty" (2011). Scholars of childhood tend to draw a line between childhood and adolescence, which begins at puberty and follows pre-adolescence. The folklore

ELIZABETH TUCKER is Professor of English at Binghamton University

25. ARTICLE IN AN ONLINE NEWSPAPER

If the URL for the article is very long, use the URL for the newspaper's home page.

> 25. Katherine Q. Seelye, "A Heinous Crime, Secret Histories, and a Sinn Fein Leader's Arrest," *New York Times,* May 2, 2014, http://www
> .nytimes.com.

> Seelye, Katherine Q. "A Heinous Crime, Secret Histories, and a Sinn Fein
>   Leader's Arrest." *New York Times,* May 2, 2014. http://www
>   .nytimes.com.

26. NEWSPAPER ARTICLE FROM A DATABASE

> 26. Demetria Irwin, "A Hatchet, Not a Scalpel, for NYC Budget Cuts,"
> *New York Amsterdam News,* November 13, 2008, Academic Search Premier
> (35778153).

> Irwin, Demetria. "A Hatchet, Not a Scalpel, for NYC Budget Cuts." *New
>   York Amsterdam News,* November 13, 2008. Academic Search Premier
>   (35778153).

27. BOOK REVIEW

After the standard information about the book under review, provide publication information for the appropriate kind of source (see models 18–26).

> 27. Arnold Relman, "Health Care: The Disquieting Truth," review of
> *Tracking Medicine: A Researcher's Quest to Understand Health Care,* by John E.
> Wennberg, *New York Review of Books* 57, no. 14 (2010): 45.

> Relman, Arnold. "Health Care: The Disquieting Truth." Review of *Tracking
>   Medicine: A Researcher's Quest to Understand Health Care,* by John E.
>   Wennberg. *New York Review of Books* 57, no. 14 (2010): 45–48.

Other online sources

In general, include the author (if given); the title of a work from a website (in quotation marks); the name of the site (in italics if the site is an online publication, but otherwise neither italicized nor in quotation marks); the sponsor of the site, if different from the name of the site or the name of the author; the date of publication or most recent update; and a URL. If the online source does not indicate when it was published or last modified, or if your instructor requests an access date, place it before the URL.

For basic information on citing works from websites in *Chicago* style, see the source map on pp. 586–87.

28. WEBSITE

If the site does not list the date of publication or date last modified, identify your access date ("accessed March 12, 2015").

> 28. Rutgers School of Arts and Sciences, The Rutgers Oral History Archives, accessed May 6, 2015, http://oralhistory.rutgers.edu/.

> Rutgers School of Arts and Sciences. The Rutgers Oral History Archives. Accessed May 6, 2015. http://oralhistory.rutgers.edu/.

29. WORK FROM A WEBSITE

If the site does not list the date of publication or date last modified, identify your access date ("accessed March 12, 2015").

> 29. Kheel Center, "Timeline of Events," Remembering the 1911 Triangle Factory Fire, Cornell University, accessed May 5, 2015, http://www.ilr.cornell.edu/trianglefire/supplemental/timeline.html.

> Kheel Center. "Timeline of Events." Remembering the 1911 Triangle Factory Fire. Cornell University. Accessed May 5, 2015. http://www.ilr.cornell.edu/trianglefire/supplemental/timeline.html.

30. BLOG POST

Treat a blog post as a work from a website (see model 29), but italicize the name of the blog.

> 30. Kate Beaton, "Ida B. Wells," *Hark! A Vagrant* (blog), accessed May 2, 2015, http://harkavagrant.com/.

Chicago recommends that blog posts appear in the notes section only, not in the bibliography, unless the blog is cited frequently. Check your instructor's preference. A bibliography reference to an entire blog would look like this:

> Beaton, Kate. *Hark! A Vagrant* (blog). http://harkavagrant.com/.

1. **Author.** In a note, list the author(s) first name first. In a bibliographic entry, list the first author last name first, comma, first name; list additional authors first name first. Note that the host may serve as the author.

2. **Document title.** Enclose the title in quotation marks, and capitalize all major words. In a note, put a comma before and after the title. In the bibliography, put a period before and after.

3. **Title of website.** Capitalize all major words. If the site's title is analogous to a book or periodical title, italicize it. In the notes section, put a comma after the title. In the bibliography, put a period after the title.

4. **Sponsor of site.** If the sponsor is the same as the author or site title, you may omit it. End with a comma (in the note) or a period (in the bibliographic entry).

5. **Date of publication or last modification.** If no date is available, or if your instructor requests it, include your date of access (with the word *accessed*).

6. **Retrieval information.** Give the URL for the website. If you are required to include a date of access, put the word *accessed* and the date in parentheses after the URL. End with a period.

Citations for the website on p. 587 would look like this:

ENDNOTE

1. Rebecca Edwards, "The Populist Party," 1896: The Presidential Campaign: Cartoons & Commentary, Vassar College, 2000, http://projects .vassar.edu/1896/populists.html.

BIBLIOGRAPHIC ENTRY

Edwards, Rebecca. "The Populist Party." 1896: The Presidential Campaign: Cartoons & Commentary. Vassar College. 2000. http://projects.vassar .edu/1896/populists.html.

projects.**vassar**.edu/1896/populists.html

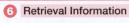 

The Populist Party •——**2** Document Title

The Rise of Populism

The People's Party (or Populist Party, as it was widely known) was much younger than the Democratic and Republican Parties, which had been founded before the Civil War. Agricultural areas in the West and South had been hit by economic depression years before industrial areas. In the 1880s, as drought hit the wheat-growing areas of the Great Plains and prices for Southern cotton sunk to new lows, many tenant farmers fell into deep debt. This exacerbated long-held grievances against railroads, lenders, grain-elevator owners, and others with whom farmers did business. By the early 1890s, as the depression worsened, some industrial workers shared these farm families' views on labor and the trusts.

 In 1890 Populists won control of the Kansas state legislature, and Kansan **William Peffer** became the party's first U.S. Senator. Peffer, with his long white beard, was a humorous figure to many Eastern journalists and politicians, who saw little evidence of Populism in their states and often treated the party as a joke. Nonetheless, Western and Southern Populists gained support rapidly. In 1892 the national party was officially founded through a merger of the Farmers' Alliance and the Knights of Labor. In that year the Populist presidential candidate, James B. Weaver, won over one million votes. Between 1892 and 1896, however, the party failed to make further gains, in part because of fraud, intimidation, and violence by Southern Democrats.

By 1896 the Populist organization was in even more turmoil than that of Democrats. Two main factions had appeared.
organizati
"fused"--c
third party

Homepage •——**3** Title of Website

© 2000, Rebecca Edwards, Vassar College

5 Date of Publication   **1** Author   **4** Sponsor of Site

31. EMAIL, FACEBOOK, TWITTER, AND PERSONAL COMMUNICATIONS

Chicago style recommends that email and communications that are not archived and accessible to all readers, such as Facebook and Twitter posts and telephone calls, be cited in notes only, not in the bibliography. If you cite a public Facebook page, give both the access date and the URL; for an individual's account, omit the URL. (Note that *Chicago* style recommends hyphenating *e-mail*.)

> 31. Kareem Adas, e-mail message to author, February 11, 2015.

> 31. Supraja Iyer, Facebook post, accessed March 1, 2015.

> 31. U.S. Department of Education, Twitter feed, accessed April 24, 2015, https://twitter.com/usedgov.

32. PODCAST

Treat a podcast as a work from a website (see model 29), and give as much of the following information as you can find: the author or speaker, the title or a description of the podcast, the title of the site, the site sponsor (if different from the author or site name), the type of podcast or file format, the date of posting or access, and the URL.

> 32. Rob Attar, "Victorian Burials and the History of Psychology," History Extra, podcast audio, May 1, 2015, http://www.historyextra.com/podcast/victorian-burials-and-history-psychology.

> Attar, Rob. "Victorian Burials and the History of Psychology." History Extra. Podcast audio. May 1, 2015. http://www.historyextra.com/podcast/victorian-burials-and-history-psychology.

33. ONLINE AUDIO OR VIDEO

Treat an online audio or video source as a work from a website (see model 29). If the source is downloadable, give the medium or file format before the URL (see model 32).

> 33. Alyssa Katz, "Did the Mortgage Crisis Kill the American Dream?" NYCRadio, June 24, 2009, http://www.youtube.com/watch?v=uivtwjwd_Qw.

> Katz, Alyssa. "Did the Mortgage Crisis Kill the American Dream?" NYCRadio. June 24, 2009. http://www.youtube.com/watch?v=uivtwjwd_Qw.

Other sources

34. PUBLISHED OR BROADCAST INTERVIEW

> 34. Nina Totenberg, interview by Charlie Rose, *The Charlie Rose Show,* PBS, June 29, 2010.

> Totenberg, Nina. Interview by Charlie Rose. *The Charlie Rose Show.* PBS, June 29, 2010.

Any interviews you conduct are considered personal communications (see model 31).

35. VIDEO, DVD, OR BLU-RAY DISC

35. Edward Norton and Edward Furlong, *American History X,* directed by Tony Kaye (1998; Los Angeles: New Line Studios, 2002), DVD.

Norton, Edward, and Edward Furlong. *American History X.* Directed by Tony Kaye, 1998. Los Angeles: New Line Studios, 2002. DVD.

36. SOUND RECORDING

36. Paul Robeson, *The Collector's Paul Robeson,* recorded 1959, Monitor MCD-61580, 1989, compact disc.

Robeson, Paul. *The Collector's Paul Robeson.* Recorded 1959. Monitor MCD-61580, 1989, compact disc.

37. WORK OF ART

Begin with the artist's name and the title of the work. If you viewed the work in person, give the medium, the date the work was created, and the name and location of the place where you saw it.

37. Mary Cassatt, *The Child's Bath,* oil on canvas, 1893, The Art Institute of Chicago, Chicago, IL.

Cassatt, Mary. *The Child's Bath.* Oil on canvas, 1893. The Art Institute of Chicago, Chicago, IL.

If you refer to a reproduction, give the publication information.

37. Mary Cassatt, *The Child's Bath,* oil on canvas, 1893, on *Art Access,* The Art Institute of Chicago, August 2004, http://www.artic.edu/artaccess /AA_Impressionist/pages/IMP_6.shtml#.

Cassatt, Mary. *The Child's Bath.* Oil on canvas, 1893. On *Art Access,* The Art Institute of Chicago. August 2004. http://www.artic.edu/artaccess /AA_Impressionist/pages/IMP_6.shtml#.

38. PAMPHLET, REPORT, OR BROCHURE

Information about the author or publisher may not be readily available, but give enough information to identify your source.

38. Jamie McCarthy, *Who Is David Irving?* (San Antonio, TX: Holocaust History Project, 1998).

McCarthy, Jamie. *Who Is David Irving?* San Antonio, TX: Holocaust History Project, 1998.

39. GOVERNMENT DOCUMENT

39. U.S. House Committee on Ways and Means, *Report on Trade Mission to Sub-Saharan Africa,* 108th Cong., 1st sess. (Washington, DC: Government Printing Office, 2003), 28.

U.S. House Committee on Ways and Means. *Report on Trade Mission to Sub-Saharan Africa.* 108th Cong., 1st sess. Washington, DC: Government Printing Office, 2003.

67 An Excerpt from a Student Research Essay, *Chicago* Style

Student Writer

Amanda Rinder

On the following pages is an excerpt from an essay by Amanda Rinder that conforms to the *Chicago* guidelines described in this chapter. Her complete project can also be found with an activity at **macmillanhighered.com/everyday6e**.

Student Writing
Chicago

Sweet Home Chicago: Preserving the Past,
Protecting the Future of the Windy City

Title announces topic clearly and succinctly

Amanda Rinder

Title and writer's name centered

Twentieth-Century U.S. History
Professor Goldberg
November 27, 2006

Course title, instructor's name, and date centered at bottom of title page

Annotations indicate effective choices or *Chicago*-style formatting.

Rinder 2

First page of
body text is
p. 2

Paper refers to
each figure by
number

Thesis
introduced

Double-spaced
text

Source
cited using
superscript
numeral

Only one city has the "Big Shoulders" described by Carl
Sandburg: Chicago (fig. 1). So renowned are its skyscrapers and
celebrated building style that an entire school of architecture is
named for Chicago. Presently, however, the place that Frank Sinatra
called "my kind of town" is beginning to lose sight of exactly what
kind of town it is. Many of the buildings that give Chicago its
distinctive character are being torn down in order to make room
for new growth. Both preserving the classics and encouraging new
creation are important; the combination of these elements gives
Chicago architecture its unique flavor. Witold Rybczynski, a professor
of urbanism, told Tracie Rozhon of the *New York Times,* "Of all the
cities we can think of . . . we associate Chicago with new things,
with building new. Combining that with preservation is a difficult
task, a tricky thing. It's hard to find the middle ground in Chicago."[1]
Yet finding a middle ground is essential if the city is to retain the
original character that sets it apart from the rest. In order to

Figure caption
includes
number, short
title, and
source

Fig. 1. Chicago skyline, circa 1940s. (Postcard courtesy of Minnie
Dangburg.)

maintain Chicago's distinctive identity and its delicate balance between the old and the new, the city government must provide a comprehensive urban plan that not only directs growth, but calls for the preservation of landmarks and historic districts as well.

Chicago is a city for the working man. Nowhere is this more evident than in its architecture. David Garrard Lowe, author of *Lost Chicago,* notes that early Chicagoans "sought reality, not fantasy, and the reality of America as seen from the heartland did not include the pavilions of princes or the castles of kings."[2] The inclination toward unadorned, sturdy buildings began in the late nineteenth century with the aptly named Chicago School, a movement led by Louis Sullivan, John Wellborn Root, and Daniel Burnham and based on Sullivan's adage, "Form follows function."[3] The early skyscraper, the very symbol of the Chicago style, represents the triumph of function and utility over sentiment, America over Europe, and perhaps, as Daniel Bluestone argues, even the frontier over the civilization of the East Coast.[4] These ideals of the original Chicago School were expanded upon by architects of the Second Chicago School. Frank Lloyd Wright's legendary organic style and the famed glass and steel constructions of Mies van der Rohe are often the first images that spring to mind when one thinks of Chicago.

Yet the architecture that is the city's defining attribute is being threatened by the increasing tendency toward development. The root of Chicago's preservation problem lies in the enormous drive toward economic expansion and the potential in Chicago for such growth. The highly competitive market for land in the city means that properties sell for the highest price if the buildings on them can be obliterated to make room for newer, larger developments. Because of this preference on the part of potential buyers, the label "landmark" has become a stigma for property owners. "In other cities, landmark . . .

Opening paragraph concludes with formal thesis statement

Second paragraph provides background

Clear transition from previous paragraph

Notes

Newspaper article in database

1. Tracie Rozhon, "Chicago Girds for Big Battle over Its Skyline," *New York Times,* November 12, 2000, Academic Search Premier (28896783).

Print book

2. David Garrard Lowe, *Lost Chicago* (New York: Watson-Guptill, 2000), 123.

3. *Columbia Encyclopedia,* 6th ed., s.v. "Louis Sullivan."

4. Daniel Bluestone, *Constructing Chicago* (New Haven: Yale University Press, 1991), 105.

Indirect source

5. Alan J. Shannon, "When Will It End?" *Chicago Tribune,* September 11, 1987, quoted in Karen J. Dilibert, *From Landmark to Landfill* (Chicago: Chicago Architectural Foundation, 2000), 11.

6. Steve Kerch, "Landmark Decisions," *Chicago Tribune,* March 18, 1990, sec. 16.

7. John W. Stamper, *Chicago's North Michigan Avenue* (Chicago: University of Chicago Press, 1991), 215.

Newspaper article online

8. Alf Siewers, "Success Spoiling the Magnificent Mile?" *Chicago Sun-Times,* April 9, 1995, http://www.sun-times.com/.

9. Paul Gapp, "McCarthy Building Puts Landmark Law on a Collision Course with Developers," *Chicago Tribune,* April 20, 1986, quoted in Karen J. Dilibert, *From Landmark to Landfill* (Chicago: Chicago Architectural Foundation, 2000), 4.

Reference to previous source

10. Ibid.

11. Rozhon, "Chicago Girds for Big Battle."

Second reference to source

12. Kerch, "Landmark Decisions."

13. Robert Bruegmann, *The Architects and the City* (Chicago: University of Chicago Press, 1997), 443.

Bibliography

Bluestone, Daniel. *Constructing Chicago.* New Haven: Yale
    University Press, 1991.

Bruegmann, Robert. *The Architects and the City.* Chicago: University
    of Chicago Press, 1997.

Dilibert, Karen J. *From Landmark to Landfill.* Chicago: Chicago
    Architectural Foundation, 2000.

Kerch, Steve. "Landmark Decisions." *Chicago Tribune,* March 18,
    1990, sec. 16.

Lowe, David Garrard. *Lost Chicago.* New York: Watson-Guptill, 2000.

Rozhon, Tracie. "Chicago Girds for Big Battle over Its Skyline."
    New York Times, November 12, 2000. Academic Search Premier
    (28896783).

Siewers, Alf. "Success Spoiling the Magnificent Mile?" *Chicago
    Sun-Times,* April 9, 1995. http://www.sun-times.com/.

Stamper, John W. *Chicago's North Michigan Avenue.* Chicago:
    University of Chicago Press, 1991.

Bibliography
starts on new
page

Print book

Pamphlet

Newspaper
article

Article from
database

Bibliography
entries use
hanging indent
and are not
numbered

Glossary of Usage

Conventions of usage might be called the "good manners" of discourse. And just as manners vary from culture to culture and time to time, so do conventions of usage. Matters of usage, like other language choices you must make, depend on what your purpose is and on what is appropriate for a particular audience at a particular time.

a, an   Use *a* with a word that begins with a consonant (*a book*), a consonant sound such as "y" or "w" (*a euphoric moment, a one-sided match*), or a sounded *h* (*a hemisphere*). Use *an* with a word that begins with a vowel (*an umbrella*), a vowel sound (*an X-ray*), or a silent *h* (*an honor*).

accept, except   The verb *accept* means "receive" or "agree to." *Except* is usually a preposition that means "aside from" or "excluding." *All the plaintiffs except Mr. Kim decided to accept the settlement.*

advice, advise   The noun *advice* means "opinion" or "suggestion"; the verb *advise* means "offer advice." *Doctors advise everyone not to smoke, but many people ignore the advice.*

affect, effect   As a verb, *affect* means "influence" or "move the emotions of"; as a noun, it means "emotions" or "feelings." *Effect* is a noun meaning "result"; less commonly, it is a verb meaning "bring about." *The storm affected a large area. Its effects included widespread power failures. The drug effected a major change in the patient's affect.*

aggravate   The formal meaning is "make worse." *Having another mouth to feed aggravated their poverty.* In academic and professional writing, avoid using *aggravate* to mean "irritate" or "annoy."

all ready, already   *All ready* means "fully prepared." *Already* means "previously." *We were all ready for Lucy's party when we learned that she had already left.*

all right, alright   Avoid the spelling *alright*.

all together, altogether   *All together* means "all in a group" or "gathered in one place." *Altogether* means "completely" or "everything considered." *When the board members were all together, their mutual distrust was altogether obvious.*

allude, elude   *Allude* means "refer indirectly." *Elude* means "avoid" or "escape from." *The candidate did not even allude to her opponent. The suspect eluded the police for several days.*

allusion, illusion   An *allusion* is an indirect reference. An *illusion* is a false or misleading appearance. *The speaker's allusion to the Bible created an illusion of piety.*

a lot   Avoid the spelling *alot*.

already   See *all ready, already.*

alright   See *all right, alright.*

altogether   See *all together, altogether.*

among, between   In referring to two things or people, use *between*. In referring to three or more, use *among. The relationship between the twins is different from that among the other three children.*

amount, number   Use *amount* with quantities you cannot count; use *number* for quantities you can count. *A small number of volunteers cleared a large amount of brush.*

an   See *a, an.*

and/or   Avoid this term except in business or legal writing. Instead of *fat and/or protein*, write *fat, protein*, or *both.*

any body, anybody, any one, anyone   *Anybody* and *anyone* are pronouns meaning "any person." *Anyone* [or *anybody*] *would enjoy this film. Any body* is an adjective modifying a noun. *Any body of water has its own ecology. Any one* is two adjectives or a pronoun modified by an adjective. *Customers could buy only two sale items at any one time. The winner could choose any one of the prizes.*

anyplace   In academic and professional discourse, use *anywhere* instead.

anyway, anyways   In writing, use *anyway*, not *anyways*.

apt, liable, likely   *Likely to* means "probably will," and *apt to* means "inclines or tends to." In many instances, they are interchangeable. *Liable* often carries a more negative sense and is also a legal term meaning "obligated" or "responsible."

as   Avoid sentences in which it is not clear if *as* means "when" or "because." For example, does *Carl left town as his father was arriving* mean "at the same time as his father was arriving" or "because his father was arriving"?

as, as if, like   In academic and professional writing, use *as* or *as if* instead of *like* to introduce a clause. *The dog howled as if* [not *like*] *it were in pain. She did as* [not *like*] *I suggested.*

assure, ensure, insure   *Assure* means "convince" or "promise"; its direct object is usually a person or persons. *She assured voters she would not raise taxes. Ensure* and *insure* both mean "make certain," but *insure* usually refers specifically to protection against financial loss. *When the city rationed water to ensure that the supply would last, the Browns could no longer afford to insure their car-wash business.*

as to   Do not use *as to* as a substitute for *about*. *Karen was unsure about* [not *as to*] *Bruce's intentions.*

at, where   See *where*.

awhile, a while   Always use *a while* after a preposition such as *for*, *in*, or *after*. *We drove awhile and then stopped for a while.*

bad, badly   Use *bad* after a linking verb such as *be*, *feel*, or *seem*. Use *badly* to modify an action verb, an adjective, or another verb. *The hostess felt bad because the dinner was badly prepared.*

bare, bear   Use *bare* to mean "uncovered" and *bear* to refer to the animal or to mean "carry" or "endure": *The walls were bare. The emptiness was hard to bear.*

because of, due to   Use *due to* when the effect, stated as a noun, appears before the verb *be*. *His illness was due to malnutrition.* (*Illness*, a noun, is the effect.) Use *because of* when the effect is stated as a clause. *He was sick because of malnutrition.* (*He was sick*, a clause, is the effect.)

being as, being that   In academic or professional writing, use *because* or *since* instead of these expressions. *Because* [not *being as*] *Romeo killed Tybalt, he was banished to Padua.*

beside, besides   *Beside* is a preposition meaning "next to." *Besides* can be a preposition meaning "other than" or an adverb meaning "in addition." *No one besides Francesca would sit beside him.*

between   See *among, between*.

brake, break   *Brake* means "to stop" and also refers to a stopping mechanism: *Check the brakes. Break* means "fracture" or an interruption: *The coffee break was too short.*

breath, breathe   *Breath* is a noun; *breathe*, a verb. *"Breathe," said the nurse, so June took a deep breath.*

bring, take   Use *bring* when an object is moved from a farther to a nearer place; use *take* when the opposite is true. *Take the box to the post office; bring back my mail.*

but that, but what   Avoid using these as substitutes for *that* in expressions of doubt. *Hercule Poirot never doubted that* [not *but that*] *he would solve the case.*

but yet   Do not use these words together. *He is strong but* [not *but yet*] *gentle.*

can, may   *Can* refers to ability and *may* to possibility or permission. *Since I can ski the slalom well, I may win the race.*

can't hardly   *Hardly* has a negative meaning; therefore, *can't hardly* is a double negative. This expression is commonly used in some varieties of English but is not used in academic English. *Tim can* [not *can't*] *hardly wait.*

can't help but   This expression is redundant. Use *I can't help going* rather than *I can't help but go.*

censor, censure   *Censor* means "remove that which is considered offensive." *Censure* means "formally reprimand." *The newspaper censored stories that offended advertisers. The legislature censured the official for misconduct.*

compare to, compare with   *Compare to* means "regard as similar." *Jamie compared the loss to a kick in the head. Compare with* means "examine to find differences or similarities." *Compare Tim Burton's films with David Lynch's.*

complement, compliment   *Complement* means "go well with." *Compliment* means "praise." *Guests complimented her on how her earrings complemented her gown.*

comprise, compose   *Comprise* means "contain." *Compose* means "make up." *The class comprises twenty students. Twenty students compose the class.*

conscience, conscious   *Conscience* means "a sense of right and wrong." *Conscious* means "awake" or "aware." *Lisa was conscious of a guilty conscience.*

consensus of opinion   Use *consensus* instead of this redundant phrase. *The family consensus was to sell the old house.*

consequently, subsequently   *Consequently* means "as a result"; *subsequently* means "then." *He quit, and subsequently his wife lost her job; consequently, they had to sell their house.*

continual, continuous   *Continual* means "repeated at regular or frequent intervals." *Continuous* means "continuing or connected without a break." *The damage done by continuous erosion was increased by the continual storms.*

could of   *Have,* not *of,* should follow *could, would, should,* or *might. We could have* [not *of*] *invited them.*

criteria, criterion   *Criterion* means "standard of judgment" or "necessary qualification." *Criteria* is the plural form. *Image is the wrong criterion for choosing a president.*

data   *Data* is the plural form of the Latin word *datum,* meaning "fact." Although *data* is used informally as either singular or plural, in academic or professional writing, treat *data* as plural. *These data indicate that fewer people are smoking.*

different from, different than   *Different from* is generally preferred in academic and professional writing, although both phrases are widely used. *Her lab results were no different from* [not *than*] *his.*

discreet, discrete   *Discreet* means "tactful" or "prudent." *Discrete* means "separate" or "distinct." *The leader's discreet efforts kept all the discrete factions unified.*

disinterested, uninterested   *Disinterested* means "unbiased." *Uninterested* means "indifferent." *Finding disinterested jurors was difficult. She was uninterested in the verdict.*

distinct, distinctive   *Distinct* means "separate" or "well defined." *Distinctive* means "characteristic." *Germany includes many distinct regions, each with a distinctive accent.*

doesn't, don't   *Doesn't* is the contraction for *does not.* Use it with *he, she, it,* and singular nouns. *Don't* stands for *do not;* use it with *I, you, we, they,* and plural nouns.

due to   See *because of, due to.*

each other, one another   Use *each other* in sentences involving two subjects and *one another* in sentences involving more than two.

effect   See *affect, effect*.

elicit, illicit   The verb *elicit* means "draw out." The adjective *illicit* means "illegal." *The police elicited from the criminal the names of others involved in illicit activities.*

elude   See *allude, elude*.

emigrate from, immigrate to   *Emigrate from* means "move away from one's country." *Immigrate to* means "move to another country." *We emigrated from Norway in 1999. We immigrated to the United States.*

ensure   See *assure, ensure, insure*.

enthused, enthusiastic   Use *enthusiastic* rather than *enthused* in academic and professional writing.

equally as good   Replace this redundant phrase with *equally good* or *as good*.

every day, everyday   *Everyday* is an adjective meaning "ordinary." *Every day* is an adjective and a noun, meaning "each day." *I wore everyday clothes almost every day.*

every one, everyone   *Everyone* is a pronoun. *Every one* is an adjective and a pronoun, referring to each member of a group. *Because he began after everyone else, David could not finish every one of the problems.*

except   See *accept, except*.

explicit, implicit   *Explicit* means "directly or openly expressed." *Implicit* means "indirectly expressed or implied." *The explicit message of the ad urged consumers to buy the product, while the implicit message promised popularity if they did so.*

farther, further   *Farther* refers to physical distance. *How much farther is it to Munich? Further* refers to time or degree. *I want to avoid further delays.*

fewer, less   Use *fewer* with nouns that can be counted. Use *less* with general amounts that you cannot count. *The world needs fewer bombs and less hostility.*

finalize   *Finalize* is a pretentious way of saying "end" or "make final." *We closed* [not *finalized*] *the deal.*

firstly, secondly, etc.   *First, second,* etc., are more common in U.S. English.

flaunt, flout   *Flaunt* means to "show off." *Flout* means to "mock" or "scorn." *The drug dealers flouted authority by flaunting their wealth.*

former, latter   *Former* refers to the first and *latter* to the second of two things previously mentioned. *Kathy and Anna are athletes; the former plays tennis, and the latter runs.*

further   See *farther, further*.

good, well   *Good* is an adjective and should not be used as a substitute for the adverb *well. Gabriel is a good host who cooks well.*

good and   *Good and* is colloquial for "very"; avoid it in academic and professional writing.

hanged, hung   *Hanged* refers to executions; *hung* is used for all other meanings.

hardly   See *can't hardly.*

herself, himself, myself, yourself   Do not use these reflexive pronouns as subjects or as objects unless they are necessary. *Jane and I* [not *myself*] *agree. They invited John and me* [not *myself*].

he/she, his/her   Better solutions for avoiding sexist language are to write out *he or she*, to eliminate pronouns entirely, or to make the subject plural. Instead of writing *Everyone should carry his/her driver's license,* try *Drivers should carry their licenses* or *People should carry their driver's licenses.*

himself   See *herself, himself, myself, yourself.*

hisself   Use *himself* instead in academic and professional writing.

hopefully   *Hopefully* is often used informally to mean "it is hoped," but its formal meaning is "with hope." *Sam watched the roulette wheel hopefully* [not *Hopefully, Sam will win*].

hung   See *hanged, hung.*

illicit   See *elicit, illicit.*

illusion   See *allusion, illusion.*

immigrate to   See *emigrate from, immigrate to.*

impact   Some readers object to the colloquial use of *impact* or *impact on* as a verb meaning "affect." *Population control may reduce* [not *impact*] *world hunger.*

implicit   See *explicit, implicit.*

imply, infer   To *imply* is to suggest indirectly. To *infer* is to guess or conclude on the basis of an indirect suggestion. *The note implied they were planning a small wedding; we inferred we would not be invited.*

inside of, outside of   Use *inside* and *outside* instead. *The class regularly met outside* [not *outside of*] *the building.*

insure   See *assure, ensure, insure.*

interact, interface   *Interact* is a vague word meaning "do something that somehow involves another person." *Interface* is computer jargon; when used as a verb, it means "discuss" or "communicate." Avoid both verbs in academic and professional writing.

irregardless, regardless   *Irregardless* is a double negative. Use *regardless.*

is when, is where   These vague expressions are often incorrectly used in definitions. *Schizophrenia is a psychotic condition in which* [not *is when* or *is where*] *a person withdraws from reality.*

its, it's   *Its* is the possessive form of *it. It's* is a contraction for *it is* or *it has. It's important to observe the rat before it eats its meal.*

kind, sort, type   These singular nouns should be modified with *this* or *that*, not *these* or *those*, and followed by other singular nouns, not plural nouns. *Wear this kind of dress* [not *those kind of dresses*].

kind of, sort of   Avoid these colloquialisms. *Amy was somewhat* [not *kind of*] *tired.*

know, no   Use *know* to mean "understand." *No* is the opposite of *yes*.

later, latter   *Later* means "after some time." *Latter* refers to the second of two items named. *Juan and Chad won all their early matches, but the latter was injured later in the season.*

latter   See *former, latter* and *later, latter*.

lay, lie   *Lay* means "place" or "put." Its main forms are *lay, laid, laid*. It generally has a direct object, specifying what has been placed. *She laid her books on the desk. Lie* means "recline" or "be positioned" and does not take a direct object. Its main forms are *lie, lay, lain. She lay awake until two.*

leave, let   *Leave* means "go away." *Let* means "allow." *Leave alone* and *let alone* are interchangeable. *Let me leave now, and leave* [or *let*] *me alone from now on!*

lend, loan   In academic and professional writing, do not use *loan* as a verb; use *lend* instead. *Please lend me your pen so that I may fill out this application for a loan.*

less   See *fewer, less*.

let   See *leave, let*.

liable   See *apt, liable, likely*.

lie   See *lay, lie*.

like   See *as, as if, like*.

likely   See *apt, liable, likely*.

literally   *Literally* means "actually" or "exactly as stated." Use it to stress the truth of a statement that might otherwise be understood as figurative. Do not use *literally* as an intensifier in a figurative statement. *Mirna was literally at the edge of her seat* may be accurate, but *Mirna is so hungry that she could literally eat a horse* is not.

loan   See *lend, loan*.

loose, lose   *Lose* is a verb meaning "misplace." *Loose* is an adjective that means "not securely attached." *Sew on that loose button before you lose it.*

lots, lots of   Avoid these informal expressions meaning "much" or "many" in academic and professional discourse.

man, mankind   Replace these terms with *people, humans, humankind, men and women*, or similar wording.

may   See *can, may*.

may be, maybe   *May be* is a verb phrase. *Maybe* is an adverb that means "perhaps." *He may be the head of the organization, but maybe someone else would handle a crisis better.*

media   *Media* is the plural form of the noun *medium* and takes a plural verb. *The media are* [not *is*] *obsessed with scandals.*

might of   See *could of*.

moral, morale   A *moral* is a succinct lesson. *The moral of the story is that generosity is rewarded. Morale* means "spirit" or "mood." *Office morale was low.*

myself   See *herself, himself, myself, yourself*.

no   See *know, no*.

nor, or   Use *either* with *or* and *neither* with *nor*.

number   See *amount, number*.

off, of   Use *off* without *of*. *The spaghetti slipped off* [not *off of*] *the plate*.

OK, O.K., okay   All are acceptable spellings, but avoid the term in academic and professional discourse.

on account of   Use this substitute for *because of* sparingly or not at all.

one another   See *each other, one another*.

or   See *nor, or*.

outside of   See *inside of, outside of*.

owing to the fact that   Avoid this and other wordy expressions for *because*.

passed, past   Use *passed* to mean "went by" or "received a passing grade": *The marching band passed the reviewing stand*. Use *past* to refer to a time before the present: *Historians study the past*.

per   Use the Latin *per* only in standard technical phrases such as *miles per hour*. Otherwise, find English equivalents. *As mentioned in* [not *As per*] *the latest report, the country's average food consumption each day* [not *per day*] *is only 2,000 calories*.

percent, percentage   Use *percent* with a specific number; use *percentage* with an adjective such as *large* or *small*. *Last year, 80 percent of the members were female. A large percentage of the members are women*.

plenty   *Plenty* means "enough" or "a great abundance." *They told us America was a land of plenty*. Colloquially, it is used to mean "very," a usage you should avoid in academic and professional writing. *He was very* [not *plenty*] *tired*.

plus   *Plus* means "in addition to." *Your salary plus mine will cover our expenses*. In academic writing, do not use *plus* to mean "besides" or "moreover." *That dress does not fit me. Besides* [not *Plus*], *it is the wrong color*.

precede, proceed   *Precede* means "come before"; *proceed* means "go forward." *Despite the storm that preceded the ceremony, the wedding proceeded on schedule*.

pretty   Except in informal situations, avoid using *pretty* as a substitute for "rather," "somewhat," or "quite." *Bill was quite* [not *pretty*] *disagreeable*.

principal, principle   When used as a noun, *principal* refers to a head official or an amount of money; when used as an adjective, it means "most significant." *Principle* means "fundamental law or belief." *Albert went to the principal and defended himself with the principle of free speech*.

proceed   See *precede, proceed*.

quotation, quote   *Quote* is a verb, and *quotation* is a noun. *He quoted the president, and the quotation* [not *quote*] *was preserved in history books*.

raise, rise   *Raise* means "lift" or "move upward." (Referring to children, it means "bring up.") It takes a direct object; someone raises something. *The guests raised their glasses to toast*. *Rise* means "go upward." It does not take a direct object; something rises by itself. *She saw the steam rise from the pan*.

rarely ever   Use *rarely* by itself, or use *hardly ever*. *When we were poor, we rarely went to the movies.*

real, really   *Real* is an adjective, and *really* is an adverb. Do not substitute *real* for *really*. In academic and professional writing, do not use *real* or *really* to mean "very." *The old man walked very* [not *real* or *really*] *slowly.*

reason is because   Use either *the reason is that* or *because* — not both. *The reason the copier stopped is that* [not *is because*] *the paper jammed.*

reason why   This expression is redundant. *The reason* [not *reason why*] *this book is short is market demand.*

regardless   See *irregardless, regardless.*

respectfully, respectively   *Respectfully* means "with respect." *Respectively* means "in the order given." *Karen and David are, respectively, a juggler and an acrobat. The children treated their grandparents respectfully.*

rise   See *raise, rise.*

set, sit   *Set* usually means "put" or "place" and takes a direct object. *Sit* refers to taking a seat and does not take an object. *Set your cup on the table, and sit down.*

should of   See *could of.*

since   Be careful not to use *since* ambiguously. In *Since I broke my leg, I've stayed home*, the word *since* might be understood to mean either "because" or "ever since."

sit   See *set, sit.*

so   In academic and professional writing, avoid using *so* alone to mean "very." Instead, follow *so* with *that* to show how the intensified condition leads to a result. *Aaron was so tired that he fell asleep at the wheel.*

someplace   Use *somewhere* instead in academic and professional writing.

some time, sometime, sometimes   *Some time* refers to a length of time. *Please leave me some time to dress. Sometime* means "at some indefinite later time." *Sometime I will take you to London. Sometimes* means "occasionally." *Sometimes I eat sushi.*

sort   See *kind, sort, type.*

sort of   See *kind of, sort of.*

stationary, stationery   *Stationary* means "standing still"; *stationery* means "writing paper." *When the bus was stationary, Pat took out stationery and wrote a note.*

subsequently   See *consequently, subsequently.*

supposed to, used to   Be careful to include the final *-d* in these expressions. *He is supposed to attend.*

sure, surely   Avoid using *sure* as an intensifier. Instead, use *certainly. I was certainly glad to see you.*

take   See *bring, take.*

than, then   Use *than* in comparative statements. *The cat was bigger than the dog.* Use *then* when referring to a sequence of events. *I won, and then I cried.*

that, which A clause beginning with *that* singles out the item being described. *The book that is on the table is a good one* specifies the book on the table as opposed to some other book. A clause beginning with *which* may or may not single out the item, although some writers use *which* clauses only to add more information about an item being described. *The book, which is on the table, is a good one* contains a *which* clause between the commas. The clause simply adds extra, nonessential information about the book; it does not specify which book.

theirselves Use *themselves* instead in academic and professional writing.

then See *than, then.*

thorough, threw, through *Thorough* means "complete": *After a thorough inspection, the restaurant reopened. Threw* is the past tense of *throw*, and *through* means "in one side and out the other": *He threw the ball through a window.*

to, too, two *To* generally shows direction. *Too* means "also." *Two* is the number. *We, too, are going to the meeting in two hours.* Avoid using *to* after *where. Where are you flying* [not *flying to*]?

two See *to, too, two.*

type See *kind, sort, type.*

uninterested See *disinterested, uninterested.*

unique Some people argue that unique means "one and only" and object to usage that suggests it means merely "unusual." In formal writing, avoid constructions such as *quite unique.*

used to See *supposed to, used to.*

very Avoid using *very* to intensify a weak adjective or adverb; instead, replace the adjective or adverb with a stronger, more precise, or more colorful word. Instead of *very nice*, for example, use *kind, warm, sensitive, endearing*, or *friendly.*

way, ways When referring to distance, use *way. Graduation was a long way* [not *ways*] *off.*

well See *good, well.*

where Use *where* alone, not with words such as *at* and *to. Where are you going* [not *going to*]?

which See *that, which.*

who, whom Use *who* if the word is the subject of the clause and *whom* if the word is the object of the clause. *Monica, who smokes incessantly, is my godmother.* (*Who* is the subject of the clause; the verb is *smokes.*) *Monica, whom I saw last winter, lives in Tucson.* (*Whom* is the object of the verb *saw.*)

who's, whose *Who's* is a contraction for *who is* or *who has. Who's on the patio? Whose* is a possessive form. *Whose sculpture is in the garden? Whose is on the patio?*

would of See *could of.*

yet See *but yet.*

your, you're *Your* shows possession. *Bring your sleeping bag along. You're* is the contraction for *you are. You're in the wrong sleeping bag.*

yourself See *herself, himself, myself, yourself.*

Index

Words in blue are followed by a definition. **Boldface** terms in definitions are themselves defined elsewhere in this index.

A

O

W

Acknowledgments

Derek Bok. "Protecting Freedom of Expression at Harvard." First published in *The Boston Globe*, March 25, 1991, p. 15. Reprinted with permission of the author.

Emily Dickinson. "A Little Madness in the Spring." From *The Poems of Emily Dickinson*, edited by Thomas H. Johnson, Cambridge, MA: The Belknap Press of Harvard University Press. Copyright © 1951, 1955, 1979, 1983 by the President and Fellows of Harvard College.

Langston Hughes. "Harlem—A Dream Deferred." From *The Collected Poems of Langston Hughes*, edited by Arnold Rampersad with David Roessel, Associate Editor. Copyright © 1994 by the Estate of Langston Hughes. Used by permission of Alfred A. Knopf, a division of Random House, Inc., and Harold Ober Associates, Ltd.

James Hunter. "Outlaw Classics: The Albums That Kept Nashville Real in the Sixties and Seventies." From *Rolling Stone*, March 9, 2006, p. 95. Copyright © 2006 Rolling Stone LLC. All rights reserved. Used by permission.

Andrea A. Lunsford and Karen J. Lunsford. "Mistakes Are a Fact of Life: A National Comparative Study." From *CCC* 59.4 (2008): 781–806. Used by permission of the National Council of Teachers of English.

Joshua Oppenheimer. Director's Statement, "The Act of Killing." Used by permission of Final Cut for Real.

Directories

Storyboard Art and Online Activities

Go to **macmillanhighered.com/everyday6e** for all online activities.

Storyboard Art (print and online)

Rhetorical situations   *23, 24, 26*
Working thesis   *39, 40, 41*
Peer review: Work with a writer   *68*
Peer review: Work with reviewers   *72*
Revising and editing   *75, 76, 78*
Critical reading   *92, 96, 98, 100*
Synthesis   *170, 171*

Top Twenty Editing Quizzes (online)

Editing quiz 1
Editing quiz 2

Tutorials (online)

DRAFTING

Word processing

CRITICAL READING

Active reading
Reading visuals for audience
Reading visuals for purpose

PRESENTATIONS

Presentations

PUBLIC, PROFESSIONAL, AND DIGITAL WRITING

Audio editing with Audacity
Job search and personal branding
Photo editing with GIMP

RESEARCH

Do I need to cite that?
Online research tools

DOCUMENTATION

How to cite a book in MLA style
How to cite an article in MLA style
How to cite a database in MLA style
How to cite a website in MLA style
How to cite a database in APA style
How to cite a website in APA style

LearningCurve Adaptive Quizzing (online)

Go to **macmillanhighered.com/everyday6e** to test yourself on these topics.

DRAFTING

Topic sentences and supporting details

CRITICAL READING

Critical reading
Topics and main ideas

ARGUMENT

Argument

RESEARCH

Evaluating, integrating, and acknowledging sources (MLA)
Evaluating, integrating, and acknowledging sources (APA)

LANGUAGE

Word choice

STYLE

Active and passive voice
Coordination and subordination
Parallelism
Shifts

GRAMMAR

Articles and nouns
Comma splices and fused (run-on) sentences

Video Prompts (online)

Go to **macmillanhighered.com/everyday6e,** and click on the Resources tab in LaunchPad Solo for these short videos of student writers.

REVIEWING AND REVISING

Lessons from being a peer reviewer
Lessons from peer review
Revision happens
Something to learn from each other

ARGUMENT

Facing a challenging argument

PRESENTATIONS

If I were in the audience
Presentation is performance
You want them to hear you

PUBLIC, PROFESSIONAL, AND DIGITAL WRITING

Improving with practice
Writing for the real world

RESEARCH

Researching something exciting
When to stop researching

LANGUAGE

Correctness in context

Student Writing

Go to **macmillanhighered.com/everyday6e** for complete versions of these student models with assignable activities. Click on the Resources tab in LaunchPad Solo for the full list.

Advice for Multilingual Writers

Multilingual   Look for the "Multilingual" icon to find advice of special interest to international students and others whose home language is not English.

Form verb phrases appropriately (38b)
Use verb tenses appropriately (38e)
Understand mood and conditional sentences (38h)
Nouns and noun phrases (Chapter 39)
Understand adjectives ending in *-ed* and *-ing* (42f)
Put adjectives in order (42g)
Prepositions and prepositional phrases (Chapter 44)

Boxed Tips

Considering Disabilities

Talking the Talk

Revision Symbols

Some instructors use these symbols as a kind of shorthand to guide you in revision. The numbers refer to a chapter number or a section of a chapter.

abb	abbreviation **54a–g**	*para*	paraphrase **14d, 15**
ad	adjective/adverb **42**	*pass*	inappropriate passive **33c, 38g**
agr	agreement **40, 41f**		
awk	awkward	*ref*	unclear pronoun reference **41g**
cap	capitalization **53**		
case	case **41c–d**	*run-on*	run-on (fused) sentence **45**
cliché	cliché **7e, 29d**		
co	coordination **30a**	*sexist*	sexist language **27b, 41f**
coh	coherence **6e**	*shift*	shift **33**
com	incomplete comparison **31e**	*slang*	slang **29a**
		sp	spelling **29f–g**
concl	weak conclusion **6f, 16b**	*sub*	subordination **30b**
cs	comma splice **45**	*sum*	summarize **14d, 15, 18b**
d	diction (word choice) **29**	*t*	tone **7d, 14c, 29a, 29d**
def	define **6c**	*trans*	transition **6e, 35b**
dm	dangling modifier **43c**	*u*	unity **6a**
doc	documentation **57–67**	*vague*	vague statement
emph	emphasis unclear **30**	*verb*	verb form **38a–d**
ex	example needed **6b–c**	*vt*	verb tense **38e–h**
frag	sentence fragment **46**	*wv*	weak verb **38**
fs	fused sentence **45**	*wrdy*	wordy **34**
hyph	hyphen **56**	*ww*	wrong word **1, 7e, 29a–b**
inc	incomplete construction **31**	*,*	comma **47**
intro	weak introduction **6f, 16b**	*;*	semicolon **48**
it	italics (or underlining) **55**	*. ? !*	period, question mark, exclamation point **49**
jarg	jargon **29a**	*'*	apostrophe **50**
lc	lowercase letter **53**	*" "*	quotation marks **51**
lv	language variety **28**	*( ) [ ] —*	parentheses, brackets, dash **52a–c**
mix	mixed construction **31a**		
mm	misplaced modifier **43**	*: / ...*	colon, slash, ellipsis **52d–f**
ms	manuscript form		
no ,	no comma **47j**	*^*	insert
num	number **54h–j**	*⌒*	transpose
¶	paragraph **6**	*⌣*	close up
//	faulty parallelism **6e, 32**	*X*	obvious error

Contents